Handbook of Research on AI-Based Technologies and Applications in the Era of the Metaverse

Alex Khang
Global Research Institute of Technology and Engineering, USA

Vrushank Shah
Institute of Technology and Engineering, Indus University, India

Sita Rani
Department of Computer Science and Engineering, Guru Nanak Dev Engineering College, India

A volume in the Advances in Computational
Intelligence and Robotics (ACIR) Book Series

Published in the United States of America by
IGI Global
Engineering Science Reference (an imprint of IGI Global)
701 E. Chocolate Avenue
Hershey PA, USA 17033
Tel: 717-533-8845
Fax: 717-533-8661
E-mail: cust@igi-global.com
Web site: http://www.igi-global.com

Library of Congress Cataloging-in-Publication Data

Names: Khang, Alex, editor. | Shah, Vrushank Manharlal, 1985- editor. |
  Rani, Sita, editor.
Title: Handbook of research on AI-based technologies and applications in the
  era of the metaverse / edited by: Alex Khang, Vrushank Manharlal Shah, and Sita Rani.
Description: Hershey, PA : Engineering Science Reference, [2023] | Includes
  bibliographical references and index. | Summary: "AI-Based Technologies
  and Applications in the Era of the Metaverse discusses essential
  components of the metaverse ecosystem such as concepts, methodologies,
  technologies, modeling, designs, statistics, implementation, and
  maintenance. Covering key topics such as machine learning, deep
  learning, quantum computing, and blockchain, this premier reference
  source is ideal for computer scientists, industry professionals,
  researchers, academicians, scholars, practitioners, instructors, and
  students"-- Provided by publisher.
Identifiers: LCCN 2023008214 (print) | LCCN 2023008215 (ebook) | ISBN
  9781668488515 (hardcover) | ISBN 9781668488539 (ebook)
Subjects: LCSH: Metaverse. | Machine learning. | Blockchains (Databases)
Classification: LCC TK5105.8864 A43 2023 (print) | LCC TK5105.8864
  (ebook) | DDC 006.3/1--dc23/eng/20230323
LC record available at https://lccn.loc.gov/2023008214
LC ebook record available at https://lccn.loc.gov/2023008215

This book is published in the IGI Global book series Advances in Computational Intelligence and Robotics (ACIR) (ISSN:
2327-0411; eISSN: 2327-042X)

British Cataloguing in Publication Data
A Cataloguing in Publication record for this book is available from the British Library.

All work contributed to this book is new, previously-unpublished material. The views expressed in this book are those of the
authors, but not necessarily of the publisher.

For electronic access to this publication, please contact: eresources@igi-global.com.

Advances in Computational Intelligence and Robotics (ACIR) Book Series

Ivan Giannoccaro
University of Salento, Italy

ISSN:2327-0411
EISSN:2327-042X

MISSION

While intelligence is traditionally a term applied to humans and human cognition, technology has progressed in such a way to allow for the development of intelligent systems able to simulate many human traits. With this new era of simulated and artificial intelligence, much research is needed in order to continue to advance the field and also to evaluate the ethical and societal concerns of the existence of artificial life and machine learning.

The **Advances in Computational Intelligence and Robotics (ACIR) Book Series** encourages scholarly discourse on all topics pertaining to evolutionary computing, artificial life, computational intelligence, machine learning, and robotics. ACIR presents the latest research being conducted on diverse topics in intelligence technologies with the goal of advancing knowledge and applications in this rapidly evolving field.

COVERAGE

- Computer Vision
- Computational Logic
- Artificial Intelligence
- Cyborgs
- Synthetic Emotions
- Artificial Life
- Intelligent Control
- Heuristics
- Pattern Recognition
- Adaptive and Complex Systems

IGI Global is currently accepting manuscripts for publication within this series. To submit a proposal for a volume in this series, please contact our Acquisition Editors at Acquisitions@igi-global.com or visit: http://www.igi-global.com/publish/.

Titles in this Series

For a list of additional titles in this series, please visit: www.igi-global.com/book-series

Scalable and Distributed Machine Learning and Deep Learning Patterns
J. Joshua Thomas (UOW Malaysia KDU Penang University College, Malaysia) S. Harini (Vellore Institute of Technology, India) and V. Pattabiraman (Vellore Institute of Technology, India)
Engineering Science Reference • ©2023 • 300pp • H/C (ISBN: 9781668498040) • US $270.00

Application and Adoption of Robotic Process Automation for Smart Cities
R. K. Tailor (Manipal University Jaipur, India)
Engineering Science Reference • ©2023 • 320pp • H/C (ISBN: 9781668471937) • US $270.00

Handbook of Research on Advancements in AI and IoT Convergence Technologies
Jingyuan Zhao (University of Toronto, Canada) V. Vinoth Kumar (Jain University, India) Rajesh Natarajan (University of Applied Science and Technology, Shinas, Oman) and T.R. Mahesh (Jain University, India)
Engineering Science Reference • ©2023 • 415pp • H/C (ISBN: 9781668469712) • US $380.00

Stochastic Processes and Their Applications in Artificial Intelligence
Christo Ananth (Samarkand State University, Uzbekistan) N. Anbazhagan (Alagappa University, India) and Mark Goh (National University of Singapore, Singapore)
Engineering Science Reference • ©2023 • 325pp • H/C (ISBN: 9781668476796) • US $270.00

Applying AI-Based IoT Systems to Simulation-Based Information Retrieval
Bhatia Madhulika (Amity University, India) Bhatia Surabhi (King Faisal University, Saudi Arabia) Poonam Tanwar (Manav Rachna International Institute of Research and Studies, India) and Kuljeet Kaur (Université du Québec, Canada)
Engineering Science Reference • ©2023 • 229pp • H/C (ISBN: 9781668452554) • US $270.00

AI-Enabled Social Robotics in Human Care Services
Sandeep Kautish (Lord Buddha Education Foundation, Nepal) Nirbhay Kumar Chaubey (Ganpat University, India) S.B. Goyal (City University, Malaysia) and Pawan Whig (Vivekananda Insitute of Professional Studies, India)
Engineering Science Reference • ©2023 • 321pp • H/C (ISBN: 9781668481714) • US $270.00

Handbook of Research on AI and Knowledge Engineering for Real-Time Business Intelligence
Kamal Kant Hiran (Aalborg University, Denmark) K. Hemachandran (Woxsen University, India) Anil Pise (University of the Witwatersrand, South Africa) and B. Justus Rabi (Christian College of Engineering and Technology, India)
Engineering Science Reference • ©2023 • 359pp • H/C (ISBN: 9781668465196) • US $380.00

701 East Chocolate Avenue, Hershey, PA 17033, USA
Tel: 717-533-8845 x100 • Fax: 717-533-8661
E-Mail: cust@igi-global.com • www.igi-global.com

List of Contributors

Table of Contents

Detailed Table of Contents

Chapter 1

Aakansha C. Saxena, Rashtriya Raksha University, India
Adhishree Ojha, Rashtriya Raksha University, India
Daksh Sobti, Rashtriya Raksha University, India
Alex Khang, Global Research Institute of Technology and Engineering, USA

Metaverse is a prodigy that combines the real and digital worlds, enabling avatars to participate in a variety of activities. AI will have an influential impact on the future of Metaverse, as it will enable Metaverse to be user-centric by introducing features like augmented reality and virtual reality. This chapter will provide insights about how AI-centric modeling and AI concepts can boost the emerging world of Metaverse. AI will be an indispensable component of Metaverse, from the foundational layer to the experiential layer. AI will enable Metaverse to be user-centric by introducing features like augmented reality and virtual reality, creating an immersive experience for the user.

Chapter 2

Alex Khang, Global Research Institute of Technology and Engineering, USA
Kali Charan Rath, GIET University, Odisha, India
Suresh Kumar Satapathy, Galler India Group, Gurgaon, India
Amaresh Kumar, National Institute of Technology, Jamshedpur, India
Sudhansu Ranjan Das, Veer Surendra Sai University of Technology, India
Manas Ranjan Panda, GIET University, Odisha, India

The integration of robotics and the internet of things (IoT) has emerged as a crucial aspect in the development of smart factory infrastructure within the context of Industry 4.0. This chapter explores the synergistic potential of combining these two transformative technologies to enable the future of smart IoT technologies. Firstly, the chapter provides an overview of the fundamental concepts of IoT and robotics, highlighting their respective contributions to the Industry 4.0 paradigm. It discusses the key characteristics and challenges associated with IoT-enabled smart factories, emphasizing the need for efficient data collection, processing, and decision-making in dynamic manufacturing environments. In conclusion, this chapter highlights the immense potential of integrating robotics and IoT in smart factory infrastructure, paving the way for increased automation, efficiency, and productivity. It underscores the importance of addressing the associated challenges to unlock the full benefits of this integration and enable the future of smart IoT technologies.

Chapter 3

Albérico Travassos Rosário, GOVCOPP, IADE, Universidade Europeia, Portugal
Paula Rosa Lopes, Universidade Lusófona, Portugal
Filipe Sales Rosário, Universidade Europeia, Portugal

The metaverse is a shared, virtual space where users can interact with each other and digital objects in real time. It has the potential to revolutionize the way we do business by providing a new platform for conducting transactions, collaborating on projects, and connecting with customers. Metaverse can benefit businesses by providing a new platform for virtual events. The metaverse also has the potential to revolutionize the way businesses collaborate and work with each other. Overall, the metaverse has the potential to be a powerful tool for businesses, providing a new platform for conducting transactions, collaborating on projects, and connecting with customers. More research is needed to provide reliable data for decision-making by managers, so based on these research gaps, this study aims to assess the challenges and opportunities, thus building a benchmark on how the metaverse can leverage the business world.

Chapter 4

Alex Khang, Global Research Institute of Technology and Engineering, USA
Muthmainnah Muthmainnah, Universitas Al Asyariah Mandar, Indonesia
Prodhan Mahbub Ibna Seraj, American International University-Bangladesh, Dhaka, Bangladesh
Ahmad Al Yakin, Universitas Al Asyariah Mandar, Indonesia
Ahmad J. Obaid, Department of Computer Science, Faculty of Computer Science and Mathematics, University of Kufa, Iraq

In the educational setting, artificial intelligence (AI) technology, notably chatbots, has made substantial improvements in English learning. This study aims to determine the effectiveness of using the Artificial Intelligence Virtual Dream Friend and John English Boot applications on learning English in the 5.0 revolution era in English courses for first-semester students at university. The assessment method used is a quantitative research method and research design (quasi-experiment design). Based on the results of the study, it can be concluded that the results of the comparison test showed that My Virtual Dream Friend and John English Bot were both effective for use as computer tutoring in English courses and also increased interest in learning English in the 5.0 revolution era compared to previous conventional methods. The outcomes of this study might be used to direct future research into utilizing chatbots outside of the classroom as learning companions, and educators could use them to adapt evaluation and feedback procedures.

Muthmainnah Muthmainnah, Universitas Al Asyariah Mandar, Indonesia
Alex Khang, Global Research Institute of Technology and Engineering, USA
Ahmad Al Yakin, Universitas Al Asyariah Mandar, Indonesia
Ibrahim Oteir, Batterjee Medical College, Jeddah, Saudi Arabia
Abdullah Nijr Alotaibi, Majmaah University, Majmaah, Saudi Arabia

The degree to which a virtual content layer exists between the viewer and the real world, and how the real world is augmented, can vary greatly across tools, and use cases, but is essential to all forms of virtual reality (VR). The degree of overlap with the real world, as well as the importance of location, cooperation, and mobility, can vary dramatically from one VR experience to the next. Teachers will need support in figuring out how to best utilize AI for the benefit of student learning because of the plethora of available AI options. In this chapter, the authors share the results of a poll of students, both in the field and those hoping to enter it, to learn their thoughts on VR in the classroom. To gauge participants' thoughts on VR potential in the classroom, they gave them the VR platform and had them create a VR experience on their mobile devices. In virtual classrooms, 165 students can interact with the VR and other students as avatars, ask questions, write conversations, identify vocabulary connected between VR and material, and provide suggestions for improving classroom management.

Jyoti Gupta, Chitkara Institute of Engineering and Technology, India
Lekha Rani, Chitkara Institute of Engineering and Technology, India
Maninder Kaur, Chitkara Institute of Engineering and Technology, India

Imagine living in a virtual environment where millions of individuals can communicate among themselves, explore, shop, and have a comfortable life on their couches. In this universe, the computer displays have transformed portals into a physical, three-dimensional digital realm that is superior and more expansive than the real world. Digital avatars that are representations of us roam between experiences while carrying our identities. Putting the sensationalism aside, this is known as the "metaverse." The metaverse is an idea that describes a virtual universe composed of a couple of interconnected virtual spaces or worlds. It is an imaginative immersion in which the digital and bodily worlds converge, creating a widespread and interconnected network of virtual environments that can be accessed globally. It can boost employment opportunities by supplementing individuals with practical training and ensures that the individuals with disabilities can also be incorporated in this marathon of growth by leveraging these technologies.

Hakan Altinpulluk, Anadolu University, Turkey
Yusuf Yıldırım, Anadolu University, Turkey

The aim of this chapter is to identify and introduce the most preferred applications by analyzing augmented reality applications used in master's theses and doctoral dissertations in Turkey. In order to achieve this aim, first of all, the concepts related to the Metaverse, which constituted the conceptual framework of the chapter, were explained by supporting them with the research findings obtained from the literature. Then, the AR development platforms, AR software development kits, AR applications, and the devices on which AR applications were run were examined in thesis studies within the scope of augmented reality accessed from the Council of Higher Education Thesis Archive. At the end of this chapter, Vuforia, ARCore, and Artivive Bridge software development kits are briefly introduced as the first three most frequently used AR software development kits in thesis studies accessed from the National Thesis Center Archive of the Council of Higher Education of Turkey.

Chapter 8

Vrushank Shah, Electronics and Communication Engineering, Indus Institute of Technology and Engineering, Indus University, India
Alex Khang, Global Research Institute of Technology and Engineering, USA

Combining the Metaverse and IoT has huge potential to change healthcare systems. In this chapter, the authors look at how the internet of things (IoT) is changing healthcare by focusing on two key areas: telemedicine and remote patient monitoring. Remote patient monitoring is enabled through internet of things (IoT) devices and wearables. These devices collect data on vital signs, activity levels, and other health metrics in order to remotely monitor patients and discover abnormalities or changes in health conditions. By facilitating remote medical consultations and virtual doctor-patient interactions, the internet of things also improves healthcare's accessibility and convenience.

Chapter 9

Shyam Sihare, Dr. A.P.J. Abdul Kalam Government College, Silvassa, India
Alex Khang, Global Research Institute of Technology and Engineering, USA

This chapter explores the impact of quantum technology on the metaverse, revolutionizing performance and security. Quantum computing enables faster processing, advanced simulations, and sophisticated AI interactions. Integrating it with the metaverse poses technical challenges and requires addressing ethical considerations. Quantum tech benefits blockchain-based cryptocurrencies, enabling decentralized ownership and secure transactions. Regulatory frameworks are needed. Future internet technologies like 5G, edge computing, and IoT play a vital role, providing high-speed connectivity and enhanced immersion. Overcoming challenges such as limited resources and interdisciplinary expertise is crucial. Addressing ethical concerns and establishing standards and regulations are necessary. This research aims to understand quantum's effects, develop strategies, and foster collaboration for a responsible and equitable integration in the metaverse, shaping a transformative digital future.

Chapter 10

Albérico Travassos Rosário, GOVCOPP, IADE, Universidade Europeia, Portugal
Paula Rosa Lopes, CICANT, Universidade Lusófona, Portugal
Filipe Sales Rosário, University Europeia, Portugal

The term metaverse refers to a collective virtual shared space created by the convergence of virtually enhanced physical reality and physically persistent virtual space, including the sum of all virtual worlds, augmented reality, and the internet. In the context of marketing, the metaverse can be thought of as a new platform for brands to engage with consumers and create immersive, interactive experiences. Brands can use the metaverse to create virtual events, product demonstrations, and other interactive experiences that allow consumers to engage with the brand in a more meaningful way. The metaverse offers new and exciting opportunities for brands to connect with consumers and create engaging, interactive experiences that drive brand awareness and loyalty. As a result, more research is needed to provide reliable and accurate data on Metaverse in marketing. This study aims to assess the challenges and opportunities, thus building a frame of reference on metaverse in marketing.

Pooja Kulkarni, Vishwakarma University, Pune, India
Babasaheb Jadhav, Global Business School and Research Centre, Dr. D.Y. Patil Vidyapeeth, Pune, India
Ashish Kulkarni, Dr. D.Y. Patil B-School, Pune, India
Alex Khang, Global Research Institute of Technology and Engineering, USA
Sagar Kulkarni, MIT World Peace University, Pune, India

Metaverse is a virtual world based on AR and VR. The word Metaverse comprises "meta," which means beyond, and "verse," which means universe, which combines world beyond imagination. Today's Z generation wants everything over the tip of their fingers, even if they don't want to step out for purchasing groceries or daily household items and hang out with buddies. The Metaverse can provide a solution to this problem. Without stepping out of their home, they can virtually cheat and chat with friends and have a party with food and drink by sitting at their own homes by purchasing through virtual currency, own virtual assets including house, jewelry, etc. by creating their avatar using AR and VR technology. The use of blockchain technology solves the decentralization issue, maintenance of cryptocurrency, and other applications. Hence, the use of blockchain in the Metaverse ecosystem can benefit financial, non-financial, and privacy issues that may occur due to the described framework of the Metaverse ecosystem.

Nilamadhab Mishra, VIT Bhopal University, India
Basanta Kumar Padhi, Balasore College of Engineering and Technology, India
Banaja Basini Rath, Balasore College of Engineering and Technology, India

Mobile cloud computing (MCC), which combines mobile computing and cloud computing, has become one of the industry's most common terms and a major topic of discussion in the IT world. Mobile clients are becoming popular clients for consuming any web resources, particularly web services (WS), as mobile network infrastructures improve. However, there are problems connecting mobile devices to existing WS. This research focuses on three of the following challenges: loss of connection, bandwidth, latency, and limited resources. This research proposes to develop and implement a cross-platform architecture for connecting mobile devices to the web. The architecture includes mobile service clients that work on any platform and a Metaverse ecosystem that makes it easier for mobile clients and WS to talk to each other. Finally, the Metaverse ecosystem can be deployed on the cloud metaverse platform, which may create more immersive and dynamic virtual worlds that are accessible to a wider audience by utilizing the power of the cloud.

Chapter 13
    Özen Özer, Kırklareli University, Turkey
    Biswadip Basu Mallik, Institute of Engineering and Management, Kolkata, India
    Gunjan Mukherjee, Brainware University, India

Linear algebra is a branch of mathematics that is widely used throughout science and engineering. Linear algebra includes arithmetic operations with notation sharing. We can be able to have a better understanding of machine learning algorithms only after having a good understanding of linear algebra. Sometimes, machine learning might be pure linear algebra, involving many matrix operations; a dataset itself is often represented as a matrix. Linear algebra is used in data pre-processing, data transformations, and model evaluation. In this chapter, the basic importance of linear algebra has been discussed, and the close liaison of the subject with current research domain in machine learning and data science has been explored in the light of application of the same in solving some critical issues.

Chapter 14
    Chitra Devi Nagarajan, Vellore Institute of Technology, Chennai, India
    Mohd Afjal, Vellore Institute of Technology, Vellore, India

Blockchain use in various industries improves the standard of services provided to end users and benefits society as a whole. The chapter discusses the innovative use of blockchain technology in the financial sector, including know your customer, cross-border payments, clearing and settlements in the insurance sector, trade finance platforms, and digital identity verification. On the other hand, while blockchain technology has the potential to be a very competitive and "imaginative" technology, it is important to address concerns with its implementation, such as the cost of adoption, energy consumption, cybersecurity, interoperability, scalability, latency, and so on. The findings of this study will give the required information to the government, decision-makers, and consumers to help them understand the applications and difficulties of implementing blockchain technology in the financial sector.

Chapter 15
    N. Ambika, St. Francis College, India

The work centers around a connected viewpoint intended for the problematic information interface between blockchain and IoT for further developing information provenance and uprightness. The examination draws on the author's industry-based experience driving a two-year AUD 1.5 million undertaking that elaborates on the coordination of IoT and blockchain to follow and safeguard the legitimacy of Australian meat in the quickly developing Chinese market. The plan drove the system to direct the improvement of the food production network project as a particular mix of IoT and blockchain to a specific food store network context. The presentation can change the prophet's personality. The information legitimacy rehearses instead of looking for the unadulterated fact of the matter and crypto financial aspects. The suggestion uses a different methodology to enhance the traceability of the product. It uses a Merkle tree to generate hash keys. It detects security breaches by 2.93% and improves client satisfaction by 9.96% compared to previous work.

The emergence of Metaverse has presented new opportunities and possibilities for the advancement of intelligent libraries. However, it also brings new challenges to the professional competencies of librarians. This chapter examines the potential of Metaverse as an enabling technology for intelligent libraries, focusing on how it can be used to drive innovation and improve library services. The chapter also delves into the advantages and underlying technologies of Metaverse, as well as its theoretical foundations for application in libraries. It is argued that Metaverse and its related technologies are crucial for transforming libraries into fully intelligent ones, and that the concept of Metaverse can also provide benefits for library collection management, reading spaces, cultural promotion, reading experiences, and special user services. Intelligent libraries must seize this opportunity to create a new form of immersive experience and achieve breakthroughs in their digital transformations, driven by the diverse technologies of Metaverse.

People who have difficulty hearing can use speech recognition software to communicate differently. The task is audio-visual speech recognition for better lip-reading comprehension. Audio speech recognition is the process of turning spoken words into text. The neural network model is trained using the Librispeech dataset. The input sound signal creates sound frames with a stride of 10 milliseconds and a window size of 20-25 milliseconds. It uses audio as the input, and feature extraction extracts information from features. A visual speech recognition system automatically recognizes spoken words by observing how the speaker moves their lips. The suggestion considers body language to understand the communicator's spoken words, increasing interpretation accuracy by 5.05%.

Facial gesture recognition (FGR) is widely regarded as an effective means of displaying and communicating human emotions. This chapter provides a comprehensive review of FGR as a biometric marker technology for detecting facial emotions, encompassing the identification of the six basic facial expressions: happiness, sadness, anger, surprise, fear, and disgust. FGR utilizes advanced algorithms to accurately identify and classify facial emotional states from images, audio, or video captured through various devices such as cameras, laptops, mobile phones, or digital signage systems. Given the importance of accuracy, computational efficiency, and mitigating overfitting, this review also discusses the diverse range of methods and models developed in facial expression recognition research. These advancements aim to enhance the accuracy of the models while minimizing computational resource requirements and addressing overfitting challenges encountered in previous studies.

This chapter presents a concise bibliometric analysis of the intersection between artificial intelligence (AI) and smart vehicles. Through systematic literature review and analysis, key research trends and themes were identified, including AI-driven autonomous driving, intelligent transportation systems, machine learning algorithms, and human-machine interaction. The analysis highlights the growing interest in the field and identifies influential research works, contributors, and collaborative networks. This bibliometric analysis provides valuable insights into the research landscape and offers directions for future studies in AI and smart vehicles.

This chapter introduces data privacy and its significance in the metaverse to the readers. It introduces several data privacy policies, privacy enhancing techniques (PET), and discusses some existing literatures on data privacy issues in the metaverse. This chapter seeks to educate readers on the various methods and technologies available to protect personal and sensitive data throughout the entire data lifecycle (collection, storage, use, and transmission). In addition, it discusses how these privacy-preserving techniques can be used to secure metaverse data and describes the most recent findings from studies conducted on the PET methods to improve these practices. The chapter also includes suggestions for additional research and development that will help readers take the first step toward enhancing data privacy techniques in the metaverse or incorporating existing technologies into privacy-enhancing metaverse applications.

Large-scale electronic databases are being maintained by businesses and can be accessed via the internet or intranet. Employing data mining techniques, significant information was extracted from the data. The privacy of the data is inherently at risk while data mining operations are being carried out. All users shouldn't have access to the private information stored in the database. Methods for protecting privacy have been suggested in the literature. Algorithms used in privacy-preserving data mining (PPDM) on private data are unknown even to the algorithm operator. Personal information about users and data on their collective behaviour are the two main aspects of privacy preservation. The majority of privacy-preserving techniques rely on reducing the level of granularity used to represent the data. Although privacy is improved, information is lost as a result. As a result, with PPDM, there is a trade-off between privacy and information loss. Effective methods that don't undermine the security defences are needed.

Visually challenged people form a large population segment, with estimates starting from tens of millions to hundreds of millions worldwide. Integration into society is a major and current goal for them. A substantial attempt has been taken into ensuring a healthcare system. To aid visually impaired people to live a usual life, several guidance system strategies are created. These systems are oftentimes created for a single purpose. The internet has become a necessary means for people to acquire knowledge and information. Today, unfortunately, the advantages of this mighty tool are still away from visually impaired people, and they find difficulty in accessing the web. Over the years, people built different technologies and tools that can help the visually impaired in reaching out to the outside world.

Chapter 23

Security in the Metaverse is a critical concern as virtual worlds continue to expand and evolve. With an increasing number of users engaging in immersive experiences, safeguarding personal information, assets, and digital identities becomes paramount. Robust security measures are essential to protect against hacking, identity theft, and fraudulent activities. Technologies like blockchain and encryption play a crucial role in ensuring secure transactions, while identity verification systems help authenticate users. Additionally, monitoring and moderation tools are necessary to combat harassment, hate speech, and inappropriate content. As the Metaverse becomes more integrated into our lives, a comprehensive approach to security is vital to foster trust and safeguard the virtual realm. This chapter aims to provide an overview of cybersecurity in Metaverse. It discussed the various cyber stacks in detail along with solutions to manage these attacks. The authors have also discussed the various challenges in securing metaverse, and possible future research directions.

Smart cities have benefited greatly from the quick development of information technology, such as cloud computing, sensors, and the IoT. Smart cities improve living services and analyze massive amounts of data, which increases privacy and security concerns. But managing security and privacy issues is crucial for a smart city that encourages businesses to adopt new computing paradigms. In recent years, there has been a proliferation of literature on security and privacy, covering topics like end-to-end security, reliable data acquisition, transmission, and processing, legal service provisioning, and privacy of personal data, as well as the application of bio inspired computing techniques to system design and operation. Effective computing systems have been developed by utilizing bio-inspired computing approaches for intelligent decision support. The indicator-based threat detection system with BAAA algorithm is the quickest and most efficient way to scope an environment after observation, and its usefulness is greatly influenced by the adversary rate of change.

Preface

The rapid advancement of technology in recent years has paved the way for the emergence of the metaverse, a virtual reality space where individuals interact with digital representations of the real world and other users. This concept, popularized by science fiction, is becoming a tangible reality as advancements in artificial intelligence (AI) continue to shape and redefine our digital experiences. AI-based technologies are playing a pivotal role in unlocking the full potential of the metaverse, enabling immersive and intelligent interactions that were once only a dream.

The metaverse is characterized by its vastness, interconnectedness, and ability to seamlessly blend the virtual and physical realms. It offers limitless possibilities for communication, collaboration, entertainment, education, and more. However, the true power of the metaverse lies in the integration of AI, which enables intelligent agents, personalized experiences, and dynamic content creation.

AI technologies such as virtual assistants, natural language processing, computer vision, generative models, and personalized recommender systems are driving the evolution of the metaverse. Virtual assistants and intelligent agents enhance user interactions by understanding and responding to voice commands, providing contextual information, and offering personalized recommendations.

Natural language processing enables users to communicate with the metaverse through speech and text, breaking down language barriers and enabling real-time language translation. Computer vision technologies enhance visual experiences by enabling object recognition, augmented reality overlays, and facial recognition capabilities.

Generative models, powered by AI, facilitate the creation of virtual worlds, avatars, and dynamic content. This allows for procedurally generated environments, personalized avatars, and interactive narratives that adapt to user preferences and behaviors. Personalized experiences and recommender systems leverage AI algorithms to deliver tailored content, recommendations, and adaptive interfaces based on individual user profiles and preferences.

As we delve into the era of the metaverse, it is essential to explore the applications of AI in various domains. From virtual collaboration and communication to entertainment and gaming, education and training, healthcare and well-being, and business and commerce, AI is revolutionizing these sectors within the metaverse. These applications bring forth new opportunities for innovation, creativity, and enhanced human-machine interaction.

However, the integration of AI and the metaverse also raises significant societal implications and challenges. Privacy and security concerns, inequalities in accessibility, ethical considerations, and potential economic disruptions and job transformations must be carefully addressed as AI and the metaverse become more intertwined.

This book aims to delve into the AI-based technologies and applications that are shaping the metaverse. It will explore the potential, challenges, and opportunities that arise from this integration, ultimately envisioning the future prospects and implications of AI in the era of the metaverse.

There are many metaverse enabling technologies discussed below:

Virtual Assistants and Intelligent Agents: One of the key AI-based technologies driving the evolution of the metaverse is virtual assistants and intelligent agents. These agents enhance user interactions by providing assistance, information, and personalized experiences.

Powered by AI, virtual assistants leverage voice recognition, natural language understanding, and contextual understanding to interpret user queries and provide relevant responses. They can perform tasks such as answering questions, scheduling appointments, recommending content, and even simulating realistic conversations. Virtual assistants enable users to interact with the metaverse in a more natural and intuitive manner, making it easier to navigate and access its vast resources.

Virtual assistants like Siri, Alexa, and Google Assistant have already gained popularity in our daily lives, but their integration into the metaverse takes their capabilities to a whole new level. In the metaverse, virtual assistants can guide users through virtual environments, provide real-time information and recommendations, and even facilitate social interactions by simulating conversations with other users. They act as intelligent guides and companions, making the metaverse more accessible and engaging for users.

Natural Language Processing (NLP): NLP is another crucial AI technology that plays a significant role in the metaverse. NLP allows computers to understand, interpret, and generate human language, enabling seamless communication between users and the metaverse.

Language translation is a prominent application of NLP in the metaverse, breaking down language barriers and facilitating global interactions. Users can communicate with others in different languages, and NLP algorithms can translate their conversations in real-time, making cross-cultural collaboration and communication possible.

Sentiment analysis is another application of NLP in the metaverse. By analyzing the sentiment expressed in user interactions, the metaverse can adapt and tailor experiences based on individual emotional states. This can enhance the overall user experience by providing content and interactions that are more aligned with users' emotional needs and preferences.

Chatbots, powered by NLP, provide automated and interactive conversational experiences in the metaverse. These chatbots can simulate realistic conversations and provide support and information to users. They can assist users in navigating the metaverse, answering questions, and providing recommendations. Chatbots enhance the metaverse's interactivity and accessibility, providing a personalized and responsive user experience.

Computer Vision: Computer vision technologies are instrumental in enhancing visual experiences within the metaverse. Object recognition algorithms enable the metaverse to identify and interact with virtual and real-world objects, enriching users' interactions and enabling seamless integration between the physical and virtual realms. With computer vision, the metaverse can recognize objects in users' surroundings and provide relevant virtual overlays or interactions.

Augmented reality (AR) is another application of computer vision in the metaverse. By overlaying virtual elements on the real world, AR enhances users' perception and interaction with their surroundings. The metaverse can use computer vision to precisely detect and track objects and surfaces in real-time, allowing virtual objects to interact with the physical environment realistically. This opens up possibilities for immersive AR experiences in various domains, such as gaming, education, and commerce, within the metaverse.

Facial recognition capabilities powered by computer vision enhance social interactions within the metaverse. Users can create personalized avatars that reflect their real-time facial expressions and emotions. This adds a layer of authenticity and emotional connection to virtual interactions, making the metaverse more immersive and engaging.

Generative Models and Content Creation: Generative models, such as generative adversarial networks (GANs) and variational autoencoders (VAEs), are revolutionizing content creation in the metaverse. These models can generate realistic and diverse virtual worlds, objects, and characters, enabling dynamic and ever-evolving metaverse experiences. Procedural generation techniques allow for the creation.

AI and Metaverse are playing a significant role in a variety of application domains, discussed below:

Virtual Collaboration and Communication: AI-powered technologies are transforming virtual collaboration and communication within the metaverse. Virtual meetings in the metaverse provide immersive and interactive experiences that go beyond traditional video conferencing. AI algorithms enable features like real-time language translation, sentiment analysis, and gesture recognition, making communication between users from different backgrounds more seamless.

Intelligent agents can assist with scheduling, note-taking, and facilitating discussions, enhancing productivity and collaboration in virtual workspaces. Furthermore, telepresence technologies allow users to project their virtual avatars into the metaverse, enabling a sense of presence and facilitating more natural interactions.

Entertainment and Gaming: The entertainment and gaming industry is one of the key beneficiaries of AI in the metaverse. AI algorithms enhance gaming experiences by generating dynamic and adaptive content. AI-powered game characters can exhibit realistic behaviors and respond intelligently to player actions, creating more immersive and challenging gameplay.

AI-generated narratives enable personalized storytelling, where the plot and outcomes adapt based on player choices and preferences. Additionally, AI-powered content curation and recommendation systems deliver personalized gaming experiences, suggesting games, challenges, and virtual events that align with individual player preferences.

Education and Training: AI-based technologies in the metaverse have the potential to revolutionize education and training. Virtual classrooms offer immersive learning experiences, where students can interact with virtual objects and simulations to enhance understanding and engagement. AI-powered intelligent tutors provide personalized guidance and adaptive learning paths, catering to individual learning styles and pace.

Moreover, virtual reality and augmented reality technologies integrated into the metaverse can create realistic and interactive training simulations for various industries, such as healthcare, aviation, and engineering. AI algorithms can analyze learner performance data to provide real-time feedback and optimize learning experiences.

Healthcare and Well-Being: AI-enabled healthcare services in the metaverse have the potential to improve access to medical resources, facilitate remote consultations, and enhance mental well-being. Telemedicine platforms within the metaverse enable users to connect with healthcare professionals virtually, reducing geographical barriers and improving healthcare accessibility. AI algorithms can assist in diagnosing medical conditions, analyzing medical images, and providing personalized treatment recommendations. Additionally, the metaverse can offer virtual environments for mental health support, providing immersive experiences for therapy, stress relief, and relaxation.

Business and Commerce: AI-powered technologies are transforming business and commerce within the metaverse. Virtual marketplaces within the metaverse enable users to buy and sell virtual assets, digital goods, and services. AI algorithms can facilitate personalized advertising by analyzing user preferences and behaviors, delivering targeted and relevant advertisements within the metaverse.

Customer analytics in the metaverse provide valuable insights into user behavior, enabling businesses to optimize their products, services, and marketing strategies. AI-powered virtual shopping assistants can assist users in finding products, making recommendations, and enhancing the overall shopping experience.

The applications of AI in the metaverse extend beyond the mentioned domains, with potential in areas such as social networking, travel and exploration, art and creativity, and environmental simulations.

As AI continues to advance, new applications and use cases will emerge, further enriching the metaverse experience and expanding its possibilities. However, as with any technology, there are challenges and considerations that need to be addressed to ensure ethical, inclusive, and responsible integration of AI in the metaverse.

There are many societal implications and challenges of AI in the metaverse, presented below:

Privacy and Security Concerns: The integration of AI in the metaverse raises significant privacy and security concerns. As AI-powered technologies gather and analyze vast amounts of user data, there is a risk of unauthorized access, data breaches, and misuse of personal information. Safeguarding user privacy becomes crucial, as the metaverse collects data on user behaviors, preferences, and interactions.

Striking a balance between personalized experiences and protecting user privacy is a challenge that must be addressed to build trust in the metaverse ecosystem. Robust security measures, data encryption, and transparent data usage policies are essential to ensure the privacy and security of users within the metaverse.

Inequalities in Accessibility: The metaverse has the potential to amplify existing inequalities if not addressed properly. Access to the metaverse requires internet connectivity, hardware devices, and technical literacy, which may exclude individuals from marginalized communities or those with limited resources. It is important to bridge the digital divide and ensure equitable access to the metaverse.

Efforts should be made to provide affordable and accessible hardware devices, internet connectivity, and educational resources to underserved populations. Moreover, designing user interfaces and experiences that are inclusive and accommodating to diverse abilities and needs is crucial to prevent exclusion and ensure equal participation in the metaverse.

Ethical Considerations: AI technologies in the metaverse raise ethical considerations that need careful attention. Bias in AI algorithms can perpetuate societal inequalities and discrimination. When AI algorithms make decisions or provide recommendations, they must be designed and trained to be fair, transparent, and accountable.

Transparent AI systems can provide explanations for their decisions, allowing users to understand how their data is being used and enabling accountability. Additionally, AI algorithms should be continuously monitored and evaluated to detect and mitigate bias. Ethical frameworks and guidelines for AI development and deployment in the metaverse must be established to ensure responsible and ethical use of AI technologies.

Economic Disruptions and Job Transformations: The integration of AI in the metaverse may lead to economic disruptions and job transformations. While AI technologies can automate certain tasks and improve efficiency, they may also replace human labor in certain industries. This can result in job displacement and require the workforce to acquire new skills to adapt to the changing job market.

To mitigate the negative impacts, reskilling and upskilling programs should be implemented to enable individuals to transition into new roles that complement AI technologies. Additionally, policies and regulations that address the social and economic implications of AI integration should be developed to ensure a fair and inclusive labor market within the metaverse.

Cognitive and Psychological Effects: The immersive and interactive nature of the metaverse, coupled with AI technologies, may have cognitive and psychological effects on users. Spending prolonged periods in virtual environments may lead to decreased real-world social interactions and potential addiction to the metaverse. It is important to promote digital well-being and find a balance between virtual and physical experiences. User education and awareness programs can provide guidance on responsible and healthy metaverse usage, promoting mindful engagement and maintaining a healthy lifestyle.

Misinformation and Manipulation: AI-powered technologies in the metaverse can also be susceptible to misinformation and manipulation. The spread of fake news, deep fakes, and AI-generated content may lead to the erosion of trust and the distortion of reality within the metaverse.

Robust content moderation mechanisms and fact-checking processes are essential to combat misinformation and ensure the integrity of information within the metaverse. User education on critical thinking, media literacy, and responsible content consumption is crucial to empower users to discern between authentic and manipulated content.

To bring advanced AI-Based technologies and applications in the era of the metaverse, the following topics will be introduced in this book:

Chapter 1: Artificial Intelligence (AI)-Centric Model in Metaverse Ecosystems

Metaverse is a 3D concept that facilitates the technology to map or draw virtual avatars parallels and acts as a bridge between the users and the digital world. It can be understood as the virtual cyberspace which mixes up the real and digital world and converges the two by providing the facility of internet and other technologies. It can be understood as an infinite universe where communities of people can collaborate together and enjoy the mechanism of augmented reality, virtual reality, extended reality, online life and much more.

Artificial Intelligence based theories and equipment along with deep learning concepts are needed for metaverse's better development to provide more powerful features of computation, perception, interaction, cooperation, reconstruction, virtual identities and assets, life similar experiences, dialogues and other different features.

Although the AI concepts being used in Metaverse has to acquire and understand more of improvisational and human like qualities to thrive, it still remains a software program that relies a lot on real human interactions to achieve successful operations and thus even the AI thriving in Metaverse will require to learn about how efficiently it could improvise itself and be more and more human-like, thus it needs real people to succeed.

A basic metaverse platform consists of seven layers, including infrastructure, human interface, decentralization, spatial computing, creator economy, discovery, and experience. AI algorithms and techniques are used in each layer to make the processing easier, favorable, and user friendly. Infrastructure provides the different options of infrastructure available, while human interface directs to various devices and technologies. Decentralization provides technologies like blockchain, AI agents, edge computing, spatial computing, creator economy, discovery, and experience. AI algorithms and techniques are used in each layer to make the processing easier, favorable, and user friendly.

Chapter 2: Enabling the Future of Manufacturing – Integration of Robotics and IoT to Smart Factory Infrastructure in Industry 4.0

Smart factory infrastructure forms the backbone of Industry 4.0, providing the necessary framework for integrating robotics, IoT, and other advanced technologies. This infrastructure encompasses a network of interconnected devices, including sensors, actuators, control systems, and data storage facilities. It facilitates the collection, storage, and analysis of vast amounts of data generated by various manufacturing processes, enabling real-time monitoring, control, and optimization.

The integration of robotics, IoT, and smart factory infrastructure in Industry 4.0 enables manufacturers to achieve greater flexibility, customization, and responsiveness to market demands. By harnessing the power of data-driven insights and automation, manufacturers can optimize production schedules, adapt to changing customer preferences, and efficiently manage inventory. Furthermore, the ability to quickly reconfigure production lines and adapt to new product designs is enhanced, enabling rapid innovation and reduced time to market.

This convergence of technologies empowers manufacturers to achieve higher levels of efficiency, productivity, and flexibility while driving innovation. By embracing these advancements, manufacturers can position themselves at the forefront of the evolving manufacturing landscape, capitalizing on the opportunities presented by the digital age.

Chapter 3: How the Metaverse Can Leverage the Business World

Metaverse is a popular concept nowadays. It is recognized as the next generation of the internet, comprising a virtual, interconnected reality seamlessly connected to the physical world. It combines virtual reality (VR), augmented reality (AR), and mixed reality (MR) to create a parallel reality where people can work, communicate, and play. The metaverse promotes innovative entrepreneurship by causing radical transformations in various sectors, such as marketing, training, education, retail, and sales. It provides technologies and platforms for users to interact in real-time, the potential for revolutionizing the business sector.

Traditionally, the metaverse definitions and user descriptions were limited to their links to computers and video games. However, when Facebook rebranded to Meta Platforms, the concept gained more public attention and has increasingly been embraced by business leaders and target customers. Brands are realizing metaverse technologies' potential and leveraging them to improve efficiency and competitive advantage. For instance, the metaverse helps improve communication and interaction between brands and their customers through virtual worlds. Since users tend to be immersed in these experiences, brands can leverage this opportunity to promote their products or services as long as they match users' interests.

Metaverse provides experiences beyond what can be achieved through conventional internet tools. For instance, while e-commerce allows customers to buy products online, the metaverse enables them to test and try them out before completing the transaction. For example, an internet user within the metaverse world can try different types of clothes or makeup on their avatars. They can change colors and designs before making a purchasing decision to ensure that they buy a product that matches their desires. Similarly, a car manufacturer can hold a virtual launching event allowing potential customers to test drive the new car model in a controlled virtual environment. These opportunities create an immersed customer experience and may lead to higher satisfaction and loyalty and increased sales.

Chapter 4: AI-Aided Teaching Model in Education 5.0

Education has undergone profound changes as a result of the widespread use of digital technologies and the proliferation of connected information networks. Better tools are becoming available to facilitate the more complex activities that have traditionally been a part of the educational process.

Giving students timely feedback like this helps them assess their progress and learn more efficiently. Technology's contribution to bettering the teaching and learning process is growing in significance as educational models adapt to new learning technologies. One of the most pressing concerns of the last decade has been the use of technology to improve the teaching and learning process and numerous learning management systems (LMS) that accomplish this goal keep being proposed to do so in a variety of ways.

With the rise of mobile and social media, it is essential for language instructors to integrate IT into their classrooms to keep students engaged and improve the quality and efficiency of the learning process. An empirical research was conducted utilizing AI chatbots like "My Virtual Dream Friend", "John English Bot", and "ChatGPT" to teach undergraduate students about "self-introduction" as well as self-paced learning of industry-based skills in not only foreign language but also other classes.

Chapter 5: An Innovative Teaching Model – The Potential of Metaverse for English Learning

A "Metaverse" is a different kind of virtual reality. It is a combination of the Latin word for "world" (universe) with the Greek prefix "meta," which signifies "beyond" or "virtual." Metaverse is defined the "digitized globe" as a new world made possible by electronic methods like mobile phones and the internet. There was a lot of research and development done to create a Metaverse once the concept was initially introduced.

A premier Metaverse research group, the Acceleration Studies Foundation (ASF) unveiled the Metaverse road map at the Metaverse Road Summit (2006). It defined the term "Metaverse" and its four variations and proposed seeing it as the point where "real life" and "virtual reality" meet. Here, we see how the digital world is being integrated with the physical one, and how regular activities and the economy are being brought online.

Since the Metaverse is rapidly being integrated into modern life, some applications have been used in the classroom. Therefore, it is crucial to get knowledge of the many forms of Metaverses and their potential educational applications. Many researchers and educators have already considered the implications of virtual worlds, or "Metaverses," for the not foreign language classroom but also other multidisciplinary classes.

Chapter 6: AR/VR Technologies in the Metaverse Ecosystem

Imagine living in a virtual environment where millions of individuals can communicate among themselves, explore, shop, and have a comfortable life on their couches. In this universe, the computer displays have transformed portals into a physical, three-dimensional digital realm that is more superior and expansive than the real world.

Digital avatars that are representations of us roam between experiences while carrying our identities. Putting the sensationalism aside, this is known as the "metaverse". The metaverse is an idea that describes a virtual universe composed of a couple of interconnected virtual spaces or worlds. It is an imaginative immersion in which the digital and bodily worlds converge, creating a widespread and interconnected network of virtual environments that can be accessed globally. It can boost employment opportunities by supplementing individuals with practical training and ensures that the Individuals with disabilities can also be incorporated in this marathon of growth by leveraging these technologies.

Chapter 7: Augmented Reality Applications and Usage Examples in the Metaverse Age

The notion of a "metaverse" links the real world and the internet. A virtual world that closely matches its actual counterpart is what the Metaverse aims to create. The objective is to create a social interaction that combines gaming, simulation, and social media to develop a made-up world that is similar to the actual one. The creation of the metaverse is the aim of Facebook and other more decentralized organizations like Decenterland. Quantum computing will without a doubt contribute to the development of the metaverse. By employing quantum randomness, developers can be assured that the laws used to protect the metaverse are not being used dishonestly.

With the usage of video, augmented reality, and virtual reality, consumers may connect more deeply inside a digital world attributable to Web 3.0. Regardless of where they are in the real world, users may interact electronically, travel, and share information. In the midst of the biggest cryptographic migration in history, quantum-resistant security approaches are without a doubt at the forefront of protecting the internet of the future.

Quantum computing has a wide range of significant applications that may ultimately enter the metaverse. To safeguard transactions from algorithms like Shor's Algorithm, it could be required to deploy quantum resistant technology. Consider about blockchains that can withstand quantum effects. Now that the metaverse blue touch-paper has been illuminated, businesses will be looking for tools and technologies they can use that will offer them a distinct advantage as they try to comprehend Facebook's news. Regardless of what happens to the Metaverse, it appears that the world's technical enterprises are now focused on this new paradigm and potential internet expansion.

Chapter 8: Metaverse-Enabling IoT Technology for a Futuristic Healthcare System

The Internet of Things (IoT) and the Metaverse are converging, bringing together the virtual world's immersive and interactive capabilities with the physical world's huge network of interconnected objects. Connecting digital content and physical information is made possible with the incorporation of IoT into the Metaverse.

IoT devices in a Metaverse-enabled IoT ecosystem can exchange data with virtual worlds in real time, resulting in richer, more interactive experiences. Wearable gadgets, for instance, can collect and send biometric data to virtual health assistants, letting virtual doctors keep tabs on their patients' health and make tailored recommendations. In the same way, Internet of Things (IoT) sensors built into smart healthcare infrastructure can share in-the-moment information about the status of individual pieces of equipment, the flow of patients, and the use of resources to enhance healthcare delivery in the Metaverse.

Incorporating Internet of Things (IoT) technologies into the Metaverse paves the way for more life-like and contextually aware simulated environments. It improves user interactions and opens up new opportunities for the healthcare, entertainment, education, collaboration, and other industries present in the Metaverse by bridging the gap between the real and virtual worlds.

Chapter 9: Effects of Quantum Technology on the Metaverse

This research paper explores the impact of quantum technology on the metaverse, revolutionizing performance and security. Quantum computing enables faster processing, advanced simulations, and sophisticated AI interactions.

Integrating it with the metaverse poses technical challenges and requires addressing ethical considerations. Quantum tech benefits blockchain-based cryptocurrencies, enabling decentralized ownership and secure transactions. Regulatory frameworks are needed. Future internet technologies like 5G, edge computing, and IoT play a vital role, providing high-speed connectivity and enhanced immersion. Overcoming challenges such as limited resources and interdisciplinary expertise is crucial. Addressing ethical concerns and establishing standards and regulations are necessary.

This chapter aims to understand quantum's effects, develop strategies, and foster collaboration for a responsible and equitable integration in the metaverse, shaping a transformative digital future.

Chapter 10: Metaverse in Marketing – Challenges and Opportunities

The metaverse comprises various technologies, such as augmented reality (AR) and virtual reality (VR), facilitating multimodal interactions with digital products, virtual settings, and people. Although the concept gained much attention in 2020-2021, the term was coined by Neal Stephenson in his 1992 novel Snow Crash. Marketers are exploring opportunities to integrate metaverse in marketing. Scientists indicate that the social dimension represents the actual value of the metaverse.

In this topic, certain activities that people engage in the internet alone can be improved through metaverse technologies. For example, shopping in a virtual store can be better than shopping on a website since the customer can use the avatar to try on the products and add customizations before making the purchase decisions. In addition, companies can leverage these innovations to create interactive experiences such as virtual events and product demonstrations. As a result, metaverse can potentially improve customer experience and satisfaction, which are critical in marketing.

Metaverse provides multiple opportunities that can help improve marketing initiatives. For instance, it provides large amounts of data and insights that can be used to optimize marketing strategies. Brands can observe user behavior and engagement in real-time, enabling them to gather data to improve their marketing campaigns and adjust the messaging.

Chapter 11: Blockchain Applications in the Metaverse Ecosystem

Metaverse is a virtual world based on AR & VR. The word Metaverse comprises Meta means beyond, and Verse means universe which combines world beyond imagination. Today's Z generation wants everything over the tip of their fingers, even if they don't want to step out for purchasing groceries or daily household items and hang out with buddies. The Metaverse can provide a solution to this problem, without stepping out of their home, they can virtually cheat and chat with friends and have a party with food and drink by sitting at their own homes by purchasing through virtual currency, own virtual assets including house, Jewelry, etc. by creating their Avatar using AR & VR technology.

Looking towards this massive use of Metaverse, in reality, arises many issues and concerns like feasibility, privacy, user safety, social issues, etc. In addition, if we figure out and store this entire data in a database like SQL or No SQL leads to many additional problems due to the decentralization of data and involvement of yourself in different activities at the same time.

The use of blockchain technology solves the decentralization issue, maintenance of cryptocurrency, and other applications. Hence, the use of blockchain in the Metaverse ecosystem can benefit financial, non-financial, and privacy issues that may occur due to the described framework of the Metaverse ecosystem.

Chapter 12: Mobile Cloud Computing Framework for an Android-Based Metaverse Ecosystem Platform

Virtual worlds, or the metaverse, are become easier for the general public to access as technology develops. The term "metaverse" describes a virtual environment where users can interact, communicate, and take part in a variety of activities in a 3D setting. Cloud computing is one of the main technologies that has made this possible.

The development of cloud computing has made it possible to create and maintain virtual worlds on a much bigger scale. Developers may create more immersive and dynamic virtual worlds that are accessible to a wider audience by utilizing the power of the cloud. In this blog article, we'll look at how cloud computing is opening up the metaverse and its advantages for both users and developers.

The combination of mobile computing with cloud computing (CC) has resulted in the development of a more advanced technological strategy known as mobile cloud computing (MCC). MCC can be defined as nothing more than cloud computing with mobile devices acting as thin clients. To support mobile clients using Web services, this research paper suggests a mobile cloud computing architecture that makes use of a cloud-hosted metaverse ecosystem (cloud services). The architecture offers a framework for personal service mash-ups for mobile clients and improves the interaction between mobile clients and Web services.

Chapter 13: Application of Mathematical Model in Linear Algebra to Metaverse Ecosystem

Linear algebra is the branch of mathematics concerning linear equations, linear functions and their representations through matrices and vector spaces. It helps us to understand geometrical terms in higher dimensions, and execute mathematical operations on them. By definition, algebra deals in primarily with scalars (one-dimensional entities), but Linear Algebra has vectors and matrices (entities which possess two or more dimensional components) to deal with linear equations and functions. Linear Algebra is the heart to almost all areas of mathematics like geometry and functional analysis. Its concepts are crucial prerequisite for understanding the theory behind Data Science and Machine learning. It is necessary to understand how the different algorithms really work.

Data science is the field of study that combines domain expertise, programming skills, and knowledge of mathematics and statistics to extract meaningful perception from data. Data science practitioners apply machine learning algorithms to numbers, text, images, video, audio, and more to produce artificial intelligence systems to perform tasks that regularly be in need of human intelligence. In turn, these systems generate insights which analysts and business users can translate into appreciable business value. Mathematics in data science is playing very crucial role as this branch is providing not only the data analysis but the data manipulation too.

Machine learning is the branch of artificial intelligence and is based on the principle that the systems learn from data and pattern, identifies the several patterns and can be able to make decisions with the nominal human intervention. Machine learning is chiefly based on the data analysis and so is connected to the data science. The machine learning involves some tasks, set of experiences and performance. The main objective of the machine learning trend is to enhance the performance of any tasks by means of the experiences. In the machine learning trends, multiple inputs are read and analyzed statistically to produce the output. So machine learning introduced the automation in performing the decision making process on the data received and siphon the same for the purpose of modelling.

Chapter 14: Innovative Applications and Implementation Challenges of Blockchain Technology in the Financial Sector

A new era of business models is dawning with the advent of digital technology, and the financial sector has been exploring better ways of increasing transaction speed and efficiency to improve customer service. Easy access to digital technology through Financial Technology companies (Fintechs) has transformed the entire banking and financial industry.

As digital technology has increasingly been used over the past few decades, financial institutions and banks have embraced the adaptation of technology to meet the fast-changing expectations of their customers. There are, however, challenges that need to be overcome for technology to be effectively implemented. Banks and financial institutions have many concerns regarding the adaptation of new technology, including high transaction costs, intermediary roles, cyber fraud, and regulatory compliance, the use of big data, artificial intelligence, and customer retention.

The profitability of banks and financial institutions is determined by the implementation of digital technology that enables them to provide better services and meet customer demands. A bank or fintech company that is not able to comply with these standards is unlikely to sustain its profitability over the long term.

The sustainable financial sector is an engine for the development of an economy because it encourages balanced, and inclusion and facilitates the growth of the commercial sector. Adopting and integrating new digital technologies such as the Internet of Things (IoT), 5G networks, artificial intelligence (AI), big data, and cloud computing at the right time is crucial to enhancing customer service and operations and, in turn, ensuring sustainable profitability of banks and fintech companies.

Chapter 15: Enhancing Traceability in Food Supply Chains Using Blockchain and IoT Technologies

The capabilities to sense, actuate, and communicate over the Internet are provided by a collection of technology. It is known as the Internet of Things. These technologies range from Radio Frequency Identification to Wireless Sensor Networks. The Internet of Things is crucial to transforming conventional cities into smart cities, electrical grids into smart grids, and homes into smart homes—and this is just the beginning. The Internet of Things (IoT) depicts a world in which everything is connected and can exchange measured data with one another. Many areas use the IoT solutions to improve production and digitize industries.

The mechanism that enables transactions to be verified by a group of unreliable actors is called the blockchain. A distributed, immutable, transparent, secure, and auditable ledger is provided by it. Access to all transactions that have taken place since the system's initial transaction is made available to anyone, and the blockchain can be verified and compiled at any time. Information is organized by the blockchain protocol in a chain of blocks, with each block storing a set of Bitcoin transactions performed at a specific time. A reference to the previous block links blocks together to form a chain.

Chapter 16: Unleashing the Power of the Metaverse in Intelligent Libraries

In today's world, a new wave of technological revolution and industrial change is emerging. Virtual reality (VR) technology is a representative technology of this new revolution in science and technology and is considered a key technology to promote the development of the digital economy, industrial transformation, and upgrade. The VR industry has a vast space and great potential for growth, as was emphasized at the World VR Industry Conference on October 20, 2021. It is believed that further "VR+" actions should be taken to enrich terminal products and content services, and to promote the industrialization of VR technology and industrial scale up.

The innovation and development of virtual and reality industries have brought about significant changes to the services offered by traditional cultural venues, such as libraries, museums and galleries. The use of VR technology in these venues allows for a more immersive and interactive experience for the visitors, bringing the exhibits and collections to life in a way that was not previously possible. Additionally, the use of VR in education and training has been gaining traction as it enables students to explore and learn in a virtual environment that simulates real-world scenarios. Furthermore, the emergence of metaverse technology has also brought new opportunities to libraries.

Metaverse is a virtual shared space where users can interact with each other and with virtual objects in a way that resembles the real world. The use of metaverse technology in libraries can enable the creation of virtual reading rooms and libraries, providing users with access to a vast collection of books and resources in a virtual environment. Additionally, the use of metaverse technology can enable the creation of virtual events, such as book clubs and author talks, providing a new way for libraries to engage with their communities.

This chapter aims to explore the potential of Metaverse technology in driving the transformation of intelligent library services. It will analyze the development opportunities of Metaverse and its application prospects in intelligent libraries, with the goal of promoting innovation and optimization of library services. The chapter will also discuss the advantages of Metaverse and its underlying technologies, as well as the theoretical logic of Metaverse application in libraries.

Chapter 17: Enhanced Assistive Technology on Audio Visual Speech Recognition for the Hearing Impaired

Natural language processing, signal processing, and artificial intelligence all play a role in the field of speech recognition systems, which is interdisciplinary. Discourse is a ceaseless sound sign with a succession of phonemes and the critical method of human communication through hearing disabled individuals perceive words verbally expressed by perusing a lip.

The variety of hearing inside the gathering is partially settled by the sound they can see. This sound is estimated in decibels (dB), laying out a breaking point inside, which is considered a solid level of sound that doesn't surpass 85 dB during a particular timeframe. The consultation limit alludes to the base power apparent by the ear. Between 40 and 70 dB of hearing loss, a language delay will affect how we communicate with the students, classmates, friends, or colleagues.

One of the most intricate mechanisms of human sensation ability is found in the auditory system. The mechanical energy of sound waves is converted into electrical stimuli by the fluid-filled inner ear, which the brain will eventually translate. Physically, the internal ear is partitioned into the hearable and vestibular frameworks. The vestibular system is responsible for three-dimensional orientation and gravity perception, while the auditory system is responsible for good sensation.

Hearing-impaired individuals frequently develop balance disorders due to the similarities between these two systems. A cochlea in the shape of a snail makes up the auditory system. The cochlea is a fluid-filled tube that wraps around the modulus in a spiral.

Chapter 18: Facial Gesture Recognition for Emotion Detection – A Review of Methods and Advancements

Facial gesture recognition (FGR) is widely regarded as an effective means of displaying and communicating human emotions. This chapter provides a comprehensive review of FGR as a biometric marker technology for detecting facial emotions, encompassing the identification of the six basic facial expressions: happiness, sadness, anger, surprise, fear, and disgust.

FGR utilizes advanced algorithms to accurately identify and classify facial emotional states from images, audio, or video captured through various devices such as cameras, laptops, mobile phones, or digital signage systems. Given the importance of accuracy, computational efficiency, and mitigating overfitting, this review also discusses the diverse range of methods and models developed in Facial Expression Recognition research.

These advancements aim to enhance the accuracy of the models while minimizing computational resource requirements and addressing overfitting challenges encountered in previous studies.

Chapter 19: Analyzing Bibliometrics of AI and Smart Vehicles

The intersection of artificial intelligence and smart vehicles is a rapidly evolving area of research and development. The use of AI in smart vehicles has the potential to revolutionize the automotive industry, making vehicles safer, more efficient, and more convenient for drivers.

Some recent studies in this area have focused on the use of AI for driver assistance, autonomous driving, and vehicle-to-vehicle communication. Additionally, there has been research on the ethical and social implications of AI in smart vehicles, including issues related to privacy, security, and liability. The research on artificial intelligence and smart vehicles is ongoing and constantly evolving as new technologies and applications are developed. There are numerous studies in the Scopus database on Artificial Intelligence and Smart Vehicles.

The authors conducted a systematic review of existing literature on this topic, and they analyzed and summarized the findings. The research method involves collecting data from various sources, including academic papers, conference proceedings, and technical reports. The study concludes that AI plays a critical role in the development of autonomous vehicles, and it is used in areas such as perception, decision-making, and control.

This chapter highlight the potential benefits of AI in enhancing the safety, efficiency, and sustainability of smart vehicles. They also discuss the challenges and limitations associated with the adoption of AI in this field, such as the need for large amounts of data and the need for reliable and robust AI algorithms. Overall, the studies suggest that the application of AI in smart vehicles has significant potential for improving transportation systems and promoting sustainable mobility.

Chapter 20: Data Privacy in the Metaverse Ecosystem

The metaverse which is a complex immersive 3D digital space with collapsed virtual and real realms, is set to become the next major evolution in the web. The potential application of such cross-platform physical-virtual reality interactions is huge and includes usage in such disciplines as education, healthcare, marketing, and tourism. But despite the transformative nature of the continued evolution of the metaverse and how it is set to positively impact people in their occupational, social, and leisure interaction, transforming, in the process, the way we conduct business, interact with ourselves and others. It is leading to develop shared experiences by the progressive blurring the gap between physical and digital world. However, this results in extensive data sharing, which raises fundamental privacy and security concerns that has attracted mounting scholarly and public policy scrutiny.

Data privacy is a major concern in the metaverse. To deal with this problem, it requires a combination of clear regulations, secure storage and transfer solutions, user control and education, and responsible use of data by metaverse platforms.

Protecting users' privacy in the metaverse's melting pot of regulatory regimes is thus critical. A number of studies have proposed solutions for safeguarding users' privacy and ensuring their security in such scenarios. Some of these privacy-enhancing technologies (PETs) include intrinsic protection, data aggregation, protected rendering and sharing, and authentication. These PETs can collectively work to obfuscate any of the users' sensible or private data from the sensors before being uploaded or shared online. However, creating a tailored privacy policy is perhaps the most effective way of mitigating privacy and security concerns in the metaverse. Thus this chapter will delve into these details on the current challenges, current research and potential solutions related to data privacy in Metaverse.

Chapter 21: Hybrid Optimization Techniques for Data Privacy Preserving in the Metaverse Ecosystem

Since computer technology affects and enhances social connections, communication, and touch, it has a tremendous impact on daily life. From the viewpoint of final customers, three main waves of technical advancement have been noted. During these waves, the development of mobiles, personal computers, and the internet technologies received more and more attention. Innovators in the fourth wave of computers are two spatial, immersive technologies called augmented reality (AR) and the virtual reality (VR).

The next paradigm for ubiquitous computing, which has the potential to alter (online) business, education, remote labor, and entertainment, is expected to be produced by this wave. This new paradigm is the metaverse. The word "metaverse" is derived from the Greek word Meta, which means beyond, beyond, or after, and universe. In alternative words, an after-reality universe is the Metaverse. Where the real world and digital virtually are continuously combined among numerous people. In order to solve the underlying issues with web-based 2D e-learning technologies, online distance education can use Metaverse.

While social networks only permit users to create messages, the Earth 3D map4 offers picture frames of the real world but lacks any physical features other than GPS information. Photos, and videos with a limited number of user involvement options (like liking a post, for example). Video games are improving and becoming more impressive. Users can enjoy stunning visuals and in-game physics in games like Call of Duty: Black Ops Cold War, which creates a sense of realism that closely mirrors the real world.

Chapter 22: Advancements in Guidance Systems and Assistive Technologies for Visually Impaired Individuals

The developed system is a self-innovative idea that aims to assist visually impaired people in accessing web pages and advanced technology with the help of voice assistance. The system is different from the email and web pages currently in use, and emphasizes reliability and user-friendliness as key features of the proposed architecture. The authors have identified that visually impaired people have trouble using the current systems, and the proposed system can be beneficial for them.

The system utilizes three different technologies: Speech-to-Text (STT), screen tapping to reload the main page, and Text-to-Speech (TTS). The authors have included features such as weather forecasts, location, date, time, emergency SMS, and e-mail notifications to enhance the system's usefulness for visually impaired users. The authors have used several Python libraries to build the system, including Beautiful Soup, Google Text-to-Speech (gTTS), Speech recognition, Open Weather API, Twilio, and Geo IP Lite. Beautiful Soup is a Python library used for pulling data out of HTML and XML files, and works with parser algorithms to provide various ways of navigating, searching, and modifying the parse tree. Other libraries like FFmpeg are also used to extract the voice and convert it into a text format. The system also uses express.js for better assistance.

The authors have used audio.py as a tool for voice recognition, and the developed system can notify visually impaired users about weather broadcasts using the open weather API. Twilio is used to initiate an emergency SMS, and Geo IP Lite is used to discover the location of an IP address in the real world.

Chapter 23: Cyber Security in the Metaverse

Security in the Metaverse is a critical concern as virtual worlds continue to expand and evolve. With an increasing number of users engaging in immersive experiences, safeguarding personal information, assets, and digital identities becomes paramount. Robust security measures are essential to protect against hacking, identity theft, and fraudulent activities.

Technologies like blockchain and encryption play a crucial role in ensuring secure transactions, while identity verification systems help authenticate users. Additionally, monitoring and moderation tools are necessary to combat harassment, hate speech, and inappropriate content. As the Metaverse becomes more integrated into our lives, a comprehensive approach to security is vital to foster trust and safeguard the virtual realm.

This chapter aims to provide an overview of the cybersecurity in metaverse. It discussed the various cyber stacks in detail along with solutions to manage these attacks. Authors have also discussed the various challenges in securing metaverse and possible future research directions.

Chapter 24: Smart Cities Data Indicator-Based Cyber Threats Detection Using Bio-Inspired Artificial Algae Algorithm

Smart cities have benefited greatly from the quick development of information technology, such as cloud computing, sensors, and the Internet of Things (IoT). Smart cities improve living services and analyze massive amounts of data, which increases privacy and security concerns. But managing security and privacy issues is crucial for a smart city that encourages businesses to adopt new computing paradigms.

In recent years, there has been a proliferation of literature on security and privacy, covering topics like end-to-end security, reliable data acquisition, transmission, and processing, legal service provisioning, and privacy of personal data, as well as the application of bioinspired computing techniques to system design and operation. Effective computing systems have been developed by utilizing bio-inspired computing approaches (such as evolutionary computation, particle swarm optimization, ant colony optimization, etc.) for intelligent decision support.

The indicator-based threat detection system with BAAA algorithm is the quickest and most efficient way to scope out an environment after observation, and its usefulness is greatly influenced by the adversary rate of change.

Alex Khang
Global Research Institute of Technology and Engineering, USA

Vrushank Shah
Institute of Technology and Engineering, Indus University, India

Sita Rani
Department of Computer Science and Engineering, Guru Nanak Dev Engineering College, India

Acknowledgment

The book *Handbook of Research on AI-Based Technologies and Applications in the Era of the Metaverse* is based on the design and implementation of Metaverse Ecosystem, Artificial Intelligence (AI), Machine Learning (ML), Data Science, Internet of Things (IoT), Big Data Solutions, Cloud platforms, Cybersecurity Technology, and AI-Based Technologies and Applications in the Era of the Metaverse.

Preparing and designing a book outline to introduce to readers across the globe is the passion and noble goal of the editorial team. To be able to make ideas to a reality and the success of this book, the biggest reward belongs to the efforts, experiences, enthusiasm, and trust of the contributors.

To all contributors, we really say big thanks for high quality chapters that we received from our experts, professors, scientists, engineers, scholars, Ph.D., postgraduate students, educators, and academic colleagues.

To all the reviewers with whom we have had the opportunity to collaborate and monitor their hard work remotely, we acknowledge their tremendous support and valuable comments not only for the book but also for future book projects.

We also express our deep gratitude for all the pieces of advice, support, motivation, sharing, collaboration, and inspiration we received from our faculty, contributors, educators, professors, scientists, scholars, engineers, and academic colleagues.

Last but not least, we are really grateful to our publisher IGI Global for the wonderful support in making sure the timely processing of the manuscript and bringing out this book to the readers soonest.

Thank you, everyone.

Chapter 1
Artificial Intelligence (AI)– Centric Model in the Metaverse Ecosystem

Aakansha C. Saxena
Rashtriya Raksha University, India

Adhishree Ojha
Rashtriya Raksha University, India

Daksh Sobti
Rashtriya Raksha University, India

Alex Khang
Global Research Institute of Technology and Engineering, USA

ABSTRACT

Metaverse is a prodigy that combines the real and digital worlds, enabling avatars to participate in a variety of activities. AI will have an influential impact on the future of Metaverse, as it will enable Metaverse to be user-centric by introducing features like augmented reality and virtual reality. This chapter will provide insights about how AI-centric modeling and AI concepts can boost the emerging world of Metaverse. AI will be an indispensable component of Metaverse, from the foundational layer to the experiential layer. AI will enable Metaverse to be user-centric by introducing features like augmented reality and virtual reality, creating an immersive experience for the user.

INTRODUCTION

Metaverse is a 3D concept that facilitates the technology to map or draw virtual avatars parallelly and acts as a bridge between the users and the digital world. It can be understood as virtual cyberspace which mixes up the real and digital world and converges the two by providing the facility of internet and other technologies. It can be understood as an infinite universe where communities of people can collaborate

DOI: 10.4018/978-1-6684-8851-5.ch001

and enjoy the mechanism of augmented reality, virtual reality, extended reality, online life and much more. Artificial Intelligence based theories and equipment along with deep learning concepts are needed for metaverse's better development to provide more powerful features of computation, perception, interaction, cooperation, reconstruction, virtual identities and assets, life similar experiences, dialogues, and other different features.

In Ready Player One, Wade Watt says," A gifted human player could always triumph over the game's AI because software couldn't improvise" (Forbes, 2022). Although the AI concepts being used in Metaverse has to acquire and understand more of improvisational and human like qualities to thrive, it still remains a software program that relies a lot on real human interactions to achieve successful operations and thus even the AI thriving in Metaverse will require to learn about how efficiently it could improvise itself and be more and more human-like, thus it needs real people to succeed.

AI modeling stays as the most crucial force behind Metaverse because Metaverse can't function without using the different fields of AI be it speech recognition, machine learning, robotics, reasoning, neural networks, expert systems, planning, etc. enabling the existence of interfaces, avatars, chatbots, and much more. Metaverse is today's emerging hype and it will take immersive and reckless research in the field of AI to make it more useful and fruitful for the users and as gradually this is achieved we will witness this new technology which can be the next Facebook but much more reciprocal, helping the people engaged in business by generating enormous virtual events, enabling the companies to advertise and sell their goods to great extent hence evolving a new media expertise in advertising, boosting up the cryptocurrency, e-transactions, e-wallets thus easing out everything. AI modeling is definitely the 'head honcho' in the emergence of Metaverse and a lot will depend on AI in the future success of Metaverse. The different domains of AI mutually contributes to the development of a proper functioning metaverse. Speech recognition enables to recognize the user's speech convert icontcontributext and do the required natural language processing on it. While the Computer Vision is used in playing with the images and the videos in the world of metaverse. Virtual reality for making the virtual environment and augmented reality for making the user able to work with the digital information. Data collection and sharing is used to gather information from various aspects and either store it or share it on the need basis. Even the AI driven bots are used to enable users to do various tasks including giving instructions, performing transactions, providing answers to various questions and much more. Concepts of Deep Learning are used to create the twins by giving it a real touch.

A basic metaverse platform consists of seven layers, including infrastructure, human interface, decentralization, spatial computing, creator economy, discovery, and experience. AI algorithms and techniques are used in each layer to make the processing easier, favorable, and user friendly. Infrastructure provides the different options of infrastructure available, while human interface directs to various devices and technologies. Decentralization provides technologies like blockchain, AI agents, edge computing, spatial computing, creator economy, discovery, and experience (Artificial intelligence for the Metaverse, n.d.). AI algorithms and techniques are used in each layer to make the processing easier, favorable, and user friendly.

Figure 1. AI domains used in Metaverse

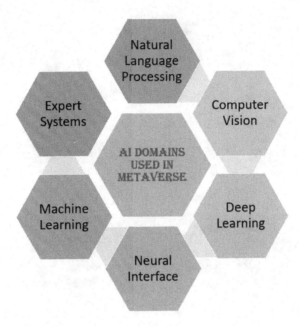

Figure 2. The different layers of a basic Metaverse platform

RESEARCH METHODOLOGY

Research is the pursuit of knowledge; it is a form of scientific inquiry. Research involves certain challenges. The processes for data collecting and information analysis that are pertinent to the issue are aesthetically stated in the study design. The area of logic called methodology is concerned with the application of the reasoning principle to research in philosophy and science. The approach taken to do research is known as methodology, and it depends on the kind and type of study being conducted. In this paper we have tried our best to investigate and explore the importance and expansion of AI in the world of metaverse and at the same time have focused on its potential in bringing a revolution in the processing and functioning of the metaverse. At the beginning of our work we tried explaining what metaverse is all about and how AI can be related to it. What are the various domains of AI playing a role in the metaverse at each and every layer and application. Subsequently we have talked about the various AI algorithms, concepts and technologies being used, the role of AI in facilitating easy workflow of metaverse. Further we have emphasized the surveys, findings, market size, challenges, applications related to the same. At last we have tried to deal with some real case studies and understand them. Figure 3 depicts a general flow of research methodology.

Figure 3. The progress cycle of a general research methodology

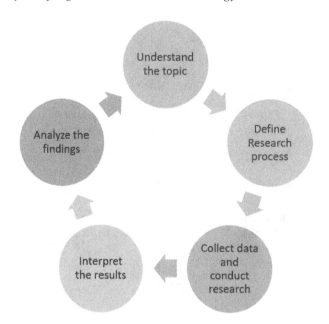

LITERATURE REVIEW TABLE

For our research paper we have referred to several papers and according to that we have made the Literature Review Table for this paper.

ALGORITHM, TECHNOLOGIES, AND CONCEPTS USED

VR, AR, MR, XR have proved to be life transforming factors and these should be empowered more. Our everyday life has become so breathtaking and have been socialized a lot. The number of people being engaged in screen platforms and remotely working has increased abruptly and just here the road for the metaverse world has paved from. The mesmerizing and socializing world of metaverse is liked by all as it helps people to collaborate and do whatever they want to do, be it shopping, playing, or exploring any several other things. Figure 4 depicts the different applications using the various technologies being modeled in the metaverse.

Table 1. Literature review

Sr. no	Name of the Paper	Publication	Paper Summary	Performance Evaluation	Advantages	Disadvantages
1	Artificial Intelligence For Metaverse: A Framework (Guo, 2022).	CAAI Artificial Intelligence Research1 VOL. 1 NO.1 2022| https://doi.org/10.26599/AIR.2022.9150004	In this paper the authors have emphasized on finding out the framework which includes various technologies to capture the features and significance of real world, large computation requirements, reconstruction to build virtual world, facilitation of long distance communication and the interaction system. It also includes how AI can be promoted to develop the world of Metaverse. In the survey they did they have mentioned the recent achievements of AI in producing framework which includes the different aspects of computation, perception, cooperation, reconstruction and interaction. They have talked about the holographic display technology which will help the metaverse.	The authors have successfully reviewed the different progress that AI has achieved in recent times to facilitate a smooth and feasible framework. They have also discussed the various challenges and potential future work nicely. The technologies or algorithms discussed like compressive imaging, total variation, sparsity priors, Gaussian Mixture Model, decompress-snapshot-compressive imaging, near-sensor-CNN accelerator, bi-nary occupancy grid, probabilistic occupancy grid, signed distance function and truncated signed distance function,3D neural radiance field, orthogon-al frequency-division multiplexing systems, RNN, stacked autoencoder (SAE), deep belief network (DBN),deep feedforward neural network (DFNN) gives really good percentage of accuracy, for e.g., the RNN used in decoding gives online raw accuracy rate of about 94.1%, and the offline automatic correction accuracy rate exceeds 99% even. Also the intracranial electroencephalography (iEEG) Translation used for synthesis of speech gives an accuracy of 61% and 76% for question and answer respectively	The expected framework discussed in this paper ensures larger computations, including good technologies of perception to ensure better capturing of features of the real world. The paper discuss about the contribution of AI to the framework in various ways which includes the detailed explanation of AI and imaging, AI and multi modality sensors, AI and different types of computing including cloud, in-memory, optoelectronic and edge computing, AI and reconstruction which further includes deep learning based 3D reconstruction, neural rendering, AI and Communication, AI and blockchain, AI and CyberSecurity, Neural modulation, neural decoding, AI for brain computation interface, AI for human computer interaction, multi modal active perception technology, holographic display technology.	Among the various different AI technologies being discussed in the papers, some are the ones which are yet far away from the practical uses whereas metaverse is all about practical aspects and real time experiences. Therefore more work can be done towards the enhancement of those technologies.
2	MetaAID: A Flexible Framework for Developing Metaverse Applications via AI Technology and Human Editing (Zhu, 2022).	Hongyin Zhu Department of Computer Science and Technology, Tsinghua University, Beijing, ChinaIarXiv:2204.01614v1 [cs. CL] 4 Apr 2022	This paper revolves around producing an AI enabled flexible framework for Metaverse "MetaAID" whose aim is to help in making digital twins and virtual humans by using semantic and language related concepts and technologies. The framework mentioned by the authors combines the common AI technologies and the application development templates with very common interfaces and functional modules. They claim that the framework promoted by them will facilitates various applications in developing metaverse.	The framework idea proposed here is absolutely wonderful ,highly technological and will probably will be a very high boost up in the world of metaverse. The only problem with the proposed framework is that it's development is quite time consuming, if this problem is dealt, it will be very easy to take the collaboration of AI and metaverse to new heights. If the cons are removed then this framework will definitely facilitate the information exchange and data analysis in a very good manner and also the expansion of this framework may result in scalable and robust web architectures and distributed systems.	The technologies proposed for making the framework are really technology rich and appreciable which includes the MetaAID framework which aims at the collaborative development of metaverse using AI technologies and human editing, formation of repositories for human machine content creation, creation of five applications in three industries throwing light on enhancing the relationship between domestic demand and the internal economic circulation chain. Apart from this to evaluate the framework developed by them they have made these application- s on different platforms like iOS apps, online websites and WeChat mini programs. The framework proposed includes all the major domains of AI like NLP, Computer Vision and Deep learning which can process the textual data also in a very efficient manner. The key advantage is the mixing up of different technologies which includes App development, AI technologies and Human editing which ensures a very strong framework	The framework that they have mentioned can face three major challenges which may take a very long time to get resolved. The first one talks about the implementation and the accumulation of the tech stack to make the application where one needs to compare all the possible options and then select the most feasible, agile and extensible approach. The second one talks about the making of the templates, code snippets and repositories needed for running many different programming languages and the last challenge is developing online applications for direct generation of results.

continues on following page

Table 1. Continued

Sr. no	Name of the Paper	Publication	Paper Summary	Performance Evaluation	Advantages	Disadvantages
3	Machine Learning for Metaverse-enabled Wireless Systems: Vision, Requirements, and Challenges (Khan, 2022a).	IEEE Network magazinearXiv:2211.03703v1 [cs.NI] 7 Nov 2022	This paper mainly focuses on the role of ML in enabling metaverse based wireless systems. The authors have discussed the major requirements for the advancement of ML technologies in the metaversed based wireless systems. A case study has also been specified which talks about the distributed split federated learning for the efficient training of metaspace models. They have even talked about the various challenges in this process. They have even used graphs for showing the working and the results of the models. The key requirements from the production of such systems have also been covered. Emphasis on proactive learning has also been mentioned in the paper.	The paper is very well enriched with various ML techniques which can ease the work of making metaverse enabled wireless systems. The pros and cons of centralized and decentralized training of agents is very well explained along with the common training design challenges. Data homogenization has been very well explained including the use of sensory data, sensor capacity, sensory APIs, Actuator commands, actuator capacity and actuator APIs. The case study of non-IID distribution using MNIST dataset has been very well explained.	The authors have very well explained about the two different aspects which are wireless for metaverse and metaverse for wireless. The paper has discussed the overview of metaverse and it's architecture where a high level architecture is explained which is a combination of both physical space and meta space. The various wireless KPIs and design trends focussing towards the proactive learning and self sustaining wireless system have also been discussed. The various concepts like partial local model training, edge aggregation, handling of service requests, semantic reasoning and centralized and distributed systems have broaden up the aspects nicely. The case study mentioned focuses on the system model, latency, performance evaluation, signal to interference plus noise ratio, local accuracy.	The paper has been written very well including all the various aspects and has even mentioned the various challenges that are being and will be faced in future. The challenges are that we need to find scalable ML techniques for handling of larger datasets, we even have to look for resource optimization, context awareness(local and global) is another aspect, noise reduction and noiseless data are also to be concerned about. Even the security aspects have to be fulfilled as ML enabled metaverse is quite prone to security attacks. Training fashion is also to be seen and standardization is another important aspect to be looked around. If these points are been worked upon then the idea jotted in this paper is quite useful.
4	Metaverse for Wireless Systems: Vision, Enablers, Architecture, and Future Directions (Khan, 2022b).	Latif U. Khan, Zhu Han, Fellow, IEEE, Dusit Niyato, Fellow, IEEE, Ekram Hossain, Fellow, IEEE, and Choong Seon Hong, Senior Member, IEEEarXiv:2207.00413v1 [cs.NI] 20 June 2022	This paper is about the vision of metaverse for enabling the development of a 6G wireless system efficiently. The paper also talks about the general architecture for metaverse based wireless system. Apart from this the design trends, key driving applications, and key enablers of this task are also been discussed. At last the authors have also thrown up some open challenges and their potential solutions.	The authors have very nicely talked about the major six technical aspects which will definitely enhance the metaverse which are NLP, blockchain, networking, machine vision, digital twin and neural interface. Along with this they have also presented an architecture using the example of wireless systems. They even have claimed that they are the first one to adopt the newly emerging technology of metaverse and even have talked about the potential for improving the wireless systems and mobile services by using key enablers like the digital twins and avatars. The enablers have been very well explained and the architecture is a very feasible one that assures the combination of meta and physical space, even there key roles have been very well explained using examples which makes the concepts more clear. The implementation aspects are another concepts which has been mentioned and described so that the reader get to know the whole idea of implementation of these systems. The various use cases and technologies to be used are very well explained and elaborated.	The paper has been very well designed and the flow of the paper is very systematic. All the proposals have been very well explained using examples and use cases which makes it easy for the reader to understand the objective of this paper. The concepts of AR, VR, XR, MR, Smart Industry, self configuring and proactive online learning based wireless systems, blockchain, mathematical, simulation, experimental modeling, and data-driven modeling, physical world, twins and avatars, interfaces security, edge based metaspace have been emphasized. They have even talked about how the roadside units and the other objects of environment could be presented as digital twins and how the scenario of real accidents can be captured.	The technologies, concepts and architecture mentioned in the paper require quite a good amount of novel resources which need to be accumulated for the designing of the systems. The other challenge is to handle the huge data sets which will be used in the distributed learning. Even the metaverse requires the interaction of a variety of players and thus facilitating their interaction is also a huge task. The algorithms which are to be used need to be highly scalable and sustainable and rather should have less computational delay, these algorithms needs to be found. Next the players of metaverse needs to be trained for the working of environment for which we need a data driven modeling. For this we need servers and other devices for the effective simulation which further could be expensive. Lastly integrating different needs and models for creation of base stations, channel for propagating the communication and other things is another challenging, time consuming and big task.

continues on following page

Table 1. Continued

Sr. no	Name of the Paper	Publication	Paper Summary	Performance Evaluation	Advantages	Disadvantages
5	Artificial Intelligence for the Metaverse: A Survey (Ghandar et al., 2021).	Thien Huynh-The. Member, IEEE, Quoc-Viet Pham, Member, IEEE, Xuan-Qui Pham, Thanh Thi Nguyen, Zhu Han, Fellow, IEEE, and Dong-Seong Kim, Senior, IEEE]arXiv:2202.10336v1 [cs. CY] 15 Feb 2022	This paper majorly talks about the survey conducted to understand and explore the beneficial impact of AI in developing and expanding the metaverse. Firstly the authors have explained the concepts and domains of AI, its related architectures and its roles. Then they have shared a comprehensive result of investigation done regarding the AI methodology in six major technical field. Furthermore the major application area of AI in metaverse is also discussed and elaborated. At last the authors have summed up the survey findings and have given some future challenges, in the direction of which further research work could be done, thus making the collaborative world of AI and Metaverse more strong and promising.	The paper has been systematically written and is enriched with statistical data and findings. Apart from a large number of algorithms and technologies the paper even includes some Metaverse projects like the Decentraland (a virtual land) have also been discussed along with the general flow of processing of conversational AI. The comprehensive and detailed research about the role of AI in metaverse has been emphasized and subsequently several key techniques related to NLP, blockchain, DT, machine vision, etc. has been discussed upon. The paper consists of review of AI based solutions which promises to produce a strong infrastructure of the system.better experience of the 3D world and built in services related to the virtual world. At last the authors have even made an outline for the further research directions which includes the enhancement of solutions for the different fields like protection from security threats, increasing the efficiency of the operations, management of dialogs, auditability of the model, mitigation of legal risks and guarantee of better user experience.	The paper starts with a very detailed explanation of how the metaverse has evolved with time and which all technologies have joined hands in shaping it. Besides the virtual world and its construction the paper also involves the various other entities like the object and users entities which would facilitate in the making of the meta world. The references to recent developments have been given, compared and explained very effectively. The infrastructure of the metaverse platform is the another major aspects explained. The different algorithms related to ML like supervised and unsupervised learning, regression models, classification and other voice recognition models are elaborated effectively. DL architecture technology has even been expanded in the paper. Further the AI aided methods related to the various applications have also been discussed to enhance the applications. The paper consists of a detailed summary of all the algorithms and concepts like k-nearest neighbors, random forest, Naive Bayes, support vector machine, association analysis, clustering, dimensionality reduction, graph based model, boosting techniques, self training, generative models, RL model, RNN, CNN, autoencoders, SOM, LSTM, GRU networks, AR, VR, NLP, XR, VR, Computer Vision methodology, convolutional sampling, blockchain based IoT framework, uRLLC, eMBB, MCNet, SCGNet, CSI prediction, etc. been mentioned in the paper. The paper even consists of various figures which elaborates the explanation of various domains of AI and application areas of AI in metaverse. The role of AI along with metaverse in making up of smart cities and establishing gaming culture is also elaborated in the paper.	Various techniques and methodologies described in the paper are not so popularly being used till date. Also the current metaverse projects being worked upon doesn't give the users a bigger picture by putting up limitations to exploration, owning and customization of things. The another drawback is that the users should be allowed to create hyperreal objects and contents so that the idea of unique experiences and exciting creations can be facilitated. Another issue is sometimes the AI agents put the security and operability on the verge of attacks related to security which needs to be looked upon. Sometimes the metaverse developers, designers, and users doesn't understand the decision making processes which needs to be corrected and simplified.

Figure 4. Metaverse: Combination of AR, VR, MR, and XR

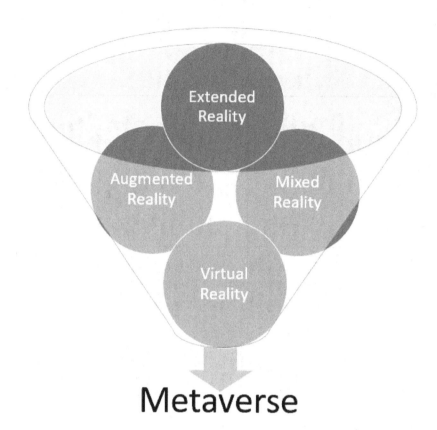

Virtual Reality (VR): Another World Within Sight

A virtual reality (VR) environment provides the user with the feeling of being completely immersed in their surroundings with visuals and objects that seem real (Artificial intelligence for the Metaverse, n.d.). The three primary components of VR are visualization, interactivity, and immersion (Krishnamurthy et al., 2023). Interactivity is the main distinction between a VRT system and a conventional three-dimensional animation, as it allows users to actively affect the world. The VRT system is made up of a professional picture disposal computer, utility software system, input unit, and demonstration apparatus (Khan, 2022b).

Augmented Reality (AR)

Augmented Reality is the art of merging a user's environment with digital particulars in real time. It is used to blend a user's perception and vision with the digital world, including the 3D effect, components and environment. It is taken with glasses or smartphones, and contact lenses are also being used to facilitate the experience. AR technology requires processors, sensors, display and input devices, as well as GPS, solid state compass and accelerometers. Figure 5 shows different usages of AR including its use for entertainment, decision making, home tours, and cycling, etc.

Figure 5. Various application area of Metaverse

MR (Mixed Reality)

The combination of the real and virtual worlds to create a new environment where it is possible for virtual and real-world items to interact in real-time is known as MR, also known as hybrid reality. MR devices continuously capture fresh information happening in the surroundings, unlike VR, which completely immerses users in a virtual environment, and AR, which effectively overlays digital content on top of the real environment without addressing its unique and dynamic composition (Khan, 2022b). For people to interact with digital content, such knowledge is required to blend it with the actual world.MR blends the physical and digital worlds in circumstances where they are intertwined.

Figure 6. AR, MR, VR blended together

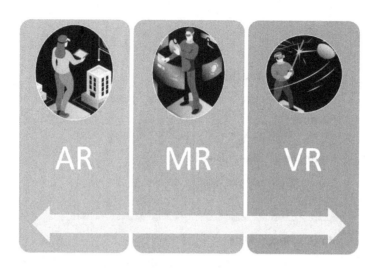

How Does AI Facilitate the Functioning of the Metaverse?

1. **Creating Tremendously Accurate Avatar:** Avatar are used in metaverse to display the visual representation of the different elements of the metaverse. AI ensures better user experience by uplifting and advancing the different features of the avatar (What is Metaverse, n.d.). The largely simulated avatar created by the AI algorithms Ensures variety of facial expressions, emotions, aging and much more.AI produces the best 3D animated figure.
2. **Intuitive Interface:** User interfaces created by AI are very intuitive which means they are very much closer to the user's expectation. It does not specify the mechanism and procedures behind the various features available through the interface and that is what the user wants. Be it the sense of touch, voice recognition, sophisticated AR enabled headset, or other things the interface is kept very user friendly.
3. **Self-Supervised Learning:** AI has the facility of self-supervised learning which means the process of learning oneself using the various input and output values. The output labels are given with the input labels hence acting as a whole one single input. Thus, self-learning models ensure the automation feature in the metaverse creation. It will allow the different algorithms used in metaverse to learn things on its own without the need of any supervisor.
4. **Expansion of VR:** Using AI, the metaverse ensures a virtual world that is exact to the real world virtually. Creation, training, and practicing are the key steps for ensuring real life like humans and environment in the world of metaverse.
5. **Linguistic Accessibility:** Metaverse ensures that language should not turn out as a barrier for the users. And thus, the metaverse allows multi linguistic accessibility to the users. The better part of this is the very fast execution of the whole process.
6. **Digital Humans:** Using the entire concepts of AI, digital humans like chatbots and automated assistants are created in the Metaverse. Many companies have invested solely in this field only like the companies Soul Machines, Unreal Engine, Unity, Amazon Lumberyard, etc.

AI CONCEPTS AND TECHNOLOGIES USED

We tried to compile several areas where AI can be useful for the metaverse's future, both from a product aspect and in terms of how AI could make the Metaverse more inclusive, using Jon's layer schema.

AIOps

Keep in mind that, according to Coinbase, the platform required to support the Metaverse must be always on and massively scalable. AIOps will play an important role in managing all of the necessary infrastructure, including hardware, base software, and communications, in such a demanding scenario. But what exactly are AIOps? According to Gartner, it is the use of "big data and machine learning to automate IT operations processes such as event correlation, anomaly detection, and causality determination." The availability of these capabilities will be critical not only for ensuring the Metaverse infrastructure's robustness, but also for providing activity insights relevant to the upper layers (Hwang & Chien, 2022).

Machine Vision

Machine vision, which combines computer vision and XR, is one of the main technologies used to build the metaverse. It enables XR devices to study and comprehend human behaviors based on significant visual data. Extended Reality (XR) is a general term that encompasses VR, AR, mixed reality (MR), and everything in between. VR gives viewing experiences in a completely immersive digital environment, while AR delivers graphics, video streams, and holograms in the real world (How AI and Metaverse Are Shaping the Future?, n.d.). Human users have access to these reality technologies as well as the metaverse and a variety of services in the real and virtual worlds. XR and AI may be integrated to provide a completely immersive metaverse experience.

Figure 7. Image processing

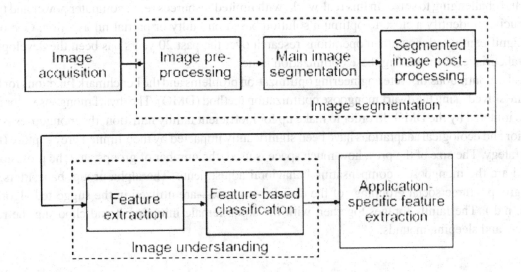

The metaverse is a virtual environment built using machine vision and extended reality (XR) technology. It allows users to interact with digital things and each other in both the real and virtual worlds. Computer vision technology enables XR devices to analyze and understand user behaviors using relevant visual data. VR headsets are designed to satisfy consumer performance and comfort requirements. AI algorithms have been used in VR systems to improve user-machine interaction based on visual data. Deep learning frameworks have been used to predict user fixations, identify and verify users, and modify virtual objects. Other devices such as triboelectric gloves, hand-held touchscreen devices, and tabletops have been proposed to access the metaverse's contents. A 3D CNN architecture has been developed to assess VR quality.

Inclusive User Interfaces

One of the cornerstones to the Metaverse's potential success is the promise of extremely immersive experiences. While this may help some individuals interact more socially, it could make it more difficult for those who have limitations to access the future digital world. Additionally, those who lack basic computer skills may be left out of this new social economy and experience. AI for accessibility should therefore be a key component of the effort to guarantee that everyone, regardless of ability, has access to the Metaverse. Image recognition for those with visual impairments, automatic translation, intelligent exoskeletons to connect with the digital world, and brain computer interfaces for the most vulnerable (like Cognixion) are some key innovations in this field (Guo, 2022).

AI ALGORITHMS

Dwarf Mongoose Optimization Algorithm

It is a type of metaheuristic algorithm, so now what is this metaheuristic algorithm? A metaheuristic algorithm is a search method created to locate a suitable answer to an optimization issue that is complicated and challenging to solve. In this real-world with limited resources (e.g., computer power and time), it is crucial to identify a close to optimum solution based on faulty or partial information. One of the most significant developments in operations research over the past 20 years has been the development of metaheuristics for resolving these optimization issues.

Twelve continuous/discrete engineering optimization problems and the benchmark functions for CEC 2020 are solved using the dwarf mongoose optimization method (DMO). The dwarf mongoose's foraging style is imitated by the DMO. In order to make up for inefficient family nutrition, the mongooses' social behavior and ecological adaptations have been significantly impacted by their limited prey capture (feeding) strategy. The size of the prey, how much space is used, the number of groups, and the provisioning of food are the mongoose's compensating behavioral adjustments. The alpha group, babysitters, and scout group—three social groupings of the dwarf mongoose—are utilized in the suggested algorithm (IEEE, n.d.). The family forages together, with the alpha female initiating it and choosing the route, distance, and sleeping mounds.

Figure 8. The working of dwarf mongoose optimization

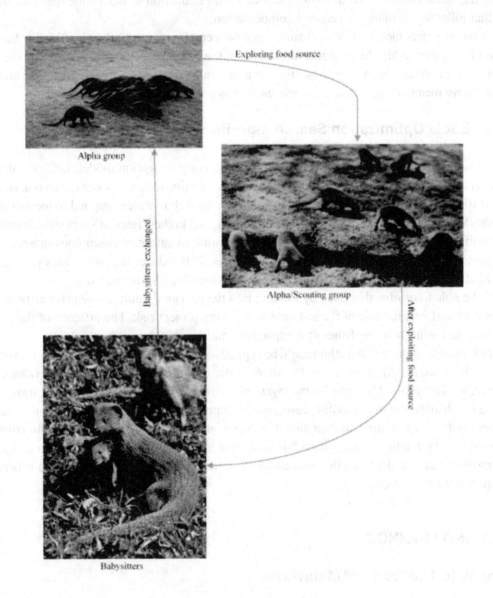

Random Forest

A well-liked ensemble learning technique for classification and regression is random forest. Through ensemble learning techniques, which combine numerous machine learning (ML) algorithms to produce a superior model, the wisdom of crowds is applied to data science (Krishnamurthy et al., 2023). They are based on the hypothesis that a team of people with different levels of competence may solve a problem more successfully than a single person with more experience.

Random forest includes decision trees, a popular metaphor for solving issues. Decision trees employ a series of true/false questions on different parts of a data collection to determine the answer. In the example that follows, calculating a person's compensation.

A decision considers factors (features) such a person's employment status (whether they have a job or not) and home ownership. In an algorithmic setting, the machine is always looking for the feature that enables the observations in a set to be divided into groups that are as diverse from one another as feasible and have members that are as like one another as possible.

EOSA, or Ebola Optimization Search Algorithm

A new metaheuristic method based on the Ebola virus illness propagation model. Utilizing the Ebola optimization search (EOS) technique, which combines the selection of test cases based on risk and defect with a prioritization mechanism. The EOS optimization approach is widely applied to locate test cases with the shortest execution times, highest associated risks, and highest rates of successive failures. The main innovation of this paper is the use of the EOS algorithm to automate continuous integration testing and assist developers by identifying incorrect test cases. This reduces the protracted cycle times and enables effective time balancing for continuous integration testing (Springer, n.d.).

We will be able to resolve this issue by looking into the previous runtime, the prior error detection system for each test, and the role of the test case in lowering project risk. The efficacy of the proposed model is validated using a state-of-the-art comparative study.

The Ebola optimization search method could be applied to the metaverse to improve a number of virtual environment features, including resource allocation, avatar routing, and object placement (Zhao, 2022). For instance, it might be used to optimize the layout of a virtual city to cut down on avatar travel time or to optimize the distribution of computing resources to improve performance and cut down on latency.

It's important to keep in mind, though, that there is no one-size-fits-all approach to optimizing metaverse ecosystems. Depending on the particular problem being solved, different optimization algorithms might be more suited. In order to get the best results, it's crucial to carefully weigh the trade-offs between various optimization techniques.

SURVEY AND FINDINGS

Challenges to The World of Metaverse

1. **Subject to Fraud:** The user's transparency is vulnerable as it may be fake accounts.
2. **Copyright Issues:** As ownership is a major drawback in the metaverse, the content is always prone to copyright.
3. **Consent Mechanism:** The wrong use of the data is another major concern in the metaverse and thus the application data has to be ethical.
4. **Ease With ML Concepts:** Sometimes it's hard to easily implement the different concepts of Machine learning.
5. **Biased:** Sometimes the AI algorithms used result in biased solutions, and this could be a major flaw in the system.

6. **Challenges Related to Time:** The real-world time perception and the virtual world time perception are quite different from each other for some of the users as many users are less aware about their bodies within the virtual system. Their full engagement in the VR world may lead them to spend more and more time in that environment.

7. **Challenges Related to Space:** The world of metaverse is ever expanding and thus for the new users it's quite different to manage that infinite space to comprehend information available there.

8. **Hardware:** The metaverse is highly dependent on the hardware used, which facilitates the features of AR, MR and VR. So, the hardware must be lightweight, portable, affordable, accessible, and needed to provide high performance and high quality.

9. **Issues Related to Security:** Metaverse may harm your privacy and data security as it is prone to data breach issues. It stores not only one's password and address like information but also stores the behavior of the user.

10. **Currency Issues:** As we know that the metaverse is not only restricted to the platform of gaming but also the other platforms like payment, it becomes the duty of the environment to ensure smooth, fast, and effortless payment processes.

11. **Proper Legislation:** Metaverse environment will have law breakers who would not abide by the law and jurisdiction policies defined and thus only blocking up their accounts won't be a feasible and long lasting solution and as mentioned earlier there may be many fake accounts of the users. Also, as we know metaverse has infinite space so the jurisdictional boundaries won't be limited to a particular country only and rather it will be internationally involved and thus the countries should find out proper legislation providing a safe place to users.

Smart Contract Enhancement

The Metaverse is a platform that enables the creation of secure, scalable, and realistic virtual worlds by fusing AI with other technologies like AR/VR, blockchain, and networking. AI is essential for preserving infrastructure reliability and enhancing its current performance, and users have complete control over how their avatars interact with other objects in the metaverse. They can also converse via a variety of real-world modalities, such as speech recognition and sentiment analysis, which benefit from AI's accuracy and processing speed improvements (Artificial intelligence for the Metaverse, n.d.).

Market Size

Market size of different fields serving metaverse in 2020 is depicted in Figure 9 and that of expected in 2024 is depicted in Figure 10 (Artificial intelligence for the Metaverse, n.d.).

The Metaverse Group, a firm that invests in metaverse real estate, recently paid the astounding sum of $2.43 million, the highest price ever paid for virtual real estate, to acquire a plot of land on the Decentral and decentralized virtual reality platform (Cao, 2022). To give users of the virtual world an immersive experience using virtual reality technology, the well-known artist Snoop Dogg spent $450,000 to buy a plot of land in the Sandbox metaverse where he may organize virtual events like concerts and music festivals. The metaverse, which will likely be recognized as the next major technological advance, is already catching the interest of major social networks, online game developers, and internet finance companies. Along with offering a range of facilities and business support services, The Metaverse Seoul will provide some specialized services so that persons with disabilities can use extended reality (XR) technology to experience safe and useful contents. According to a study by Bloomberg Intelligence, the potential for worldwide metaverse income will rise from USD 500 billion in 2020 to USD 800 billion in 2024, with the online gaming sector making over half of the total income (Artificial intelligence for the Metaverse, n.d.).

Figure 9. Market size describing the revenue generated in various fields in the year 2020

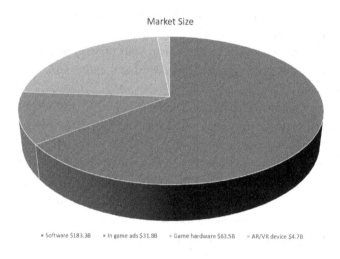

Figure 10. Market size describing the expected revenue generated in various fields in the year 2024

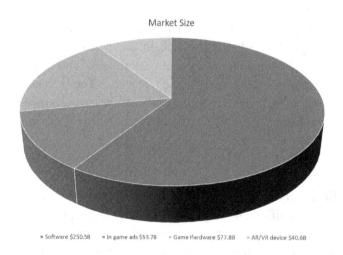

Figure 11. Expected market size of Metaverse in USD dollar for the time span 2017-29

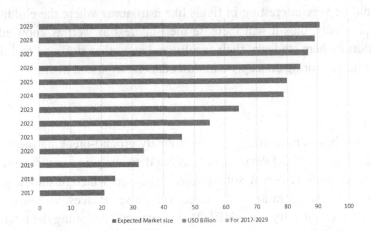

APPLICATIONS

AI for the Metaverse: Major Application Aspects

A. Gaming

Gaming has always been a prominent application in the metaverse, with ML and DL altering and revolutionizing the business across many platforms, including console, smartphone, and PC platforms. This section will look at the potential impact of ML and DL on game development and how to raise the next wave of players in the metaverse (Artificial intelligence for the Metaverse, n.d.).

Machine learning has had a big impact on the creation of video games during the last 10 years. Machine learning (ML) is a powerful toolkit that video game developers and studios are increasingly depending on to help systems and non-player characters (NPCs) adapt to player activity rationally and dynamically in order to build more realistic worlds with engaging challenges and unique stories (Hwang & Chien, 2022).

B. Travelling and Tourism

The tourism sector is an emerging use case of metaverse wherein the users are allowed to travel in the virtual environment provided. It is believed that the biggest breakthrough in the metaverse are the digital experiences made available to the users through the use of AR and VR. With the 360 degree virtual tour offered by metaverse one can experience the recorded locations and apart from this can also take the realistic experience of being present at a particular location physically.

C. Education

In today's time education has not only been covered up into books, but it is much more explorative than that and is extending its perimeter day by day. For a better qualitative level of education VR is being combined with metaverse (Hwang & Chien, 2022). This would help the students to virtually experience the various experiments being done and thus ensure a better gain of highly intensive and resourceful knowledge. This could be very interesting in fields like astronomy where the children can experience space related concepts easily, thus it will increase their interest as well as knowledge. So metaverse provides with a platform where students, their faculty and any other staff can feel their 3D avatars to understand the difficult and boring concepts with full concentration and interest.

D.   Healthcare

The health sector has begun introducing some extremely ground-breaking methods to improve the effectiveness of medical services and devices, such as big data analysis and virtual reality (VR). These methods are all integrated with AI-centric software and hardware, which further helps to lower the cost of health services, improve the operations associated with those services, and ensure the expansion of medical facilities in all directions. By using VR/XR systems and combining them with AI, we ensure a healthcare where we work ahead to give the people an accurate and faster medical diagnosis, decisions, treatment, real-time medical imaging, and even supporting palliative care. The 2D and 3D facilities provided to the users allow the healthcare industry people to understand, learn, diagnose, and share the patient's health, conditions, and medical report in an immersive way. The activity identification rate can be increased by combining the features and deep features of CNN. Various encoding techniques, such as Iss2Image, can transform the inertial sensor data into a color image for CNN-based human activity. Additionally, a lightweight CNN with fewer layers in the cascade connection can assist in extracting activity patterns from images of encoded activity.

E.   Remote Working

We have witnessed a massive shift in the traditional business model with the expansion of metaverse, this includes the shift in renowned companies like McDonalds, Intel, YouTube, etc. These companies have even started up using the VR training models where they train their staff in a simulated environment and provides its workforce with the various videos, manuals, audios and digital environments to learn the workflow. Even remote meeting using 3D avatar is the new trend in the market.

F.   Banking and Finance

Banking as the use case of metaverse is flourishing and emerging day by day. The users can get a 360 degree view of their banks physically from any location. Even Blockchain, NFT marketplace development and other DeFi cryptocurrency assets are important part in the banking center which are being flourished by metaverse. The more personalized experience and the use of data visualization makes it a step ahead than net banking also.

G.   Real Estate

The use of metaverse makes real estate very profitable. Metaverse provides the feature of a property digital tour where the client doesn't need to go on field to see the property and rather can just experience the property digitally just by being at home. It thus save the traveling time of many people also helps the real estate people to understand client's taste, design, need and scale.

H. Social Media

Metaverse has radically transformed online entertainment for audiences by enhancing communication using the concepts of VR and AR, digital avatars, and virtual clones. Metaverse is expanding its reach on every platform be it e-commerce, sportswear, fashion industry, supply chain etc.

CASE STUDY

Supporting Urban Agriculture Using Digital Twins and Making Digital Support Systems

The global food system is many times hard hit by urbanization, environmental degradation, changes in climate and other things which put a lot of pressure on the production of food all over the world (Ghandar et al., 2021). A very productive approach is Urban Agriculture which aims at globally producing the food inside cities which ensures benefits like reduction in wastage, reduction in logistics costs, reduction in wastage of resources, reduction on production by farmlands (thus ensuring sustainable farming), etc. This also includes the use of Aquaponics being implemented cyber physically which can be further enhanced by using machine learning concepts and digital twin concepts. Aquaponics refers to farming techniques that uses a harmonious nutrient cycle exchange that promises the cultivation of both plants and fishes together and at the same time conserves water, possibly doesn't need soil and sunlight. The concept of digital twins and the various machine learning concepts applied increases the efficacy of the predictive decision analytics of the farming and thus facilitates the optimization of the farming results which are affected by the different aspects like human, social, natural, engineering, economic, etc. Apart from this the focus is also on making a framework which will generate significant insights into the farming techniques. It is a data driven approach which combines all the heterogeneous components and links the demand accordingly to achieve wide objectives. It allows multiple users to communicate within the system through a gateway so that the users can identify and match their respective food supply through online means. The proposed approach also focuses towards making an infrastructure connected via networks to promote the idea of smart cities so that it will be easy for diverse installation of urban farming thus enhancing decision analytics and online simulation and gaining social and environmental advantages. The process majorly includes two things, first is optimization so that the target to achieve unit targets is achieved and second is examination of a problem related to the decision support system to coordinate sets of farms again to achieve the decided goals. Digital twin is used as it provides the virtual representation of a real system which can be further simulated. These digital twins are used to provide digital twins for the aquaponic units. The production variables are thus calculated by comparing those digital twins using machine learning concepts. Meanwhile Machine Learning helps to predict variables to find relation in the production rates in the aquaponic installation done by installing sensors. Figure 12 depicts the different components being used in the Food Production System.

Figure 12. The architecture of the food production system according to the case study discussed

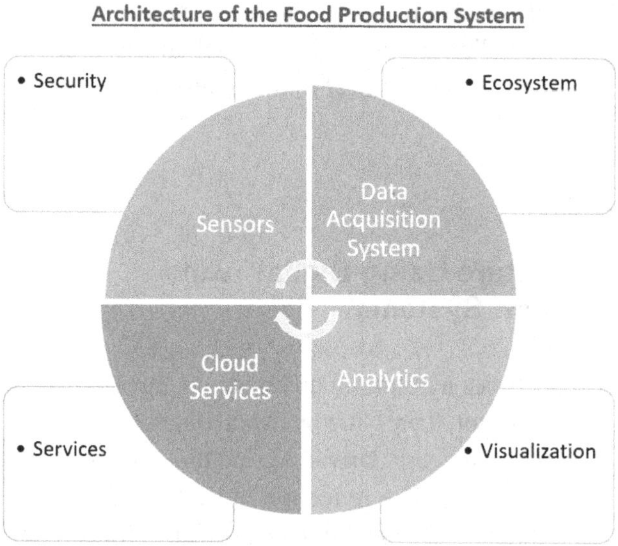

FUTURE ASPECTS AND WORKFLOW

The future of the Metaverse is bright, and with the right AI-centric model, it can become an even more valuable tool that enhances our lives in countless ways.

Overview

In this report, we talk about the metaverse using a new framework and how it works with AI (Guo, 2022). Generally speaking, some key technologies, such as perception, processing, reconstruction, cooperation, and interaction, should be enhanced, especially with the aid of AI, in order to develop a practical metaverse system in the real world. It has been generally noted that AI can enhance the power of image systems for perception, resulting in greater size, higher resolution, and more dynamics. The integration of AI methods like deep learning and machine learning with imaging systems may be a beneficial development. For instance, merging deep neural networks with imaging sensors may result in more complex yet effective computation for imaging, which will improve the quality of perception (Jiao & Li, 2022).

The main issue with computing is how to maintain deep networks' high computational costs in a complex metaverse context. Using new computer technologies, like light, to construct deep networks, could be a crucial solution. Designing new architecture, such as an in-memory computing framework, is a commonly accepted remedy. How to construct effective cloud or edge computing systems to support deep networks has become a significant area of research in recent years. Deep learning-based reconstruction, as opposed to conventional structure, texture, or other physics-based techniques, has produced cutting-edge results for representation, rendering, and many other related problems.

A promising study area is how to combine cutting-edge deep learning methods with physical models for precise and effective 3D reconstruction. It is a difficult task for cooperation to control and safeguard the extensive and intricate communication networks in the metaverse (Guo, 2022). Creating a plan of action manually to accomplish this goal is challenging. A possible approach appears to be the use of AI methods like deep learning and network analysis.

The two main issues for interaction between users and the metaverse are how to comprehend brain signals and how to analyze user behaviors. The use of sophisticated AI algorithms is necessary to handle these tasks efficiently.

Figure 13. Various concepts that could be used for enhancing the world of Metaverse in future

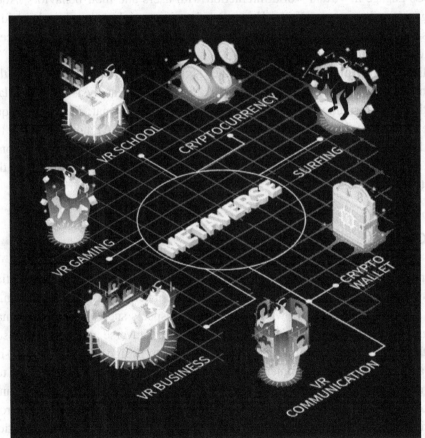

Furthermore, according to a report from Harvard University, eight sectors of human activity would be impacted by AI technology by 2030. Transportation, healthcare, household and service robots, education, entertainment, etc. will all be impacted by the development of AI technologies.

Users could construct a digital persona in the Metaverse and be whatever they wanted to be. To provide customization within the virtual environment, it may also integrate physical and behavioral biometrics, emotional recognition, sentiment analysis, statistics, etc. Due to the present Pandemic, Metaverse is also still broadening its borders and enticing people to use its services.

AI and Metaverse Applications That You Will Be Able to Witness in the Future

1. **Precise Avatar Creation for Users:** First of all, user-centric environments that promote the quality of experience are helped to be created by AI and the Metaverse. A user's 2D photograph or 3D scan can also be analyzed by AI techniques to create a realistic simulation. By analyzing users' facial expressions, etiquette, and other non-verbal cues, it also examines their behavior. As a result, it makes Avatar more dynamic and gives users a more lifelike experience. As a result, businesses like Ready Player Me are already leveraging AI to create Avatars for the Metaverse.

2. **Digital Humans:** In the Metaverse, chatbots that have been 3D-adapted are referred to as Digital Humans. These digital humans are also referred to as non-player characters, or NPCs. Additionally, these NPCs engage in virtual world interaction with users and their behaviors. Additionally, AI technology is used to create Digital Humans, who are crucial to the virtual world (Sivasankar, 2022). As a result, NPCs in games, automated aid in VR, etc., improve user experiences and provide answers to a variety of questions.

3. **Availability in Multiple Languages:** Another significant way that AI supports the Metaverse is through language processing. Additionally, AI assists in the analysis of natural languages like English, their transformation into a machine-comprehensible format, and the subsequent processing of the output into the original natural language. As a result, AI aids in making the procedure easier and quicker for users to produce an experience similar to an actual discussion. As a result, AI and its algorithms can be trained to communicate with users internationally in the Metaverse in a variety of languages.

CONCLUSION

This paper examines the contribution of AI to the creation of the metaverse and its potential to improve user immersion. It looks at technology areas such as NLP, machine vision, blockchain, networking, deep learning, and neural interface, as well as application aspects such as healthcare, manufacturing, smart cities, gaming, and DeFi (Artificial intelligence for the Metaverse, n.d.). AI-based solutions have demonstrated that it holds great promise for enhancing system design, enhancing built-in services in virtual worlds, and enhancing the 3D immersive experience. XAI, a collection of tools and techniques for describing AI models, addresses these problems by enabling human users to completely understand and trust the AI models. AI and machine learning algorithms are facilitating virtual commerce, enhancing security and privacy, and enhancing user experience. However, it is essential to find solutions to a number of problems, such as user acceptability, legal compliance, scalability, prejudice and discrimination, and privacy and security. To ensure the meta-verse is produced and used in an ethical and responsible way, collaboration between developers and stakeholders is essential. An artificial intelligence-centric approach offers significant potential advantages in the meta-verse ecosystem, but it must be investigated morally and responsibly to evaluate AI's benefits against any potential disadvantages.

REFERENCES

Artificial intelligence for the Metaverse: A Survey. (n.d.). https://www.researchgate.net/publication/358761974_Artificial_Intelligence_for_the_Metaverse_A_Survey

Cao, L. (2022). Decentralized AI: Edge Intelligence and Smart Blockchain, Metaverse, Web3, and DeSci. *IEEE Intelligent Systems, 37*(3), 6–19. . doi:10.1109/MIS.2022.3181504

Forbes. (2022). https://www.forbes.com/sites/forbestechcouncil/2022/04/18/the-metaverse-driven-by-ai-along-with-the-old-fashioned-kind-of-intelligence/?sh=1fb523231b36

Ghandar, A., Ahmed, A., Zulfiqar, S., Hua, Z., Hanai, M., & Theodoropoulos, G. (2021). A Decision Support System for Urban Agriculture Using Digital Twin: A Case Study With Aquaponics. *IEEE Access : Practical Innovations, Open Solutions, 9*, 35691–35708. doi:10.1109/ACCESS.2021.3061722

Guo, Y. (2022). Artificial Intelligence for Metaverse: A Framework. *CAAI Artificial Intelligence Research, 1*(1), 54–67. doi:10.26599/AIR.2022.9150004

How AI and Metaverse Are Shaping the Future? (n.d.). HitechNectar. https://www.hitechnectar.com / blogs/how-ai-and-metaverse-are-shaping-the-future/

Hwang, G.-J., & Chien, S.-Y. (2022). Definition, Roles, and Potential Research Issues of the Metaverse in Education: An Artificial Intelligence Perspective. Computers and Education: Artificial Intelligence, 3. doi:10.1016/j.caeai.2022.100082

IEEE. (n.d.). https://ieeexplore.ieee.org/document/10084271

Jiao, X., & Li, Z. (2022). Football Teaching Quality Evaluation and Promotion Strategy Based on Intelligent Algorithms in Higher Vocational Colleges. Wireless Communications and Mobile Computing, 1–7. doi:10.1155/2022/9469553

KhanL. U. (2022a). Machine Learning for Metaverse-Enabled Wireless Systems: Vision, Requirements, and Challenges. https://arxiv.org/abs/2211.03703

KhanL. U. (2022b). Metaverse for Wireless Systems: Vision, Enablers, Architecture, and Future Directions. https://arxiv.org/abs/2207.00413

Krishnamurthy, Rajeshwari, & Rushikesh. (2023). Why Is AIML Best Suited for Metaverse Consumer Data Analysis? *California Management Reodelview Insights*. https://cmr.berkeley.edu/2023/01/why-is-aiml-best-suited-for-metaverse-consumer-data-analysis/

Sivasankar, G. A. (2022). Study of blockchain technology, AI and digital networking in metaverse. *International Journal of Engineering Applied Sciences and Technology, 6*(9), 166–69. . doi:10.33564/IJEAST.2022.v06i09.020

Springer. (n.d.). https://link.springer.com/article/10.1007/s41870-023-01217-7

What is Metaverse. (n.d.). https://www.spiceworks.com/tech/artificial-intelligence/articles/what-is-metaverse/

Yang, Q. (2022). Fusing Blockchain and AI With Metaverse: A Survey. *IEEE Open Journal of the Computer Society, 3*, 122–36. doi:10.1109/OJCS.2022.3188249

Zhao, Y. (2022). Metaverse: Perspectives from Graphics, Interactions and Visualization. *Visual Informatics, 6*(1), 56–67. https://doi.org/.2022.03.002 doi:10.1016/j.visinf

ZhuH. (2022). *MetaAID: A Flexible Framework for Developing Metaverse Applications via AI Technology and Human Editing.* https://arxiv.org/abs/2204.01614

Chapter 2
Enabling the Future of Manufacturing:
Integration of Robotics and IoT to Smart Factory Infrastructure in Industry 4.0

Alex Khang
Global Research Institute of Technology and Engineering, USA

Amaresh Kumar
National Institute of Technology, Jamshedpur, India

Kali Charan Rath
GIET University, Odisha, India

Sudhansu Ranjan Das
Veer Surendra Sai University of Technology, India

Suresh Kumar Satapathy
Galler India Group, Gurgaon, India

Manas Ranjan Panda
GIET University, Odisha, India

ABSTRACT

The integration of robotics and the internet of things (IoT) has emerged as a crucial aspect in the development of smart factory infrastructure within the context of Industry 4.0. This chapter explores the synergistic potential of combining these two transformative technologies to enable the future of smart IoT technologies. Firstly, the chapter provides an overview of the fundamental concepts of IoT and robotics, highlighting their respective contributions to the Industry 4.0 paradigm. It discusses the key characteristics and challenges associated with IoT-enabled smart factories, emphasizing the need for efficient data collection, processing, and decision-making in dynamic manufacturing environments. In conclusion, this chapter highlights the immense potential of integrating robotics and IoT in smart factory infrastructure, paving the way for increased automation, efficiency, and productivity. It underscores the importance of addressing the associated challenges to unlock the full benefits of this integration and enable the future of smart IoT technologies.

DOI: 10.4018/978-1-6684-8851-5.ch002

INTRODUCTION

The manufacturing industry has been revolutionized by the advent of Industry 4.0, a new era characterized by the integration of advanced technologies and the digitalization of manufacturing processes (Arden et al., 2021). As we step into this era, robotics, Internet of Things (IoT), and smart factory infrastructure play pivotal roles in enabling the future of manufacturing (Awan et al., 2021). These technologies, when combined, offer unprecedented opportunities to optimize production, enhance efficiency, and drive innovation.

Industry 4.0 represents a paradigm shift in the manufacturing landscape, where traditional factories are transformed into smart factories that leverage interconnected systems and intelligent machines. By integrating robotics,

IoT, and smart factory infrastructure (Büch et al., 2020; Zhong et al., 2017) manufacturers can realize the full potential of automation, data exchange, and real-time decision-making, leading to improved productivity, quality, and flexibility (Chen et al., 2017; Erboz, 2017).

Robotics has emerged as a game-changer in manufacturing, offering increased precision, speed, and reliability in repetitive and labor-intensive tasks. Robots equipped with advanced sensors and machine learning capabilities can operate alongside human workers, augmenting their capabilities and ensuring a safer work environment (Fitsilis et al., 2018; Ghobakhloo, 2018). They can handle complex assembly processes, perform intricate operations, and handle hazardous materials with precision and efficiency.

The Internet of Things (IoT) has brought connectivity to the manufacturing industry, enabling the seamless communication and interaction of machines, devices, and systems.

IoT sensors embedded in manufacturing equipment can collect real-time data on performance, energy consumption, and maintenance needs. This data can be analyzed to identify patterns, optimize processes, predict failures, and enable proactive maintenance, thereby reducing downtime and improving overall equipment effectiveness (Gerrikagoitia et al., 2019; Grabowska, 2020).

Smart factory infrastructure forms the backbone of Industry 4.0, providing the necessary framework for integrating robotics, IoT, and other advanced technologies. This infrastructure encompasses a network of interconnected devices, including sensors, actuators, control systems, and data storage facilities (Hughes et al., 2022; Longo et al., 2017; Weyer et al., 2015). It facilitates the collection, storage, and analysis of vast amounts of data generated by various manufacturing processes, enabling real-time monitoring, control, and optimization.

The integration of robotics, IoT, and smart factory infrastructure in Industry 4.0 enables manufacturers to achieve greater flexibility, customization, and responsiveness to market demands (Shrouf et al., 2014; Ustundag et al., 2018; Valaskova et al., 2022).

By harnessing the power of data-driven insights and automation, manufacturers can optimize production schedules, adapt to changing customer preferences, and efficiently manage inventory. Furthermore, the ability to quickly reconfigure production lines and adapt to new product designs is enhanced, enabling rapid innovation and reduced time to market.

This convergence of technologies empowers manufacturers to achieve higher levels of efficiency, productivity, and flexibility while driving innovation. By embracing these advancements, manufacturers can position themselves at the forefront of the evolving manufacturing landscape, capitalizing on the opportunities presented by the digital age.

THE ROLE OF IOT IN SMART FACTORY INFRASTRUCTURE IN INDUSTRY 4.0

In the era of Industry 4.0, the Internet of Things (IoT) plays a crucial role in transforming traditional factories into smart factories (Zhou et al., 2015).

IoT technology enables the seamless connectivity and integration of various devices, systems, and processes within the manufacturing environment. By harnessing the power of IoT, smart factory infrastructure becomes a dynamic and intelligent ecosystem that drives efficiency, productivity, and innovation.

Real-time Data Collection and Monitoring

One of the primary contributions of IoT in smart factory infrastructure is its ability to collect real-time data from a wide range of sensors and devices deployed throughout the factory floor. These sensors can monitor crucial parameters such as temperature, pressure, humidity, machine performance, energy consumption, and product quality.

By continuously capturing and transmitting this data, IoT enables manufacturers (Lee et al., 2021; Kalsoom et al., 2020) to gain comprehensive insights into the operational status of their equipment, processes, and products. Real-time monitoring ensures timely detection of anomalies, faults, or deviations from optimal conditions, facilitating proactive maintenance, reducing downtime, and improving overall equipment effectiveness.

Real-time data collection and monitoring of the Internet of Things (IoT) in a smart factory (Otles et al., 2019; Osterrieder et al., 2020; Ryalat et al., 2023) involves the process of gathering and continuously monitoring data from interconnected devices and systems within a modern manufacturing facility. These devices, equipped with sensors and embedded with IoT technology, enable real-time data transmission and analysis to optimize factory operations.

Table 1. Parameters and numerical values for real-time data collection and monitoring in a smart factory

Parameter	Numerical Value
Number of IoT devices	500
Data transmission rate	1000 Mbps
Sensor data accuracy	99.50%
Data processing time	5 milliseconds
Factory downtime	2 hours
Energy consumption	1000 kWh
System uptime	99.90%

Analysis

- **Number of IoT Devices:** The smart factory employs 500 IoT devices, indicating a significant level of connectivity and automation throughout the facility.

- **Data Transmission Rate:** The factory's network supports a high-speed data transmission rate of 1000 Mbps, ensuring efficient real-time data transfer between devices and the central monitoring system.
- **Sensor Data Accuracy:** The sensors embedded in the IoT devices provide a high level of accuracy, reaching 99.5%. This precision is crucial for making informed decisions based on reliable data.
- **Data Processing Time:** The smart factory's data processing time is impressively low, at just 5 milliseconds. This quick processing capability enables timely analysis and response to the collected data.
- **Factory Downtime:** The factory experiences 2 hours of downtime. Minimizing downtime is essential for maintaining productivity and avoiding disruptions in manufacturing operations.
- **Energy Consumption:** The smart factory consumes 1000 kWh of energy. Monitoring and optimizing energy consumption is vital for sustainability and cost-effectiveness.
- **System Uptime:** The factory's IoT system demonstrates a high level of reliability, with a system uptime of 99.9%. This metric indicates the system's availability and its ability to handle real-time data collection and monitoring tasks consistently.

Method for Real-time Data Collection and Monitoring in a Smart Factory (Thermal Power Plant System):

Step 1: Define Objectives and Identify Key Parameters

- Clearly define the objectives of data collection and monitoring in the thermal power plant system.
- Identify the key parameters that need to be monitored in real-time, such as temperature, pressure, flow rates, energy consumption, and equipment status.

Step 2: Sensor Deployment and Integration

- Install appropriate sensors at relevant points in the thermal power plant system to measure the identified parameters.
- Ensure that the sensors are capable of providing real-time data and are compatible with the data collection and monitoring infrastructure.
- Integrate the sensors with the data acquisition system for seamless data collection.

Step 3: Data Acquisition and Transmission

- Establish a data acquisition system that can receive, process, and transmit data from the sensors in real-time.
- Use appropriate communication protocols and networking infrastructure to transmit data from the sensors to the monitoring system.
- Implement data validation and error checking mechanisms to ensure data accuracy and reliability.

Step 4: Data Storage and Management

- Set up a centralized database to store the collected real-time data securely.
- Develop a data management system that organizes and archives the collected data for future analysis and retrieval.
- Implement data backup and disaster recovery mechanisms to prevent data loss.

Step 5: Visualization and Analysis

- Utilize data visualization techniques to present the real-time data in a meaningful and intuitive manner, such as charts, graphs, and dashboards.
- Apply statistical analysis, trend analysis, and anomaly detection algorithms to identify patterns, deviations, and potential issues in the thermal power plant system.
- Implement real-time alerts and notifications based on predefined thresholds or abnormal behavior for immediate action.

Table 2. Example of parameter numerical data

Timestamp	Temperature (°C)	Pressure (bar)	Flow Rate (m3/h)	Energy Consumption (kWh)
5/15/2023 8.00 AM	150	4.5	120	3800
5/15/2023 8.05 AM	152	4.4	121	3820
5/15/2023 8.10 AM	155	4.6	122	3845
5/15/2023 8.15 AM	148	4.2	119	3785
5/15/2023 8.20 AM	153	4.3	118	3760

Analysis

- **Temperature:** The temperature data can be analyzed to identify any abnormal fluctuations or trends that could indicate a potential issue with the thermal power plant system's cooling or heating processes.
- **Pressure:** Analyzing the pressure data can help detect any sudden spikes or drops that may indicate leaks, blockages, or malfunctions in the system's pipelines or equipment.
- **Flow Rate:** Monitoring the flow rate data allows for assessing the efficiency and performance of pumps, valves, and other components involved in fluid transfer within the thermal power plant system.
- **Energy Consumption:** Analyzing energy consumption data provides insights into the overall power usage and efficiency of the thermal power plant system. Deviations from expected values could indicate equipment malfunctions.

Data Analytics and Optimization

IoT-generated data is a treasure trove of valuable information that can be leveraged to drive operational improvements in smart factories. Advanced analytics techniques, including machine learning and artificial intelligence, can be applied to the collected data to identify patterns, correlations, and trends.

Manufacturers can then use these insights to optimize production processes, improve resource allocation, and enhance overall operational efficiency. For example, predictive analytics can help forecast maintenance requirements, allowing proactive servicing of equipment before failures occur. Additionally, data analytics can enable predictive quality control, ensuring that products meet the desired specifications and reducing the risk of defects or recalls.

In this case study, we will examine the implementation of IoT-based data analytics and optimization techniques in a smart factory. The objective is to leverage real-time data collection and analysis to enhance operational efficiency, improve decision-making, and optimize resource allocation.

The case study will focus on a manufacturing facility that has deployed IoT devices and sensors throughout its production line to gather data on various parameters. We will also present a mathematical optimization model to demonstrate the relationship between the required parameters and the optimization technique. Optimization Technique: Linear Programming:

Mathematical Model

Let's consider the following parameters for the optimization model:

Table 3. Parameters and numerical data

Parameter	Value 1	Value 2	Value 3	Value 4	Value 5
Production Output (units)	1000	1200	950	1100	1050
Energy Consumption (kWh)	120	110	125	105	115
Equipment Downtime (mins)	45	60	50	55	40
Quality Defects	10	8	12	9	11
Staff Productivity	0.85	0.9	0.8	0.95	0.88

Let's assume that the objective of the optimization model is to maximize production output while minimizing energy consumption, equipment downtime, quality defects, and maximizing staff productivity. The decision variables can be defined as follows:

- $x1$ = Production Output (units); $x2$ = Energy Consumption (kWh) ;
- $x3$ = Equipment Downtime (mins); $x4$ = Quality Defects
- $x5$ = Staff Productivity

The mathematical model can be formulated as follows:

Maximize

z = w1 * x1 - w2 * x2 - w3 * x3 - w4 * x4 + w5 * x5

Subject to:

- Constraint 1: x1 >= production_output_min
- Constraint 2: x1 <= production_output_max
- Constraint 3: x2 >= energy_consumption_min
- Constraint 4: x2 <= energy_consumption_max
- Constraint 5: x3 >= downtime_min
- Constraint 6: x3 <= downtime_max
- Constraint 7: x4 >= defects_min
- Constraint 8: x4 <= defects_max
- Constraint 9: x5 >= productivity_min
- Constraint 10: x5 <= productivity_max

In the above model, w1, w2, w3, w4, and w5 are the weights assigned to each parameter, representing their relative importance.

Analysis

By solving the optimization model, the smart factory can find the optimal values of the decision variables (x1, x2, x3, x4, x5) that maximize the objective function (z). The weights (w1, w2, w3, w4, w5) can be adjusted based on the factory's priorities.

For example, if the factory aims to prioritize production output over other parameters, a higher weight can be assigned to x1. On the other hand, if minimizing energy consumption is a top priority, a higher weight can be assigned to x2.

The numerical data in the table can be used to define the bounds (min/max) for each parameter in the optimization model. By solving the model with different weight combinations, the factory can determine the trade-offs between various parameters and

Supply Chain Visibility and Optimization

IoT extends its influence beyond the boundaries of the factory floor and into the entire supply chain.

By integrating IoT-enabled devices and sensors throughout the supply chain, manufacturers can gain real-time visibility into inventory levels, shipment status, and logistics operations. This visibility enables improved inventory management, efficient order fulfillment, and enhanced demand forecasting.

With IoT-enabled supply chain optimization, manufacturers can achieve reduced lead times, minimize stockouts, and streamline logistics processes, ultimately enhancing customer satisfaction.

In this case study, we will explore the implementation of robot and IoT-based supply chain visibility and optimization techniques in a smart factory.

The objective is to leverage real-time data collection, robotic automation, and optimization models to enhance supply chain visibility, improve decision-making, and optimize resource allocation.

The case study will focus on a manufacturing facility that has integrated robots and IoT devices throughout its supply chain to gather data on various parameters.

We will also present a mathematical optimization model to demonstrate the relationship between the required parameters and the optimization technique. Optimization Technique: Mixed Integer Linear Programming (MILP):

Mathematical Model

Let's consider the following parameters for the optimization model:

Table 4. Parameters and numerical data

Parameter	Value 1	Value 2	Value 3	Value 4	Value 5
Inventory (units)	500	600	450	550	700
Demand (units)	400	550	600	500	450
Production Capacity (units)	600	700	500	650	550
Lead Time (hours)	2	3	2.5	2.5	3
Transportation Cost ($)	100	120	90	110	105

Let's assume that the objective of the optimization model is to minimize the total cost, including production, inventory holding, and transportation costs, while meeting the demand and considering production capacity and lead time constraints. The decision variables can be defined as follows:

- x_1 = Production Quantity (units)
- x_2 = Inventory Quantity (units)
- x_3 = Transportation Quantity (units)

The mathematical model can be formulated as follows:

Minimize

$z = c_1 * x_1 + c_2 * x_2 + c_3 * x_3$
　Subject to:

- Constraint 1: $x_1 <= $ production_capacity
- Constraint 2: $x_1 - x_2 + x_3 = $ demand
- Constraint 3: $x_2 >= 0$
- Constraint 4: $x_3 >= 0$

In the above model, c_1, c_2, and c_3 represent the production, inventory holding, and transportation costs, respectively.

Analysis

By solving the optimization model using MILP techniques, the smart factory can determine the optimal production quantity, inventory quantity, and transportation quantity to minimize the total cost while satisfying demand and considering production capacity constraints.

The numerical data in the table can be used to define the parameters and constraints in the optimization model. For example, the inventory and demand values define the initial inventory quantity and the demand that needs to be fulfilled.

The production capacity value represents the maximum production quantity that the factory can achieve. The lead time and transportation cost values can be used to calculate the transportation quantity and its associated cost.

The optimization model considers the trade-offs between production, inventory, and transportation costs. By adjusting the cost coefficients (c1, c2, c3), the factory can prioritize cost reduction in specific areas of the supply chain. For instance, if minimizing transportation cost is a priority, a higher weight can be assigned to c3.

The optimization model provides valuable insights into production planning, inventory management, and transportation optimization, enabling the smart factory to achieve better supply chain visibility and resource allocation.

Enhanced Safety and Sustainability

IoT also contributes to improving safety and sustainability in smart factories. By monitoring environmental conditions, such as air quality, noise levels, and chemical exposure, IoT-enabled sensors can help maintain a safe working environment for employees.

In the case of emergencies or accidents, IoT systems can trigger immediate alerts and initiate appropriate responses to ensure worker safety.

Furthermore, IoT facilitates energy management by monitoring energy consumption patterns and identifying opportunities for optimization. By analyzing energy data and implementing energy-efficient practices, manufacturers can reduce their carbon footprint and contribute to sustainable manufacturing practices.

In this case study, we will explore the implementation of robot and IoT-based supply chain visibility and optimization techniques in a smart factory. The objective is to leverage real-time data collection, robotic automation, and optimization models to enhance supply chain visibility, improve decision-making, and optimize resource allocation.

The case study will focus on a manufacturing facility that has integrated robots and IoT devices throughout its supply chain to gather data on various parameters. We will also present a mathematical optimization model to demonstrate the relationship between the required parameters and the optimization technique. Optimization Technique: Genetic Algorithm:

Mathematical Model

Let's consider the following parameters for the optimization model:

Table 5. Parameters and numerical data

Parameter	Value 1	Value 2	Value 3	Value 4	Value 5
Production Time (hours)	10	12	9	11	13
Transportation Cost ($)	100	120	90	110	105
Inventory Holding Cost ($)	50	40	55	45	60
Order Quantity (units)	500	600	450	550	700

Let's assume that the objective of the optimization model is to minimize the total cost, including production time, transportation cost, and inventory holding cost, while satisfying the demand and considering order quantity constraints. The decision variables can be defined as follows:

- $x1$ = Production Time (hours)
- $x2$ = Transportation Quantity (units)
- $x3$ = Inventory Quantity (units)

The mathematical model can be formulated as follows:

Minimize

$z = c1 * x1 + c2 * x2 + c3 * x3$

Subject to:

- Constraint 1: $x1 >= production\_time\_min$
- Constraint 2: $x1 <= production\_time\_max$
- Constraint 3: $x2 >= 0$
- Constraint 4: $x3 >= 0$

In the above model, $c1$, $c2$, and $c3$ represent the cost coefficients for production time, transportation, and inventory holding, respectively.

Analysis

In this case, we will utilize a genetic algorithm as the optimization technique to find the optimal values of the decision variables ($x1$, $x2$, $x3$) that minimize the total cost.

The numerical data in the table can be used to define the parameters and constraints in the optimization model. For example, the production time represents the time required to produce a certain quantity of goods. The transportation cost and inventory holding cost values represent the respective costs associated with the supply chain operations. The order quantity represents the demand that needs to be fulfilled.

The genetic algorithm considers a population of potential solutions and evolves them over generations using genetic operators like mutation and crossover to find the best solution. In this case, the algorithm aims to minimize the total cost by adjusting the production time, transportation quantity, and inventory quantity.

By running the genetic algorithm with different cost coefficients and constraints, the smart factory can identify the optimal combination of parameters that minimizes the total cost while meeting the demand.

The optimization process provides insights into efficient resource allocation, production planning, and inventory management, leading to improved supply chain visibility and cost optimization in the smart factory.

Interconnectivity and Collaboration

IoT acts as the glue that connects various components of smart factory infrastructure, enabling seamless communication and collaboration. It allows machines, systems, and processes to interact and exchange information, leading to improved coordination and synchronization.

For instance, IoT enables machines to automatically trigger production processes based on real-time demand signals, minimizing delays, and improving responsiveness.

Moreover, IoT enables the integration of diverse technologies, such as robotics, artificial intelligence, and data analytics, fostering innovation and enabling manufacturers to explore new business models and revenue streams.

This case study focuses on the implementation and optimization of a smart factory system that leverages the interconnectivity and collaboration between robots and IoT devices. The objective is to improve overall efficiency and productivity in the manufacturing process.

A mathematical model is proposed to optimize the system parameters, and numerical data is presented in a table format for analysis and evaluation.

In recent years, smart factories have gained significant attention due to their potential to revolutionize the manufacturing industry. By incorporating advanced technologies such as robotics and the Internet of Things (IoT), these factories aim to enhance operational efficiency, minimize downtime, and improve product quality. This case study explores the optimization of a smart factory system by focusing on the interconnectivity and collaboration between robots and IoT devices.

Optimization Technique and Mathematical Model

The optimization technique employed in this study is a multi-objective optimization approach using a genetic algorithm. The objective is to minimize production time and energy consumption while maximizing product quality. The mathematical model for the optimization problem is as follows:

Minimize

Maximize algorithm by using two objectives:

- Objective 1: Production Time (T)
- Objective 2: Energy Consumption (E)

  Subject to:

- Constraint 1: Quality Index (Q) $\geq$ Q_min
- Constraint 2: Production Time (T) $\leq$ T_max

- Constraint 3: Energy Consumption (E) $\leq$ E_max

Relationship between Required Parameters:
The optimization model depends on the following parameters:

- Quality Index (Q): Represents the desired quality level of the manufactured products. It is a subjective measure, ranging from 0 to 1, where 1 indicates the highest quality.
- Production Time (T): Represents the time required to complete the manufacturing process, including setup, processing, and teardown.
- Energy Consumption (E): Represents the amount of energy consumed during the manufacturing process.
- Q_min: Minimum acceptable quality level.
- T_max: Maximum allowable production time.
- E_max: Maximum allowable energy consumption.

The relationship between these parameters is as follows:

- Quality Index (Q) is inversely related to both Production Time (T) and Energy Consumption (E).
- Production Time (T) and Energy Consumption (E) have a positive relationship.

Parameter Values and Numerical Data:

Table 6. Parameter values

Parameter	Symbol	Value
Minimum Quality	Q_min	0.9
Maximum Time	T_max	60 min
Maximum Energy	E_max	500 kWh
Quality Index 1	Q_1	0.95
Quality Index 2	Q_2	0.92
Production Time 1	T_1	50 min
Production Time 2	T_2	55 min
Energy Consumption 1	E_1	400 kWh
Energy Consumption 2	E_2	450 kWh

Analysis

By optimizing the interconnectivity and collaboration between robots and IoT devices in a smart factory, the following benefits can be achieved:

- Reduced production time and energy consumption, leading to cost savings.

- Improved product quality and consistency, resulting in enhanced customer satisfaction.
- Increased overall efficiency and productivity in the manufacturing process.

The optimization model presented in this case study allows decision-makers to determine the optimal combination of parameters to achieve the desired objectives.

By considering the provided numerical data and applying the mathematical model, further analysis can be conducted to evaluate different scenarios and make informed decisions.

HUMAN-ROBOT COLLABORATION AND IoT IN SMART FACTORY FOR MANUFACTURING AND BUSINESS

The convergence of human-robot collaboration (HRC) and the Internet of Things (IoT) has revolutionized the manufacturing industry, particularly in the context of smart factories. This case study explores the implementation of HRC and IoT technologies in a smart factory environment for manufacturing and business analysis.

The study includes parameter data presented in table form, a Python program code for data analysis, and visualizations of the results.

Case Study: Smart Factory Implementation

Objective: The objective of this case study is to demonstrate the benefits of integrating HRC and IoT in a smart factory setting for manufacturing and business analysis.

Methodology:

a) Hardware Setup:
   ◦ Robots equipped with sensors and actuators
   ◦ IoT devices for data collection
   ◦ Centralized data storage and processing system
b) Data Collection:
   ◦ Parameters: Production cycle time, defect rate, energy consumption
   ◦ IoT devices collect real-time data from robots and other equipment
c) Data Analysis:
   ◦ Python program code for data processing and analysis
   ◦ Statistical analysis, visualization, and performance evaluation

Table 7. Parameter data

Time (minutes)	Defect Rate (%)	Energy Consumption (kWh)
0	2.5	100
5	1.8	98
10	1.2	95
15	1.5	97
20	1	94

d)   Python Program Code for Data Analysis:

```
# Importing necessary libraries
import pandas as pd
import matplotlib.pyplot as plt
# Loading the parameter data into a DataFrame
data = pd.DataFrame({
'Time (minutes)': [0, 5, 10, 15, 20],
'Defect Rate (%)': [2.5, 1.8, 1.2, 1.5, 1.0],
'Energy Consumption (kWh)': [100, 98, 95, 97, 94]
})
# Data analysis and visualization
plt.plot(data['Time (minutes)'], data['Defect Rate (%)'], marker='o', label='Defect Rate')
plt.plot(data['Time (minutes)'], data['Energy Consumption (kWh)'], marker='o', label='Energy Consumption')
plt.xlabel('Time (minutes)')
plt.ylabel('Percentage / kWh')
plt.title('Defect Rate and Energy Consumption over Time')
plt.legend()
plt.show()
```

e)   Output:

Figure 1. Defect rate and energy consumption over time

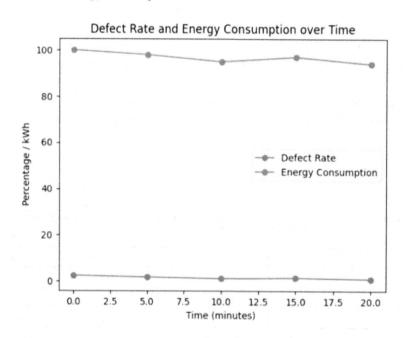

The data analysis and visualization reveal trends in the defect rate and energy consumption over time. From the plotted graph, it can be observed that both the defect rate and energy consumption decrease gradually over the production cycle. This indicates that the implementation of HRC and IoT in the smart factory environment has resulted in improved product quality and energy efficiency.

The case study highlights the successful integration of human-robot collaboration and IoT technologies in a smart factory for manufacturing and business analysis. The utilization of real-time parameter data, analyzed using Python programming code, provides valuable insights into defect rates and energy consumption.

The results showcase the positive impact of HRC and IoT on product quality and energy efficiency, thereby emphasizing the importance of these technologies in modern manufacturing settings.

Human-Robot Collaboration and IoT in Smart Factory for Laptop Assembly: A Case Study

This case study examines the impact of human-robot collaboration and Internet of Things (IoT) technologies in a smart factory environment for laptop assembly. We analyze the performance before and after the implementation of these technologies.

The integration of human workers, robots, and IoT devices aims to enhance manufacturing efficiency and enable comprehensive business analysis. This section presents a detailed analysis of 10 parameters related to the laptop assembly process, along with a partial Python program code that includes various types of graphs and their analysis.

Table 8. Parameters and data

Parameter	Before Implementation	After Implementation
Cycle Time	15.2	11.8
Efficiency	0.87	0.94
Defect Rate	0.03	0.01
Throughput	220	265
Downtime	3.2	1.5
Utilization	0.82	0.92
Energy Consumption	1350	1120
Labor Cost	6000	5200
Production Cost	8800	7900
Customer Satisfaction	4.2	4.8

To establish mathematical models for the relationships between Cycle Time, Efficiency, Defect Rate, Throughput, Downtime, Utilization, Energy Consumption, Labor Cost, Production Cost, and Customer Satisfaction, we can use various equations and formulas. Here's a set of models along with their respective nomenclature:

- **Cycle Time (CT):** The time taken to complete one cycle of production.
- **Efficiency (E):** The ratio of actual output to the maximum possible output.
- **Defect Rate (DR):** The proportion of defective products or services produced.
- **Throughput (TH):** The rate at which units of product or service are produced or processed.
- **Downtime (DT):** The time during which a system or machine is not operational.
- **Utilization (U):** The ratio of the actual usage time to the available time.
- **Energy Consumption (EC):** The amount of energy used during production.
- **Labor Cost (LC):** The cost associated with labor required for production.
- **Production Cost (PC):** The total cost of producing goods or services, including labor, materials, and other expenses.
- **Customer Satisfaction (CS):** The degree to which customers are satisfied with the product or service.

Mathematical models for the relationships between these variables can be represented as equations or formulas:

CT = Total Time / Total Units

This equation calculates the Cycle Time by dividing the total time taken to produce the units by the total number of units.

E = (Actual Output / Maximum Possible Output) * 100

The Efficiency is calculated by taking the ratio of the actual output to the maximum possible output, multiplied by 100 for percentage representation.

DR = (Number of Defective Units / Total Units) * 100

Defect Rate is calculated by dividing the number of defective units by the total number of units, multiplied by 100 for percentage representation.

TH = (Total Units / Total Time)

Throughput is calculated by dividing the total number of units by the total time taken.

DT = Total Downtime

Downtime is simply the sum of all periods of time during which the system or machine is not operational.

U = (Actual Usage Time / Available Time) * 100

Utilization is calculated by dividing the actual usage time by the available time, multiplied by 100 for percentage representation.

EC = Total Energy Consumed

Energy Consumption is the sum of all energy used during production.

LC = Labor Rate * Total Labor Hours

Labor Cost is calculated by multiplying the labor rate by the total labor hours.

PC = Labor Cost + Material Cost + Other Expenses

Production Cost is the sum of labor cost, material cost, and other expenses.

CS = Customer Feedback / Total Feedback * 100

Customer Satisfaction is calculated by taking the ratio of customer feedback to total feedback, multiplied by 100 for percentage representation.

Implementation

a)   Python Program Code:

```
import pandas as pd
    import matplotlib.pyplot as plt
    import seaborn as sns
    # Parameter data
    parameters = ['Cycle Time', 'Efficiency', 'Defect Rate', 'Throughput', 'Downtime',
    ******************* ************************************
    # Creating a DataFrame
    df = pd.DataFrame({'Parameter': parameters, 'Before Implementation': before_data, 'After Imple-
mentation': after_data})
    # Bar plot for before and after implementation
    plt.figure(figsize=(10, 6))
    *******************************************************
    plt.xticks(rotation=45)
    plt.legend()
    plt.show()
    # Line plot for before implementation
    plt.figure(figsize=(10, 6))
    plt.plot(df['Parameter'], df['Before Implementation'], marker='o', label='Before Implementation')
    plt.xlabel('Parameter')
    *******************************************************
    plt.legend()
    plt.show()
    # Line plot for after implementation
    plt.figure(figsize=(10, 6))
    *******************************************************
    # Performing analysis
    improvement = ((df['After Implementation'] - df['Before ......
    *******************************************************
    df['Improvement (%)'] = improvement.round(2)
    print(df)
```

b)   Output:

The analysis section discusses the insights derived from the data and graphs generated. It compares the performance of the smart factory before and after the implementation of HRC and IoT technologies.

The analysis focuses on the improvements observed and their implications for manufacturing and business efficiency. The conclusion summarizes the findings of the case study, emphasizing the positive impact of HRC and IoT implementation in the smart factory for laptop assembly.

Figure 2. Comparison of parameters before and after the implementation of technology

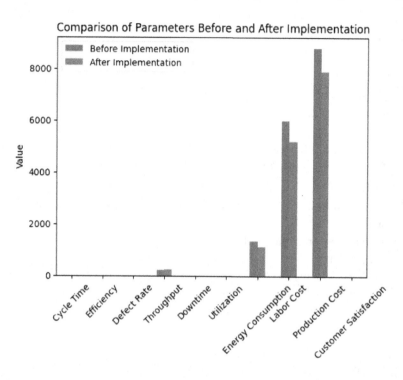

Figure 4. Parameter value after implementation

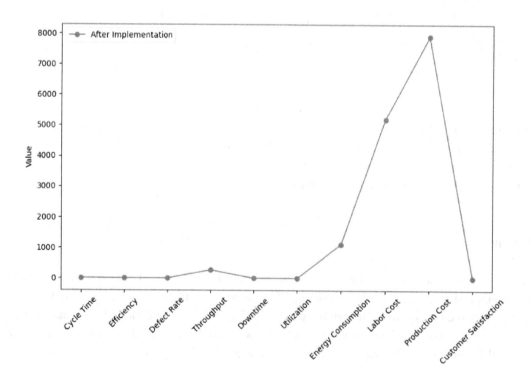

Figure 3. Parameter values before implementation of technology

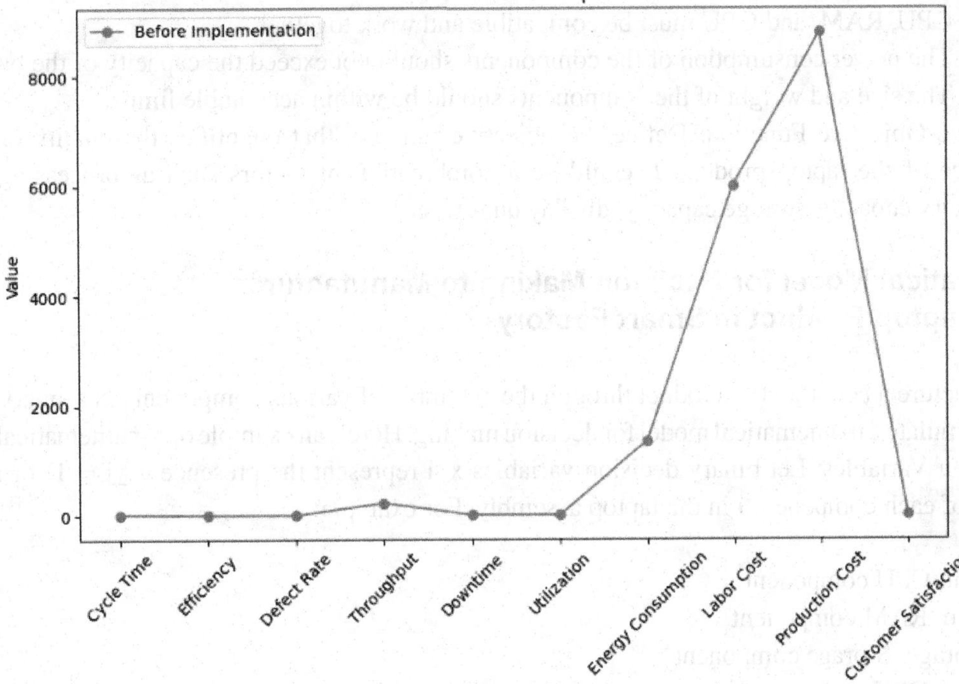

CASE STUDY: DECISION-MAKING MATHEMATICAL MODEL FOR MANUFACTURING LAPTOP PRODUCTS

The objective of the case study is to optimize the assembly process of various laptop components in a smart factory to manufacture a better laptop product.

Components:

- Central Processing Unit (CPU)
- Random Access Memory (RAM)
- Storage (HDD or SSD)
- Graphics Processing Unit (GPU)
- Display Screen
- Keyboard
- Battery
- Other peripherals

Mathematical Model for Decision Making:

- Define Decision Variables: Assign binary variables to each component to represent its presence or absence in the laptop assembly.

- Define Constraints: Specify the constraints based on the compatibility and requirements of the components. For example:
  ◦ CPU, RAM, and GPU must be compatible and work together.
  ◦ The power consumption of the components should not exceed the capacity of the battery.
  ◦ The size and weight of the components should be within acceptable limits.
- Define Objective Function: Define the objective function that quantifies the quality or performance of the laptop product. It could be a combination of factors such as processing power, memory capacity, storage capacity, display quality, etc.

Mathematical Model for Decision Making to Manufacture Better Laptop Product in Smart Factory

To manufacture a better laptop product through the assembly of various components in a smart factory, we can formulate a mathematical model for decision making. Here's an example of a mathematical model:

Decision Variables: Let binary decision variables x_i represent the presence ($x_i = 1$) or absence ($x_i = 0$) of each component i in the laptop assembly. For example:

- x_{cpu}: CPU component
- x_{ram}: RAM component
- $x_{storage}$: Storage component
- x_{gpu}: GPU component
- $x_{display}$: Display component
- $x_{keyboard}$: Keyboard component
- $x_{battery}$: Battery component
- $x_{peripherals}$: Other peripherals component

Maximize the objective function that represents the quality or performance of the laptop product. This can be a weighted sum of various performance metrics, such as processing power, memory capacity, storage capacity, display quality, etc. The objective function can be represented as: maximize f (x_{cpu}, x_{ram}, $x_{storage}$, x_{gpu}, $x_{display}$, $x_{keyboard}$, $x_{battery}$, $x_{peripherals}$)

- Constraints: Compatibility Constraints: Ensure that certain components are compatible and work together. For example, if a dedicated GPU is selected, it may require a compatible CPU and sufficient RAM. This can be represented as:
  ◦ $x_{cpu} + x_{gpu} <= 1$ (Mutual exclusion between integrated and dedicated GPU)
  ◦ Compatibility constraints for other components as per specific requirements.
- Power Consumption Constraint: Ensure that the power consumption of the components does not exceed the capacity of the battery. This can be represented as:
  ◦ power_cpu * x_{cpu} + power_ram * x_{ram} + power_storage * $x_{storage}$ + power_gpu * x_{gpu} + ... <= battery_capacity
- Size Constraint: Ensure that the size of the assembled laptop is within acceptable limits. This can be represented as:
  ◦ size_cpu * x_{cpu} + size_ram * x_{ram} + size_storage * $x_{storage}$ + size_gpu * x_{gpu} + ... <= max_size

- Weight Constraint: Ensure that the weight of the assembled laptop is within acceptable limits. This can be represented as:
  - weight_cpu * x_cpu + weight_ram * x_ram + weight_storage * x_storage + weight_gpu * x_gpu + ... <= max_weight
- Other Constraints: Additional constraints based on specific requirements, specifications, and limitations of the components and the smart factory. These can include thermal constraints, cost constraints, performance constraints, etc.

This mathematical model provides a framework to optimize the assembly process of laptop components in a smart factory based on various factors and constraints. Depending on the specific requirements and specifications, additional variables and constraints may need to be incorporated into the model.

Advantages of Integration of Robotics, IoT, and Smart Factory

Smart Factory Infrastructure in Industry 4.0 refers to the advanced technological systems and interconnected network of devices, sensors, and machinery that enable efficient and autonomous operations within a manufacturing facility, leveraging cutting-edge technologies like the Internet of Things (IoT), artificial intelligence (AI), and data analytics to optimize productivity, improve decision-making processes, and enhance overall manufacturing performance.

Advantages of Integration of Robotics, IoT, and Smart Factory Infrastructure in Industry 4.0:

- **Increased Productivity:** Integration of robotics, IoT, and smart factory infrastructure allows for enhanced automation and efficiency in manufacturing processes, leading to increased productivity levels.
- **Cost Savings:** By automating repetitive tasks and optimizing resource utilization, companies can significantly reduce operational costs, including labor and energy expenses.
- **Improved Product Quality:** Smart factories equipped with robotics and IoT technologies enable real-time monitoring and data analysis, ensuring consistent quality control and minimizing defects in the production process.
- **Enhanced Safety:** Collaborative robots and IoT-enabled safety systems help create a safer working environment by reducing the risk of accidents and injuries for human workers.
- **Higher Flexibility:** The integration of robotics and IoT enables the customization of manufacturing processes, allowing for quick adaptation to changing market demands and customer preferences.
- **Efficient Inventory Management:** IoT sensors and RFID technology can track and manage inventory levels in real-time, optimizing supply chain operations and reducing stockouts or excess inventory.
- **Predictive Maintenance:** IoT-enabled sensors and analytics can monitor equipment and machinery performance, detecting potential faults or maintenance needs in advance, which helps prevent unexpected breakdowns and costly downtime.
- **Real-Time Data Analytics:** Integration of robotics, IoT, and smart factory infrastructure facilitates the collection, analysis, and visualization of real-time data, enabling better decision-making and process optimization.

- **Increased Scalability:** Smart factories equipped with robotics and IoT technologies can easily scale production capacity to meet market demands without compromising efficiency or quality.
- **Reduced Time-to-Market:** Streamlined production processes, automated workflows, and real-time monitoring enable faster product development and shorter time-to-market, giving companies a competitive edge.
- **Energy Efficiency:** IoT-enabled sensors and smart devices help monitor energy consumption, enabling companies to identify and implement energy-saving measures, leading to reduced environmental impact and lower operational costs.
- **Improved Supply Chain Visibility:** Integration of robotics, IoT, and smart factory infrastructure provides end-to-end visibility across the supply chain, allowing companies to track and manage inventory, logistics, and delivery processes more effectively.
- **Enhanced Collaboration:** Collaborative robots (cobots) can work alongside human workers, assisting them in tasks that require strength, precision, or speed, fostering a more collaborative and efficient working environment.
- **Remote Monitoring and Control:** IoT-enabled devices and robotics systems can be monitored and controlled remotely, allowing for real-time oversight, troubleshooting, and optimization of operations even from remote locations.
- **Enhanced Customer Satisfaction:** By leveraging robotics, IoT, and smart factory infrastructure, companies can improve product quality, shorten lead times, and offer greater customization options, leading to higher customer satisfaction levels.
- **Better Resource Allocation:** Real-time data analytics and predictive modeling enable companies to allocate resources optimally, ensuring efficient utilization of materials, equipment, and manpower.
- **Improved Maintenance Planning:** IoT-enabled sensors and predictive analytics enable proactive maintenance planning, allowing companies to schedule maintenance tasks during planned downtime, and minimizing disruptions to production.
- **Reduced Waste and Environmental Impact:** Automation and optimization of manufacturing processes help minimize waste generation, promote recycling, and reduce the environmental impact associated with production activities.
- **Competitive Advantage:** Companies that successfully integrate robotics, IoT, and smart factory infrastructure gain a competitive advantage by staying at the forefront of technological advancements and driving innovation in their industries.
- **Workforce Upskilling:** Integration of robotics and IoT technologies requires a skilled workforce to operate, maintain, and manage these systems, providing opportunities for upskilling and career advancement for employees.

Disadvantages of Integration of Robotics, IoT, and Smart Factory

Potential disadvantages of integrating robotics, IoT, and smart factory technologies:

- High initial investment costs for implementing and maintaining the integrated systems.
- Complex integration process requiring significant expertise and resources.
- Increased vulnerability to cybersecurity threats due to interconnected devices and networks.
- Dependence on technology, making the system more susceptible to malfunctions or breakdowns.

- Disruption caused by system failures or glitches, leading to production downtime.
- Need for regular software updates and compatibility issues between different components.
- Reduced job opportunities for manual laborers as automation takes over certain tasks.
- Potential job losses due to the replacement of human workers by robots.
- Concerns about data privacy and the security of sensitive manufacturing information.
- Higher training and skill requirements for workers to adapt to new technologies.
- Resistance from employees due to fear of job displacement or changes in work dynamics.
- Difficulty in managing and coordinating multiple interconnected systems.
- Increased complexity in troubleshooting and maintenance procedures.
- Dependence on a stable and reliable power supply for uninterrupted operation.
- Limited flexibility in adapting to rapid changes in production demands or market trends.
- Risk of over-reliance on technology, leading to reduced human oversight and decision-making.
- Potential for increased environmental impact due to the energy consumption of integrated systems.
- Lack of standardized protocols and interoperability between different manufacturers' systems.
- Difficulty in finding skilled professionals capable of maintaining and repairing advanced technologies.
- Potential social and ethical concerns regarding the impact on employment and the future of work.

Integration of Robotics, IoT, and Smart Factory Infrastructure: Challenges and Their Overcomes

Here are few challenges that can arise in the integration of robotics, IoT, and smart factory technologies, along with potential solutions to overcome them:

- **Challenges:** Interoperability: Integrating different technologies from various manufacturers may result in compatibility issues.
- **Solution:** Prioritize the selection of standardized and interoperable technologies to ensure seamless integration.
- **Scalability:** Adapting integrated systems to accommodate future growth and expansion can be challenging.
- **Solution:** Design the infrastructure with scalability in mind, allowing for easy integration of additional components or technologies.
- **Data Management:** Managing and analyzing large volumes of data generated by interconnected devices can be overwhelming.
- **Solution:** Implement advanced data analytics and management tools to streamline data processing, storage, and analysis.
- **Training and Skill Gaps:** Integrating new technologies requires skilled personnel capable of managing and maintaining them.
- **Solution:** Invest in training programs for existing employees or hire skilled professionals experienced in robotics, IoT, and smart factory technologies.
- **Security Risks:** Increased connectivity increases the potential for cybersecurity threats and data breaches.
- **Solution:** Implement robust security protocols, including encryption, access controls, regular vulnerability assessments, and employee training on cybersecurity best practices.

- **Reliability and Downtime:** Technical failures or system disruptions can lead to production downtime and financial losses.
- **Solution:** Implement redundancy measures, perform regular maintenance and updates, and establish backup systems to minimize downtime.
- **Cost-Effectiveness:** Integrating technologies may require significant upfront investments.
- **Solution:** Conduct a thorough cost-benefit analysis to identify areas where automation and integration will provide the most significant returns on investment.
- **Change Management:** Resistance to change among employees and stakeholders can hinder the integration process.
- **Solution:** Involve employees early on, provide comprehensive training, and communicate the benefits of the integrated systems to gain buy-in and support.
- **Regulatory Compliance:** Adhering to industry regulations and standards in an integrated environment can be complex.
- **Solution:** Stay updated on relevant regulations and standards, work closely with regulatory bodies, and implement compliance measures as part of the integration process.
- **Supplier and Partner Collaboration:** Coordinating efforts and ensuring smooth collaboration among different suppliers and partners can be challenging.
- **Solution:** Establish clear communication channels, define responsibilities and expectations, and foster strong partnerships to facilitate effective collaboration.

It's important to note that these challenges and solutions are general in nature and may vary depending on the specific context and industry.

CONCLUSION

In conclusion, the integration of robotics, IoT, and smart factory infrastructure in Industry 4.0 presents a transformative opportunity for the manufacturing sector. This study has provided insights into the remarkable advantages and challenges associated with this integration, emphasizing the potential for enhanced efficiency, productivity, and innovation.

Moving forward, future endeavours should focus on optimizing human-machine collaboration, fortifying cybersecurity measures to safeguard sensitive data, and exploring the untapped possibilities of emerging technologies such as artificial intelligence and blockchain within the realm of Industry 4.0. By addressing these areas, we can unlock unprecedented avenues for growth and establish a sustainable and intelligent future for the manufacturing industry.

Looking ahead, the future scope of research in the integration of robotics, IoT, and smart factory infrastructure in Industry 4.0 lies in exploring advanced algorithms and machine learning techniques to optimize the decision-making process and predictive maintenance systems, developing standardized protocols for seamless interoperability between different manufacturing systems, and investigating the potential of edge computing and decentralized architectures to enhance real-time data processing and reduce latency.

Additionally, further investigations into the ethical, social, and environmental implications of Industry 4.0 technologies are crucial for ensuring responsible and sustainable implementation in the future of manufacturing.

REFERENCES

Arden, N. S., Fisher, A. C., Tyner, K., Lawrence, X. Y., Lee, S. L., & Kopcha, M. (2021). Industry 4.0 for pharmaceutical manufacturing: Preparing for the smart factories of the future. *International Journal of Pharmaceutics, 602*, 120554. doi:10.1016/j.ijpharm.2021.120554 PMID:33794326

Awan, U., Sroufe, R., & Shahbaz, M. (2021). Industry 4.0 and the circular economy: A literature review and recommendations for future research. *Business Strategy and the Environment, 30*(4), 2038–2060. doi:10.1002/bse.2731

Büchi, G., Cugno, M., & Castagnoli, R. (2020). Smart factory performance and Industry 4.0. *Technological Forecasting and Social Change, 150*, 119790. doi:10.1016/j.techfore.2019.119790

Chen, B., Wan, J., Shu, L., Li, P., Mukherjee, M., & Yin, B. (2017). Smart factory of industry 4.0: Key technologies, application case, and challenges. *IEEE Access : Practical Innovations, Open Solutions, 6*, 6505–6519. doi:10.1109/ACCESS.2017.2783682

Erboz, G., 2017). How to define industry 4.0: main pillars of industry 4.0. *Managerial trends in the development of enterprises in globalization era*, 761-767.

Fitsilis, P., Tsoutsa, P., & Gerogiannis, V., 2018). Industry 4.0: Required personnel competences. *Industry 4.0, 3*(3), 130-133.

Gerrikagoitia, J. K., Unamuno, G., Urkia, E., & Serna, A. (2019). Digital manufacturing platforms in the industry 4.0 from private and public perspectives. *Applied Sciences (Basel, Switzerland), 9*(14), 2934. doi:10.3390/app9142934

Ghobakhloo, M. (2018). The future of manufacturing industry: A strategic roadmap toward Industry 4.0. *Journal of Manufacturing Technology Management, 29*(6), 910–936. doi:10.1108/JMTM-02-2018-0057

Grabowska, S., 2020). Smart factories in the age of Industry 4.0. *Management Systems in Production Engineering, 28*(2), 90-96.

Hughes, L., Dwivedi, Y. K., Rana, N. P., Williams, M. D., & Raghavan, V. (2022). Perspectives on the future of manufacturing within the Industry 4.0 cra. *Production Planning and Control, 33*(2-3), 138–158. doi:10.1080/09537287.2020.1810762

Kalsoom, T., Ramzan, N., Ahmed, S., & Ur-Rehman, M. (2020). Advances in sensor technologies in the era of smart factory and industry 4.0. *Sensors (Basel), 20*(23), 6783. doi:10.339020236783 PMID:33261021

Lee, C., & Lim, C. (2021). From technological development to social advance: A review of Industry 4.0 through machine learning. *Technological Forecasting and Social Change, 167*, 120653. doi:10.1016/j.techfore.2021.120653

Longo, F., Nicoletti, L., & Padovano, A. (2017). Smart operators in industry 4.0: A human-centered approach to enhance operators' capabilities and competencies within the new smart factory context. *Computers & Industrial Engineering, 113*, 144–159. doi:10.1016/j.cie.2017.09.016

Osterrieder, P., Budde, L., & Friedli, T. (2020). The smart factory as a key construct of industry 4.0: A systematic literature review. *International Journal of Production Economics, 221*, 107476. doi:10.1016/j.ijpe.2019.08.011

Otles, S., & Sakalli, A. 2019). Industry 4.0: The smart factory of the future in beverage industry. In Production and management of beverages (pp. 439-469). Woodhead Publishing.

Ryalat, M., ElMoaqet, H., & AlFaouri, M. (2023). Design of a smart factory based on cyber-physical systems and internet of things towards industry 4.0. *Applied Sciences (Basel, Switzerland), 13*(4), 2156. doi:10.3390/app13042156

Shrouf, F., Ordieres, J., & Miragliotta, G., 2014, December). Smart factories in Industry 4.0: A review of the concept and of energy management approached in production based on the Internet of Things paradigm. In *2014 IEEE international conference on industrial engineering and engineering management* (pp. 697-701). IEEE.

Ustundag, A., Cevikcan, E., Bayram, B., & İnce, G., 2018). Advances in Robotics in the Era of Industry 4.0. *Industry 4.0: Managing the Digital Transformation*, 187-200.

Valaskova, K., Nagy, M., Zabojnik, S., & Lăzăroiu, G. (2022). Industry 4.0 wireless networks and cyber-physical smart manufacturing systems as accelerators of value-added growth in Slovak exports. *Mathematics, 10*(14), 2452. doi:10.3390/math10142452

Weyer, S., Schmitt, M., Ohmer, M., & Gorecky, D. (2015). Towards Industry 4.0-Standardization as the crucial challenge for highly modular, multi-vendor production systems. *IFAC-PapersOnLine, 48*(3), 579–584. doi:10.1016/j.ifacol.2015.06.143

Zhong, R. Y., Xu, X., Klotz, E., & Newman, S. T. (2017). Intelligent manufacturing in the context of industry 4.0: A review. *Engineering (Beijing), 3*(5), 616–630. doi:10.1016/J.ENG.2017.05.015

Zhou, K., Liu, T., & Zhou, L. 2015, August). Industry 4.0: Towards future industrial opportunities and challenges. In *2015 12th International conference on fuzzy systems and knowledge discovery (FSKD)* (pp. 2147-2152). IEEE.

Chapter 3
How the Metaverse Can Leverage the Business World

Albérico Travassos Rosário
GOVCOPP, IADE, Universidade Europeia, Portugal

Paula Rosa Lopes
Universidade Lusófona, Portugal

Filipe Sales Rosário
Universidade Europeia, Portugal

ABSTRACT

The metaverse is a shared, virtual space where users can interact with each other and digital objects in real time. It has the potential to revolutionize the way we do business by providing a new platform for conducting transactions, collaborating on projects, and connecting with customers. Metaverse can benefit businesses by providing a new platform for virtual events. The metaverse also has the potential to revolutionize the way businesses collaborate and work with each other. Overall, the metaverse has the potential to be a powerful tool for businesses, providing a new platform for conducting transactions, collaborating on projects, and connecting with customers. More research is needed to provide reliable data for decision-making by managers, so based on these research gaps, this study aims to assess the challenges and opportunities, thus building a benchmark on how the metaverse can leverage the business world.

INTRODUCTION

Metaverse is a popular concept nowadays. It is recognized as the next generation of the internet, comprising a virtual, interconnected reality seamlessly connected to the physical world. It combines virtual reality (VR), augmented reality (AR), and mixed reality (MR) to create a parallel reality where people can work, communicate, and play (Gursoy et al., 2022). The metaverse promotes innovative entrepreneurship by causing radical transformations in various sectors, such as marketing, training, education,

DOI: 10.4018/978-1-6684-8851-5.ch003

retail, and sales. It provides technologies and platforms for users to interact in real-time, the potential for revolutionizing the business sector (Yemenici, 2022). Traditionally, the metaverse definitions and user descriptions were limited to their links to computers and video games. However, when Facebook rebranded to Meta Platforms, the concept gained more public attention and has increasingly been embraced by business leaders and target customers (Periyasami & Periyasamy, 2022). Brands are realizing metaverse technologies' potential and leveraging them to improve efficiency and competitive advantage. For instance, the metaverse helps improve communication and interaction between brands and their customers through virtual worlds. Since users tend to be immersed in these experiences, brands can leverage this opportunity to promote their products or services as long as they match users' interests.

Metaverse provides experiences beyond what can be achieved through conventional internet tools. For instance, while eCommerce allows customers to buy products online, the metaverse enables them to test and try them out before completing the transaction (Yemenici, 2022). For example, an internet user within the metaverse world can try different types of clothes or makeup on their avatars. They can change colours and designs before making a purchasing decision to ensure that they buy a product that matches their desires. Similarly, a car manufacturer can hold a virtual launching event allowing potential customers to test drive the new car model in a controlled virtual environment. These opportunities create an immersed customer experience and may lead to higher satisfaction and loyalty and increased sales. In addition, the metaverse allows businesses to collect real-time data that can aid informed decision-making (Dwivedi et al., 2022). For instance, a company running a virtual storefront in the metaverse can collect consumer behaviour and engagement data, which can be used to improve marketing strategies and optimize the store layout and product placement. However, leveraging opportunities in the metaverse has raised concerns over issues such as security and privacy, technical complexity, and interoperability (Gursoy et al., 2022). These challenges can slow its adoption and application in business, thus slowing development. Therefore, this bibliometric literature review identifies opportunities and challenges in the metaverse to aid business leaders' and decision-makers efforts to incorporate these emerging innovations to improve efficiency and productivity.

METHODOLOGICAL APPROACH

A systematic bibliometric literature review (LRSB) was conducted to identify and synthesize data on how the metaverse can leverage the business world. This comprehensive and rigorous methodology allows the researcher to identify the key trends, patterns, and knowledge gaps in the literature related to the study topic. With the exponential expansion of academic knowledge, thousands of journal articles and reports are published daily. This has negatively affected the quality of research and information published. For instance, Linnenluecke et al. (2022) indicated that the number of published journal articles surpassed 50 million in 2009 due to increased predatory journals publishing high volumes of low-quality research. This situation reflects the importance of using the systematic review of the bibliometric literature methodology since it depends on rigorous scientific methods and transparent reporting.

The LRSB helped filter the most relevant and quality sources for analysis and reporting. Consequently, the methodology can be used to decipher and map cumulative scientific knowledge and emerging variations of a well-established topic (Rosário & Dias, 2023; Rosário, 2021; Rosário & Dias, 2022; Rosário, et al., 2021).

Thus, the use of bibliometric analysis can help understand its how the metaverse can leverage the Business World. The use of the LRSB review process is divided into 3 phases and 6 steps (Table 1), as proposed by Rosário and Dias (2023); Rosário (2021); Rosário and Dias (2022); Rosário, et al. (2021).

Table 1. Process of systematic LRSB

Phase	Step	Description
Exploration	Step 1	formulating the research problem
	Step 2	searching for appropriate literature
	Step 3	critical appraisal of the selected studies
	Step 4	data synthesis from individual sources
Interpretation	Step 5	reporting findings and recommendations
Communication	Step 6	presentation of the LRSB report

Source: Rosário and Dias (2023), Rosário (2021), Rosário and Dias (2022)

Within the scope of this investigation, the database of scientific and/or academic documents indexed by Scopus, recognized as the most important peer review in the scientific and academic world, was used. However, we consider that the study has the limitation of considering only the Scopus decomposition database, excluding other scientific and academic bases. The literature search includes peer-reviewed scientific and/or academic documents published up to March 2023.

The process began with identifying the academic database for searching relevant literature. In this case, the Scopus database was selected. The second stage was a comprehensive literature search using the keyword "metaverse," which resulted in 1,086 document results. In order to narrow down the search results to the most relevant sources, the researcher limited the search to the subject area "Business, Management and Accounting," reducing the original number to 974. This was followed by a thorough screening of the retrieved studies based on their relevance to the research topic. The exact keyword "Business" was added to ensure that the selected sources explain the significance of the metaverse in the business world. This process resulted in 123 document results (N=123) that were synthesized to identify common themes and trends that present opportunities and challenges for the metaverse in business applications, which are synthesized in the final report Table 2.

Table 2. Screening methodology

Database Scopus	Screening	Publications
Meta-search	keyword: metaverse	1,086
First Inclusion Criterion	keyword: metaverse, marketing Subject area "business, management and accounting	974
Screening	keyword: metaverse, marketing keyword: metaverse, marketing Subject area "business, management and accounting Exact keyword: business Published until March 2023	123

Source: Own elaboration

Finally, content and theme analysis techniques were used to identify, analyze and report the various documents as proposed by Rosário and Dias (2023), Rosário (2021), Rosário and Dias (2022), Rosário, et al. (2021).

The 123 scientific and/or academic documents indexed in Scopus are later analyzed in a narrative and bibliometric way to deepen the content and possible derivation of common themes that directly respond to the research question (Rosário & Dias, 2023; Rosário, 2021; Rosário & Dias, 2022; Rosário, et al., 2021). Of the 123 selected documents, 87 articles, 16 are conferences, 11 are book series, and 9 are books.

PUBLICATION DISTRIBUTION

Peer-reviewed articles on Metaverse in marketing until March 2023. The year 2022 had the highest number of peer-reviewed publications on the subject, reaching 70. Figure 1 summarizes the peer-reviewed literature published in March 2023. The publications were sorted out as follows: Technological Forecasting And Social Change (5); Springer Proceedings In Business And Economics (5); Lecture Notes In Business Information Processing (5); with 3 (Psychology And Marketing; Journal Of Business Strategy; Journal Of Business Research; International Journal Of Information Management; Immersive Internet Reflections On The Entangling Of The Virtual With Society Politics And The Economy; Business Horizons); with 2 (Technovation; Proceedings Of The International Conference On Electronic Business Iceb; Palgrave Studies In Practice Global Fashion Brand Management; Journal Of Theoretical And Applied Electronic Commerce Research; Journal Of The Academy Of Marketing Science; International Journal Of Health Geographics; International Journal Of Contemporary Hospitality Management; International Journal Of Advertising; I Com; Fashion Style And Popular Culture; and the remaining publications with 1.

Figure 1. Documents by year
Source: Own elaboration

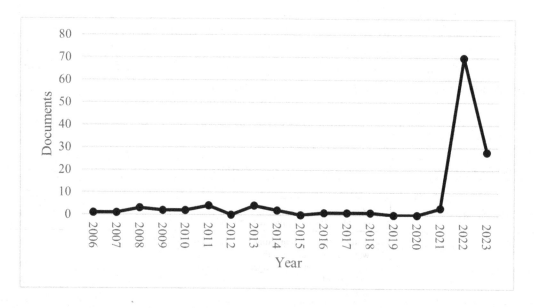

Table 3 presents the analysis performed on the Scimago Journal & Country Rank (SJR), which registers the Journal Of Marketing in the position of best quartile and H index per publication, which is the most cited publication with 7,460 (SJR), Q1 and H Index 6.

There are a total of 32 publications in Q1, 3 in Q2 and 4 in Q3 and 4 in Q4. Publications in the best Q1 quartile represent 67% of publications in titles; best quartile Q2 represents 6%, best quartile Q3 represents 8% and best Q4 represents 8% of each of the titles of 48 publications, finally, 5 publications still do not have available data, representing 10% of publications. The significant majority of publications are in the best Q1 quartile, according to the information presented in Table 3.

Table 3. Scimago journal and country rank impact factor

Title	SJR	Best Quartile	H Index
International Journal Of Information Management	4.58	Q1	132
Journal Of The Academy Of Marketing Science	4.43	Q1	183
Journal Of Strategic Information Systems	4.02	Q1	94
Tourism Management	3.38	Q1	216
Journal Of Service Management	2.85	Q1	69
Journal Of Advertising	2.7	Q1	119
Journal Of Business Ethics	2.44	Q1	208
Business Horizons	2.38	Q1	97
Technological Forecasting And Social Change	2.34	Q1	134
Journal Of Business Research	2.32	Q1	217
International Journal Of Contemporary Hospitality Management	2.29	Q1	100
International Journal Of Operations And Production Management	2.29	Q1	146
Technovation	2.07	Q1	140
Journal Of Hospitality Marketing And Management	2	Q1	59
Current Issues In Tourism	1.84	Q1	82
Journal Of Interactive Advertising	1.81	Q1	11
Service Industries Journal	1.8	Q1	70
International Journal Of Advertising	1.74	Q1	67
Journal Of Business Venturing Insights	1.72	Q1	25
Tourism Review	1.48	Q1	38
Accounting Auditing And Accountability Journal	1.47	Q1	105
Journal Of Marketing Management	1.24	Q1	75
International Journal Of Entrepreneurial Behaviour And Research	1.21	Q1	75
Psychology And Marketing	1.2	Q1	124
Technology In Society	1.14	Q1	58
International Journal Of Tourism Research	1.14	Q1	67
International Conference On Information And Knowledge Management Proceedings	1.14	-*	127
International Journal Of Health Geographics	1.05	Q1	81

continues on following page

Table 3. Continued

Title	SJR	Best Quartile	H Index
Tourism Economics	1.04	Q1	64
Research In International Business And Finance	1.04	Q1	51
Journal Of Vacation Marketing	0.96	Q1	68
Journal Of Brand Management	0.94	Q1	55
Journal Of Internet Commerce	0.93	Q2	31
Research Technology Management	0.9	Q1	73
Service Business	0.88	Q1	36
Big Data And Cognitive Computing	0.83	Q1	18
International Journal Of Management Education	0.82	Q1	34
Journal Of Tourism Futures	0.81	Q1	21
International Journal Of Lean Six Sigma	0.79	Q1	43
Operational Research	0.68	Q2	22
Journal Of Theoretical And Applied Electronic Commerce Research	0.57	Q2	33
Data Base For Advances In Information Systems	0.57	Q2	58
European Journal Of Futures Research	0.51	Q1	18
Strategic Change	0.5	Q2	20
Organizational Dynamics	0.49	Q2	68
Journal Of Cases On Information Technology	0.46	Q2	15
Journal Of Business Strategy	0.42	Q2	42
Risks	0.4	Q2	18
Management And Marketing	0.37	Q2	14
ZWF Zeitschrift Fuer Wirtschaftlichen Fabrikbetrieb	0.34	Q2	16
Journal Of Financial Reporting And Accounting	0.34	Q2	10
Journal Of Cultural Heritage Management And Sustainable Development	0.33	Q1	18
Pakistan Journal Of Commerce And Social Science	0.32	Q3	12
Lecture Notes In Business Information Processing	0.3	Q3	52
Journal Of System And Management Sciences	0.28	Q3	7
Journal Of Enabling Technologies	0.27	Q3	21
EC Tax Review	0.27	Q2	4
International Journal Of Electronic Marketing And Retailing	0.26	Q3	13
Nanoethics	0.23	Q2	31
Fashion Style And Popular Culture	0.19	Q2	4
Journal Of Distribution Science	0.18	Q4	11
Strategic Direction	0.11	Q4	14
Textile View Magazine	0.1	Q4	1
Proceedings Of The International Conference On Electronic Business Iceb	0	-*	9
Proceedings International Conference On Education And Technology ICET	0	-*	12

Table 3. Continued

Title	SJR	Best Quartile	H Index
Picmet Portland International Center For Management Of Engineering And Technology Proceedings	0	-*	11
PC World San Francisco CA	0	-*	6
IEEE International Conference On Industrial Engineering And Engineering Management	0	-*	21
Advances In Transdisciplinary Engineering	0	-*	12
Springer Proceedings In Business And Economics	-*	-*	-*
Immersive Internet Reflections On The Entangling Of The Virtual With Society Politics And The Economy	-*	-*	-*
Palgrave Studies In Practice Global Fashion Brand Management	-*	-*	-*
I Com	-*	-*	-*
Virtual Social Identity And Consumer Behavior	-*	-*	-*
Springer Series In Design And Innovation	-*	-*	-*
Routledge Handbook Of Digital Consumption	-*	-*	-*
Proceedings Vrcai 2022 18th ACM SIGGRAPH International Conference On Virtual Reality Continuum And Its Applications In Industry	-*	-*	-*
Proceedings Of The 2022 IEEE International Conference On Dependable Autonomic And Secure Computing International Conference On Pervasive Intelligence And Computing International Conference On Cloud And Big Data Computing International Conference On Cyber Science And Technology Congress Dasc Picom Cbdcom Cyberscitech 2022	-*	-*	-*
Palgrave Studies Of Cross Disciplinary Business Research In Association With Euromed Academy Of Business	-*	-*	-*
Leadership Strategies For The Hybrid Workforce Best Practices For Fostering Employee Safety And Significance	-*	-*	-*
Journal Of Risk And Financial Management	-*	-*	-*
Journal Of Global Scholars Of Marketing Science Bridging Asia And The World	-*	-*	-*
Interdisciplinary Aspects Of Information Systems Studies The Italian Association For Information Systems	-*	-*	-*
Handbook Of Research On The Future Of Advertising And Brands In The New Entertainment Landscape	-*	-*	-*
Handbook Of Research On Interdisciplinary Reflections Of Contemporary Experiential Marketing Practices	-*	-*	-*
Developments In Marketing Science Proceedings Of The Academy Of Marketing Science	-*	-*	-*
Anticipation Science	-*	-*	-*
2022 IEEE Technology And Engineering Management Conference Societal Challenges Technology Transitions And Resilience Virtual Conference Temscon Europe 2022	-*	-*	-*
2022 IEEE European Technology And Engineering Management Summit E Tems 2022 Conference Proceedings	-*	-*	-*

Note: *data not available.

Source: Own elaboration

The subject areas covered by the 123 scientific and/or academic documents were: Business, Management and Accounting (123); Social Sciences (38); Computer Science (33); Economics, Econometrics and Finance (26); Decision Sciences (21); Engineering (17); Psychology (13); Mathematics (8); Arts and Humanities (8); Medicine (3); Materials Science (2); Environmental Science (2); and Physics and Astronomy (1).

The most cited article was "Web GIS in practice V: 3-D interactive and real-time mapping in second life", by Boulos & Burden (2007) with 94 citations published in the International Journal of Health 1,050 (SJR), the best quartile (Q1) and with an H index (81), this article explores "the geo-data display potential of virtual worlds and their likely convergence with mirror worlds in the context of the future 3-D Internet or Metaverse, and reflect on the potential of such technologies and their future possibilities, e.g. their use to develop emergency/public health virtual situation rooms to effectively manage emergencies and disasters in real time".

In Figure 2 we can analyze the evolution of citations of the documents published until March 2023. The number of citations shows a positive net growth with R2 of 31% for the period ≤2013-2023, with 2022 reaching 450 citations.

Figure 2. Evolution of citations between ≤2013 and 2023
Source: own elaboration

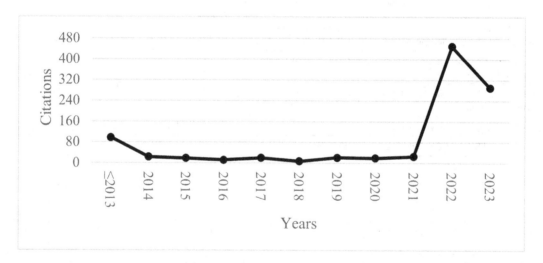

The h-index was used to ascertain the productivity and impact of the published work, based on the largest number of articles included that had at least the same number of citations. Of the documents considered for the h-index, 17 have been cited at least 17 times.

Citations of all scientific and/or academic documents from the period ≤2013 to March 2032, with a total of 980 citations, of the 123 documents 57 were not cited.

This research work is based on a bibliometric study that was carried out to find and discover indicators of the evolution and dynamics of scientific and/or academic information in published articles based on the main keywords (Figure 3).

In order to accomplish these results, was used VOSviewe, a scientific software, which allowed to extract the relevant information. This software allows you to find and identify the main search keywords "metaverse, marketing".

Figure 3. A network of all keywords

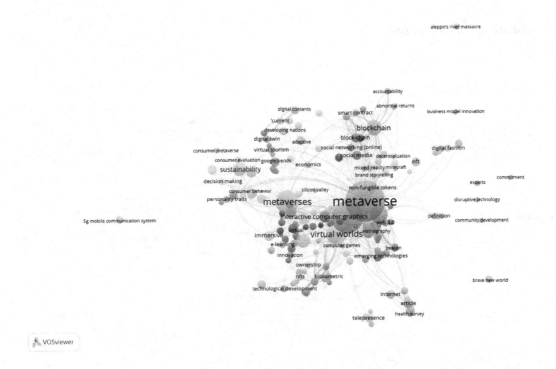

To make this study feasible, a survey was carried out based on scientific and/or academic documents that address the topic of *How the Metaverse Can Leverage the Business World*. Figure 4 presents the analysis of linked keywords to highlight the network of keywords that appear together/linked in each scientific article, leading to the recognition of the topics studied and the identification of trends in future research. Ultimately, Figure 5 presents a wealth of bibliographic coupling, including a unit of analysis of the cited references.

THEORETICAL PERSPECTIVES

The metaverse is a virtual world that allows users to interact with each other and digital objects in a shared space. It can potentially transform business practices and performance through its applications in critical areas such as marketing, customer engagement, and even product development (Aharon et al., 2022).

One of its major benefits is that it allows companies to create immersive experiences that help them differentiate themselves from competitors (Owens et al., 2011). In addition, it can improve collaboration and productivity through virtual meetings and workspaces that enable employees to communicate and work together in real time regardless of the physical distance (Lee & Kim, 2022; Marmaridis & Griffith, 2009).

Therefore, the metaverse can be a crucial tool for facilitating remote working as businesses accommodate employees' demand for flexible working conditions.

This literature review explores the metaverse concept, its significance in the business sector, and potential opportunities and challenges.

Figure 4. A network of linked keywords

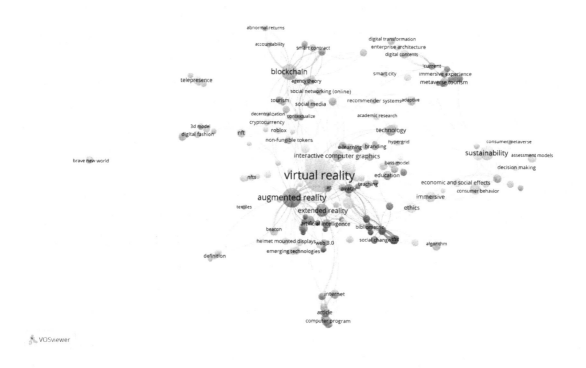

Background and Context of the Metaverse

Science fiction author Neal Stephenson coined the metaverse in his 1992 novel Snow Crash. It refers to a virtual universe characterized by immersive, interactive, shared environments and experiences accessible to millions of users worldwide (Ampountolas et al., 2023).

Over the years, technological advancements, such as augmented reality (AR) and virtual reality (VR), have evolved the metaverse concept from a purely fictional idea to a tangible reality (Pamucar et al., 2022; Prodinger & Neuhofer, 2023).

As a result, the metaverse has become a rapidly growing market that features various platforms, such as video games, social networks, and virtual reality environments (Papagiannidis et al., 2008). It can transform many aspects of people's lives, including education and entertainment, and shape the global business landscape as businesses strive to embrace technologies to increase efficiency, performance, and productivity.

Figure 5. A network of bibliographic coupling

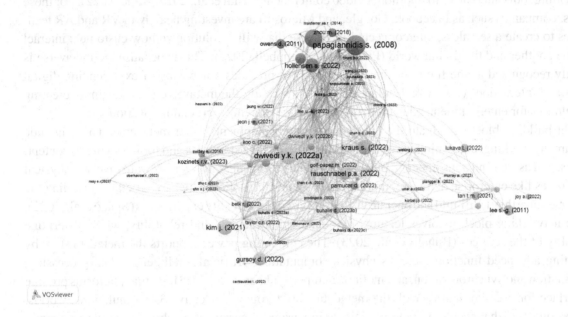

Definition of the Metaverse

The term metaverse describes an advanced form of virtual reality that integrates multiple digital platforms, environments, and experiences into an interconnected, seamless, and immersive universe.

Abbate et al. (2022) define it as a virtual space that allows users to interact with each other and with virtual objects and environments using advanced technologies such as VR, AR, and artificial intelligence (AI).

The science fiction writer Neal Stephenson introduced the metaverse concept in his 1992 novel Snow Crash (Queiroz et al., 2023; Kappe & Steurer, 2010). The author described a futuristic virtual reality environment that combined elements of the internet, video games, and immersive storytelling. However, the origin of the metaverse can be traced back to the 1980s and 1990s when computer networks and online communities were developed (Khan et al., 2022).

During this period, people had more access to the internet, which enabled the creation of online communities such as Usenet, MUDs, and MMORPGs that offered users access to shared virtual space. They could use these platforms to interact, communicate, and collaborate (Shah, 2022). Although the currently shared environments within the metaverse are more advanced due to new innovative technologies, these early online communities laid the foundation for the metaverse.

Over the years, the video game industry, social media platforms, and technology companies continued to popularize the metaverse, resulting in massive adoption in the business sector. For instance, companies in the gaming industry are leveraging the metaverse to create new gaming experiences that are more immersive and social (Koo et al., 2022). Similarly, those in the entertainment industry recognize that the metaverse can create interactive shows and experiences that can help maintain an active and engaged audience (Kozinets, 2023). In the education sector, metaverse technologies provide opportunities for creating immersive learning environments that improve student engagement and understanding. Finally, the metaverse in the business sector is facilitating innovations such as remote work and virtual meetings by providing tools alternative to traditional video conferencing (Ahn et al., 2022; Bojic, 2022). For these reasons, companies such as Facebook, Google, and Microsoft are investing heavily in VR and AR technologies to create a seamless, interconnected metaverse that will revolutionize how customers interact with one another and the digital world (Plangger & Campbell, 2022). This is because the metaverse is currently recognized as the future of the internet since it provides a new way of experiencing digital content and interactions (Power & Teigland, 2013). As a result, the metaverse is increasingly creating opportunities for entertainment, education, and commerce, making a crucial innovation.

Eight building blocks facilitate the emergence and development of the metaverse. These include hardware, networking, computing, virtual platforms, interchange standards and tools, payment, content, services, and assets, and consumer and business behavior (Yemenici, 2022). Hardware involves physical technologies like enterprise hardware, mobile phones, and tactile gloves that are crucial in enabling the Metaverse since they help build and operate virtual and augmented reality experiences (Spanò et al., 2022).

The networking block involves features like bandwidth, latency, and reliability, which determine the quality of the services (Buhalis et al., 2023). The computing power supports the metadata store by facilitating advanced functions such as physics computation, artificial intelligence, data processing, reconciliation and synchronization, and motion capture (Syuhada et al., 2023). Virtual platforms provide an interface for users to interact with the metadata store through immersive 3-D simulations, worlds, and environments that enable users to participate in various experiences, such as shopping or playing games (Calongne et al., 2013).

While blockchain coins are believed to be the most common payment systems in the metaverse, some companies incorporate other payments such as barter, NFTs, or cryptocurrencies (Smith, 2022; Belk et al., 2022). The content, services, and assets reflect brands and other businesses' role as content providers, while consumer and business behavior indicate observable behavioral changes among users as they adapt to the Metaverse.

These blocks show that the metaverse involves an interplay of various innovations and stakeholders' behaviors (Figure 1).

Figure 6. The eight building blocks of the metaverse
Source: Yemenici (2022)

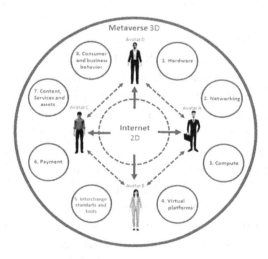

Types of Metaverse Platforms

Many companies are leveraging the metaverse to improve their user experience. As a result, multiple types of the metaverse exist as businesses design these virtual worlds to meet the specific needs of their target customers (Buchholz et al., 2022). For example, the Roblox Metaverse provides an immersive 3D virtual space for gamers to experience different games and interact with each other. On the contrary, AltspaceVR by Microsoft was a social VR platform that enabled users to host live virtual events such as meetings and business conferences. Therefore, this section explores the various types of a metaverse in detail.

Gaming Platforms

Gaming platforms are among the most popular metaverse platforms designed to target enthusiastic gamers. These platforms are characterized by various virtual worlds and games with sophisticated graphics and game mechanics, enabling users to explore and play (Reay & Wanick, 2023). An example of a popular gaming platform is Second Life by Linden Lab, which provides tools for users to create their avatars, explore virtual worlds, and engage in various activities such as shopping, socializing, and gaming (Spivey & Munson, 2009; Cagnina & Poian, 2008; Boulos & Burden, 2007). Roblox is another gaming platform that provides an immersive 3D virtual space consisting of various virtual games and immersive spaces. Besides playing games, Roblox enables users to engage in other virtual activities, such as hosting and attending virtual events, including concerts and ceremonies (Boulos et al., 2008). Many tech companies have recognized the significance of gaming platforms as the foundation for developing the metaverse (Wanick & Stallwood, 2023). Most games such as Roblox, Minecraft, and Fortnite have the infrastructure and large user bases that facilitate the development of the metaverse. For instance, Wiederhold (2022) found that in 2020 consumers spent $178 billion on video games. In addition, approximately 75% of revenues in the gaming industry are generated from the sale of virtual products, such as clothes for users' avatars. Most gamers are ready to spend money on virtual properties. Thus, tech companies are leveraging these gaming platforms to develop their metaverse technologies instead of starting from scratch.

Social Platforms

Social platforms are metaverse platforms designed to facilitate socializing and networking. They allow users to interact with each other in a virtual environment (Tan et al., 2022). One major differentiating factor for these platforms is that they strongly emphasize creating user-generated content and encourage users to customize their virtual spaces and avatars (Chen & Yang, 2022; Zhan et al., 2023). For example, VRChat allows users to join virtual worlds and engage in activities such as gaming, socializing, and attending events (Hennig-Thurau et al., 2022). Similarly, the high-Fidelity social platform provides tools for building and scripting custom content, thus allowing users to create and share virtual reality experiences (Solomon & Wood, 2014). As a result, social platforms are popular among internet users looking for opportunities for creativity and expression since they can create and share experiences impossible to develop in the physical world, such as virtual buildings, objects, and even entire virtual worlds (Kraus et al., 2023; Tan & Salo, 2021). In addition, the social aspect of these metaverse platforms makes them useful for entrepreneurship (Jaung, 2022). For instance, brands selling virtual products such as fashion and accessories can engage users in virtual events such as product launches and meet-and-greets with influencers with the goal of marketing and selling these products. Therefore, social metaverse platforms can be designed to support personal and commercial purposes.

Education Platforms

Education platforms provide immersive learning environments through tools designed for educators to create and deliver engaging content to students. Contreras et al. (2022) explained that the metaverse could be applied to develop virtual educational centers with classrooms, dining rooms, and teachers' rooms. This virtual replica of an institution can allows students, teachers, and other employees to communicate and interact in a way that imitates in-person interactions, including video calls or videoconferences (Praherdhiono et al., 2022; Lee, 2023). While this can be applied in various institutions, it would be beneficial for institutions focused on e-learning or online training since it can humanize the interactions and make them feel more interactive and engaging (Ratten, 2023). Moreover, educational metaverse platforms provide virtual tools such as whiteboards, simulations, and 3D models since they often strongly emphasize collaboration and interactivity (Hines & Netland, 2022; Masferrer et al., 2014). For example, Unimersiv is an education platform that offers VR educational experiences. It covers various subjects ranging from history and science to art and literature (Tan & Saraniemi, 2022). These educational platforms prove that the metaverse can be used for purposes beyond gaming and entertainment, including making learning fun to help students use VR to learn faster.

Business Platforms

Business platforms facilitate business-related activities such as virtual meetings and remote work. They provide tools that enable employees to communicate and collaborate throughout projects, thus enhancing productivity and efficiency (Murray et al., 2023). These professional business activities are conducted using virtual tools such as whiteboards, document sharing, and video conferencing (Lee et al., 2011). An example of these platforms is Engage VR, a professional metaverse for enterprise businesses. The platform is designed for corporations, education organizations, professionals, and event organizers and provides tools that enable them to deliver their services directly to customers (Taylor, 2022; Kshetri & Dwivedi, 2023). It also allows them to engage their employees, suppliers, and other stakeholders, thus streamlining business activities and communication (Kraus et al., 2022). In addition, these platforms provide an immersive environment for employee training and development, allowing them to learn and practice desired skills (Hollensen et al., 2022; Golf-Papez et al., 2022). As a result, the organization can leverage these platforms to ensure that its workforce possesses in-demand skills and knowledge needed to adopt emerging innovations. As a result, the business can adapt to changing market conditions and respond quickly to customer needs.

Mixed-Use Platforms

Mixed-use platforms combine elements from gaming, socializing, education, and business platforms. They are designed to be flexible and adaptable to different applications. These platforms are defined by various characteristics, such as high customization, collaboration, multi-purpose, and the use of immersive technologies (Giang Barrera & Shah, 2023). By combining features from other types of the metaverse, mixed-use platforms facilitate socializing, entertainment, education, and business activities (Koay et al., 2022).

As a result, they are associated with multiple benefits, including increased engagement and creativity, high levels of productivity and collaboration, increased learning opportunities, and cost savings (Gauttier et al., 2022; Festa et al., 2022).

Companies aiming to provide diverse virtual experiences ranging from gaming to networking and shopping can leverage mixed-use platforms since they offer higher flexibility and agility.

Key Features and Technologies of the Metaverse

The metaverse is a convergence of multiple features and technologies that support its development. These include the metaverse worlds (M-Worlds), the augmented, virtual, and mixed-reality (AR, VR, and MR) technologies, and Web3/Virtual Assets (Figure 7).

Figure 7. The intersection of the key features and technologies of the metaverse
Source: Bobier et al. (2022)

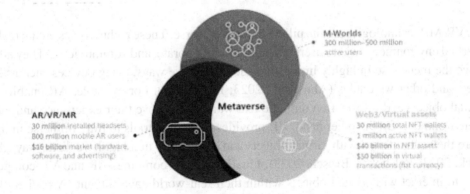

1)   M-Worlds

The M-Worlds are immersive and interactive virtual environments accessible to users from anywhere in the world. They consist of applications run on mobile phones, tablets, PC browsers, and AR or VR headsets to enable brands to reach new audiences, especially Gen Zs, who are considered digital natives (Wallace, 2006). Each M-World is characterized by unique communities, content, rules, business models, and user accounts. Bobier et al. (2022) identified six other defining characteristics of the M-Worlds, as shown in Figure 3, which include persistent, synchronous and live, concurrent, immersive, functioning economy, and multiple contributors. In addition, the author explained that these M-Worlds are designed to be highly realistic and immersive (Tlili et al., 2023; Umar, 2022).

Thus, they often use advanced graphics and rendering technologies to create a seamless and believable virtual experience (Oxford Analytica, 2022).

Although most M-Worlds start as gaming applications, they often add features and attractions such as virtual concerts and map creation tools that keep users engaged within the metaverse environment.

In addition, they customize their avatars and virtual spaces using apparel and accessories sold in the virtual environment (Figure 8).

Figure 8. Characteristics of the m-worlds
Source: Bobier et al. (2022)

2) AR/VR/MR

The AR/VR/MR technologies are the pillars of the metaverse. These technologies create realistic and engaging virtual environments where users can interact, collaborate, and communicate. They allow them to experience the metaverse in highly immersive and interactive ways, using devices such as headsets, smartphones, and other wearables (Ahn et al., 2023; Kim, 2021). For example, AR enables users to overlay virtual objects and information onto the real world to improve their experience and interaction with their environment. On the other hand, VR provides them with tools to fully immerse in the digital world, where they can interact with virtual objects and other users in a highly realistic way (Alcantara & Michalack, 2023; Volchek & Brysch, 2023). Finally, the MR combines AR and VR components to enable users to interact with virtual objects within their real-world environment (Arpaci et al., 2022). Mobile technologies continue to facilitate the transition to the metaverse, as Bobier et al. (2022) note that approximately 6 billion mobile phones in use today are powerful enough to enable AR. In addition, Apple's iOS and Google's Android can be extended to AR and VR development. As a result, it is estimated that 800 million users actively use mobile AR, projected to reach 1.7 billion in 2025. These numbers reflect the growth potential of the metaverse and its foundational technologies. The AR/VR/MR technologies have numerous applications within the metaverse, such as creating interactive advertisements, immersive gaming, virtual assistants, and training experiences.

3) Web3/Virtual Assets

While Web3 is still at an early stage, it is powering a vibrant virtual asset economy, causing major global hype. Examples of these virtual assets includes cryptocurrencies, NFTs, and smart contracts (Belk et al., 2022). One major differentiating aspect of Web3 is that it is more decentralized and secure. It improves Web2 increasing user involvement in content and value creation. For instance, Web2 allowed consumers to be creators and consumers of online content (Lukava et al., 2022; Llamas & Belk, 2022). However, centralized systems continued to control and benefit from its distribution. Web3 solves this problem by allowing users to consume, create, and own content (Zhou et al., 2018). It is characterized by decentralized networks and money exchange, thus ensuring that users benefit from these systems (Murray et al., 2023). For example, virtual assets can be bought, sold, and traded within the metaverse, including virtual currency, real estate, clothing, and accessories for virtual avatars (Belei et al., 2011). Blockchain technology helps secure these digital assets, thus ensuring their authenticity and security. Examples of popular virtual assets include Cryptocurrency such as Bitcoin, Non-Fungible Tokens (NFTs), and virtual real estate within platforms like Decentraland. Users can benefit from owning and trading these assets since they are valuable in virtual and real-world environments. Users can improve their social status and profit from buying and selling virtual assets.

Leveraging the Metaverse in the Business World

The metaverse is transforming how businesses operate by providing a unique platform for companies to create immersive experiences. These experiences attract new customers, improve engagement, and drive revenue growth (Gadalla et al., 2013). Businesses achieve these benefits primarily by creating immersive experiences for customers within the metaverse (Bonales-Daimiel, 2023; Joy et al., 2022). For example, they engage in virtual showrooms, which enable customers to explore products in 3D, or virtual events, which allow customers to interact with each other and company representatives in a virtual environment (Korbel et al., 2022). Businesses can leverage these opportunities to showcase their products and services in interactive and innovative ways (Wang & Medvegy, 2022). Such immersive experiences create memorable brand experiences that enhance customer engagement and loyalty, consequently increasing sales and revenue.

Additionally, business leaders can leverage the Metaverse by creating virtual workplaces. In the current competitive business environment, it has become critical for businesses to provide flexible and healthy working environments that enable employees to perform and develop (Go & Kang, 2022; Weiss, 2022). Most employees consider virtual working spaces flexible and convenient since they allow better work-life balance than traditional office working. For example, remote working through virtual workplaces reduces commute times and costs (Dwivedi et al., 2022). Employees can use this time to engage in other activities, including spending time with their families or a hobby. Moreover, virtual workplaces benefit companies in various ways, including reducing overhead costs, increasing productivity, and the ability to hire talent from anywhere in the world (Englisch, 2022; Weking et al., 2023). It enables seamless collaboration since employees can collaborate in real time, share files, and access tools and resources from anywhere in the world with an internet connection (Branca et al., 2023). Besides, virtual workplaces can be designed to reflect a company's brand and culture by creating content that reinforces these values and enhances employee engagement.

Finally, the Metaverse allows businesses to expand their revenue streams. For example, a company could create a virtual marketplace where users can buy and sell virtual goods, such as in-game items or digital art (Darwish & Hassanien, 2022). Companies can create virtual versions of their products, such as clothing, accessories, and furniture, for users to buy using digital currencies (Buhalis et al., 2023; Hirsch, 2022). In addition, brands can leverage the metaverse as an advertising platform by placing virtual billboards or product placements (Zainurin et al., 2023). The resulting experience can influence the users' purchasing decisions, leading to sales of real or virtual products (Chan et al., 2023). Companies can also charge for virtual experiences such as virtual events, concerts, or guided tours. These additional income streams can increase a brand's competitiveness and stability, thus leading to long-term success.

Opportunities and Benefits of the Metaverse in Business

The metaverse provides multiple opportunities for business growth and expansion. For instance, businesses can use metaverse technologies to expand their market reach since the metaverse is accessible globally (Zarka & Hajismail, 2022). In addition, companies can improve teamwork and collaboration by setting up virtual working spaces, thus improving performance and productivity. This section explores other opportunities and benefits of the metaverse in business.

Marketing and Customer Engagement

One major defining characteristic of the metaverse is its ability to improve social interactions and networking. This feature creates opportunities for businesses to enhance their marketing strategies and promote customer engagement (Chen & Yao, 2022). There are two primary ways of achieving this identified in research: i) virtual events and product launches, ii) interactive shopping experiences.

i)   Virtual events and product launches

The metaverse provides a platform for businesses to host virtual events and product launches. The metaverse is characterized by interactive features such as demos, Q&A sessions, polls, multimedia continent, and customizable environments that enable brands to engage their customers in virtual events and hold product launches (Cheah & Shimul, 2023). Customers in these digital worlds can use their avatars to try new products or attend events, including business conferences, concerts, and meet-and-greets (Tsai, 2022). This feature is particularly effective for businesses in the gaming, technology, and entertainment industries, where customers are highly engaged with virtual experiences. Furthermore, virtual events and product launches conducted in the metaverse are more cost-effective and accessible than physical events (Sartamorn & Oe, 2022; Rauschnabel et al., 2022). This means businesses can leverage these opportunities to reach a larger audience without needing physical space, logistics, and other expenses associated with traditional events. As a result, the metaverse provides new and innovative ways of engaging with customers while saving on costs.

ii)   Interactive shopping experiences

Interactivity is a major characteristic of the metaverse. Businesses adopting metaverse technologies leverage this feature to create interactive shopping experiences (Swilley, 2016). For example, companies can use the metaverse to create virtual stores and showrooms that enable users to explore and interact with products in a highly immersive way. Although companies in multiple sectors can apply this opportunity, it can be particularly effective for companies in the fashion, home decor, and automotive industries (Lee et al., 2011; Hassani et al., 2022). Customers in these industries value seeing and iterating with products before purchasing. Besides, the metaverse empowers businesses with tools to personalize and customize interactive shopping experiences (Durukal, 2022). In this case, companies can create virtual shopping experiences tailored to customers' needs and interests by leveraging customer data and preferences (Buhalis et al., 2023). As a result, they are more likely to experience higher engagement and conversion rates since customers are more likely to purchase when they feel personally connected to the product and brand.

Employee Collaboration and Productivity

The metaverse provides opportunities for improving employee collaboration and production, thus enhancing organizational productivity and success. This is because collaboration improves communication, creativity, knowledge sharing, and problem-solving, resulting in higher job satisfaction and more tremendous organizational growth. The two major opportunities for employee collaboration and productivity in the metaverse are i) virtual meetings and workspaces and ii) remote work and telecommuting.

i)   Virtual meetings and workspaces

Businesses can use the metaverse to create virtual environments that enable employees to collaborate and communicate in real time. After the COVID-19 pandemic, most companies adopted remote working structures, resulting in multiple businesses with distributed teams (Reed, 2022). These companies can leverage the metaverse to build virtual workspaces that allow employees to seamlessly and efficiently work together, irrespective of their physical location (Cerniauskas & Werth, 2022). Besides, these virtual meetings and workspaces are highly immersive and engaging, which can increase employees' engagement, motivation, and productivity.

ii)   Remote work and telecommuting

With the metaverse, businesses have access to a vast pool of talents from all over the world. For instance, a US company can hire competent employees from Asia at a relatively low cost due to the differences in living costs and standard market salaries. This opportunity can help companies attract and retain top talent since employees can work from anywhere worldwide while collaborating and communicating effectively with their colleagues. In addition, metaverse technologies make remote work and telecommuting highly flexible and customizable (Michalikova et al., 2022). By leveraging VR and other advanced technologies, businesses can create virtual workspaces customized to each employee's needs and preferences (Chinie et al., 2022). As a result, they are likely to have higher levels of employee satisfaction and retention since employees' satisfaction and engagement are more likely to increase when they feel supported and valued by their employer.

Product Development and Innovation

The metaverse provides opportunities for improving employee collaboration and production, thus enhancing organizational productivity and success. This is because collaboration improves communication, creativity, knowledge sharing, and problem-solving, resulting in higher job satisfaction and more tremendous organizational growth. The two major opportunities for employee collaboration and productivity in the metaverse are i) virtual meetings and workspaces and ii) remote work and telecommuting.

i)   Digital prototyping and testing

The metaverse enables businesses to create digital prototypes and conduct testing in virtual environments. Brands can test and iterate on product designs with the metaverse before committing to physical production (Choi & Kim, 2017). This opportunity is particularly beneficial for businesses in the manufacturing, automotive, and aerospace industries, where the cost and time for physical prototyping can be high. In addition, metaverse technologies, including 3D modelling and simulation, AR, and VR, can help businesses create highly realistic and accurate digital prototypes, allowing them to identify and address design issues early in development (Dincelli & Yayla, 2022; Lee & Wong, 2022). For example, VR can help designers and engineers replicate conditions in the real world and provide insights regarding product performance and user experience (Zhu et al., 2023). AR, on the other hand, allows designers to overlay digital content in the real world, thus visualizing how the product will look and function (Wang et al., 2022). These technologies can enable designers and engineers to gain insights and feedback that can be implemented to improve the product's design, performance, and functionality before proceeding with mass manufacturing. As a result, companies are likely to have higher levels of product quality and faster time-to-market.

ii)   Real-time customer feedback and insights

    The metaverse enables companies access to real-time customer feedback and insights. For instance, virtual environments allow customers to interact with products and provide feedback in real-time (Ober-hauser et al., 2022). Companies can leverage analytics tools in the metaverse to monitor and track these customer interactions to gain insights or ask customers for feedback (Pham et al., 2022). This real-time customer feedback and insights in the metaverse can be highly valuable and actionable since they enable businesses to make informed decisions about product development and marketing strategies (Dator, 2022). This can lead to higher levels of customer satisfaction and loyalty, as companies can meet the needs and preferences of their customers more effectively.

Challenges and Limitations of the Metaverse in Business

While the metaverse provides multiple opportunities and benefits for businesses, it also presents various challenges that hinder its adoption. For instance, some users are concerned about their privacy and data safety, given the increased cases of cybersecurity attacks and data misuse by corporations (Dai, 2022). Therefore, businesses must address these concerns to achieve the maximum benefits of integrating the metaverse into their systems.

Technology and Infrastructure Limitations

The metaverse relies on advanced technology and infrastructure, which can be a barrier for some businesses, particularly SMEs with limited resources. To fully leverage the metaverse, enterprises need powerful computing devices, high-speed internet, and advanced virtual reality technologies (Huvila, 2013; Grinbaum & Adomaitis, 2022). These technologies and devices can be expensive to acquire and maintain, making them unaffordable for businesses with limited resources (Firmansyah et al., 2022). Moreover, the metaverse is still a relatively new and evolving innovation, and companies may find it challenging to integrate it into their existing IT infrastructure and workflows (Filimonau et al., 2022). For instance, developing the metaverse may require acquiring new hardware and software and significant investments in training to ensure access to necessary talents.

Privacy and Security Concerns

Privacy and security concerns are major challenges within the metaverse. The data collected in the metaverse is massive as the technology transitions its users from the physical world to the digital realm (Guo & Hou, 2022). While this creates opportunities for personalization and improved products and services, it also exposes users to higher security threats. Chen et al. (2022) identifies two primary challenges; difficulties authenticating and security of user identity in the virtual world, and large amounts of data in the interactive technology increase the likelihood of theft. Thus, cybersecurity issues such as identity theft, phishing, and social engineering are more likely to increase (Gursoy et al., 2022). Di Pietro and Cresci (2021) further note the increased cases of 'doxing' where user private information is used for extortion or online shaming. Virtual environments create new risks for data breaches, hacking, and other cybersecurity threats, which can result in adverse consequences for organizations and their customers.

Cultural and Social Barriers

Businesses may also face cultural and social barriers that may lead to resistance to the metaverse. Individuals and communities may resist virtual environments or have concerns about their impact on social interactions and relationships (Hancock, 2022). For example, some employees question the effectiveness of virtual workspaces in facilitating collaboration and creativity. At the same time, some feel that the virtual environment isolates employees and disconnects them from their colleagues (Jeon, 2021). These negative perceptions may lead to resistance and slow adoption of the technologies despite their benefits.

CONCLUSION

The metaverse has become a popular concept in business due to its potential to connect the physical and digital worlds and associated opportunities. The innovation integrates VR, AR, and MR technologies to create a parallel reality where people can work, communicate, and interact. As more people worldwide embrace new technologies, online commercial transactions and networking have significantly increased. People have fewer in-person and more online interactions due to the popularity of the internet and social media platforms. The metaverse is building on these changes by developing advanced platforms that allow people to collaborate, interact, and communicate in virtual worlds that imitate the real world. This development helps humanize these digital worlds, thus making people feel more connected. However, the nature of the connectedness and interactions depend on the type of metaverse a company develops. For example, gaming platforms incorporate game mechanics and elements to create immersive experiences that appeal to game enthusiasts. On the other hand, social platforms are developed by companies that focus on socialization and networking. Thus, they emphasize user-generated content to increase engagement and encourage virtual interactions. Educational platforms provide tools that support immersive learning environments, targeting educators, learners, and educational institutions in general. These platforms prove that the metaverse can be used beyond entertainment and gaming. Finally, mixed-use metaverse platforms combine elements from all the other types of metaverse to create multi-purpose platforms that provide diverse experiences ranging from educational, entertainment, and gaming.

The metaverse presents various opportunities that businesses can tap into to improve organizational performance and growth. For instance, the metaverse provides tools enabling firms to hold virtual events, launch products, and create interactive shopping experiences. In addition, companies can use the metaverse to improve employee collaboration and productivity through virtual shared workspaces and meetings that support remote working and telecommuting. Finally, the metaverse provides technologies that support product development and innovation. For instance, businesses can use AR and VR technologies for digital prototyping and testing. This ensures that the final product design and quality match consumer needs and expectations since designers and engineers can access feedback and insights by engaging consumers throughout the process. Despite these opportunities, the metaverse is associated with various challenges that require addressing. These include technical limitations, privacy and security concerns, and cultural and social barriers that result in resistance.

ACKNOWLEDGMENT

I would like to express gratitude to the Editor and the Arbitrators. They offered extremely valuable suggestions or improvements. The author was supported by the GOVCOPP Research Center of the University of Aveiro.

REFERENCES

Abbate, S., Centobelli, P., Cerchione, R., Oropallo, E., & Riccio, E. (2022). A first bibliometric literature review on metaverse. *2022 IEEE Technology and Engineering Management Conference: Societal Challenges: Technology, Transitions and Resilience Virtual Conference, Temscon Europe 2022*, 254-260. 10.1109/TEMSCONEUROPE54743.2022.9802015

Aharon, D. Y., Demir, E., & Siev, S. (2022). Real returns from the unreal world? market reaction to metaverse disclosures. *Research in International Business and Finance*, *63*, 101778. Advance online publication. doi:10.1016/j.ribaf.2022.101778

Ahn, S. J., Kim, J., & Kim, J. (2022). The bifold triadic relationships framework: A theoretical primer for advertising research in the metaverse. *Journal of Advertising*, *51*(5), 592–607. doi:10.1080/009133 67.2022.2111729

Ahn, S. J., Kim, J., & Kim, J. (2023). The future of advertising research in virtual, augmented, and extended realities. *International Journal of Advertising*, *42*(1), 162–170. doi:10.1080/02650487.2022.2137316

Alcantara, A. C., & Michalack, D. L. (2023). *The metaverse narrative in the matrix resurrections: A semiotic analysis through costumes*. doi:10.1007/978-3-031-09659-4_20

Ampountolas, A., Menconi, G., & Shaw, G. (2023). Metaverse research propositions: Online intermediaries. *Tourism Economics*. Advance online publication. doi:10.1177/13548166231159520

Arpaci, I., Karatas, K., Kusci, I., & Al-Emran, M. (2022). Understanding the social sustainability of the metaverse by integrating UTAUT2 and big five personality traits: A hybrid SEM-ANN approach. *Technology in Society*, *71*, 102120. Advance online publication. doi:10.1016/j.techsoc.2022.102120

Belei, N., Noteborn, G., & De Ruyter, K. (2011). It's a brand new world: Teaching brand management in virtual environments. *Journal of Brand Management, 18*(8), 611–623. doi:10.1057/bm.2011.6

Belk, R., Humayun, M., & Brouard, M. (2022). Money, possessions, and ownership in the metaverse: NFTs, cryptocurrencies, Web3 and wild markets. *Journal of Business Research, 153*, 198–205. doi:10.1016/j.jbusres.2022.08.031

Bobier, J. F., Merey, T., Robnett, S., Grebe, M., Feng, J., Rehberg, B., Woolsey, K., & Hazan, J. (2022). *The Corporate Hitchhiker's guide to the metaverse.* Boston Consulting Group. https://ismguide.com/wp-content/uploads/2022/05/bcg-the-corporate-hitchhikers-guide-to-the-metaverse-27-apr-2022.pdf

Bojic, L. (2022). Metaverse through the prism of power and addiction: What will happen when the virtual world becomes more attractive than reality? *European Journal of Futures Research, 10*(1), 22. Advance online publication. doi:10.118640309-022-00208-4

Bonales-Daimiel, G. (2023). New formulas of interactive entertainment: From advergaming to metaverse as an advertising strategy. In Handbook of research on the future of advertising and brands in the new entertainment landscape (pp. 76-103) doi:10.4018/978-1-6684-3971-5.ch004

Boulos, M., & Burden, D. (2007). Web GIS in practice V: 3-D interactive and real-time mapping in second life. *International Journal of Health Geographics, 6*(1), 51. Advance online publication. doi:10.1186/1476-072X-6-51 PMID:18042275

Boulos, M. N. K., Scotch, M., Cheung, K., & Burden, D. (2008). Web GIS in practice VI: A demo playlist of geo-mashups for public health neogeographers. *International Journal of Health Geographics, 7*(1), 38. Advance online publication. doi:10.1186/1476-072X-7-38 PMID:18638385

Branca, G., Resciniti, R., & Loureiro, S. M. C. (2023). Virtual is so real! consumers' evaluation of product packaging in virtual reality. *Psychology and Marketing, 40*(3), 596–609. doi:10.1002/mar.21743

Buchholz, F., Oppermann, L., & Prinz, W. (2022). There's more than one metaverse. *I-Com, 21*(3), 313–324. doi:10.1515/icom-2022-0034

Buhalis, D., Leung, D., & Lin, M. (2023). Metaverse as a disruptive technology revolutionising tourism management and marketing. *Tourism Management, 97*, 104724. Advance online publication. doi:10.1016/j.tourman.2023.104724

Buhalis, D., Lin, M. S., & Leung, D. (2023). Metaverse as a driver for customer experience and value co-creation: Implications for hospitality and tourism management and marketing. *International Journal of Contemporary Hospitality Management, 35*(2), 701–716. doi:10.1108/IJCHM-05-2022-0631

Buhalis, D., O'Connor, P., & Leung, R. (2023). Smart hospitality: From smart cities and smart tourism towards agile business ecosystems in networked destinations. *International Journal of Contemporary Hospitality Management, 35*(1), 369–393. doi:10.1108/IJCHM-04-2022-0497

Cagnina, M. R., & Poian, M. (2008). Second life: A turning point for web 2.0 and E-business? In Interdisciplinary aspects of information systems studies: The italian association for information systems (pp. 377-383). doi:10.1007/978-3-7908-2010-2_46

Calongne, C., Sheehy, P., & Stricker, A. (2013). Gemeinschaft identity in a gesellschaft metaverse. In The immersive internet: Reflections on the entangling of the virtual with society, politics and the economy (pp. 180-191). doi:10.1057/9781137283023

Cerniauskas, T., & Werth, D. (2022). Industry goes metaverse - the fusion of real and virtual industrial worlds exemplified by the wastewater industry. *I-Com, 21*(3), 325–329. doi:10.1515/icom-2022-0032

Chan, C., Wong, K. Y., & Lui, T. (2023). Marketing tourism products in virtual reality: Moderating effect of product complexity. *Springer Proceedings in Business and Economics,* 318-322. 10.1007/978-3-031-25752-0_34

Cheah, I., & Shimul, A. S. (2023). Marketing in the metaverse: Moving forward–What's next? *Journal of Global Scholars of Marketing Science: Bridging Asia and the World, 33*(1), 1–10. doi:10.1080/216 39159.2022.2163908

Chen, B., & Yang, D. (2022). User recommendation in social metaverse with VR. *International Conference on Information and Knowledge Management, Proceedings,* 148-158. 10.1145/3511808.3557487

Chen, C., & Yao, M. Z. (2022). Strategic use of immersive media and narrative message in virtual marketing: Understanding the roles of telepresence and transportation. *Psychology and Marketing, 39*(3), 524–542. doi:10.1002/mar.21630

ChenZ.WuJ.GanW.QiZ. (2022). *Metaverse security and privacy: An overview.* doi:10.1109/BigData55660.2022.10021112

Chinie, C., Oancea, M., & Todea, S. (2022). The adoption of the metaverse concepts in Romania. *Management and Marketing, 17*(3), 328–340. doi:10.2478/mmcks-2022-0018

Choi, H., & Kim, S. (2017). A content service deployment plan for metaverse museum exhibitions—Centering on the combination of beacons and HMDs. *International Journal of Information Management, 37*(1), 1519–1527. doi:10.1016/j.ijinfomgt.2016.04.017

Contreras, G. S., González, A. H., Fernández, M. I. S., Martínez, C. B., Cepa, J., & Escobar, Z. (2022). The importance of the application of the metaverse in education. *Modern Applied Science, 16*(3), 1–34. doi:10.5539/mas.v16n3p34

Dai, W. (2022). Optimal policy computing for blockchain based smart contracts via federated learning. *Operations Research, 22*(5), 5817–5844. doi:10.100712351-022-00723-z

Darwish, A., & Hassanien, A. E. (2022). Fantasy magical life: Opportunities, applications, and challenges in metaverses. *Journal of System and Management Sciences, 12*(2), 411–436. doi:10.33168/JSMS.2022.0222

Dator, J. (2022). *Destination identities.* doi:10.1007/978-3-031-11732-9_7

Di Pietro, R., & Cresci, S. (2021, December). Metaverse: security and privacy issues. In *2021 Third IEEE International Conference on Trust, Privacy and Security in Intelligent Systems and Applications (TPS-ISA)* (pp. 281-288). IEEE. https://arxiv.org/pdf/2205.07590.pd

Dincelli, E., & Yayla, A. (2022). Immersive virtual reality in the age of the metaverse: A hybrid-narrative review based on the technology affordance perspective. *The Journal of Strategic Information Systems*, *31*(2), 101717. Advance online publication. doi:10.1016/j.jsis.2022.101717

Durukal, E. (2022). Customer online shopping experience. In Handbook of research on interdisciplinary reflections of contemporary experiential marketing practices (pp. 60-77). doi:10.4018/978-1-6684-4380-4.ch004

Dwivedi, Y. K., Hughes, L., Baabdullah, A. M., Ribeiro-Navarrete, S., Giannakis, M., Al-Debei, M. M., Dennehy, D., Metri, B., Buhalis, D., Cheung, C. M. K., Conboy, K., Doyle, R., Dubey, R., Dutot, V., Felix, R., Goyal, D. P., Gustafsson, A., Hinsch, C., Jebabli, I., ... Wamba, S. F. (2022). Metaverse beyond the hype: Multidisciplinary perspectives on emerging challenges, opportunities, and agenda for research, practice and policy. *International Journal of Information Management*, *66*, 102542. Advance online publication. doi:10.1016/j.ijinfomgt.2022.102542

Dwivedi, Y. K., Hughes, L., Wang, Y., Alalwan, A. A., Ahn, S. J., Balakrishnan, J., Barta, S., Belk, R., Buhalis, D., Dutot, V., Felix, R., Filieri, R., Flavián, C., Gustafsson, A., Hinsch, C., Hollensen, S., Jain, V., Kim, J., Krishen, A. S., ... Wirtz, J. (2022). Metaverse marketing: How the metaverse will shape the future of consumer research and practice. *Psychology and Marketing*, *40*(4), 750–776. doi:10.1002/mar.21767

Englisch, J. (2022). VAT goes virtual: Security tokens. *EC Tax Review*, *31*(5), 232–237. doi:10.54648/ECTA2022022

Festa, G., Melanthiou, Y., & Meriano, P. (2022). *Engineering the metaverse for innovating the electronic business: A socio-technological perspective.* doi:10.1007/978-3-031-07765-4_4

Filimonau, V., Ashton, M., & Stankov, U. (2022). Virtual spaces as the future of consumption in tourism, hospitality and events. *Journal of Tourism Futures.* doi:10.1108/JTF-07-2022-0174

Firmansyah, E. A., Wahid, H., Gunardi, A., & Hudaefi, F. A. (2022). A scientometric study on management literature in southeast asia. *Journal of Risk and Financial Management*, *15*(11), 507. Advance online publication. doi:10.3390/jrfm15110507

Gadalla, E., Keeling, K., & Abosag, I. (2013). Metaverse-retail service quality: A future framework for retail service quality in the 3D internet. *Journal of Marketing Management*, *29*(13-14), 1493–1517. doi:10.1080/0267257X.2013.835742

Gauttier, S., Simouri, W., & Milliat, A. (2022). When to enter the metaverse: Business leaders offer perspectives. *The Journal of Business Strategy.* Advance online publication. doi:10.1108/JBS-08-2022-0149

Giang Barrera, K., & Shah, D. (2023). Marketing in the metaverse: Conceptual understanding, framework, and research agenda. *Journal of Business Research*, *155*, 113420. Advance online publication. doi:10.1016/j.jbusres.2022.113420

Go, H., & Kang, M. (2022). Metaverse tourism for sustainable tourism development: Tourism agenda 2030. *Tourism Review.* Advance online publication. doi:10.1108/TR-02-2022-0102

Golf-Papez, M., Heller, J., Hilken, T., Chylinski, M., de Ruyter, K., Keeling, D. I., Grinbaum, A., & Adomaitis, L. (2022). Moral equivalence in the metaverse. *NanoEthics, 16*(3), 257–270. doi:10.100711569-022-00426-x

Guo, X., & Hou, L. (2022). Key technology research of digital fashion based on virtual technology. *Advances in Transdisciplinary Engineering, 20,* 894-903. 10.3233/ATDE220093

Gursoy, D., Malodia, S., & Dhir, A. (2022). The metaverse in the hospitality and tourism industry: An overview of current trends and future research directions. *Journal of Hospitality Marketing & Management, 31*(5), 527–534. doi:10.1080/19368623.2022.2072504

Hancock, J. H. II. (2022). Merchandising technologies: It is still all about people; thank goodness. *Fashion, Style & Popular Culture, 9*(4), 433–435. doi:10.1386/fspc_00154_2

Hassani, H., Huang, X., & MacFeely, S. (2022). Enabling digital twins to support the UN SDGs. *Big Data and Cognitive Computing, 6*(4), 115. Advance online publication. doi:10.3390/bdcc6040115

Hennig-Thurau, T., Aliman, D. N., Herting, A. M., Cziehso, G. P., Linder, M., & Kübler, R. V. (2022). Social interactions in the metaverse: Framework, initial evidence, and research roadmap. *Journal of the Academy of Marketing Science.* Advance online publication. doi:10.100711747-022-00908-0

Hines, P., & Netland, T. H. (2022). Teaching a lean masterclass in the metaverse. *International Journal of Lean Six Sigma.* Advance online publication. doi:10.1108/IJLSS-02-2022-0035

Hirsch, P. B. (2022). Adventures in the metaverse. *The Journal of Business Strategy, 43*(5), 332–336. doi:10.1108/JBS-06-2022-0101

Hollensen, S., Kotler, P., & Opresnik, M. O. (2022). Metaverse – The new marketing universe. *The Journal of Business Strategy.* Advance online publication. doi:10.1108/JBS-01-2022-0014

Huvila, I. (2013). Sorting out the metaverse and how the metaverse is sorting us out. In The immersive internet: Reflections on the entangling of the virtual with society, politics and the economy (pp. 192-203). doi:10.1057/9781137283023

Jaung, W. (2022). Digital forest recreation in the metaverse: Opportunities and challenges. *Technological Forecasting and Social Change, 185,* 122090. Advance online publication. doi:10.1016/j.techfore.2022.122090

Jeon, J. (2021). The effects of user experience-based design innovativeness on user– metaverse platform channel relationships in south korea. *Journal of Distribution Science, 19*(11), 81–90. doi:10.15722/jds.19.11.202111.81

Joy, A., Zhu, Y., Peña, C., & Brouard, M. (2022). Digital future of luxury brands: Metaverse, digital fashion, and non-fungible tokens. *Strategic Change, 31*(3), 337–343. doi:10.1002/jsc.2502

Kappe, F., & Steurer, M. (2010). *The open metaverse currency (OMC) - A micropayment framework for open 3D virtual worlds.* doi:10.1007/978-3-642-15208-5_9

Khan, S. W., Raza, S. H., & Zaman, U. (2022). Remodeling digital marketplace through metaverse: A multi-path model of consumer neuroticism, parasocial relationships, social media influencer's credibility, and openness to metaverse experience. *Pakistan Journal of Commerce and Social Science, 16*(3), 337–365.

Kim, J. (2021). Advertising in the metaverse: Research agenda. *Journal of Interactive Advertising, 21*(3), 141–144. doi:10.1080/15252019.2021.2001273

Koay, K. Y., Tjiptono, F., Teoh, C. W., Memon, M. A., & Connolly, R. (2022). Social media influencer marketing: Commentary on the special issue. *Journal of Internet Commerce*. Advance online publication. doi:10.1080/15332861.2022.2128277

Koo, C., Kwon, J., Chung, N., & Kim, J. (2022). Metaverse tourism: Conceptual framework and research propositions. *Current Issues in Tourism*, 1–7. Advance online publication. doi:10.1080/13683500.2022.2122781

Korbel, J. J., Siddiq, U. H., & Zarnekow, R. (2022). Towards virtual 3D asset price prediction based on machine learning. *Journal of Theoretical and Applied Electronic Commerce Research, 17*(3), 924–948. doi:10.3390/jtaer17030048

Kozinets, R. V. (2023). Immersive netnography: A novel method for service experience research in virtual reality, augmented reality, and metaverse contexts. *Journal of Service Management, 34*(1), 100–125. doi:10.1108/JOSM-12-2021-0481

Kraus, S., Kanbach, D. K., Krysta, P. M., Steinhoff, M. M., & Tomini, N. (2022). Facebook and the creation of the metaverse: Radical business model innovation or incremental transformation? *International Journal of Entrepreneurial Behaviour & Research, 28*(9), 52–77. doi:10.1108/IJEBR-12-2021-0984

Kraus, S., Kumar, S., Lim, W. M., Kaur, J., Sharma, A., & Schiavone, F. (2023). From moon landing to metaverse: Tracing the evolution of technological forecasting and social change. *Technological Forecasting and Social Change, 189*, 122381. Advance online publication. doi:10.1016/j.techfore.2023.122381

Kshetri, N., & Dwivedi, Y. K. (2023). Pollution-reducing and pollution-generating effects of the metaverse. *International Journal of Information Management, 69*, 102620. Advance online publication. doi:10.1016/j.ijinfomgt.2023.102620

Lee, C., & Wong, K. D. (2022). Towards self-adaptive/Reflective co-managed open generativity to augment absorptive-multiplicative-relational Capabilities/Capacities. *IEEE International Conference on Industrial Engineering and Engineering Management, 2022-December* 52-56. 10.1109/IEEM55944.2022.9989957

Lee, S., Domina, T., & MacGillivray, M. (2011). Exploring consumers' flow experiences in virtual shopping: An exploratory study. *International Journal of Electronic Marketing and Retailing, 4*(2-3), 165–182. doi:10.1504/IJEMR.2011.043046

Lee, S., Trimi, S., Byun, W. K., & Kang, M. (2011). Innovation and imitation effects in metaverse service adoption. *Service Business, 5*(2), 155–172. doi:10.100711628-011-0108-8

Lee, U., & Kim, H. (2022). UTAUT in metaverse: An "Ifland" case. *Journal of Theoretical and Applied Electronic Commerce Research, 17*(2), 613–635. doi:10.3390/jtaer17020032

Linnenluecke, M. K., Marrone, M., & Singh, A. K. (2020). Conducting systematic literature reviews and bibliometric analyses. *Australian Journal of Management*, *45*(2), 175–194. doi:10.1177/0312896219877678

Llamas, R., & Belk, R. (2022). The Routledge handbook of digital consumption. doi:10.4324/9781003317524

Lukava, T., Morgado Ramirez, D. Z., & Barbareschi, G. (2022). Two sides of the same coin: Accessibility practices and neurodivergent users' experience of extended reality. *Journal of Enabling Technologies*, *16*(2), 75–90. doi:10.1108/JET-03-2022-0025

Mahr, D. (2022). Embracing falsity through the metaverse: The case of synthetic customer experiences. *Business Horizons*, *65*(6), 739–749. doi:10.1016/j.bushor.2022.07.007

Marmaridis, I., & Griffith, S. (2009). *Metaverse services: Extensible learning with mediated teleporting into 3D environments.* doi:10.1007/978-3-642-01112-2_24

Masferrer, J. Á. R., Sánchez, F. E., & Hernández, D. F. (2014). Experiences complementing classroom teaching with distance seminars in metaverses and videos. *Journal of Cases on Information Technology*, *16*(4), 1–12. doi:10.4018/jcit.2014100101

Michalikova, K. F., Suler, P., & Robinson, R. (2022). Virtual Hiring and Training Processes in the Metaverse: Remote Work Apps, Sensory Algorithmic Devices, and Decision Intelligence and Modeling. *Psychosociological Issues in Human Resource Management*, *10*(1), 50–63. doi:10.22381/pihrm10120224

Murray, A., Kim, D., & Combs, J. (2023). The promise of a decentralized internet: What is Web3, and how can firms prepare? *Business Horizons*, *66*(2), 191–202. doi:10.1016/j.bushor.2022.06.002

Oberhauser, R., Baehre, M., & Sousa, P. (2022). *VR-EA+TCK: Visualizing enterprise architecture, content, and knowledge in virtual reality.* doi:10.1007/978-3-031-11510-3_8

Owens, D., Mitchell, A., Khazanchi, D., & Zigurs, I. (2011). An empirical investigation of virtual world projects and metaverse technology capabilities. *The Data Base for Advances in Information Systems*, *42*(1), 74–101. doi:10.1145/1952712.1952717

Oxford Analytica. (2022). Commercial metaverse to expand fast but unevenly. *Emerald Expert Briefings*. doi:108/OXAN-DB271953

Pamucar, D., Deveci, M., Gokasar, I., Tavana, M., & Köppen, M. (2022). A metaverse assessment model for sustainable transportation using ordinal priority approach and aczel-alsina norms. *Technological Forecasting and Social Change*, *182*, 121778. Advance online publication. doi:10.1016/j.techfore.2022.121778

Papagiannidis, S., Bourlakis, M., & Li, F. (2008). Making real money in virtual worlds: MMORPGs and emerging business opportunities, challenges and ethical implications in metaverses. *Technological Forecasting and Social Change*, *75*(5), 610–622. doi:10.1016/j.techfore.2007.04.007

Periyasami, S., & Periyasamy, A. P. (2022). Metaverse as future promising platform business model: Case study on the fashion value chain. *Businesses*, *2*(4), 527–545. doi:10.3390/businesses2040033

Pham, V. C., Luu, Q. K., Nguyen, T. T., Nguyen, N. H., Tan, Y., & Ho, V. A. (2022). *Web of Tactile things: Towards an Open and Standardized platform for Tactile things via the W3C web of Things.* doi:10.1007/978-3-031-07481-3_11

Plangger, K., & Campbell, C. (2022). Managing in an era of falsity: Falsity from the metaverse to fake news to fake endorsement to synthetic influence to false agendas. *Business Horizons, 65*(6), 713–717. doi:10.1016/j.bushor.2022.08.003

Power, D., & Teigland, R. (2013). Postcards from the metaverse: An introduction to the immersive internet. In The immersive internet: Reflections on the entangling of the virtual with society, politics and the economy (pp. 1-12). doi:10.1057/9781137283023

Praherdhiono, H., Adi, E. P., Prihatmoko, Y., Abidin, Z., Nindigraha, N., Hidayati, A., & Muttaqin, A. (2022). Synchronization of virtual and real learning patterns in E-learning systems with metaverse concept. *Proceedings - International Conference on Education and Technology, ICET,* 185-189. 10.1109/ICET56879.2022.9990891

Prodinger, B., & Neuhofer, B. (2023). Never-ending tourism: Tourism experience scenarios for 2030. *Springer Proceedings in Business and Economics,* 288-299. 10.1007/978-3-031-25752-0_31

Queiroz, M. M., Fosso Wamba, S., Pereira, S. C. F., & Chiappetta Jabbour, C. J. (2023). The metaverse as a breakthrough for operations and supply chain management: Implications and call for action. *International Journal of Operations & Production Management.* Advance online publication. doi:10.1108/IJOPM-01-2023-0006

Ratten, V. (2023). The post COVID-19 pandemic era: Changes in teaching and learning methods for management educators. *International Journal of Management Education, 21*(2), 100777. Advance online publication. doi:10.1016/j.ijme.2023.100777

Rauschnabel, P. A., Babin, B. J., tom Dieck, M. C., Krey, N., & Jung, T. (2022). What is augmented reality marketing? its definition, complexity, and future. *Journal of Business Research, 142,* 1140–1150. doi:10.1016/j.jbusres.2021.12.084

Reay, E., & Wanick, V. (2023). *Skins in the game: Fashion branding and commercial video games.* doi:10.1007/978-3-031-11185-3_5

Reed, D. (2022). The new rules of engagement: Hearts and minds in turbulent times. In Leadership strategies for the hybrid workforce: Best practices for fostering employee safety and significance (pp. 50-59). doi:10.4018/978-1-6684-3453-6.ch004

Rosário, A., Vilaça, F., Raimundo, R., & Cruz, R. (2021). Literature review on Health Knowledge Management in the last 10 years (2009-2019). *The Electronic Journal of Knowledge Management, 18*(3), 338-355. doi:10.34190/ejkm.18.3.2120

Rosário, A. T. (2021). The Background of artigicial intelligence applied to marketing. *Academy of Strategic Management Journal, 20*(6), 1–19.

Rosário, A. T., & Dias, J. C. (2022). Sustainability and the Digital Transition: A Literature Review. *Sustainability (Basel), 14*(7), 4072. doi:10.3390u14074072

Rosário, A. T., & Dias, J. C. (2023). How Industry 4.0 and Sensors Can Leverage Product Design: Opportunities and Challenges. *Sensors (Basel), 23*(3), 1165. doi:10.339023031165 PMID:36772206

Sartamorn, S., & Oe, H. (2022). Metaverse marketing for community development: Revitalization of traditional industrial sectors in Thailand. *Springer Proceedings in Business and Economics,* 121-126. 10.1007/978-3-031-06581-1_16

Shah, D. R. (2022). Textiles in the metaverse. *Textile View Magazine,* (137), 24-25+288.

Smith, R. (2022). NPD with the metaverse, NFTs, and crypto. *Research Technology Management,* 65(5), 54–56. doi:10.1080/08956308.2022.2090182

Solomon, M. R., & Wood, N. T. (2014). Introduction: Virtual social identity: Welcome to the metaverse. *Virtual Social Identity and Consumer Behavior,* vii-xv.

Spanò, R., Massaro, M., Ferri, L., Dumay, J., & Schmitz, J. (2022). Blockchain in accounting, accountability and assurance: An overview. *Accounting, Auditing & Accountability Journal,* 35(7), 1493–1506. doi:10.1108/AAAJ-06-2022-5850

Spivey, W. A., & Munson, J. M. (2009). Mot: Technology entrepreneurs in second life. *PICMET: Portland International Center for Management of Engineering and Technology, Proceedings,* 2200-2221. 10.1109/PICMET.2009.5262553

Swilley, E. (2016). *Moving virtual retail into reality: Examining metaverse and augmented reality in the online shopping experience.* doi:10.1007/978-3-319-24184-5_163

Syuhada, K., Tjahjono, V., & Hakim, A. (2023). Dependent metaverse risk forecasts with heteroskedastic models and ensemble learning. *Risks,* 11(2), 32. Advance online publication. doi:10.3390/risks11020032

Tan, T. M., Makkonen, H., Kaur, P., & Salo, J. (2022). How do ethical consumers utilize sharing economy platforms as part of their sustainable resale behavior? the role of consumers' green consumption values. *Technological Forecasting and Social Change,* 176, 121432. Advance online publication. doi:10.1016/j.techfore.2021.121432

Tan, T. M., & Salo, J. (2021). Ethical marketing in the blockchain-based sharing economy: Theoretical integration and guiding insights. *Journal of Business Ethics.* Advance online publication. doi:10.100710551-021-05015-8

Tan, T. M., & Saraniemi, S. (2022). Trust in blockchain-enabled exchanges: Future directions in blockchain marketing. *Journal of the Academy of Marketing Science.* Advance online publication. doi:10.100711747-022-00889-0

Taylor, C. R. (2022). Research on advertising in the metaverse: A call to action. *International Journal of Advertising,* 41(3), 383–384. doi:10.1080/02650487.2022.2058786

Tlili, A., Huang, R., & Kinshuk. (2023). Metaverse for climbing the ladder toward 'Industry 5.0' and 'Society 5.0'? [元宇宙是否为迈向"工业5.0"和"社会5.0"的阶梯?]. *Service Industries Journal,* 43(3-4), 260–287. Advance online publication. doi:10.1080/02642069.2023.2178644

Tsai, S. (2022). Investigating metaverse marketing for travel and tourism. *Journal of Vacation Marketing.* Advance online publication. doi:10.1177/13567667221145715

Umar, A. (2022). A digital transformation lab for developing countries and small to medium enterprises. *2022 IEEE European Technology and Engineering Management Summit, E-TEMS 2022 - Conference Proceedings,* 160-165. 10.1109/E-TEMS53558.2022.9944423

Volchek, K., & Brysch, A. (2023). Metaverse and tourism: From a new niche to a transformation. *Springer Proceedings in Business and Economics,* 300-311. 10.1007/978-3-031-25752-0_32

Wallace, M. (2006). Virtual worlds, virtual lives. *PC World (San Francisco, CA), 24*(11), 133–136.

Wang, A., Gao, Z., Wang, Z., Hui, P., & Braud, T. (2022). Envisioning A hyper-learning system in the age of metaverse. *Proceedings - VRCAI 2022: 18th ACM SIGGRAPH International Conference on Virtual-Reality Continuum and its Applications in Industry,* 10.1145/3574131.3574427

Wang, J., & Medvegy, G. (2022). Exploration the future of the metaverse and smart cities. *Proceedings of the International Conference on Electronic Business (ICEB), 22,* 106-115.

Wanick, V., & Stallwood, J. (2023). *Brand storytelling, gamification and social media marketing in the "Metaverse": A case study of the Ralph Lauren winter escape.* doi:10.1007/978-3-031-11185-3_3

Weiss, C. (2022). Fashion retailing in the metaverse. *Fashion, Style & Popular Culture, 9*(4), 523–538. doi:10.1386/fspc_00159_1

Weking, J., Desouza, K. C., Fielt, E., & Kowalkiewicz, M. (2023). Metaverse-enabled entrepreneurship. *Journal of Business Venturing Insights, 19,* e00375. Advance online publication. doi:10.1016/j.jbvi.2023.e00375

Wiederhold, B. K. (2022). Metaverse games: Game changer for healthcare? [editorial]. *Cyberpsychology, Behavior, and Social Networking, 25*(5), 267–269. doi:10.1089/cyber.2022.29246.editorial PMID:35549346

Yemenici, A. D. (2022). Entrepreneurship in the world of Metaverse: Virtual or real? *Journal of Metaverse, 2*(2), 71–82. doi:10.57019/jmv.1126135

Zainurin, M. Z. L., Haji Masri, M., Besar, M. H. A., & Anshari, M. (2023). Towards an understanding of metaverse banking: A conceptual paper. *Journal of Financial Reporting and Accounting.* doi:10.1108/JFRA-12-2021-0487

Zarka, W., & Hajismail, S. (2022). Prospects of negative heritage management in syria. *Journal of Cultural Heritage Management and Sustainable Development.* Advance online publication. doi:10.1108/JCHMSD-08-2021-0139

Zhan, Y., Xiong, Y., & Xing, X. (2023). A conceptual model and case study of blockchain-enabled social media platform. *Technovation, 119,* 102610. Advance online publication. doi:10.1016/j.technovation.2022.102610

Zhou, M., Leenders, M. A. A. M., & Cong, L. M. (2018). Ownership in the virtual world and the implications for long-term user innovation success. *Technovation, 78,* 56–65. doi:10.1016/j.technovation.2018.06.002

Zhu, C., Wu, D. C. W., Hall, C. M., Fong, L. H. N., Koupaei, S. N., & Lin, F. (2023). Exploring non-immersive virtual reality experiences in tourism: Empirical evidence from a world heritage site. *International Journal of Tourism Research*, 25(3), 372–383. Advance online publication. doi:10.1002/jtr.2574

KEY TERMS AND DEFINITIONS

Augmented Reality: Augmented reality (AR), different from virtual reality, is a technology that, when applied, allows us to superimpose virtual elements on our view of reality. This integration of virtual information to real-world visualizations can be simulated and generated by a computer of a three-dimensional image or environment that can be interacted with in an apparently real or physical way by a person wearing special electronic equipment.

Business Platforms: They facilitate business-related activities such as virtual meetings and remote work and, in this scenario, enterprises will provide better engagement, collaboration and connection to their employees through immersive workspaces in virtual offices. These professional business activities are conducted using virtual tools such as whiteboards, document sharing, and video conferencing. It also allows them to engage their employees, suppliers, and other stakeholders, thus streamlining business activities and communication.

Metaverse: Constitutes a computer-mediated environment where people engage in social activities through avatars in 360-degree virtual worlds. It is an interactive, immersive, and collaborative virtual 3D world inhabited by avatars of real people. This social dimension in a three-dimensional virtual world allows companies to create interactive experiences such as virtual events and product demonstrations, improving customer experience which are critical in marketing.

Mixed Reality (MR): Mixed reality is the technology that combines features of virtual reality with augmented reality, revealing natural and intuitive 3D human, computational and environmental interactions. This inserts virtual objects into the real world and allows the user to interact with the objects, producing new environments in which physical and virtual items coexist and interact in real time. These new realities allow for new opportunities in the marketing, communication, and advertising of brands, not only in entertainment situations but also in interaction with consumers in online stores.

Social Platforms: Social platforms are metaverse platforms designed to facilitate socializing and networking. They allow users to interact with each other in a virtual environment and engage in activities such as gaming, socializing, and attending events. Traditional social media is mainly focused on posting, liking, and sharing content, whereas Metaverse-based social media will take it to the next level by allowing users to interact with each other and the digital environment in a more immersive way. It will enhance the social experience and allow for new forms of communication and expression.

Virtual Reality: Virtual reality (VR) is an interface technology between a user and an operating system through 3D graphics resources or 360° images whose objective is to create the sensation of presence in an environment created by computational techniques in real time. This interaction is carried out through equipment that increases the feeling of presence of the individual in the virtual environment, designated as immersion.

Chapter 4
AI–Aided Teaching Model in Education 5.0

Alex Khang

Global Research Institute of Technology and Engineering, USA

Muthmainnah Muthmainnah

Universitas Al Asyariah Mandar, Indonesia

Prodhan Mahbub Ibna Seraj

ⓘD https://orcid.org/0000-0002-4483-6059

American International University-Bangladesh, Dhaka, Bangladesh

Ahmad Al Yakin

Universitas Al Asyariah Mandar, Indonesia

Ahmad J. Obaid

ⓘD https://orcid.org/0000-0003-0376-5546

Department of Computer Science, Faculty of Computer Science and Mathematics, University of Kufa, Iraq

ABSTRACT

In the educational setting, artificial intelligence (AI) technology, notably chatbots, has made substantial improvements in English learning. This study aims to determine the effectiveness of using the Artificial Intelligence Virtual Dream Friend and John English Boot applications on learning English in the 5.0 revolution era in English courses for first-semester students at university. The assessment method used is a quantitative research method and research design (quasi-experiment design). Based on the results of the study, it can be concluded that the results of the comparison test showed that My Virtual Dream Friend and John English Bot were both effective for use as computer tutoring in English courses and also increased interest in learning English in the 5.0 revolution era compared to previous conventional methods. The outcomes of this study might be used to direct future research into utilizing chatbots outside of the classroom as learning companions, and educators could use them to adapt evaluation and feedback procedures.

DOI: 10.4018/978-1-6684-8851-5.ch004

INTRODUCTION

Education has undergone profound changes as a result of the widespread use of digital technologies and the proliferation of connected information networks. Better tools are becoming available to facilitate the more complex activities that have traditionally been a part of the educational process (Wright et al., 2023; Fullan, 2023).

Giving students timely feedback like this helps them assess their progress and learn more efficiently (Huang et al., 2023). Technology's contribution to bettering the teaching and learning process is growing in significance as educational models adapt to new learning technologies. One of the most pressing concerns of the last decade has been the use of technology to improve the teaching and learning process (Ekin et al., 2023) and numerous learning management systems (LMS) that accomplish this goal keep being proposed (Alfalah, 2023) to do so in a variety of ways (Anderson, 2023).

Academics have stressed that while learning technologies can significantly improve learning and teaching, they will also produce a range of issues related to student-system interactions due to their many forms and sizes (Elme et al., 2022). Students' learning processes and outcomes with the help of modern learning aids are strongly influenced by their attitudes, emotions, and learning experiences (Kuleto et al., 2022).

A growing body of research has sought to clarify the ways in which educational chatbots can enhance learning in a variety of contexts, such as language learning (Kuhail, M. A., et al., 2022), vocabulary acquisition (Yunjiu et al., 2022; Huang & Wang, 2021), the development of communicative competence (Kim et al., 2022; Hu & Hu, 2020; Mohammed Mahmoud Ghoneim, & Elsayed Abdelsalam Elghotmy, 2021).

These chatbots used a question-and-answer format to motivate students to put in the effort required to acquire the requisite information or skill. In the same way that human reading companions may accompany and give emotional supports to help students read actively, chatbots can act like them and inspire students to think about the tales they are reading (Liu et al., 2022; Zhang et al., 2022).

Student responses to chatbots may differ from those to humans, according to the literature (Winkler & Söllner, 2018; Hill et al., 2015). The literature is silent on how students evaluate the chatbot's usefulness as a reading companion. The research isn't clear on whether or whether students believe chatbots made with modern natural language processing techniques, such co-reference resolution and dependency parsing approaches, to have intelligence about the books they've read and act like a human reading partner.

Scholars and professionals in the field of language study and teaching have started looking into Intelligent Computer Assisted Language Learning (ICALL) because of the promising future it holds for AI in education (Weng & Chiu, 2023). This topic expands Computer Assisted Language Learning (CALL) by introducing artificial intelligence (AI) into the language learning environment (Huang et al., 2023).

Differentiating itself from other LMSs, ICALL makes use of a number of different artificial intelligence (AI) techniques, including natural language processing (NLP) (Pokriváková, S. 2019), intelligent tutoring systems (ITS), and others to facilitate complex interactions between students and their learning environment (Swartz & Yazdani, 2012). These interactions were developed using automated feedback (Huang et al., 2023), intelligent tutoring (Furlan et al., 2021), and customization (Huang et al., 2022).

The best learning outcomes for students (Mitra & Banerjee, 2022) and 21st century skills may be achieved through their flexibility and adaptability, which allows them to meet the demands of each individual student (Muthmainnah et al., 2022).

For an ICALL environment to be successful, it must adhere to sound instructional design principles that direct learning practice and optimize student growth (Muthmainnah et al., 2023). For this purpose,

Merrill's suggested First Principles of Education (FPI) are adequate since they may be used to design instructional materials for any type of learning activity or program (Merrill, 2002).

Computers and Education: Artificial Intelligence suggests studying FPI's integration into the ICALL setting as part of AI in education research to reveal the associated pedagogical advances. Learning environments as diverse as flipped classrooms (Weng & Chiu, 2023) and video-based physics instructional games have been found to benefit from the implementation of the five FPI principles, which include problem-centered, activation, demonstration, application, and integration (Kuba, Rahimi, Smith, Shute, & Dai, 2021).

Most language classes have four distinct parts: the warm-up, the pre-practice, the control exercises, and the post-practice. For students who have already understood or mastered the procedures involved, this method's constant repetition from lesson to lesson can quickly become tedious. It's time for college and university language instructors to reevaluate their methods of instruction in light of recent developments in the use of technology in language learning. As a matter of fact, there is a wealth of information in the pedagogical sector from ITC applications utilized in the context of language teaching and learning.

Anastasios Karakas and George Kartal (2020). In order to improve language teaching and learning, ELT educational applications have made use of a wide range of information and communication technologies (ICTs), such as the interactive web, ELT software, synchronous chat, etc. (Huang et al., 2023). To distinguish themselves from other types of software, chatbot developers focused on creating applications that could hold an intelligent conversation with human users using either speech or text (Zhou, 2023; Lin & Wu, 2023).

In reality, AI chatbots can aid education by allowing instructors to customize lessons to individual students' linguistic abilities. The development of an AI chatbot is a sophisticated and large-scale undertaking that calls for a lot of expertise in the field of information technology. For this reason, it has been accepted by certain language instructors for classroom usage.

A learner who wants to use an AI chatbot for instruction must also have the patience to react to the chatbot's predetermined series of automated questions. Students at the university level are of an age when they may be motivated to study independently, thus the idea of utilizing technology to teach a foreign language makes sense.

With the rise of mobile and social media, it is essential for language instructors to integrate IT into their classrooms to keep students engaged and improve the quality and efficiency of the learning process. An empirical research was conducted utilizing AI chatbots like "My Virtual Dream Friend" and "John English Bot" to teach undergraduate students about "self-introduction" in a foreign language.

ICALL INSTRUCTIONAL DESIGN

CALL is a well-established area with documented application outcomes in boosting student engagement and delivering improved language acquisition before AI was integrated into language teaching (Zhang & MacWhinney, 2023).

Both wide and narrow CALL review studies have been conducted by researchers. Topic modeling analysis was used by Chen, Zou, Xie, and Su (2021) to learn more about the topics and technologies that have caught the attention of CALL researchers. In particular, the researchers (Chen, Zou, Xie, & Cheng, 2021) investigated students' customized language learning in the context of technology-enhanced language learning and the use of artificial intelligence (AI) in the classroom.

However, ICALL breaks through the generic and one-size-fits-all instructional philosophy, offering new opportunities for providing learners with seamless intelligent support/feedback and catering to student differences in proficiency levels and learning preferences, as was found in the review study by Huang et al. (2021). With the use of NLP and ITS in AI, for instance, students are able to use language in more organic contexts (Shardlow, Sellar, & Rousell, 2022).

Artificial intelligence techniques like machine learning, data mining, and deep learning make possible personalized learning systems that cater to each learner's unique needs, interests, learning style, and speed.

There are three ways in which artificial intelligence (AI) aids language activities: (1) automated feedback in the form of corrections and prompt responses; (2) intelligent tutoring in the form of answers to questions and explanations of concepts; and (3) customization in the form of information tailored to the specific needs of users.

ICALL settings were developed to accommodate students from a wide range of linguistic backgrounds and interests. Several studies have shown that instructors and students in ICALL settings have different perspectives on the learning processes and results that are optimal for each (De la Vall & Araya, 2023).

Weng and Chiu (2023), for example, revealed the use of the concept of activation in intelligent tutoring, the principle of problem-centeredness in individualized instruction, and the principle of demonstration in automatic feedback.

In the meanwhile, we talked about the difficulties encountered in these research endeavors and provided some insights into instructional design as well as some empirical ideas for use in ICALL classrooms. De la Vall and Araya (2023) examine the pros, cons, and potential future developments of ICALL language learning technologies, such as the dependence on enormous amounts of data for training, the need for greater human contact, and the contextual nuances of language.

There are a number of ways that these AI tools could improve in the future. These include the incorporation of virtual reality and augmented reality technologies, the development of better natural language processing algorithms, and the creation of more sophisticated adaptive learning algorithms.

AI learning systems have the potential to become even more powerful and impactful tools for language learning if these problems and limitations are resolved, and their integration is essential for developing more efficient and effective learning user experience solutions.

Freeman (2023) shows that educators value classroom activities that encourage students to actively participate in learning grammatical concepts both internationally and in Sweden particularly. Furthermore, Blake (2023) conducted an ICALL study to assist and engaged in their work with ICALL tools, Question Generator is a first of its kind online application as it allows students to construct questions based on user input.

Previous reports of a variety of ICALL learning objectives/contexts and associated learning results proved the usefulness of ICALL applications. Positive results cannot be achieved just by using technological applications; their implementation is what makes the difference (Kale, Roy, & Yuan, 2020; Marek & Wu, 2020; Kuosa, 2014). Therefore, it is important to examine the instructional design for ICALL as a factor that influences the results of ICALL applications.

Instructional design for AI-based language learning (ICALL) is the process of developing instructional strategies, resources, and activities that help students learn a language in an artificial intelligence (AI) setting (Shu & Gu, 2023).

Instructional designers at ICALL will use methods including need analysis, environment design, system development, and evaluation to build and test their environments and ensure they provide the desired effects on students' learning (Archuby, Sanz, & Manresa-Yee, 2023). To make their lessons more successful and flexible, instructional designers developed these steps into a number of different instructional design models and concepts.

The principles and ideas of instructional design may be applied in an ICALL context since they are consistent with technology-supported learning methods (Koszalka et al., 2013). For instance, Johnson (2019) used the Data-Driven Development method as the instructional design principles of the artificial intelligence (AI) driven system eSkill, and found that students who practiced with the system had improved their public speaking abilities.

An intelligent tutoring system was developed by Fang et al. (2022) to facilitate the PACES curriculum for students with low reading competence (e.g., predicting, acquiring, clarifying, evaluating, and summarizing).

They found that the method led to the greatest comprehension increases among careful readers. In addition, Huang and Wang (2021) combined Total Physical Response (TPR) language teaching instruction with artificial intelligence in their creation of the TPRAI motion sensing teaching system for learning French vocabulary. Academic performance on the delay exam was high in the experimental groups, according to the study's findings.

Researchers have reported their hands-on experiences with ICALL instructional design, and several instructional design strategies for ICALL have been proposed. Unfortunately, there hasn't been a lot of research done to systematically look at how different pedagogical approaches may improve ICALL.

Even fewer scholars have looked at a single instructional framework for ICALL and all the challenges that come with it in terms of implementation.

CHATBOTS AS COMPUTER TUTORING IN LANGUAGE TEACHING

Artificial intelligence (AI) chatbots are information applications that can understand human speech using natural language processing (NLP) methods and respond accordingly (Zhong, Scarinci, & Cicirello, 2023). Thanks to developments in natural language processing (NLP), Chatbots have progressed from simple pattern matching to coping with increasingly complex interactions and reasoning, even replacing certain discussions with human beings.

Users were satisfied and positive about chatbots because of their practicality, simplicity of use, entertainment value, aesthetic appeal, and socializing capabilities (Shum et al., 2018). There has been a lot of focus on how useful chatbots can be in the classroom.

According to the studies conducted, the majority of the learning systems out there have interfaces that are set in format, limiting the user's ability to be creative and interactive. Students are less engaged when they are required to follow a set method or respond in a predetermined way (Mukhiya et al., 2020).

Edwards et al. (2018) found that students' attitudes toward learning and their interactions with social robots were correlated with how quickly teachers provided teaching. When compared to interactions with teachers, both verbal and nonverbal, learning system exchanges feel fake and distant (Kim et al., 2020).

Unlike learning management systems (LMSs), chatbots allow for both human and automated direction of the interaction. Having a discourse like this with their peers is a great way for students to feel like they belong in a community (Jiang, Yang, & Zheng, 2023).

Even if chatbots' vocabularies are limited, people are nevertheless interested in and eager to have conversations with them because of how easy they are to engage with and how they make them feel like they are part of the conversation (Fryer et al., 2019).

Additionally, chatbots can provide interactive messages similar to real conversations in order to encourage students to access online materials (Pham et al., 2018). Thus, chatbots may now function as equals in the classroom (Neto & Fernandes, 2019).

Naturalistic dialogue with chatbots has been found by several academics to make students feel less alone and separated from their learning in conventional LMSs (Shamsi, 2021). Students are commonly involved in studying with chatbots because of how novel and interesting they find it to be (Kerly, Hall, & Bull, 2007).

Some students would rather communicate with a chatbot than a human teacher or other student (Kim, 2021; Zamora, 2017). Students' engagement, motivation, and teamwork can all benefit from the use of chatbots as a medium for education (Kumar, 2021).

Kohnke (2023) for example, employed chatbots to promote student interactions in online courses, and their findings showed that chatbots not only increased the percentage of students completing learning activities, but that most of students wished to use chatbots in additional courses as well.

Messenger bots, or "chatbots," are software programs that aim to simulate human conversation. Yildiz Durak (2022) stated in the field of education, chatbots present exciting new possibilities.

Chatbots have many potentials uses in the classroom, including the facilitation of interaction, the dissemination of information (of varying forms), and the provision of direction. It's true that chatbots have the potential to improve education by introducing more interaction into the classroom.

Students who reported more happiness with their chatbot experiences also reported greater competence in visual design. The extent to which you enjoy using the chatbot will have a favorable effect on how satisfied you are with many facets of the course.

User happiness with a chatbot has a bearing on how often it is used. Implications for future investigation and clinical use were highlighted. In this respect, the use of chatbots in education is gaining popularity and is regarded as a significant development trend.

METHOD

This study used a quasi-experimental design because it took samples from two classes at random (randomly) (Campbell & Stanley, 1966). Both groups were called "experimental classes," but they were given different ways to learn English. Quasi-experimental studies are used in educational research when random assignment of participants is impractical or unethical. These studies allow comparative research to be carried out in real-world contexts (Campbell & Stanley, 1966).

In addition, conducting quasi-experiments in outcome evaluation using a historical cohort control group design is a feasible approach that requires few resources and causes little disruption to daily classroom activities (Walser, 2014). In this study, we ensured that the experimental group and the control group were in the same position by selecting classes given by the same instructor and lasting for two consecutive semesters with identical curricula, course materials, and activities.

In this study, students in the experimental group in the Agribusiness study program (hereinafter referred to as the "AI-John English Bot group") and their colleagues in the control group in the government science study program (so referred to as the "AI-My Virtual Dream Friend group") used artificial intelligence applications during language learning, as many as four meetings.

The goal of this study is to find out what happens when first-year college students learn English with the help of AI and how the application affects their motivation to learn English. Among the many tools used in this study, one is observation, which is the act of looking at an object to learn about a phenomenon or event.

Data collection technique Researchers use a data collection technique to get the information they need to solve problems. In this study, the following methods were used to gather data:

1.   Pre-test

A pre-test is an observation made before the experiment. This is done to get some initial data. Researchers make observations by giving tests to find out how well people learn English on average before they are treated or do anything else.

2.   Treatment

After giving students their first test (pretest), the next step is to give them treatment or treatment to see how well artificial intelligence helps them learn English. Both classes got the same treatment and learned the same things, like how to use the contractions am/is/are, how to introduce yourself, how to say hello and goodbye, how to tell time, how to talk about countries and nationalities, and how to use position adjectives and possessive adjectives. The two classes will be taught in the following ways:

After installing artificial intelligence on their student devices, they then practice self-introduction gradually with their AI. The lecturer monitors and observes the class carefully. The two applications have advantages and disadvantages based on the observations of the two classes.

Figure 1. Teaching model using Artificial Intelligence
Source: Muthmainnah et al. (2022)

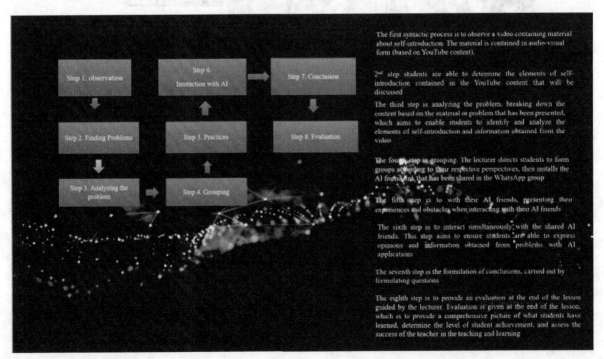

Figure 2. My virtual dream app

In the My Virtual Dream Friend group, students must discuss with their group mates to determine who they will choose to interact with or practice with, and of course this takes time. However, the excitement was found when they discussed with each other which robot to choose in terms of appearance, gender, and hair color.

Figure 3. My virtual dream friend feature

Meanwhile, in the John English Bot class, there were no other robot options to be found, only John English Bot. After installed, the students asked to choose native language or students' language (Indonesian)

Figure 4. John English Bot feature

During the activity, students are allowed to use Google Translate or e-dictionary tools; besides that, they are also asked to connect the material obtained before to their artificial intelligence. During the interaction activities, the lecturer asks students to record their experiences and obstacles when interacting with artificial intelligence. Simultaneous interaction occurs with the shared AI.

In this finding, each group found that when they interacted, AI could facilitate their English practice activities, but AI My Virtual Dream Friend did not correct grammar mistakes made by undergraduate students. While in the John English Bot group, they found that the AI provided sample answer facilities and having corrected feedback to students.

At this stage, the lecturer ensures that students can express their English without feeling anxious or afraid of being wrong.

Figure 5. Corrected feedback by John English Bot

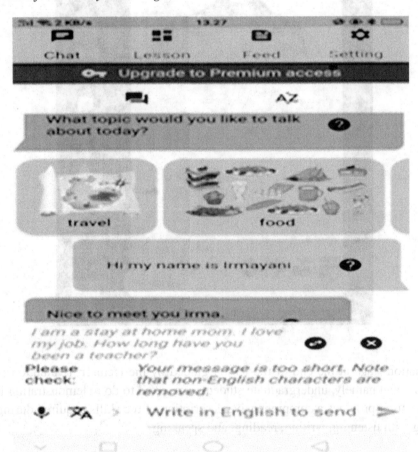

At the conclusion formulation stage, it is carried out by formulating the results of the script that has been created while interacting with AI and before logging out so that students do screen screening. This stage is carried out to measure the level of student understanding after the learning process when practicing with AI, correcting mistakes made, and providing reflection.

Figure 6. Chatbots scan screening of artificial intelligence
Source: https://youtube.com/shorts/rNnGPJT6_ao?feature=share

At the evaluation stage at the end of the lesson guided by the lecturer. Evaluation is given at the end of the lesson, and namely, undergraduate students are asked to do a demonstration in the form of speaking. The lecturer provides a comprehensive description of the skills acquired during the learning process, starting with listening, writing, reading, and speaking.

3.   Post-test

The post-test is the opposite of the pre-test. If the pre-test is done before a treatment or action is taken, then the post-test is done after the treatment or action has been taken.

INSTRUMENTS

1. Test

In the experimental class, a pre-test and a post-test are used to find out how well students could do before and after learning.

2. Observation

Rosenbaum, Rosenbaum, and Briskman (2010) says that observation is making direct observations of research objects to look closely at what is going on and consists of all activities in the class. If the goal of the research is to find out about behavior and actions, small respondents use natural phenomena, which are things that happen in the natural world.

The goal of this observation is to find out how My Virtual Dream Friend and John English Bot are used in English classes.

Figure 7. Class observation

DATA ANALYSIS TECHNIQUE

In this study, the collected data were analyzed using descriptive statistical techniques and inferential statistical analysis. The data processing procedures used are:

1. Descriptive Statistical Analysis

Descriptive statistics are statistics that are used to analyze data by describing data or describing data that has been collected as it is without intending to make general conclusions or generalizations (Nardi, 2018). Descriptive statistics are used to describe student activity scores, student responses, and scores of Indonesian language learning outcomes obtained from each class.

The next procedure calculates the sample frequency in each category using the formula:

$P = f\,x/n\,100$

Keterangan:

P = percentage

f = frequency

n = sum

INFERENTIAL STATISTICAL ANALYSIS

Inferential statistical analysis was used to test the research hypothesis using the t-test. However, before testing the hypothesis, the normality and homogeneity tests were first performed.

The normality test used is the Kolmogrov Smirnov to find out whether the data follows a normally distributed population. The criteria used for learning outcomes are said to follow a normally distributed population if the value of p > a = 0.05.

The description of the research data presented below is a description of the experimental and control group data. The description of the data for each group consists of initial ability data (pre-test) and final ability data (post-test) comparisons of My Virtual Dream Friend and John English Bot.

RESULTS OF THE DESCRIPTIVE STATISTICAL ANALYSIS OF THE MY VIRTUAL DREAM FRIEND GROUP AND JOHN ENGLISH BOT

Based on the analysis of descriptive statistical data using the computerized system program SPSS version 21.0 for Windows and frequency descriptive statistics, the following will present the results of the scores for the My Virtual Dream Friends group.

Table 1. Mean score of before and after treatment using Artificial Intelligence

Statistics		Pretest John English Bot Group	Pos Test John English Bot Group	Pretest My Virtual Dream Friend	Pos Test My Virtual Dream Friend
N	Valid	21	21	15	15
	Missing	0	0	6	6
Mean		65.67	71.71	65.33	85.20
Median		65.00	70.00	65.00	87.00
Mode		60[a]	65	65[a]	83[a]
Std. Deviation		7.559	7.309	8.338	8.436
Variance		57.133	53.414	69.524	71.171
Range		25	31	25	30
Minimum		50	60	50	65
Maximum		75	91	75	95
Sum		1379	1506	980	1278
a. Multiple modes exist. The smallest value is shown					

On Table 1 it is known that the two groups, after receiving treatment to learn English using artificial intelligence, experienced a significant increase in English learning outcomes. In the trial group using the Pretest My Virtual Dream Friend with a pretest of 65.67 and a post test of 71.71. while the John English Bot group had a pre-test of 65.33 and a post-test of 85.20.

Based on the trials of the two artificial intelligence applications, it is known that John English Bot contributes more to improving English learning outcomes due to the superiority of the grammar feedback feature during undergraduate interactions.

When compared to My Virtual Dream Friend, which does not provide feedback to undergraduate students and is only comfortable for chatting. The results of learning English using artificial intelligence My virtual dream friend and John English Bot are then assessed based on the assessment criteria that have been prepared by the researcher.

The categories of learning outcomes for writing, listening, reading, and speaking experienced an increase, and grammar improvements occurred in the John English Bot group. This is caused by; (1) A desire to learn, succeed, be appreciated, and engage in engaging activities are all necessary components of a learning environment, as are (2) a desire to do so, (3) encouragement from others, (4) future hopes and aspirations, (5) an appreciation for learning, and (6) interesting learning activities.

Inferential Statistical Analysis Results

Inferential statistics are statistics used to analyze sample data, and the results are applied to the population. As previously stated in the previous section for hypothesis testing using inferential statistics, in this case the t-test with a significant level of = 0.05, the conditions that must be met for hypothesis testing are that the data obtained is normally distributed and has a homogeneous variance. Therefore, the normality test and homogeneity test were first carried out.

1. Normality Test.

Normality test to see whether the population seen is normally distributed or not. The normality test was carried out on the data of each of the two groups; all calculations were carried out with the help of the Statistical Package for Social Science (SPSS) version 22.0 for Windows, which showed that the John English Bot and My Virtual Dream Friend groups were normally distributed. The acceptance criteria that determine whether a data set is normally distributed or not are as follows:

If it is significant at 0.05, then the data is not normally distributed.

If significant $\geq$ 0.05, then the data is normally distributed.

Table 2. Estimated distribution parameters

		Pretest John English Bot Group	Pos Test John English Bot Group	Pretest My Virtual Dream Friend	Pos Test My Virtual Dream Friend
Normal Distribution	Location	65.67	71.71	65.33	85.20
	Scale	7.559	7.309	8.338	8.436
The cases are unweighted.					

a)   Homogeneity test.

The homogeneity test was carried out for two groups, namely the experimental group data and the control group data, by testing the similarity of the variances of the two groups. All calculations were carried out using the SPSS (Structural Package for Social Studies) computer program, version 22 for Windows, where hypothesis formula.

H0: Variance of two groups of homogeneous data.
H1: The variances of the two groups are not homogeneous.

The results of the calculation of the homogeneity test for the pre-test experimental pre-test control values and the results of the post-test experimental post-test control values can be seen in Table 3.

Table 3. Test of homogeneity of variance

		Levene Statistic	df1	df2	Sig.
Outcome	Based on Mean	.119	1	34	.732
	Based on Median	.022	1	34	.884
	Based on Median and with adjusted df	.022	1	31.863	.884
	Based on trimmed mean	.076	1	34	.784

Based on Table 3, the results of the calculation of the average homogeneity test for the two groups using SPSS were significant: 0.732 based on mean, 0.884 based on median, and 0.784 based on trimmed mean greater than 0.05, then H0 is accepted, so it can be concluded that both variants were significant.
Determine table at a significance level of 0.05; $2 = 0.025$ (2-sided test) with DF (degree of cleanliness).

Table 4. Paired sample test

		Paired Differences					t	df	Sig. (2-tailed)
		Mean	Std. Deviation	Std. Error Mean	95% Confidence Interval of the Difference				
					Lower	Upper			
Pair 1	Before trearment – after treatment	-19.867	6.664	1.721	-23.557	-16.176	-11.546	14	.000

3.   Testing criteria
   ○   If table is true, then H0 is accepted and H1 is rejected.
   ○   If table, then H0 is rejected and H1 is accepted

Based on significance
If significance is > 0.05, then H0 is accepted.

If the significance is 0.05, then H0 is rejected.

The results of the paired sample test showed that the use of artificial intelligence by the two groups effectively increased the English learning outcomes of undergraduate students at Universitas Al Asyariah Mandar.

Table 4 presents that there are differences in students' abilities results between the John English Bot and My Virtual Dream Friend groups with the chatbot application, for each English class.

For the three topic units Self Introduction, Telling Time and Hobbies, which shows the John English Bot group does a better job than the My Virtual Dream Friend group with an average difference rating from 65 to 85, based on a rating scale of 100.

From these statistics, the chatbots in the John English Bot group are very useful because of the availability of feature lessons so that they can help lecturers design teaching materials based on Artificial Intelligence. These findings contribute to the conclusion that chatbots are not only used to _assess academic progress, predict future performance and see potential problem' but can be used to design teaching materials for students in tertiary institutions.

DISCUSSION

The purpose of this study is to answer the question, "How is the effectiveness of AI in language learning?" by utilizing two AI applications, AI-My Virtual Dream Friend and AI-John English Bot. The results show that both applications make use of chatbot features, and that there is a significant performance gap between the two groups of students when it comes to improving their command of English.

When comparing the post-test scores of the two AIs, however, it becomes clear that the AI-John English Bot makes a more significant impact on undergraduates' proficiency in English. The findings demonstrate that AI-John English Bot offers both lesson and grammar feedback options. As can be shown in Table 1, these resources allow undergraduates to learn, and they have also boosted their sense of self-efficacy.

Chou and Zou (2020) dug into the literature and found that students need external feedback to help them reflect on their learning performance and adjust their learning accordingly. The findings of this study have important implications for students' abilities to self-regulate and their approaches to learning a second language.

Students can better gauge their progress toward goals and get extra support if they're falling behind when they use data visualizations to track their progress. Figure 4 from the AI-John English Bot shows that the availability of a variety of materials and instructional material subjects also influenced the learning behavior of undergraduate students, suggesting that chatbot representations alone are not enough to assist students develop their language skills.

Instructors can use the provided content visualization and lesson options to train their materials using AI. Data visualization, as shown by Minovi'c et al. (2015), aids students in making sense of their coursework and enhancing their capacity for self-regulation.

According to Sun et al. (2023), students are more likely to reach their educational objectives when they use data visualizations created with those objectives in mind. For this instance's data-visualization capabilities. References can be found in the study and creation of sentences, paragraphs, and dialogue scripts when doing so, students are more likely to be successful in their pursuit of their academic goals.

Regarding assistance requests, the system does not have a built-in mechanism for keeping track of such actions. We observed that when both groups had difficulties, they turned to third-party tools for aid, such as Google Translate or Editing, or looked for answers elsewhere on the Internet.

Visualizations of chatbot robots, such as AI-My Virtual Dream, are proposed. Figure 2 shows how glad a group of students are to see the kind face of AI robot AI-John English Bot after the latter inspires them to study by keeping tabs on their online conversation activity.

The goal of the management strategy for these two AI features is to pique students' curiosity about education and encourage them to take charge of their own education based on the feedback they receive from the technology. It confirms the findings of a previous study by Nicol, Yilmaz-Na, and Sönmez (2023) that found that students who received feedback on their learning performance also showed increased levels of self-regulation.

Although there are numerous potential benefits to AI-assisted language learning, little is known about how students interact with AI agents for language learning or whether there are variances in human-AI interaction based on student demographics.

For this reason, we still don't know much about how AI aids in language learning; specifically, while research has looked at students' beginning and end-of-course language skills, the middle ground remains largely unexamined. Thus, it is necessary to develop suitable instructional design based on student learning needs in order to advance the pedagogy and design of AI agents for language acquisition.

It is possible that students and AI will form learning communities where the presence social, cognitive, and teaching that students feel in interacting with AI will form meaningful learning experiences and assist in mastering the target language (Yu, Lu, Yu, & Lu, 2021).

Hsu, Chang, and Jen (2023)'s findings may be used to investigate the nature of human-AI interactions, which in turn provide light on how AI-supported language acquisition works (Schmidt & Strasser, 2022; Tsvilodub et al., 2022).

While it's commonly assumed that today's young people are fluent in technology matters, this study reveals that they may lack the expertise required to effectively use digital technologies, especially artificial intelligence (AI) in the classroom.

CONCLUSION

The aim of this study was to examine the various chatbots out there and determine whether or not they can be used as a useful tool for language training. We now know that there are three different types of chatbots, each with their own strengths and weaknesses, thanks to these findings.

Many bots provide synthesized text and speech, allowing students to practice listening and reading skills; (4) Bots are new and interesting for students; (5) students have the opportunity to use various language structures.

However, there are also complaints that the novelty of the chatbot is flawed and needs improvement. My Virtual Dream Friend and John English Bot, the chatbot-based English learning platform, was also evaluated as part of this study.

Based on these findings, further research and development is needed into the technology and features of both of the AI-John English Bot so it can fulfill its promise as a tool for teaching English, especially grammar.

REFERENCES

Alfalah, A. A. (2023). Factors influencing students' adoption and use of mobile learning management systems (m-LMSs): A quantitative study of Saudi Arabia. *International Journal of Information Management Data Insights, 3*(1), 100143. doi:10.1016/j.jjimei.2022.100143

Anderson, C. R. (2023). *Traditional Versus Modern Teaching Methods amongst Special Education Students and Enhancing Students' Self-Concept: A Comprehensive Literature Review* [Doctoral dissertation]. The Chicago School of Professional Psychology.

Archuby, F., Sanz, C., & Manresa-Yee, C. (2023). DIJS: Methodology for the Design and Development of Digital Educational Serious Games. *IEEE Transactions on Games*, 1–9. doi:10.1109/TG.2022.3217737

Blake, J. (2023, February). Intelligent CALL: Individualizing Learning Using Natural Language Generation. In *The Post-pandemic Landscape of Education and Beyond: Innovation and Transformation: Selected Papers from the HKAECT 2022 International Conference* (pp. 3-18). Springer Nature Singapore.

Campbell, D. T., & Stanley, J. C. (1966). Experimental and Quasi-Experimental Designs for Research, Rand Mc. *Nally Coll. Publ. Chicago, 47*, 1.

Chen, X., Zou, D., Xie, H. R., & Su, F. (2021). *Twenty-five years of computer-assisted language learning: A topic modeling analysis.* Academic Press.

de la Vall, R. R. F., & Araya, F. G. (2023). Exploring the Benefits and Challenges of AI-Language Learning Tools. *International Journal of Social Sciences and Humanities Invention, 10*(01), 7569–7576. doi:10.18535/ijsshi/v10i01.02

Edwards, C., Edwards, A., Spence, P. R., & Lin, X. (2018). I, teacher: Using artificial intelligence (AI) and social robots in communication and instruction. *Communication Education, 67*(4), 473–480. doi:10.1080/03634523.2018.1502459

Ekin, C. C., Polat, E., & Hopcan, S. (2023). Drawing the big picture of games in education: A topic modeling-based review of past 55 years. *Computers & Education, 194*, 104700. doi:10.1016/j.compedu.2022.104700

Elme, L., Jørgensen, M. L., Dandanell, G., Mottelson, A., & Makransky, G. (2022). Immersive virtual reality in STEM: Is IVR an effective learning medium and does adding self-explanation after a lesson improve learning outcomes? *Educational Technology Research and Development, 70*(5), 1601–1626. doi:10.100711423-022-10139-3 PMID:35873274

Fang, Y., Lippert, A., Cai, Z., Chen, S., Frijters, J. C., Greenberg, D., & Graesser, A. C. (2021). Patterns of adults with low literacy skills interacting with an intelligent tutoring system. *International Journal of Artificial Intelligence in Education*, 1–26.

Freeman, N. (2023). *Teaching L2 grammar: A study of teachers' beliefs on frequency, methods and approaches of teaching English grammar in Swedish schools.* Academic Press.

Fryer, L. K., Nakao, K., & Thompson, A. (2019). Chatbot learning partners: Connecting learning experiences, interest and competence. *Computers in Human Behavior*, *93*, 279–289. doi:10.1016/j.chb.2018.12.023

Fullan, M. (2023). *The Principal 2.0: Three Keys to Maximizing Impact.* John Wiley & Sons.

Furlan, R., Gatti, M., Menè, R., Shiffer, D., Marchiori, C., Giaj Levra, A., Saturnino, V., Brunetta, E., & Dipaola, F. (2021). A natural language processing–based virtual patient simulator and intelligent tutoring system for the clinical diagnostic process: Simulator development and case study. *JMIR Medical Informatics*, *9*(4), e24073. doi:10.2196/24073 PMID:33720840

Hill, J., Ford, W. R., & Farreras, I. G. (2015). Real conversations with artificial intelligence: A comparison between human–human online conversations and human–chatbot conversations. *Computers in Human Behavior*, *49*, 245–250. doi:10.1016/j.chb.2015.02.026

Hsu, T. C., Chang, C., & Jen, T. H. (2023). Artificial Intelligence image recognition using self-regulation learning strategies: Effects on vocabulary acquisition, learning anxiety, and learning behaviours of English language learners. *Interactive Learning Environments*, 1–19. doi:10.1080/10494820.2023.2165508

Hu, J., & Hu, X. (2020, November). The Effectiveness of Autonomous Listening Study and Pedagogical Implications In the Module of Artificial Intelligence. *Journal of Physics: Conference Series*, *1684*(1), 012037. doi:10.1088/1742-6596/1684/1/012037

Huang, A. Y., Lu, O. H., & Yang, S. J. (2023). Effects of artificial Intelligence–Enabled personalized recommendations on learners' learning engagement, motivation, and outcomes in a flipped classroom. *Computers & Education*, *194*, 104684. doi:10.1016/j.compedu.2022.104684

Huang, T. H., & Wang, L. Z. (2021). Artificial intelligence learning approach through total physical response embodiment teaching on French vocabulary learning retention. *Computer Assisted Language Learning*, 1–25. doi:10.1080/09588221.2021.2008980

Huang, W., Hew, K. F., & Fryer, L. K. (2022). Chatbots for language learning—Are they really useful? A systematic review of chatbot-supported language learning. *Journal of Computer Assisted Learning*, *38*(1), 237–257. doi:10.1111/jcal.12610

Huang, X., Zou, D., Cheng, G., Chen, X., & Xie, H. (2023). Trends, research issues and applications of artificial intelligence in language education. *Journal of Educational Technology & Society*, *26*(1), 112–131.

Huang, Y. M., Chan, H. Y., Wang, Y. H., & Ho, Y. F. (2023). Effects of a blended multimedia teaching approach on self-efficacy and skills in over-the-counter medication counselling versus a lecture-based approach: Protocol for a prospective cohort study of undergraduate students from a pharmacy school in Taiwan. *BMJ Open*, *13*(1), e068738. doi:10.1136/bmjopen-2022-068738 PMID:36697044

Jiang, Y., Yang, X., & Zheng, T. (2023). Make chatbots more adaptive: Dual pathways linking human-like cues and tailored response to trust in interactions with chatbots. *Computers in Human Behavior*, *138*, 107485. doi:10.1016/j.chb.2022.107485

Johnson, W. L. (2019). Data-driven development and evaluation of Enskill English. *International Journal of Artificial Intelligence in Education*, *29*(3), 425–457. doi:10.100740593-019-00182-2

Kale, U., Roy, A., & Yuan, J. (2020). To design or to integrate? Instructional design versus technology integration in developing learning interventions. *Educational Technology Research and Development, 68*(5), 2473–2504. doi:10.100711423-020-09771-8

Karakas, A., & Kartal, G. (2020). Pre-Service Language Teachers' Autonomous Language Learning with Web 2.0 Tools and Mobile Applications. *International Journal of Curriculum and Instruction, 12*(1), 51–79.

Kerly, A., Hall, P., & Bull, S. (2007). Bringing chatbots into education: Towards natural language negotiation of open learner models. *Knowledge-Based Systems, 20*(2), 177–185. doi:10.1016/j.knosys.2006.11.014

Kim, H., Hwang, S., Kim, J., & Lee, Z. (2022). Toward Smart Communication Components: Recent Advances in Human and AI Speaker Interaction. *Electronics (Basel), 11*(10), 1533. doi:10.3390/electronics11101533

Kim, H. S., Kim, N. Y., & Cha, Y. (2021). Is It Beneficial to Use AI Chatbots to Improve Learners' Speaking Performance? *Journal of Asia TEFL, 18*(1), 161–178. doi:10.18823/asiatefl.2021.18.1.10.161

Kim, J., Merrill, K., Xu, K., & Sellnow, D. D. (2020). My teacher is a machine: Understanding students' perceptions of AI teaching assistants in online education. *International Journal of Human-Computer Interaction, 36*(20), 1902–1911. doi:10.1080/10447318.2020.1801227

Kohnke, L. (2023). L2 learners' perceptions of a chatbot as a potential independent language learning tool. *International Journal of Mobile Learning and Organisation, 17*(1-2), 214–226. doi:10.1504/IJMLO.2023.128339

Koszalka, T. A., Russ-Eft, D. F., & Reiser, R. (2013). *Instructional designer competencies: The standards*. IAP.

Kuba, R., Rahimi, S., Smith, G., Shute, V., & Dai, C. P. (2021). Using the first principles of instruction and multimedia learning principles to design and develop in-game learning support videos. *Educational Technology Research and Development, 69*(2), 1201–1220. doi:10.100711423-021-09994-3

Kuhail, M. A., Alturki, N., Alramlawi, S., & Alhejori, K. (2022). Interacting with educational chatbots: A systematic review. *Education and Information Technologies*, 1–46.

Kuleto, V., Ilić, M. P., Bucea-Manea-Țoniş, R., Ciocodeică, D. F., Mihălcescu, H., & Mindrescu, V. (2022). The Attitudes of K–12 Schools' Teachers in Serbia towards the Potential of Artificial Intelligence. *Sustainability (Basel), 14*(14), 8636. doi:10.3390u14148636

Kumar, J. A. (2021). Educational chatbots for project-based learning: Investigating learning outcomes for a team-based design course. *International Journal of Educational Technology in Higher Education, 18*(1), 1–28. doi:10.118641239-021-00302-w PMID:34926790

Kuosa, T. (2014). *Towards strategic intelligence: foresight, intelligence, and policy-making*. Dynamic Futures.

Lin, C. J., & Mubarok, H. (2021). Learning analytics for investigating the mind map-guided AI chatbot approach in an EFL flipped speaking classroom. *Journal of Educational Technology & Society, 24*(4), 16–35.

Lin, J. S. E., & Wu, L. (2023). Examining the psychological process of developing consumer-brand relationships through strategic use of social media brand chatbots. *Computers in Human Behavior, 140,* 107488. doi:10.1016/j.chb.2022.107488

Liu, C. C., Liao, M. G., Chang, C. H., & Lin, H. M. (2022). An analysis of children'interaction with an AI chatbot and its impact on their interest in reading. *Computers & Education, 189,* 104576. doi:10.1016/j.compedu.2022.104576

Marek, M. W., & Wu, P. H. N. (2020). Digital learning curriculum design: Outcomes and affordances. In *Pedagogies of digital learning in higher education* (pp. 163–182). Routledge. doi:10.4324/9781003019466-9

Merrill, M. D. (2002). First principles of instruction. *Educational Technology Research and Development, 50*(3), 43–59. doi:10.1007/BF02505024

Minović, M., Milovanović, M., Šošević, U., & González, M. Á. C. (2015). Visualisation of student learning model in serious games. *Computers in Human Behavior, 47,* 98–107. doi:10.1016/j.chb.2014.09.005

Mitra, N., & Banerjee, A. (2022). A Study on Using AI in Promoting English Language Learning. *Proceedings of IEMIS, 2,* 287–297.

Mohammed Mahmoud Ghoneim, N., & Elsayed Abdelsalam Elghotmy, H. (2021). *Using an Artificial Intelligence Based Program to Enhance Primary Stage Students' EFL Listening Skills.* المجلة التربوية.

Mukhiya, S. K., Wake, J. D., Inal, Y., Pun, K. I., & Lamo, Y. (2020). Adaptive elements in internet-delivered psychological treatment systems: Systematic review. *Journal of Medical Internet Research, 22*(11), e21066. doi:10.2196/21066 PMID:33245285

Muthmainnah, P. M. I. S., & Oteir, I. (2022). Playing with AI to Investigate Human-Computer Interaction Technology and Improving Critical Thinking Skills to Pursue 21st Century Age. Education Research International. doi:10.1155/2022/6468995

Muthmainnah, S. G., Al Yakin, A., & Ghofur, A. (2023). An Effective Investigation on YIPe-Learning Based for Twenty-First Century Class. *Digital Learning based Education: Transcending Physical Barriers, 21.*

Nardi, P. M. (2018). *Doing survey research: A guide to quantitative methods.* Routledge. doi:10.4324/9781315172231

Neto, A. J. M., & Fernandes, M. A. (2019, July). Chatbot and conversational analysis to promote collaborative learning in distance education. In *2019 IEEE 19th International Conference on Advanced Learning Technologies (ICALT)* (Vol. 2161, pp. 324-326). IEEE.

Nguyen, M. H. (2023). Academic writing and AI: Day-1 experiment. *Center for Open Science 2023.*

Pham, X. L., Pham, T., Nguyen, Q. M., Nguyen, T. H., & Cao, T. T. H. (2018, November). Chatbot as an intelligent personal assistant for mobile language learning. In *Proceedings of the 2018 2nd International Conference on Education and E-Learning* (pp. 16-21). 10.1145/3291078.3291115

Pokrivčáková, S. (2019). Preparing teachers for the application of AI-powered technologies in foreign language education. *Journal of Language and Cultural Education*.

Rosenbaum, P. R., Rosenbaum, P., & Briskman. (2010). *Design of observational studies* (Vol. 10). New York: Springer.

Schmidt, T., & Strasser, T. (2022). Artificial intelligence in foreign language learning and teaching: A CALL for intelligent practice. *Anglistik: International Journal of English Studies*, *33*(1), 165–184. doi:10.33675/ANGL/2022/1/14

Shamsi, U. R. (2021). *Role of mobile technology in enabling learning and EFL learning: an ecological account of the pedagogical decisions of Pakistani lecturers* [Doctoral dissertation]. ResearchSpace@ Auckland.

Shardlow, M., Sellar, S., & Rousell, D. (2022). Collaborative augmentation and simplification of text (CoAST): Pedagogical applications of natural language processing in digital learning environments. *Learning Environments Research*, *25*(2), 1–23. doi:10.100710984-021-09368-9

Shu, X., & Gu, X. (2023). An Empirical Study of A Smart Education Model Enabled by the Edu-Metaverse to Enhance Better Learning Outcomes for Students. *Systems*, *11*(2), 75. doi:10.3390ystems11020075

Shum, H. Y., He, X. D., & Li, D. (2018). From Eliza to XiaoIce: Challenges and opportunities with social chatbots. *Frontiers of Information Technology & Electronic Engineering*, *19*(1), 10–26. doi:10.1631/FITEE.1700826

Sun, J. C. Y., Tsai, H. E., & Cheng, W. K. R. (2023). Effects of integrating an open learner model with AI-enabled visualization on students' self-regulation strategies usage and behavioral patterns in an online research ethics course. *Computers and Education: Artificial Intelligence*, *4*, 100120. doi:10.1016/j.caeai.2022.100120

Swartz, M. L., & Yazdani, M. (Eds.). (2012). *Intelligent tutoring systems for foreign language learning: The bridge to international communication* (Vol. 80). Springer Science & Business Media.

Tsvilodub, P., Chevalier, E., Klütz, V., Oberbeck, T., Sigetova, K., & Wollatz, F. (2022, December). Improving a Gamified Language Learning Chatbot through AI and UX Boosting. In *Innovative Approaches to Technology-Enhanced Learning for the Workplace and Higher Education: Proceedings of 'The Learning Ideas Conference'2022* (pp. 557–569). Springer International Publishing.

Walser, T. M. (2014). Quasi-experiments in schools: The case for historical cohort control groups. *Practical Assessment, Research & Evaluation*, *19*(1), 6.

Weng, X., & Chiu, T. K. (2023). Instructional design and learning outcomes of intelligent computer assisted language learning: Systematic review in the field. *Computers and Education: Artificial Intelligence*, 100117.

Winkler, R., & Söllner, M. (2018). Unleashing the potential of chatbots in education: A state-of-the-art analysis. *Academy of management annual meeting (AOM)*. 10.5465/AMBPP.2018.15903abstract

Wright, A. M., Munz, S. M., & McKenna-Buchanan, T. (2023). Triage Teaching: Exploring Teacher Self-Efficacy during COVID-19. In Pandemic Pedagogies (pp. 96-111). Routledge.

Yildiz Durak, H. (2022). Conversational agent-based guidance: Examining the effect of chatbot usage frequency and satisfaction on visual design self-efficacy, engagement, satisfaction, and learner autonomy. *Education and Information Technologies*, 1–18.

Yilmaz-Na, E., & Sönmez, E. (2023). Unfolding the potential of computer-assisted argument mapping practices for promoting self-regulation of learning and problem-solving skills of pre-service teachers and their relationship. *Computers & Education, 193*, 104683. doi:10.1016/j.compedu.2022.104683

Yu, S., Lu, Y., Yu, S., & Lu, Y. (2021). Intelligent learning environments. *An Introduction to Artificial Intelligence in Education*, 29-52.

Yunjiu, L., Wei, W., & Zheng, Y. (2022). Artificial Intelligence-Generated and Human Expert-Designed Vocabulary Tests: A Comparative Study. *SAGE Open, 12*(1). doi:10.1177/21582440221082130

Zamora, J. (2017, October). I'm sorry, dave, i'm afraid i can't do that: Chatbot perception and expectations. In *Proceedings of the 5th international conference on human agent interaction* (pp. 253-260). 10.1145/3125739.3125766

Zhang, Y., & MacWhinney, B. (2023). The role of novelty stimuli in second language acquisition: Evidence from the optimized training by the Pinyin Tutor at TalkBank. *Smart Learning Environments, 10*(1), 1–19. doi:10.118640561-023-00223-3

Zhang, Z., Xu, Y., Wang, Y., Yao, B., Ritchie, D., Wu, T., ... Li, T. J. J. (2022, April). Storybuddy: A human-ai collaborative chatbot for parent-child interactive storytelling with flexible parental involvement. In *Proceedings of the 2022 CHI Conference on Human Factors in Computing Systems* (pp. 1-21). 10.1145/3491102.3517479

Zhao, X. (2022). Leveraging artificial intelligence (AI) technology for English writing: Introducing wordtune as a digital writing assistant for EFL writers. *RELC Journal*. doi:10.1177/00336882221094089

Zhong, S., Scarinci, A., & Cicirello, A. (2023). Natural Language Processing for systems engineering: Automatic generation of Systems Modelling Language diagrams. *Knowledge-Based Systems, 259*, 110071. doi:10.1016/j.knosys.2022.110071

Zhou, J. (2020). *Foreign-Language Teachers' Needs to Achieve Better Results: The Role of Differentiated Instruction* [Doctoral dissertation]. University of Southern California.

Zhou, Q., Li, B., Han, L., & Jou, M. (2023). Talking to a bot or a wall? How chatbots vs. human agents affect anticipated communication quality. *Computers in Human Behavior, 143*, 107674. doi:10.1016/j.chb.2023.107674

Chapter 5
An Innovative Teaching Model:
The Potential of Metaverse for English Learning

Muthmainnah Muthmainnah
Universitas Al Asyariah Mandar, Indonesia

Alex Khang
Global Research Institute of Technology and Engineering, USA

Ahmad Al Yakin
Universitas Al Asyariah Mandar, Indonesia

Ibrahim Oteir
Batterjee Medical College, Jeddah, Saudi Arabia

Abdullah Nijr Alotaibi
Majmaah University, Majmaah, Saudi Arabia

ABSTRACT

The degree to which a virtual content layer exists between the viewer and the real world, and how the real world is augmented, can vary greatly across tools, and use cases, but is essential to all forms of virtual reality (VR). The degree of overlap with the real world, as well as the importance of location, cooperation, and mobility, can vary dramatically from one VR experience to the next. Teachers will need support in figuring out how to best utilize AI for the benefit of student learning because of the plethora of available AI options. In this chapter, the authors share the results of a poll of students, both in the field and those hoping to enter it, to learn their thoughts on VR in the classroom. To gauge participants' thoughts on VR potential in the classroom, they gave them the VR platform and had them create a VR experience on their mobile devices. In virtual classrooms, 165 students can interact with the VR and other students as avatars, ask questions, write conversations, identify vocabulary connected between VR and material, and provide suggestions for improving classroom management.

DOI: 10.4018/978-1-6684-8851-5.ch005

INTRODUCTION

The use of visual aids in the classroom has improved both lecture-based and hands-on learning. Education has improved greatly because of the widespread use of media like movies, pictures, graphics, and animation-aided materials in lecture halls and laboratories.

In a similar vein, incorporating technological tools into the classroom increases productivity and ultimately benefits students' learning. It also reduces the amount of time spent in lecture and lab, making room for greater practice in the real world. But a technical breakthrough that will be even more helpful is on the horizon.

In other words, it's a type of VR hardware (VR). It's probable that new methods of teaching and learning will emerge as a result of virtual reality's varied applications and capabilities (Alam, 2022; Wang, Wu, Wang, Chi, & Wang, 2018).

Participating in a real-time, computer-generated 3D environment via a controller is essential to the concept of virtual reality. Its interface transports users to a simulated, computer-generated third space, where they can engage in real-time interaction using a wide range of control devices and their senses (Ausburn & Ausburn, 2008); Chalmers, 2022). So, this is the stuff that allows us to feel like we're really there when we're interacting with 3D computer animations and graphics. Therefore, the high degree of realism in this context allows for more effective answers to real-world situations.

In order for virtual reality (VR) to be useful in language classes, instructors must be confident and knowledgeable about the medium (such as Google Cardboard). Due to their major responsibilities in introducing VR technology to the classroom, language teachers are ideally suited to make use of VR and VR apps in their teaching.

For teachers to effectively incorporate virtual reality (VR) into their classes, they must have a deep understanding of the medium. Although the potential benefits of using virtual reality (VR) in the classroom for teaching languages are clear, doing so may prove challenging. As a result, it's crucial to foresee and address potential difficulties that language teachers may have while incorporating VR into the classroom.

As specialists in the humanities, language teachers may face skepticism and resistance when it comes to using virtual reality (VR) software. According to a report by Bacalja, (2022), digital game literacy not only presents an opportunity to help us satisfy the long-standing demand to teach English, but also to provide fresh techniques to assisting students in forming a sense of identity and place in the world.

Learning about digital games in English has been shown to help students relate to the realities of being a student, to foster the growth of both traditional and cutting-edge skill sets, to prompt critical reflection on the text's own representations, and to bolster the aesthetic dimension of textual experience.

In addition, there is a scarcity of VR-based classroom materials, and it is the responsibility of teachers to adapt potential assets to suit classroom use, which adds extra labor.

Therefore, it is important to study and improve these attitudes to achieve an agreement on which features of VR technology could be considered as an educational tool for language acquisition, and how much of an impact these features should have in the actual classroom setting.

In this light, the study's investigator is keen to collect feedback from EFL students who have used Metaverse technology in the classroom. Researchers can learn more about the possible uses of VR devices in the classroom by studying students' perspectives on the issue and what professionals in the field of language learning are doing with VR technologies.

METAVERSE IN EDUCATION

The American science fiction author Neal Stephenson coined the term "Metaverse" in his novel Snow Crash, published in 1992. The main characters in Snow Crash don avatars and conduct their daily lives in a Metaverse, a type of virtual 3D world where they can communicate with one another.

A "Metaverse" is a different kind of virtual reality. It is a combination of the Latin word for "world" (universe) with the Greek prefix "meta," which signifies "beyond" or "virtual." Schlichting, Füchter, Schlichting, and Alexander (2022) define the "digitized globe" as a new world made possible by electronic methods like mobile phones and the internet. There was a lot of research and development done to create a Metaverse once the concept was initially introduced.

A premier Metaverse research group, the Acceleration Studies Foundation (ASF) unveiled the Metaverse road map at the Metaverse road summit (2006). It defined the term "Metaverse" and its four variations and proposed seeing it as the point where "real life" and "virtual reality" meet. Here, we see how the digital world is being integrated with the physical one, and how regular activities and the economy are being brought online.

One's virtual self, or avatar, serves as a representation of oneself in the Metaverse. Avatars participate in the social, cultural, and economic activities of the Metaverse. The term "Metaverse" refers to a parallel universe in which actual and virtual worlds coexist and generate value through human interactions and the exchange of goods and services.

The phrase "Metaverse" can be used to describe a world where work and play are not just combined, but also interactively mash up with one another. As defined by Go SY, Jeong, Kim, and Sin, "3D-based VR in which real-world activities and economic life are carried out via avatars portraying the real themselves" (2021).

The idea of the Metaverse has been around for a while; it was featured in the novel Snow Crash (Stephenson, 1992) and the subsequent film version, Ready Player One (Cline, 2011). Massive multi-player online role-playing games (MMORPGs) like World of Warcraft and Second Life were already drawing in millions of users (Wiederhold, 2022).

In contrast, Mark Zuckerberg's official introduction of the word "Metaverse" in October 2021 led to its widespread use. Multiple potential future ideas and tactics for usage in classroom instruction have been outlined by educators and academics. It is possible that the social aspects of teaching and learning can be enhanced by adopting a virtual environment, which gives accurate representations of selves and other circumstances.

However, given the relative unfamiliarity of the phrase "Metaverse," it's worth looking at the current state of study on the topic.

The prefix "meta," which means "beyond," and the word "universe," which implies "a parallel or virtual environment related to the actual world," combine to form the term "Metaverse."

As a successor to the Internet, Neal Stephenson's "Metaverse" described in his 1992 science fiction novel Snow Crash is built on a combination of virtual reality and the Internet. The heroes of this narrative escape the pain of the real world by assuming the identities of digital avatars and venturing across that realm (Stephenson, 1992).

In the time afterwards, it has been called many things, including a post-reality universe (Mystakidis et al., 2021), a mirror world (Lee et al., 2021) and a new sort of Internet application and social form that incorporates a wide range of new technologies (Ning et al., 2021; Bruun & Stentoft, 2019).

Since the Metaverse is rapidly being integrated into modern life, some applications have been used in the classroom. Therefore, it is crucial to get knowledge of the many forms of Metaverses and their potential educational applications. Many researchers and educators have already considered the implications of virtual worlds, or "Metaverses," for the classroom.

For instance, Kemp and Livingstone (2006) discussed how incorporating Metaverse using Second Life with LMS could improve the learning experience. From a virtuality standpoint, Collins (2008) argued, the Metaverse has the potential to become the next venue where people may connect and socially interact; this suggests higher education should take the initiative to use it for instructional purposes. It's arguable that having an avatar around makes a 3D digital virtual world feel more interactive and welcoming (Schlemmer & Backes, 2015).

The development of Metaverse technology was also discussed at a summit held at Stanford Research Institute International in 2006. The future decade of the Internet was imagined and predicted by a group of diverse academics, technological architects, businesspeople, and futurists (Metaverse Roadmap Summit, 2006).

Kye et al. (2021) defined the four Metaverse variations presented at the Roadmap Summit from a pedagogical perspective, considering both their potential and inherent restrictions, despite the roadmap's focus on technology. Table 1 depicts the four distinct categories of Metaverse technology: augmented reality (AR), lifelogging, mirror worlds, and virtual worlds.

The four types can be thought of along two axes: augmentation vs simulation (A versus S) and openness versus exclusivity (P versus S) (E vs I). Augmentation technology enables us to do previously impossible visual tasks by superimposing digital data on top of our perceptual view of the physical world.

However, simulation technology may build and modify models of the real-world physical environment to create virtual interactions and experiences. The other part of the paper focuses on the contrast between internal and external factors.

Providing information about one's immediate surroundings and how to exercise influence over them is important to the technology, indicating its focus on the external realm.

In contrast, in the Intimate world, technology is utilized to build interior worlds of avatars or digital profiles where people have agency in the digital environment, centered on the identity and conduct of individuals or things. The merging of data along these two dimensions produced four distinct flavors of the Metaverse.

Using augmented reality (AR), users can create their own "smart settings" that are aware of their current position, like what is shown in Pokémon Go. Lifelogging Metaverse allows its users to keep track of the people and locations in their lives using augmented reality apps like Facebook or Instagram.

The GPS in programs like Google Earth and Google Maps is what the technology in Mirror Worlds' Metaverse uses to build digital representations of the real world. The "Metaverse" of massively multiplayer online games relies on avatars, digital representations of players.

Increased support for Metaverse in a range of educational settings is a direct result of the popularity of immersive technologies like VR, MR, AR, and XR. The Metaverse can help students because it functions similarly to a traditional classroom.

In the Metaverse, students can interact with their teachers and classmates using fictional characters. This could lead to a more interesting and inspiring learning environment for the kids. For example, Siyaev and Jo (2021) explored the use of mixed reality in aviation maintenance to produce an engaging learning experience.

Crespo et al. (2013) analyzed the effectiveness of using Open Sim in the classroom using open educational resources like MOOCs. With the help of augmented reality and mobile learning.

Conversely, the Metaverse can be conceptualized as comprising both an inside and outer reality. Information about one's own nature and activities is processed in the mind. With the aid of technology, the inner reality of the Metaverse can be realized to its full potential.

When users act in their virtual worlds, be it through an avatar, digital profile, or by influencing the system itself, they are exercising control. To the contrary, in the external world, the user (the Metaverse's subject) is usually the focus of attention. For this reason, it includes aids for displaying the user's surroundings and guiding them through interacting with them.

These frameworks provide additional dimension for classifying applications, whether they employ Metaverse technology that emphasizes the user's inner world or their outer environment.

The Metaverse roadmap divides the Metaverse into four categories based on these two dimensions: augmented reality (AR), lifelogging (LL), the mirror world (MW), and virtual reality (VR). Table 1 provides a summary of the definitions, characteristics, application domains, and examples of use for each kind.

Table 1. Four types of Metaverse

Type	Augmented Reality	Lifelogging	Mirror World	Virtual Reality
Definition	Building a smart environment by utilizing location-based technologies and networks.	Capturing, storing, and disseminating information on commonplace things and people.	The plethora of social media applications today includes not only Facebook and Instagram but also the Apple Watch, Samsung Health, and Nike+.	A computer-generated environment that can be explored digitally.
Features	Smart environment construction via networked location-based technologies	Keeping track of object details	Computer-generated geographic models based on GPS data.	Each user's unique personality shines through in the way their avatars interact with one another.
Applications	Devices such as smartphones and head-up displays in cars	gadgets you wear and mysterious boxes	Location based services maps	Competing with others in real time online
Use Cases	Realistic Content, Digital Textbook, and Pokemon Go	Social media apps such as Facebook, Instagram, Apple Watch, Samsung Health, and Nike+	Space, maps, and lodging bookings on Google, Naver, and Google Earth; Airbnb;	Comparison of Second Life, Minecraft, Roblox, and Zepeto

Source: Lee (2020)

VIRTUAL REALITY IN EFL CLASSROOMS

Virtual reality is the most versatile and widely adopted Metaverse technology for classroom use. In the current unacted era, virtual reality has becoming increasingly popular because it can be accessible from any location.

The "5 Cs" were proposed by Kye, Han, Kim, Park, and Jo (2021) to distinguish the VR Metaverse from existing platform services. The Metaverse has many functions: as a canon, designers and participants work together to construct and expand the Metaverse's space-time; as a creator, anyone in the Metaverse can make content; as a digital currency, production and consumption are possible through the creation of various contents; as a foundation for daily life, the Metaverse guarantees stability; and as a bridge between the physical and the digital, the Metaverse connects the Metaverse (avatars).

Book (2004) proposes the following six characteristics for virtual reality: First, users in a virtual reality environment should be able to interact with one another in real time; second, the virtual reality experience is typically expressed and implemented in a two- or three-dimensional graphical user interface; third, immediacy means that users' interactions within the virtual reality take place in real time; and fourth, interactivity means that users can manipulate and create content within the virtual reality.

Wearable Virtual Reality systems that give a completely interactive environment entirely disguising the physical world are not included in educational studies for practical reasons such as cost and size A. Pack, Barrett, Liang, and D. (2020) for the most part, virtual environments are used in virtual reality studies, with people communicating with one another through computer displays.

However, as VR/VEs can be tailored to any setting with the right programming (Park, 2018); Kozlova and Priven, 2015), language study benefits greatly from their use. In their article, Riley and Stacy (2008) highlight the many benefits of VR learning environments, including their flexibility, focus on the individual learner, and adoption of the "learning by doing" pedagogical tenet.

Using 360-degree movies to shadow presentation skills, creating virtual reality role-playing videos to encourage learning verbs, and creating a virtual reality city all these things constitute (Wang et al., 2017) Virtual Reality language class activity. For a deeper insight into how students of English in a 3D Virtual World are experiencing the language, Virtual City design yields useful insights.

Students can learn to improve their listening skills with a virtual world created by Garrido-Iigo and Rodrguez-Moreno (2015) The Virtual World was proposed by Garrido-Iigo and Rodrguez-Moreno as a match consisting of a series of examinations. The users had to complete the process in five stages.

There are three stages to the procedures: training, testing of participants, and a community test of listening comprehension. Grammar (syntax, morphology, verb conjugation), spelling, and the usual vocabulary of an airport conversation (which the student has studied on the learning island) all play a role in the examination.

In this research, students focused intently on the grammatical structures they were supposed to create. Students do not view their use of this virtual environment as a competitive activity when it comes to the realm of collaboration. They were primarily concerned with finishing the panel.

A further VR implementation was carried out by Levak and Son (2017) combined the usage of Skype and Virtual World to instruct students on the importance of attentive listening. Users will listen to the directions through Skype and then follow them on the map.

Assignments like "Shopping" and "At the Cafe" required users to travel to Virtual World versions of real-world establishments. Communicating and learning via Skype is facilitated using authentic resources (such as excerpts from real shopping catalogues and actual menus).

Participants described a 3D virtual representation of an object or event in Virtual World, and a 2D visual depiction of the same in the Skype version of the assignment.

Listeners who took part in this study found both facilitation methods to be helpful in improving their listening skills. Participants valued the ability to communicate with native speakers through themed exercises that reflected their actual needs.

The features of Second Life include the ability to overhear and read the text messages of other users in cyberspace, to interact with random avatars, to visit and learn about virtual cultural locations, to view music and artwork, to engage in role-playing, and to have access to the virtual world around the clock.

One of Skype's most interesting features is the ability to observe a user's companions. Effectiveness of tasks appears to be affected by the capabilities of online tools and how well they correspond with the pedagogical goals of activities.

Bonner and Reinders (2018) conducted research to determine the feasibility of augmented and virtual reality (AR/VR) for use in language instruction.

Having seen the good effects that AR and VR have had in fields such as engineering, medicine, and history education, they reasoned that these technologies could be applied to the teaching of languages as well.

They used AR to lead students to the tour schedule or entice them to play location-based games by having them roam around a town in search of story-related clues. This study demonstrates how AR and VR may be included into standard language schools without requiring instructors to acquire any additional specialist knowledge. Its use is also thought to lessen the likelihood of interruptions.

Bonner and Reinders (2018) argue that using virtual reality (VR) video content can assist students better understand the relevance of what they are learning to the real world. In addition, augmented reality has a few standout characteristics, including:

(1) Various forms of mobile technology may be included;
(2) Facilitating communication and group study;
(3) It gives students the opportunity to see how content in a foreign language adapts to the learner's situation; and
(4) In addition to facilitating personalized learning, the ease of connectivity and access to resources like knowledge is another key benefit.

Kassim, Witkin, and Stone (2019) also investigated the effectiveness of VR for enhancing language instruction. Results showed that students had more pleasant emotions and had greater gains in speaking ability when utilizing VR in Immersion-Prompted Contact. Wang et al. found similar results (2017).

VILLAGE (Virtual Immersive Language Learning and Gaming Environment) was created as an online environment meant to mimic traditional classrooms and universities. The target audience was educators and their students, who were experiencing some trepidation about entering the Virtual World.

Education in this area always opens up opportunities for pupils to talk to one another. Students can build their own talks, adapt the sample conversations provided in Moodle, or model their own conversations after the ones provided by the instructor.

The goal of this activity is to train students to use the present tense while writing and speaking, and to help them differentiate between liaison verbs, action verbs, and participatory verbs.

VILLAGE's primary focus was on developing students' verbal skills, including their ability to recognize and use the tenses present, past, and future, as well as their command of active and passive voice in their writing.

The research demonstrates that learners experience a sense of realism when interacting with learning artifacts like chatbots and time machines. Using chatbots and time machines, students are completely submerged in a virtual 3D world.

Increased exposure to language learning in virtual environments improves students' sense of agency and community. The study also provides theoretical and empirical frameworks for understanding the phenomena of immersion and presence (Wang, Petrina, and Feng, 2017).

The use of Chatbots and time machines in real time promotes a feeling of realism. How well a student can apply what they've learned in a 3D virtual environment to the actual world depends on how real and present the environment feels to them.

Furthermore, Chen (2016) advocates for the usage of Virtual World in language classrooms to improve students' spoken communication skills. Avatars, he believes, not only give inhabitants the opportunity to communicate with one another in the target language, but also to do so in a more natural, conversational manner, as if they were in a real-world setting situation.

Students of foreign languages can develop their linguistic abilities in Virtual World through a variety of Real-Life simulation games involving voice and text conversation.

The Virtual World's features will inspire task-based experiences and keep users committed to their goals. In the end, it enhances the encoding and functioning of the language being learned.

Using photo libraries and other digital platforms where storytellers may track their characters' actions and build stories using real-world props, Liang (2019) included virtual reality multimodality into her research, drawing parallels between traditional storytelling and digital storytelling.

According to Liang (2019), while virtual world story simulations can assist students communicate ideas and build stories, training on embodied and digital activities may be necessary to help people learning a second language fully explore virtual world skills.

METAVERSE'S PEDAGOGICAL POTENTIAL IS LIMITED DUE TO ITS DESIGN FLAWS

Real-world responses to the COVID-19 epidemic have included "social distancing" policies that make it more difficult for people with common interests to meet and form communities.

Nonetheless, the Metaverse has enabled users to engage in "social connection" by offering a platform where those with common interests may meet and talk to one another.

However, social bonds in the virtual world are less solid than in the real one. As an alternative to "myself, as I am," users in the Metaverse can select which aspects of their identities to highlight.

The risk of having one's privacy compromised is an extra consideration when partaking in social activities in the Metaverse, as various sorts of data that were not generated in real-world interactions are collected and analyzed in real-time (Kye, Han, Kim, Park, & Jo, 2021).

Tlili et al. (2022) along with Metaverse users are riskier than those who use preexisting online services and games due to the large degree of flexibility that is a benefit of the Metaverse. The high degree of freedom makes it impossible for the administrator to foresee all the users' behaviors.

Because of the Metaverse's virtual nature and the anonymity it affords users, offenders feel less remorse over their actions there. Anxiety has been raised over the potential emergence of new crimes that are much more heinous and technologically advanced than those already seen in the actual world.

While the 'I' that takes part in the virtual world may share some physical characteristics with the 'I' that does the same thing in the actual world, the 'I' that takes part in the virtual world may have a completely different appearance and perspective on the world. Avatar is one possible meaning of the phrase sub-character (extra character). In a future where blending the virtual and real worlds is the norm, users can expect to have more leeway to be themselves in a setting where they remain anonymous online. Identification of individuals is restricted in comparison to reality.

Be wary, as a greater degree of anonymity in the Metaverse can make one more vulnerable to criminal activity. There can be no selective censorship of the vast volumes of user-generated and shared data in a free-minded Metaverse. That's why anarchy is a distinct possibility there.

Caution is warranted here because of the potential danger it poses to prepubescent children who have not yet developed a strong sense of their own identity and have little social experience. Citizenship in the virtual world will need to be nurtured, and this will necessitate an ethical curriculum.

As the lines between the digital and physical worlds continue to blur, people may begin to question who they really are. It's possible that they won't be able to adjust to VR.

There is a risk that one's real-world relationships will suffer if he or she spends too much time in a virtual environment, either because of a dissatisfaction with one's current connections or an obsession with the possibility of finding a better one (Table 2).

Table 2. EFL teaching model through Metaverse

Metaverse Characteristic	Merit	Shortcomings
a brand-new medium for group dialogue	Extremely Lifelike Virtual Reality (VR)	Play-based relationships are less robust than face-to-face interactions, and privacy issues arise as a result of the collecting and processing of numerous types of personal information.
Abundant freedom	Facilitating greater independence in the classroom by connecting content users and producers through shared experiences.	Due to the open nature of the platform, administrators are at risk of being victimized by a wide range of crimes that would be impossible to foresee in a more restricted environment.
High-Immersion Virtual Reality (VR)	Providing a novel, out-of-this-world experience can pique students' curiosity and keep their attention for longer, leading to more engaged learning.	For students whose sense of self is still developing, this can lead to a clouding of their sense of identity, an avoidance of reality, and a failure to adapt to the actual world.

Source: Kye et al. (2021)

METHOD

Participants and Setting

Given the wide variety of Virtual reality (VR) tools already on the market, the intention of the researcher to capitalize on the constructivist and constructionist aspects of using the tool for learning, and the study's focus on the Metaverse as an illustrative case, the main question investigated in this article is: How do students perceive when integrate Virtual Reality (Metaverse) technology into their language learning classes? This makes us wonder whether students have previous experience with VR other than language learning which is different from English courses which integrate VR in their Metaverse classes.

We conducted a quantitative and qualitative survey to gain insight into this issue. Participants' platform VR content creation was also observed for qualitative data. This research involved 165 students at universitas Al Asyariah Mandar consisting of representatives from the computer science faculties, public health faculty, teacher training and education faculty and agriculture faculty.

Verbal and nonverbal communication skills, as well as reading, writing, speaking, and listening, were all covered. To conduct research, we integrated Virtual Reality into language learning for three weeks. Participants were taken from a sample of undergraduate students participating in English I courses in semester 1 of the 2022 academic year.

Figure 1. Demographic information

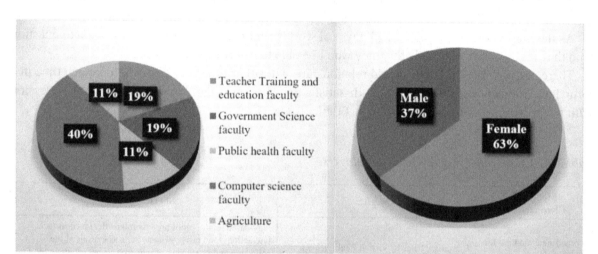

Research Procedures

The three sets of meetings are treated equally. They may engage in language learning with Virtual Reality (VR). Each undergraduate student meeting is asked to determine the work team and given the opportunity to discuss the material they will study by accessing the VR link https://edu.cospaces.io/Studio/Classes with material telling the chronology of Harry Potter Adventure using the past tense, writing paragraphs based on lord of the flies and describing Shelly and her Grandmom's house and describing dinosaurs based on the Jurassic Museum using the simple present tense.

Students who attended each VR material were given the opportunity to fill out a survey which was shared using the Google form in their WhatsApp group afterwards. Only information from those who actively interact with VR Metaverse is relevant to this page.

Before participants were involved in research activities, they were given a brief introduction explaining virtual reality and giving examples of how this technology is currently being used to assist language learning and providing examples of sentences according to their target language.

Instructional Teaching Model

First, the lecturer explains material regarding describing things, and undergraduate students are asked to listen to definitions, example sentences, and elements of describing things: quantity, opinion, size, shape, color, origin, or material + adjective.

The students were then asked to describe in simple terms their friends who sat on their right and left sides. Next, the lecturer introduced virtual reality and asked them to access, observe, and be involved in the VR. Then, lecturers asked undergraduate students to form a work team.

Second step, they were given the opportunity to try the Metaverse VR experience, which was accessed using the link that had been shared via the WhatsApp group. In the first set of instructions, students learn how to access the VR platform (login), then observe the platform and analyze the content and make connections with the material (describing things) then they write down the main sentences based on VR until they design a descriptive text.

Participants were asked to describe the virtual objects provided by Metaverse to explore how Metaverse enables the integration of virtual objects into real-world experiences.

Figure 2. VR gallery of co-space edu platform

The second set requires undergraduate students to work in groups to complete drafts of describing things (describing dinosaurs) to create their Metaverse adventures using VR.

Participants were assigned to proofread their manuscripts; the lecturer asked them to access Google Translate and the Grammarly application. Then in groups, they practice reading and correcting their pronunciation. The exercises are designed to be quick and simple so that participants can get a feel for the tools and how they can be used.

The third set, namely, the lecturer asks individual undergraduate students to speak in front of the class, and because time is limited, they are asked to record a video of their speech using a smartphone, upload it to their YouTube account, and provide feedback.

Lecturers and students reflect. After the VR implementation was carried out for four meetings, the lecturer conducted a survey. The main aim of this survey was to determine how undergraduate students feel about their time in the Metaverse, how they feel it influences their language learning, and how confident they are using various technology tools.

In addition, they were asked to consider how much they liked social/collaborative learning and 21st century skills, and how much they enjoyed actively incorporating technology into their English lessons.

Figure 3. Students joining VR by grouping

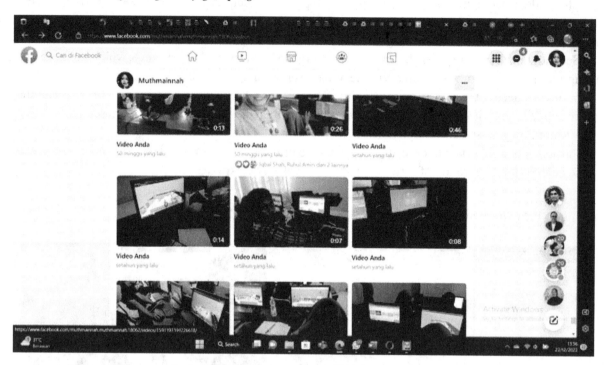

Figure 4. Students speaking performance

Data Collecting Procedure

To collect information for this quantitative study, two instruments were used. A 35-item survey was used in the first survey (adapted from Mahmoud, 2014). All of them were asked to rate their agreement with the statements using a five-point Likert scale, where 1 indicated strongly disagree, 2 indicated somewhat disagree, 3 indicated did not know, 4 indicated agreed to some extent, and 5 indicated strongly agreed.

After completing the survey, participants met for a round of discussions and were interviewed using open-ended questions. Since the responses are short, the transcription procedure takes very little time. Interviews are trusted because the same or comparable questions are asked many times.

RESULTS

The purpose of this study was to collect feedback on virtual reality (VR) from undergraduate students of English as a foreign language. Meanwhile, 165 out of 181 experienced students responded to a survey about their use of Metaverse.

The remainder refused to participate in the research or decided to focus solely on different virtual reality activities. Apart from that, quota and network constraints have caused them not to participate in filling out the link survey according to a predetermined time limit. The table below provides a synopsis of student opinions.

Figure 5. Metaverse technology improve students English skill

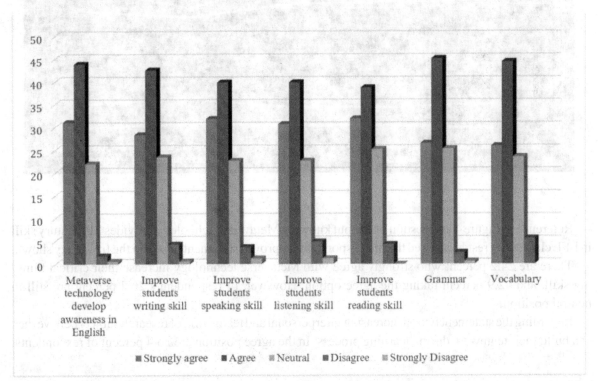

Regarding the data on Table 3 due the most popular use Metaverse technology in EFL learning we investigate further the use of this technology by students in 2022 academic year.

The results showed most of the students believe Metaverse technology help them to increase their English skill and awareness in English of 165 student's 31.1 percent took strongly agree and 43.9 percent agree followed by separate language skill most of them felt their writing, speaking, listening, reading increase by this technology.

On grammar and vocabulary here the data show 26.5 percent respondent believe their grammar knowledge can be categorized very good and 45.1 percent in good categories.

The reassuring news is only 0.6 percent categorized himself or herself as having insufficient knowledge about English. The survey on Metaverse technology provides 21st skill covers five research questions and data findings can see below.

Figure 6. Metaverse technology provides 21st skill

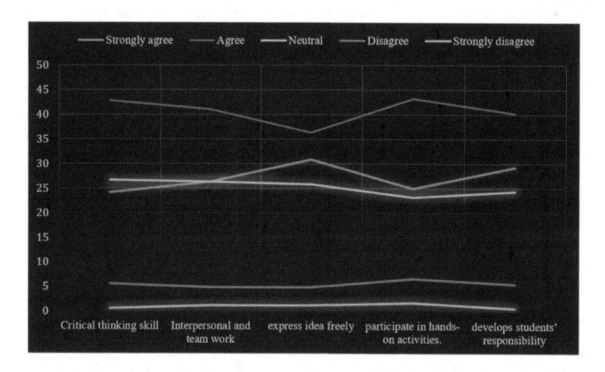

Reference as Figure 4, in question one about knowing Metaverse technology provides 21st century skill in EFL classroom, results showed that the respondents approved statement based on the frequency shown.

There are 24.2 percent who strongly agree with Metaverse technology increase their critical thinking skill, and 42.9 percent taking the agree option. However, of respondent's 26.7 percent are still in neutral position.

Regarding the statement two on increasing interpersonal and teamwork, of research subject believe they can build their teamwork during learning process. In the agree position are 26.4 percent of respondents.

On the item concerning express idea freely, of respondents say they can express idea without anxiety and 41.1 took agree.

The next survey item is the students provides participate in hands on activities in the chart, it is clearly displayed that 30.9 percent respondents strongly agree with the statement, and 36.4 percent of them agree on it.

The last question is by using Metaverse technology it can develop students' responsibility not only for learning what is being taught, but also for helping teammates learn 29.3 percent of respondents agree and 40.2 percent took agree position.

In this session, the core question is experience in learning through Metaverse technology for EFL by research subject and reference Figure 5 is here.

Figure 7. Experience in learning

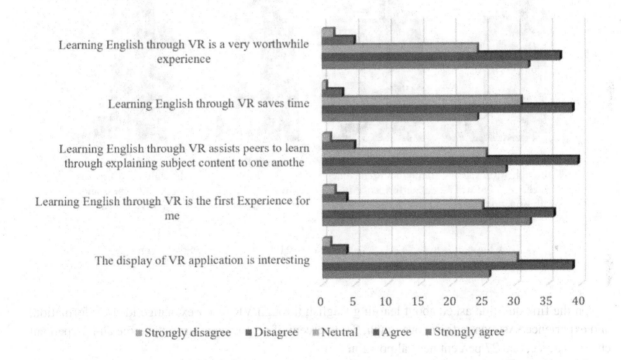

Based on the table shown learning English through VR is very worthwhile experience by himself or herself, with 31.9 percent responding strongly agree and 36.8 percent respondent answering agree.

Concerning the statement learning English through VR saves time most of respondent's 23.9 percent strongly agree and 38.7 percent agreed with the statement. The third statement concern learning English through VR assists peer to learn through explaining subject content to one another. Most of respondents strongly agree 28.4 percent with the statement and 39.5 percent respondents chose to agree.

The next question is learning English through VR is the first experience for those 32.1 of respondents strongly agree and 35.8 percent of respondents opted agree. The last question asked the display of VR (Metaverse) app is interesting.

In this finding, subject opted for strongly agree 38.7 percent, and agree 30.1 percent of respondents. Here all the respondents have ability to play and access Metaverse technology better.

The instructional design of Metaverse technology in EFL classroom as the last session of the survey. It consists of four statements, and it is about respondent stimulate to acquire more knowledge. Reference Figure 6 is here.

Figure 8. Metaverse technology stimulate students to acquire more knowledge

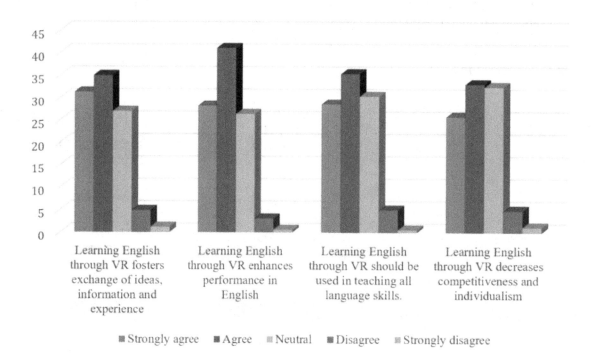

On the first question asked about learning English through VR foster exchange ideas, information, and experience. As seen in the above graph, 31.3 percent of respondents strongly agree and 35 percent chose to agree, and 27 percent neutral position.

The second question concerns the Metaverse technology enhances performance in English 28.2 percent of respondents chose strongly to agree and 41.1 took agree position.

Regarding statement one and two on EFL class they recommended to use Metaverse technology in teaching all language skill, 28. 1 percent of the research subjects who strongly agree with the statement and 37.5 percent taking the agree option.

DISCUSSION

In the modern era of computer-assisted language learning (CALL), anyone who desire to study a foreign or second language can do so with the help of a machine in place of traditional classroom instruction (Yaman & Ekmekçi, 2016; Zhang & Zou, 2022). Learners were able to find information on their own.

Using CALL, instructors can direct students to online resources where they can learn more about a topic or supplement what they've already learned. As time has passed, the computer has shrunk into more portable forms, changing CALL into MALL (Mobile-assisted Language Learning).

The MALL has expanded into VR because of this time. Virtual reality (VR) in the classroom is one of the most obvious extensions of computer-assisted instruction (CAI) and computer-based training (CBT).

In this study students in English as a Foreign Language lesson are given a blank questionnaire to fill out (google form) which is distributed using WhatsApp group after learning English using Metaverse technology is carried out.

Using Metaverse technology, we conducted an objective sample of a group of high school students who had expressed an interest in enrolling in an English 1 course. The procedures used for data conformed to statistical norms. Parametric statistics are used because they best fit the conceptual model of the research.

Data processing was carried out, namely: each part of the developed questionnaire underwent data collection. Qualitative and quantitative data were analyzed descriptively using procedural statistics; Following are some of the principles and procedures used when analyzing qualitative data. Information tabulation; reduce it through classification; interpret findings; make a conclusion.

Additional analysis of the respondent's attributes was carried out based on the results of data processing. The survey found that women accounted for 63% of participants and men 37%.

Based on their experience using Metaverse technology based on virtual reality, students reported that they found it very useful to improve their English mastery, writing skill, speaking (Kassim, Witkin, & Stone, 2019), reading skill, listening skill, grammar and vocabulary.

These findings also support those of related study that reported students' English skills improve by this Metaverse technology (VR) by Pantelidis (2010) said that virtual reality was seen as helpful by all respondents in improving their communication skills.

This shows that the pedagogical approach adopted was successful in improving English proficiency and creating a relaxed learning environment. Virtual reality has carried on the trend, which is seen in many kinds of technological implements.

Using the Metaverse as a teaching model has resulted in improvements not only in English proficiency, but also in critical thinking, interpersonal and teamwork skills, the ability to express ideas openly, engagement in experiential learning, and instilling a sense of personal responsibility (table 5). Based on this study, virtual reality exercises can be tailored to the needs of individual students.

In the 21st century, student-centered learning has emerged as a key pedagogical principle. This study also finds from Thurairasu (2022) research that learning language and critical thinking skills simultaneously is possible using a virtual learning community in which students work together to overcome challenges presented in the target language, if the avatars' role in mediating interactions affected students' ability to work together effectively, undergraduate students agreed unequivocally that they saw themselves in the avatars' portrayals.

Avatars are seen as helpful for collaborative learning because they provide a sense of anonymity, which increases students' engagement with tasks and willingness to take risks while also reducing the anxiety and inherent self-awareness associated with revealing their imperfect command of a second language (Duffy, Stone, Townsend, & Cathey, 2022).

Using this Metaverse technology has undoubtedly made learning English as a second language more interesting and enjoyable (EFL). Based on the findings shown in table 6, it is suggested that implementing this Metaverse technology will improve English proficiency and encourage greater opportunities for teamwork. This study is related with Yeh and Lan (2018) research.

They claim that virtual reality provides the opportunity for hands-on training. Virtual reality (VR) allows students to have hands-on experience with cutting-edge technologies, and they in turn build their understanding of these tools as they use them.

As an illustration, Yeh and Lan developed a virtual 3D environment where users may quickly and simply build their own virtual 3D background by selecting elements from a catalog of virtual objects and placing them where they like.

Users have complete control over the environment, including the ability to reposition and reorient objects at will.

Additionally, VR provides a way to acquire material that has traditionally been inaccessible via distance education. Students can get data simply by looking at the 3D model and the virtual setting.

According to Bogusevschi, Muntean, and Muntean (2020), the use of virtual reality in the classroom has enormous potential and many pedagogical benefits.

Virtual reality (VR) provides a realistic 3D multimedia simulation, encourages participation in the simulated environment, and enables sensory experiences.

The applications of virtual reality span a wide range of fields. Education also makes use of VR because some courses need students to do experiments.

Using VR, students can design and conduct their own experiments in a safe, controlled setting before seeing the results in a 3D simulation.

This technology provides students with an enjoyable method to gain the problem-solving, computer literacy, and practical skills that are essential for their future success in school and in life.

Using a three-dimensional item and virtual 360 degrees of expertise, the instructors will provide students with real-world context.

When it comes to the third pillar of education, "learning to be," virtual reality can boost student motivation (Bogusevschi, Muntean, & Muntean, 2020; Chen, 2016).

As mentioned in Hussein and Nätterdal (2015) and Cowie and Alizadeh (2022) virtual reality works best when employed in a visually appealing setting.

Teachers have the freedom to select engaging lessons that will help students achieve their potential. Another study using Google Street View for a virtual trip found that students who participated in the activity developed a more accepting and accepting attitude toward cultural differences and a greater desire to learn about them in the context of the target culture (Pilgrim & Pilgrim, 2016); Chabot, Drozdal, Zhou, Su, & Braasch, 2019).

Learning how to get along with others is the final objective. Using VR in the classroom encourages more student participation and engagement (Koşar, 2022).

CONCLUSION

This study concludes that EFL students at specific universities are the ones who claim to have never used Metaverse technology for language instruction before. Despite their frequent usage of mobile devices in everyday life, they have never tried virtual reality (VR) for language study.

They conclude that the Metaverse is an effective tool for language study and advocate its adoption in similar programs. They were open to trying out EFL instruction via Metaverse technology and expressed a favorable outlook on the practice.

This could be interpreted as a call to action for policymakers and teachers to take advantage of the Metaverse environment, employ teaching models that are tailored to the needs, characteristics, skills, and attitudes of undergraduate students, and make the most of learning technology and games while also designing affordable options for Metaverse technology-assisted language learning and promoting language learning beyond the classroom.

However, students' use of the findings is restricted to the most fundamental aspects of VR, and there is still VR content on the CoSpaceEdu platform that uses languages other than English, meaning that not all content on the platform can be developed into teaching materials. This, along with difficulties reported in technical support and facilitation conditions, suggests that users of certain smartphones will need to upgrade their hardware to run this application.

Aside from that, students' access to cutting-edge technology is hampered by a lack of institutional support, understanding, and infrastructure. If teachers in Indonesia are going to help their students master the language with the help of this Metaverse technology, this issue must be resolved.

The institution's leader can use this information to better equip their students with technology, allowing them to adopt cutting-edge methods of language study more easily.

Research has certain limitations, and they must be acknowledged. There are more women than men involved because they tend to learn the subject matter (i.e., language programmers). Hence, it is not possible to study how gender differences use and view the Metaverse of technology in higher education.

To avoid this bias in future studies, it may be important to have a balanced sample of males and females. In addition, the online survey instrument is the only important instrument for research findings.

The results are presented without participant subjective explanation. To provide more thorough and insightful information, future researchers may want to think about integrating participant insights and using different Metaverse technology platforms.

REFERENCES

Alam, A. (2022). Employing Adaptive Learning and Intelligent Tutoring Robots for Virtual Classrooms and Smart Campuses: Reforming Education in the Age of Artificial Intelligence. In *Advanced Computing and Intelligent Technologies* (pp. 395–406). Springer. doi:10.1007/978-981-19-2980-9_32

Ausburn, L. J., & Ausburn, F. B. (2008). Effects of desktop virtual reality on learner performance and confidence in environment mastery: Opening a line of enquiry. *Journal of Industrial Teacher Education*, *45*(1), 54–87.

Bacalja, A. (2022). A critical review of digital game literacies in the English classroom. *L1-Educational Studies in Language and Literature*, 1–28. doi:10.21248/l1esll.2022.22.2.370

Bogusevschi, D., Muntean, C., & Muntean, G. M. (2020). Teaching and learning physics using 3D virtual learning environment: A case study of combined virtual reality and virtual laboratory in secondary school. *Journal of Computers in Mathematics and Science Teaching*, *39*(1), 5–18.

Book, B. (2004). Moving beyond the game: Social virtual worlds. State of Play, 2.

Chabot, S., Drozdal, J., Zhou, Y., Su, H., & Braasch, J. (2019, July). Language learning in a cognitive and immersive environment using contextualized panoramic imagery. In *International Conference on Human-Computer Interaction* (pp. 202-209). Springer. 10.1007/978-3-030-23525-3_26

Chalmers, D. J. (2022). Reality+: Virtual worlds and the problems of philosophy. Penguin UK.

Chen, J. C. (2016). EFL learners' strategy use during task-based interaction in Second Life. *Australasian Journal of Educational Technology*, *32*(3). Advance online publication. doi:10.14742/ajet.2306

Chen, Y. L. (2016). The Effects of Virtual Reality Learning Environment on Student Cognitive and Linguistic Development. *The Asia-Pacific Education Researcher*, *25*(4), 637–646. doi:10.100740299-016-0293-2

Cline, E. (2011). *Ready player one*. Crown Publishing Group.

Collins, C. (2008). Looking to the future: Higher education in the Metaverse. *EDUCAUSE Review*, *43*(5), 51–63.

Cowie, N., & Alizadeh, M. (2022). The affordances and challenges of virtual reality for language teaching. *International Journal of TESOL Studies*, *4*(3), 50–56.

Crespo, R. G., Escobar, R. F., Aguilar, L. J., Velazco, S., & Sanz, A. G. C. (2013). Use of ARIMA mathematical analysis to model the implementation of expert system courses by means of free software OpenSim and Sloodle platforms in virtual university campuses. *Expert Systems with Applications*, *40*(18), 7381–7390. doi:10.1016/j.eswa.2013.06.054

Duffy, L. N., Stone, G. A., Townsend, J., & Cathey, J. (2022). Rethinking curriculum internationalization: Virtual exchange as a means to attaining global competencies, developing critical thinking, and experiencing transformative learning. *SCHOLE: A Journal of Leisure Studies and Recreation Education*, *37*(1-2), 11-25.

Hussein, M., & Nätterdal, C. (2015). *The benefits of virtual reality in education-A comparison Study*. Academic Press.

Kassim, S., Witkin, N., & Stone, A. (2019). Student perceptions of virtual reality use in a speaking activity. *CALL and Complexity*, 223.

Kemp, J., & Livingstone, D. (2006). Putting a Second Life "Metaverse" skin on learning management systems. In *Proceedings of the Second Life education workshop at the Second Life community convention* (Vol. 20). The University of Paisley.

Koşar, G. (2022). A Comparative Study of the Attitudes of EFL Student and Practicing Teachers towards First Language Use. *Journal of Language Teaching and Learning*, *12*(1), 28–43.

Kozlova, I., & Priven, D. (2015). ESL teacher training in 3D virtual worlds. *Language Learning & Technology, 19*(1), 83–101.

Kye, B., Han, N., Kim, E., Park, Y., & Jo, S. (2021). Educational applications of Metaverse: Possibilities and limitations. *Journal of Educational Evaluation for Health Professions, 18*, 18. doi:10.3352/jeehp.2021.18.32 PMID:34897242

Lee, S. (2020). *Log in Metaverse: Revolution of Human Space Time.* Issue Report.

Levak, N., & Son, J. B. (2017). Facilitating second language learners' listening comprehension with Second Life and Skype. *ReCALL, 29*(2), 200–218. doi:10.1017/S0958344016000215

Liang, M. Y. (2019). Beyond elocution: Multimodal narrative discourse analysis of L2 storytelling. *ReCALL, 31*(1), 56–74. doi:10.1017/S0958344018000095

Mahmoud, M. M. A. (2014). The effectiveness of using the cooperative language learning approach to enhance EFL writing skills among Saudi university students. *Journal of Language Teaching and Research, 5*(3), 616. doi:10.4304/jltr.5.3.616-625

Martínez-Hernández, C., Yubero, C., Ferreiro-Calzada, E., & Mendoza-de Miguel, S. (2020). *Didactic use of GIS and Street View for Tourism Degree students: Understanding commercial gentrification in large urban destinations.* Academic Press.

Metaverse Roadmap Summit 2006. (n.d.). *Elon University.* https://www.elon.edu/u/imagining/event-coverage/Metav erse/

Mystakidis, S., Christopoulos, A., & Pellas, N. (2022). A systematic mapping review of augmented reality applications to support STEM learning in higher education. *Education and Information Technologies, 27*(2), 1883–1927. doi:10.100710639-021-10682-1

Ning, H., Wang, H., Lin, Y., Wang, W., Dhelim, S., Farha, F., & Daneshmand, M. (2021). *A Survey on Metaverse: the State-of-the-art, Technologies, Applications, and Challenges.* https://doi.org//arXiv.2111.09673 doi:10.48550

Pack, A., Barrett, A., Liang, H. N., & Monteiro, D. V. (2020). University EAP students' perceptions of using a prototype virtual reality learning environment to learn writing structure. *International Journal of Computer-Assisted Language Learning and Teaching, 10*(1), 27–46. doi:10.4018/IJCALLT.2020010103

Pantelidis, V. S. (2010). Reasons to use virtual reality in education and training courses and a model to determine when to use virtual reality. *Themes in Science and Technology Education, 2*(1-2), 59–70.

Park, M. (2018). Innovative assessment of aviation English in a virtual world: Windows into cognitive and metacognitive strategies. *ReCALL, 30*(2), 196–213. doi:10.1017/S0958344017000362

Park, S. M., & Kim, Y. G. (2022). A Metaverse: Taxonomy, components, applications, and open challenges. *IEEE Access, 10*, 4209–4251. doi:10.1109/ACCESS.2021.3140175

Park, S., Min, K., & Kim, S. (2021). Differences in learning motivation among Bartle's player types and measures for the delivery of sustainable gameful experiences. *Sustainability, 13*(16), 9121. https://doi.org/ doi:10.1109/ACCESS.2021.3140175

Pilgrim, J. M., & Pilgrim, J. (2016). The use of virtual reality tools in the reading-language arts classroom. *Texas Journal of Literacy Education, 4*(2), 90–97.

Riley, S. K. L., & Stacy, K. (2008). Teaching in virtual worlds: Opportunities and challenges. *Setting Knowledge Free: The Journal of Issues in Informing Science and Information Technology, 5*(5), 127–135.

Schlemmer, E., & Backes, L. (2015). *Learning in Metaverses: Co-existing in real virtuality.* IGI Global. doi:10.4018/978-1-4666-6351-0

Schlichting, M. S., Füchter, S. K., Schlichting, M. S., & Alexander, K. (2022, September). Metaverse: Virtual and Augmented Reality Presence. In *2022 International Symposium on Measurement and Control in Robotics (ISMCR)* (pp. 1-6). IEEE.

Siyaev, A., & Jo, G. S. (2021). Towards aircraft maintenance Metaverse using speech interactions with virtual objects in mixed reality. *Sensors (Basel), 21*(6), 2066. doi:10.339021062066 PMID:33804253

Stephenson, N. (1992). *Snow crash: A novel.* Spectra.

Thurairasu, V. (2022). Gamification-Based Learning as the Future of Language Learning: An Overview. *European Journal of Humanities and Social Sciences, 2*(6), 62–69. doi:10.24018/ejsocial.2022.2.6.353

Tlili, A., Huang, R., Shehata, B., Liu, D., Zhao, J., Metwally, A. H. S., Wang, H., Denden, M., Bozkurt, A., Lee, L.-H., Beyoglu, D., Altinay, F., Sharma, R. C., Altinay, Z., Li, Z., Liu, J., Ahmad, F., Hu, Y., Salha, S., ... Burgos, D. (2022). Is Metaverse in education a blessing or a curse: A combined content and bibliometric analysis? *Smart Learning Environments, 9*(1), 1–31. doi:10.118640561-022-00205-x

Wang, P., Wu, P., Wang, J., Chi, H. L., & Wang, X. (2018). A critical review of the use of virtual reality in construction engineering education and training. *International Journal of Environmental Research and Public Health, 15*(6), 1204. doi:10.3390/ijerph15061204 PMID:29890627

Wang, Y. F., Petrina, S., & Feng, F. (2017). VILLAGE—Virtual Immersive Language Learning and Gaming Environment: Immersion and presence. *British Journal of Educational Technology, 48*(2), 431–450. doi:10.1111/bjet.12388

Wiederhold, B. K. (2022). Ready (orNot) player one: Initial musings on the Metaverse. *Cyberpsychology, Behavior, and Social Networking, 25*(1), 1–2. doi:10.1089/cyber.2021.29234.editorial PMID:34964667

Yaman, I., & Ekmekçi, E. (2016). A shift from CALL to MALL? *Participatory Educational Research, 4*(2), 25–32.

Zhang, R., & Zou, D. (2022). Types, purposes, and effectiveness of state-of-the-art technologies for second and foreign language learning. *Computer Assisted Language Learning, 35*(4), 696–742. doi:10.1080/09588221.2020.1744666

Chapter 6
AR/VR Technologies in the Metaverse Ecosystem

Jyoti Gupta
Chitkara Institute of Engineering and Technology, India

Lekha Rani
Chitkara Institute of Engineering and Technology, India

Maninder Kaur
Chitkara Institute of Engineering and Technology, India

ABSTRACT

Imagine living in a virtual environment where millions of individuals can communicate among themselves, explore, shop, and have a comfortable life on their couches. In this universe, the computer displays have transformed portals into a physical, three-dimensional digital realm that is superior and more expansive than the real world. Digital avatars that are representations of us roam between experiences while carrying our identities. Putting the sensationalism aside, this is known as the "metaverse." The metaverse is an idea that describes a virtual universe composed of a couple of interconnected virtual spaces or worlds. It is an imaginative immersion in which the digital and bodily worlds converge, creating a widespread and interconnected network of virtual environments that can be accessed globally. It can boost employment opportunities by supplementing individuals with practical training and ensures that the individuals with disabilities can also be incorporated in this marathon of growth by leveraging these technologies.

INTRODUCTION

The utilization of the term "metaverse" (Mystakidis, 2022) has expanded in technological know-how fiction literature and films, and "Snow Crash" by Neal Stephenson is a tremendous instance of this trend. With advancements in virtual and augmented truth technology, on-line gaming, and social networking structures, the idea of a metaverse is steadily transforming into a tangible fact. The metaverse is expected as a totally immersive and interactive surroundings that merges the physical and digital worlds. Various

DOI: 10.4018/978-1-6684-8851-5.ch006

digital territories or nation-states will represent the metaverse (Zvarikova et al., 2022), each having its unique characteristics, regulations, and targets. These virtual worlds can be created through individuals or groups and might serve exceptional purposes, along with gaming, socializing, education, and greater. In the metaverse, verbal exchange among customers could be facilitated via avatars that represent their online personas. Users may be able to interact, collaborate and have interaction in sports simply as they could in actual lifestyles. The metaverse stands other than traditional environments in that customers have surely no limitations on their moves or studies. The metaverse has the capacity to revolutionize various factors of human existence, ranging from enjoyment, education, healthcare, to trade. It will be utilized for numerous functions such as online purchasing, product showcases, sensible education simulations, and scientific interventions. Developing a versatile and adaptable foundation able to accommodate a plethora of applications and studies is one of the foremost demanding situations in building the metaverse. Establishing protocols and conventions to make certain seamless verbal exchange between diverse virtual nation-states and selling cooperation amongst specific entities, including corporations, programmers, and companies, is critical in reaching this purpose.

Another impediment is ensuring identical get entry to the metaverse for all, no matter their financial fame, bodily area, or capabilities. Achieving these calls for the development of low cost and on hand hardware and software solutions whilst addressing concerns about privacy, safety, and moral considerations. Despite the challenges, the metaverse holds tremendous capacity to foster novel and innovative connections amongst humans internationally. It has the potential to generate clean potentialities for commerce, change, social interplay, enjoyment, and schooling.

Although still in its early stages, the improvement of the metaverse has the ability to seriously transform many sides of our life and unveil new avenues for progress. In building the metaverse, it is essential to prioritize openness, inclusivity, and ethical concerns to make certain that it acts as a positive pressure for societal, economic, and cultural development.

WORKING OF METAVERSE

The term "Metaverse" describes a shared virtual area in which customers can have interaction with each different and digital item (O'Brien & Chan, 2021). While popularized by technological know-how fiction literature and movies, the metaverse is turning into increasingly viable with advancements in digital and augmented fact, on-line gaming, and social networking structures. Users can get entry to the digital worlds inside the metaverse through a number of hardware and software technologies, consisting of net browsers, virtual truth headsets, and augmented reality glasses. By the use of those tools, customers can interact with the virtual realm through their avatar, a digital illustration of their identity within the metaverse.

Avatars can be customized to appear to be something, from a human to a fantastical creature. Through avatars, users can explore the metaverse and have interaction with others inside a digital surroundings, permitting them to pass and have interaction with the virtual world in a comparable manner to their physical selves in the real world.

Real-time consumer collaboration and interaction is an essential component of the metaverse, allowing individuals to participate in organization activities similar to they could in the physical world. The metaverse offers quite a number of opportunities for customers to engage in sports collectively, such as attending virtual activities, taking lessons, gambling video games, and accomplishing business.

Digital items have inherent worth inside the metaverse and may be bought and sold. Virtual economies have sprung from this, allowing customers to alternate virtual products like virtual money, clothes for his or her avatars, and virtual actual estate. There need to be perfect conversation across extraordinary digital worlds for the metaverse to be characterized as an individual entity. This necessitates the improvement of structures and requirements which might be at the same time interoperable and permit the switching of facts among various digital environments.

The metaverse also is predicated substantially on user-generated content. Users have to be capable of creating and sharing their own material for you to ensure a diverse and thriving ecology. This consists of the whole lot from on-line conversations to video games and digital worlds. To attain its complete potential, the metaverse should get over a number of challenges as it's miles still in its infancy. The major hassle is developing an independent platform that is adaptable and can help more than a few apps and reports. To enable ideal communique throughout digital worlds, this calls for collaboration among groups, programmers, and companies further to the creation of requirements and protocols.

Another challenge is to ensure that the metaverse is available to all and sundry, irrespective of their economic, geographical, or bodily constraints Creating lower priced and without difficulty reachable hardware and software solutions will be crucial, at the side of addressing troubles of privacy, security, and ethics in order to make certain that the metaverse is available to all of us, irrespective of their economic situation, geography, or physical competencies. The metaverse has the potential to introduce new possibilities for trade and exchange, in addition to new avenues for social interaction, amusement, and education. Ultimately, the metaverse is a network of interconnected virtual worlds that lets in customers speak with each other and with virtual entities in a shared environment. Thanks to improvements in the digital and augmented truth era, online gaming, and social media structures, this idea is now starting to take shape.

ACCESSING THE METAVERSE

People can interact with digital items and different human beings in the metaverse, a shared digital environment. By using numerous hardware and software technologies, customers can access the metaverse and immerse themselves in the virtual world even as they interact with it through their digital avatar or persona.

One of the most famous methods to reach the metaverse is through virtual reality (VR) headsets (Hennig-Thurau, 2022). These gadgets generate an immersive, 3-d virtual surroundings that can be explored through head and hand moves employing modern-day motion sensors, displays, and audio structures. From cheaper cell alternatives to high-cease, PC-powered headsets that offer the very best degrees of immersion and interactivity, VR headsets range in price and complexity.

Through augmented truth (AR) glasses or different gadgets, there are other ways to go into the metaverse. This equipment enables users to interact with digital entities and other users in a more natural way by superimposing virtual objects and facts onto the consumer's real environment. Mobile phones and pills, in addition to specialized glasses and headsets, are examples of AR gadgets.

The metaverse also can be accessed through mobile apps and internet browsers.

These attributes give users a more convenient and adaptable method to engage with other customers and discover digital worlds. Users can create and explore digital worlds using web-primarily based metaverse systems like Second Life, High Fidelity, and Sansar, even as mobile programs like AltspaceVR and

VRChat provide an extra immersive and sociable cellular experience. Facebook, Instagram, and Twitter are only some of the social media websites which are starting to have an impact on the metaverse. These platforms allow customers to have interaction with each other in clean and immersive methods by way of incorporating AR and VR talents into their merchandise. For instance, Instagram's Spark AR permits customers to create and percentage AR outcomes and filters, whilst Facebook's Horizon Workrooms (Kraus et al., 2022) is a VR platform that permits humans to meet and collaborate in a virtual setting.

There are also increasingly systems and gear that are being created specifically for the metaverse in addition to those hardware and software program solutions. These include movement capture devices, haptic remarks suits, and designated hardware and software for constructing and growing virtual environments.

Although still in its infancy, the metaverse can now be accessed and interacted with via a huge type of tools and platforms. As the metaverse keeps on developing, we might assume ever more creative and approachable approaches to go into and discover this virtual world.

METAVERSE TECHNOLOGIES

Everybody on the planet can access and explore the shared, interactive, three-dimensional metaverse. It integrates elements of immersive technology including augmented reality (AR), virtual reality (VR), and others. A wide range of metaverse technologies, including social VR platforms, gaming engines, blockchain-based virtual real estate, and AI-powered avatars, are being developed (Ning, 2021; Owens et al., 2011) to make this practical. We shall examine some of the major metaverse technologies that are promoting the growth of this new digital horizon in this post.

SOCIAL VR PLATFORMS

One of the important things in technology riding the metaverse is social VR systems. These are digital fact environments in which humans can have interaction with every different in real time, the use of three-D avatars. VRChat, Rec Room, and AltspaceVR are a number of the social VR structures which might be most usually used. Users of these systems can perform digital job interviews, attend digital meetings, and interact in casual socializing all of the way as much as professional networking.

The capability to set up social relationships and create communities in a way that isn't always possible with conventional net structures is one of the principal blessings of social VR systems. People can talk with one another effectively and pleasingly in the metaverse by means of the use of gestures and frame language, as well as by touring around digital worlds collectively.

GAME ENGINES

Another key metaverse-allowing era is game engines. Computer programs known as "Game Engines" offer developers with the sources they want to create and control video games. Two of the most famous sports engines are Singularity and Unreal Engine. The immersive settings that make up the metaverse, consisting of digital cities and landscapes and immersive game worlds, are created deploying those engines.

The capability to generate realistic and immersive settings that may be skilled in actual time is one of the most important advantages of recreation engines. This is critical for the metaverse as it allows humans to discover virtual worlds and have interaction in intuitive, natural interactions with each other.

VIRTUAL REAL ESTATE

There is a growing demand for virtual actual estate as the metaverse grows (Yemenici, 2022). The digital lands and assets that make up the metaverse are examples of virtual real property. Everything from digital houses and office homes to digital music halls and different venues may be protected on this.

Blockchain is one of the predominant technologies promoting the boom of virtual real estate (Hutson, 2023). Secure and open transactions are made viable by using an era called blockchain that is designed in addition. A secure, open, and decentralized gadget of virtual land ownership is being evolved inside the metaverse the usage of blockchain era. This is critical for the metaverse as it makes it possible for users to soundly and reliably own and sell virtual real estate.

AI-POWERED AVATARS

Finally, AI-powered avatars are any other key technology driving the metaverse. Avatars powered through AI may be created to engage with the environment and other characters within the metaverse. They are virtual representations of real humans. From digital personal assistants and social media influencers to digital customer service and technical assist, these avatars are harnessed for the entirety.

One of the key advantages of AI-powered avatars is their ability to facilitate greater herbal, intuitive, and easy interactions with the metaverse. This is important for the metaverse because it allows individuals to interact and labor collectively in a manner that is greater like real lifestyles.

In conclusion, plenty of immersive and interactive technologies are enabling the metaverse, a new frontier in the digital world.

From social VR platforms and recreation engines to digital real property and AI-powered avatars, these technologies are growing a shared, immersive, and interactive digital area that is reworking the manner we live, paintings, and engage with each other.

SOCIAL VR PLATFORMS

Social VR structures are virtual reality (VR) environments designed to facilitate social interaction among users. Through using speech and hand gestures, users of these structures can communicate with different customers in actual time even as growing virtual versions of themselves, or avatars.

The following are some of the maximum properly-appreciated social VR structures:

VRChat: VRChat is a social VR platform that enables customers to explore and have interaction with each other's creations in addition to their personal digital worlds and avatars. Voice and text chat, as well as some interactive functions and items, are all supported via VRChat.

Rec Room is a social VR platform that is proficient in producing pleasing, sensible, and engaging video games and activities.

Users can create their personal video games and environments, or they could join in with others in video games like paintball, dodgeball, or laser tag.

NeosVR: NeosVR is a social VR platform created mainly for gatherings and social occasions. Users can compile occasions and invite others to attend them, or they can attend digital activities like concert events, comedies, and panel discussions.

Sansar is a social VR platform created mainly for artists and creators. Users can create their very own digital environments and stories, share them with others, and collaborate on community initiatives.

NeosVR: NeosVR is a social VR platform that is centered on providing a particularly customizable and flexible surroundings for customers. Users can create and proportion their very own virtual environments and avatars, in addition to building their very own interactive items and stories.

As a device for users to have interaction with others in a virtual setting that can be extra engaging and immersive than conventional social networking or video conferencing systems, social VR platforms are growing in reputation. Additionally, those systems present sparkling possibilities for groups, marketers, and creators to have interaction with consumers and convey collaborative experiences.

GAME ENGINES

Games are created and run on software program systems referred to as "recreation engines." They provide a comprehensive range of sport improvement gear, libraries, and frameworks, together with the ones for networking, pics, sound, and sport physics. Game engines offer pre-constructed modules and components that can be designed to match the unique desires of a sport undertaking, permitting developers to design and prototype video games more swiftly and efficaciously.

Here are a number of the most famous sport engines currently in use:

Unity: A popular cross-platform game engine known as Unity is used to create 2D and 3-d video games for smartphones, gaming consoles, and computing device PCs. It offers a wealth of tools for building video games with sophisticated physics, pix, and AI and helps a wide style of scripting languages.

Unreal Engine: High-cease AAA video games for consoles and PC are often evolved using the sturdy and adaptable Unreal Engine. It has a strong physics engine, rich tools for constructing immersive reviews, and superior pix capabilities.

CryEngine: The sport engine CryEngine is famous for its cutting-edge visual capabilities, which encompass practical lighting, physics, and particle effects. High-stop video games and digital truth stories regularly employ it.

Godot: Godot is an open-supply recreation engine that is designed to be lightweight and bendy. It is regularly used for developing 2D games, however it also supports 3D recreation development.

GameMaker Studio: Popular recreation engine GameMaker Studio is regularly used to provide 2D video games for consoles, PCs, and cellular gadgets. It offers a simple consumer interface and a number of included tools for rapidly and without difficulty constructing video games.

Since they may drastically speed up the introduction technique and give creators the sources they want to make difficult and compelling games, game engines are regularly hired in the sport development enterprise. Game engines are also increasingly being employed to create immersive and interactive reviews outside of conventional video games such as virtual reality and the metaverse is benefitted in terms of recognition.

VIRTUAL REAL ESTATE

Digital residences or belongings located in virtual environments like the metaverse or digital truth systems are referred to as virtual real property. There are many one-of-a-kind varieties of digital actual estate, along with digital towns, buildings, and land. Virtual actual property may have big economic and cultural value, and it can be bought, sold, evolved, and leased just like traditional real estate.

Second Life, which debuted in 2003, is one of the most well-known digital worlds that includes virtual actual estate. Users can purchase and sell digital land in Second Life, and they can dwell on it via setting up digital homes, companies, or even whole towns. In Second Life, where digital actual estate has been known to exchange for tens of heaps of greenbacks, some users have even made their entire dwelling by way of buying and selling digital homes.

Decentraland, a blockchain-based virtual world constructed on the Ethereum network, is another famous virtual surroundings with digital real property. Users should purchase virtual land in Decentraland the usage of the platform's cryptocurrency, MANA. Then, customers can assemble whatever they want on their virtual land, from houses and agencies to entire cities. In Decentraland, investing in digital homes has grown substantially, with a few promoting for tens of millions of bucks.

In virtual fact systems like VRChat, where customers may additionally create and proportion their own virtual spaces, virtual actual estate is also turning into extra accepted. Users can design and create virtual worlds and rooms in VRChat, which can be used for something from gaming to engaging. Some users have even established fictional organizations within VRChat, including fictitious shops and art galleries.

Within the metaverse, virtual real property has grown to be a significant region for investment and enterprise. As the cost of digital real property keeps to boom, some investors are purchasing digital homes with the intention of selling them for income. Others are making an investment within the development of digital corporations, together with virtual shops and entertainment venues, that can be worthwhile inside the virtual surroundings.

A vast tool for expressing one's social and cultural identity is digital actual estate. Virtual nightclubs and artwork galleries, as an example, have served as the muse for sure online groups. These online environments give people a platform to express themselves and interact with others in clean and unique approaches.

Virtual real property is probably going to come to be an even more treasured and vast asset elegance as the metaverse develops and will become extra state-of-the-art.

EDUCATION AND TRAINING IN AR/VR TECHNOLOGIES

In the metaverse ecosystem, schooling and education in AR/VR technologies have become more and more vital. There is a growing desire for people having hands-on experience in designing AR/VR content material as virtual environments become more complicated and sensible. Education and education in AR/VR technology in this context can be resourceful in making ready human beings for professions in this discipline (Park, 2019).

The capacity to narrow the shortage of qualified manpower that now exists in this industry is one of the key blessings of inculcating competence in AR/VR generation. There is a lack of certified experts who can produce this content as the call for AR/VR content rises. People can accumulate the skills and expertise important to satisfy this need through receiving schooling and palms-on schooling in the AR/VR era, with the intention to increase career possibilities (Ardiny & Khanmirza, 2018).

There are numerous ways to obtain education and schooling in AR/VR technologies. Programs in AR/VR layout and improvement are available at some universities and schools. These courses can deliver to college students radical information of the technical components of AR/VR as well as the design concepts and inventiveness required to produce fascinating and immersive content (Sharma et al., 2021). There also are a ton of online assets that offer instruction and lessons on designing and developing AR/VR.

There are several alternatives for human beings to acquire experience with AR/VR technologies via internships and apprenticeships further to legit education and schooling. These types of programs are supplied by way of a number of companies inside the AR/VR zone, and they can deliver participants practical know-how in order to run actual AR/VR tasks.

Businesses and enterprises wishing to integrate AR/VR into their operations must foreground tutelage and education within the area. For instance, education courses can be created to train personnel contributors how to use AR/VR devices and software programs. This can be specifically beneficial for companies in sectors like manufacturing and logistics, in which making use of AR and VR technologies can grow production and performance.

The benefits of training and edification in AR/VR technology cross past just getting ready people for careers in this sector. In numerous sectors, such as healthcare, education, and enjoyment, AR/VR technologies are gaining significance. Individuals may be better prepared to work in these organizations and to use AR/VR technologies in innovative ways via receiving training and education in those fields.

In the metaverse ecosystem, training and schooling in AR/VR technologies are getting increasingly critical. The want for knowledgeable professionals on this difficulty is projected to increase as digital environments continue to broaden and become extra complicated. People can accumulate the competencies and understanding required to fulfill this demand and flourish on this fascinating and quickly increasing enterprise via receiving schooling and education in AR/VR technology.

HEALTH AND WELLNESS

In the metaverse surroundings, AR/VR technologies have the potential to absolutely transform the medical sector. These technologies may be harnessed to develop immersive reviews that improve patient consequences, promote fitness and wellness, and lift the quality of care as a whole.

The capacity to supply realism and immersion in simulations is one of the key blessings of AR/VR technologies for the health and wellness stratum (). For example, virtual reality can be used to create correct simulations of medical methods, allowing healthcare experts to increase their capabilities in a safe surroundings. This may be quite beneficial for techniques which can be tough, dangerous, or unusual. Patients can also utilize AR and VR to relieve their pain and anxiety.

For patients experiencing uncomfortable or painful scientific tactics, digital truth environments can be created to encourage relaxation and lower anxiety. Additionally, patients can be distracted with the aid of AR/VR technologies throughout those remedies, which can reduce their sense of pain.

The field of mental health is one greater place where AR/VR technology might be incorporated in the fitness and wellness sector. Virtual environments that sell stress reduction, mindfulness, and rest are achievable. For those who are struggling with tension, unhappiness, or different mental fitness troubles, those traits may be extraordinarily useful. In addition, AR/VR era may be utilized to broaden simulations that help patients in facing and overcoming their phobias or fears, for instance apprehensions of heights or flying.

The improvement of patient involvement and edification is some other utility for AR/VR generation. Virtual worlds may be used to interactively and engagingly recommend sufferers regarding their scientific circumstance or treatment plan. Patients who've trouble comprehending complex medical data or who are not gifted within the language of their healthcare provider may also find this to be of unique benefit.

Finally, patients who live in faraway or impoverished areas may additionally recognize it as pretty useful to employ far off healthcare reports made viable by AR/VR technology. Virtual reality may be used to create immersive telemedicine stories that provide patients a connection to medical experts that can simulate that of being there in person. This may be especially useful for the afflicted who have mobility issues, or who're not able to tour to a healthcare facility.

In end, the health and wellbeing zone within the metaverse environment has the ability to go through a revolution thanks to AR/VR technologies. These equipment can be deployed to develop practical simulations, lessen discomfort and tension in sufferers, enhance patient participation and understanding, and broaden remote healthcare reports. These technologies have the capacity to improve affected person effects and lift the excellence of care completely as they expand and grow to be extra sophisticated.

CHALLENGES AND FUTURE DIRECTIONS

There are some challenges that should be triumphed over earlier than AR/VR technology are extensively followed in a variety of corporations, regardless of the many capability advantages of these technologies within the metaverse surroundings. The following are a number of the main problems and capability instructions for AR and VR within the metaverse habitat:

Technical restrictions: The technological limits of AR/VR technology are one in all their key obstacles. Particularly, problems with decision, latency, and discipline of view can sabotage the usefulness of digital experiences with the aid of making them feel artificial. However, it's widely predicted that these technical obstacles may be removed as technology develops, allowing more engaging and useful virtual reports.

Accessibility: The accessibility of AR/VR technologies presents another issue. Many AR/VR technologies are currently out of reach for many human beings and organizations due to the fact they require high priced hardware or specialized equipment. But as they improve and become inexpensive, these technologies can be availed by a wide variety of consumers.

Privacy and Security: The metaverse environment increases privateness and security problems, as with any futuristic advancement. The utilization of AR/VR technology particularly raises apprehensions regarding statistics amassing and ownership (Di Pietro & Cresci, 2021), in addition to the opportunity of cyberattacks and hacking. To ease these concerns, it will be important for builders to place privateness and safety first when constructing and enforcing AR/VR generation.

Content Creation: It may be difficult to supply tremendous content for AR/VR technology, mainly for organizations which might be just getting commenced with them. AR/VR stories ought to be created with a thorough hold of consumer needs and alternatives in addition to the technical skills of the supporting hardware and software program with a purpose to achieve success. As an end result, it's workable that sparkling establishments specializing in the improvement of AR/VR content material will sprout up.

Ethical Considerations: The ethical ramifications of AR/VR technology will need to be taken under consideration as these technologies spread. The ability for addiction, desensitization, and social isolation that might result from excessive usage of virtual environments is of unique concern. It can be crucial for builders to not forget the effect of AR/VR technology on customers' bodily, mental, and social properly-being on the way to allay these worries.

The future of AR/VR technology within the metaverse surroundings is promising regardless of those problems. These technologies have the capability to revolutionize a number of industries, from health-care and schooling to enjoyment and gaming, as they broaden and become extra superior. However, it'll be critical for builders to present user demands, privateness, safety, and moral problems with pinnacle precedence whilst designing and implementing AR/VR reviews with a view to fully recognise the capacity of those technologies. As they come to be extra generally on hand and used, these breakthroughs will virtually have a sizable impact on how we stay, work, and have interaction with each other within the metaverse and beyond.

USES OF METAVERSE IN CONTEMPORARY WORLD

Although the word "metavers" has been in the picture since the 1990s, current breakthroughs in virtual and augmented truth technologies have introduced it to new attention and significance. The time period "metaverse" is used to explain a very immersive virtual realms this is related to the physical environment via more than a few equipment and interfaces.

There are many approaches the idea of the metaverse is applied nowadays, in particular in the fields of gaming, social networking, and digital reality studies, even though it is nevertheless by and large limited to technological know-how fiction and speculation.

The most obvious and well-known use case for the metaverse is probably gaming. Users can construct and customize avatars, connect with different players, and discover massive virtual worlds in online multiplayer video games like World of Warcraft, Fortnite, and Second Life.

Social media is one of the metaverse's key use instances. Users can already have interaction with each other through avatars, stickers, and filters on social media platforms like Facebook, Snapchat, and Instagram. We can also expect to see even greater superior social media reviews that enable users to speak with every different in absolutely immersive and interactive digital worlds as virtual fact generation advances.

The metaverse is being utilized for a huge range of other purposes outdoor gaming and social networking, together with digital purchasing, education, and teleconferencing. For instance, organizations are developing digital stores that permit clients to browse and purchase things in a totally immersive set up. Students can take part in lectures and speak with lecturers and classmates, certainly due to the development of digital school rooms. Additionally, because of the COVID-19 epidemic, technology for digital teleconferencing, like Zoom and Microsoft Teams, have grown in importance as a method of connecting individuals at some stage in a length of social isolation.

In well known, the metaverse is a hastily developing concept that is but in its infancy. While the metaverse already has a number of charming and current packages, we can also count on seeing even greater authentic and extensive applications emerge within the future years as the generation underlying it advances.

NFTs AND METAVERSE

Non-fungible tokens (NFTs) are virtual assets saved on a blockchain that act rather for a particular object or piece of content, this sort of artwork, a chunk of music, or a film. NFTs have gained popularity as a manner for creators to monetize their virtual creations in latest years, and they're now starting to infiltrate the metaverse (Di Pietro & Cresci, 2021).

NFTs are used to symbolize digital assets, that is one way they integrate into the metaverse. Players might also purchase and gather virtual goods consisting of clothes, weaponry, and homes in digital worlds. These matters frequently have a connection to a particular recreation or platform and are vain someplace else.

Nevertheless, with the aid of presenting these items as NFTs, game enthusiasts can now own a special, verifiable asset with monetary worth outside of the virtual universe. This creates new chances for each game enthusiasts and artists to make cash off of their digital items.

NFTs can also function as a method of representing land ownership in the metaverse. Players should purchase and own virtual land in digital worlds, which they can later develop and monetize. Players can acquire a special piece of digital assets with real worth out of doors of the digital international through expressing this virtual land as an NFT. As an end result, there are more opportunities for manufacturers and players to benefit from their virtual creations. Unique virtual stories can also be represented using NFTs. A virtual live performance or occasion, as an instance, may be represented as an NFT, giving the owner access to the occasion and a unique object of digital memorabilia. As an end result, there at the moment are greater ways for both producers and fanatics to profit from their virtual reports. Finally, ownership of virtual identities can be represented through NFTs (Vidal-Tomás, 2022).

Players may also layout and personalize their avatars, which act as their virtual identities inside the metaverse. Players can possess a unique, verifiable asset that symbolizes their digital self by reflecting their identity as an NFT. Both the improvement of recent virtual identity systems and the commercialization of individuals' on-line presence are now made possible. NFTs offer a fresh method for representing and creating wealth from virtual goods, stories, and identities within the metaverse. As the metaverse grows and evolves, we should expect new extraordinarily bizarre NFT programs that push the boundaries of what is viable inside the virtual global.

METAVERSE COMPANIES

The metaverse is a young zone that has attracted a great deal of engrossment and investment recently. The following organizations are engaged within the metaverse marketplace:

Roblox: On the web gaming platform called Roblox, customers may also create and play video games in a digital environment. The website online now has over 150 million active customers and is well-favored by younger gamers.

Epic Games: Epic Games is the maker of the Unreal Engine, a nicely-liked gaming engine that is hired to produce stunning visuals and engrossing gameplay in video games. Fortnite, a highly successful video game that has prompted lifestyle, was advanced by this commercial enterprise.

Decentraland: A decentralized digital environment named Decentraland was built on the Ethereum blockchain. Users of the platform can also buy and build virtual land, produce and sell content material, and interact in absolutely immersive user interactions.

High Fidelity: A software referred to as High Fidelity allows customers to create and take part in social VR reviews.

Somnium Space is a decentralized virtual global that was sculpted deploying the Ethereum blockchain. The platform allows customers to buy and develop digital land, create, and monetize content, and interact with other customers in completely certain surroundings. One of the maximum installed virtual worlds is Second Life, which was added in 2003. Users of the platform can also design their personal avatars, buy and assemble digital property, and interact in absolutely immersive user interactions.

Facebook: With intentions to build a very immersive virtual sphere that may be accessed via its many systems, which include Oculus VR and Messenger, Facebook is making tremendous investments in the metaverse. The company is trying to broaden new systems for users to communicate and engage with one another in a virtual environment as it views the metaverse as a brand new frontier for social media.

These are just a handful of the corporations that are engaged in the metaverse industry. As the market continues to develop and evolve, we might also count on the creation of new organizations and systems that push the boundaries of what is feasible within the digital arena.

FULL-FLEDGED METAVERSE ARRIVAL PREDICTION

Since the infrastructure and technology required to maintain this type of giant and complex digital surroundings are nevertheless being constructed, it's arduous to mention decisively that when a fully whole metaverse will be forged. A metaverse is, although, predicted to come into limelight within the near future, in keeping with some of variables:

First off, it is now feasible to construct more immersive and sensible digital reviews thanks to trends in haptic feedback technology and digital reality. The concept of a fully advanced metaverse that is equal to the real world is becoming increasingly more possible as this technology advances.

Second, new avenues for getting, promoting, and owning virtual property are being spread out by way of the improvement of the blockchain era and non-fungible tokens (NFTs). The potential to own and trade digital items is a critical aspect of a metaverse, making this a full-size step closer to its development.

Thirdly, huge laptop organizations are spending a lot of money generating virtual and augmented truth, which is anticipated to be a critical step within the advent of a metaverse. These organizations include Microsoft, Google, and Facebook. These groups are already growing gear and systems that permit customers to construct and proportion virtual worlds, and it is probable that their development will speed up in the upcoming years.

The COVID-19 epidemic has also introduced attention to the blessings of distant and digital reports, which may additionally spur further interest and funding for the creation of a metaverse. The attractiveness of a completely realized metaverse grows increasingly apparent as people are looking for new approaches to have interaction and engage with others in the virtual realm.

While it's laborious to forecast with conviction that when a totally developed metaverse will materialize, it is apparent that the infrastructure and era required to preserve this type of sphere are growing quickly. We can be closer than ever to the established order of a completely realized metaverse as extra agencies and people invest inside the manufacturing of digital reports and the specified infrastructure.

IMPACT OF METAVERSE ON THE FUTURE

Many areas of our future, including how we exert, learn, play, and engage with others, might be impacted with the aid of the metaverse. Here are some forthcoming implications of the metaverse:

- Work: By promoting remote collaboration and creating new possibilities for virtual workspaces, the metaverse can also remodel the way we labor. Businesses may organize digital conferences, schooling classes, and even complete conferences employing the metaverse, doing away with the requirement for commercial enterprise tour and fostering new forms of conversation and collaboration.
- Education: By delivering immersive and engrossing educational experiences, the metaverse has the capability to revolutionize the way we learn. Teachers may design on-line learning environments that allow students to explore and engage with the content they may be gaining knowledge of in fresh and interesting approaches.
- Entertainment: By establishing new possibilities for immersive and interactive stories, the metaverse has the potential to completely remodel the enjoyment quarter. People can be capable of engaging with their favored performers and entertainers in novel and thrilling ways through virtual concerts, films, and other activities.
- Socializing: By presenting new options for socializing and connection, the metaverse may additionally modify the manner we have interaction with others. People may have interaction with people in manners which are now impractical inside the actual world through attending digital occasions, exploring digital environments, and attending digital parties.
- Economy: By permitting users to buy, sell, and alternate digital belongings, the metaverse can also open up new financial opportunities. This may include digital property with real-international value like in-game goods, digital real property, and others ().
- Environment: The metaverse can also have a wonderful environmental impact through lowering corporal tours and enhancing digital stories. This may want to assist in lowering carbon emissions and decreasing the outcomes of climatic reform.

The metaverse has the potential to open up sparkling avenues for conversation, teamwork, and creative expression whilst additionally providing fresh answers to some of the issues we come across within the actual world. The metaverse's subsequent development continues to be quiet in question, however it's apparent that this current technology has the capability to have a significant effect on it.

BUSINESS PREPARATION FOR THE METAVERSE

Businesses of all types will need to adjust as the metaverse develops and expands in order to remain relevant and competitive. Here are a few ways companies may get ready for the metaverse:

- Knowing the generation is important for companies. Blockchain, augmented fact, digital reality, and other technology that underpin the metaverse must all be updated.
- Try Out Virtual Studies: Businesses can also engage in experimenting with virtual stories to analyze more about what capabilities conduct nicely within the metaverse and what doesn't. This can

entail protecting online gatherings, putting in place online businesses, or using augmented reality to enhance the customer's enjoyment.

- Invest in Talent: Organizations that wish to compete inside the metaverse ought to hire or train employees with expertise in blockchain, digital and augmented reality, and other contemporary technology. This will assure that they own the abilities and statistics necessary to provide unique and compelling virtual reviews.
- Think Regarding Statistics and Privacy: A s with any new advancement, firms have to consider how they may gather, keep, and use information in the metaverse. They ought to additionally consider customer privacy concerns and try to use data in a transparent and moral way.
- Create a Metaverse Method: Finally, businesses need to develop a metaverse strategy that describes their goals and top priorities for interacting with the metaverse. This should entail determining prospective use cases, defining spending limits, and forming alliances with different companies and businesses.

Overall, staying educated and being open to trying new things are essential to become ready for the metaverse. Businesses may put themselves in a position to take advantage of possibilities by understanding technology and investing in personnel.

METAVERSE PROS AND CONS, CHALLENGES

A fascinating and unexpectedly evolving era, the metaverse has the potential to basically change an amazing deal of our everyday lives. As with each freshly created technology, there are pros and cons, in addition to some demanding situations that have to be triumphed over (Xu, 2022). Here are a number of the principle blessings, drawbacks, and difficulties of the metaverse:

Pros:

- New Possibilities for Interplay: The metaverse has the energy to provide new opportunities for human beings to engage and have interaction with one another, regardless of where they are physically located.
- Accessibility: People who're unable to have interaction in real locations due to any incapability or for other reasons can also locate new possibilities inside the metaverse.
- Enhanced Creativity: People may additionally explore and experiment with new virtual environments and can get involved in the metaverse, which opens up new possibilities for creative expression and invention.
- Increased Productivity: The metaverse should make it viable for brand new types of remote jobs and cooperation, which might enhance output and effectiveness.

Cons:

- Addiction Threat: Users of the metaverse might, like every other person who uses technology, get addicted and spend immoderate quantities of time in digital worlds at the detriment of their physical health and well-being.

- Potential for Social Isolation: Although the metaverse can open up new doorways for interplay, it might also make humans perceive more alienation.
- Data Protection and Privacy Concerns: As with any technology, there may be dangers related to those issues in the metaverse.

Challenges:

- Interoperability: The metaverse is made of a wide variety of virtual worlds and reports, some of which may not be capable of interacting with one another. This should make it hard for users to navigate the metaverse's many regions.
- Standardization: To assure interoperability and promote creativity, as the metaverse develops, it could be important to standardize technology, systems, and protocols.
- Infrastructure: A big quantity of infrastructure, inclusive of speedy net connections, processing electricity, and garage area, can be required for the metaverse. Cost and availability troubles could get up as an end result.
- Regulation: As the metaverse expands, policies may be required to deal with concerns like information privacy, protection, and accessibility.

Overall, the metaverse has the potential to be highly beneficial, but it also presents important problems that need to be solved if it is to be a technology that is secure, inclusive, and available to everyone.

BENEFITS OF BUYING LAND WITHIN THE METAVERSE

Purchasing digital land in the metaverse can have a number of advantages, especially as technology advances and undergoes modifications. Some of the main benefits of purchasing land inside the metaverse are as follows:

- Investment Potential: Virtual land inside the metaverse is probably viewed as a funding possibility, much like traditional real estate. The cost of digital actual estate is projected to rise as the metaverse expands and gains popularity, supplying profits to buyers. Virtual land offers a clean canvas for innovative expression, permitting customers to assemble and design one-of-a-type virtual places that show off their personalities, pastimes, and sense of favor. Particularly for people with an interest in layout, architecture, or the humanities, this can be a pleasant and fulfilling creative outlet.
- Social Interaction: Virtual areas may also function as amassing spots for human beings to get to recognize each other and shape communities. Users may also organize events or gatherings, invite guests over, and work together on creative tasks of their virtual spaces.
- Opportunities for Enterprise: Virtual land can be utilized to construct digital galleries, stores, and other establishments. With the upward push of on-line purchasing and digital experiences because of the worldwide pandemic, this may provide a new channel for marketers and small organization owners to connect with clients.

- Access to Strange Reviews: By making an investment in virtual land in the metaverse, one would possibly accumulate access to rare stories that might now not be viable inside the actual domain. Users can produce digital replicas of exotic locales or innovative environments, as an example, which can be impractical to supply in the real domain.

Overall, buying virtual assets inside the metaverse can offer a variety of blessings, from financial potentialities to social connection and artistic expression. It is likely that the blessings of proudly owning virtual assets will grow with the development of the metaverse.

CONCLUSION

AR/VR technologies have the capability to greatly alter the way we have interaction with different customers of virtual environments and the metaverse atmosphere. These technologies can alternate the manner we research, learn and play in the digital world. They can be utilized in various fields which include training, healthcare, entertainment, and social interplay (Mystakidis, 2022). Although there are still problems to be resolved before these technologies can be widely used, along with technical limitations, accessibility, privacy and safety, content creation and ethical issues, there's no question that AR/VR technology will keep on evolving in the coming years. As this technology advances, higher and greater immersive digital experiences with higher decision, lower latency and more interactivity are in all likelihood on the horizon. More people may have access to these technologies as greater person-friendly and cheaper hardware and software programs are developed, and the emergence of recent sectors focused on the design and introduction of AR/VR content will force innovation and growth. It is crucial to prioritize personal requirements, privateness, protection and moral troubles whilst designing and imposing AR/VR reviews as these technologies turn out to be extensively adopted. It fosters innovation and improvement in a metaverse surroundings by means of making sure that new technology has a fine impact on the bodily, mental and social well-being of customers.

REFERENCES

Allam, Z., Sharifi, A., Bibri, S. E., Jones, D. S., & Krogstie, J. (2022). The metaverse as a virtual form of smart cities: Opportunities and challenges for environmental, economic, and social sustainability in urban futures. *Smart Cities*, 5(3), 771–801. doi:10.3390martcities5030040

Ardiny, H., & Khanmirza, E. (2018). The role of AR and VR technologies in education developments: opportunities and challenges. In *2018 6th rsi international conference on robotics and mechatronics (icrom)*. IEEE. 10.1109/ICRoM.2018.8657615

Di Pietro, R., & Cresci, S. (2021). Metaverse: security and privacy issues. In *2021 Third IEEE International Conference on Trust, Privacy and Security in Intelligent Systems and Applications (TPS-ISA)*. IEEE.

Filipova, I. A. (2023). Creating the Metaverse: Consequences for Economy, Society, and Law. *Journal of Digital Technologies and Law*, 1(1), 1. doi:10.21202/jdtl.2023.1

Fu, Y. (2021). *A Survey of Possibilities and Challenges with AR/VR/MR and Gamification Usage in Healthcare.* HEALTHINF. doi:10.5220/0010386207330740

Hennig-Thurau, T. (2022). *The Value of Real-time Multisensory Social Interactions in the Virtual-Reality Metaverse: Framework, Empirical Probes, and Research Roadmap.* Academic Press.

Hsieh & Lee. (2018). Preliminary study of VR and AR applications in medical and healthcare education. *J Nurs Health Stud, 3*(1).

Hutson, J. (2023). Architecting the Metaverse: Blockchain and the Financial and Legal Regulatory Challenges of Virtual Real Estate. *Journal of Intelligent Learning Systems and Applications, 15.*

Kraus, S., Kanbach, D. K., Krysta, P. M., Steinhoff, M. M., & Tomini, N. (2022). Facebook and the creation of the metaverse: Radical business model innovation or incremental transformation? *International Journal of Entrepreneurial Behaviour & Research, 28*(9), 52–77. doi:10.1108/IJEBR-12-2021-0984

Mystakidis, S. (2022). Metaverse. *Encyclopedia, 2*(1), 486–497. doi:10.3390/encyclopedia2010031

Ning, H. (2021). *A Survey on Metaverse: the State-of-the-art, Technologies, Applications, and Challenges.* arXiv preprint arXiv:2111.09673

O'Brien & Chan. (2021). *Explainer: What is the metaverse and how will it work?* AP News.

Owens, D., Mitchell, A., Khazanchi, D., & ZIgurs, I. (2011). An empirical investigation of virtual world projects and metaverse technology capabilities. *The Data Base for Advances in Information Systems, 42*(1), 74–101. doi:10.1145/1952712.1952717

Park, M. (2019). A study on the development direction of education and training system based on AR/VR technology. *Journal of the Korea Institute of Military Science and Technology, 22*(4), 545–554.

Sharma, B., Mantri, A., Singh, N. P., Sharma, D., Gupta, D., & Tuli, N. (2022, October). EduSense-AR: A Sensory Learning Solution for Autistic Children. In *2022 10th International Conference on Reliability, Infocom Technologies and Optimization (Trends and Future Directions) (ICRITO)* (pp. 1-4). IEEE. 10.1109/ICRITO56286.2022.9964860

Sharma, B., Singh, N. P., Mantri, A., Gargrish, S., Tuli, N., & Sharma, S. (2021, October). Save the Earth: Teaching Environment Studies using Augmented Reality. In *2021 6th International Conference on Signal Processing, Computing and Control (ISPCC)* (pp. 336-339). IEEE.

Vidal-Tomás, D. (2022). The new crypto niche: NFTs, play-to-earn, and metaverse tokens. *Finance Research Letters, 47*, 102742. doi:10.1016/j.frl.2022.102742

Xu, M. (2022). A full dive into realizing the edge-enabled metaverse: Visions, enabling technologies, and challenges. *IEEE Communications Surveys and Tutorials.*

Yemenici, A. D. (2022). Entrepreneurship in the world of Metaverse: Virtual or real? *Journal of Metaverse, 2*(2), 71–82. doi:10.57019/jmv.1126135

Zvarikova, K., Michalikova, K. F., & Rowland, M. (2022). Retail data measurement tools, cognitive artificial intelligence algorithms, and metaverse live shopping analytics in immersive hyper-connected virtual spaces. *Linguistic and Philosophical Investigations, 21*(0), 9–24. doi:10.22381/lpi2120221

Chapter 7
Augmented Reality Applications and Usage Examples in the Metaverse Age

Hakan Altinpulluk
https://orcid.org/0000-0003-4701-1949
Anadolu University, Turkey

Yusuf Yıldırım
https://orcid.org/0000-0003-4475-4923
Anadolu University, Turkey

ABSTRACT

The aim of this chapter is to identify and introduce the most preferred applications by analyzing augmented reality applications used in master's theses and doctoral dissertations in Turkey. In order to achieve this aim, first of all, the concepts related to the Metaverse, which constituted the conceptual framework of the chapter, were explained by supporting them with the research findings obtained from the literature. Then, the AR development platforms, AR software development kits, AR applications, and the devices on which AR applications were run were examined in thesis studies within the scope of augmented reality accessed from the Council of Higher Education Thesis Archive. At the end of this chapter, Vuforia, ARCore, and Artivive Bridge software development kits are briefly introduced as the first three most frequently used AR software development kits in thesis studies accessed from the National Thesis Center Archive of the Council of Higher Education of Turkey.

INTRODUCTION

In this chapter, augmented reality applications used in master's theses and doctoral dissertations in Turkey were examined, and the programs and software used in the development of augmented reality applications were introduced. In the first part, concepts related to Metaverse (augmented reality, virtual reality, mixed reality, Web 3.0, blockchain, NFT, 5G) were explained by supporting the research findings from the literature.

DOI: 10.4018/978-1-6684-8851-5.ch007

In the second part of the chapter, the method of the research to be carried out in order to realize the purpose of the chapter were given. In the method section, the research model and the methods used in determining the researches included in the study were included. In this section, master's theses and doctoral dissertations carried out within the scope of augmented reality accessed from the Higher Education Council Thesis Archive were examined.

In the third part of the chapter, the findings obtained as a result of the research carrying out, software, programs and mobile tools that develop augmented reality applications used in theses were introduced briefly in tables. Augmented reality applications used in master's theses and doctoral dissertations in Turkey were introduced through screenshots.

In the conclusion part of the chapter, augmented reality technologies, one of the three-dimensional technology components of the Metaverse concept with the research results obtained from the master's theses and doctoral dissertations were briefly mentioned.

CONCEPTS ASSOCIATED WITH THE METAVERSE ECOSYSTEM

In the 21st century, with the increase in mobile technology ownership and the intensive use of web technologies internationally for communication purposes, individuals started to use digital environments to communicate. With the COVID-19 pandemic, interest in digital environments increased, it was seen that digital environments are a great necessity, and the effects of digital transformation began to be felt in social life. Digital transformation has facilitated the adoption of virtual environments in individual and community life. When virtual environments are used for educational purposes, they are transformed into virtual learning environments. Virtual learning environments are computer-designed environments where learners interact with the instructor, other learners or 3D virtual objects simultaneously through their avatars (Mroz, 2012).

The metaverse is an umbrella concept for the virtual environments that individuals use today for education, health, entertainment, shopping, marketing and communication purposes and can be defined as a fictional virtual reality universe (Yıldırım, 2021). In order to make sense of the metaverse, it is necessary to have knowledge about the concepts and technologies related to the metaverse. In the literature, 3D technologies can be associated with the metaverse. In this section, three-dimensional technologies such as augmented, virtual and mixed reality, blockchain, NFT, 5G and Web 3.0 technologies were mentioned.

Three Dimensional (3D) Technologies

As a result of the enrichment and widespread use of 3D technologies over time, the reduction of necessary hardware and software costs, and the increase in access to mobile technologies, the number of applications that will run 3D technologies and users who will use these technologies has increased (Broll et al., 2008). In this section, augmented reality (AR), virtual reality (VR) and mixed reality (MR) technologies as 3D technologies were mentioned in the following headings, supported by the findings obtained from the literature.

Augmented Reality (AR)

Augmented reality (AR) technology, which is one of the 3D technologies (Küçük-Avcı, 2018), is defined by Azuma (1997) as the technology that enables the display of computer-generated virtual objects on the real world environment; Azuma et al. (2001) as the technology that enables the display of real and virtual objects simultaneously and in the real world environment by enriching the real environment with computer-generated virtual objects; Yuen, Yaoyuneyong, and Johnson (2011) as the technology that enables the enrichment of the real world environment with computer-generated objects through special actions. When the definitions are examined, AR enriches the real environment with computer-generated 3D virtual objects, enabling real and virtual images to be displayed simultaneously in the real environment, and enabling interaction with virtual objects by communicating with virtual data in the real environment. Therefore, AR means the perception of reality by individuals in the real environment by augmenting it with visual, auditory or tactile (haptic) stimuli produced in the computer environment (Lamata et al., 2010). When the definitions of AR in the literature are examined, augmented reality can be redefined as a technology that combines reality and virtuality by adding 3D virtual objects to the real environment and allows simultaneous interaction with virtual 3D objects.

As AR technologies, mobile devices such as smartphones and tablets, wearable technologies such as smart glasses, smart wristbands, smart watches, GPS, camera, digital compass, and internet are used extensively in AR applications (Altınpulluk, 2018; Pence, 2010). AR applications, on the other hand, are defined as 3D technology applications that enable individuals to enrich activities in which they can exhibit affective, psychomotor and cognitive behaviors by combining and blending real and virtual images (Hugues, Fuchs, & Nannipieri, 2011). Examples of the widespread use of AR applications include the enrichment of photographs with virtual animations and objects through applications installed on smartphones, in-service training applications prepared by multinational companies for the professional development of their employees, and many applications applied in the fields of education, art, clothing, make-up, production and marketing.

There are research findings that the use of AR applications in educational environments provides benefits in academic achievement (Akın, 2022; Gökçe, 2022) and skill development (Avcı, 2022), permanent learning (Onur, 2021), and increasing motivation (Çiloğlu, 2022). Based on these findings obtained from the literature, since augmented reality technologies have many positive benefits on learning, it can be ensured to conduct survey and experimental research on the use of augmented reality technologies in distance education environments, and to integrate augmented reality technologies into distance learning environments by developing policies related to distance education according to the research results.

Virtual Reality (VR)

The term virtual reality (VR), which was first used by Jaron Lanier in 1989 (Oppenheim, 1993), is defined as a 3D technology that allows people to interact with computer-generated three-dimensional objects as well as giving the feeling of being in a virtual environment that is not real in their minds by using head mounted displays, wearable technologies, glasses surrounding the eyes or smart contact lenses (Altınpulluk et al., 2021). In another definition, VR is defined as a 3D technology that enables individuals to establish rich interactions with computer-generated three-dimensional objects (Ryan, 2015), where reality is experienced by replacing reality with fictional virtual environments and objects that are not completely real (Altınpulluk, 2018).

As VR technologies, wearable technologies such as HTC Vive, Meta Quest smart glasses, special gloves, hand touch controllers are widely used in VR applications. Examples of the widespread use of VR applications include virtual reality tours, virtual museum visits, VR games, and many other applications in education, health, art, production and marketing.

In the literature, the advantages offered by VR technologies are reported as providing experiences close to real life without jeopardizing human health in a virtual environment (Şimşek & Can, 2019) and giving individuals the feeling of telepresence (being in a real environment) (Altınpulluk et al., 2021). As an example of the benefits provided by VR technologies in the field of education, Altınpulluk et al. (2021) compiled findings from the literature, according to the findings of Altınpulluk et al. (2021), while VR technologies facilitate learning, they enable students to be active, facilitate the transfer of learning to real life by supporting learning by doing and experiencing, and increase students' creativity and interest thanks to the fun environments they offer. Çoruh (2011) stated that the VR technologies support distance education by enabling instructors and learners, who are physically distant, to interact and communicate in a virtual environment.

According to the findings obtained from the literature, since VR technologies support distance education, provide tele-presence to distance learners and have many positive benefits on learning, it can be ensured that survey and experimental researches are conducted on the use of VR technologies in distance education environments, and according to the research results, policies related to distance education are developed and integrated into distance learning environments.

Mixed Reality (MR)

Milgram and Kishino (1994) defined mixed reality (MR) as the broadest cluster encompassing AR and VR environments. MR can be expressed as an umbrella concept that encompasses the concepts of AR and VR. Therefore, mixed reality can be defined as the continuum of reality and virtuality, encompassing all AR and VR technologies from real to virtual environments.

The MR-supported smart glasses called HoloLens with hologram technology produced by Microsoft is one of the examples of the use of mixed reality technologies that offer MR environment by covering augmented and virtual reality (Microsoft, 2017). One of the examples where mixed reality technologies are used is Mat Collishaw's Thresholds exhibition held in Istanbul in 2018.

Blockchain

The blockchain technology, which was first used in the literature in the article "Bitcoin: A Peer-to-Peer Electronic Cash System" to realize online payments without intermediary institutions (Nakamoto, 2008), has been accepted as the fifth disruptive technology in the field of technology today (Wu & Tran, 2018). Blockchain is defined as a database consisting of decentralized ledgers thanks to its distributed data structure, where data is stored in a single block, which cannot be changed or lost (Anascavage & Davis, 2018). Blockchain technology works on the principle that digital data is permanently recorded by identifying and copying digital data in blocks with crypto tags with timestamps in all nodes (nodes) in the blockchain database. The fact that blockchain technology is secure, unalterable and unforfeitable has made it potential for use in many areas such as education, health and entertainment.

Blockchain technology has taken its place in the Horizon Reports published in 2019 as the current technological trends in the field of education (Alexander et al., 2019). In the field of education, blockchain technology can be used in the near future so that individual development reports and student portfolios can be securely stored, recognized and used in all educational institutions in all countries throughout the lifelong education of the individual from kindergarten age; learning records such as diplomas, badges and certificates can be recognized and used securely on all platforms. It also has the potential to be used securely in the near future for the recognition of microcredits obtained through distance education through massively open online courses by all educational institutions or professional institutions in all international platforms by recording them in the blockchain database. With the use of the Metaverse universe as virtual learning environments for educational purposes in the near future, it is foreseen that the badges and microcredits obtained through the trainings carried out through virtual learning environments can also be officially recognized and used by all educational and professional institutions.

NFT

NFT (non fungible token) is a digital data unit that can be stored in blockchain technology and is a concept that expresses the uniqueness and interchangeability of digital assets (Wang et al., 2021). In the Gartner Hype technological progress cycle published in 2022, it is among the critical technologies under the theme of evolving and expanding immersive experiences (Perri, 2022).

In the Gartner Hype technological progress cycle, NFT technology has taken its place among the current technologies that have the potential to be used in many fields such as education, health and entertainment. In the field of education, it is foreseen that NFT technology will be used extensively in virtual learning environments and especially in the metaverse universe as the digital data equivalent of all products of students in the near future, and that NFT products will be recognized and used by all educational and vocational training institutions in the near future as the equivalent of all digitized products of students.

5G

The fifth generation 5G technology used in wireless communication is the next generation of mobile networks (Haas, 2018). 5G technology, which will form the internet and mobile network infrastructure of digital transformation and metaverse environments, is predicted to be used intensively in virtual environments such as the metaverse thanks to its features such as connecting people through their avatars, controlling internet-connected smart devices, objects and machines. By providing high-speed mobile network infrastructure to the metaverse and virtual environments, 5G technologies are planned to find application areas,

- In metaverse environments in the future in critical intervention applications that are vital in the field of health,
- In augmented reality (AR) and virtual reality (VR) applications in entertainment, culture, arts and education,
- In Internet of Things applications such as smart homes, smart cities, smart agriculture and autonomous driving,
- In machine learning and artificial intelligence applications (Dangi et al., 2022).

For these reasons mentioned above, it can be said that 5G technology will be used in virtual learning environments in the metaverse to communicate and interact in real time by processing high-resolution graphic data between learners and objects in the field of education. When machine learning and artificial intelligence technologies are supported by 5G mobile network infrastructure, it can be easily used in realizing instant and uninterrupted interactions of augmented and virtual reality technologies with 3D virtual objects, in designing individualized and adaptive activities and learning processes specific to the learner by processing real-time instant data of learners in distance education environments with learning analytics.

Web 3.0

Web 3.0 can be defined as an internet network technology that will be used for the network infrastructure of metaverse environments with artificial intelligence supported automatic coding system known as semantic web. Web 3.0 provides internet services that utilize AI-supported intelligent search applications, AI-supported advanced mobile software tools, data mining, web analytics, AR, VR and MR applications that provide recommendations on the searched word when a keyword is typed into a search engine (Kapan & Üncel, 2020). Considering that the network infrastructure of Metaverse environments is provided by Web 3.0 technologies, it can be said that Web 3.0 technologies are an important technology for Metaverse environments.

METHOD

The research for this chapter was conducted as a systematic review study of master's thesis and doctoral dissertation studies prepared within the scope of augmented reality accessed in the National Thesis Center of the Council of Higher Education of Turkey.

Including and Excluding Criteria

The inclusion and exclusion criteria for the theses selected for this chapter are shown in Figure 1.

Before conducting the systematic review of master's thesis and doctoral dissertation studies published in the National Thesis Center Archive of the Council of Higher Education of Turkey, 3 criteria were determined to determine which thesis studies would be included in the review. Within the scope of this research, the archive of the National Thesis Center of the Council of Higher Education of Turkey was used as a data collection tool. As the keyword to be scanned in this archive, the theses containing "Augmented Reality" in the title were listed. The last 5-year period was selected as the time interval and theses between 2018 and 2022 were targeted. At the time of scanning, the year 2023 was not included in the research as it had not yet been completed. Among the 282 theses that met the above criteria, 207 theses that were approved for open access were filtered and 173 theses prepared in Turkish among 207 theses were included in the document review in the research.

Within the scope of the research, the AR development platforms, AR software development kits, AR applications and the devices on which the AR applications were run were examined in 173 theses. These examinations are given under the following headings.

Figure 1. Including and excluding criteria

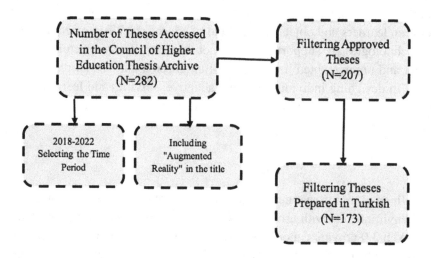

FINDINGS

AR Development Platforms Used in the Theses

In the research we conducted in the National Thesis Center Archive of the Council of Higher Education of Turkey, it was determined that Unity was used in 61 theses, Blender 3D in 4 theses, Sketchfab in 3 theses, SketchUP in 3 theses and 3ds Max in 3 theses as AR development platforms in master's theses and doctoral dissertations prepared in Turkey.

Table 1. AR development platforms used in the theses

AR Development Platforms	*f*	%
Unity	61	82,5
Blender 3D	4	5,5
Sketchfab	3	4
SketchUP	3	4
3ds Max	3	4
Total	**74**	**100**

AR Software Development Kits (SDK) Used in Theses

In the literature, tools that can be used as AR software development kits are ARCore, ARKit, Artivive, ARToolKit, Augment, LayAR (BlippAR), WikitTude, Vuforia and Kudan AR (Türksoy, 2019; Ulusoy, 2022). In the research conducted in the National Thesis Center Archive of the Council of Higher Education in Turkey, it was determined that Vuforia Engine was used in 45 theses, ARCore in 8 theses,

Artivive in 3 theses, ARKit in 1 thesis, ARToolKit in 1 thesis, and WikiTude in 1 thesis as AR software development kits in master's theses and doctoral dissertations prepared in Turkey.

Table 2. AR software development kits (SDK) used in theses

AR Software Development Kits (SDK)	f	%
Vuforia	45	76,2
ARCore	8	13,6
Artivive	3	5,1
ARKit	1	1,7
ARToolKit	1	1,7
WikiTude	1	1,7
Total	**59**	**100**

AR Applications Used in Theses

In the research conducted in the National Thesis Center Archive of the Council of Higher Education in Turkey, the AR applications used in master's theses and doctoral dissertations prepared in Turkey were HP Reveal in 18 theses, Space4D in 10 theses, Our Body 4D in 6 theses, Quiver Vision in 4 theses, Anotomy 4D in 4 theses, and Cell AR application in 2 theses. Other applications used in theses are shown in Table 3.

Devices on Which AR Applications Are Run in Theses

In the literature, the devices on which AR applications are run are Epson AR glasses, Google Glass, Contact Lens, Meta, Microsoft HoloLens MR glasses, mobile device (smartphone, tablet), projection, Sony Smart Eyeglass AR glasses and Vuzix AR glasses (Ulusoy, 2022). In the research conducted in the National Thesis Center Archive of the Council of Higher Education in Turkey, it was determined that 119 theses used mobile devices, 2 theses used Microsoft HoloLens MR glasses and 2 theses used Sony Smart Eyeglass AR glasses as the devices used in the master's theses and doctoral dissertations in Turkey.

Learning Benefits of AR Applications Used in Theses

In the research conducted in the National Thesis Center Archive of the Council of Higher Education of Turkey, it was found that the AR applications used in master's theses and doctoral dissertations in Turkey were beneficial in increasing academic achievement, improving attitudes, increasing motivation, increasing learning retention, developing spatial skills, reducing cognitive load, increasing satisfaction levels, increasing self-efficacy, language and concept development, developing self-confidence, developing 21st century skills and increasing course participation.

Table 3. AR applications used in theses

AR Applications	f	%
HP Reveal (Aurasma)	18	26
Space 4D	10	14,4
Our Body 4D	6	8,6
Quiver Vision (ColAR Mix)	4	5,7
Anatomy 4D	4	5,7
Cell AR	2	2,8
AR Bilim	1	1,5
AR-Flute	1	1,5
AR Foundation	1	1,5
Atoms Revealed AR	1	1,5
ATPAG	1	1,5
Bilim 4d	1	1,5
Chemistry AR	1	1,5
Cinema 4D	1	1,5
EfesAR	1	1,5
Elements 4D	1	1,5
Fotosentez AG	1	1,5
Geogebra 3D Hesap Makinası	1	1,5
Human Anatomy 4D	1	1,5
KemosentezAG	1	1,5
Metaverse Studio	1	1,5
Mapbox Studio	1	1,5
MoleculAR Experience	1	1,5
Moverio AR SDK	1	1,5
Solar System 3D	1	1,5
Space Craft 4D	1	1,5
SpatioAR	1	1,5
StudioART Tool	1	1,5
UzayAG	1	1,5
Zappar	1	1,5
3D Sınıfı	1	1,5
Total	**69**	**100**

Table 4. Devices on which AR applications are run in theses

Devices Running AR Applications	f	%
Mobile Device (smartphone, tablet)	119	96,8
Microsoft HoloLens	2	1,6
Sony SmartEyeglass SED-E1	2	1,6
Total	**123**	**100**

Table 5. Learning benefits of AR applications used in theses

Learning Benefits of AR Applications Used in Theses	f	%
Increasing academic achievement	45	41,6
Improving attitudes	23	21,3
Increasing motivation	15	13,9
Increasing the retention of learning	8	7,4
Developing spatial skills	5	4,6
Reducing cognitive load	3	2,7
Increasing satisfaction levels	2	1,8
Increasing self-efficacy	2	1,8
Language and concept development	2	1,8
Developing self-confidence	1	1
Developing 21st century skills	1	1
Increasing class participation	1	1
Total	**108**	**100**

AR SOFTWARE DEVELOPMENT KITS

When it is aimed to develop a product in researches in the fields of education, science and social sciences, it is seen that design-based research, in which a new application is produced by researchers, designers and practitioners, is used as a method (Fırat, 2022). The product to be developed in design-based research goes through cyclical processes consisting of design-application-analysis-redesign. Another method used to develop products or projects in research is the agile project development method, which was used by a group of 17 engineers led by Kent Beck in 2001 to define better software development methods. The application to be developed with agile project development method goes through analysis, design, production, testing and maintenance processes (Akbayır, 2010). While developing an augmented reality (AR) application, researchers, practitioners and designers develop their products by going through a similar product development process. AR application development stages consist of content and scope determination, development of the application, testing the developed application, evaluating the test results and noting the feedback, and finally, improvement and development studies for the AR application (Emreli, 2019; Ulusoy, 2022).

When the master's and doctoral thesis studies in the National Thesis Center Archive of the Council of Higher Education of Turkey were examined, it was found that the following strategies were frequently followed by researchers and practitioners in order to produce an AR application. First of all, the necessary hardware and software must be procured to create a virtual object that can be transferred to the real environment to be used in the AR application. Which software or which hardware is preferred is a matter for the application developer to decide.

In the research conducted in the National Thesis Center Archive of the Council of Higher Education of Turkey, it was determined that in 119 thesis studies, mobile devices (smartphones, tablets...) that have the potential to be owned by everyone in terms of accessibility, can be carried, cost less, and can work compatible with augmented reality application development kits were preferred by the researchers. In 2 thesis studies, Microsoft HoloLens and in 2 thesis studies Sony Smart Eyeglass AR glasses were used.

In the research conducted in the National Thesis Center Archive of the Council of Higher Education of Turkey, it was determined that 3D virtual objects were developed through Blender 3D software in 4 thesis studies, 3ds Max software in 3 thesis studies, and in other theses, 3D ready-made virtual objects were used. When the software development kits used to provide users with augmented reality experience with 3D virtual objects on the screens of mobile devices were examined, it was determined that Vuforia Engine, which offers an augmented reality platform in 45 thesis studies, Google ARCore in 8 thesis studies, and Artivive in 3 thesis studies, provided 3D virtual objects with augmented reality features, and mobile applications that can run on mobile devices were developed with software used as AR development platforms such as Unity, Android Studio, XCode and Visual Studio, which are used to develop mobile applications.

After deciding on the hardware and software to be used by the implementers to produce an AR application, another situation to be decided is to decide on a tracking method that can control the user's position. With the tracking method to be used, the relationship between the changes in the user's position and the 3D virtual object can be maintained without interruption. In order for the user to experience a sense of reality in the interaction with the 3D virtual object, the position of the 3D virtual object marker should be taken as a reference. In this way, as the user moves in the real environment while using the application, it will enable the 3D virtual object to react by adapting to this positional change and the user to experience augmented reality. Finally, in order to provide users with a real augmented reality experience, users should be able to interact with 3D virtual objects and the control of 3D virtual objects should be given to the user.

In the research conducted in the National Thesis Center Archive of the Council of Higher Education of Turkey, when the AR software development kits used to provide users with augmented reality experience with 3D virtual objects on the screens of mobile devices were examined, it was determined that Vuforia Engine, which offers an augmented reality platform in 45 thesis studies, Google ARCore in

8 thesis studies, and Artivive software development kits in 3 thesis studies provided 3D virtual objects with augmented reality features.

In the literature, the most preferred kits for AR software development can be listed as ARCore, ARKit, Artivive, ARToolKit, Augment, LayAR (BlippAR), WikitTude, Vuforia and Kudan AR (Türksoy, 2019; Ulusoy, 2022). Below, the first three AR software development kits that were frequently used in 173 thesis studies accessed from the National Thesis Center Archive of the Council of Higher Education of Turkey will be briefly introduced in order of preference.

Vuforia

Vuforia is an AR software development kit developed for mobile environments that can be easily added to the Unity game engine. With Unity Vuforia integration, AR applications can be created for Android or IOS mobile platforms. In the research we conducted in the National Thesis Center Archive of the Council of Higher Education of Turkey, we determined that the Unity platform, which is frequently used to develop mobile applications, was used in AR application development research using Vuforia. Vuforia has 4 tools for 4 different purposes: Vuforia Chalk, Vuforia Studio, Vuforia Expert Capture and Vuforia Engine.

Vuforia Chalk can be defined as AR technology superimposed on video chat technology. It is mostly used in industrial environments where experts and employees are in different environments to provide interactive support to employees with AR technologies on the job through the expert.

In the field of education, in distance learning environments, a Chalk call between the instructor and the learner can be used to get support on the subject matter in practical trainings, and the distance learner can be used to get simultaneous guidance from the instructor on the application. During the call, Vuforia Chalk can also record the screenshots of the application and provide the learner with an asynchronous repetition and reinforcement while working on the subject again.

Vuforia Expert Capture is used to prepare a training content through markers and video content, respectively, related to the work and operations related to the work to be performed by the employee with expert wearable AR glasses in the training processes of new employees in industrial environments such as Vuforia Chalk. The prepared content is processed through the Vuforia Editor and the application to be used by the new employee is developed. The new personnel learns the work and operations related to the work they will do through wearable AR glasses or mobile smartphones or tablet devices on the job.

In the field of education, content prepared through Vuforia Expert Capture can be used in distance learning environments, on-the-job in-service training for distance learners or applied vocational training. Distance learners can realize their practical trainings through this application via their AR glasses or mobile devices.

Vuforia Studio can be used in production, service, sales and marketing. The AR application developed through Vuforia Studio can be used to familiarize and train employees with an industrial product and its components, or to introduce a new product to customers in marketing processes. Through Vuforia View, employees or customers can use the application produced through Vuforia Studio on their mobile devices or AR glasses.

In the field of education, in distance learning environments, distance learners can use this application to recognize the product by disassembling it on the screens of their mobile devices, and to provide practical training on how to operate the product gradually and sequentially.

Vuforia Engine is a product that provides an AR experience based on customer or end-user satisfaction and is used for mobile application development. In the research conducted in the National Thesis Center Archive of the Council of Higher Education of Turkey, it was determined that Vuforia Engine was used in the theses.

After registering in the Vuforia Engine portal, creating and downloading a database by uploading target images into the database is explained below in 4 steps in Figure 2, Figure 3, Figure 4, and Figure 5.

Figure 2. License key generation step in the Vuforia Engine development portal

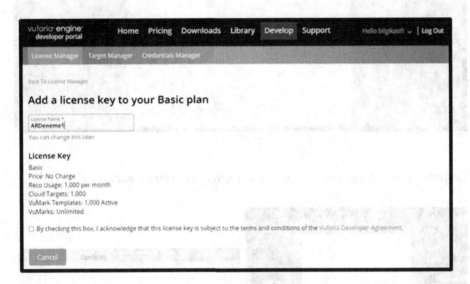

In step 1, a license key is created in the license manager through the Vuforia Engine portal by entering the develop menu on the official website of Vuforia (https://developer.vuforia.com/vui/develop/licenses).

In step 2, by entering the develop menu on the official website of Vuforia (https://developer.vuforia.com/vui/develop/databases), a database named ARDeneme1 is created by clicking the Add Database button in the target manager through the Vuforia Engine portal. In the created file, a pointer is defined for a 3D object named 3D_skeleton for this application with the help of the "add target" button. For other applications, pointers can be defined for different objects on this button.

In the 3rd step, the target setting process is performed to add AR features to our 3D virtual picture. For this application, in this step, the image defined as a marker in the Vuforia Engine portal was downloaded as a package for transfer to Unity and added to the project. For this process, in the "target manager" tab under the "develop" menu, the Download Database (AII) button on the right side of the screen was clicked and the Unity Editor section was selected in the popup screen and the download process was performed.

In the 4th step, through the Vuforia Engine portal, the database created by using our 3D virtual objects using the Licence Manager and Target Manager application steps can be used as a marker in the mobile application development tool. A marker is an object that will be recognized by the camera of the mobile device or the AR goggle that has a physical counterpart. After the marker is recognized by the camera of the mobile device or the AR goggles, the 2D or 3D object defined to this marker is displayed on the user's mobile device screen.

Figure 3. Database creation step in the Vuforia Engine development portal

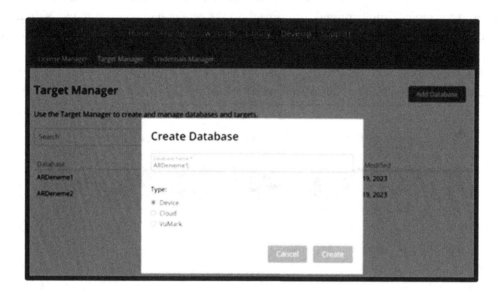

Figure 4. 3D virtual image targeting step in Vuforia Engine development portal

The markers produced through the Vuforia Engine SDK can be developed as mobile applications that can run on mobile devices with software used as AR development platforms such as Unity, Android Studio, XCode and Visual Studio. Figure 6 shows the mobile device screenshots of the mobile application example developed on the Unity platform for a 3D object with AR features in the Vuforia Engine SDK environment.

In distance learning environments in the field of education, it can be ensured that abstract content can be made concrete with 3D objects by providing AR experience through the Vuforia Engine application for distance learners, and for learners who cannot think spatially, it can be ensured that AR technologies can associate learning contents more easily with 3D modeling and permanent learning can be realized.

Figure 5. Step of downloading the database created on the Vuforia Engine development portal

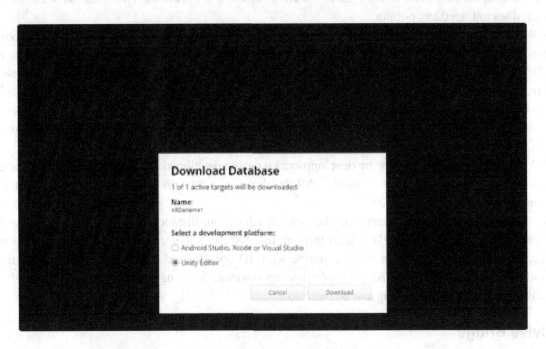

Figure 6. Mobile device screenshots of the AR application sample

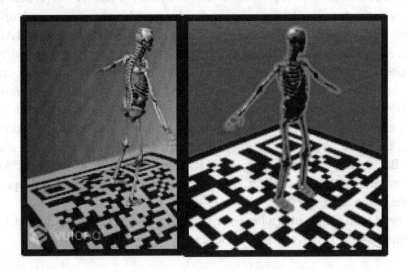

ARCore

ARCore software development kit was released by Google in 2017 as free and open source. When ARCore is run on a mobile device, it scans all the surfaces detected by the mobile device's camera and places a 3D object on a surface area determined by the user as a result of a double click. Unlike the Vuforia software development kit, ARCore uses the movement of the camera in the environment, the flat surfaces in the environment, the light of the environment and the location information of the device. Thus, it does not need any pointer.

ARCore uses motion tracking, surface detection and real-world light detection to place the 3D object on the surface in the real world environment (ARCore, 2023; Papakçı, 2022; Türksoy, 2019; Ulusoy, 2022). Motion tracking enables the mobile phone or tablet to understand and track its actual position relative to the world. Surface detection allows the mobile phone or tablet to detect the size and position of any horizontal, vertical and angled surface, such as a real object (sofa, armchair, table...) or walls seen in its camera. Ambient light detection allows the mobile phone or tablet to estimate the current lighting conditions of the environment (Papakçı, 2022; Türksoy, 2019).

3D objects with ARCore software development kit can be developed as mobile applications that can run on mobile devices with software used as AR development platforms such as Unity, Android Studio, XCode and Unreal (ARCore, 2023).

In distance learning environments in the field of education, distance learners can experience AR experience by interacting with 3D objects through the ARCore software development kit for distance learners, abstract content can be made concrete with 3D objects, and for learners who cannot think spatially, it can be ensured that AR technologies can associate learning contents more easily with 3D modeling and permanent learning can be realized.

Artivive Bridge

Artivive Bridge software development kit was developed by Artivive in 2017 for artists to enrich their products by adding AR features to their products in a digital environment (Artivive, 2023). For AR applications produced with the Artivive Bridge software development kit, there is no need for Unity, Android Studio, XCode and Unreal mobile application development platforms as in Vuforia and ARCore software development kits. Artists share their works through their Artivive accounts. There is no need to develop separate applications for different platforms such as Android and IOS through the Artivive software development kit, and users are provided with common use for all platforms via https://artivive.com. Users only need to download and run the Artivive application on their mobile devices to experience AR.

Artivive Bridge kit is used for museums, exhibitions, galleries and other art institutions to enable audiences to have an AR experience by interacting with artworks on mobile device screens. By clicking on the Go to Bridge link from the Create AR ART tab on the official website of Artivive (https://bridge.artivive.com/editor), the AR application examples shown in Figure 7 can be produced through the interface of the Artivive Bridge portal shown in Figure 6.

Visitors only need to use their smartphones or tablets to experience the augmented reality layer in applications developed with Artivive Bridge in museums, exhibitions or galleries.

CONCLUSION

This chapter aims to analyze the AR applications used in master's theses and doctoral dissertations in Turkey, to identify the most preferred AR applications in theses and to introduce these applications. For this purpose, in the first part of the chapter, 3D technologies (AR, VR, MR, blockchain, NFT, 5G, Web 3.0) that can be associated with the metaverse in the literature are conceptualized by associating them with the environment in which they are used.

Figure 7. Artivive Bridge screenshot

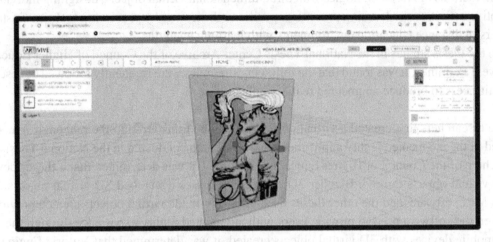

In the master's theses and doctoral dissertations prepared in Turkey, it was found that AR applications used in master's and doctoral dissertations provide benefits in increasing academic achievement, improving attitudes, increasing motivation, increasing retention of learning, developing spatial skills, reducing cognitive load, increasing satisfaction levels, increasing self-efficacy, language and concept development, developing self-confidence, developing 21st century skills, and increasing participation in the stream. Based on these findings obtained from master's theses and doctoral dissertations, since augmented reality technologies have many positive benefits on learning, it can be ensured to conduct survey and experimental research on the use of augmented reality technologies in distance education environments, and to integrate augmented reality technologies into distance learning environments by developing policies related to distance education according to the research results.

In the field of education, blockchain technology can be used in the near future so that individual development reports and student portfolios can be securely stored, recognized and used in all educational institutions in all countries throughout the lifelong education of the individual from kindergarten age; learning records such as diplomas, badges and certificates can be recognized and used securely on all platforms. It also has the potential to be used securely in the near future for the recognition of microcredits obtained through distance education through massively open online courses by all educational institutions or professional institutions in all international platforms by recording them in the blockchain database. With the use of the Metaverse universe as virtual learning environments for educational purposes in the near future, it is foreseen that the badges and microcredits obtained through the trainings carried out through virtual learning environments can also be officially recognized and used by all educational and professional institutions.

In the field of education, it is foreseen that in the near future, NFT technology will be used intensively in virtual learning environments and especially in the metaverse universe as the digital data equivalent of all products of students, and that NFT products will be recognized and used by all educational and vocational training institutions in the near future as the equivalent of all digitized products of students.

In the field of education, it can be said that 5G technology will be used to communicate and interact in real time by processing high-resolution graphic data between learners and objects in the metaverse universe. When Web 3.0 technologies using machine learning and artificial intelligence applications are supported by 5G mobile network infrastructure, it can be easily used in realizing instant and uninterrupted interactions of AR technologies with three-dimensional virtual objects, designing individualized and adaptive activities and learning processes specific to the learner by processing real-time instant data of learners in distance education environments with learning analytics.

When the thesis studies in the National Thesis Center Archive of the Council of Higher Education of Turkey were examined, it was found that the following strategies were frequently followed by researchers and practitioners to produce augmented reality applications.

- The researchers first created a virtual object that can be transferred to the real environment to be used in the augmented reality application. In the research conducted in the National Thesis Center Archive of the Council of Higher Education of Turkey, it was determined that 4 theses developed 3D virtual objects through Blender 3D software, 3 theses developed 3D virtual objects through 3ds Max software, and the other theses used 3D ready-made virtual objects created previously.
- When the software used to provide users with augmented reality experience through the screens of mobile devices with 3D virtual objects created, it was determined that Vuforia Engine, which offers an augmented reality platform in 45 thesis studies, Google ARCore in 8 thesis studies, and Artivive software development kits in 3 thesis studies were used to provide augmented reality features to 3D virtual objects, and mobile applications that can run on mobile devices were developed with software used as AR development platforms such as Unity, Android Studio, XCode and Visual Studio used to develop mobile applications.
- The last decision to be made by researchers and practitioners when creating an augmented reality application is to determine a tracking method that can control the user's location. With the tracking method to be used, the relationship between the changes in the user's position and the 3D virtual object can be maintained without interruption. In order for the user to experience a sense of reality in the interaction with the 3D virtual object, the position of the 3D virtual object marker (marker) should be taken as a reference. In this way, as the user moves in the real environment while using the application, it will enable the 3D virtual object to react by adapting to this positional change and the user to experience augmented reality. Finally, in order to provide users with a real augmented reality experience, users should be able to interact with 3D virtual objects and the control of 3D virtual objects should be given to the user.

Conclusions about Vuforia and ARCore kits as AR software development kits frequently used in master's and doctoral thesis studies in Turkey are given below.

- In the field of education, a Chalk call between the instructor and the learner in distance learning environments can be used in practical trainings to get support on the subject, and the distance learner can be used to get simultaneous guidance from the instructor on the application. During the call, Vuforia Chalk can record the screenshots of the application and provide the learner with an asynchronous repetition and reinforcement opportunity while working on the subject again.
- In the field of education, content prepared through Vuforia Expert Capture can be used in distance learning environments, on-the-job in-service trainings for distance learners or applied vocational trainings. Distance learners can carry out their practical trainings through this application via their AR glasses or mobile devices.
- In distance learning environments in the field of education, it can be ensured that abstract content can be made concrete with 3D objects by providing AR experience through the Vuforia Engine

application for distance learners, and for learners who cannot think spatially, it can be ensured that AR technologies can associate learning contents more easily with 3D modeling and permanent learning can be realized.

- In distance learning environments in the field of education, distance learners can experience AR by interacting with 3D objects through the ARCore software development kit for distance learners, abstract content can be made concrete with 3D objects, 3D modeling for learners who cannot think spatially, and AR technologies can be associated with learning content more easily and permanent learning can be achieved.

REFERENCES

Akbayır, D. (2010). *Implementation and tailoring of agile software development process* (Publication No. 266136) [Master's thesis, Maltepe University]. Higher Education Council Thesis Archive. https://tez.yok.gov.tr

Akın, Ö. (2022). *The effects of activities organized with augmented reality applications on the academic achievement of 4th grade students in mathematics lesson* (Publication No. 714589) [Master's Thesis, Çanakkale Onsekiz Mart University]. Higher Education Council Thesis Archive. https://tez.yok.gov.tr

Alexander, B., Ashford-Rowe, K., Barajas-Murph, N., Dobbin, G., Knott, J., McCormack, M., Pomerantz, J., Seilhamer, R., & Weber, N. (2019). EDUCAUSE Horizon Report: 2019 Higher Education Edition. Louisville, CO: EDUCAUSE 2019.

Altınpulluk, H. (2018). *Açık ve uzaktan öğrenmede evrensel tasarım ilkeleri çerçevesinde artırılmış gerçekliğin kullanılabilirliği* [Usability of augmented reality within the framework of universal design principles in open and distance learning] (Publication No. 531761) [Doctoral Disertation, Anadolu University]. Higher Education Council Thesis Archive. https://tez.yok.gov.tr

Altınpulluk, H., Demirbağ, İ., Ertan, S., Yıldırım, Y., Koçak, A., Yıldız, T., Yıldırım, M., Köse, B. S., Özer Taylan, G., Karagil, S. D., Helvacı Aydın, E., Güven, K., Türktan, O., & Tabak, B. (2021). Examination of postgraduate theses on virtual reality in the field of social sciences in Turkey. *Asian Journal of Distance Education*, 171-193. doi:10.5281/zenodo.4895633

AnascavageR.DavisN. (2018). *Blockchain technology: A literature review*. doi:10.2139/ssrn.3173406

ARCore. (2023). *ARCore overview*. https://developers.google.com/ar

Artivive. (2023). *About artivive*. https://artivive.com/about

Avcı, M. (2022). *The effect of augmented reality application on nursing students' intravenous catheterization application skill, level of satisfaction in learning and perception of self-confidence* (Publication No. 716102) [Doctoral Disertation, İnönü University]. Higher Education Council Thesis Archive. https://tez.yok.gov.tr

Azuma, R. (1997). A survey of augmented reality. *Presence (Cambridge, Mass.), 6*(4), 355–385. doi:10.1162/pres.1997.6.4.355

Azuma, R., Baillot, Y., Behringer, R., Feiner, S., Julier, S., & MacIntyre, B. (2001). Recent advances in augmented reality. *IEEE Computer Graphics and Applications, 21*(6), 34–47. doi:10.1109/38.963459

Broll, W., Lindt, I., Herbst, I., Ohlenburg, J., Braun, A. K., & Wetzel, R. (2008). Toward next-gen mobile AR games. *IEEE Computer Graphics and Applications, 28*(4), 40–48. doi:10.1109/MCG.2008.85

Çiloğlu, T. (2022). *Augmented reality based learning environment: Effects of augmented reality on high school students' motivation, attitude and self-efficacy in biology education* (Publication No. 718957) [Master's Thesis, Bartın University]. Higher Education Council Thesis Archive. https://tez.yok.gov.tr

Çoruh, L. (2011). *Assessment of the effectiveness of virtual reality applications in art history course as a learning model (An example of Erciyes University Architecture & Fine Arts Faculties)* (Publication No. 279715) [Doctoral Dissertation, Gazi University]. Higher Education Council Thesis Archive. https://tez.yok.gov.tr

Dangi, R., Lalwani, P., Choudhary, G., You, I. & Pau, G. (2022). Study and investigation on 5G technology: A systematic review. *Sensors, 22.* doi:10.3390/s22010026

Emreli, D. (2019). *Investigation of the effects of use virtual & augmented reality (V/AR) applications in technical drawing training for machine manufacturing sector on learning performance* (Publication No. 595467) [Master's thesis, Bursa Uludağ University]. Higher Education Council Thesis Archive. https://tez.yok.gov.tr

Fırat, M. (2022). *Karma yöntem araştırmaları: Yöntembilimde açıklığın yükselişi.* Nobel Yayıncılık.

Gökçe, S. (2022). *The effect of augmented reality supported history lesson books on spatial thinking ability and academic success of students* (Publication No. 707107) [Master's Thesis, Ankara University]. Higher Education Council Thesis Archive. https://tez.yok.gov.tr

Haas, H. (2018). LiFi is a paradigm-shifting 5G technology. *Reviews in Physics, 3,* 26–31. doi:10.1016/j.revip.2017.10.001

Hughes, C. E., Stapleton, C. B., Hughes, D. E., & Smith, E. M. (2005). Mixed reality in education, entertainment, and training. *IEEE Computer Graphics and Applications, 25*(6), 24–30. doi:10.1109/MCG.2005.139 PMID:16315474

Hugues, O., Fuchs, P., & Nannipieri, O. (2011). New augmented reality taxonomy: technologies and features of augmented environment. In B. Furth (Ed.), *Handbook of Augmented Reality* (pp. 47–63). Springer. doi:10.1007/978-1-4614-0064-6_2

İpek, A. R. (2020). Artırılmış gerçeklik, sanal gerçeklik ve karma gerçeklik kavramlarında isimlendirme ve tanımlandırma sorunları. *İdil Sanat ve Dil Dergisi, 9*(71), 1061-1072. doi:10.7816/idil-09-71-02

Kapan, K., & Üncel, R. (2020). Gelişen web teknolojilerinin (web 1.0- web 2.0- web 3.0) Türkiye turizmine etkisi. *Safran Kültür ve Turizm Araştırmaları Dergisi, 3*(3), 276-289. https://dergipark.org.tr/en/pub/saktad/issue/59328/756788

Küçük Avcı, Ş. (2018). *The impact of three dimensional virtual environments and augmented reality applications on learning achievement: A meta-analysis study* (Publication No. 493087) [Doctoral Dissertation, Necmettin Erbakan University]. Higher Education Council Thesis Archive. https://tez.yok.gov.tr

Lamata, P., Ali, W., Cano, A., Cornella, J., Declerck, J., Elle, O. J., & Gomez, E. J. (2010). Augmented reality for minimally invasive surgery: Overview and some recent advances. In S. Maad (Ed.), *Augmented Reality* (pp. 73–98). InTech. doi:10.5772/7128

Microsoft. (2017). *Why hololens.* https://www.microsoft.com/microsofthololens/en-us/why-hololens

Milgram, P., & Kishino, F. (1994). A taxonomy of mixed reality visual displays. *IEICE Transactions on Information and Systems, 77*(12), 1321–1329.

Nakamoto, S. (2008). Bitcoin: A peer-to-peer electronic cash system. *Decentralized Business Review, 21260.* https://bitcoin.org/bitcoin.pdf

Onur, M. (2021). *The effect of augmented reality-supported teaching on students' academic achievement, level of learning permanence, and learning motivation in the solar system and beyond unit* (Publication No. 704680) [Master's Thesis, Mustafa Kemal University]. Higher Education Council Thesis Archive. https://tez.yok.gov.tr

Oppenheim, C. (1993). Virtual Reality and the Virtual Library. *Information Services & Use, 13*(3), 215–227. doi:10.3233/ISU-1993-13303

Pan, Z., Cheok, A. D., Yang, H., Zhu, J., & Shi, J. (2006). Virtual reality and mixed reality for virtual learning environments. *Computers & Graphics, 30*(1), 20–28. doi:10.1016/j.cag.2005.10.004

Papakçı, E. (2022). *Developing a mobile application for the basic education of mentally handicapped individuals using augmented reality technology* (Publication No. 759743) [Master's thesis, Kocaeli University]. Higher Education Council Thesis Archive. https://tez.yok.gov.tr

Perri, L. (2022, Aug 10). *What's new in the 2022 gartner hype cycle for emerging technologies?* https://www.gartner.com/en/articles/what-s-new-in-the-2022-gartner-hype-cycle-for-emerging-technologies

Ryan, M. L. (2015). *Narrative as virtual reality 2: revisiting immersion and interactivity in literature and electronic media.* John Hopkins University Press. doi:10.1353/book.72246

Şimşek, B. (2022). *The effect of augmented reality supported texts on students' reading comprehension and examining students' attitudes* (Publication No. 753803) [Doctoral Dissertation, Akdeniz University]. Higher Education Council Thesis Archive. https://tez.yok.gov.tr

Şimşek, İ. & Can, T. (2019). Examination of virtual reality usage in higher education in terms of different variables. *Folklor/edebiyat, 97*(1), 77-90. doi:10.22559/folklor.928

Türksoy, E. (2019). *The effect of teaching methods integrated with augmented reality and online materials on achievement and retention in science lesson: Mixed design* (Publication No. 600062) [Doctoral Dissertation, Burdur Mehmet Akif Ersoy University]. Higher Education Council Thesis Archive. https://tez.yok.gov.tr

Ulusoy, Ç. S. (2022). *An augmented reality application using unity and vuforia* (Publication No. 712152) [Master's thesis, Trakya University]. Higher Education Council Thesis Archive. https://tez.yok.gov.tr

Wang, Q., Li, R., Wang, Q., & Chen, S. (2021). *Non-fungible token (NFT): Overview, evaluation, opportunities and challenges.* https://doi.org//arXiv.2105.07447 doi:10.48550

Wu, J., & Tran, N. K. (2018). Application of blockchain technology in sustainable energy systems: An overview. *Sustainability (Basel)*, *10*(9), 3067. doi:10.3390u10093067

Yıldırım, Y. (2021, Nov 11). Social media and virtual lives before the Metaverse. *Eskişehir Ekspres*. https://www.eskisehirekspres.net/metaverse-oncesi-sosyal-medya-ve-sanal-yasamlar-1

Yuen, S., Yaoyuneyong, G., & Johnson, E. (2011). Augmented reality: An overview and five directions for AR in education. *Journal of Educational Technology Development and Exchange*, *4*(1), 119–140. doi:10.18785/jetde.0401.10

KEY TERMS AND DEFINITIONS

AR Development Platform: Software for developing three-dimensional virtual objects and mobile augmented reality content.

AR Software Development Kit: Software that develops AR applications used to provide users with an augmented reality experience with 3D virtual objects on the screens of mobile devices.

Augmented Reality: 3D technology that combines reality and virtuality by adding 3D virtual objects to the real environment and allows simultaneous interaction with virtual 3D objects.

Metaverse: Fictional virtual reality universe.

Mixed Reality: The continuum of reality and virtuality, encompassing all AR and VR technologies from real to virtual environments.

Virtual Reality: 3D technology that allows people to interact with computer-generated three-dimensional objects as well as giving the feeling of being in a virtual environment that is not real in their minds by using head mounted displays, wearable technologies, glasses surrounding the eyes or smart contact lenses.

Chapter 8
Metaverse–Enabling IoT Technology for a Futuristic Healthcare System

Vrushank Shah
Electronics and Communication Engineering, Indus Institute of Technology and Engineering, Indus University, India

Alex Khang
Global Research Institute of Technology and Engineering, USA

ABSTRACT

Combining the Metaverse and IoT has huge potential to change healthcare systems. In this chapter, the authors look at how the internet of things (IoT) is changing healthcare by focusing on two key areas: telemedicine and remote patient monitoring. Remote patient monitoring is enabled through internet of things (IoT) devices and wearables. These devices collect data on vital signs, activity levels, and other health metrics in order to remotely monitor patients and discover abnormalities or changes in health conditions. By facilitating remote medical consultations and virtual doctor-patient interactions, the internet of things also improves healthcare's accessibility and convenience.

INTRODUCTION

The term "Metaverse" is used to describe a shared digital environment that combines elements of "regular" (or "physical") reality with "augmented" (or "virtual") reality. Virtual reality (VR) is an immersive and interactive digital environment in which users can interact with digital objects, other users, and computer-generated simulations of either familiar or alien environments (Wang & Kung, 2018). As a new level of human connection and digital experiences, the Metaverse seeks to create a seamless and integrated experience across numerous devices, platforms, and applications.

DOI: 10.4018/978-1-6684-8851-5.ch008

Virtual reality, augmented reality, mixed reality, artificial intelligence, the Internet of Things, and blockchain are just a few of the technologies that have come together to form what is known as the Metaverse. The virtual environment it creates is dynamic and interconnected because to the incorporation of real-time data, simulated items, social interactions, and full-immersion experiences.

The Internet of Things (IoT) is a global network of computing devices, automobiles, appliances, and other everyday items equipped with sensors, software, and network connectivity. Through the internet, these devices can automatically and invisibly share information with one another and with other systems. The Internet of Things (IoT) paves the way for frictionless connection and communication across the digital and real worlds (Bhattacharya & Sasi, 2021).

Sensors in IoT devices monitor and collect information about things like temperature, humidity, motion, location, and biometrics. This information can be shared, analyzed, and put to use in a variety of ways. Efficiency, convenience, and quality of life are all boosted by the Internet of Things' ability to automate, remotely operate, and monitor equipment and systems.

The Internet of Things (IoT) has the potential to revolutionize sectors and disrupt established procedures, including the healthcare sector. IoT allows for real-time data collection, remote monitoring, predictive analytics, and individualized healthcare solutions by linking medical devices, wearables, and healthcare infrastructure.

The Internet of Things (IoT) and the Metaverse are converging, bringing together the virtual world's immersive and interactive capabilities with the physical world's huge network of interconnected objects. Connecting digital content and physical information is made possible with the incorporation of IoT into the Metaverse.

IoT devices in a Metaverse-enabled IoT ecosystem can exchange data with virtual worlds in real time, resulting in richer, more interactive experiences. Wearable gadgets, for instance, can collect and send biometric data to virtual health assistants, letting virtual doctors keep tabs on their patients' health and make tailored recommendations. In the same way, Internet of Things (IoT) sensors built into smart healthcare infrastructure can share in-the-moment information about the status of individual pieces of equipment, the flow of patients, and the use of resources to enhance healthcare delivery in the Metaverse.

Incorporating Internet of Things (IoT) technologies into the Metaverse paves the way for more life-like and contextually aware simulated environments. It improves user interactions and opens up new opportunities for healthcare, entertainment, education, collaboration, and other industries present in the Metaverse by bridging the gap between the real and virtual worlds.

Significance of IoT in Healthcare Transformation

IoT is very important to the transformation of healthcare because it offers a lot of benefits and chances to improve patient care, operational efficiency, and health results. Here are some key points that show how important IoT is in transforming healthcare:

Remote Patient Monitoring: The Internet of Things (IoT) lets wearable devices, sensors, and medical equipment work together to receive real-time health data from patients. This lets doctors check patients' vital signs, make sure they take their medicine, and check on their general health from a distance. It makes it easier to be engaged in health care, find health problems early, and go to the hospital less often.

Telemedicine and virtual consultations are made possible by IoT technology, which removes geographical obstacles and makes healthcare more accessible. Patients who live in remote places or have trouble getting around can connect with doctors and nurses online to get diagnoses and treatment plans.

It gives healthcare services to people who don't have access to them, reducing differences and making access to healthcare better generally.

Efficient Healthcare Operations: IoT-enabled technology in healthcare improves the efficiency of operations. Medical devices, equipment, and assets that are connected to the internet can be checked online for performance, maintenance, and inventory management. Real-time data analytics and predictive maintenance cut down on downtime, make better use of resources, and improve workflow. This saves money, makes people more productive, and makes patients safer.

Personalized and Preventive Care: The Internet of Things (IoT) makes it possible for healthcare treatments and preventive care to be tailored to the person. By keeping an eye on patient data all the time, healthcare workers can tailor treatment plans and interventions to each person's health profile. AI algorithms and real-time data analysis can find trends, predict health risks, and make proactive suggestions for preventing and treating diseases. This personalized method makes patients more interested, happier, and healthier overall.

Patient Safety and Managing Medications: IoT devices are very important for patient safety and managing medications. Smart pill dispensers and medication tracking systems make sure that medicines are given correctly, cut down on mistakes, and remind people to take their medicines as prescribed. IoT-enabled patient safety solutions include devices that identify falls, alarms that can be worn, and real-time monitoring of a patient's movements. This makes it possible to respond quickly to emergencies and makes sure that the patient is safe.

Data-Driven Decision Making and Research: The Internet of Things (IoT) creates a lot of healthcare data that can be used to make decisions and do research that is based on the data. When applied to IoT data, real-time data analytics, machine learning, and AI algorithms can give useful insights for disease surveillance, population health management, evaluating the effectiveness of treatments, and planning healthcare resources. This makes it possible to make decisions based on facts, improve health care, and make progress in medical studies.

In short, IoT technology has big effects on the way healthcare is changing. It gives healthcare providers access to real-time data, connectivity, and insights, which allows for remote patient monitoring, personalized care, operational efficiency, and better health results. When IoT is used in healthcare, it improves access, safety, and the way decisions are made, which leads to a more patient-centered and efficient system.

METAVERSE-ENABLED IoT APPLICATIONS IN FUTURISTIC HEALTHCARE

Remote Patient Monitoring and Telemedicine

Telemedicine and remote patient tracking are two important uses of IoT in healthcare that have changed the way services are given in a big way. Using IoT sensors and wearables makes real-time health tracking possible, so doctors and nurses always have access to important health parameters. Wearable devices, like smartwatches and biosensors, take measurements of your heart rate, blood pressure, temperature, oxygen saturation, and exercise level. This information is then sent wirelessly to your doctor. This real-time data analysis makes it possible to keep an eye on a patient's health from afar, allowing for early discovery of abnormalities or worsening health and quick action to stop medical emergencies. Patients can also access their own health information through mobile apps or online sites. This gives them the power to take an active role in managing their own healthcare.

IoT technology makes it possible for doctors and patients to talk to each other virtually and have remote appointments. With video conferencing, messaging platforms, or specific telemedicine platforms, doctors and nurses can talk to patients in real time, despite the fact that they are in different places. Virtual appointments let people get medical advice, diagnoses, and treatment plans without having to go to a hospital or clinic in person. Doctors can look at a patient's symptoms, look at visual clues, and talk about their medical history from a distance, which is often easier and more convenient for the patient. This method also makes it possible for patients to talk to specialists, get second views, and coordinate care across multiple disciplines. This leads to better health outcomes and less travel for patients.

Telemedicine and remote patient tracking are very important in health care. These IoT-enabled apps make healthcare services easier to get to, especially for people who live in remote places or have trouble moving around. They also help lower the cost of health care and save time by getting rid of the need to travel. Also, early detection and treatment of health problems that are getting worse because of real-time tracking improves patient outcomes and cuts down on hospital readmissions. Access to real-time health data and online services give patients the tools they need to take charge of their own health. Telemedicine also makes it easier for care to be given quickly, for people from different fields to talk to each other, and for healthcare workers to work together better. Overall, IoT-based remote patient tracking and telemedicine have changed healthcare by making it more accessible, convenient, and effective, especially for people who live in remote or underserved areas.

Remote Patient Monitoring and Telemedicine

Augmented reality (AR) and virtual reality (VR) are both powerful technologies that have a lot of promise in the healthcare field. These immersive tools offer new ways to train doctors and nurses and make surgeries and other medical interventions better. Simulation-based training has become an important part of medical education, and AR and VR are key to making training settings that are realistic and immersive. Virtual simulations of complicated medical situations can be done by medical professionals. This lets them practice and improve their skills in a safe and controlled environment. AR and VR let medical students see and interact with virtual patient models, anatomy, and medical equipment, giving them important hands-on experience without putting real patients at risk. This simulation-based training helps medical workers improve not only their technical skills, but also their ability to make decisions, think critically, and work as a team.

AR and VR have also changed the way surgery and other medical treatments are done. Surgeons can plan and practice hard surgeries before going into the operating room with these interactive technologies. AR and VR help doctors plan the best way to do surgery by showing them detailed 3D images of the patient's body and surgical tools. This improves accuracy and reduces risks during the procedure. During surgeries, virtual overlays can help guide the surgeon by putting important information right in his or her line of sight. Virtual reality can also be used during minimally invasive surgeries to help doctors see and understand the patient's body better and move around it more easily.

AR and VR technologies have also made it easier for doctors and surgeons to work together and discuss from far away. Surgeons in different places can work together and share their knowledge during complicated procedures by using these immersive technologies. This makes it easier to share information, gives people better access to specialized care, and makes it possible for medical experts to help people in more places.

When AR and VR are used together in healthcare, there are many perks. It improves medical education and training by giving doctors and nurses the chance to learn and practice skills in a realistic but risk-free setting. By making surgical planning and accuracy better, these tools make patients safer and improve the results of surgery. AR and VR also make it easier for people from different fields to work together, share information, and get access to specialized care, which improves the way healthcare is given and how patients feel about it.

As AR and VR technologies continue to improve, they are likely to change how doctors are trained, how surgeries are done, and how patients are cared for. With ongoing improvements and more people using them, AR and VR have a lot of potential to change the way healthcare is done, leading to better outcomes and a higher standard of care overall.

Smart Healthcare Infrastructure

The Internet of Things (IoT) is enabling a new generation of healthcare infrastructure that will transform the way hospitals and clinics function and provide treatment. Several Internet of Things (IoT) applications improve healthcare operations by facilitating real-time monitoring of medical equipment and facilities and streamlining hospital administration systems. Hospital management systems with Internet of Things integration simplify many facets of healthcare delivery, raising both productivity and satisfaction. Patient flow, bed occupancy, and resource utilization data are collected and analyzed by IoT through the use of networked devices and sensors. Decisions, resource allocation, and workflow optimization in the healthcare industry can all be improved with the help of this data-driven strategy. The Internet of Things also makes it possible for healthcare facilities to implement automated systems for inventory management, medication tracking, and patient scheduling, all of which serve to cut down on human error, waste, and inefficiency.

Internet of Things applications in smart healthcare infrastructure also include real-time monitoring of medical equipment and facilities. The performance, status, and usage of medical devices like imaging machines, patient monitors, and infusion pumps are continuously monitored by Internet of Things (IoT) sensors. By sending this information wirelessly to a central monitoring system, medical professionals can check the status of their equipment from afar, spot any problems before they become serious, and schedule maintenance accordingly. Improvements in patient safety and continuity of care can be realized through the use of real-time monitoring to forestall equipment failures, guarantee prompt repairs, and reduce downtime.

The Internet of Things also provides real-time monitoring of infrastructure, including temperature, humidity, and other factors vital to infection control and patient well-being. These factors are monitored by sensors installed throughout healthcare facilities, which report any significant changes to healthcare providers. By keeping an eye on things in real time, hospitals can make sure patients are safe and healthy in their surroundings.

There are many advantages of using IoT in smart healthcare infrastructure. It improves productivity by maximizing returns on investments and cutting down on waste. By keeping tabs on machines in real time, hospitals can make sure nothing goes wrong and patients are safer. In addition, IoT-driven solutions make hospitals and clinics safer and more pleasant places to be by constantly monitoring and adjusting settings to prevent complications.

The potential for better healthcare operations and patient outcomes is growing as more and more healthcare facilities deploy IoT-enabled technology. By boosting care quality, streamlining processes, and making the most of available resources, smart healthcare infrastructure helps create a more efficient and patient-focused healthcare system. Constant improvements in IoT technology are allowing hospitals to evolve into smart, networked ecosystems that will dramatically alter the way patients receive and interact with medical treatment.

Virtual Health Assistants and Personalized Medicine

Artificial intelligence (AI) is revolutionizing the healthcare industry by facilitating developments like virtual health assistants and personalized treatment. Virtual healthcare assistants driven by artificial intelligence play an important part in offering personalized care, which also includes individualized treatment regimens and prescription reminders.

Virtual health assistants use artificial intelligence (AI) algorithms and natural language processing to communicate with patients, share health information, and give individualized medical assistance. These digital assistants can help with a wide variety of healthcare-related duties, including question answering, prescription reminders, lifestyle advice, and symptom triage. Virtual health assistants can learn about their users and tailor their responses to each person's unique profile, medical history, and preferences. This individualized strategy encourages patient participation and gives people more control over their healthcare.

However, the goal of personalized medicine is to individualize medical care based on the specifics of each patient. Massive volumes of patient data, such as genetic information, medical history, lifestyle factors, and treatment outcomes, are analyzed by AI to find patterns and make predictions. As a result of these discoveries, doctors may tailor a patient's treatment to their unique condition, genetic predispositions, and drug interactions. Medication reminders and adherence assistance are also a part of personalized medicine since they increase treatment efficacy and decrease the likelihood of medication errors by making sure patients take their prescriptions as prescribed and as scheduled.

There are many advantages to combining AI-driven virtual health aides with personalized medicine. Health information, assistance, and directions may now be accessed whenever a user needs it thanks to virtual health assistants. Virtual health assistants promote a patient-centered, individualized approach to care by allowing for the customization of interactions and responses. In contrast, personalized medicine improves health outcomes by tailoring care to each patient, reducing the need for "trial and error" methods, and encouraging more consistent pharmaceutical use. These developments aid in better health outcomes, happier patients, and better use of healthcare dollars.

The promise for improved healthcare experiences and results grows as AI technologies advance and healthcare systems incorporate virtual health assistants and personalized medicine approaches. Healthcare is being revolutionized into a more individualized and precise field because of the rise of personalized medicine and virtual health assistants. These AI-driven solutions have the potential to radically alter the healthcare system by giving patients individualized assistance and helping medical professionals provide more efficient, precise treatment.

CONCLUSION

The potential for the Internet of Things to improve healthcare systems is enormous, and it holds the promise of radically altering both the delivery of healthcare and the patient's overall experience of receiving it. The field of medicine has the potential to evolve into one that is more suited to the individual, productive, and open to participation if immersive capabilities of the Metaverse are combined with the connection and data-driven insights offered by Internet of Things technology.

The combination of the Metaverse with the Internet of Things in the healthcare industry has the potential to solve significant problems and improve many facets of the delivery of healthcare. Sharing of data in a smooth manner, monitoring in real time, and intelligent analysis of data pertaining to one's health are all made possible by the capacity to connect many systems, sensors, and devices in a single network. This enables earlier diagnosis of health problems, more individualized treatment regimens, and enhanced decision-making by medical experts. Immersive experiences, such as those provided by the Metaverse, make it possible to improve patient education, conduct remote consultations, and train medical personnel in surroundings that are as close to reality as possible.

However, deploying IoT in healthcare that is enabled by the Metaverse presents some problems and calls for careful assessment of those challenges. Concerns of privacy and security need to be addressed in order to safeguard the confidentiality of patient data and provide adequate defense against cyberattacks. It is necessary to have interoperability between the various IoT devices and systems in order to achieve fluid data exchange and integration. Additionally, in order to achieve successful uptake and optimal utilization, training for healthcare professionals on how to make efficient use of Metaverse and IoT technologies is required (Wang, 2019).

When seen in the long term, the future of the Metaverse and the Internet of Things in healthcare looks positive. The continued developments in technology, such as 5G connection, edge computing, and artificial intelligence, will significantly boost the possibilities of Metaverse-enabled IoT applications in the healthcare industry (Topol, 2019). IoT devices and wearables are becoming more widely available, and at the same time, more affordable. This will allow for their increased adoption and incorporation into routine healthcare practices. The Metaverse will continue to develop, eventually providing experiences that are more immersive and engaging, paving the way for virtual collaborations, and enlarging the pool of people who can access healthcare services (Kazmi & Xue, 2020).

In the field of medicine, the Internet of Things that is enabled by Metaverse will have a significant and far-reaching impact. It will make it possible to provide care that is more individualized and focused on the patient, enabling individualized treatment regimens, proactive monitoring, and remote consultations (da Silva, 2018). Accessibility and convenience, given by a Metaverse-enabled Internet of Things, will help to cross geographical barriers and deliver medical services to previously unreached and underserved places. When it comes to healthcare, more productivity and coordination among providers will lead to more effective use of available resources, lower overall costs, and better patient outcomes. In addition, the information gathered by Internet of Things (IoT) devices and the Metaverse will contribute to the evolution of healthcare delivery models, as well as medical research and the management of populations' health (Hassanalieragh et al., 2015).

In summing up, the convergence of the Metaverse and the Internet of Things (IoT) technology presents the possibility of revolutionary change in the medical field. It has the potential to reimagine healthcare delivery models, making them more patient-centered, resource-conscious, and broadly available. It is possible to revolutionize healthcare by utilizing the immersive experiences of the Metaverse and the interconnection of the Internet of Things (IoT). This will ultimately result in improved patient outcomes, enhanced healthcare experiences, and will shape the future of the healthcare business. As we continue on this transformative path, tackling obstacles, guaranteeing privacy and security, and making the most of future breakthroughs will be essential if we are to realize the full potential of the Internet of Things in healthcare that is allowed by the Metaverse.

REFERENCES

Bhattacharya, S., Sasi, P., Sankaranarayanan, V., & Woungang, I. (2019). Internet of Things and healthcare: An overview. *Future Generation Computer Systems*, *94*, 849–861.

Cai, C., Xue, M., Chen, J., Xue, Z., & Hu, J. (2020). Virtual reality in healthcare: State-of-the-art and future challenges. *IEEE Transactions on Industrial Informatics*, *16*(8), 5152–5161.

Cheng, X., Deng, Y., Xiong, R., & Xu, X. (2021). A review of artificial intelligence in healthcare: Challenges, opportunities, and implementation strategies. *Journal of Healthcare Engineering*.

da Silva, R. B., de Castro, L. N., & Costa, C. A. (2018). Internet of Things and augmented reality applied to the healthcare area: A systematic review. *Journal of Biomedical Informatics*, *87*, 73–86.

Dascalu, M., Bodea, C. N., & Nechifor, S. (2019). Augmented reality in healthcare: A systematic literature review. *Sensors (Basel)*, *19*(19), 4172. PMID:31561481

Grustam, A. S., Fountoukidou, P., Tsiropoulou, E. E., & Dimitriou, N. (2020). Internet of Things (IoT) in healthcare: A comprehensive survey. *Journal of Network and Computer Applications*, *154*, 102570.

Halamka, J. D., & Mandl, K. D. (2019). Making healthcare IT sustainable. *The New England Journal of Medicine*, *381*(26), 2497–2499. PMID:31733140

Hassanalieragh, M. (2015). Health monitoring and management using internet-of-things (IoT) sensing with cloud-based processing: Opportunities and challenges. In *2015 IEEE International Conference on Services Computing (SCC)* (pp. 285-292). IEEE. 10.1109/SCC.2015.47

Iyawa, G., Dwolatzky, B., & De Vries, J. (2020). Telemedicine and the COVID-19 pandemic in sub-Saharan Africa: A comprehensive overview. *EMHJ-Eastern Mediterranean Health Journal*, *26*(9), 973–981.

Kazmi, S., & Xue, Y. (2020). Internet of Things (IoT) enabled healthcare applications, architectural elements, and security: A comprehensive survey. *Future Generation Computer Systems*, *106*, 1109–1127.

Kocaballi, A. B., Laranjo, L., & Coiera, E. (2019). The use of virtual reality in clinical applications: A systematic review and meta-analysis. *Human Factors*, *61*(6), 811–831.

Majeed, S., & Goyal, R. K. (2020). Internet of Things (IoT) in healthcare: Applications, benefits, and challenges. In *Advances in computer and computational sciences* (pp. 119–129). Springer.

Oudshoorn, N., & Pinch, T. (Eds.). (2003). *How users matter: The co-construction of users and technology*. MIT Press. doi:10.7551/mitpress/3592.001.0001

Poulson, M. E., Balcom Raleigh, D., Ghosh, T., Johnson, D. C., & Patel, V. L. (2019). The potential of virtual reality and augmented reality for healthcare applications. *Journal of Digital Imaging*, *32*(4), 469–479.

Prabhakaran, R. T. (2020). Augmented reality and virtual reality in healthcare—A brief survey. In *2020 11th International Conference on Computing, Communication and Networking Technologies (ICCCNT)* (pp. 1-7). IEEE.

Swenson, D. L. (2018). Internet of Things in healthcare: Information technology architecture to enhance patient outcomes. *Journal of Medical Internet Research*, *20*(2), e25. PMID:29396387

Topol, E. J. (2019). High-performance medicine: The convergence of human and artificial intelligence. *Nature Medicine*, *25*(1), 44–56. doi:10.103841591-018-0300-7 PMID:30617339

Wang, C., & Hsu, M. C. (2019). Exploring the potential of virtual reality in medical education: A systematic review of VR applications used in medical education. *Journal of Medical Systems*, *43*(4), 1–13. PMID:30820676

Wang, Y., Kung, L., & Byrd, T. A. (2018). Big data analytics: Understanding its capabilities and potential benefits for healthcare organizations. *Technological Forecasting and Social Change*, *126*, 3–13. doi:10.1016/j.techfore.2015.12.019

World Health Organization. (2021). *Telemedicine: Opportunities and developments in Member States: Report on the second global survey on eHealth*. Retrieved from https://www.who.int/health-topics/ehealth#tab=tab_1

Chapter 9
Effects of Quantum Technology on the Metaverse

Shyam Sihare
Dr. A.P.J. Abdul Kalam Government College, Silvassa, India

Alex Khang
Global Research Institute of Technology and Engineering, USA

ABSTRACT

This chapter explores the impact of quantum technology on the metaverse, revolutionizing performance and security. Quantum computing enables faster processing, advanced simulations, and sophisticated AI interactions. Integrating it with the metaverse poses technical challenges and requires addressing ethical considerations. Quantum tech benefits blockchain-based cryptocurrencies, enabling decentralized ownership and secure transactions. Regulatory frameworks are needed. Future internet technologies like 5G, edge computing, and IoT play a vital role, providing high-speed connectivity and enhanced immersion. Overcoming challenges such as limited resources and interdisciplinary expertise is crucial. Addressing ethical concerns and establishing standards and regulations are necessary. This research aims to understand quantum's effects, develop strategies, and foster collaboration for a responsible and equitable integration in the metaverse, shaping a transformative digital future.

INTRODUCTION

Quantum metaverse delves into the connection between the real world and the internet through the concept of the metaverse, a virtual realm that aims to closely mirror reality (Choi et al., 2022). It seeks to create a social environment that combines elements of gaming, simulation, and social media to construct a fictional world resembling our own. Facebook and decentralized organizations like Decenterland are actively working towards the realization of the metaverse (Damodaran, 2023).

DOI: 10.4018/978-1-6684-8851-5.ch009

Quantum computing is poised to play a pivotal role in the development of the metaverse. By harnessing quantum randomness, developers can ensure the integrity of the protective measures employed within the metaverse (Bhattacharya et al., 2023). This technology holds tremendous potential for enhancing security and furthering the metaverse's evolution (Duan et al., 2021).

The advent of Web 3.0 technologies, including video, augmented reality, and virtual reality, enables users to immerse themselves more deeply in a digital world, irrespective of their physical location (Billewar et al., 2022). This connectivity empowers users to engage in electronic interactions, travel, and information sharing. As the world witnesses the largest cryptographic migration in history, quantum-resistant security approaches take center stage in safeguarding the future internet (Alladi et al., 2022; Wang et al., 2022; Sihare & Nath, 2017a).

Quantum computing boasts a wide range of significant applications that may eventually integrate into the metaverse. Deploying quantum-resistant technology may be necessary to protect transactions from algorithms like Shor's Algorithm (Perlner et al., 2009; Allende et al., 2023). Considerations about blockchain systems that can withstand quantum effects also arise. With the metaverse gaining momentum, businesses are actively seeking tools and technologies that provide a competitive advantage and enable them to navigate the metaverse's landscape, spurred by the recent developments surrounding Facebook's initiatives (Allam et al., 2022; Dwivedi et al., 2022; Julian et al., 2023). This newfound focus on the metaverse indicates a shift in attention among global technical enterprises towards this emerging paradigm and the potential expansion of the internet (Cook, 2008; Sihare & Nath, 2017b).

Unlike conventional supercomputers, quantum computers possess working memory capable of storing diverse data combinations to solve real-world problems (Gill et al., 2022). Embracing ecosystem-based tactics recognizes the collaborative nature required to satisfy customers, acknowledging that no single business can fully meet all their needs (Layzer, 2008).

The quantum metaverse environment is poised to bring significant changes to various fields in the future, including security, computation, simulation, machine learning, and communication (Zhao et al., 2023). Quantum computing has revolutionized processing power, paving the way for a new golden age of software engineering. Currently valued at \$47.69 billion, the Metaverse market is projected to grow at a CAGR of 43.3% until 2028[1]. The technological advancements in the Metaverse and Omniverse parallel those depicted in recent science fiction works (Ning et al., 2023). Quantum computing offers the potential for swift tracking of ESG metrics and contributes to the pursuit of UN SDGs (Bonime-Blanc, 2019). Accenture Ventures has strategically invested in The Good Chemistry Company, while Pascal excels in atom-neutral quantum computing, partnering with Microsoft to make its technologies accessible (Nassimbeni et al., 2008).

Pasqal utilizes optical "tweezers" and laser light to control atoms with an equal number of protons and electrons (Padgett et al., 2010). NVIDIA revealed advancements in quantum computing during their GTC conference, and Maybelle introduced the Quantum Icebox, a cutting-edge quantum technology[2]. La Trobe University, Australian National University, and Quantum Brilliance have collaborated in the development of manufacturing techniques for quantum computer qubits through the Research Hub for Diamond Quantum Materials[3]. This initiative builds upon an existing partnership with ETH Zurich and the establishment of a quantum computing center in May 2021[4].

The notion of a "metaverse" links the real world and the internet, aiming to create a virtual world that closely resembles its physical counterpart. This research chapter explores the effects of quantum technology on the metaverse, focusing on its potential to revolutionize performance and security. Quantum computing enables faster processing speeds, advanced simulations, and sophisticated AI interactions within virtual environments. Integrating quantum computing with the metaverse poses technical challenges such as software development, hardware optimization, and system integration. Ethical considerations, including privacy, security, and equitable access, must also be addressed for responsible deployment (Nieminen, 2001).

The research objectives of this study are to analyze the impact of quantum technology on the metaverse and identify the challenges and opportunities it presents. By examining the merits, demerits, and future challenges, the study aims to develop strategies to overcome technical obstacles and address ethical concerns. The research also aims to explore the potential applications of quantum computing in areas such as security, computation, simulation, machine learning, and communication within the metaverse (Figure 1).

Figure 1. Quantum computing, AI algorithms, blockchain, quantum teleportation, enhancing efficiency, realism, security, and seamless experiences in virtual environments
Source: Ali et al. (2023)

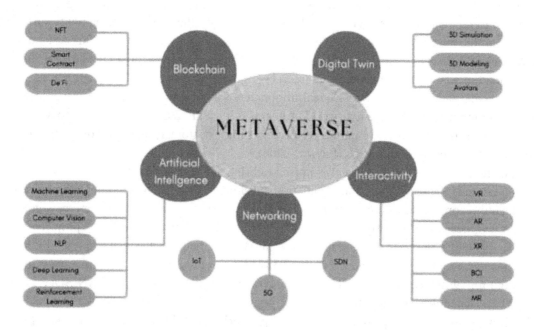

The significance of this study lies in its contribution to understanding the transformative potential of quantum technology in the metaverse. By uncovering the implications of quantum computing and its integration with virtual environments, policymakers, developers, and researchers can make informed decisions regarding the responsible and equitable deployment of quantum technology. This study will inform the development of standards, regulatory frameworks, and collaborative efforts among stakeholders to shape a responsible integration of quantum computing in the metaverse. Ultimately, this research aims to pave the way for a transformative future in digital experiences.

LITERATURE REVIEW

Quantum mechanics, a fundamental theory of physics, describes events at atomic and subatomic scales, where physical quantities have discrete values and objects exhibit characteristics of both particles and waves (Capellmann, 2021; Di Sia, 2021). Predicting exact values is constrained, but probabilities can be determined through complex calculations. Quantum phenomena such as tunneling, interference, and entanglement play important roles in understanding the behavior of quantum systems (Dergachev et al., 2023; Dewdney, 2023, Avner, 2021).

Quantum mechanics, the only theory capable of describing small-scale interactions, has found applications in various modern technologies (Dawson et al., 2022). Quantum chaos investigates the connection between classical and quantum descriptions, addressing the challenges of chaotic systems (Mohamed, 2021). Quantum decoherence can cause quantum systems to lose coherence and behave classically. Quantum field theory is used to describe charged particles influenced by electromagnetic fields (Sugiyama et al., 2022).

The wave theory of light explains its wavelike and particle-like properties, while the photoelectric effect and atomic models proposed by Planck, Einstein, Bohr, and others contribute to our understanding of quantum behavior (Mbagwu et al., 2020). The exclusion principle prohibits identical fermions from occupying the same quantum state. Concepts such as tunneling and measurement are essential to quantum mechanics (Thompson, 2023; Jacak, 2023; Piela, 2020).

Throughout history, significant contributions from scientists like von Laue, Compton, and de Broglie further expanded our knowledge of quantum phenomena (Brock, 2021). The wave equations developed by Schrödinger and Dirac played crucial roles in unifying quantum mechanics with relativity (Kholodenko, 2023). The intricate nature of quantum systems and the diverse outcomes of repeated measurements on identical systems are fundamental principles in quantum mechanics (Renou et al., 2021; Sihare & Nath, 2017c).

Quantum mechanics makes precise predictions about the interaction between electrons and radiation based on Maxwell's field equations and Dirac's relativistic theory (Oldani, 2023). The Heisenberg uncertainty principle sets a limit on the simultaneous measurement of an object's location and momentum, becoming increasingly significant for smaller particles (Gampel & Gajda, 2023). The Copenhagen interpretation acknowledges quantum indeterminacy as inherently random, rejecting the concept of hidden variables (Del Santo & Gisin, 2019).

When measuring the angular momentum component of two particles in the same direction, the outcomes are equal and opposite, resulting in a system with zero overall angular momentum (Forbes & Andrews, 2021). The Schrödinger equation accurately calculates the time variation of a system's wave function, while quantum mechanics approaches measurement differently (Dall'Osto & Corni, 2022). Friction, wear, lubrication, and phenomena like the AC Josephson effect and Fock's Hartree-Fock equation are explored within the context of quantum mechanics (Wang et al., 2020).

Statistical mechanics combines classical and quantum mechanics with statistical concepts to predict and explain the quantifiable properties of macroscopic systems. Symmetry plays a fundamental role in physics, governing conservation laws and determining permissible particle interactions (Liu, 2023; Brown, 2020).

The concept of the "quantum myth" is introduced, referring to the potential of quantum technology to create a virtual world. Ongoing research and studies investigate the development of safer and more effective virtual environments for quantum computing and quantum cryptography (Zable et al., 2020; Brijwani et al., 2023; Chaubey & Prajapati, 2020; Kan & Une, 2021; Sihare & Nath, 2016).

The integration of quantum technology in the Metaverse offers several advantages, such as the ability to perform multiple calculations simultaneously, resulting in faster processing of large data volumes (Chengoden et al., 2023). Quantum algorithms can optimize the performance of virtual environments by reducing latency and improving network traffic management (Gill, 2021).

Quantum computing can also play a significant role in enhancing the security of the Metaverse through quantum encryption. Quantum encryption technologies, due to their resistance to detection and data manipulation, can provide a higher level of security compared to traditional cryptographic methods. (Ren et al., 2023; Kumar et al., 2022)

Research has explored the use of quantum technologies to create more specialized virtual worlds. For instance, the establishment of intricate non-local connections between different areas of the virtual world, such as through quantum blending, can provide users with a more immersive and dynamic experience (Seskir et al., 2022; Kaur & Venegas-Gomez, 2022).

While the concept of quantum computer software remains largely theoretical, there is considerable interest in developing more advanced and secure virtual environments. Future investigations and experiments are expected to be conducted as quantum computing and quantum cryptography continue to advance.

WEB 3.0, OR THE "METAVERSE"

The "quantum metaverse," which describes the synergy between quantum and metaverse technologies. The Metaverse represents a virtual world that combines virtual and augmented reality elements to create an immersive digital environment. Quantum technology, on the other hand, leverages the laws of quantum physics to unlock new possibilities in information processing.

The theory of the quantum metaverse suggests that by combining quantum technology with the Metaverse, a new and more powerful form of digital reality can be achieved. This integration has the potential to enable previously unimaginable forms of communication, collaboration, and discovery within the virtual realm. By leveraging the unique capabilities of quantum technology, the Metaverse can be enhanced with more intricate synergies, elaborate systems, and advanced machine operations. Additionally, the application of predictive analytics in this context can facilitate more perceptive and intelligent interactions with virtual entities.

While the concept of the quantum metaverse holds great promise, further research and development are required to fully comprehend its possibilities. Currently, the idea of the quantum metaverse is relatively nascent and requires extensive exploration to unlock its full potential. Nevertheless, the fusion of quantum technology and the Metaverse represents an exciting technological frontier, offering a wide range of new opportunities and prospects within the digital landscape (Figure 1).

Figure 2. Synergy between quantum and metaverse technologies. It shows the integration of quantum technology and the metaverse, enabling enhanced communication, collaboration, and discovery within a more powerful digital reality. Ongoing research and development are exploring the vast possibilities of this exciting technological frontier.

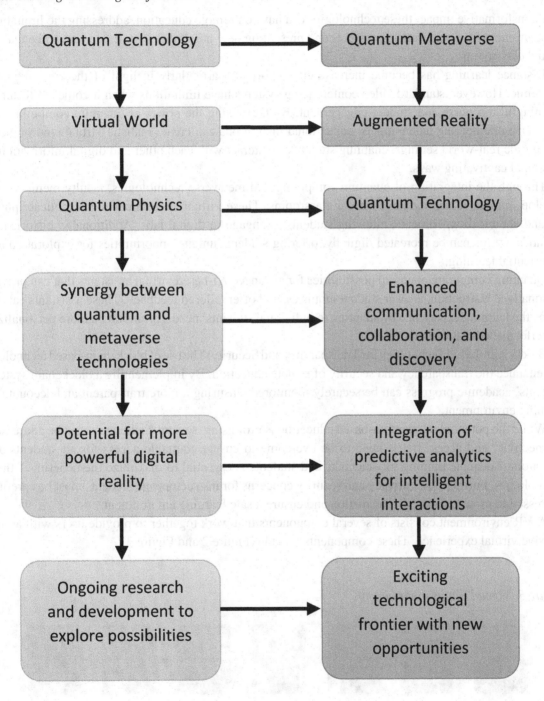

REALISTIC VIRTUAL ENVIRONMENT APPLICATIONS

Unlocking the Potential of Immersive Virtual Classrooms

The transformative impact these technologies can have on remote education, addressing the limitations of traditional video conferencing systems and presenting new possibilities for immersive and engaging virtual classrooms.

Distance learning has become increasingly important, particularly in light of the current global pandemic. However, standard video conferencing systems have limitations when it comes to fostering meaningful discourse and student engagement. By harnessing the power of quantum computing and metaverse engineering technologies, educational institutions can create realistic virtual environments that mimic real-world settings, enabling students to interact with each other and digital information in novel and captivating ways.

Through the integration of quantum computing and metaverse technologies, faculty members can develop immersive and dynamic virtual classrooms. These virtual environments can replicate physical and chemical experiments, allowing students to engage in digital labs. Additionally, historical or scientific events can be recreated digitally, offering students unique opportunities for exploration and experiential learning.

Quantum computing opens up possibilities for advanced AI-based virtual assistants that can provide personalized instruction, answer student inquiries, and offer tailored feedback. These assistants can enhance the learning experience by adapting to individual students' needs, promoting a more personalized and effective educational approach.

Blockchain-based Technology for Transparency and Security: The use of blockchain-based technology can enhance the transparency and security of remote education. By implementing a blockchain system, students' academic progress can be securely monitored, ensuring a more transparent and accountable learning environment.

While the potential of quantum-based education is promising, several challenges must be addressed. Connectivity and access issues need to be overcome to ensure equitable access for all students and educators. Adequate training for scientists and students is essential to maximize the benefits of these technologies. Furthermore, privacy and security concerns for instructors and students must be carefully addressed to protect sensitive information and ensure a safe learning environment.

A VR environment consists of several components that work together to provide users with an immersive virtual experience. These components include (Figure 2 and Figure 3):

Figure 3. Virtual reality environment

Figure 4. Virtual environment-associated components form the Quantum Metaverse, creating a seamless virtual classroom for effective teaching and learning. The Quantum Metaverse utilizes quantum technology to enhance the educational experience, ensuring a smooth and immersive learning environment.

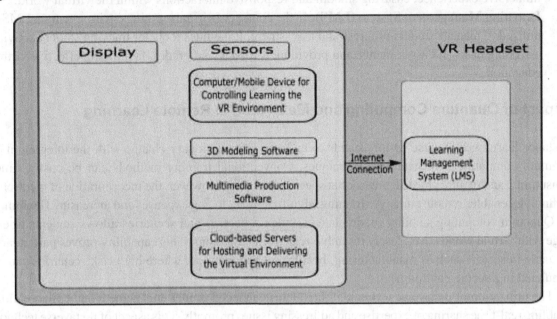

1. **VR Headset:** The VR headset is a wearable device that is worn on the head to immerse the user in the virtual environment. It typically comprises a screen, lenses, and motion sensors, enabling the user to see and interact with the virtual world.

2. **Display:** The display is a crucial part of the VR headset that showcases the virtual environment to the user. It renders the immersive visuals and ensures that the user perceives the virtual world with clarity and detail.

3. **Sensors:** Motion sensors integrated into the VR headset track the user's movements and orientation. These sensors capture the user's motions and adjust the view of the virtual environment accordingly, enhancing the sense of presence and interactivity.

4. **Control Device:** A control device, such as a gamepad or joystick, is used to navigate and interact with the virtual environment. It enables users to control their movements, actions, and interactions within the virtual world, providing a means for user input and engagement.

5. **3D Modeling Software:** 3D modeling software plays a crucial role in creating and modifying the 3D objects and scenes within the virtual environment. This software enables designers and developers to build immersive virtual worlds with intricate details and realistic elements.

6. **Multimedia Production Software:** Multimedia production software is employed to create and edit various forms of multimedia content, including audio and video, which are integrated into the virtual environment. This software enhances the sensory experience within the virtual world by incorporating realistic sound effects and visual elements.

7. **Internet Connection:** An internet connection is essential for remote access to the virtual environment from anywhere in the world. It enables users to connect to cloud-based servers and access the VR content seamlessly.

8. **Cloud-Based Servers:** Cloud-based servers host and deliver the virtual environment to users over the internet. These servers provide the computational power and storage necessary to support the immersive experience, ensuring smooth and responsive interactions within the virtual world.
9. **Learning Management System (LMS):** In the context of virtual learning environments, a LMS is utilized to manage student progress and assessment. It includes tools for tracking student activity, assigning tasks and assessments, and providing feedback and grades, facilitating effective virtual education.

Impact of Quantum Computing and Metaverse in Remote Learning

Distance learning in diverse sectors stands to undergo a revolutionary change with the integration of quantum computing and metaverse techniques. Conventional training methods can be costly, time-consuming, and require physical presence at specific locations. However, the incorporation of metaverse technology enables remote employee training, significantly reducing expenses and increasing flexibility.

Quantum computing's ability to simulate complex processes and scenarios allows students to engage with virtual worlds that closely resemble real-world situations. This capability proves particularly valuable in sectors such as manufacturing, healthcare, and aviation, where high-risk scenarios can be simulated in a secure environment.

The utilization of metaverse technology facilitates enhanced trainer engagement and collaboration, enabling real-time sharing of expertise and addressing issues promptly. This aspect of metaverse technology proves especially beneficial in fields like emergency response or military training, where teamwork and coordinated actions are paramount.

Nevertheless, quantum computing, like any emerging technology, faces challenges in fully comprehending its potential applications for diverse training needs. These concerns encompass the necessity of ensuring confidentiality, security, and equitable access for all participants. Additionally, there are challenges related to access, connectivity, and providing adequate training to both trainers and participants.

The fusion of metaverse technology and quantum computing presents a range of new opportunities for remote learning, paving the way for the development of more captivating and efficient training programs tailored to the demands of contemporary industries.

The integration of metaverse technology and quantum computing holds immense promise for remote training in various sectors. By leveraging the capabilities of quantum computing to simulate complex processes and scenarios, combined with the immersive nature of metaverse technology, remote training programs can provide engaging and realistic learning experiences (Figure 4).

Unleashing the Prospective of Quantum Computing and Metaverse in Entertainment

Quantum computing, in conjunction with metaverse technology, has the potential to revolutionize the entertainment sector. While virtual reality and augmented reality have gained popularity in entertainment, the incorporation of quantum computing can advance the simulation of interactions between physics, natural phenomena, and sophisticated artificial intelligence, resulting in even more immersive and engaging experiences for users.

Figure 5. The integration of quantum computing and metaverse techniques for distance learning, creating a virtual environment with enhanced training programs, realistic simulations, and collaborative learning opportunities

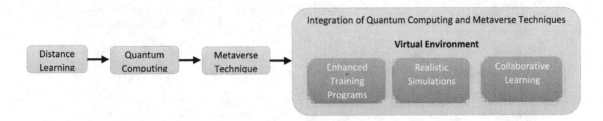

Metaverse technology enables the development of virtual worlds and environments where users can explore and interact with digital information in real time, offering new and exciting entertainment experiences. Users can participate in virtual concerts, sporting events, or social gatherings that closely resemble real-world settings.

Furthermore, quantum computing can enhance AI interactions in these virtual environments, providing users with more personalized and appealing experiences. This could involve creating more naturalistic and comprehensible virtual animations that engage with users and applying predictive analytics to tailor content to specific users' preferences.

The fusion of metaverse technology and quantum computing presents a wide range of exciting possibilities for the entertainment sector, ultimately leading to the development of more immersive and captivating user experiences. By leveraging quantum computing's capabilities and the immersive nature of metaverse technology, the entertainment industry can offer groundbreaking and tailored entertainment experiences to audiences worldwide (Figure 5).

Unleashing the Potential of Quantum Computing and Metaverse in Multiplayer Gaming

The fusion of quantum computing and metaverse technology has the potential to revolutionize multiplayer gaming by creating more realistic and immersive virtual worlds. Quantum computing enables more complex physical simulations, allowing players to move and interact with the game world in more lifelike ways. This enhanced realism makes the gaming experience more engaging and immersive.

Metaverse technology facilitates the creation of novel social gaming experiences by enabling real-time player interaction in virtual gaming environments. Players can interact with virtual items, participate in virtual social events, or embark on joint explorations of virtual worlds. This fosters a sense of community and socialization among players, enhancing the multiplayer gaming experience.

Quantum computing can also enable more sophisticated AI-based game processes, leading to more dynamic and challenging gaming experiences. Predictive algorithms can be employed to tailor the game for individual players, offering personalized challenges and experiences. Virtual agents can be developed to communicate with players in a more intelligent and natural manner, enhancing the overall immersion and interactivity of the game.

Figure 6. Integration of quantum computing and metaverse technology in the entertainment sector, offering immersive virtual reality and augmented reality experiences, enhanced simulations, and personalized AI interactions

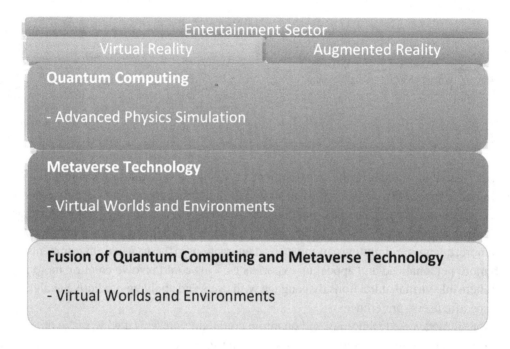

Quantum-Enhanced Virtual Workspaces

The advent of technology and quantum computing has paved the way for flexible and remote work environments. Employees can access virtual workplaces from anywhere in the world, reducing the need for physical office spaces and enabling more flexible work schedules. This shift results in increased productivity and reduced costs associated with renting office spaces and commuting.

Quantum computing enables more complex process simulations, improving the accuracy of digital representations of real-world settings. This advancement facilitates the creation of virtual workspaces that closely resemble actual office environments. As a result, the virtual workspace becomes more engaging, appealing, and conducive to productivity.

Metaverse technology allows team members to work together remotely in real-time. This technology enables seamless communication and sharing of workspaces, enhancing collaboration and information exchange among team members. The ability to collaborate effectively in virtual workspaces leads to increased productivity and better outcomes.

Impact of Quantum Computing and Switching Technology on DeFi

Quantum computing has the potential to significantly improve the security and effectiveness of DeFi platforms. Due to the computational power of quantum computers, traditional security mechanisms used in DeFi platforms become more vulnerable to hacking attacks. Implementing quantum-resistant security measures becomes essential to ensure the integrity of the DeFi platform.

Metaverse technology can play a crucial role in developing decentralized virtual markets for DeFi trading. These virtual markets enable the creation and exchange of new financial services and goods on an international scale. Real-time peer-to-peer trading within virtual markets reduces transaction costs and enhances overall efficiency.

The combination of quantum computing and switching technology empowers the DeFi platform to leverage more sophisticated predictive analysis and machine learning algorithms. This enables better decision-making and the provision of personalized financial products and services to users.

EXAMPLES OF QUANTUM METAVERSE

Harnessing Quantum Computing in Real-Time Collaboration Within the Metaverse

The quantum metaverse empowers individuals to collaborate and interact in real time while tackling complex issues, creating designs, or conducting scientific research. By harnessing the computational power of quantum computing, multiple users can actively collaborate and solve problems more quickly than traditional computing methods.

Traditional collaboration technologies, such as video conferencing or chat applications, often face limitations in communication due to bandwidth and latency restrictions. Quantum computing in the metaverse mitigates these challenges, enabling fluid and immersive real-time collaboration experiences (Figure 6).

With quantum metaverse technology, users can collaborate on virtual projects or designs in real time, making instant changes and observing their effects. This feature proves particularly valuable in fields like engineering or construction, where teams must work together on intricate designs and make adjustments on the fly.

Quantum computing opens up new avenues for in-the-moment cooperation, such as virtual reality experiences that allow users to interact with tangible objects or engage in collaborative simulations for scientific research or teaching purposes.

Quantum Metaverse and Multi-State Objects: Enhancing Dynamic Virtual Experiences

In the quantum metaverse, the superposition principle allows for the creation of virtual objects that can exist in multiple states simultaneously. Unlike traditional computers where objects are represented as bits in either the 0 or 1 state, quantum bits (qubits) can describe objects in a superposition of states. This enables the development of more sophisticated and dynamic virtual objects that can adapt and evolve based on human interactions and other factors.

Virtual objects in the quantum metaverse can be designed to exist in multiple states, reflecting various developmental, physiological, or contextual conditions. For example, virtual trees could have different states representing different growth stages or respond to human inputs such as watering or chopping. Similarly, virtual characters could have multiple states that convey different emotions or actions based on user interactions (Figure 7).

Figure 7. The quantum metaverse branches into real-time collaboration and quantum computing. Real-time collaboration includes tackling complex issues, creating designs, and offers fluid and immersive collaboration, mitigating communication limitations. Quantum computing focuses on harnessing computational power and faster problem solving. metaverse technology is a separate branch.

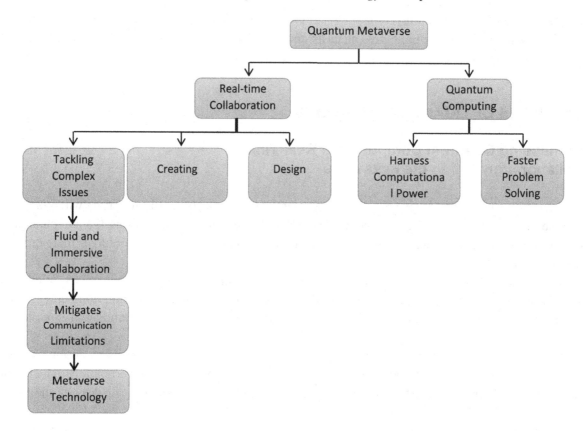

By incorporating multi-state objects in the quantum metaverse, virtual environments can offer a richer and more dynamic user experience. Users can interact with objects that evolve and respond to their actions, creating a sense of realism and immersion. The ability of multi-state objects to reflect various conditions and contexts adds depth and complexity to virtual spaces, stimulating imagination and encouraging innovative interactions.

The integration of multi-state objects in the quantum metaverse unlocks new avenues for imagination and innovation. Designers and developers can create virtual worlds with objects that behave in ways previously unimaginable, allowing users to explore and interact with dynamic and ever-changing environments. This opens up possibilities for novel applications in fields such as gaming, simulation, and creative expression.

Figure 8. The relationship between the quantum metaverse, superposition principle, multi-state virtual objects, and integration of multi-state objects, leading to a richer user experience and new avenues for imagination and innovation in dynamic environments and novel applications

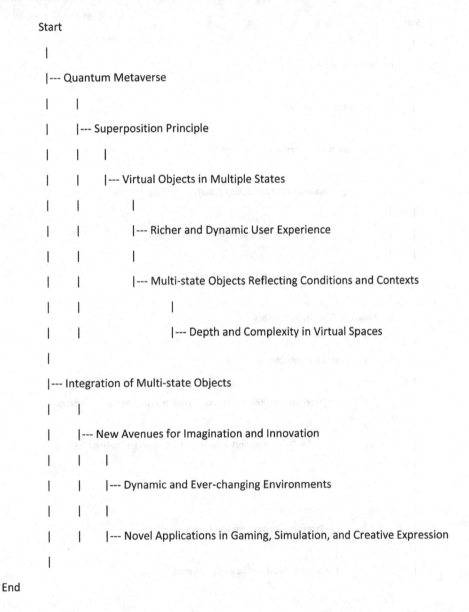

Quantum Entanglement for Secure Communication in the Quantum Metaverse

In the quantum metaverse, secure communication can be achieved through a combination of encryption techniques and quantum computing. Quantum encryption methods utilize the principles of quantum mechanics to provide secure communication channels within the virtual environment or metaverse.

Figure 9. The relationship between the quantum metaverse, secure communication, enhanced security and privacy, and user trust and confidence in the virtual environment through quantum encryption techniques and cryptography

```
Start
 |
 |--- Quantum Metaverse
 |    |
 |    |--- Secure Communication
 |    |    |
 |    |    |--- Quantum Encryption Techniques
 |    |    |
 |    |    |--- Quantum Key Distribution (QKD)
 |    |    |
 |    |    |--- Secure Distribution of Encryption Keys
 |    |    |
 |    |    |--- Verifiably Secure Communication
 |    |
 |    |--- Enhanced Security and Privacy
 |         |
 |         |--- Quantum Cryptography
 |         |    |
 |         |--- Safeguard Sensitive Interactions, Transactions, and Communications
 |         |         |
 |         |         |--- Defense against Attacks on Traditional Encryption Methods
 |         |
 |         |--- User Trust and Confidence
 |              |
 |              |--- Protected Interactions and Communications
 |              |
 |              |--- Sense of Trust and Open Communication
 |
End
```

Quantum computing can enhance security in the quantum metaverse by employing quantum key distribution (QKD). QKD enables the secure distribution of encryption keys that are virtually impossible to crack. With QKD, two parties can communicate in a manner that is verifiably secure, as any attempt to intercept the communication would disrupt the entanglement, alerting the communicating parties to potential eavesdropping.

By implementing quantum cryptography techniques within the quantum metaverse, sensitive interactions, transactions, and private communications can be safeguarded from unauthorized access. Quantum encryption provides a higher level of defense against attacks that could compromise traditional encryption methods, enhancing the security and privacy of user interactions in the virtual world.

Utilizing quantum computing and encryption in the metaverse bolsters users' security and instills confidence in the integrity of their communications. By ensuring that their interactions within the virtual environment are protected from interference and intrusion, users can engage in secure and confidential exchanges, fostering a sense of trust and enabling more open communication (Figure 8).

ENHANCING REAL-TIME PROCESSING IN VIRTUAL WORLDS THROUGH QUANTUM COMPUTING AND METAVERSE TECHNOLOGIES

Quantum computing can provide faster processing rates and more efficient algorithms for creating and modeling virtual worlds. This leads to more responsive and fluid experiences for users, as computations and rendering can be performed at a significantly accelerated pace.

Quantum computing enables the creation of more sophisticated models of physics and other natural processes within virtual worlds. This enhances the realism of user-digital object interactions, allowing for more lifelike and dynamic experiences.

The integration of quantum computing can facilitate the development of intelligent agents or chatbots within virtual worlds. These agents can interact with users in real-time, providing more personalized and natural experiences. Quantum computing's computational power enables advanced AI algorithms that can adapt and respond intelligently to user input.

Quantum computing allows virtual environments to handle data more quickly and effectively. For example, user behavior analysis or sensor data processing can be performed in real-time, enabling interactive and customized experiences for users based on their actions or environment.

Quantum computing can also contribute to improved security in virtual environments. With faster and more effective data encryption and decryption algorithms, as well as advanced authentication and access control techniques, the integrity and confidentiality of user interactions can be strengthened.

QUANTUM COMPUTING AND VIRTUAL REALISTIC ENVIRONMENTS: UNLOCKING NOVEL OUTCOMES

Quantum computing enables more effective and rapid VRE simulations, resulting in lifelike and immersive experiences for users. This includes improvements in aesthetics, faster rendering times, and more intricate physics simulations, creating a heightened sense of realism within VRE environments.

By leveraging quantum computing, VRE environments can employ advanced artificial intelligence algorithms to create realistic interactions between humans and digital objects. These interactions can closely resemble real-world experiences, contributing to more engaging and immersive VRE environments. Quantum computing provides a more powerful platform for training and running AI systems, further enhancing their capabilities.

Blockchain-based technology, in conjunction with quantum computing, can enable secure transfer and storage of VRE assets, such as virtual homes or avatars. This opens up possibilities for a decentralized and democratic VRE economy, where users have greater control over their digital assets and can freely exchange them within a secure framework.

Quantum teleportation techniques can allow users to move between VRE settings instantaneously, providing a seamless and immersive experience. This capability is particularly beneficial for applications such as virtual travel, training simulations, and remote collaboration, where users can effortlessly navigate and interact within various VRE environments.

Quantum computing's ability to handle complex calculations makes it possible to simulate intricate physics phenomena within VREs. This includes simulations of quantum systems or challenging chemical processes, which can have significant implications for areas like medicine development, materials research, and advancements in quantum computing itself.

VR, AR, AND VIDEO WITHIN DIGITAL UNIVERSE

Quantum Computing and Virtual Reality: Expanding the Frontiers of Immersive Experiences

Quantum computing can enhance the efficiency and speed of VR simulations, enabling more realistic and immersive experiences. This includes advancements in graphics, faster rendering times, and more sophisticated physics simulations, resulting in a heightened sense of presence and immersion within VR environments.

Leveraging quantum computing, VR environments can leverage advanced AI algorithms to create more lifelike interactions between users and digital objects. This integration can lead to more intelligent and responsive virtual characters, improving the overall realism and engagement of VR experiences.

Blockchain-based technologies, in conjunction with quantum computing, can provide secure storage and transfer of VR assets, such as digital avatars or virtual real estate. This enables a decentralized and transparent VR ecosystem, empowering users with greater control over their virtual possessions.

Quantum teleportation techniques can enable near-instantaneous movement between VR environments, eliminating the need for manual transitions and providing users with a seamless and immersive experience. This capability has implications for remote collaboration, virtual tourism, and training simulations.

Quantum computing's computational power can facilitate more complex physics simulations within VR environments. This includes simulations of quantum systems or intricate chemical reactions, offering opportunities for scientific research, materials science, and advancements in quantum computing itself.

Quantum Computing and Augmented Reality: Pioneering Immersive Experiences

Quantum computing can improve the efficiency and speed of AR simulations, delivering more immersive experiences. This includes advancements in graphics rendering, faster processing times, and sophisticated physics simulations, resulting in heightened realism and interactivity within AR environments.

Algorithm 1. An algorithm for initialize VR environment, enhance efficiency with quantum computing, incorporate AI, secure assets with blockchain, enable seamless movement, optimize, explore, evaluate, refine

1. Initialize VR simulation environment.

2. Apply quantum computing techniques for enhanced efficiency and speed.

3. Enhance graphics rendering and physics simulations using quantum computing.

4. Incorporate advanced AI algorithms powered by quantum computing for lifelike interactions.

5. Integrate blockchain-based technologies with quantum computing for secure storage and transfer of VR assets.

6. Implement quantum teleportation techniques for seamless movement between VR environments.

7. Utilize quantum computing's power for complex physics simulations.

8. Continuously update and optimize the VR simulation based on user feedback and advancements in quantum computing.

9. Explore scientific research opportunities in quantum systems and chemical reactions within VR environments.

10. Evaluate and refine the algorithm based on performance, user experience, and advancements in quantum computing.

Leveraging quantum computing, AR environments can incorporate advanced AI algorithms to create lifelike interactions between users and digital objects. This integration enables more intelligent and responsive virtual elements, enhancing the overall realism and engagement of AR experiences.

Blockchain-based technologies, in conjunction with quantum computing, can provide secure storage and transfer of AR assets, such as digital overlays or virtual real estate. This ensures decentralized and transparent asset management, empowering users with greater control over their digital possessions.

Quantum computing's computational power enables more complex physics simulations within AR environments. This includes simulations of quantum systems or intricate chemical reactions, offering opportunities for scientific research, materials science, and advancements in quantum computing itself.

AR can be utilized for educational and training purposes, such as medical training or industrial maintenance. By leveraging quantum computing, AR simulations and training environments can become more advanced, leading to better outcomes for trainees in various fields.

Quantum Computing and Mixed Reality: Advancing Immersive Digital Experiences

Quantum computing can enhance the efficiency and speed of MR simulations, resulting in more realistic and immersive experiences. This includes advancements in graphics rendering, faster processing times, and sophisticated physics simulations, allowing users to engage with virtual environments in a more authentic manner.

By leveraging quantum computing, MR environments can incorporate advanced AI algorithms to enhance realism and create more lifelike interactions between users and digital objects. This integration enables intelligent and responsive virtual elements, further blurring the line between the physical and digital worlds.

The utilization of blockchain-based technologies, combined with quantum computing, can provide secure storage and transfer of MR assets, such as digital overlays or virtual real estate. This fosters a decentralized and transparent ecosystem, empowering users with increased control over their digital assets.

Quantum teleportation holds the potential to enable near-instantaneous movement between MR environments, offering users a seamless and immersive experience. This capability can facilitate remote collaboration, virtual tourism, and other applications that require fluid transitions between different virtual spaces.

Quantum computing's computational power can support more complex physics simulations within MR environments. This includes simulations of quantum systems or intricate chemical reactions, opening up possibilities for scientific research, materials science, drug discovery, and advancements in quantum computing itself.

QUANTUM COMPUTING, METAVERSE, AND FUTURE INTERNET: TRANSFORMING THE DIGITAL LANDSCAPE

Quantum computing can greatly impact network communication within the metaverse and future internet technologies. By leveraging quantum algorithms and encryption techniques, it can improve the efficiency and security of data transmission, ensuring faster and more secure interactions between users and digital objects.

Metaverse technologies, in combination with quantum computing, can create highly immersive and interactive virtual environments. Users can engage with realistic simulations, interact with virtual objects, and collaborate with others in shared digital spaces. Blockchain integration can enable decentralized ownership and governance of digital assets, fostering a more inclusive and democratic metaverse ecosystem.

The metaverse relies on future internet technologies to deliver its full potential. High-speed 5G networks provide the necessary bandwidth and low latency for seamless and immersive virtual experiences. Edge computing brings processing power closer to users, reducing latency and enabling real-time interactions. The Internet of Things (IoT) connects physical and virtual worlds, enhancing the metaverse with smart and interconnected devices.

The integration of quantum computing, metaverse technologies, and future internet technologies can unlock new levels of creativity, collaboration, and innovation. Users can engage in immersive experiences, create and trade digital assets securely, and explore novel applications across industries. This convergence opens doors for advancements in fields such as gaming, education, healthcare, architecture, and more.

Quantum Computing, Metaverse, and Blockchain: Advancing Decentralized Digital Economies

The advancement of quantum computing poses a threat to the cryptographic algorithms used in blockchain-based cryptocurrencies. To ensure future security, it is crucial to develop quantum-resistant cryptographic algorithms. This will safeguard the integrity and confidentiality of transactions and user data within blockchain networks.

The metaverse empowers individuals by enabling the creation of virtual assets that can be owned and controlled directly, bypassing centralized entities. Blockchain-based cryptocurrencies provide a secure means for transferring and exchanging these virtual assets, fostering decentralized ownership and governance models.

The metaverse facilitates the emergence of tokenized economies, where virtual assets are represented by tokens. Blockchain-based cryptocurrencies offer secure recording and verification of transactions within these economies. This allows for efficient exchange and trading of virtual assets, fostering a vibrant and liquid digital marketplace.

As the metaverse grows and accommodates an increasing number of users and transactions, scalability becomes a critical challenge. Addressing this challenge requires innovative solutions to ensure blockchain-based systems can handle the demands of a large-scale metaverse environment, maintaining transaction efficiency and responsiveness.

The utilization of blockchain-based cryptocurrencies in the metaverse introduces regulatory challenges. Taxation, anti-money laundering measures, and consumer protection regulations must adapt to the unique characteristics of virtual assets and transactions within the metaverse. Striking the right balance between regulations and fostering innovation is key.

INTEGRATION OF QUANTUM TECHNOLOGY IN THE METAVERSE

Enhancing Security in the Metaverse

This research focuses on the integration of quantum technology to enhance security in the metaverse. It explores the potential of quantum computing for cryptographic algorithms, authentication, and access control mechanisms in virtual environments. The study investigates how quantum encryption and secure communication protocols can protect sensitive data and transactions within the metaverse. It also examines the challenges and opportunities of implementing quantum security measures in a decentralized and distributed environment.

Quantum Computing for Simulations and Virtual Environments

This case study explores the use of quantum computing for simulations and virtual environments in the metaverse. It investigates how quantum algorithms and quantum simulations can enable more realistic physics simulations, advanced graphics rendering, and immersive user experiences. The research explores the potential of quantum-enhanced algorithms to accelerate complex computations and enable more efficient processing in virtual environments. It also discusses the technical challenges and limitations of integrating quantum computing into existing metaverse platforms.

Quantum Machine Learning in the Metaverse

This research examines the application of quantum machine learning techniques in the metaverse. It explores how quantum computing can enhance machine learning algorithms and enable more advanced AI interactions within virtual environments. The study investigates the potential of quantum-inspired algorithms for personalized recommendations, intelligent agents, and natural language processing in the metaverse. It also discusses the challenges of integrating quantum machine learning models into the metaverse infrastructure.

Quantum Communication and Networking

This case study focuses on the integration of quantum communication and networking technologies in the metaverse. It explores how quantum communication protocols, such as quantum teleportation and entanglement, can enable secure and efficient communication between users and digital objects in virtual environments. The research investigates the potential of quantum networks to support large-scale metaverse applications and the challenges of scalability, synchronization, and interoperability. It also examines the implications of quantum communication for remote collaboration and virtual social interactions.

Quantum Encryption and Cryptocurrencies in the Metaverse

This research examines the integration of quantum encryption and blockchain-based cryptocurrencies in the metaverse. It explores how quantum-resistant cryptographic algorithms can secure digital assets, transactions, and virtual economies within the metaverse. The study investigates the potential of quantum-safe blockchain protocols for decentralized ownership and governance of virtual assets. It also discusses the challenges and regulatory considerations associated with the use of quantum-secure cryptocurrencies in the metaverse.

CASE STUDIES AND RESEARCH FINDINGS

Quantum Metaverse

This case study provides a comprehensive review of the integration of quantum computing and metaverse technologies. It examines the potential benefits, challenges, and applications of quantum-powered metaverse platforms. The study explores the impact of quantum computing on rendering, simulation, AI interactions, and cryptography within the metaverse, highlighting the advancements and limitations of existing research and implementations.

Quantum Computing in Virtual Reality

This research study presents a survey of the current state of quantum computing in the context of virtual reality (VR). It investigates the intersection of these two technologies and explores the potential synergies and challenges. The study covers various aspects such as quantum algorithms for VR simulations, quantum-enhanced graphics rendering, and quantum cryptography in immersive environments. It provides insights into the progress made in this field and identifies key areas for further research.

Quantum Metaverse

This case study examines the emergence of the quantum metaverse as a new paradigm in immersive technologies. It explores the integration of quantum computing and metaverse technologies, discussing the potential implications and future prospects. The study investigates the advancements in quantum simulations, AI interactions, and blockchain-based virtual asset management within the metaverse. It also analyzes the impact on user experience and the challenges that need to be addressed for widespread adoption.

Quantum Metaverse

This research study delves into the intersection of quantum computing and virtual reality, exploring the potential synergies and applications. It investigates the role of quantum algorithms in enhancing VR simulations, graphics rendering, and physics-based interactions. The study also examines the challenges associated with hardware requirements, scalability, and user acceptance. It provides insights into ongoing research and highlights the possibilities for future development and collaboration.

Quantum-Enhanced Metaverse

This systematic review focuses on the quantum-enhanced metaverse, analyzing the existing literature and research findings in this field. It evaluates the impact of quantum computing on various aspects of the metaverse, including simulations, AI interactions, cryptography, and blockchain-based virtual economies. The study identifies the key advancements, challenges, and potential applications, offering a comprehensive overview of the current state of quantum-powered metaverse technologies.

MERITS, DEMERITS AND FUTURE CHALLENGES

Merits

1. **Improved Performance:** Quantum computing can enhance the efficiency and speed of simulations, graphics rendering, and physics simulations in the metaverse, resulting in more realistic and immersive experiences for users.
2. **Advanced AI Interactions:** Quantum computing can enable more complex and intelligent AI interactions in the metaverse, leading to personalized and responsive experiences for users.
3. **Enhanced Security:** Quantum computing can strengthen security measures in the metaverse through faster encryption, authentication, and access control mechanisms, ensuring the protection of user data and assets.
4. **Innovation Opportunities:** The combination of quantum computing and metaverse technologies opens up new possibilities for innovation in entertainment, scientific research, education, and training.

Demerits

1. The integration of quantum computing and metaverse technologies is a complex and emerging field, and there are technical challenges related to software development, hardware optimization, and system integration that need to be overcome.

2. Ensuring privacy, security, and equitable access for all users in the metaverse presents ethical challenges that require careful attention and mitigation.
3. Cost and Resource Intensity: Developing and deploying quantum-powered metaverse technologies require significant investment in research, development, and infrastructure, which may pose financial barriers for some organizations.
4. The scarcity of accessible quantum computing resources may restrict the development and deployment of quantum-powered metaverse technologies for organizations that lack the necessary resources.
5. Integrating quantum computing with metaverse technologies demands specialized technical expertise, which may be a challenge for organizations with limited experience in these domains.

Challenges

1. Overcoming software development, hardware optimization, and system integration challenges is crucial to realize the full potential of the combination of quantum computing and metaverse technologies.
2. Expanding the availability of quantum computing resources and making them accessible to a broader range of organizations is essential to drive the development and deployment of quantum-powered metaverse technologies.
3. Developing quantum-powered metaverse technologies requires collaboration between experts in quantum computing, metaverse technologies, and other relevant fields to bridge knowledge gaps and foster innovation.
4. Addressing privacy, security, and equitable access concerns is crucial in the development and deployment of quantum-powered metaverse technologies to ensure responsible and inclusive use.
5. Establishing common standards and protocols that enable interoperability and compatibility between different metaverse platforms and quantum computing systems is necessary for seamless integration and widespread adoption.
6. There is a shortage of experts skilled in both quantum computing and metaverse technologies, necessitating investments in education and training programs to cultivate the required talent.

CHALLENGES AND FUTURE DIRECTIONS

The combination of quantum computing and metaverse technologies faces several technological limitations and roadblocks that need to be addressed. These include software development challenges, hardware optimization, system integration complexities, and scalability issues. Further research and development efforts are needed to overcome these obstacles and create efficient, seamless, and user-friendly quantum-powered metaverse platforms.

The integration of quantum computing and metaverse technologies raises ethical and privacy concerns that must be carefully addressed. As the metaverse becomes more immersive and interconnected, ensuring privacy, security, and equitable access for all users becomes paramount. Transparent data handling practices, robust encryption algorithms, and user-centric policies should be developed to protect user information and prevent unauthorized access or misuse. Additionally, ethical considerations should be taken into account when designing AI interactions and virtual environments to ensure they adhere to ethical guidelines and respect user autonomy and well-being.

To fully unlock the potential of the combination of quantum computing and metaverse technologies, several promising research directions can be pursued:

a)   Further explore the specific applications and benefits of quantum computing in enhancing metaverse technologies. This includes developing quantum algorithms tailored for virtual environment simulations, AI interactions, and cryptography within the metaverse.

b)   Investigate and develop quantum-resistant cryptographic algorithms to safeguard blockchain-based cryptocurrencies and protect the privacy and security of metaverse users in a post-quantum computing era.

c)   Establish common standards, protocols, and interoperability frameworks to enable seamless integration and interaction between different metaverse platforms and quantum computing systems. This will foster collaboration, innovation, and a more interconnected metaverse ecosystem.

d)   Focus on improving user experience and accessibility within the metaverse, ensuring that these technologies are inclusive and accessible to individuals of all abilities and backgrounds. This includes addressing issues such as motion sickness, latency, device compatibility, and designing intuitive user interfaces.

e)   Conduct research on the ethical and societal implications of the metaverse, such as its potential effects on social interactions, mental health, privacy, and equality. Develop guidelines and policies that promote responsible and ethical use of metaverse technologies, balancing innovation with societal well-being.

CONCLUSION

Quantum computing has the potential to enhance the performance and realism of metaverse technologies by enabling faster processing speeds, advanced simulations, and more complex AI interactions. The combination of quantum computing and metaverse technologies can enable decentralized ownership, tokenized economies, and secure transactions through blockchain-based cryptocurrencies. The integration of quantum computing and metaverse technologies brings both merits and demerits, including technical challenges, ethical considerations, and resource limitations. Addressing these challenges requires collaboration, innovation, and investments in research, education, and infrastructure. The combination of quantum computing and metaverse technologies can lead to the creation of immersive and interactive virtual environments that revolutionize fields such as entertainment, scientific research, education, and training. Decentralized ownership and tokenized economies within the metaverse can provide new opportunities for individuals to create, trade, and exchange virtual assets. The integration of quantum computing can enhance security, privacy, and authentication mechanisms in the metaverse, ensuring a safe and trustworthy digital environment. Further research is needed to develop quantum-resistant cryptographic algorithms that can secure blockchain-based cryptocurrencies against potential threats from quantum computing advancements. Continued research and development efforts are required to overcome technical challenges related to software development, hardware optimization, and system integration in quantum-powered metaverse technologies. Ethical considerations, including privacy, security, and equitable access, should be at the forefront of future research to ensure responsible and fair deployment of quantum computing and metaverse technologies. Collaboration between academia, industry, and policymakers is crucial to establish standards, regulations, and frameworks that govern the integration of quantum computing and metaverse technologies, fostering innovation while addressing societal concerns.

REFERENCES

Alladi, T., Chamola, V., Sahu, N., Venkatesh, V., Goyal, A., & Guizani, M. (2022). A comprehensive survey on the applications of blockchain for securing vehicular networks. *IEEE Communications Surveys and Tutorials*, *24*(2), 1212–1239. doi:10.1109/COMST.2022.3160925

Allam, Z., Sharifi, A., Bibri, S. E., Jones, D. S., & Krogstie, J. (2022). The metaverse as a virtual form of smart cities: Opportunities and challenges for environmental, economic, and social sustainability in urban futures. *Smart Cities*, *5*(3), 771–801. doi:10.3390martcities5030040

Allende, M., León, D. L., Cerón, S., Pareja, A., Pacheco, E., Leal, A., Da Silva, M., Pardo, A., Jones, D., Worrall, D. J., Merriman, B., Gilmore, J., Kitchener, N., & Venegas-Andraca, S. E. (2023). Quantum-resistance in blockchain networks. *Scientific Reports*, *13*(1), 5664. doi:10.103841598-023-32701-6 PMID:37024656

Avner, S. (2021). Conceiving particles as undulating granular systems allows fundamentally realist interpretation of quantum mechanics. *Entropy (Basel, Switzerland)*, *23*(10), 1338. doi:10.3390/e23101338 PMID:34682062

Bhattacharya, P., Saraswat, D., Savaliya, D., Sanghavi, S., Verma, A., Sakariya, V., Tanwar, S., Sharma, R., Raboaca, M. S., & Manea, D. L. (2023). Towards future internet: The metaverse perspective for diverse industrial applications. *Mathematics*, *11*(4), 941. doi:10.3390/math11040941

Billewar, S. R., Jadhav, K., Sriram, V. P., Arun, D. A., Mohd Abdul, S., Gulati, K., & Bhasin, D. N. K. K. (2022). The rise of 3D E-Commerce: The online shopping gets real with virtual reality and augmented reality during COVID-19. *World Journal of Engineering*, *19*(2), 244–253. doi:10.1108/WJE-06-2021-0338

Bonime-Blanc, A. (2019). *Gloom to Boom: How Leaders Transform Risk Into Resilience and Value*. Routledge. doi:10.4324/9780429287787

Brijwani, G. N., Ajmire, P. E., & Thawani, P. V. (2023). Future of Quantum Computing in Cyber Security. In *Handbook of Research on Quantum Computing for Smart Environments* (pp. 267–298). IGI Global. doi:10.4018/978-1-6684-6697-1.ch016

Brock, R. (2021). *Stories from physics 8: Quantum Nuclear and Particle Physics*. Academic Press.

Brown, H. R. (2020). *Do symmetries "explain" conservation laws? The modern converse Noether theorem vs pragmatism*. arXiv preprint arXiv:2010.10909.

Capellmann, H. (2021). Space-time in quantum theory. *Foundations of Physics*, *51*(2), 1–34. doi:10.100710701-021-00441-0

Chaubey, N. K., & Prajapati, B. B. (Eds.). (2020). *Quantum Cryptography and the Future of Cyber Security*. IGI Global. doi:10.4018/978-1-7998-2253-0

Chengoden, R., Victor, N., Huynh-The, T., Yenduri, G., Jhaveri, R. H., Alazab, M., Bhattacharya, S., Hegde, P., Maddikunta, P. K. R., & Gadekallu, T. R. (2023). Metaverse for healthcare: A survey on potential applications, challenges and future directions. *IEEE Access : Practical Innovations, Open Solutions, 11*, 12765–12795. doi:10.1109/ACCESS.2023.3241628

Choi, M., Azzaoui, A. E., Singh, S. K., Salim, M. M., Jeremiah, S. R., & Park, J. H. (2022). The Future of Metaverse: Security Issues, Requirements, and Solutions. *Human-Centric Computing and Information Sciences, 12*.

Cook, N. (2008). *Enterprise 2.0: How social software will change the future of work*. Gower Publishing, Ltd.

Dall'Osto, G., & Corni, S. (2022). Time Resolved Raman Scattering of Molecules: A Quantum Mechanics Approach with Stochastic Schroedinger Equation. *The Journal of Physical Chemistry A, 126*(43), 8088–8100. doi:10.1021/acs.jpca.2c05245 PMID:36278928

Damodaran, A. (2023). From non fungible tokens to metaverse: Blockchain based inclusive innovation in arts. *Innovation and Development*, 1–20. doi:10.1080/2157930X.2023.2180709

Dawson, W., Degomme, A., Stella, M., Nakajima, T., Ratcliff, L. E., & Genovese, L. (2022). Density functional theory calculations of large systems: Interplay between fragments, observables, and computational complexity. *Wiley Interdisciplinary Reviews. Computational Molecular Science, 12*(3), e1574. doi:10.1002/wcms.1574

Del Santo, F., & Gisin, N. (2019). Physics without determinism: Alternative interpretations of classical physics. *Physical Review. A, 100*(6), 062107. doi:10.1103/PhysRevA.100.062107

Dergachev, I. D., Dergachev, V. D., Rooein, M., Mirzanejad, A., & Varganov, S. A. (2023). Predicting Kinetics and Dynamics of Spin-Dependent Processes. *Accounts of Chemical Research, 56*(7), 856–866. doi:10.1021/acs.accounts.2c00843 PMID:36926853

Dewdney, C. (2023). Rekindling of de Broglie–Bohm Pilot Wave Theory in the Late Twentieth Century: A Personal Account. *Foundations of Physics, 53*(1), 24. doi:10.100710701-022-00655-w

Di Sia, P. (2021). Birth, development and applications of quantum physics: A transdisciplinary approach. *World Scientific News, 160*, 232–246.

Duan, H., Li, J., Fan, S., Lin, Z., Wu, X., & Cai, W. (2021, October). Metaverse for social good: A university campus prototype. In *Proceedings of the 29th ACM international conference on multimedia* (pp. 153-161). 10.1145/3474085.3479238

Dwivedi, Y. K., Hughes, L., Baabdullah, A. M., Ribeiro-Navarrete, S., Giannakis, M., Al-Debei, M. M., Dennehy, D., Metri, B., Buhalis, D., Cheung, C. M. K., Conboy, K., Doyle, R., Dubey, R., Dutot, V., Felix, R., Goyal, D. P., Gustafsson, A., Hinsch, C., Jebabli, I., ... Wamba, S. F. (2022). Metaverse beyond the hype: Multidisciplinary perspectives on emerging challenges, opportunities, and agenda for research, practice and policy. *International Journal of Information Management, 66*, 102542. doi:10.1016/j. ijinfomgt.2022.102542

Forbes, K. A., & Andrews, D. L. (2021). Orbital angular momentum of twisted light: Chirality and optical activity. *JPhys Photonics, 3*(2), 022007. doi:10.1088/2515-7647/abdb06

Gampel, F., & Gajda, M. (2023). Continuous simultaneous measurement of position and momentum of a particle. *Physical Review. A, 107*(1), 012420. doi:10.1103/PhysRevA.107.012420

Gill, S. S. (2021). Quantum and blockchain based Serverless edge computing: A vision, model, new trends and future directions. *Internet Technology Letters, 275*. doi:10.1002/itl2.275

Gill, S. S., Kumar, A., Singh, H., Singh, M., Kaur, K., Usman, M., & Buyya, R. (2022). Quantum computing: A taxonomy, systematic review and future directions. *Software, Practice & Experience, 52*(1), 66–114. doi:10.1002pe.3039

Jacak, J. E. (2023). *Topological hint to the information paradox and firewall concept for black holes.* arXiv preprint arXiv:2304.10384.

Julian, H. L. C., Chung, T., & Wang, Y. (2023). Adoption of Metaverse in South East Asia: Vietnam, Indonesia, Malaysia. In *Strategies and Opportunities for Technology in the Metaverse World* (pp. 196–234). IGI Global. doi:10.4018/978-1-6684-5732-0.ch012

Kan, K., & Une, M. (2021). *Recent trends on research and development of quantum computers and standardization of post-quantum cryptography.* Academic Press.

Kaur, M., & Venegas-Gomez, A. (2022). Defining the quantum workforce landscape: A review of global quantum education initiatives. *Optical Engineering (Redondo Beach, Calif.), 61*(8), 081806–081806. doi:10.1117/1.OE.61.8.081806

Kholodenko, A. L. (2023). *Maxwell-Dirac isomorphism revisited: from foundations of quantum mechanics to geometrodynamics and cosmology.* arXiv preprint arXiv:2304.01211.

Kumar, A., Ottaviani, C., Gill, S. S., & Buyya, R. (2022). Securing the future internet of things with post-quantum cryptography. *Security and Privacy, 5*(2), e200. doi:10.1002py2.200

Layzer, J. A. (2008). *Natural experiments: ecosystem-based management and the environment.* MIT Press. doi:10.7551/mitpress/9780262122986.001.0001

Liu, Z. K. (2023). *Next fifty years of thermodynamics and its modeling: Integrating quantum, statistical, classical, and irreversible thermodynamics for prediction of transformative properties.* arXiv preprint arXiv:2301.02132.

Mbagwu, J. P. C., Madububa, B. I., & Onwuemeka, J. I. (2020). Article on basics of quantum theory. *Int. J. Sci. Res. in Physics and Applied Sciences, 8*(3).

Mohamed, M. (2021). *Quantum Annealing: Research and Applications* [Master's thesis]. University of Waterloo.

Nassimbeni, G., Sartor, M., Nassimbeni, G., & Sartor, M. (2008). The Case Studies. *Sourcing in India: Strategies and Experiences in the Land of Service Offshoring*, 173-252.

Nieminen, R. M. (2001). From number crunching to virtual reality: mathematics, physics and computation. *Mathematics Unlimited—2001 and Beyond*, 937-959.

Ning, H., Wang, H., Lin, Y., Wang, W., Dhelim, S., Farha, F., Ding, J., & Daneshmand, M. (2023). A Survey on the Metaverse: The State-of-the-Art, Technologies, Applications, and Challenges. *IEEE Internet of Things Journal*, 1. doi:10.1109/JIOT.2023.3278329

Oldani, R. (2023). *The Influence of Time in a Theory of Nature*. Academic Press.

Padgett, M. J., Molloy, J., & McGloin, D. (Eds.). (2010). *Optical Tweezers: methods and applications*. CRC Press. doi:10.1201/EBK1420074123

Perlner, R. A., & Cooper, D. A. (2009, April). Quantum resistant public key cryptography: a survey. In *Proceedings of the 8th Symposium on Identity and Trust on the Internet* (pp. 85-93). 10.1145/1527017.1527028

Piela, L. (2020). Ideas of Quantum Chemistry: Volume 1: From Quantum Physics to Chemistry. Elsevier.

Ren, X., Xu, M., Niyato, D., Kang, J., Xiong, Z., Qiu, C., & Wang, X. (2023). *Building Resilient Web 3.0 with Quantum Information Technologies and Blockchain: An Ambilateral View*. arXiv preprint arXiv:2303.13050.

Renou, M. O., Trillo, D., Weilenmann, M., Le, T. P., Tavakoli, A., Gisin, N., Acín, A., & Navascués, M. (2021). Quantum theory based on real numbers can be experimentally falsified. *Nature*, 600(7890), 625–629. doi:10.103841586-021-04160-4 PMID:34912122

Seskir, Z. C., Migdał, P., Weidner, C., Anupam, A., Case, N., Davis, N., Decaroli, C., Ercan, İ., Foti, C., Gora, P., Jankiewicz, K., La Cour, B. R., Yago Malo, J., Maniscalco, S., Naeemi, A., Nita, L., Parvin, N., Scafirimuto, F., Sherson, J. F., ... Chiofalo, M. (2022). Quantum games and interactive tools for quantum technologies outreach and education. *Optical Engineering (Redondo Beach, Calif.)*, 61(8), 081809–081809. doi:10.1117/1.OE.61.8.081809

Sihare, S., & Nath, V. (2017). Revisited quantum protocols. *International Journal of Mathematical Sciences and Computing*, 3(2), 11–21. doi:10.5815/ijmsc.2017.02.02

Sihare, S., & Nath, V. V. (c) (2017, January). Multiple Entities Search through Simon's Quantum Algorithm. In *2017 IEEE 7th International Advance Computing Conference (IACC)* (pp. 789-792). IEEE.

Sihare, S. R., & Nath, V. V. (2016, December). Application of quantum search algorithms as a web search engine. In *2016 International Conference on Global Trends in Signal Processing, Information Computing and Communication (ICGTSPICC)* (pp. 11-17). IEEE. 10.1109/ICGTSPICC.2016.7955261

Sihare, S. R., & Nath, V. V. (2017). Analysis of quantum algorithms with classical systems counterpart. *International Journal of Information Engineering and Electronic Business*, 9(2), 20. doi:10.5815/ijieeb.2017.02.03

Sugiyama, Y., Matsumura, A., & Yamamoto, K. (2022). Consistency between causality and complementarity guaranteed by the Robertson inequality in quantum field theory. *Physical Review. D, 106*(12), 125002. doi:10.1103/PhysRevD.106.125002

Thompson, R. B. (2023). *A Holographic Principle for Non-Relativistic Quantum Mechanics.* arXiv preprint arXiv:2301.04180.

Wang, H., Liang, X., Wang, J., Jiao, S., & Xue, D. (2020). Multifunctional inorganic nanomaterials for energy applications. *Nanoscale, 12*(1), 14–42. doi:10.1039/C9NR07008G PMID:31808494

Wang, Y., Su, Z., Zhang, N., Xing, R., Liu, D., Luan, T. H., & Shen, X. (2022). A survey on metaverse: Fundamentals, security, and privacy. *IEEE Communications Surveys and Tutorials.*

Zable, A., Hollenberg, L., Velloso, E., & Goncalves, J. (2020, November). Investigating immersive virtual reality as an educational tool for quantum computing. In *Proceedings of the 26th ACM Symposium on Virtual Reality Software and Technology* (pp. 1-11). 10.1145/3385956.3418957

Zhao, N., Zhang, H., Yang, X., Yan, J., & You, F. (2023). Emerging information and communication technologies for smart energy systems and renewable transition. *Advances in Applied Energy, 9*, 100125. doi:10.1016/j.adapen.2023.100125

ADDITIONAL READING

Azuma, R. T. (1997). A survey of augmented reality. *Presence (Cambridge, Mass.), 6*(4), 355–385. doi:10.1162/pres.1997.6.4.355

Gubbi, J., Buyya, R., Marusic, S., & Palaniswami, M. (2013). Internet of Things (IoT): A vision, architectural elements, and future directions. *Future Generation Computer Systems, 29*(7), 1645–1660. doi:10.1016/j.future.2013.01.010

Kshetri, N. (2017). Blockchain's roles in meeting key supply chain management objectives. *International Journal of Information Management, 37*(2), 150–160.

KEY TERMS AND DEFINITIONS

Augmented Reality: A technology that overlays digital information and virtual objects onto the real world, enhancing the user's perception and interaction with their surroundings.

Blockchain: A decentralized and transparent digital ledger technology that securely records and verifies transactions across multiple computers or nodes.

Cryptocurrency: Digital or virtual currency that uses cryptography for secure transactions and operates independently of a central bank.

Internet of Things: The network of interconnected physical devices and objects that can collect and exchange data over the internet, enabling them to communicate and interact with each other.

Quantum Metaverse: A virtual space where users interact with digital objects and each other, leveraging the power of quantum computing for enhanced performance and experiences.

Virtual Reality: An immersive technology that creates a simulated environment, allowing users to interact with and experience computer-generated content in a realistic and interactive way.

ENDNOTES

[1] https://blog.shi.com/digital-workplace/how-the-metaverse-can-transform-your-business-for-the-better/#:~:text=The%20global%20metaverse%20market%20was,(CAGR)%20of%2043.3%25.

[2] https://nvidianews.nvidia.com/news/nvidia-announces-new-system-for-accelerated-quantum-classical-computing

[3] https://www.rmit.edu.au/news/all-news/2022/apr/diamond-quantum-computing-hub

[4] https://ethz.ch/en/news-and-events/eth-news/news/2021/05/eth-zurich-and-psi-found-quantum-computing-hub.html

Chapter 10
Metaverse in Marketing:
Challenges and Opportunities

Albérico Travassos Rosário
GOVCOPP, IADE, Universidade Europeia, Portugal

Paula Rosa Lopes
CICANT, Universidade Lusófona, Portugal

Filipe Sales Rosário
University Europeia, Portugal

ABSTRACT

The term metaverse refers to a collective virtual shared space created by the convergence of virtually enhanced physical reality and physically persistent virtual space, including the sum of all virtual worlds, augmented reality, and the internet. In the context of marketing, the metaverse can be thought of as a new platform for brands to engage with consumers and create immersive, interactive experiences. Brands can use the metaverse to create virtual events, product demonstrations, and other interactive experiences that allow consumers to engage with the brand in a more meaningful way. The metaverse offers new and exciting opportunities for brands to connect with consumers and create engaging, interactive experiences that drive brand awareness and loyalty. As a result, more research is needed to provide reliable and accurate data on Metaverse in marketing. This study aims to assess the challenges and opportunities, thus building a frame of reference on metaverse in marketing.

INTRODUCTION

Since 2020, the term "metaverse" has increasingly gained traction in the tech world, with world tech giants such as Facebook leading the wave. Kim (2021) defines the metaverse as "a three-dimensional virtual world inhabited by avatars of real people" (p. 141). It constitutes a computer-mediated environment where people engage in social activities through avatars in virtual 360-degree worlds. In addition, a metaverse can be defined as an interactive, immersive, and collaborative virtual 3D world that allows

DOI: 10.4018/978-1-6684-8851-5.ch010

people or their avatars to interact in real-time. The metaverse comprises various technologies, such as augmented reality (AR) and virtual reality (VR), facilitating multimodal interactions with digital products, virtual settings, and people. Although the concept gained much attention in 2020-2021, the term was coined by Neal Stephenson in his 1992 novel Snow Crash. Marketers are exploring opportunities to integrate metaverse in marketing. Hennig-Thurau and Ognibeni (2022) indicate that the social dimension represents the actual value of the metaverse. In this case, certain activities that people engage in the internet alone can be improved through metaverse technologies. For example, shopping in a virtual store can be better than shopping on a website since the customer can use the avatar to try on the products and add customizations before making the purchase decisions. In addition, companies can leverage these innovations to create interactive experiences such as virtual events and product demonstrations. As a result, metaverse can potentially improve customer experience and satisfaction, which are critical in marketing.

Metaverse provides multiple opportunities that can help improve marketing initiatives. For instance, it provides large amounts of data and insights that can be used to optimize marketing strategies. Brands can observe user behavior and engagement in real-time, enabling them to gather data to improve their marketing campaigns and adjust the messaging (Buhalis et al., 2022). Moreover, metaverse in marketing allows brands to reach a global audience in a highly targeted way. The metaverse is accessible worldwide, allowing companies to use highly localized and relevant content to reach consumers in different countries or regions. However, metaverse in marketing is associated with various challenges, such as privacy and user-consent concerns and consumers' access to technologies (Bushell, 2022). These challenges can undermine or slow its adoption in marketing practice. As a result, this systematic bibliometric literature review integrates data from multiple sources to provide insights on opportunities and challenges of using metaverse in marketing to build a framework of reference for marketers, decision- and policy-makers.

METHODOLOGICAL APPROACH

A systematic bibliometric literature review (LRSB) was conducted to identify relevant sources and synthesize data for final reporting on the opportunities and challenges of the metaverse in marketing. The method was selected since it enables the researcher to explore and analyze large volumes of data and unpack evolutionary nuances in the emergence of the metaverse and its integration into marketing. In addition, it uses a replicable, scientific, and transparent process that helps the researcher eliminate bias through a comprehensive literature search of published and unpublished studies (Linnenluecke et al., 2020). Due to the rigorous approach used and the large amount of data analyzed, this methodology helps uncover emerging themes and topics, map the evolution of a specific topic, and identify gaps in research and practice. With the metaverse still an emerging innovation, this methodology will help gather relevant data that can help enhance its integration into marketing strategies and campaigns, thus bridging the transfer from the research to practice gap.

The LRSB helped filter the most relevant and quality sources for analysis and reporting. Consequently, the methodology can be used to decipher and map cumulative scientific knowledge and emerging variations of a well-established topic (Rosário & Dias, 2023; Rosário, 2021; Rosário & Dias, 2022; Rosário, et al., 2021).

Thus, the use of bibliometric analysis can help understand its development and adoption in businesses to identify potential challenges. The use of the LRSB review process is divided into 3 phases and 6 steps (Table 1), as proposed by Rosário and Dias (2023), Rosário (2021), Rosário and Dias (2022), Rosário, et al. (2021).

Table 1. Process of systematic LRSB

Phase	Step	Description
Exploration	Step 1	formulating the research problem
	Step 2	searching for appropriate literature
	Step 3	critical appraisal of the selected studies
	Step 4	data synthesis from individual sources
Interpretation	Step 5	reporting findings and recommendations
Communication	Step 6	presentation of the LRSB report

Source: Rosário and Dias (2023), Rosário (2021), Rosário and Dias (2022)

Within the scope of this investigation, the database of scientific and/or academic documents indexed by Scopus, recognized as the most important peer review in the scientific and academic world, was used. However, we consider that the study has the limitation of considering only the Scopus decomposition database, excluding other scientific and academic bases. The literature search includes peer-reviewed scientific and/or academic documents published up to March 2023.

The literature search process began with identifying the appropriate database, which in this case was Scopus. The initial keyword "metaverse" was used, resulting in 1,086 document results. These sources evaluated the development of the metaverse and its application in various fields, making some sources irrelevant to this study. Therefore, the exact keyword "marketing" was added to filter the search to document results relevant to the study topic. As a result, 55 document results were identified (N=55), which are synthesized in the final report Table 2.

Table 2. Screening methodology

Database Scopus	Screening	Publications
Meta-search	keyword: metaverse	1,086
First Inclusion Criterion	keyword: metaverse, marketing	
Screening	keyword: metaverse, marketing Published until March 2023	55

Source: Own elaboration

Finally, content and theme analysis techniques were used to identify, analyze and report the various documents as proposed by Rosário and Dias, (2023), Rosário (2021), Rosário and Dias (2022), Rosário, et al. (2021).

The 55 scientific and/or academic documents indexed in Scopus are later analyzed in a narrative and bibliometric way to deepen the content and possible derivation of common themes that directly respond to the research question (Rosário & Dias, 2023; Rosário, 2021; Rosário & Dias, 2022; Rosário et al., 2021). Of the 55 selected documents, 26 Articles, 15 are conferences, 4 are reviews, 2 are editorial, and 1 is a book chapter.

PUBLICATION DISTRIBUTION

Peer-reviewed articles on Metaverse in marketing until March 2023. The year 2022 had the highest number of peer-reviewed publications on the subject, reaching 35. Figure 1 summarizes the peer-reviewed literature published in March 2023. The publications were sorted out as follows: Journal Of Cosmetic Dermatology (3); with 2 publications (Sustainability Switzerland; Springer Proceedings In Business And Economics; Smart Innovation Systems And Technologies; Psychology And Marketing; Proceedings Of The International Conferences On E Health 2015 Eh 2015 E Commerce And Digital Marketing 2015 EC 2015 And Information Systems Post Implementation And Change Management 2015 Ispcm 2015 Part Of The Multi Conference On Computer Science And Information Systems 2015; Journal Of Business Research; and ACM International Conference Proceeding Series); and the remaining publications with 1.

Figure 1. Documents by year
Source: Own elaboration

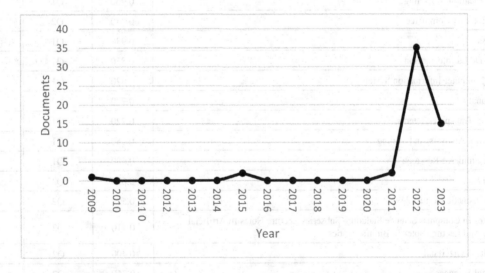

In Table 3 we analyze the Scimago Journal & Country Rank (SJR), which registers the Journal Of Marketing in the position of best quartile and H index per publication, which is the most cited publication with 7,460 (SJR), Q1 and H Index 6.

There is a total of 32 publications in Q1, 3 in Q2 and 4 in Q3 and 4 in Q4. Publications from best quartile Q1 represent 67% of the publications on titles; best quartile Q2 represents 6%, best quartile Q3 represents 8%, and best Q4 represents 8% of each of the titles of 48 publications, finally, 5 publications still do not have data available, representing 10% of publications. As shown in Table 3, the significant majority of publications are in the best quartile Q1.

Table 3. Scimago journal and country rank impact factor

Title	SJR	Best Quartile	H Index
International Journal Of Information Management	4.580	Q1	132
Journal Of The Academy Of Marketing Science	4.430	Q1	183
Tourism Management	3.380	Q1	216
Journal Of Business Ethics	2.440	Q1	208
Journal Of Business Research	2.320	Q1	217
International Journal Of Contemporary Hospitality Management	2.290	Q1	100
Journal Of Hospitality Marketing And Management	2.000	Q1	59
Data Analysis And Knowledge Discovery	1,400	Q4	3
Psychology And Marketing	1.20	Q1	124
International Journal Of Tourism Research	1.140	Q1	67
Journal Of Vacation Marketing	0.960	Q1	68
Journal Of Internet Commerce	0.930	Q2	31
IEEE Access	0.930	Q1	158
Profesional De La Informacion	0.830	Q1	33
Journal Of Computer Information Systems	0.820	Q1	66
IT Professional	0.770	Q2	54
Iet Intelligent Transport Systems	0.720	Q1	51
Social Network Analysis And Mining	0.680	Q1	38
Electronic Commerce Research	0.680	Q1	43
Information Switzerland	0.620	Q2	36
Journal Of Cosmetic Dermatology	0.570	Q2	49
Lecture Notes In Computer Science Including Subseries Lecture Notes In Artificial Intelligence And Lecture Notes In Bioinformatics	0.410	Q2	415
Sustainability Switzerland	0.400	Q2	11
Cogent Social Sciences	0.360	Q2	15
Management And Marketing	0.320	Q2	14
Fashion Practice	0.310	Q1	9
Studies In Computational Intelligence	0.240	Q4	73
ACM International Conference Proceeding Series	0.230	-*	128
Smart Innovation Systems And Technologies	0.220	Q3	27
Communications In Computer And Information Science	0.210	Q4	55

continues on following page

Table 3. Continued

Title	SJR	Best Quartile	H Index
Journal Of Distribution Science	0.180	Q4	11
Journal Of Content Community And Communication	0.170	Q3	6
Proceedings Of The International Conferences On E Health 2015 Eh 2015 E Commerce And Digital Marketing 2015 EC 2015 And Information Systems Post Implementation And Change Management 2015 Ispcm 2015 Part Of The Multi Conference On Computer Science And Information Systems 2015	0	-*	2
Springer Proceedings In Business And Economics	-*	-*	-*
Software Impacts	-*	-*	-*
Proceedings Web3d 2022 27th ACM Conference On 3D Web Technology	-*	-*	-*
Proceedings Of The Laccei International Multi Conference For Engineering Education And Technology	-*	0	6
Proceedings 2022 IEEE Conference On Virtual Reality And 3D User Interfaces Abstracts And Workshops Vrw 2022	-*	-*	-*
Palgrave Studies In Practice Global Fashion Brand Management	-*	-*	-*
Ismsit 2022 6th International Symposium On Multidisciplinary Studies And Innovative Technologies Proceedings	-*	-*	-*
I Com	-*	-*	-*
Computers	-*	-*	-*
2022 IEEE Global Communications Conference Globecom 2022 Proceedings	-*	-*	-*
2022 IEEE 13th Annual Ubiquitous Computing Electronics And Mobile Communication Conference Uemcon 2022	-*	-*	-*
2022 Asu International Conference In Emerging Technologies For Sustainability And Intelligent Systems Icetsis 2022	-*	-*	-*
2022 10th International Conference On Orange Technology Icot 2022	-*	-*	-*

Note: *data not available.

Source: own elaboration

The subject areas covered by the 55 scientific and/or academic documents were: Computer Science (30); Business, Management and Accounting (19); Social Sciences (17); Engineering (11); Decision Sciences (7); Economics, Econometrics and Finance (6); Energy (5); Environmental Science (4); Mathematics (4); Medicine (4); Psychology (3); Arts and Humanities (2); and Materials Science (1).

The most cited article was "A metaverse: Taxonomy, components, applications, and open challenges", by Park and Kim (2022) with 158 citations published in the IEEE Access 0,930 (SJR), the best quartile (Q1) and with an H index (158), this article "divides the concepts and essential techniques necessary for realizing the Metaverse into three components (i.e., hardware, software, and contents) and three approaches (i.e., user interaction, implementation, and application) rather than marketing or hardware approach to conduct a comprehensive analysis".

In Figure 2 we can analyze the evolution of citations of the documents published until March 2023. The number of citations shows a positive net growth with R2 of 39% for the period ≤2013-2023, with 2022 reaching 268 citations.

Figure 2. Evolution of citations between ≤2013 and 2023
Source: Own elaboration

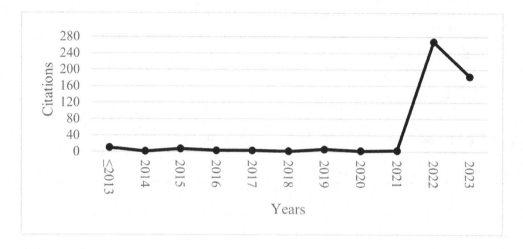

The h-index was used to ascertain the productivity and impact of the published work, based on the largest number of articles included that had at least the same number of citations. Of the documents considered for the h-index, 10 have been cited at least 10 times.

Citations of all scientific and/or academic documents from the period ≤2013 to March 2032, with a total of 487 citations, of the 55 documents 29 were not cited. The self-citation of documents in the period ≤2013 to March 2032, 2022 was self-cited 60 times.

This investigation is based on a bibliometric study that was carried out to research and discover indicators of the evolution and dynamics of scientific and/or academic information in published articles based on the main keywords (Figure 3).

The results were extracted from VOSviewe, a scientific software, which aims to find and identify the main search keywords "metaverse, marketing".

To conduct this study, a survey was carried out based on scientific and/or academic documents that address the topic of Influencer Marketing in the Digital Ecosystem. Figure 4 allows examining the linked keywords with the aim of highlighting the keywords network that appears together/linked in each scientific article, leading to the recognition of the studied topics and the identification of trends in future research. Finally, in Figure 5, a profusion of bibliographic coupling is presented, including a unit of analysis of the cited references.

Figure 3. A network of all keywords

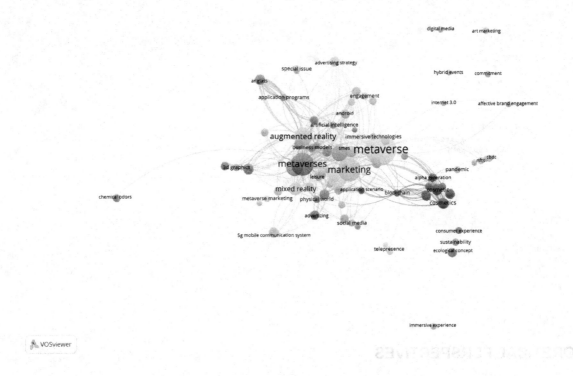

Figure 4. A network of linked keywords

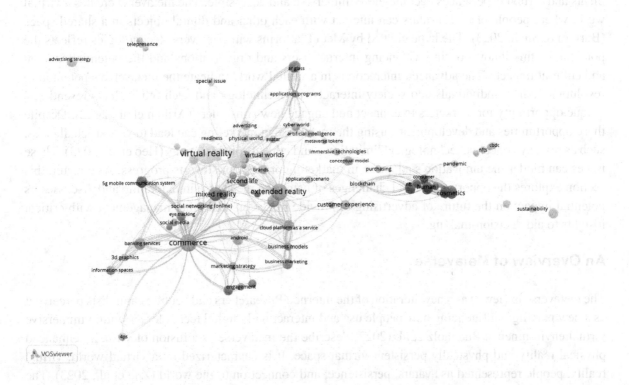

Figure 5. A network of bibliographic coupling

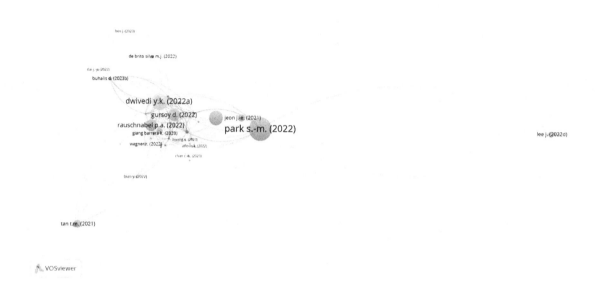

THEORETICAL PERSPECTIVES

The metaverse concept has increasingly gained attention in recent years as technological advancements and virtual experiences become more immersive and accessible. The metaverse creates a virtual world where people or their avatars can interact with each other and digital objects in a shared space (Barrera & Shah, 2023). The hype created by Meta Platforms with metaverse technologies reflects the potential of this innovation in influencing internet users and organizations and the potential societal and cultural impacts. The advanced interactions in a virtual world indicate the metaverse's potential to revolutionize how individuals and society interact with technology and each other, thus presenting a unique opportunity for marketers to connect and engage new consumers (Arikan et al., 2022). Despite these opportunities and developments, using the metaverse in marketing can lead to various challenges, such as privacy concerns, technological limitations, and ethical considerations (Heo et al., 2023). These issues can hinder the innovation's adoption in marketing practice or slow its progress. As a result, this section explores the opportunities and challenges of using the metaverse in marketing and discusses its potential impact on the future of advertising to provide marketers and other management with critical insights to aid decision-making.

An Overview of Metaverse

The metaverse is viewed as a new iteration of the internet. Researchers and venture capitalists perceive it as a new paradigm influencing how people use and interact with digital technologies within immersive virtual environments. Buchholz et al. (2022) describe the metaverse as a fusion of virtually enhanced physical reality and physically persistent virtual space. It is characterized by a virtual world, virtual reality, people represented as avatars, persistence, and connection to the world (Zhe et al., 2023). The virtual world can be explored through gaming consoles, computers, wearable technology, and mobile technologies. They allow users to experience 3D graphics and sound, making them feel more present in the metaverse despite being physically in the real world (Buhalis et al., 2023). Although there lacks a universally or scientifically-accepted definition of the metaverse, it is represented in research as a social medium combining virtual worlds and augmented real worlds to enable people to interact, communicate, collaborate, own property, and trade (Tsai, 2022). The information, interactions, and activities facilitated in the metaverse combine real and digital influences, creating an integrated system.

The metaverse concept has been increasingly gaining popularity among businesses considering it a lucrative opportunity to achieve organizational growth in this digital era. It is characterized by two technological breakthroughs: wearable technology and immersive experiences (Ricoy-Casas, 2023). The wearable technology includes the virtual reality headset. Immersive experiences refer to the perceptions of being in a continuous digital environment, different from the one experience in day-to-day life (Bourlakis et al., 2009). Although popularized by tech and gaming companies like Meta Platforms (formerly Facebook Inc.) and Fortnite, the metaverse is not limited to any location or individuals. This is evidenced in Buchholz et al.'s (2022, p.316) research which indicates that the metaverse can be experienced "synchronously and persistently by an effectively unlimited number of users with an individual sense of presence and with continuity of data, such as identity, history, entitlements, objects, communications, and payments." This broad reach ensures global reach and access to the metaverse.

Many businesses perceive the metaverse as a cutting-edge technological market that can be leveraged as a platform for producing, trading, and buying things. As a result, they are increasing investments in metaverse technologies and infrastructure to enhance their ability to develop virtual objects and engage customers through virtual environments and experiences (Buhalis et al., 2023). While these organizations are applying this innovation in multiple sectors, it has become exciting in marketing due to its ability to enhance customer experiences and engagement (Havele et al., 2022). This makes it essential to study and explore how the metaverse can be leveraged in marketing to enhance the performance and outcomes of marketing initiatives and campaigns.

Metaverse and Marketing

The metaverse is a term used to describe a virtual world created by combining augmented and virtual reality technologies. It can potentially revolutionize how marketers interact with consumers by creating immersive experiences where customers join events or experience products in a virtual world. The rapid growth of the metaverse in marketing is evidenced in Dwivedi et al.'s (2022) research, which found that the direct-to- avatar transactions are estimated at US $54 billion. Companies are setting up shops in the Roblox gaming platform to promote and sell products relevant to their target customers. Examples include "Walmart Land," launched in September 2022, and Gucci-Town. These platforms sell digital twins of real products, such as clothes and jewelry, allowing customers to experience the product before making an actual purchase. However, some digital shops, such as Gucci-Town, sell limited products. An example of this sale strategy is the "Gucci Virtual 25" shoes selling for under €20, which can be used in the Gucci app or as a digital product in Roblox (Buchholz et al., 2022). Another example was the Gucci Dionysus bag sold at $4115, a price exceeding the cost of the physical bag (Dwivedi et al., 2022). These examples demonstrate that marketers and brands can create virtual spaces that consumers can explore and interact with, enabling them to experience products and services more engagingly than simply viewing an advertisement.

Additionally, the metaverse allows for more personalized marketing experiences. Personalization in the metaverse is facilitated by the ability to collect customer behavior, such as behaviors and interests, which can empower brands to tailor their messages and experiences to individual consumers (Hazan et al., 2022). For example, a clothing brand that runs a virtual store that allows users to try on clothes and accessories in a virtual fitting room can collect customer data on their preferences, such as colors, styles, and types of clothes. This data can be used to offer personalized recommendations and marketing experiences (Chan et al., 2023). Tracking how consumers interact with ads or products can be difficult in traditional marketing. Thus, the metaverse helps marketers and brands overcome this challenge by providing detailed analytics and data on how consumers interact with virtual spaces and products (Giang Barrera & Shah, 2023). In addition, the real-time interactions between consumers and brands in the metaverse allow for immediate feedback, enabling quick campaign adjustments. Therefore, data and analytics in the metaverse create an opportunity in marketing for refining marketing strategies and creating more effective campaigns.

Interactive Advertising in the Metaverse

The metaverse is interactive in nature, making it an effective advertising tool. The strategies used to facilitate consumer-brand interactions in the metaverse can influence how consumers process, perceive and respond to advertising. One major way the metaverse supports interactive advertising is by facilitating two-way communication between the brand and the consumer (Du et al., 2022). Unlike in traditional marketing, where customers were passive, and advertising was largely one-sided, the metaverse provides an interactive experience that allows meaningful engagement. Moreover, it has a higher level of interactivity availed through tools such as virtual reality headsets, haptic feedback devices, and motion sensors (Enriquez et al., 2022). Companies using the metaverse as an advertising tool leverage these features to create more immersive and interactive experiences (Hastuti et al., 2023). For example, a car manufacturer can use the metaverse to create a virtual driving experience that allows customers to test-drive cars in a safe and controlled environment. These experiences are more likely to leave a lasting impression on consumers (Gursoy et al., 2022). Moreover, they are not available in other forms of digital or traditional advertising, making interactive advertising in the metaverse unique. Therefore, brands can use the metaverse to create more engaging advertising campaigns that capture consumers' attention and keep them engaged.

Flow Theory and the Metaverse in Marketing

The concept of flow can help brands understand user experience in the digital world and improve their digital products or services. The flow theory reflects a situation in which people are in an optimal state of mind, thus fully immersed in a single task; they feel in control (An et al., 2021). In this case, they are involved and concentrating on the activity for optimal experiences. As a result, the flow concept involves analyzing the user's cognitive, emotional, sensory, behavioral, and social components (Dwivedi et al., 2022). With the evolution of the internet and the increased access to information and channels, people can engage in a wide range of activities, thus influencing their flow experiences. For example, research shows that users' attention span has significantly decreased, with more people preferring short videos over long ones or short posts over long blogs (Demir et al., 2023). However, the metaverse can help overcome this challenge by seamlessly blending people's digital and physical lives into a single immersive experience. The metaverse features enhance users' deep involvement in an activity, resulting in flow experiences. In the marketing context, the flow experiences in the metaverse can be used to improve consumer engagement and involvement in meaningful brand interactions that influence their behaviors, attitudes, and emotions.

The flow theory suggests that user engagement and satisfaction increase when they are in a state of flow. This occurs when they fully concentrate on an activity and feel a sense of control over their environment. Flow experiences can be created in the metaverse by providing users with challenging tasks and goals requiring full attention and involvement (Dwivedi et al., 2022). For example, brands can create challenges within the metaverse that require increased skill and concentration to achieve specific points that can be exchanged with rewards such as bonuses or discounts. As users strive to achieve these points, they will enter a state of flow, feeling fully engaged and in control of their experience (Demir et al., 2023). Furthermore, companies can create collaborative activities within the metaverse to leverage its social nature, thus creating flow experiences that require group effort and coordination. For instance, a virtual team-building activity could encourage users to work together to solve a problem, complete a task, or achieve a goal (Hassouneh & Brengman, 2015). As they participate in this collaborative exercise, they will enter a state of flow characterized by absolute concentration and enjoyment and complete engagement and connection to the task. These activities can be replicated in marketing, where customers engage in activities such as product demonstrations to improve experience co-creation and brand interaction (An et al., 2021). Positive flow experiences can result in positive outcomes such as sales, customer acquisition, and retention. Therefore, the flow theory in the metaverse demonstrates the significance of immersive, interactive activities and experiences that capture users' attention and influence their emotional, mental, and behavioral responses to marketing initiatives.

Opportunities of Metaverse in Marketing

The metaverse presents opportunities for marketers to improve engagement and customer interaction in digital environments. For instance, running a virtual store within the metaverse allows marketers to interact with customers in real-time or demonstrate product usage, thus improving customer experience and satisfaction. Consequently, this use can result in positive outcomes such as increased sales and brand perception. This section explores these opportunities to provide insights that can help marketing professionals improve their strategies and campaigns.

Increased Brand Awareness

Marketers can use the metaverse presents to increase brand awareness and engagement with their target audience. For instance, the metaverse facilitates virtual events and experiences, allowing brands to engage with their audience within the digital environment (Bousba & Arya, 2022). These events can include product launches, concerts, or even meet-and-greets with influencers and other brand ambassadors. For example, a makeup brand can organize and host a virtual beauty product launch event featuring makeup artists and influencers. During the event, the customers can interact with these experts and participate in product demonstrations showcasing how each product works or is applied. Such an experience is more likely to leave a positive impression on the customer and increase their satisfaction and the likelihood of purchasing the products (Lee & Kwon, 2022). Therefore, hosting virtual events creates memorable experiences that can result in positive brand associations and increase brand awareness. Moreover, the metaverse can increase brand awareness by facilitating virtual product placement, where products are placed within virtual environments (Zhu et al., 2023). This approach enables brands to showcase their products within the metaverse for online customers. For example, companies set up shops in the Roblex metaverse environment, selling digital and physical products (Ario et al., 2022). These aspects show that the metaverse creates unique opportunities for businesses to increase brand awareness by targeting potential customers in various digital environments.

Other opportunities for increasing brand awareness identified in metaverse research include virtual advertising and gamification. The metaverse facilitates virtual advertising by providing virtual ad placements through billboards, posters, and other advertising opportunities within virtual environments (Wagner & Cozmiuc, 2022). This new, unique advertising strategy creates an opportunity for brands to reach consumers in a new and immersive way. On the other hand, gamification as a marketing strategy involves leveraging game design principles to engage and motivate people to achieve specific goals (Chen & Yao, 2022). Brands embracing the metaverse as a marketing channel create games and challenges to provide their target audiences with a more engaging experience that results in higher brand awareness. From these perspectives, it is evident that the metaverse can be used to increase brand awareness.

Enhanced Tracking and Monitoring

The metaverse enhances marketers' tracking and monitoring capabilities to optimize marketing campaigns. The metaverse achieves this by providing real-time data on user behavior and interactions (Chinie et al., 2022). As a result, this capability allows marketers to track and monitor campaign performance in real-time, creating an opportunity to identify potential areas that need adjustments. In addition, knowing what is working and what is not helps improve campaign performance and results by continuously refining the marketing messages and targeting strategies (Njoku et al., 2023). Furthermore, the metaverse is characterized by advanced analytics capabilities, which enable marketers to measure the effectiveness of their campaigns with greater precision (Dai & Zhao, 2022). Data analytics is crucial in marketing since they enable marketers and brands to understand the market and their customers, leading to greater personalization, efficiency, and customer satisfaction. For instance, advanced analytics in the metaverse can provide deeper insights into user behavior, preferences, and interests. This information can be used to optimize campaigns for better performance and personalization.

Additionally, the metaverse provides audience-targeting capabilities that allow marketers to target specific demographics and psychographics. Audience targeting empowers marketers to create more relevant and personalized campaigns that resonate with their target users, thus driving better results (Zhe et al., 2023). In addition, the metaverse provides an ideal platform for A/B testing, which enables marketers to test different variations of marketing campaigns to determine the one that can perform better. A/B testing enables marketers to measure the impact of different marketing elements on user behavior and engagement (Dwivedi et al., 2022). Finally, the metaverse enhances tracking and monitoring by allowing marketers to collect real-time user feedback. This feedback provides marketers with insights into user preferences and opinions. The information gathered through user feedback and A/B testing can be used to optimize campaigns for better performance.

Improved Customer Engagement

Marketers can leverage the metaverse to improve customer engagement with their brand. For instance, the metaverse provides a more immersive and interactive consumer experience by providing an extensive, shared virtual world in real-time. Customers, through their avatars, can engage with the products or services in a virtual, controlled environment (Jeon, 2022). For example, a fashion brand can engage its customers through a virtual try-on experience that allows them to try on clothing and accessories in a virtual environment. In addition, customer engagement in the metaverse is enhanced through personalization (Bousba & Arya, 2022). The metaverse allows brands to collect customer data, such as preferences, behaviors, and interests, which can be used to improve the personalization of marketing messages. This strategy can help create a more tailored experience for the consumer, improving engagement and loyalty.

Virtual customer service, social connectivity, and brand storytelling are other capabilities that facilitate greater customer engagement in the metaverse. For instance, most organizations are increasingly adopting the metaverse as a platform to offer customer service through virtual customer service representatives (de Brito Silva et al., 2022). These virtual representatives answer customer questions and concerns, thus creating a more efficient customer service experience and improving engagement and satisfaction. Similarly, the social connectivity dimension of the metaverse can help improve customer engagement and build long-term relationships. Companies can leverage the metaverse to build virtual communities where consumers engage with each other and the brand (Jeon, 2022). This connection can build a sense of belonging and community, which improves customers' responsiveness to marketing campaigns and other initiatives. Finally, the metaverse provides a platform for brands to tell the story and promote their values. An immersive and engaging storytelling experience can help these companies improve engagement and build a stronger connection with their audience. Therefore, companies investing in the metaverse can leverage them to improve customer engagement and loyalty, which can help them improve their competitiveness.

Market Research in the Metaverse

The survival of any business in the current dynamic business environment requires a comprehensive understanding of the marketplace and customers, including emerging trends and changing customer preferences and interests. One way that businesses achieve this understanding is by conducting market research (Dwivedi et al., 2022). New technologies such as the metaverse are increasingly allowing entrepreneurs and their teams to conduct market research more immersive and engagingly. For example, the metaverse enables marketers to create virtual focus groups comprising users worldwide. Highly engaged and interactive focus groups effectively acquire in-depth insights into products, services, customer beliefs, perceptions, attitudes, and behaviors (Gao, 2022). The metaverse empowers brands to create an immersive environment that supports focus groups, thus facilitating customer and market research. In addition, the metaverse gaming platforms such as Roblox support in-game surveys that can help collect user feedback. This data is collected based on how users interact with virtual products and environments and can provide insights into user behavior, preferences, and opinions (Lee & Gu, 2022). Moreover, the virtual product testing capabilities in the metaverse by simulating real-world usage scenarios can facilitate data gathering. The information collected through these techniques can help optimize products and marketing campaigns.

Personalization of Advertising

The metaverse provides a unique opportunity for personalized advertising. It provides marketers access to user data that can be used to personalize marketing messages and strategies. For example, companies can gather user behavior, preferences, and interests' data within the metaverse to create more personalized advertising messages and targeting strategies (Rauschnabel et al., 2022). In addition, the metaverse allows users to create avatars that represent them within the virtual world. This personalization provides marketers with insights relating to users' appearance and behaviors, which can be used to enhance the personalization. Another opportunity for personalized advertising in the metaverse is evidenced in enhanced location-based advertising (Crespo-Pereira et al., 2023). Despite being a virtual world, the metaverse can simulate real-world locations, creating opportunities for companies to create location-based advertising messages. This helps ensure that the marketing content delivered in each location is relevant to the specific users in that area (Hwang & Koo, 2023). For example, brands selling different products in different regions can set up a virtual store that displays products to users depending on their location. This approach helps ensure accurate and relevant advertising messages reach the appropriate audience.

Social connectivity and real-time interactions are other opportunities in the metaverse that facilitate personalized advertising. For instance, the metaverse allows for social connections between users and brands, which can be leveraged into personalized advertising experiences (de Brito Silva et al., 2022). During the interactions, the brand can pay attention to the customers' interests and behaviors and use them to deliver personalized services and marketing messages. Similarly, real-time interactions within the metaverse allow organizations to interact with users in real-time (Hwang & Koo, 2023). As a result, they can continuously adjust the marketing campaign to accommodate the observed customer preferences, interests, and behaviors. Suppose a marketer notices a particular client is price-sensitive (Koay et al., 2022). They can adjust the marketing strategy to include personalized discounts or recommend low-priced products within the customer's budget.

Interactive and Immersive Experiences

Companies are leveraging the metaverse technology to create interactive and immersive experiences that engage users in new and exciting ways. The strong sense of realism and immersion in the metaverse environment contribute to customers' positive personal online experiences, thus boosting engaging and building loyalty (Ario et al., 2022). Customers are more interactive, fun, and highly engaged in the metaverse. This is because the virtual environment and its supporting technologies allow them to try new things and products (Zhu et al., 2023). For example, customers can try new lipstick shades or clothes and see how they look in the real world. This playful engagement with products takes customers beyond the typical eCommerce transactional experience, where they see a product and continue to pay for it without trying (Chen & Yao, 2022). As a result, personalization is more likely to increase their brand experiences, resulting in higher satisfaction, loyalty, and emotional connection. Besides virtual stores, brands can use gamification in the metaverse to create interactive and immersive customer experiences. This opportunity involves using fun games and challenges to engage customers and promote products and services.

Additionally, interactive experiences within the metaverse can be improved through virtual events, such as concerts and conferences. For example, more than 12 million people attended Travis Scott's virtual concert through Fortnite (Dwivedi et al., 2022). In addition, Kim (2021, p.142) indicated that the metaverse as a social platform enables users through their avatars to "build homes and businesses, conduct meetings, attend classes, find partners, raid 3D villages, invade planets, fly to the sun, and do all sorts of real-life impersonations and impossible stuff on a computer." These events showcase the power of the metaverse in providing interactive experiences that bring customers together and potentially build brand loyalty. The metaverse leverages storytelling to connect and communicate with target audiences (Wanick & Stallwood, 2023). According to Bian et al. (2022), brands must understand that virtual stores cannot keep customers engaged for long. These scholars indicate that brands must establish a way to communicate with customers through avatars. Storytelling has been identified as one of the main ways of communicating within the metaverse, where brands communicate their brand values, identity, and history through stories.

Expansion of Reach and Accessibility

The metaverse is not limited to a specific geographical location, thus allowing brands to expand their reach and accessibility. With the growing eCommerce sector and globalization, it has become critical for businesses to ensure presence and accessibility in the global market (Tan & Saraniemi, 2022). Customers worldwide purchase and ship desired products by leveraging the internet and advanced transportation systems. Thus, the global reach with metaverse means that brands can reach and connect with audiences in new and emerging markets to improve their accessibility and competitiveness. In addition, the metaverse ensures their 24/7 accessibility, meaning that brands leveraging the metaverse technologies can engage with users anytime (Rosnberg, 2022). This capability helps accommodate global time differences and ensures all customers can access needed support. Brands can use this feature to create always-on marketing campaigns that connect with users whenever they are active within the Metaverse (Park & Chun, 2022). This global, 24/7 accessibility enhances the marketing campaign's cost-effectiveness. This is because the technologies in the metaverse enable marketing campaigns to reach specific audiences without the need for expensive media buys or production costs (Patil et al., 2022). In addition, the metaverse facilitates cross-platform integration, meaning that it can be integrated with other platforms and technologies. This feature enables companies to expand their reach beyond the virtual world by creating cross-platform marketing campaigns connecting users across multiple channels and touchpoints.

Challenges of Metaverse in Marketing

Despite the marketing opportunities, the metaverse is associated with various challenges hindering companies' and consumers' adoption. For example, some users are concerned about data safety and privacy within virtual environments. This challenge may discourage them from using the innovations despite their associated benefits. Therefore, it is crucial to identify and analyze challenges affecting the use of the metaverse to aid organizational planning and the adoption of appropriate solutions.

Privacy and Security Concerns

The metaverse is accessed through multiple interconnected devices that generate data about individual customers and products or services promoted or offered. This interconnection and the massive customer data gathered raise security and privacy concerns (Lee & Kwon, 2022). For instance, data privacy is a significant issue where marketers must obtain consent before collecting personal data. In addition, they must be transparent about what data they are collecting and how it will be used. Dwivedi et al. (2022) explain this situation, arguing that the metaverse uses its tool-driven architecture to facilitate massive data collection, which poses data safety and privacy issues. Thus, marketers must collaborate with other organizational departments, such as the ICT, to integrate rigorous protection mechanisms to strengthen data safety and overcome cyber threats.

Consumers in virtual environments also worry about other issues, such as identity theft and harassment. The virtual identities created in the metaverse can be vulnerable to identity theft, increasing marketers' responsibilities in protecting users' virtual identities and preventing theft or comprise that may harm customers (Panagiotakopoulos et al., 2022). Moreover, cyberbullying is a major global issue affecting internet users and causing severe consequences such as mental illnesses and suicides. As a result, appropriate strategies must be embraced to reduce harassment and abuse in the metaverse, and marketers must ensure that users feel safe and comfortable in the virtual environment (Park & Kim, 2022). Marketers must comply with appropriate laws and regulations governing technology use in the metaverse, including data privacy laws, advertising regulations, and other regulatory requirements.

Ethical Considerations

The metaverse presents various ethical issues that may affect its usage in marketing. For instance, it can lead to virtual addiction, where users are addicted to highly immersive and engaging experiences (Shim et al., 2022). Marketers leveraging metaverse technologies aim to increase consumer engagement and interaction within the virtual environment. Consequently, they may unintentionally promote unhealthy addictive behavior that can severely affect the customers and the brand in the long run. Another ethical issue is the potential exploitation of vulnerable users (Tan & Salo, 2021). This problem occurs when marketers use manipulative tactics to target vulnerable users to encourage purchasing certain products or services or influence behaviors. Inaccurate representation, where brands or users create virtual representations that may not accurately reflect their real-world identities, is also a significant issue (Lee & Kwon, 2022). Finally, the blurred lines between public and private spaces in the metaverse can lead to an invasion of privacy. Brands and marketers must avoid using intrusive tactics or collecting unnecessary data to uphold ethical practices and protect their customers within virtual environments.

Technical Limitations

For companies to use metaverse in marketing, they require advanced technologies, including AR and VR, and technical skills. These technical resources require additional investments, which can be unavailable in some organizations, such as SMEs (Lee & Kwon, 2022). Moreover, bandwidth and speed are necessary to provide a seamless user experience. A slow or glitchy metaverse experience can negatively impact the user experience and, ultimately, the success of a marketing campaign (Koohang et al., 2023). In addition, many technologies are not yet integrated with metaverse platforms since it is still in their early development stages. As a result, it is increasingly difficult for marketers to integrate it with existing marketing strategies, limiting their ability to track and analyze user data (Jeon, 2021). The lack of standardization is also a significant technical challenge undermining marketers' ability to ensure their campaigns are compatible with different platforms. This issue affects tracking and measuring marketing campaigns' success across different metaverse platforms.

CONCLUSION

The metaverse concept has increasingly become popular with the rapid technological advancements in modern-day society. It refers to a 3D virtual world that allows people in the form of avatars to interact with each other and with brands and products. In addition, it uses advanced technologies such as VR and AR to facilitate real-time interactive, immersive, and collaborative experiences. While researchers and practitioners are testing its application in various fields, metaverse has gained increased adoption in marketing due to its social connectivity and increased engagement. For instance, its ability to facilitate virtual social events such as product launches and conferences has increased its use in marketing. Marketers leverage this aspect to connect and communicate with potential target customers in various ways, such as through product demonstrations and testing. For example, a car manufacturer can hold a virtual launch where users can test drive a new car model. The memorable experiences built on the virtual environment encourage customers to purchase a physical or digital product promoted within the metaverse. In addition, these positive experiences can improve customer brand perceptions, attitudes, and behaviors, thus leading to long-term relationships and brand trust.

The various opportunities of a metaverse in marketing identified in the research include increased brand awareness, enhanced tracking and monitoring, improved customer engagement, and personalized advertising. Companies using the metaverse as a marketing tool can observe customer behaviors, preferences, styles, and interests. The data collected in these processes can help adjust marketing campaigns to enhance engagement and experiences. In addition, the metaverse facilitates market research, enables brands to create interactive and immersive experiences, and expands brand reach and accessibility. The interactivity and global reach ensure that a brand's products and services are accessible in various places beyond its domestic market. In addition, the metaverse empowers brands with capabilities to deliver customized marketing campaigns refined to meet a specific region's needs and interests. In this case, the brand can deliver marketing campaigns for products or services in a specific market instead of the general campaigns targeting a mass audience. Despite these opportunities, marketing within the metaverse is limited by various challenges, including increased data safety, privacy, security concerns, and ethical considerations such as virtual addiction and exploitation of vulnerable users. Finally, the metaverse as an emerging innovation is characterized by technical limitations. For instance, it is not compatible with some technologies used in marketing, thus hindering its usability. Besides, some customers lack the skills and technologies to access the metaverse, thus limiting its accessibility to the larger global population. Thus, brands and their marketers must collaborate to establish appropriate solutions to these problems to enhance the metaverse's adoption and implementation in marketing.

ACKNOWLEDGMENT

I would like to express gratitude to the Editor and the Arbitrators. They offered extremely valuable suggestions or improvements. The author was supported by the GOVCOPP Research Center of the University of Aveiro.

REFERENCES

An, S., Choi, Y., & Lee, C. K. (2021). Virtual travel experience and destination marketing: Effects of sense and information quality on flow and visit intention. *Journal of Destination Marketing & Management, 19*, 100492. doi:10.1016/j.jdmm.2020.100492

Arikan, O. U., Ozturk, E., Duman, S., & Aktas, M. A. (2022). Conceptualization of meta-servitization: 3D case study from furniture industry. *ISMSIT 2022 - 6th International Symposium on Multidisciplinary Studies and Innovative Technologies, Proceedings, 702-706.* 10.1109/ISMSIT56059.2022.9932819

Ario, M. K., Santoso, Y. K., Basyari, F., Edbert, Fajar, M., Panggabean, F. M., & Satria, T. G. (2022). Towards an implementation of immersive experience application for marketing and promotion through virtual exhibition. *Software Impacts, 14,* 100439. Advance online publication. doi:10.1016/j.simpa.2022.100439

Barrera, K. G., & Shah, D. (2023). Marketing in the Metaverse: Conceptual understanding, framework, and research agenda. *Journal of Business Research, 155,* 113420. doi:10.1016/j.jbusres.2022.113420

Bian, Y., Leng, J., & Zhao, J. L. (2022, February). Demystifying metaverse as a new paradigm of enterprise digitization. In *Big Data–BigData 2021: 10th International Conference, Held as Part of the Services Conference Federation, SCF 2021, Virtual Event, December 10–14, 2021, Proceedings* (pp. 109-119). Cham: Springer International Publishing. 10.1007/978-3-030-96282-1_8

Bourlakis, M., Papagiannidis, S., & Li, F. (2009). Retail spatial evolution: Paving the way from traditional to metaverse retailing. *Electronic Commerce Research, 9*(1-2), 135–148. doi:10.100710660-009-9030-8

Bousba, Y., & Arya, V. (2022). Let's connect in metaverse. Brand's new destination to increase consumers' affective brand engagement & their satisfaction and advocacy. *Journal of Content. Community and Communication, 15*(8), 276–293. doi:10.31620/JCCC.06.22/19

Buchholz, F., Oppermann, L., & Prinz, W. (2022). There's more than one metaverse. *I-Com, 21*(3), 313–324. doi:10.1515/icom-2022-0034

Buhalis, D., Leung, D., & Lin, M. (2023). Metaverse as a disruptive technology revolutionising tourism management and marketing. *Tourism Management, 97,* 104724. doi:10.1016/j.tourman.2023.104724

Buhalis, D., Lin, M. S., & Leung, D. (2022). Metaverse as a driver for customer experience and value co-creation: Implications for hospitality and tourism management and marketing. *International Journal of Contemporary Hospitality Management, 35*(2), 701–716. doi:10.1108/IJCHM-05-2022-0631

Buhalis, D., O'Connor, P., & Leung, R. (2023). Smart hospitality: From smart cities and smart tourism towards agile business ecosystems in networked destinations. *International Journal of Contemporary Hospitality Management, 35*(1), 369–393. doi:10.1108/IJCHM-04-2022-0497

BushellC. (2022). The Impact of Metaverse on Branding and Marketing. doi:10.2139/ssrn.4144628

Chan, C., Wong, K. Y., & Lui, T. (2023). Marketing tourism products in virtual reality: Moderating effect of product complexity. *Springer Proceedings in Business and Economics, 318-322.* 10.1007/978-3-031-25752-0_34

Chen, C., & Yao, M. Z. (2022). Strategic use of immersive media and narrative message in virtual marketing: Understanding the roles of telepresence and transportation. *Psychology and Marketing, 39*(3), 524–542. doi:10.1002/mar.21630

Chinie, C., Oancea, M., & Todea, S. (2022). The adoption of the metaverse concepts in Romania. *Management and Marketing, 17*(3), 328–340. doi:10.2478/mmcks-2022-0018

Crespo-Pereira, V., Sánchez-Amboage, E., & Membiela-Pollán, M. (2023). Facing the challenges of metaverse: A systematic literature review from social sciences and marketing and communication. *El Profesional de la Información, 32*(1), e320102. Advance online publication. doi:10.3145/epi.2023.ene.02

Dai, J., & Zhao, L. (2022). Happiness and fashion culture of smart kidswear from the perspective of metaverse. *2022 10th International Conference on Orange Technology, ICOT 2022.* 10.1109/ICOT56925.2022.10008154

de Brito Silva, M. J., de Oliveira Ramos Delfino, L., Alves Cerqueira, K., & de Oliveira Campos, P. (2022). Avatar marketing: A study on the engagement and authenticity of virtual influencers on instagram. *Social Network Analysis and Mining, 12*(1), 130. Advance online publication. doi:10.100713278-022-00966-w

Demir, G., Argan, M., & Halime, D. İ. N. Ç. (2023). The Age Beyond Sports: User Experience in the World of Metaverse. *Journal of Metaverse, 3*(1), 19–27. doi:10.57019/jmv.1176938

Du, H., Niyato, D., Miao, C., Kang, J., & Kim, D. I. (2022). Optimal targeted advertising strategy for secure wireless edge metaverse. *2022 IEEE Global Communications Conference, GLOBECOM 2022 - Proceedings,* 4346-4351. 10.1109/GLOBECOM48099.2022.10001331

Dwivedi, Y. K., Hughes, L., Baabdullah, A. M., Ribeiro-Navarrete, S., Giannakis, M., Al-Debei, M. M., Dennehy, D., Metri, B., Buhalis, D., Cheung, C. M. K., Conboy, K., Doyle, R., Dubey, R., Dutot, V., Felix, R., Goyal, D. P., Gustafsson, A., Hinsch, C., Jebabli, I., ... Wamba, S. F. (2022). Metaverse beyond the hype: Multidisciplinary perspectives on emerging challenges, opportunities, and agenda for research, practice and policy. *International Journal of Information Management, 66,* 102542. Advance online publication. doi:10.1016/j.ijinfomgt.2022.102542

Dwivedi, Y. K., Hughes, L., Wang, Y., Alalwan, A. A., Ahn, S. J., Balakrishnan, J., Barta, S., Belk, R., Buhalis, D., Dutot, V., Felix, R., Filieri, R., Flavián, C., Gustafsson, A., Hinsch, C., Hollensen, S., Jain, V., Kim, J., Krishen, A. S., ... Wirtz, J. (2022). Metaverse marketing: How the metaverse will shape the future of consumer research and practice. *Psychology and Marketing, 40*(4), 750–776. doi:10.1002/mar.21767

Enriquez, D. R., Molero-Castillo, G., Bárcenas, E., & Pérez, R. A. (2022). Algorithm for identification and analysis of targeted advertising used in trending topics. *Proceedings of the LACCEI International Multi-Conference for Engineering, Education and Technology, 2022-July* 10.18687/LACCEI2022.1.1.57

Gao, S. (2022). Research on the innovation of the internet of things business model under the new scenario of metaverse. *ACM International Conference Proceeding Series,* 44-49. 10.1145/3545897.3545904

Giang Barrera, K., & Shah, D. (2023). Marketing in the metaverse: Conceptual understanding, framework, and research agenda. *Journal of Business Research, 155,* 113420. Advance online publication. doi:10.1016/j.jbusres.2022.113420

Gursoy, D., Malodia, S., & Dhir, A. (2022). The metaverse in the hospitality and tourism industry: An overview of current trends and future research directions. *Journal of Hospitality Marketing & Management, 31*(5), 527–534. doi:10.1080/19368623.2022.2072504

Hassouneh, D., & Brengman, M. (2015). Metaverse retailing: Are SVW users ready to buy real products from virtual world stores? *Proceedings of the International Conferences on e-Health 2015, EH 2015, e-Commerce and Digital Marketing 2015, EC 2015 and Information Systems Post-Implementation and Change Management 2015, ISPCM 2015 - Part of the Multi Conference on Computer Science and Information Systems 2015,* 104-110.10.3390/computers12010005

Hastuti, T. D., Sanjaya, R., & Koeswoyo, F. (2023). The readiness of Lasem batik small and medium enterprises to join the metaverse. *Computers, 12*(1). 10.3390/computers12010005

Havele, A., Brutzman, D., Benman, W., & Polys, N. F. (2022). The keys to an open, interoperable metaverse. *Proceedings - Web3D 2022: 27th ACM Conference on 3D Web Technology.* 10.1145/3564533.3564575

Hazan, E., Kelly, G., Khan, H., Spillecke, D., & Yee, L. (2022). Marketing in the metaverse: An opportunity for innovation and experimentation. *The McKinsey Quarterly.*

Hennig-Thurau, T., & Ognibeni, B. (2022). Metaverse marketing. *NIM Marketing Intelligence Review, 14*(2), 43–47. doi:10.2478/nimmir-2022-0016

Heo, J., Kim, D., Jeong, S. C., Kim, M., & Yoon, T. (2023). *Examining Participant's perception of SPICE factors of metaverse MICE and its impact on Participant's loyalty and behavioral intentions.* doi:10.1007/978-3-031-16485-9_14

Hwang, S., & Koo, G. (2023). Art marketing in the metaverse world: Evidence from South Korea. *Cogent Social Sciences, 9*(1), 2175429. Advance online publication. doi:10.1080/23311886.2023.2175429

Jeon, J. (2021). The effects of user experience-based design innovativeness on user– metaverse platform channel relationships in south korea. *Journal of Distribution Science, 19*(11), 81–90. doi:10.15722/jds.19.11.202111.81

Jeon, Y. A. (2022). Reading social media marketing messages as simulated self within a metaverse: An analysis of gaze and social media engagement behaviors within a metaverse platform. *Proceedings - 2022 IEEE Conference on Virtual Reality and 3D User Interfaces Abstracts and Workshops, VRW 2022,* 301-303. 10.1109/VRW55335.2022.00068

Kim, J. (2021). Advertising in the metaverse: Research agenda. *Journal of Interactive Advertising, 21*(3), 141–144. doi:10.1080/15252019.2021.2001273

Koay, K. Y., Tjiptono, F., Teoh, C. W., Memon, M. A., & Connolly, R. (2022). Social media influencer marketing: Commentary on the special issue. *Journal of Internet Commerce.* Advance online publication. doi:10.1080/15332861.2022.2128277

Koohang, A., Nord, J. H., Ooi, K., Tan, G. W., Al-Emran, M., Aw, E. C., Baabdullah, A. M., Buhalis, D., Cham, T.-H., Dennis, C., Dutot, V., Dwivedi, Y. K., Hughes, L., Mogaji, E., Pandey, N., Phau, I., Raman, R., Sharma, A., Sigala, M., ... Wong, L.-W. (2023, May 04). -., . . . Wong, L. (2023). Shaping the metaverse into reality: A holistic multidisciplinary understanding of opportunities, challenges, and avenues for future investigation. *Journal of Computer Information Systems, 63*(3), 735–765. Advance online publication. doi:10.1080/08874417.2023.2165197

Lee, H. J., & Gu, H. H. (2022). Empirical research on the metaverse user experience of digital natives. *Sustainability (Basel), 14*(22), 14747. Advance online publication. doi:10.3390u142214747

Lee, J., & Kwon, K. H. (2022). Future value and direction of cosmetics in the era of metaverse. *Journal of Cosmetic Dermatology, 21*(10), 4176–4183. doi:10.1111/jocd.14794 PMID:35073437

Lee, J., & Kwon, K. H. (2022a). Novel pathway regarding good cosmetics brands by NFT in the metaverse world. *Journal of Cosmetic Dermatology, 21*(12), 6584-6593. doi:10.1111/jocd.15277

, J., & Kwon, K. H. (2022b). Sustainable and safe consumer experience NFTs and raffles in the cosmetics market after COVID-19. *Sustainability (Switzerland), 14*(23). doi:Lee

Lee, J., & Kwon, K. H. (2022). The significant transformation of life into health and beauty in metaverse era. *Journal of Cosmetic Dermatology, 21*(12), 6575–6583. doi:10.1111/jocd.15151 PMID:35686389

Linnenluecke, M. K., Marrone, M., & Singh, A. K. (2020). Conducting systematic literature reviews and bibliometric analyses. *Australian Journal of Management, 45*(2), 175–194. doi:10.1177/0312896219877678

Njoku, J. N., Nwakanma, C. I., Amaizu, G. C., & Kim, D. (2023). Prospects and challenges of metaverse application in data-driven intelligent transportation systems. *IET Intelligent Transport Systems, 17*(1), 1–21. doi:10.1049/itr2.12252

Panagiotakopoulos, D., Marentakis, G., Metzitakos, R., Deliyannis, I., & Dedes, F. (2022). Digital scent technology: Toward the internet of senses and the metaverse. *IT Professional, 24*(3), 52–59. doi:10.1109/MITP.2022.3177292

Park, J., & Chun, J. (2022). Evolution of fashion as play in the digital space. *Fashion Practice*. Advance online publication. doi:10.1080/17569370.2022.2149837

Park, S., & Kim, Y. (2022). A metaverse: Taxonomy, components, applications, and open challenges. *IEEE Access : Practical Innovations, Open Solutions, 10*, 4209–4251. doi:10.1109/ACCESS.2021.3140175

Patil, K., Bharathi, S. V., & Pramod, D. (2022). Can metaverse retail lead to purchase intentions among the youth? A stimulus-organism-response theory perspective. *2022 ASU International Conference in Emerging Technologies for Sustainability and Intelligent Systems, ICETSIS 2022*, 314-320. 10.1109/ICETSIS55481.2022.9888929

Rauschnabel, P. A., Babin, B. J., tom Dieck, M. C., Krey, N., & Jung, T. (2022). What is augmented reality marketing? its definition, complexity, and future. *Journal of Business Research, 142*, 1140–1150. doi:10.1016/j.jbusres.2021.12.084

Ricoy-Casas, R. M. (2023). The metaverse as a new space for political communication 10.1007/978-981-19-6347-6_29

Rosário, A., Vilaça, F., Raimundo, R., & Cruz, R. (2021). Literature review on Health Knowledge Management in the last 10 years (2009-2019). *The Electronic Journal of Knowledge Management, 18*(3), 338-355. doi:10.34190/ejkm.18.3.2120

Rosário, A. T. (2021). The Background of articial intelligence applied to marketing. *Academy of Strategic Management Journal, 20*(6), 1–19.

Rosário, A. T., & Dias, J. C. (2022). Sustainability and the Digital Transition: A Literature Review. *Sustainability (Basel), 14*(7), 4072. doi:10.3390u14074072

Rosário, A. T., & Dias, J. C. (2023). How Industry 4.0 and Sensors Can Leverage Product Design: Opportunities and Challenges. *Sensors (Basel), 23*(3), 1165. doi:10.339023031165 PMID:36772206

Shim, B. K., Seo, J. Y., Na, K. Y., Lee, D. Y., Moon, M. H., & Lim, Y. K. (2022). *A study on software proposals for optimization of augmented reality glasses.* doi:10.1007/978-3-031-19679-9_73

Tan, T. M., & Salo, J. (2021). Ethical marketing in the blockchain-based sharing economy: Theoretical integration and guiding insights. *Journal of Business Ethics*. Advance online publication. doi:10.100710551-021-05015-8

Tan, T. M., & Saraniemi, S. (2022). Trust in blockchain-enabled exchanges: Future directions in blockchain marketing. *Journal of the Academy of Marketing Science*. Advance online publication. doi:10.100711747-022-00889-0

Tsai, S. (2022). Investigating metaverse marketing for travel and tourism. *Journal of Vacation Marketing*. Advance online publication. doi:10.1177/13567667221145715

Wagner, R., & Cozmiuc, D. (2022). Extended reality in Marketing—A multiple case study on internet of things platforms. *Information (Switzerland), 13*(6). doi:10.3390/info13060278

, V., & Stallwood, J. (2023). *Brand storytelling, gamification and social media marketing in the "Metaverse": A case study of the Ralph Lauren winter escape.* doi:Wanick

Zhe, C., Huilan, G., Jiang, W., & Zhongyi, H. (2023). The ideal and reality of metaverse: User perception of VR products based on review mining. *Data Analysis and Knowledge Discovery, 7*(1), 49–62. doi:10.11925/infotech.2096-3467.2022.0371

Zhu, C., Wu, D. C. W., Hall, C. M., Fong, L. H. N., Koupaei, S. N., & Lin, F. (2023). Exploring non-immersive virtual reality experiences in tourism: Empirical evidence from a world heritage site. *International Journal of Tourism Research, 25*(3), 372–383. Advance online publication. doi:10.1002/jtr.2574

KEY TERMS AND DEFINITIONS

Customer Engagement: The metaverse allows marketeers to improve brands engagement, as they can use a more immersive and interactive consumer experience by providing an extensive, shared virtual world in real-time. In this scenario customers, through their avatars, can engage with the products or services in a virtual, controlled environment. The metaverse allows brands to collect customer data, such as preferences, behaviors, and interests, which can be used to improve the personalization of marketing messages. This strategy can help create a more tailored experience for the consumer, improving engagement and loyalty.

Interactive Advertising in the Metaverse: This virtual world facilitates consumer-brand interactions influencing how consumers process, perceive and respond to advertising. The major advantage is the two-way communication between the brand and the consumer, i.e., the metaverse provides an interactive experience that allows engagement, unlike traditional advertising.

Interactive and Immersive Experiences: Experiences that engage users in new and exciting ways as the metaverse provides a strong sense of realism and immersion that contributes to customers' personal online experiences, leveraging engagement and building loyalty.

Metaverse: Constitutes a computer-mediated environment where people engage in social activities through avatars in 360-degree virtual worlds. It is an interactive, immersive, and collaborative virtual 3D world inhabited by avatars of real people. This social dimension in a three-dimensional virtual world allows companies to create interactive experiences such as virtual events and product demonstrations, improving customer experience which are critical in marketing.

Metaverse Ethics: Some ethical aspects can damage image brand and affect customers as the possible virtual addiction where users are addicted to highly immersive and engaging experiences or the potential exploitation of vulnerable users. Brands and marketeers should leverage metaverse technologies with strategies well thought.

Personalization of Advertising: The user data access to be used to personalize marketing messages and strategies in metaverse.

Chapter 11
The Role of Blockchain Technology in the Metaverse Ecosystem

Pooja Kulkarni
Vishwakarma University, Pune, India

Babasaheb Jadhav
Global Business School and Research Centre, Dr. D.Y. Patil Vidyapeeth, Pune, India

Ashish Kulkarni
Dr. D.Y. Patil B-School, Pune, India

Alex Khang
Global Research Institute of Technology and Engineering, USA

Sagar Kulkarni
MIT World Peace University, Pune, India

ABSTRACT

Metaverse is a virtual world based on AR and VR. The word Metaverse comprises "meta," which means beyond, and "verse," which means universe, which combines world beyond imagination. Today's Z generation wants everything over the tip of their fingers, even if they don't want to step out for purchasing groceries or daily household items and hang out with buddies. The Metaverse can provide a solution to this problem. Without stepping out of their home, they can virtually cheat and chat with friends and have a party with food and drink by sitting at their own homes by purchasing through virtual currency, own virtual assets including house, jewelry, etc. by creating their avatar using AR and VR technology. The use of blockchain technology solves the decentralization issue, maintenance of cryptocurrency, and other applications. Hence, the use of blockchain in the Metaverse ecosystem can benefit financial, non-financial, and privacy issues that may occur due to the described framework of the Metaverse ecosystem.

DOI: 10.4018/978-1-6684-8851-5.ch011

INTRODUCTION

Today's era is the adoption of digital technologies for improving the efficiency of the fields such as education, entertainment, marketing, human resource, business management, etc. the main reason for increasing efficiency is centralized access to data, due to the centralized access data started collecting at the server level and increase in data generate the need of Data Centers and Cloud Storage which further require to manage to have the less loaded UI and UX Interface.

After digitization the next resolution is a smartphone, people are using smartphones with an internet connection and the application develops for ease of life and changes the angle of the word digitization. Many applications in the smartphone can provide you personalize view and which is not possible without capturing all the information and finding out the trend, further the computer professional starts providing all the daily needs to the figure tip from chit chat with a friend to buying or selling household items, connecting to the world to ordering glossary and food items to a home, all can be handled over figure tip, and pandemic added flavor on to increase in the use of same.

We can do everything with the internet, smartphone, or smart gadgets, only without having a personal touch and feel, obviously technology cannot give the personal touch but it can provide you a personal feel and this can be given by the use of Augmented Reality, Virtual Reality and Extended Reality and the platform created by using all these three called as Metaverses

Metaverse is a virtual ecosystem extended from the massive use of social media, excessive use of the internet for daily use, and depending on the internet for all the necessary things majorly food, cloth, and shelter, and providing all the routine to the service provider through the various apps installed in cell phone like daily travel, call history, financial transaction, etc. almost every human being left on the planet earth depend on the internet for various of purpose still they are many things which may require physical presence, this can be resolved by creating our own AVATAR and launching them on the internet in the world of the Metaverse, the Metaverse can allow almost everything which you can do physically like attending the meeting, attending a party, the ecosystem is completely based on the technical front where the Virtual Reality and Augmented reality plays a vital role. The ecosystem is currently used majorly in game development but very soon it will be used to perform other things as well.

In this ecosystem, a digital world is developed, and you can imagine the world by keeping virtual reality glasses in front of your eyes. Through this, you can do e-commerce stuff, hang out with friends, attend meetings with teammates, can take a trip around the world by seating at your home.

The entire ecosystem is built on data and data is the center point for all the stakeholders available in this ecosystem. Which talking about the forms of data inputted for this ecosystem is as follows

1. **Data Procurement:** The collection of data and keeping the data ready for interpretation.
2. **Data Storage:** Storing of data for further use.
3. **Data Sharing:** Data sharing with multiple stakeholders of the ecosystem
4. **Data Privacy:** Protecting data from tampering or threat.

The blockchain will help in all four phases of data required for the ecosystem. Mr. Nakamoto Satoshi 2008 (Name is Misty) introduce the concept of blockchain he introduced the concept of storing the data in different places rather than one place (database) with correlation in data with a chain, each block of data connected to the adjacent block with reference link (pointer) known as the blockchain, the concept

Figure 1. Metaverse ecosystem

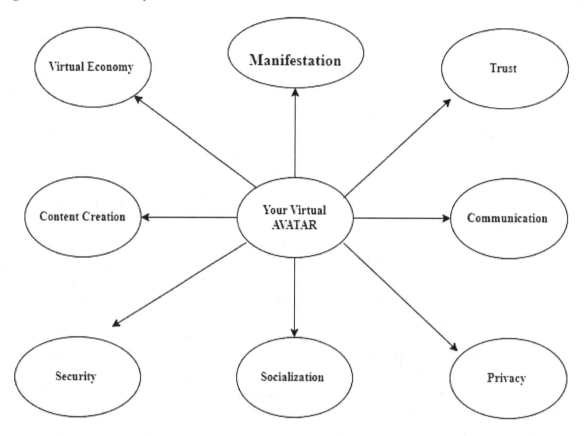

derived from the linked list in data structure and Nakamoto Satoshi used this concept for virtual currency called bitcoin.

The blockchain compressed of distributed ledger, wallet, hash, block, digital signature, etc. where elements of blockchain consist of Encryption, Distribution, Immutability, tokenization, and decentralization which provide the security and privacy support for multiple Metaverse ecosystem parameters.

The Metaverse ecosystem provides a variety of works that are related to financial transactions like purchasing and selling virtual assets, Purchasing and Selling on E-Commerce Websites, attending a virtual concert, or attending a party with friends require financial support, and the security for these financial application provided by a blockchain, in addition with this Data Procurement, Data Storage, Data Sharing can be made secure with the help of blockchain

This chapter discusses the role of the blockchain ecosystem in the Metaverse in terms of multiple parameters available for the Metaverse, a few of them enlisted in the above diagram.

LITERATURE REVIEW

The Metaverse is a permanent multiuser platform that connects a network of socially interactive, networked immersive worlds. It allows for fluid, real-time user-embodied integrated communication and

Figure 2. Blockchain ecosystem for the metaverse

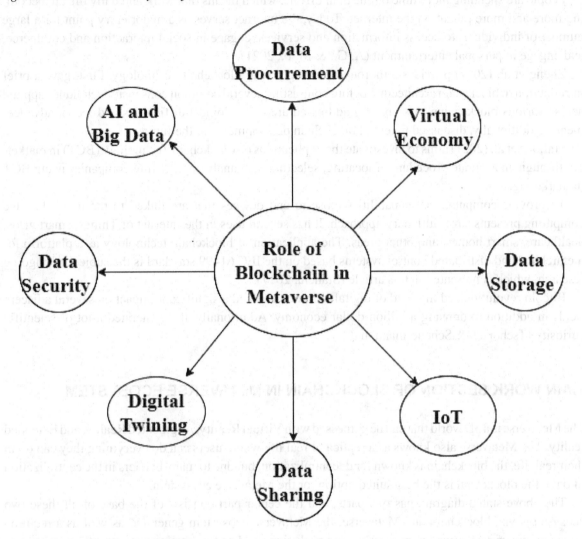

dynamic interactions with digital artifacts. Avatars could travel between several virtual worlds in their initial incarnation (Mystakidis, 2022).

A new concept of the Metaverse that is appropriate for the present and distinct from the prior Metaverse must incorporate increased social interactions and neural-net techniques. The principles and fundamental methods are necessary to realize the Metaverse are separated into three parts (hardware, software, and contents) and three approaches (user interaction, implementation, and application) in this study (Park & Kim, n.d.).

To create a completely immersive, hyper spatiotemporal, and self-sustaining virtual shared environment for people to play, work, and socialize, the Metaverse, a paradigm for the next-generation Internet, is in development. The metaverse is transitioning from science fiction to an impending reality thanks to recent developments in advanced technologies like blockchain, artificial intelligence, and extended reality (Wang et al., 2023).

People are spending more time online than offline, which means that work and daily life are becoming more and more reliant on the internet. Today, the internet serves as a major entry point for a large number of individuals to access information and services, engage in social interaction and commerce, and engage in personal entertainment (A. G., & M. F., 2021).

Zheng et al. (2017) provides a thorough introduction to blockchain technology. First, gave a brief introduction to blockchain architecture before contrasting several common consensus techniques applied across various blockchains. Also briefly addressed are technological difficulties and recent advancements. Additionally, discussed potential blockchain developments in the future.

Stallone et al. (2021) aims to investigate the applications of Blockchain Technology (BCT) in marketing through an accurate procedure of locating, selecting, and analyzing existing companies using BCT in marketing.

To provide computational capabilities close to end devices that are linked to the network, edge computing presents a revolutionary approach. It has several uses in the Internet of Things, smart grids, healthcare, smart homes, and other areas. The application of blockchain technology as a platform for hierarchical and distributed control systems based on the IEC 61499 standard is the subject of ongoing research, which is presented in this article (Stanciu, 2017).

Bitcoin revolutionized the field of digital currency and had a significant impact on several adjacent fields in addition to drawing a billion-dollar economy. Additionally, this generated a lot of scientific curiosity (Tschorsch & Scheuermann, n.d.).

MAIN WORK SECTION OF BLOCKCHAIN IN METAVERSE ECOSYSTEM

The Metaverse is a 3D world that can be witnessed with Virtual Reality, Augmented Reality, and Extended reality. The Metaverse also knows as a replica of real life where users can do everything they can do in their real life, the blockchain is known for decentralization, but due to many barriers in the centralization of data, the blockchain is the best-suited option for the Metaverse ecosystem.

The above-stated diagram has two parts, and the center part consists of the base of all these two ecosystems viz. blockchain and Metaverse, the Metaverse ecosystem generated as well as a required large volume of data as well as processing and analyzing the data for creating a strong comparative ecosystem whereas another side which is left states that the importance the role of blockchain for securing and managing the data. In the Metaverse, the data is more crucial and required to be stored for multiple purposes as well as required to have multiple faces as required in real life the safety and security of data should be more concern and this is provided by blockchain to demonstrate this we have some of the application of blockchain in the Metaverse.

Financial Application: The Metaverse is a second world so at multiple positions you are required to use cash for borrowing multiple things from drinks to clothes shoes to playing gadgets e.g., Nike launched the Shoes for Metaverse, as a virtual world you prefer to use virtual concurrency which is provided by blockchain in the form for cryptocurrency. The main advantage of the use of cryptocurrency is that it's secure and can have a unique currency worldwide.

Smart Contract: the blockchain is used to secure the content for sharing as its programmable for predefined condition and if the condition occurs then only it run, so can be considered as storage for sharing, and loading the content can be controlled which can be required at various stages of metaverse as an example to buy virtual property can be managed through a smart contract.

Figure 3. Role of blockchain in the metaverse

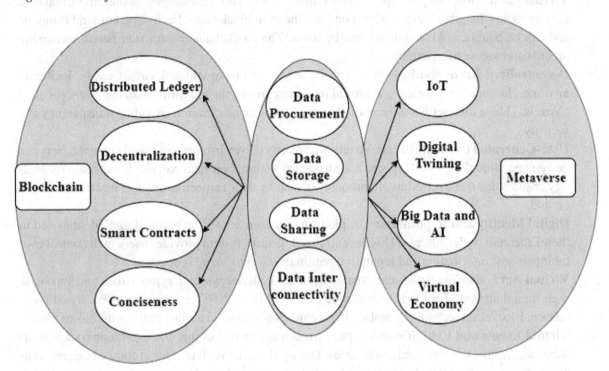

Decentralized Governance: Decentralized governance allows us to use blockchain for making the decision forming the rule and participate in decision making which is the core of the Metaverse ecosystem.

Intellectual Property Protection: Blockchain can provide a means to protect and enforce intellectual property rights within the metaverse. By using blockchain-based registries, creators can timestamp and authenticate their digital assets, such as virtual art, music, or designs. This ensures provable ownership and helps prevent unauthorized copying or distribution.

Cross-Platform Integration: Blockchain protocols can enable interoperability between different metaverses or virtual worlds. This means that users can seamlessly transfer their assets or avatars across multiple platforms, fostering a more connected and diverse Metaverse experience.

Digital Identity: Blockchain can provide a secure and decentralized identity management system for users in Metaverse. By using blockchain-based identity solutions, individuals can have control over their data and maintain privacy while participating in virtual worlds.

The following case study was picked up from CHAT GPT to show the use of Blockchain in the Metaverse areas like healthcare, social content creation, digital marketing, etc.

Case Study: Crypto Voxels

Blockchain-Based Virtual World Crypto Voxels is a blockchain-based virtual world that leverages the Ethereum blockchain to enable users to create, own, and trade virtual assets within a decentralized Metaverse. It serves as an excellent example of how blockchain technology can enhance the user experience and provide unique opportunities in a virtual environment.

Key Features and Applications:

1. **Virtual Land Ownership:** Crypto Voxels utilizes blockchain technology to represent virtual land parcels as non-fungible tokens (NFTs) on the Ethereum blockchain. Each parcel of land is unique and can be bought, sold, and developed by users. The blockchain ensures transparent ownership records and secure transactions.

2. **Decentralized Economy:** In Crypto Voxels, users can create and sell virtual assets, including artwork, clothing, accessories, and virtual real estate, using the platform's native currency, called "Voxels." These transactions are recorded on the Ethereum blockchain, providing transparency and security.

3. **User-Generated Content:** Crypto Voxels is primarily driven by user-generated content. Users can design and build their virtual spaces and structures within their land parcels. Blockchain technology ensures that these creations are probably owned by their respective creators and can be traded or sold.

4. **Digital Identity and Reputation:** The platform allows users to establish a digital identity tied to their Ethereum wallet address. This decentralized identity system provides users with control over their personal information and reputation within the Crypto Voxels ecosystem.

5. **Virtual Art Galleries:** Artists can create virtual art galleries within Crypto Voxels and showcase their digital artwork. Each art piece can be tokenized as an NFT, ensuring uniqueness and provenance. Blockchain technology enables the secure ownership and trading of these digital art pieces.

6. **Virtual Events and Exhibitions:** Crypto Voxels hosts virtual events and exhibitions, such as art showcases, music concerts, and conferences. Through blockchain-based smart contracts, event organizers can ensure ticket verification, fair distribution of rewards, and transparent event management.

7. **Governance and Decision-Making:** The development and governance of Crypto Voxels involves the community through a decentralized autonomous organization (DAO). Token holders can participate in decision-making processes, vote on proposals, and shape the future development of the virtual world. This case study demonstrates how blockchain technology, through its decentralized and transparent nature, can empower users, enable secure ownership, foster a vibrant economy, and provide unique opportunities for creativity, collaboration, and commerce within the Metaverse ecosystem.

Crypto Voxels showcases the potential for blockchain-based virtual worlds to create immersive experiences, establish digital economies, and redefine ownership and interaction in the Metaverse.

THE ROLE OF BLOCKCHAIN IN THE METAVERSE

1. **Data Procurement:** The AVTAR which is the backbone of Metaverse required data about your personal like height, width, weight etc. in addition your financial data is also required like credit card details and so on, the cameras used in Metaverse required much information. This data which is gathered at various phases is unstructured in nature as well as this data is real-time data so required Many applications that can be the integrity of data as well as duplicated data removal mechanism are also required. The adoption of blockchain technology helps to capture authenticated data as well as record every transaction. While capturing the blockchain will capture the entire hash which includes a timestamp, metadata, actual encrypted data, and link to the previous and next hash, the barrier is only to data mining the more data we capture more time spend on capturing the data.

2. **Data Storage:** As we witnessed data created by social media is very huge in nature and every individual either creates the data or makes a replica of data, here in the Metaverse is the same infect it will create far more data than social media and all the data need to store in addition this data is nonlinear in nature which make towards the reach of the capacity of data sets, in blockchain for every transaction a new block created and this new block can be stored at anywhere in the protected network space, this activity will distribute the data at various location so the program can easily clean unwanted data and linked to other places.

3. **Data Sharing:** The Metaverse is well known for creating personalize systems which leads to the creation of a variety of applications that can be given the user comfort the current example can be the True Caller app or Swiggy app etc. to gain the user preference and build a personalized product we need to have data analytics through the metaverse and shared data will help to understand the customer better in the form of requirement as well as help for personalized advertisement and personalized content. Smart contracts in blockchain uses will help to solve this problem as well as heterogeneous provide more security while sharing the data.

4. **Data Interconnectivity:** It has been said that there are 7 more persons who are your look-a-like so in the virtual world there are more chances of data getting interlinked with other applications due to this there are many places where the user need to enroll themselves again and crate the multiple access point in addition where security is more required their new access point gets created this can be resolved with blockchain by using cross-blockchain technology.

With these four important functions, the blockchain provides the solution for various other issues like the use of IoT, Big Data and AI, Digital Twining, use of AR and VR, etc. In all the blockchain has the great potential to provide a helping hand to the Metaverse ecosystem

CONCLUSION

Blockchain technology offers numerous benefits and functions within the metaverse ecosystem. By using its decentralized, transparent, and secure nature, blockchain can enhance the user experience, provide verifiable ownership of virtual assets, foster economic activity, and enable new forms of collaboration.

Key areas where blockchain can make a significant impact in the metaverse include virtual asset ownership, decentralized governance, virtual economies and digital currencies, intellectual property protection, interoperability, reputation systems, digital identity, virtual land ownership, royalty tracking, and micropayments, transparency and provenance, virtual collaboration, virtual insurance and risk management, and virtual governance and legal systems. These applications not only improve the overall functionality and trustworthiness of the metaverse but also unlock new opportunities for creators, users, and businesses.

As the Metaverse continues to evolve, blockchain technology is poised to play a vital role in shaping its future, enabling seamless and secure interactions, and empowering individuals to participate in and benefit from this immersive digital real.

REFERENCES

A. G., &. M. (2021). Metaverse: The Next Stage of Human Culture and the Internet. *International Journal of Advanced Research Trends in Engineering and Technology.*

How to use Blockchain in the Metaverse | Oodles Blockchain. (n.d.). Retrieved from https://blockchain.oodles.io/blog/how-to-use-blockchain-in-the-metaverse/

Huynh-The, T. R. (n.d.). Blockchain for the Metaverse. *RE:view.*

Mystakidis, S. (2022). *Metaverse.* Metaverse. Encyclopedia. doi:10.3390/encyclopedia2010031

Scheuermann, F. T. (2016). Bitcoin and Beyond: A Technical Survey on Decentralized Digital Currencies. *IEEE Communications Surveys and Tutorials, 18*(3), 2084–2123. doi:10.1109/COMST.2016.2535718

Stallone, V. W., Wetzels, M., & Klaas, M. (2021). Applications of Blockchain Technology in marketing systematic review of marketing technology companies. Blockchain. *Research and Applications, 2*(3), 100023. doi:10.1016/j.bcra.2021.100023

Stanciu, A. (2017). Blockchain-Based Distributed Control System for Edge Computing. *21st International Conference on Control Systems and Computer Science (CSCS),* 667-671. 10.1109/CSCS.2017.102

Thien Huynh-The a, T. R.-V. (n.d.). Blockchain for the metaverse. *RE:view.*

Wang, Y. S., Su, Z., Zhang, N., Xing, R., Liu, D., Luan, T. H., & Shen, X. (2023). A Survey on Metaverse: Fundamentals, Security, and Privacy. *IEEE Communications Surveys and Tutorials, 25*(1), 319–352. doi:10.1109/COMST.2022.3202047

What is metaverse in blockchain? A beginner's guide on an internet-enabled virtual world. (n.d.). Retrieved from https://cointelegraph.com/learn/what-is-metaverse-in-blockchain

Zheng, Z. S. X. (2017). An Overview of Blockchain Technology: Architecture, Consensus, and Future Trends. *IEEE International Congress on Big Data (BigData Congress),* 557-564.

Chapter 12
Mobile Cloud Computing Framework for an Android–Based Metaverse Ecosystem Platform

Nilamadhab Mishra
VIT Bhopal University, India

Basanta Kumar Padhi
Balasore College of Engineering and Technology, India

Banaja Basini Rath
Balasore College of Engineering and Technology, India

ABSTRACT

Mobile cloud computing (MCC), which combines mobile computing and cloud computing, has become one of the industry's most common terms and a major topic of discussion in the IT world. Mobile clients are becoming popular clients for consuming any web resources, particularly web services (WS), as mobile network infrastructures improve. However, there are problems connecting mobile devices to existing WS. This research focuses on three of the following challenges: loss of connection, bandwidth, latency, and limited resources. This research proposes to develop and implement a cross-platform architecture for connecting mobile devices to the web. The architecture includes mobile service clients that work on any platform and a Metaverse ecosystem that makes it easier for mobile clients and WS to talk to each other. Finally, the Metaverse ecosystem can be deployed on the cloud metaverse platform, which may create more immersive and dynamic virtual worlds that are accessible to a wider audience by utilizing the power of the cloud.

INTRODUCTION

DOI: 10.4018/978-1-6684-8851-5.ch012

Virtual worlds, or the metaverse, are become easier for the general public to access as technology develops. The term "metaverse" describes a virtual environment where users can interact, communicate, and take part in a variety of activities in a 3D setting. Cloud computing is one of the main technologies that has made this possible. The development of cloud computing has made it possible to create and maintain virtual worlds on a much bigger scale. Developers may create more immersive and dynamic virtual worlds that are accessible to a wider audience by utilizing the power of the cloud. In this blog article, we'll look at how cloud computing is opening up the metaverse and its advantages for both users and developers. A significant increase in application models such as cloud computing, software as a service, community networks, web stores, and others has been seen in recent years as a result of developments in network-based computing and on-demand applications. Cloud computing is frequently defined as a collection of services offered via an Internet-based cluster system. These cluster systems are made up of several inexpensive servers or personal computers (PCs), which organize their various resources following a predetermined management strategy and provide customers with secure, dependable, quick, convenient, and transparent data storage, access, and computing services. The number of smartphone users has already surpassed 1 billion at this time (Mishra, Lin, & Chang, 2014). Therefore, using mobile devices for computing has become a more practical idea than the traditional method. However, numerous shortcomings, like the lack of storage and processing capacity and the short battery life of mobile devices, have emerged as difficulties for MC technology. The cloud may offer a practical remedy for overcoming these difficulties. Software as a Service (SaaS), Platform as a Service (PaaS), and Infrastructure as a Service (IaaS) are all components of cloud computing, which combines the virtualization of numerous resources with a distributed computing model (IaaS). Numerous cloud services providers, like Microsoft Azure and Amazon EC2, offer seamless elastic processing and storage that is "on-demand" and "pay as you use" (Mishra, Chang, & Lin, 2014). Therefore, the combination of mobile computing with cloud computing (CC) has resulted in the development of a more advanced technological strategy known as mobile cloud computing (MCC). MCC can be defined as nothing more than cloud computing with mobile devices acting as thin clients. To support mobile clients using Web services, this research paper suggests a mobile cloud computing architecture that makes use of a cloud-hosted metaverse ecosystem (cloud services). The architecture offers a framework for personal service mash-ups for mobile clients and improves the interaction between mobile clients and Web services.

Motivation to Develop an Android Metaverse Ecosystem Framework

The fact that there are more mobile users nationwide than there are service providers, but the availability of services is quite limited, inspired me to create this framework for mobile cloud computing. The best server technologies are available through the Internet service provider, enabling cloud computing services. The cloud computing business will have a fantastic possibility to expand faster in the nation if the solution I'm suggesting is put into practice.

Despite heterogeneous environments and platforms, mobile cloud computing technology manages integrated elastic resources of various clouds and network technologies toward unlimited functionality, mobility, and storage to support a large number of mobile equipment anywhere and at any time through the Ethernet channel or Internet (Web Services Architecture, 2004). MCC is a system that allows data to be processed and stored in the cloud rather than on a mobile device. In MCC, computational power and data storage are transferred from mobile devices to the cloud, offering mobile cloud apps and mobile computing to a wider spectrum of mobile subscribers in addition to smartphone users (Google App

Figure 1. Consuming WS from a mobile client

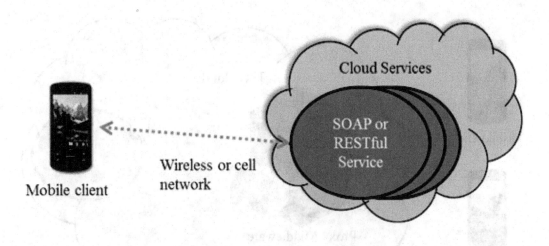

Engine, 2010). Therefore, MCC is an infrastructure that combines the cloud computing and mobile computing domains, where both data processing and data storage take place remotely.

The Modelling Narrative and Challenges

The key issue with cloud computing is its inefficient and unfair utilization, which limits opportunities for mobile users and deters the sustainable management of resources. One of the main sources of the issue is the system's inadequate design, structure, and execution, which results in signal, bandwidth, and latency issues. Everyone agrees that the current telecom system cannot comprehend consumer requirements and desires, comprehend societal demands, utilize contemporary technologies, be sufficiently adaptable, build on its successes, and go forward. Due to the following reasons (Figure 1), using Web Services via Mobile Clients is different from using Web Services in conventional settings (e.g. CPU power, screen size). Since wireless or cellular networks are used to connect clients to services, the Metaverse ecosystem is necessary to reduce bandwidth and latency. The Cloud's current web services do not support mobile clients.

The process of consuming Web Services from mobile clients is fraught with difficulties. The three listed below are the subject of this study.

A reliable connection is necessary for the interaction between the client and the service. Mobile clients, however, can be momentarily disconnected from the previously connected network and afterward may access another network due to the mobility of the clients and the wireless network configuration. In such cases, service requests or responses may not reach their intended location.

Cell networks have a finite amount of bandwidth, and they frequently charge users according to the volume of data transferred. However, even a straightforward SOAP message frequently includes a sizable amount of XML data, which uses a lot of bandwidth and can significantly increase network latency during transmission. The SOAP message also primarily uses XML tags that are not all required by mobile clients. Limited resources: "Thin clients" (Al-Turkistany, 2009) with low processing speeds are mobile clients. Mobility has inherent constraints that go beyond the limitations of present technology (Farley & Capp, 2005). For instance, a service mashup necessitates extensive computation and involves

Figure 2. Consuming WS from mobile client through client Metaverse ecosystem

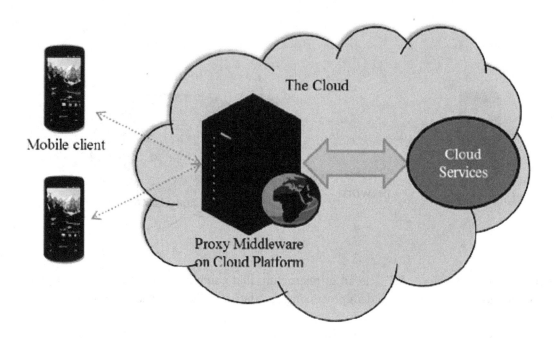

parsing and merging many WS responses. The difficulties lay in extending processing power beyond mobile clients and reducing data processing on mobile clients. In addition, several mobile systems lack the required SOAP WS libraries.

The Mobile Cloud Computing (MCC) architecture (Figure 2), which connects mobile devices to Cloud Computing, is suggested as a solution to these problems. A mobile client and a Metaverse ecosystem design are features of the MCC architecture. The mobile client can be implemented using either native programs or browser-based embedded applications. Specific programming languages that are supported by mobile platforms are used to create native applications. However, embedded browser programs can make use of the native application's available interfaces and run HTML and JavaScript in the embedded browser.

With the help of the Metaverse ecosystem (Al-Turkistany, 2009; Tian et al., 2004), which is hosted on cloud platforms, mobile clients can access cloud services. The Metaverse ecosystem facilitates better adaption, optimization, and caching between mobile clients and cloud services. The Metaverse ecosystem also offers mobile users extra features like service mashups. The usefulness, dependability, and compatibility of the interaction between mobile clients and Cloud Services are all improved by the Metaverse ecosystem. The Mobile Cloud Computing architecture offers the following characteristics to help overcome the difficulties stated in the preceding section.

Caching for clients and the Metaverse ecosystem Mobile clients and the Metaverse ecosystem both save copies of service results. The client-side cache is used when mobile clients are unable to connect to the Metaverse ecosystem. The Metaverse ecosystem delivers its cached data to the mobile clients when the WS connection to it is unavailable. Push notifications from the Metaverse ecosystem are sent instantly to mobile clients that are linked to the Metaverse ecosystem when the Metaverse ecosystem receives an update of the service result.

The mobile clients instantly connect to the Metaverse ecosystem once they identify an available network connection. Bandwidth and latency are reduced by protocol transformation, which also lowers the bandwidth used for client-to-service communications. The ecology of the Metaverse converts SOAP WS into RESTful WS. In contrast to RESTful WS, which can send messages in a lightweight format like JSON, SOAP is a verbose protocol that requires XML parsing. By switching from SOAP WS to lightweight protocols like RESTful WS, processing time and message size are both decreased. Optimizing results reduces the size of the service results, which lowers the bandwidth required to communicate with WS. The original service result's XML format is changed by the Metaverse ecosystem to JSON, and extraneous data is removed. Network latency is also decreased with fewer data transfers.

The resources of mobile clients are extended cost-effectively by connecting them to cloud computing. Internet Services The research/study will answer the following research questions: How may mobile clients' functionality be expanded while receiving computational power from cloud platforms? The Metaverse ecosystem is built to run on cloud computing infrastructure like GAE and Amazon EC2. Scalability is the ecosystem of the Metaverse's primary issue.

The Metaverse ecosystem's automatic scaling is provided through cloud platforms. The personal mashup platform enables the mobile client to mix and match various services. However, WS interaction and processing power are needed for service mashup. It is ineffective to do service mashups on mobile clients due to the resource (energy, processing power, and software libraries) restrictions of these clients. The Metaverse ecosystem offers a Personal Mashup Platform that offers mobile client mash-up services. The platform offers generic WS-defining and consuming interfaces. The services can be combined to create a workflow (a mash-up service) that offers the option of storing intermediate service outcomes because they are saved on the Metaverse ecosystem.

ü How can online services be accessed by mobile devices quickly and effectively?
ü Why don't web services support customers or users of mobile devices?
ü How can a service mashup platform be made interactive?
ü The overall goal of the project is to make mobile clients more accessible within the context of mobile cloud computing. The following are the study's precise goals.
ü To provide a scalable and effective architecture for tying mobile hardware to the mobile cloud computing environment.
ü To improve communication between the mobile cloud computing environment and clients on the go
ü To offer a service mashup platform to clients who use mobile devices
ü To suggest uncovered issues to the group and researchers.

The focus of this study/research is on mobile clients using the internet to access cloud services. The study will concentrate on mobile cloud computing and attempt to provide a prototype that embodies the majority of the characteristics listed in this paper. The prototype software won't be market-ready because it will be developed with a focus on a limited number of scenarios. Considering that the server's actual usage will be to mimic telecom servers, the server that will be utilized to provide cloud computing services may be any temporary server.

This research is based on the overall cloud computing system as there are practical application issues in the developed countries, On the other hand, there are basic issues Available alone that don't solve the problems related to mobile service. So this research work is, therefore, an eye-opener in bringing strategic value to mobile users and the service provider and overall mobile cloud computing environment process. It can also be used as a baseline for future researchers. This research is limited in terms of an empirical study of area coverage, and there is no doubt that future development works will come up with issues and problems worth investigating. Further, it is hoped that mobile users and service providers would find the findings of this study worth looking at and would initiate revision and amendments of the current working system currently in place as most of the problem is due to the current system in place. And this study is significant simply because there are several advantages of cloud computing. It helps in improving the service flow, increases efficiency, and numerous other reasons.

STUDY OF MOBILE CLOUD COMPUTING BASED METAVERSE ECOSYSTEM FRAMEWORK

This section discusses related studies in the areas of mobile web services, how mobile devices and WS interact, the Metaverse ecosystem for supporting mobile clients, and cloud computing applications. According to the study (Mishra, Alebachew, & Patnaik, 2018; Wang & Zhao, 2022), there are five fundamental aspects of cloud computing: resource self-provisioning and elasticity, pay-per-use, availability on demand, scalability, and resource pooling.

1. **Self-Provisioning of Resources and Elasticity:** With cloud computing, customers can easily add any number of computing resources. For instance, network storage, processing power, or software, all of which are always and everywhere accessible.
2. **Pay-per-Use:** The price of cloud computing services depends on how much is used. For instance, a daily or monthly rate, traffic volume, or user count.
3. **On-Demand Accessibility:** Cloud services are regularly accessed by a web browser or web service API, are constantly accessible, and are platform-independent.
4. **Scalability:** In the sense of being able to satisfy any resource requirements the user may have, computational resources are thought to be limitless. For instance, computing power, storage capacity, or bandwidth. Cloud services should be able to adjust to the requested consumption immediately.
5. **Resource Pooling:** Data and resources are distributed over numerous servers, most of which are dispersed geographically; the resources required are then allocated in accordance with the computational requirements of the service.
   Although there are many various ways to define the properties of cloud computing, they all generally cover the same ground or come to the same conclusions.

Cloud Computing Implication in Metaverse Ecosystem Platform

The resources needed for the metaverse to exist can be provided by the cloud infrastructure, and the metaverse can offer a brand-new platform for cloud computing services and applications. This is the relationship between the metaverse and cloud computing. The cloud can facilitate the hosting, distribution, and scaling of metaverse experiences, and the metaverse can create a new, significant market for cloud services. Over the past few years, we have noticed some important developments in technological advancement. Mobile and cloud computing are two examples. The widespread acceptance of these two is altering our daily interactions, including how we conduct business. The field of systems of engagement is expanding rapidly Brick-and-mortar stores and conventional browser-based web apps are no longer the only places where it may be found. Many companies are attempting to engage clients through mobile channels as mobile devices spread throughout society. Therefore, mobile cloud computing is crucial to us. The growth of mobile and handheld devices is also having a big impact on IP data traffic globally. Due to its quick scalability, widespread network access, on-demand self-service, and other qualities, cloud computing appears to be the best option to support such data demand. We want to present some facts in this study to show how important cloud computing and mobile are. The ICT industry is undergoing a once every 20–25 years move to a new technology platform for development and innovation, according to the International Data Corporation (IDC). We refer to it as the "3rd Platform," which is based on social media, cloud services, mobile broadband networks, and mobile devices and apps. IDC initially used the phrase "3rd platform" in 2007. Today's IT solutions are frequently constructed around at least one of the four pillars of cloud, analytics, mobile, and social. The Nexus of Forces is how analyst company Gartner refers to this technology mix. An overview of IDC's technology forecast for 2015 may be of interest to you. According to IDC's 2015 Technology Predictions Report, the development and contribution of mobile, cloud, big data, Internet of Things, and social will cause global IT spending to surpass 3.8 trillion USD in 2015. Additionally, the survey predicts that sales of mobile devices and application development will account for 40% of the increase in IT spending in 2015. Additionally, the enormous global expansion in wireless data will force carrier operators to offer platforms and API-based services to draw developers.

When a business outsources, it pays for another company to complete a portion of its work, according to the Cambridge Dictionary (Cambridge Dictionary – Outsourcing, 2012). An example of outsourcing is when an IT business contracts with another business to handle its customer service. There are some similarities and some differences with cloud computing. Businesses can contract out their entire IT department or just a portion of it to firms that specialize in that area. As an illustration, consider a business that outsources the installation, upkeep, and storage of its servers to avoid having to keep them on-site at its corporate grounds. This is comparable to the way cloud computing suppliers manage the platform and/or infrastructure as a service (PaaS or IaaS). The remarkable similarities are offset by the disparities in how quickly the services are provided and the associated agreements. Cloud computing delivers a preset solution that satisfies the requirements of the customer's application, in contrast to traditional outsourcing, which necessitates extensive contracts that typically merely continue as long as the contracts agree to (Dhelim et al., 2022; Papazoglou & Georgakopoulos, 2003; Wang & Zhao, 2022). The customer typically incurs no upfront costs and only pays for the services they utilize.

Major Scenarios of Cloud Computing Based on Metaverse

A new computing paradigm known as cloud computing is produced through the integration of virtualization, distributed computing, and service-oriented architecture. Cyberinfrastructure, one of the essential components of successful information technology, is embraced by cloud computing (IT). In cloud computing, three main scenarios are identified according to the level of abstraction. A service that makes users aware of hardware resources is referred to as infrastructure as a service (IaaS).

Platform as a Service (PaaS) makes computing resources available as platforms for high-level applications. An illustration of PaaS is Google App Engine (GAE) (Liu et al., 2007). Software as a Service (SaaS) aims to make software functionality available as services (i.e. WS). Many service companies offer their software capabilities as WS, including Google, Yahoo, and Amazon.

In a cloud computing system, resources are made available to local clients as needed and typically over the internet. The paradigm of cloud computing is described in the works (Jiang et al., 2022; Liu & Deters, 2007; Oliver, 2008), which moves the location of computing infrastructure to the network to cut costs related to managing hardware and software resources. The two components of cloud computing are cloud platforms (CP) and cloud services (CS). Application hosts that provide computing power, storage, and Internet connection are referred to as cloud platforms. Google App Engine and Amazon Elastic Cloud Computing (EC2) are the two well-known cloud computing platforms (GAE). According to definitions given in references 14 and 30, cloud computing is a concept that gives users the flexibility and on-demand network connectivity to quickly supply and release a shared pool of reconfigurable computing resources with little oversight from the service provider. Networks, servers, storage, applications, and services are some of these reconfigurable computing resources. Infrastructure as a Service (IaaS), Platform as a Service (PaaS), and Software as a Service are the three service models used in cloud computing (SaaS). The capacity to deploy processing, storage, networks, servers, and other computer resources within the cloud infrastructure is offered by IaaS.

Any virtualized servers, operating systems, and applications may be deployed and run by the user. Additionally, the user has some flexibility over the chosen networking components, as well as operating systems, storage, and deployed applications (e.g., host firewalls). The Amazon Elastic Compute Cloud (EC2) is an illustration of IaaS (Hevner & March, 2005; Wu et al., 2018). Applications that have been produced using the programming languages, libraries, tools, and services offered by the cloud service provider can be deployed by the user onto the cloud infrastructure utilizing PaaS. Google App Engine (Sanaei et al., 2014) and Microsoft Azure (Fernando et al., 2013) are two examples of PaaS. The utilization of apps that are running on a cloud architecture is made possible via SaaS. Through a program interface or a thin-client interface, the user can access the programs from client devices. Google Docs is an illustration of SaaS (Cai et al., 2022; Wibowo, 2018). According to (Mishra, 2019), an architecture that facilitates the offloading of data processing and data storage from mobile devices into the cloud can be referred to as mobile cloud computing. As a result, cloud computing and mobile computing are said to have been integrated (Dhelim et al., 2022; Jiang et al., 2022; Mishra, Lin, & Chang, 2014). Smaller sizes, lighter weights, longer battery lives, and other qualities are important and desirable, but they also place substantial restrictions on mobile cloud computing systems. The development of these devices' hardware and software are frequently severely constrained by this. By allowing the more resource-intensive operations to be completed on systems without these restrictions and having the results delivered to the device, cloud computing enables devices to escape these limitations. Consequently, cloud computing for mobile devices is a very appealing and perhaps advantageous trend.

Simply described, mobile cloud computing (MCC) is cloud computing with at least some mobile devices. "A software system designed to facilitate interoperable machine-to-machine interaction across a network," according to the definition given by Web Services (Mishra, 2018; Mishra, Chang, & Lin, 2014). It provides a machine-processable interface with detailed descriptions (e.g. WSDL (Wu et al., 2018)). Other systems communicate with the WS following its specifications by sending messages that are commonly transmitted over HTTP using an XML serialization in addition to other Web-related standards. The Service-oriented architecture protocol (SOAP) Web Service and RESTful WS are two WS protocol standards, according to (Dhelim et al., 2022). The message envelope for sending Web Services messages across the Internet or Internet is provided by SOAP. It is a part of the collection of standards that the W3C has established. Two components make up the SOAP envelope:

1. An optional header containing details on authentication, data encoding, or how a SOAP message's recipient should handle the message.
2. The textual portion of the communication. The WSDL specification can be used to define these messages.

The Simple Mail Transfer Protocol (SMTP) and HTTP are the two protocols that SOAP most frequently employs. Complete documents can be exchanged or a remote process can be called using SOAP. Both a web server and a mobile service client are referred to as mobile web services (Mishra, Lin, & Chang, 2014) in the mobile environment. The introduction of new mobile platforms makes implementing MWS simpler. According to the study (Mishra, Lin, & Chang, 2014), Android, BlackBerry, iPhone, Symbian (S60), and Windows Mobile, all support the idea of mobile network-based research, such as mobile service clients. All of these mobile platforms have some restrictions, according to the poll. Android 2.0 fixes issues with Android 1.0, such as the absence of Bluetooth stacks and the inability to choose network interfaces programmatically. The iPhone framework isn't open. Since RESTful WS just uses the HTTP protocol, the mobile client can use its built-in HTTP client to access RESTful WS. However, because the Android platform lacks a framework for reading and generating SOAP messages, the mobile client does not support SOAP WS. Additionally, XML messages consume more processing power and bandwidth than JSON messages. Thus, the Metaverse ecosystem offers the mobile client style change (from SOAP to RESTful), format conversion (from XML to JSON), and other modifications.

In a mobile context with limited resources, resource usage is still another issue. According to earlier studies by the work (Jiang et al., 2022) and the work (Dhelim et al., 2022), the use of XML accounts for around 400% of the processing cost of WS when compared to binary protocols. A strategy to enhance performance using dynamic compression of the WS response was proposed in the paper (Mishra et al., 2015). According to his method, the client network load as well as the server load determines whether or not compression should be applied. His investigations demonstrate that the server and client's performance only increases when the client network's bandwidth is limited and the server is not operating at full capacity. Caching is a widely used technique in server-client communication to improve user experience. Caching is essential for mobile service users because of their weak connectivity and capacity restrictions. A dual caching method was suggested in the work (Mishra, 2018) to increase the performance and dependability of WS consumption from mobile clients. Caches are installed on the server and mobile clients in this strategy. The server cache is located on a distant computer that has a dependable connection to the server, whereas the client cache is a proxy on the client devices. Dual Caching has a linear rise in overhead with request and response size, but the benefit is a notable improvement in reading operation performance. The main technology used to provide services to end users at the moment is WS. The majority of the difficulties in a mobile context are caused by platform and resource limitations. RESTful WS is more suited to the mobile environment because it only needs the HTTP protocol. Two strategies for overcoming bandwidth restrictions are caching and optimization/compression. The Metaverse ecosystem will offer RESTful interfaces for mobile clients under our strategy. Additionally, it caches and improves service outcomes from Cloud Service. A Distributed Computing (DC) system frequently uses the Metaverse ecosystem. Multiple independent processors that do not share primary memory but instead work together by delivering messages via a communications network make up DC systems (Chang, Liu, & Mishra, 2015). Mobile clients are connected to the Metaverse ecosystem by geographically dispersed computers. Five needs for the whole Metaverse ecology were outlined in the paper (Chang, Mishra, & Lin, 2015). A Metaverse ecosystem is frequently employed in mobile computing to deal with user context, and a context-aware SCaLaDE is the name of the metaverse ecosystem for Internet data services (Services with Context-awareness and Location awareness for Data Environments). Based on deployment, level of access, and cloud services, cloud computing can be segmented. There are four typical models for cloud computing implementation. They are community, hybrid, private, and public cloud models. Public clouds are held by a third-party company that provides the cloud service and are accessible to the general public or major organizations (Chang et al., 2016; Wu et al., 2018). Public cloud companies like Google, Amazon, and Microsoft provide their services to everyone (Mishra, Chang, & Lin, 2018). Customers' produced and submitted data is often stored on the third-party vendor's servers. Online software solutions are readily available through SaaS (Software as a Service). The application software is entirely under the provider of SaaS software. Online mail, project management software, CRMs, and social media platforms are a few examples of SaaS applications. The primary distinction between SaaS and PaaS is that although PaaS typically serves as a framework for application development, SaaS offers previously created internet applications (Mishra, Chang, & Lin, 2018).

MOBILE CLOUD COMPUTING FRAMEWORK FOR ANDROID-BASED METAVERSE ECOSYSTEM

Design Metaverse Ecosystem Architecture

The Metaverse ecosystem will provide the following features to improve the interaction between mobile clients and Cloud Services:

ü Metaverse ecosystem pushing
ü Protocol transformation
ü Optimizing results
ü Metaverse ecosystem Caching

Implementation of the Mobile Client and Cloud Metaverse Ecosystem

Plan to implement the proposed mobile client architecture on smartphones like Android, iPhone, HTC, etc. which have native libraries and embedded browsers.

The Metaverse ecosystem is proposed to implement and host on the telecom cloud data center, the cloud data center is expected to implement recently (Figure 3).

Client mobile apps, Proxy Metaverse ecosystem servers, and Cloud Services make up the three core layers of the Mobile Cloud Computing Architecture. Smart devices like smartphones, smart TVs, and smartwatches—basically all gadgets that can need a cloud service via the internet—are represented by the client mobile app layer. Through the proxy Metaverse ecosystem server, the mobile app will have access to a cloud service on this layer. It will be possible for the mobile app to access a RESTful cloud service. In other words, a REST request can be made to access the service, and the response data will be in JSON (JavaScript Object Notation) format.

The web-based program that is installed on a server serving as a Metaverse ecosystem between the cloud services and the client mobile app is represented by the proxy Metaverse ecosystem server layer. This server's primary function will be to display cloud services in a style that is appropriate for mobile

Figure 3. Integrated MCC frameworks for the Android Metaverse ecosystem

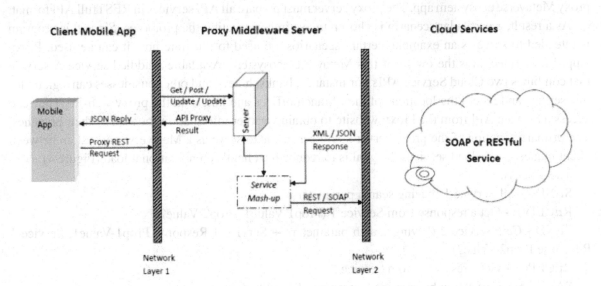

apps. The server will contain a list of APIs with specified functions called a service mash-up. These APIs can be created by combining or altering several online cloud services. Cloud services may have multiple formats during this procedure (for example SOAP and RESTfull). In this scenario, the XML result obtained from the SOAP service will be converted to a JSON format by the Metaverse ecosystem server to enable the merging process. Minimizing computation time on the client's mobile apps is the server's primary purpose. The computation time would increase if the client mobile apps had to combine these cloud services. To drastically reduce the processing load on the client's mobile apps, the Metaverse ecosystem services will be tasked with handling this operation. A RESTful request and a JSON result are used for communication between the client mobile app and the server layer of the Metaverse ecosystem. According to the type of cloud service, the communication between the cloud services layer and the Metaverse ecosystem server layer will consist of a REST or SOAP request and a JSON or XML answer. The cloud services layer represents the online cloud services. These services could be RESTful or SOAP. RESTfull cloud services produce JSON results, while SOAP cloud services produce XML outputs. Unlike the custom service mash-up option made available in the proxy Metaverse ecosystem server layer, cloud services have the nature of fulfilling a specific purpose.

DEVELOPMENT AND EXPERIMENT

This proxy metaverse ecosystem app was created to show how mobile clients and cloud services can leverage proxy servers as a metaverse ecosystem. An Android mobile app was created in addition to this web application. The processing time will be significantly reduced by the client devices sending a request that is already on this server.

The suggested system's initial requirements are as follows. A Metaverse ecosystem server with a certain set of cloud service bundles should exist. Public and management pages should be included in the proxy Metaverse ecosystem app. The proxy server must prepare all API services in RESTfull API format.

As a result, a particular scenario is chosen to use in constructing the prototype. Since this program is intended to serve as an example, certain scenarios are used to illustrate how it can be used. Proxy App: Ethio Telecom is the owner of this Metaverse ecosystem. Available muddled service A service that combines two Cloud Service APIs For instance, banks, hotels, and other businesses can sign up for this service and record the locations of their branch offices and hotels on the proxy website. They can access a Service API from the Proxy website to obtain weather information for each of their branches. The primary function of the proxy server's API service is to serve as a Metaverse ecosystem between client requests and cloud services. Its goal is to reduce the client's computational load (Figure 4).

The process:

SEND - Call Service 1 (having search parameters)

RECEIVE - Get a response from Service 1 (Prop1-Value1, Prop2-Value2)

SEND - Call Service 2 (having search parameters + Service 1 Response.Prop1-Value1, Service 1 Response.Prop2-Value2)

RECEIVE - Get a response from Service 2

SAVE - Save the action by creating a mashup URL address.

Testing the API request to the server using Postman

API Address: https://taborsolutions.com/mcc/service/mash_api/1

Request Method: GET

Request time: 7101 ms

Size: 4.92 KB

Status: 200 OK

Result Type: JSON art phone) hence reducing the bandwidth latency.

This is where the public will have access to available cloud services. As stated in Figure 5, the 'Subscribe' button is put in to indicate that any interested customer may subscribe to this service package and gets to use it. The android app is a hybrid mobile app with both web-based and native android wrappers.

1. HTML5, JavaScript, CSS3
2. Framework: Framework7 - a free and open-source mobile HTML framework to develop hybrid mobile apps or web apps with iOS & Android native look and feel.
3. OS Platform: Android

Type a quote from the document or the summary of an interesting point. You can position the text box anywhere in the document. Use the Text Box Tools tab to change the formatting of the pull quote text box as depicted in Figures 6 and 7.

Using a sandbox environment, the proxy API was tested. The desktop app Postman is utilized. Through our REST API, requests may be made and replies can be obtained using a tool called postman. It works by submitting a request to the web server and receiving a reply (Figure 6).

Users can configure all the headers and cookies the API anticipates, and it verifies the response. Some of the Postman's capabilities, including those listed below, can help you work more efficiently. A test in Postman is essentially a piece of JavaScript code that executes once a request is sent and server

Figure 4. API request testing using Postman

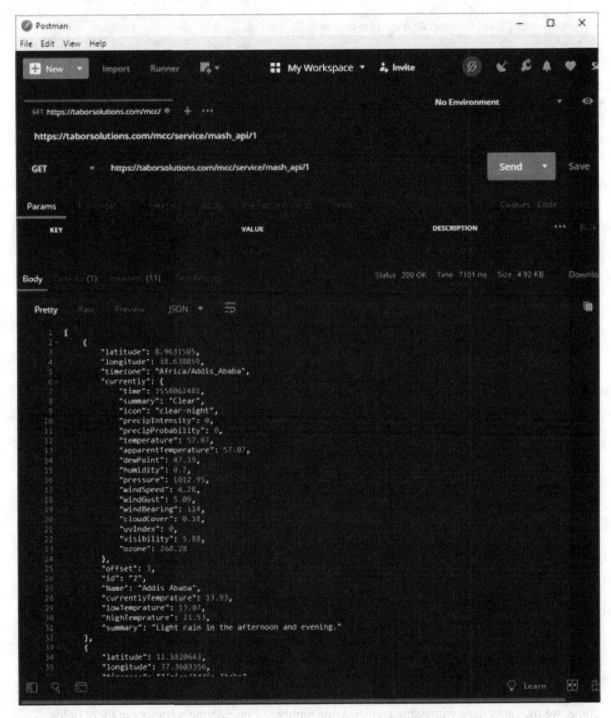

response is obtained. The following tests will be run to assess how well the Metaverse ecosystem and mobile client are designed following the study's goals.

Figure 5. Screen shots for the Proxy Metaverse ecosystem app

To improve the interaction between mobile clients and web services, the design of mobile clients' cross-platform functionality will be assessed. Utilize the ecosystem of the Metaverse to consume RESTful WS, Reduce the amount of bandwidth that mobile clients use, and Real-time push updates to mobile clients.

To make the Metaverse ecosystem more scalable and reliable by utilizing the Cloud platform:

ü Any server that mocks a telecom server can implement the Metaverse ecosystem.
ü To offer a service mashup platform to clients on mobile devices:
ü Use a mashup service offered by the Metaverse ecosystem.

The way we interact and experience virtual worlds could be completely transformed if cloud computing were to be integrated into the metaverse ecology. Cloud computing is facilitating the entry and participation of people and organizations in the metaverse by supplying scalability, accessibility, and cost-effectiveness. When powered by the cloud, the possibilities of the metaverse are limitless, ranging from immersive games to virtual events and remote work. The metaverse is still a very young and fast-developing technology, thus there are still a lot of unanswered questions regarding its long-term effects on society. However, the metaverse and cloud computing have a promising future, and in the years to come, we may anticipate witnessing an increasing number of fascinating advances in these fields.

Figure 6. Demo page for the Proxy Metaverse ecosystem app branch weather service API

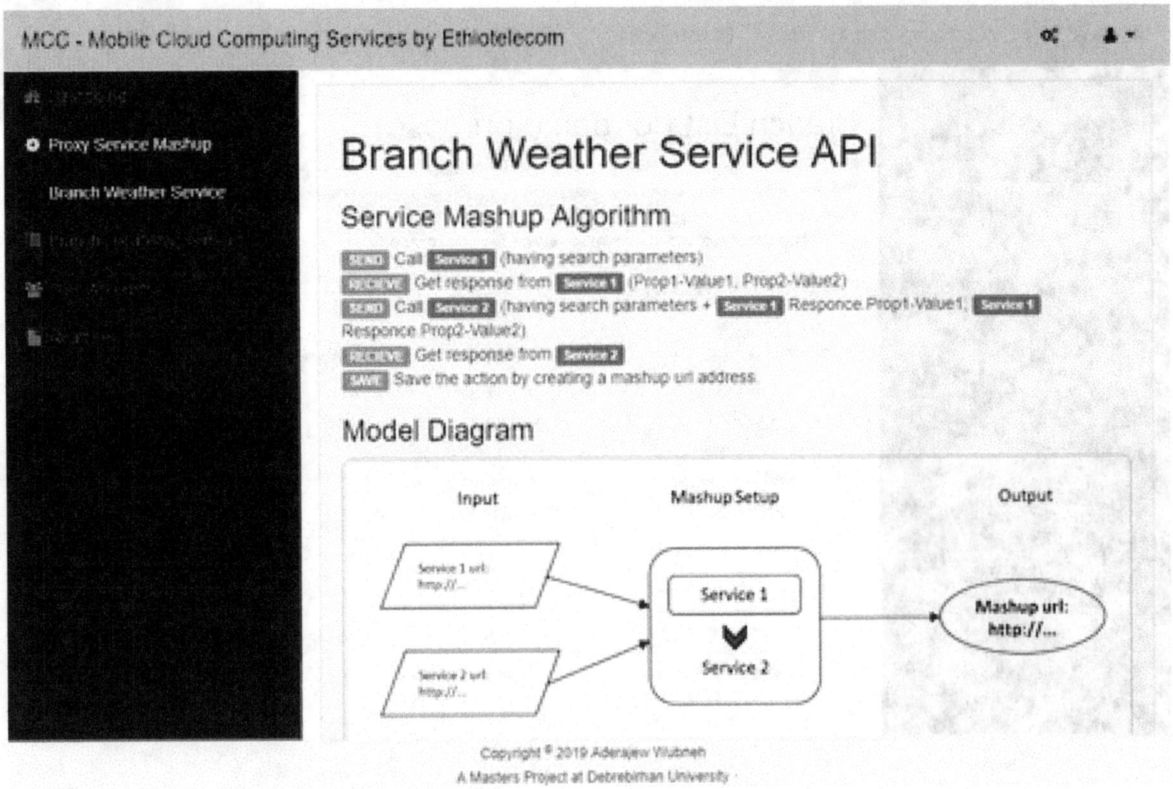

CONCLUSION AND FUTURE WORK

The post-reality world, also known as the Metaverse, is a continuously existing multiuser environment that combines physical reality and digital virtuality. It is built on the convergence of technologies, including augmented reality (AR) and virtual reality (VR), that allow for multimodal interactions with digital objects, people, and places (AR). As a result, the Metaverse is a network of persistent multi-user platforms that are socially networked and immersive. Dynamic interactions with digital artifacts are made possible by seamless embodied user communication. A web of virtual worlds with teleportation between them made up its initial edition. The modern version of the Metaverse includes social, immersive VR platforms that work with open game worlds, massively multiplayer online video games, and AR collaborative environments. We know the quality of communication in a wired network is better than in wireless networks, so reducing the proportion of data delivery in a wireless environment is an effective way to improve the quality. In addition, upgrading bandwidth is envisaged to be a simple way to increase performance but it incurs additional costs to users. There is still much work to be done for business implementation in the Metaverse through an interconnected web of social, networked immersive environments that are persistent multi-user platforms, even though some projects of mobile cloud computing have already been implemented around the world. More feature aspects will be taken into account in future work.

Figure 7. Demo page for the Proxy Metaverse ecosystem app branch list

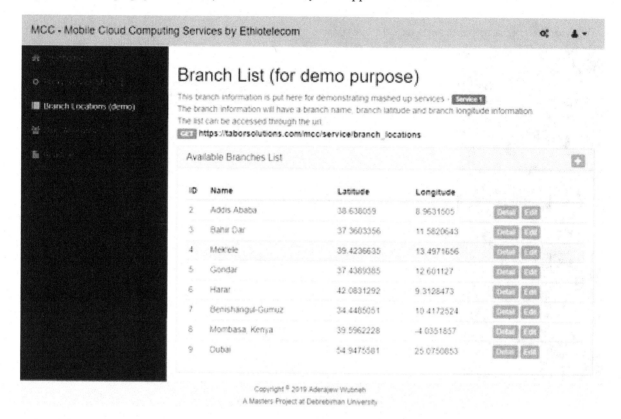

REFERENCES

Al-Turkistany, M. (2009). Adaptive wireless thin-client model for mobile computing. *Wireless Communications and Mobile Computing*, 9, 47–59. doi:10.1002/wcm.603

Backhouse, R. (1992). Should we ignore Methodology? *Royal Economic Society Newsletter*, 78, 4–5.

Cai, Y., Llorca, J., Tulino, A. M., & Molisch, A. F. (2022, July). Compute-and data-intensive networks: The key to the metaverse. In *2022 1st International Conference on 6G Networking (6GNet)* (pp. 1-8). IEEE.

Chang, Li, & Mishra. (2016). *mCAF: A Multi-dimensional Clustering Algorithm for Friends of Social Network Services*. Springer Plus.

Chang, H. T., Liu, S. W., & Mishra, N. (2015). A tracking and summarization system for online Chinese news topics. *Aslib Journal of Information Management*, 67(6), 687–699. doi:10.1108/AJIM-10-2014-0147

Chang, H.-T., Mishra, N., & Lin, C.-C. (2015). IoT Big-Data Centred Knowledge Granule Analytic and Cluster Framework for BI Applications: A Case Base Analysis. *PLoS One*, 10(11), e0141980. doi:10.1371/journal.pone.0141980 PMID:26600156

Dhelim, S., Kechadi, T., Chen, L., Aung, N., Ning, H., & Atzori, L. (2022). *Edge-enabled metaverse: The convergence of metaverse and mobile edge computing*. arXiv preprint arXiv:2205.02764.

Farley, P., & Capp, M. (2005). Mobile Web Services. *BT Technology Journal, 23*(3), 202–213. doi:10.100710550-005-0042-1

Fernando, N., Loke, S. W., & Rahayu, W. (2013). Mobile cloud computing: A survey. *Future Generation Computer Systems, 29*(1), 84–106. doi:10.1016/j.future.2012.05.023

Google App Engine. (2010). http://code.google.com/appengine/

Hevner, A.R., & March, S.T. (2005). *Integrated decision support systems: A data warehouse perspective*. Academic Press.

Jiang, Y., Kang, J., Niyato, D., Ge, X., Xiong, Z., Miao, C., & Shen, X. (2022). Reliable distributed computing for metaverse: A hierarchical game-theoretic approach. *IEEE Transactions on Vehicular Technology*.

Liu, X., & Deters, R. (2007). An efficient dual caching strategy for web service-enabled PDAs. In *SAC '07: Proceedings of the 2007 ACM symposium on applied computing*. ACM. 10.1145/1244002.1244178

Liu, X., Hui, Y., Sun, W., & Liang, H. (2007). Towards Service Composition Based on Mashup. *Services, 2007 IEEE Congress on*, 332-339. 10.1109/SERVICES.2007.67

Mishra, N. (2018). Internet of Everything Advancement Study in Data Science and Knowledge Analytic Streams. *International Journal of Scientific Research in Computer Science and Engineering, 6*(1), 30–36. doi:10.26438/ijsrcse/v6i1.3036

Mishra, N. (2019). Data Science and Knowledge Analytic Contexts on IoE Data for E-BI Application Case. In Edge Computing and Computational Intelligence Paradigms for the IoT (pp. 100-126). IGI Global. doi:10.4018/978-1-5225-8555-8.ch007

Mishra, N., Alebachew, K., & Patnaik, B. C. (2018). Knowledge Analytics in Cloud-Centric IoT Vicinities. *International Journal on Computer Science and Engineering, 6*(1), 385–390. doi:10.26438/ijcse/v6i1.385390

Mishra, N., Chang, H. T., & Lin, C. C. (2014). Data-centric Knowledge Discovery Strategy for a Safety-critical Sensor Application. *International Journal of Antennas and Propagation*. doi:10.1155/2014/172186

Mishra, N., Chang, H. T., & Lin, C. C. (2015). An IoT Knowledge Reengineering Framework for Semantic Knowledge Analytics for BI-Services. *Mathematical Problems in Engineering*.

Mishra, N., Chang, H. T., & Lin, C. C. (2018). Sensor data distribution and knowledge inference framework for a cognitive-based distributed storage sink environment. *International Journal of Sensor Networks, 26*(1), 26–42. doi:10.1504/IJSNET.2018.088387

Mishra, N., Chang, H. T., & Lin, C. C. (2018). Sensor Data Distribution and Distributed Knowledge Inference Systems. Lap Lambert Academic Publishing.

Mishra, N., Lin, C. C., & Chang, H. T. (2014). A Cognitive Oriented Framework for IoT Big-data Management Perspective. In *High-Speed Intelligent Communication Forum (HSIC) with International Conference on Computational Problem-Solving (ICCP) China, 2014, 6th International* (pp. 1-4). IEEE.

Mishra, N., Lin, C. C., & Chang, H. T. (2014). Cognitive inference device for activity supervision in the elderly. *TheScientificWorldJournal*, *2014*, 2014. doi:10.1155/2014/125618 PMID:25405211

Mishra, N., Lin, C. C., & Chang, H. T. (2014). A Cognitive Adopted Framework for IoT Big-Data Management and Knowledge Discovery Prospective. *International Journal of Distributed Sensor Networks*.

Oliver, E. (2008). A survey of platforms for mobile networks research. *SIGMOBILE Mob. Comput. Commun. Rev.*, *12*(4), 56–63. doi:10.1145/1508285.1508292

Papazoglou, M., & Georgakopoulos, D. (2003). Service-oriented Computing. *Communications of the ACM*, *46*(10), 25–65. doi:10.1145/944217.944233

Sanaei, Z., Abolfazli, S., Gani, A., & Buyya, R. (2014). Heterogeneity in mobile cloud computing: Taxonomy and open challenges. *IEEE Communications Surveys and Tutorials*, *16*(1), 369–392. doi:10.1109/SURV.2013.050113.00090

Tian, M., Voigt, T., Naumowicz, T., Ritter, H., & Schiller, J. (2004). Performance considerations for mobile web services. *Computer Communications*, *27*(11), 1097–1105. doi:10.1016/j.comcom.2004.01.015

WangY.ZhaoJ. (2022a). *A Survey of Mobile Edge Computing for the Metaverse: Architectures, Applications, and Challenges*. doi:10.1109/CIC56439.2022.00011

Wang, Y., & Zhao, J. (2022b). *Mobile Edge Computing, Metaverse, 6G Wireless Communications, Artificial Intelligence, and Blockchain: Survey and Their Convergence*. arXiv preprint arXiv:2209.14147.

Web Services Architecture. (2004). https://www.w3.org/TR/ws-arch/

Wibowo, A. (2018). Pregnancy Consultation Application Development based on Cloud Computing. Ultima Infosys. *Jurnal Ilmu Sistem Informasi*, *9*(1), 1–8.

Wu, Y., Ni, K., Zhang, C., Qian, L. P., & Tsang, D. H. (2018). NOMA-assisted multi-access mobile edge computing: A joint optimization of computation offloading and time allocation. *IEEE Transactions on Vehicular Technology*, *67*(12), 12244–12258. doi:10.1109/TVT.2018.2875337

Chapter 13
Application of Mathematical Models in Linear Algebra to the Metaverse Ecosystem

Özen Özer
Kırklareli University, Turkey

Biswadip Basu Mallik
Institute of Engineering and Management, Kolkata, India

Gunjan Mukherjee
https://orcid.org/0000-0002-3959-3718
Brainware University, India

ABSTRACT

Linear algebra is a branch of mathematics that is widely used throughout science and engineering. Linear algebra includes arithmetic operations with notation sharing. We can be able to have a better understanding of machine learning algorithms only after having a good understanding of linear algebra. Sometimes, machine learning might be pure linear algebra, involving many matrix operations; a dataset itself is often represented as a matrix. Linear algebra is used in data pre-processing, data transformations, and model evaluation. In this chapter, the basic importance of linear algebra has been discussed, and the close liaison of the subject with current research domain in machine learning and data science has been explored in the light of application of the same in solving some critical issues.

INTRODUCTION

Linear algebra is the branch of mathematics concerning linear equations, linear functions and their representations through matrices and vector spaces. It helps us to understand geometrical terms in higher dimensions, and execute mathematical operations on them. By definition, algebra deals in primarily with scalars (one-dimensional entities), but Linear Algebra has vectors and matrices (entities which possess

DOI: 10.4018/978-1-6684-8851-5.ch013

two or more dimensional components) to deal with linear equations and functions. Linear Algebra is the heart to almost all areas of mathematics like geometry and functional analysis (Strum et al., 2010). Its concepts are crucial prerequisite for understanding the theory behind Data Science and Machine learning. It is necessary to understand how the different algorithms really work.

Data science is the field of study that combines domain expertise, programming skills, and knowledge of mathematics and statistics to extract meaningful perception from data (Jones et al., 2008). Data science practitioners apply machine learning algorithms to numbers, text, images, video, audio, and more to produce artificial intelligence systems to perform tasks that regularly be in need of human intelligence (Waldrop et al., 2010). In turn, these systems generate insights which analysts and business users can translate into appreciable business value (Davenport et al., 2007). Mathematics in data science is playing very crucial role as this branch is providing not only the data analysis but the data manipulation too (Chapman et al., 2000).

Machine learning is the branch of artificial intelligence and is based on the principle that the systems learn from data and patterns, identifies the several patterns and can be able to make decisions with the nominal human intervention (Hibert & Lopez, 2011). Machine learning is chiefly based on data analysis and so is connected to data science (Philip et al., 2014). Machine learning involves some tasks, set of experiences and performance. The main objective of the machine learning trend is to enhance the performance of any tasks by means of the experiences. In the machine learning trends, multiple inputs are read and analyzed statistically to produce the output. So machine learning introduced the automation in performing the decision making process on the data received and siphon the same for the purpose of modelling.

Data manipulation is the way of manipulating and estimating data which requires the rigorous application of statistics and linear algebra (Ambrust et al., 2010). Matrix is the basic tool in algebra which stores huge amounts of information (Kakhani et al., 2015) in the field of image processing. Matrix operations including its decomposition with eigen vectors contributes a lot towards development of various data model. Similarly, the machine learning model both for the classification and regression requires in-depth knowledge of mathematics, especially linear algebra. The convolution part in the machine learning is being controlled by the algebraic equations. The optimization of model also is heavily dependent on matrix operations.

Calculus is the prime mathematical tool used as the rate measurer, In many data science and machine learning based applications, calculus plays the crucial role. Determination of the tendency in data mapping (Bollean et al., 2009), trends analysis of the regression models and optimization of machine learning models demands the huge involvements and application of calculus-based approach (Slavkovic et al., 2012). In the following sections we will look into the detailed concepts and analysis strategies using sub domain of mathematics linear algebra.

SCALARS, VECTORS, MATRICES AND TENSORS

- A scalar is a single number which may appear inside any vector also. On the other hand, any vector consists of the scalar terms. The rules for scalar terms manipulation is different from the vector operation.

Figure 1. Representation of data in data science by linear algebra

Scalar	Vector	Matrix	Tensor
1	$\begin{bmatrix} 2 \\ 4 \end{bmatrix}$	$\begin{bmatrix} 2 & 3 \\ 4 & 5 \end{bmatrix}$	$\begin{bmatrix} [3 & 1] & [1 & 2] \\ [2 & 4] & [3 & 5] \end{bmatrix}$

- A vector is an array of numbers. A vector is represented as the collections of number of scalars. Any vector can be expressed as either the row matrix or column matrix. The operation on vectors follows specialized rules for vector operations.
- A matrix is a 2-D array. It is the combination of number of vectors placed together one after another. The operation concerned are being performed on the 2D array following the rules of matrix.
- Tensor defines the n dimensional data which can be represented as the grid of numbers or called as the N way array.

The representation of the individual terms has been shown in Figure 1.

APPLICATIONS OF LINEAR ALGEBRA IN MULTIPLE ALLIED DISCIPLINES

The following diagram states the relation of linear algebra (Will, 2014) with the versatile research fields of current trends. The fields like machine learning, computer vision, optimization, AI, natural language processing seeks multiple application of the linear algebra from the fundamental levels. The following sections gloss over the different intricacies in the following domains implied by the very concepts of linear algebra. In the machine learning domain, several optimization strategies have been carried out by applying linear algebra concepts in some judicial way. Figure 2 provides us with different allied application areas related to Linear algebra.

Figure 2. Applications of linear algebra in data sciences

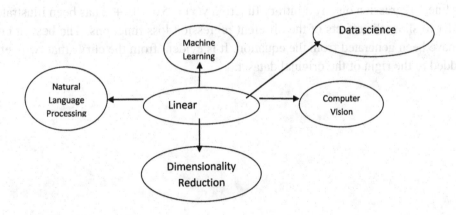

LINEAR ALGEBRA IN MACHINE LEARNING

The following are the some application parts of linear algebra in machine learning.

1. Loss Functions
2. Regularization
3. Covariance Matrix
4. Support Vector Machine Classification
5. Regression
6. ANN Classification
7. Deep Learning Model

LOSS FUNCTIONS

The loss function is termed as the difference between the actual and predicted values. The cost function is something obtained by taking average of all the loss functions. The linear regression function decides how good and efficient the model is in prediction of the future trends of any relational behavior of mutually dependent data. The regression model must fit the given set of data. The linear regression model is based on some arbitrary prediction function. The function works on the independent set of features of the data to predict the output. The regression model also calculates the independent features of data to predict the output trends. The regression model estimates the distance of how far away the estimated output is from the actual one and applies some unique strategies like Gradient Descent to minimize the distance between the twos in order to optimize the prediction process. The loss function helps in tracking the difference between the prediction and the expected output. The loss function is an application of the vector norm in Linear Algebra. The magnitude of such a vector is implied as the norm of the vector. In the domain of linear algebra, there are many such types of vector norms exists.

The regression loss function can mathematically be illustrated in terms of the error between the predictions and the observations as

$\mathbf{e(m)} = \mathbf{d} - f(\mathbf{G}, \mathbf{m}),$

where $e_u(\mathbf{m})$ is the *uth* element of the vector:and m_v is the *v*th element of the vector $\mathbf{m}$.

The linear regression on any arbitrary function $y(x) = 5x^2 - 3x + 2$ has been illustrated in the Figure 3 in order to show the effects of the different regression loss functions. The best fit curve through 19 points have been generated from the equation. It is evident from the curve that two outlier points have been added to the right of the original dataset.

Figure 3. Linear regression of any arbitrary function

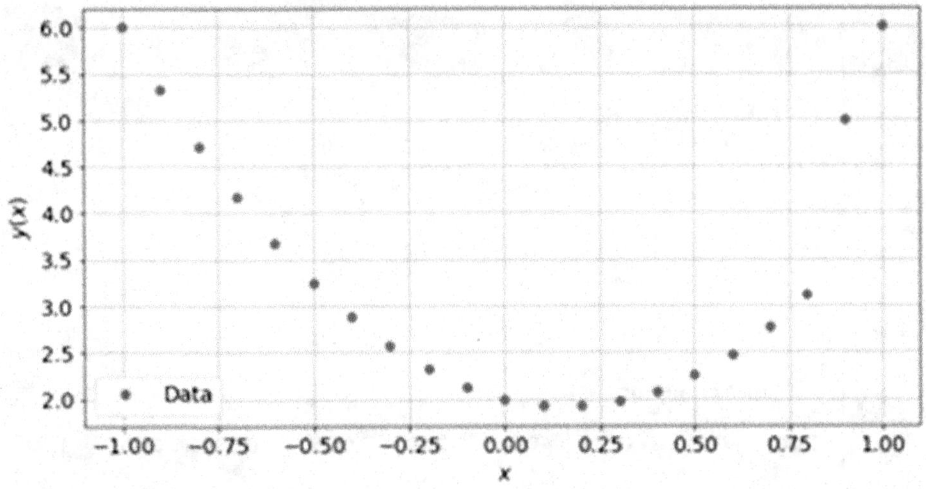

L1 NORM

The L1 norm is being defined to be the distance travelled from the origin to the vector provided that the only permitted directions are parallel to the axes of the spaces. This L1 norm also implies the Manhattan Distance or Taxicab Norm which is shown in Figure 4.

Figure 4. Manhattan distance or L1 norm
L_1 *Norm of vector* $V = (v_1, v_2..., v_n)$; $V_2 = |v_1| + |v_2| + ... + |v_n|$ *(3,4)*

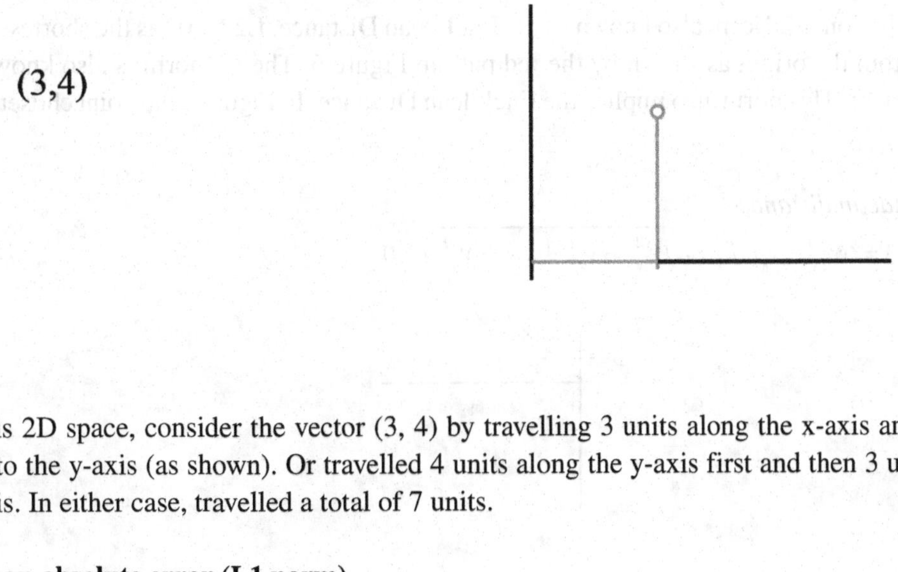

(3,4)

In this 2D space, consider the vector (3, 4) by travelling 3 units along the x-axis and then 4 units parallel to the y-axis (as shown). Or travelled 4 units along the y-axis first and then 3 units parallel to the x-axis. In either case, travelled a total of 7 units.

- **Mean absolute error (L1 norm)**

  $L(\mathbf{m}) = \Sigma_u |e_u(\mathbf{m})|.$

Figure 5. Plotting of the L1 norm

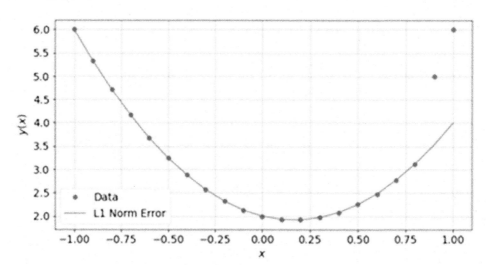

This loss function is not as widely used as the mean squared error, as it assumes that the noise in the data is drawn from the exponential distribution. As the absolute value of the error is used, this loss function is not strongly affected by outliers as can be seen in Figure 5 — the best fit curve completely ignores the two outlier points. The curve has been shown in Figure 5.

L2 NORM

This is the most widely used loss function which assumes that the noise in the data is based on the Gaussian distribution, L2 Norm also known as the Euclidean Distance. L2 Norm is the shortest distance of the vector from the origin as shown by the red path in Figure 6. The L2 norm is also known as the mean squared error. This norm also implies the Euclidean Distance. In Figure 6 the point chosen is (3,4).

Figure 6. Euclidean distance

L_2 *Norm of vector V*$= (v_1, v_2, ..., v_n)$, $V_2 = \sqrt{v_1^2 + v_2^2 + ... + v_n^2}$ *(3,4)*

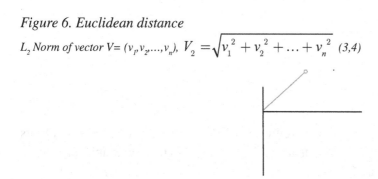

This distance is calculated using the Pythagoras Theorem as shown in Figure 6. It is the square root of (3^2+4^2), which is equal to 5. The predicted values are stored in a vector P and the expected values are stored in a vector E. Then P – E is the difference vector. And the norm of P – E is the total loss for the prediction. Due to squaring of the error, the loss function is strongly affected in presence of the outliers. Mathematically it can be expressed as $L(\mathbf{m}) = \Sigma_u(e_u(\mathbf{m}))^2$. The L2 has been shown in Figure 7.

Figure 7. Plotting of the L2 norm

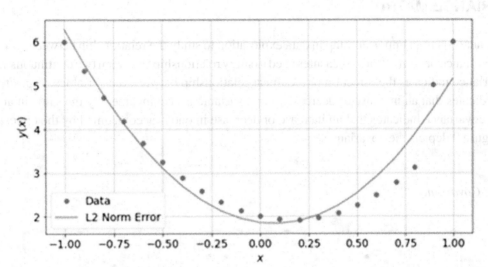

REGULARIZATION

Regularization is a very important concept in data science. It's a technique we use to prevent models from over fitting. Regularization is actually another application of the Norm. A model is said to over fit when it fits the training data too well. Such a model does not perform well with new data because it has learned even the noise in the training data. It will not be able to generalize on data that it has not seen before. The regularization curve has been shown in Figure 8.

Regularization penalizes overly complex models by adding the norm of the weight vector to the cost function. Since, we want to minimize the cost function; we will need to minimize this norm. This causes unrequited components of the weight vector to reduce to zero and prevents the function from being overly complex.

Figure 8. Regularization

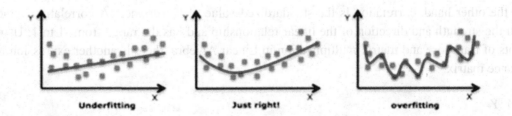

The L1 and L2 norms we discussed above are used in two types of regularization:

- L1 regularization used with Lasso Regression
- L2 regularization used with Ridge Regression

COVARIANCE MATRIX

bivariate analysis is an important step in data exploration to study the relationship between pairs of variables. covariance or correlation is measures used to study relationships between two continuous variables.

Covariance indicates the direction of the linear relationship between the variables. A positive covariance indicates that an increase or decrease in one variable is accompanied by the same in another. A negative covariance indicates that an increase or decrease in one is accompanied by the opposite in the other. Figure 9 depicts the covariance.

Figure 9. Covariance

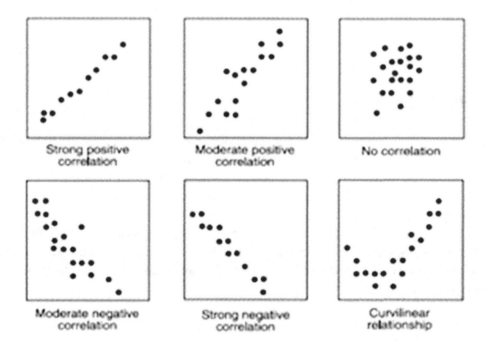

On the other hand, correlation is the standardized value of Covariance. A correlation value tells us both the strength and direction of the linear relationship and has the range from -1 to 1. Using the concepts of transpose and matrix multiplication in Linear Algebra, there is another expression for the covariance matrix:

$$cov = Y^T Y$$

Here, Y is the standardized data matrix containing all numerical features.

SUPPORT VECTOR MACHINE CLASSIFICATION

One of the most common classification algorithms that regularly produces impressive results. It is an application of the concepts of Vector Spaces in Linear Algebra. Support Vector Machine, or SVM (Cristianini & Ricci, 2008), is a discriminative classifier that works by finding a decision surface. It is a supervised machine learning algorithm. In this algorithm, we plot each data item as a point in an n-dimensional space (where n is the number of features you have) with the value of each feature being the value of a particular coordinate. Then, we perform classification by finding the hyper plane that differentiates the two classes very well i.e. with the maximum margin, which is C in this case. Out of the many decision boundaries segregating the datasets, one which fits best is chosen and termed as the best decision boundary and is known as the hyperplane of SVM as dhown in Figure 10.

Figure 10. Support vector machine

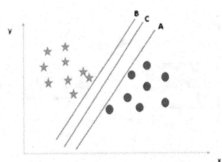

A hyper plane is a subspace whose dimensions are one less than its corresponding vector space, so it would be a straight line for a 2D vector space, a 2D plane for a 3D vector space and so on. Again, Vector Norm is used to calculate the margin.

TYPE OF SVM

1. Linear SVM works on the linearly separable data where the data are classified into two classes by using the straight line. The classifier is linear in nature and hence is called the linear SVM.
2. Nonlinear SVM works on the nonlinearly separable data i.e., the dataset is of such nature, it cannot be classified easily by means of the straight line only.

LINEAR ALGEBRA IN DIMENSIONALITY REDUCTION

1. Principal Component Analysis
2. Singular Value Decomposition

PRINCIPAL COMPONENT ANALYSIS

Principal Component Analysis, or PCA (Seghal et al., 2014) is an unsupervised dimensionality reduction technique. PCA finds the directions of maximum variance and projects the data along them to reduce the dimensions. Without going into the math, these directions are the Eigen vectors of the covariance matrix of the data. PCA is the statistical transformation which becomes functional in converting the set of corelated variables to uncorrelated variables. PCA is used for exploratory data analysis and examine the interrelationship among the set of variables. It is manifesting the general factor analysis where the best fit is determined by the regression analysis. The Eigen Vector plotting has been shown in Figure 11.

Figure 11. Eigen vectors

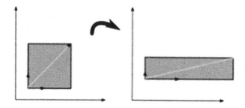

Eigen vectors for a square matrix are special non-zero vectors whose direction does not change even after applying linear transformation (which means multiplying) with the matrix. They are shown as the red colored vectors in Figure 11.

SINGULAR VALUE DECOMPOSITION

Singular Value Decomposition (SVD) (Jaradat et al., 2021), is under rated and not discussed enough. It is an amazing technique of matrix decomposition with diverse applications. This has been proved to the important tool towards the Dimensionality Reduction. Specifically, this is known as Truncated SVD. A is termed as the numerical data matrix of dimension m X n, where m is the number of features. The matrix has been decomposed into three different matrices as shown in Figure 12.

$A = USV^T$

Choose k singular values based on the diagonal matrix and truncate (trim) the 3 matrices accordingly:
Finally, the transformed matrix A-K has been obtained by means of the truncated matrices. It has the dimension $m \times k$ with k features and k < n. On applying truncated SVD to the Digits data, the plot

Figure 12. SVD decomposition

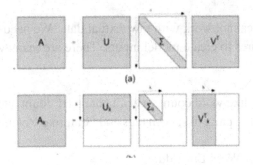

Figure 13. SVD decomposition

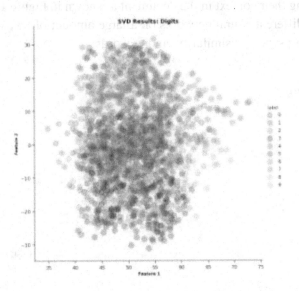

given in Figure 13 has been obtained. It has been evident from the plot shown that the clusters formed is not as distinct as that obtained in case of PCA.

NATURAL LANGUAGE PROCESSING (NLP)

Natural Language Processing (NLP) (Jiang & Lu, 2023). Is the hottest field in data science in the current scenario? This is primarily due to major breakthrough taking place in the last 18 months. Given below are the couple of interesting applications of linear algebra in NLP furnished. This should help swing your decision.

WORD EMBEDDINGS

Machine learning algorithms cannot work with raw textual data. We need to convert the text into some numerical and statistical features to create model inputs. There are many ways for engineering features from text data, such as:

1. Meta attributes of a text, like word count, special character count, etc.
2. NLP attributes of text using parts of speech tags and Grammar Relations like the number of proper nouns
3. Word Vector Notations or Word Embeddings

Word Embeddings (Jiao & Zhang, 2021) is a way of representing words as low dimensional vector of number while presenting their context in the document as shown in Figure 14. These representations are obtained by training different neural networks on a large amount of text which is called a corpus. They also help in analyzing syntactic similarity among words:

Figure 14. Word embedding

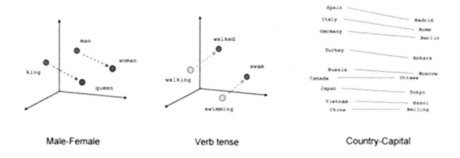

| Male-Female | Verb tense | Country-Capital |

Word2Vec and GloVe are two popular models to create word Embeddings. The model trained on the Shakespeare corpus after some light preprocessing using Word2Vec and obtained the word embedding for the word 'world': The corpus has been shown in Figure 15.

LATENT SEMANTIC ANALYSIS (LSA)

Several words uttered like "prince, royal, king, nobel" has been bearing some resemblence. These very different words are almost synonymous. Now, the following sentences have been considered

- The pitcher of the home team seemed out of form
- There is a pitcher of juice on the table for you to enjoy

The word 'pitcher' has different meaning based on the other words in the two sentences. It means a baseball player in the first sentence and a jug of juice in the second. Both these sets of wordds are easy

Figure 15. Word embedding for world

```
Word Embedding for 'world'
[-5.51259406e-02  4.12687426e-03 -3.91943246e-01  7.98276290e-02
  1.95584342e-01  1.06719201e-02 -1.80827945e-01 -1.58239201e-01
  5.25065251e-02  3.08515906e-01  7.70677403e-02  2.15309232e-01
 -1.76252797e-01  1.48237124e-01  2.26699933e-03  1.03173576e-01
  2.06766561e-01  5.34750847e-03  2.46566124e-02  2.59118438e-01
 -2.70715114e-02 -2.47280404e-01  3.82245481e-01  2.06979588e-01
 -1.11549675e-01  7.07698911e-02  2.27834001e-01  2.54352421e-01
 -5.08933328e-02 -3.22999954e-01  1.51017293e-01  1.05106058e-02
  4.48949076e-02  2.38278791e-01 -1.29405648e-01  9.35490653e-02
 -1.19607383e-02 -1.10186301e-01 -3.25406939e-01 -1.82196513e-01
 -1.57575116e-01  2.44453356e-01  2.39373803e-01 -2.29061678e-01
 -2.41212785e-01  3.77874933e-02  1.60421342e-01 -1.53848259e-02
  2.60948479e-01  2.05284163e-01 -2.95275599e-01  5.84802181e-02
  2.00317800e-01  1.51339561e-01 -4.36831564e-02 -4.72796857e-02
  1.29834697e-01 -4.44906503e-02 -2.14892551e-01 -1.72190405e-02
  2.95504004e-01  3.07721496e-02 -1.61519662e-01  1.23960808e-01
 -6.33224696e-02 -1.71648487e-01 -5.52447923e-02  2.19030678e-01
 -5.23866620e-03 -1.67808130e-01  2.32335880e-01 -1.87726706e-01
  2.10608952e-01  3.24162357e-02  1.40128642e-01  1.82926416e-01
  3.48672755e-02 -2.70526297e-02  3.66246764e-04  4.11806107e-02
 -1.21602915e-01  1.67497639e-02 -4.88639362e-02 -2.41602156e-02
  1.02392279e-01 -9.56652761e-02  1.12021834e-01  1.22618370e-01
 -2.15947643e-01 -1.21888198e-01  1.65163383e-01  6.60482198e-02
  1.46776205e-02  1.05597220e-01 -2.55980641e-01  1.78161003e-02
  6.14810875e-03  2.33961027e-02 -4.85116765e-02  1.91777591e-02]
```

for us humans to interpret with years of experience with the language. But what about machines? Here, the NLP concept of topic modeling comes into play: The same has been displayed in Figure 16.

Figure 16. Topic modeling

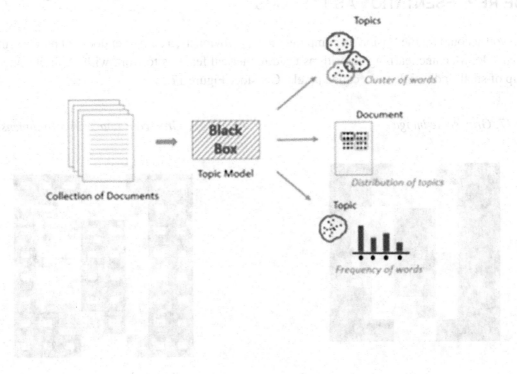

Topic modeling is an unsupervised technique to find topics across various text documents. These topics are nothing but clusters of related words. Each document can be have multiple topics. The topic model outputs the various topics, their distribution in each document, and the frequency of different words it contains. Latent semantic analysis (LSA) (Kherwa & Basant, 2017). Or latent semantic indexing, is one of thee techniques of topic modeling. It is another application of singular value decomposition.

Latent means "hidden". True to its name, LSA attempts to capture the hidden thems or topics from the documents by leveraging the context around the words. I will describe the steps in LSA in short so make sure you check out this simple introduction to topic modeling using latent semantic analysis with code in python for a proper and in depth understanding.

- First, document term matrix for data has been generated.
- SVD technique been used to decompose the matrix into 3 sub matrices:

Document topic matrix has been based on the topic importance.
Topic term matrix has been obtaned on truncating the matrices.

COMPUTER VISION

Another field of deep learning that is creating waves computer vision (Zhang et al., 2018). This focuses on the digital systems which has been engaged in the processing, analysis and making sense of visual data which may comprise of either the images or videos in the same way as the human beings do, the processing and analysis in this domain has been carried out in the pixel level.

IMAGE REPRESENTATION AS TENSORS

How do you account for the 'vision' in computer vision? Obviously, a computer does not process images as humans do. Machine learning algorithms need numerical features to work with. A digital image is made up of small indivisible units called pixels. Consider Figure 17.

Figure 17. Gray scale image

Figure 18. Grayscale image as two-dimensional matrix

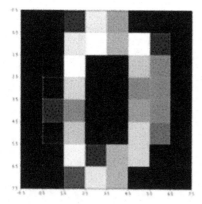

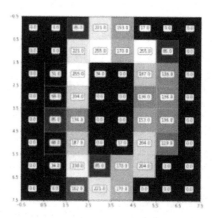

This grayscale image of thee digit zero is made of 8×8 =64 pixel has a value in the range 0 to 255. A value of 0 represents a black pixel and 255 represents a white pixel. Conveniently, an m × n grayscale images can be represented as a 2D matrix with m rows and n columns with the cells containing the respective pixel values as shown in Figure 18.

A colored image is generally stored in the RGB system. Each image can be thought of as being represented by three 2D matrices, one for each R, G and B channel. A pixel value of 0 in the R channel represented by three 2D matrices, one for each R, G and B channel. A pixel value of o on the R channel represents zero intensity of the red color and of 255 represents the full intensity of the red color.

CONVOLUTION AND IMAGE PROCESSING

2D Convolution is very important operation in image processing. It consists of the below steeps:

1.   Start with a small matrix of weights, called a kernel or a filter
2.   Slide this kernel on the 2D input data, performing element wise multiplication
3.   Add the obtained values and put the sum in a single output pixel

The function can seem a bit complex but it's widely used for performing various image processing operations like sharpening and blurring the images and edge detection. The right kernel of the task concerned should be known to us. Some of the kernels have been provided in Figure 19.

Figure 19. Kernels of the 2D convolution

Kernels	Sharpen			Box Blur		
	0	-1	0	1/9	1/9	1/9
	-1	5	-1	1/9	1/9	1/9
	0	-1	0	1/9	1/9	1/9

Sobel (Vertical Edge)			Sobel (Horizontal Edge)			Laplace (All Edges)		
-1	0	1	1	2	1	1	1	1
-2	0	2	0	0	0	1	-8	1
-1	0	1	-1	-2	-1	1	1	1

REGRESSION

Linear regression (Huang, 2020) is the commonly used data model representing a relation between the two different variables, so that the values of the variables can easily be predicted based on the values of the others. The linearity in relationship between the two variables is implied by the increase in the value of one variable with the increase of the other similarly the decrease of one variable can be associated to the decrease of the other. The formula of the line representing the linear relationship can be expressed as $Y = w1*x + w0$. In this relation x implies the independent variables and y represent the dependent variable. The slope andintercepts are respectively represented by w1 and w0 respectively. The graph given below shows the linear regression model for some fictitious data sets. The regression curve has been shown in Figure 20.

Figure 20. Regression curve

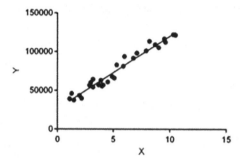

BEST FIT LINE

In order to find the perfect formula of the line, the best fit line is to be found. Given number of data, the line is to be found which fits the best possible way among all the data points present. The best fit line will be chosen to calculate the coefficients of the line. The cost of any house depends on the area in square feet. More the area covered, higher will be the cost of the house. The best fit line will determine the best presented relationship between the two variables cost and the area. The predictive nature of the line provides us with enough information to find out the price of any house any given area. The cost trends here depend on the area covered. The main objective of the regression is to reduce the gap between the actual value and the estimated value of any variables. In the above example, the linear regression has been used to have the difference between the actual prices.

SIGNIFICANCE OF THE COEFFICIENTS OF LINEAR REGRESSION

Two prime coefficients involved with the linear regression are the slope of the line and the intercept it makes on either of the axes. The slope implies the increase in the dependent variable due to the unit change in the value of independent variable. In order to draw the analogy with the above cited example for determination of the house price as per the area, the price of any house per square meter of the space provides the slope of the regression line for the cost -vs area regression plotting.

Likewise, the intercept signifies the least value of the dependent variable for the zero value of the independent variable. In the above case, the least value of the price of the house for each square area of the house provides the intercept in case of the linear regression curve.

MULTIVARIATE REGRESSION

Multilinear regression model is the generalization of the linear regression where the number of variables extends beyond more than two variables. This type of regression models also picks up more number of coefficients compared to the case of the linear model. The following multivariate expression shows for n number of variables. Two important factors attached to the multivariate regression model are the number of observation and the number of data variables. It works on the basis two assumptions:

1. The number of independent variables should be less than the number of assumptions.
2. There are no significant relationships between the independent variables.

SOME ASSUMPTIONS RELATED TO THE LINEAR REGRESSION

The main objective of the regression model is the prediction of the values of some dependent variables. In order to get the good linearity in the relation towards obtaining the effective prediction, the normal distribution of the data should be maintained. In order to make sure in the linear distribution of data, the data should not be diverted much. The removal of divergent data renders linearity in the regression.

The reliability of the model lies in maintaining the linear relationships between the dependent and independent variables involved in the linear regression.

ANN MODEL

The Neural Networks Model

Neural network (Mishra & Srivastava, 2014) model is the simulated version of the human brain structure which contains the complex nervous systems. Neuron is the basic unit of the human brain and is organized into number of layers.as shown in Figure 21.

The model network is the simplified version of the complex human brain structure and simulates the number of interconnected processing units resembling that of the abstract view of internal human brain structure.

The neural network structure consists of the three distinct layers firstly, the input layer containing number of input units with each representing the input fields. Secondly one or more hidden layers and thirdly the output layer with each unit representing the target fields. The units are all connected with the variable weight values. The input data were presented to the first layer and thereafter the values are propagated from each neuron to every neuron in the succeeding layers. Finally, the output layer produces the result. The learning phase of the network model is very important which involves examination of individual records followed by the prediction of each individual records. In case of the incorrect predic-

Figure 21. Neural network model structure

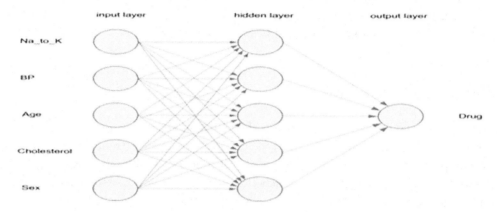

tion, the weight values are getting adjusted. The prediction gets improved through the reputation of such adjustment process till the stopping criteria have been met.

The network weight values have been initialized in some random order. Later, gradually the network learns through the training phase and the output coming out from each phase are getting repeatedly getting submitted to the network. The answers obtained are compared to the known outcomes. The information obtained through the comparison gets fed back to the network reflecting in the change of weight values. Such replication of known outcomes becomes accurate as the training progresses. Once the training phase of the network has become fully over, it can be applied to all future cases involving the known outcomes.

Perceptrons

Perceptrons, invented by Frank Rosenblatt in 1958, are the simplest neural network that consists of n number of inputs, only one neuron, and one output, where n is the number of features of our dataset. The process of passing the data through the neural network is known as forward propagation and the forward propagation carried out in a perceptron is explained in the following three steps.

The perceptron consists of n number of neurons each corresponding to individual features of the dataset engaged. The model has the n number of inputs and one single output. The passing of data through the network is termed as the forward propagation and appear in three different steps.

Step 1: The total weight value of the network is calculated by taking the sum of the products of individual inputs and its corresponding weight values as shown in Equation 1.

$$\Sigma = (x_1 \times w_1) + (x_2 \times w_2) + \ldots + (x_n \times w_n)$$

The row vectors of the inputs and weights are $x = [x_1, x_2 \ldots x_n]$ and $w = [w_1, w_2 \ldots w_n]$ respectively and their *dot product* is given by

$$x.w = (x_1 \times w_1) + (x_2 \times w_2) + \ldots + (x_n \times w_n)$$

Hence, the summation is equal to the *dot product* of the vectors *x* and *w*.

$$\sum = x.w$$

Step 2: The bias value b has been added to the multiplied value which is termed as z. to move the entire activation function to the left or right to generate the required output values.

$$z = x.w + b$$

Step 3: Pass the value of *z* to a non-linear activation function. Activation functions — are used to introduce non-linearity into the output of the neurons, without which the neural network will just be a linear function. Moreover, they have a significant impact on the learning speed of the neural network. Perceptrons have *binary step function* as their activation function. However, we shall use *sigmoid* — also known as *logistic* function as our activation function.

The activity function injects the nonlinearity and carries also some significant impacts on the rate of learning. The sigmoid known as the logistic function has been used here as the activation function.

$$\hat{y} = \sigma(z) = \frac{1}{1 + e^{-z}}$$

where **σ** denotes the *sigmoid* activation function and the output we get after the forward prorogation is known as the *predicted value* **ŷ**.

LEARNING ALGORITHM

The learning algorithm consists of two parts backpropagation and optimization.

Backpropagation: The back propagation initiates the error propagation in the backward direction. It is used to calculate the gradient of the loss function. This is explained in the following section.

Step 1: The mean squared error term has been shown in the following section. Let's take a regression problem and its loss function be mean squared error, which squares the difference between *actual* (y_i) and *predicted value* ($\hat{y}_i$).

$$MSE_i = (y_i - \hat{y}_i)^2$$

Loss function is calculated for the entire training dataset and their average is called the *Cost function* **C**.

$$C = MSE = \frac{1}{n} \sum_{i=1}^{n} (y_i - \hat{y}_i)^2$$

Step 2: The gradient is calculated in order to estimate the change in the cost function with respect to weights and bias.

Let's calculate the gradient of cost function **C** with respect to the weight w_i using *partial derivation*. Since the cost function is not directly related to the weight w_i, using the chain rule.

$$\frac{\partial C}{\partial w_i} = \frac{\partial C}{\partial \hat{y}} \times \frac{\partial \hat{y}}{\partial z} \times \frac{\partial z}{\partial w_i}$$

Now we need to find the following three gradients

$$\frac{\partial C}{\partial \hat{y}} = ? \quad \frac{\partial \hat{y}}{\partial z} = ? \quad \frac{\partial z}{\partial w_1} = ?$$

Let's start with the gradient of the *cost function (C)* with respect to the *predicted value* ($\hat{y}$)

$$\frac{\partial C}{\partial \hat{y}} = \frac{\partial}{\partial \hat{y}} \frac{1}{n} \sum_{i=1}^{n} (y_i - \hat{y}_i)^2 = 2 \times \frac{1}{n} \sum_{i=1}^{n} (y_i - \hat{y}_i)$$

Let $y = [y_1, y_2 \ldots y_n]$ and $\hat{y} = [\hat{y}_1, \hat{y}_2 \ldots \hat{y}_n]$ be the row vectors of actual and predicted values. Hence the above equation is simplified as

$$\frac{\partial C}{\partial \hat{y}} = \frac{2}{n} \times sum(y - \hat{y})$$

Now let's find the gradient of the *predicted value* with respect to the *z*. This will be a bit lengthy.

$$\frac{\partial \hat{y}}{\partial z} = \frac{\partial}{\partial z} \sigma(z)$$

$$= \frac{\partial}{\partial z} \left(\frac{1}{1+e^{-z}} \right)$$

$$= \frac{e^{-z}}{\left(1+e^{-z}\right)^2}$$

$$= \frac{1}{\left(1+e^{-z}\right)} \times \frac{e^{-z}}{\left(1+e^{-z}\right)}$$

$$= \frac{1}{\left(1+e^{-z}\right)} \times \left(1 - \frac{1}{\left(1+e^{-z}\right)}\right)$$

$$= \sigma(z) \times (1 - \sigma(z))$$

The gradient of *z* with respect to the weight w_i is

$$\frac{\partial z}{\partial w_i} = \frac{\partial}{\partial w_i}(z)$$

$$= \frac{\partial}{\partial w_i} \sum_{i=1}^{n} (x_i \cdot w_i + b)$$

$$= x_i$$

Therefore, we get,

$$\frac{\partial C}{\partial w_i} = \frac{2}{n} \times sum(y - \hat{y}) \times \sigma(z) \times (1 - \sigma(z)) \times x_i$$

What about Bias? — Bias is theoretically considered to have an input of constant value *1*. Hence,

$$\frac{\partial C}{\partial b} = \frac{2}{n} \times sum(y - \hat{y}) \times \sigma(z) \times (1 - \sigma(z))$$

OPTIMIZATION

Optimization refers to the selection of the best weight and bias of the perceptron, The gradient descent has been chosen as the optimisation algorithm, (Dean et al., 2008). The variation of the cost function with respect to the bias and weight has been shown in the equation, (Gupota et al., 2010). *Learning rate* (α) is a hyperparameter which is used to control how much the weights and bias are changed.

The weights and bias are updated as follows and the backpropagation and gradient descent is repeated until convergence.

$$w_i = w_i - \left(\alpha \times \frac{\partial C}{\partial w_i} \right)$$

$$b = b - \left(\alpha \times \frac{\partial C}{\partial b} \right)$$

DEEP LEARNING MODEL

The deep learning model, (Wuchty et al., 2007) is also another abstraction of the human brain simulating all the intricacies of the normal human brain, this typical network model consists of several layers interconnected nodes distributed over the three distinct layers namely input layer, output layer and hidden layer. The deep learning model easily extracts the high-level features from the data fed and abstracts the representation of data to the next layer with the final layer catering with human like interpretation. The deep learning model works on the large volume of labeled data The ingestion of such large volume of unstructured data with intelligence applied lead the model to perform the human like functions lie facial recognition and natural language processing.

Figure 22. Deep learning model

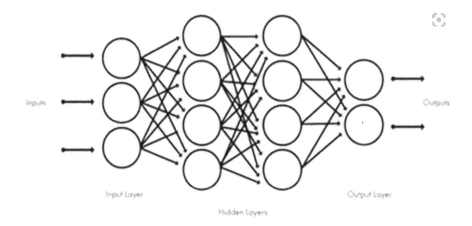

CONCLUSION

Linear algebra has vast uses in real world. Linear algebra methods are applied in the domain of data science to improve the efficiency of algorithms to attain the more accurate results obtained in respective machine learning models. In this paper the concepts of the linear algebra applications have been explored in respective fields of machine learnings and data science-based models. The machine learning domain is currently evolved into much broaden and generalized fields towards achievement of automation in the versatile fields. The steady and steep rise of the growth of such domain backed by the influences of data sciences has opened the door to much specific research fields. In this paper the machine learning model behaviors has been studied thoroughly in terms of the algebraic approach. It undoubtedly opened up the new horizon of research in current trends of recent intelligence growth and meeting particular challenge of the research field in overall quality improvement.

IMPORTANCE OF THE CHAPTER

This chapter mainly elaborates the basic ideas of the algebraic models applied in the data science and machine learning. Data science is dealing with the data analysis, data processing and manipulation, In all the aspects of such works. Machine learning is the abstraction of AI models and has profusely been used as the model structures for carrying out the classification tasks. Which can perform well and with the utmost precision with the help of the optimization of the model and scaling of the images to be experimented. The real need of the mathematical models and its appropriate applications in the field of data science and machine learning following the principles of linear algebra for meeting up all the criterions of the mentioned fields has been considered in this chapter. This chapter therefore spruce up the mathematical models in the linear algebra with the analysis of the models and its application both in the data science and machine learning fields which will be of great interest to the concerned persons.

THE BENEFICIARIES OF THIS CHAPTER

This chapter presents the basic and intricate concepts of mathematics applied in the model architecture and application fields with in-depth analysis of the concepts in the concerned areas of data science and machine learning. The volumes of information being catered in this chapter will of immense help to the researchers, scientists, academicians, mathematicians and students as well. The professionals working in the industries in the similar domain of research and development can also get much of the concerned and required information regarding mathematical concepts lying in the background of huge and promising fields of data science and machine learning unveiling the unbounded opportunities ahead.

FUTURE RESEARCH DIRECTION

The underlying platform for the data science and machine learning domain stands on the mathematical pillars. The model architecture has been fine-tuned and gradually sharpened up with introduction of many different mathematical rules and principles. With the ongoing research activities in mathematical domain provides myriad noble and multidirectional concepts. Optimization of the model is of utmost importance for obtaining more accuracy in the result of processing and classification. The presented work can provide us with future research scopes in the domain of optimization of such models.

REFERENCES

Ambrust A. Fox, R., Griffith, R., Joseph, A. D., Konwinski, A., Lee, G., Patterson, D., Rabkin, A., Stoica, I., & Zaharia, M. (2010). A view of cloud computing. *Communications of the ACM, 53*(4), 50–58. doi:10.1145/1721654.1721672

Bollean, de Sompel, Hagberg, Chute, Rodriguez, & Balakireva. (2009). Click stream Data yields High-Resolution Maps of Science. *PLoS One, 4,* 1–11.

Chapman, P., Clinton, J., Kerber, R., Shearer, C., & Wirth, R. (2000). *CRISP-DM 1.0: Step by step data mining guide.* The CRISP DM Consortium.

Davenport, T. H., & Harris, J. G. (2007). *Competing on analytics: the new Science of winning.* Harvard business school press.

Dean, J., & Ghemawat, S. (2008). Map Reduce: Simplified dataprocessing on large clusters. *Communications of the ACM, 51,* 107–113. doi:10.1145/1327452.1327492

Fan, Li, Zhang, & Feng. (2018). Data Driven Feature election for Machine Learning Algorithms in Computer Vision. *IEEE Internet of Things Journal, 5*(6), 4262-4272.

Gupota, S., Sahoo, O. P., Goel, A., & Gupta, R. (2010). A new optimized approach to face recognition using eigen faces. Global. *Journal of Computer Science and Technology.*

Hibert, M., & Lopez, P. (2011). The world's technological capacity to store, communicate and compute information. *Science.* PMID:21310967

Jones, B. F., Wuchty, S., & Uzzi, B. (2008). Multi University Research Teams: Shifting impact Geograph and Stratification in Science. *Science, 322*(5905), 1259–1262. doi:10.1126cience.1158357 PMID:18845711

Kakhani, M.K., Kakhani, S., & Biradar, S.R. (2015). Research issues in big data analytics. *International Journal of Application or Innovation in Engineering and Management, 2,* 228-232.

Mishra, M., & Srivastava, M. (2014). A view of Artificial Neural Network. *2014 International Conference on Advances in Engineering & Technology Research (ICAETR - 2014),* 1-3. 10.1109/ICAETR.2014.7012785

Philip, C. L., Chen, Q., & Zhang, C. Y. (2014). Data-intensive applications, challenges, techniques and technologies: A survey on big data. *Information Sciences, 275,* 314–347. doi:10.1016/j.ins.2014.01.015

Sehgal, S., Singh, H., Agarwal, M., Bhasker, V., & Shantanu. (2014). Data analysis using principal component analysis. *2014 International Conference on Medical Imaging, m-Health and Emerging Communication Systems (MedCom),* 45-48. . doi:10.1109/MedCom.2014.7005973

Slavkovic, M., & Jevtic, D. (2012). *Face Recognition using Eigenface Approach.* Serbian Journal of Electrical Engineering. doi:10.2298/SJEE1201121S

Sturm, P., Ramalingam, S., Tardif, J.P., Gasparini, S., & Barreto, J. (2010). *Camera models and fundamental concepts used in geometric computer Graphics and Vision algorithms and applications.* Springer.

Van Hell, J. G., Oosterveld, P., & De Groot, A. M. B. (1996). Covariance structure analysis in experimental research: Comparing two word translation models. *Behavior Research Methods, Instruments, & Computers, 28*(4), 491–503. doi:10.3758/BF03200538

Waldrop, M. M. (1992). *Complexity: The Emerging Science at the Edge of Order and Chaos.* Simon and Schuster.

Will, H. (2014). *Linear Algebra for Computer Vision.* Attribution Share Alike 4.0 International (CC BY-SA 4.0).

Wuchty, S., Jones, B. F., & Uzzi, B. (2007). The increasing dominance of teams in production of knowledge. *Science, 316*(5827), 1038–1039. doi:10.1126cience.1136099 PMID:17431139

Chapter 14
Innovative Applications and Implementation Challenges of Blockchain Technology in the Financial Sector

Chitra Devi Nagarajan
Vellore Institute of Technology, Chennai, India

Mohd Afjal
Vellore Institute of Technology, Vellore, India

ABSTRACT

Blockchain use in various industries improves the standard of services provided to end users and benefits society as a whole. The chapter discusses the innovative use of blockchain technology in the financial sector, including know your customer, cross-border payments, clearing and settlements in the insurance sector, trade finance platforms, and digital identity verification. On the other hand, while blockchain technology has the potential to be a very competitive and "imaginative" technology, it is important to address concerns with its implementation, such as the cost of adoption, energy consumption, cybersecurity, interoperability, scalability, latency, and so on. The findings of this study will give the required information to the government, decision-makers, and consumers to help them understand the applications and difficulties of implementing blockchain technology in the financial sector.

INTRODUCTION

A new era of business models is dawning with the advent of digital technology, and the financial sector has been exploring better ways of increasing transaction speed and efficiency to improve customer service. Easy access to digital technology through Financial Technology companies (Fintechs) has transformed the entire banking and financial industry (Riasanow et al., 2018). As digital technology has increasingly been used over the past few decades, financial institutions and banks have embraced the adaptation of

DOI: 10.4018/978-1-6684-8851-5.ch014

technology to meet the fast-changing expectations of their customers. There are, however, challenges that need to be overcome for technology to be effectively implemented (Swan, 2017). Banks and financial institutions have many concerns regarding the adaptation of new technology, including high transaction costs, intermediary roles, cyber fraud, regulatory compliance, the use of big data, artificial intelligence, and customer retention (Eyal, 2017).

The profitability of banks and financial institutions is determined by the implementation of digital technology that enables them to provide better services and meet customer demands. A bank or fintech company that is not able to comply with these standards is unlikely to sustain its profitability over the long term (Mishra & Kaushik, 2021; Sundarraj, 2019). The sustainable financial sector is an engine for the development of an economy because it encourages balanced, and inclusion and facilitates the growth of the commercial sector. Adopting and integrating new digital technologies such as the Internet of Things (IoT), 5G networks, artificial intelligence (AI), big data, and cloud computing at the right time is crucial to enhancing customer service and operations and, in turn, ensuring sustainable profitability of banks and fintech companies.

As one of the world's most recent technologies, blockchain has enabled several applications in financial technology, allowing finance to become more global. Blockchain is a tamper-proof digital ledger that is implemented in a distributed manner (i.e., without a central repository) and usually without any central authority (i.e., no bank, government, or company) (Yaga et al., 2019). A distributed ledger technology called blockchain enables all participants to connect, review and approve a transaction before it is included in the value chain (Walters & Novak, 2021). Due to various computer technologies, distributed data storage, point-to-point transmission, consensus mechanisms, and encryption algorithms, the application of blockchain in the financial sector has attracted a lot of attention, especially in the fintech and banking services industries (Guo & Liang, 2016a). As a component of Industry 4.0, blockchain technology has the potential to change how businesses operate in a variety of sectors. Blockchain technology is now widely employed in the banking and financial sectors. Several international institutions, including the United Nations and the International Monetary Fund, have taken note of the development of blockchains and explored their application in various fields. As well as developed nations, such as the United States, the UK, and Japan, these technologies have received considerable attention and exploration. The advantages offered by blockchain technology in the financial sector, many companies, such as Dwolla, PayPal and Square Payments, have adopted it as a means of facilitating decentralised, risk-free digital financial transactions. The technology of blockchain has the potential to revolutionize the way that money is transferred. Globally, blockchain is modernizing digital banking services. The timely evolution and adoption of the advanced technology of blockchain will add to the required economic growth (Dutra et al., 2018). Blockchain technology adoption in financial sectors comes in three flavours: distributed, decentralized, and centralized. A reliable central server that makes decisions about data storage, data integrity, and user needs is referred to as a centralized system. In this system, all financial transactions are overseen by an intermediary, and client confidence is enhanced in because of the centralised measures to safeguard user-profiles and user-generated content. In the absence of trusted intermediaries, blockchain is also considered a peer-to-peer decentralized communication system while also boosting security, trust, and data integrity.

The distributed system is helpful in the financial sector because it substantially reduces the risk of loss of asset-related information (Rechtman, 2017). Record management for every individual user ends in a decentralized scheme, making it secure and safer (Mori, 2016). The blockchain application is a distributed ledger system of transactions that is tamper-proof due to cryptographic methods (Pilkington, 2016). To construct the infrastructure required for a free, secure flow of financial transactions, understanding the fundamental differences between the various blockchain technologies and rules that govern digital ledger technology platforms is a necessary condition for the design of successful applications of blockchain technology (Saito & Yamada, 2016). All transactions and other information are bundled into 'blocks' by network participants in all blockchain systems. Upon being deemed valid by the network, a fresh block is appended ('chained') sequentially to the previously validated block. As new transactions occur this process is repeated. To maintain the integrity of a blockchain, a set of rules (a consensus mechanism) is adhered to by a distributed network of nodes.

Figure 1. Centralized, decentralized, and distributed

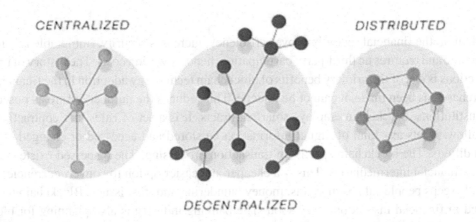

Blockchain-Based Financial Transactions

The digital transactions between two parties require an intermediary for processing any transactions. However, blockchain as a public immutable digital ledger leads to the elimination of intermediaries as a new mode of conducting transactions. The adoption of blockchain technology in fintech eliminates the need for centralized entities or intermediaries and legal enforcement (Cai, 2018). Moreover, this technology authenticates the data transfer on its autonomous process between two independent parties involved in financial transactions. Financial transactions using blockchain technology enable a safe agreement between users through a consensus mechanism, which results in the addition of a new transaction to the ledger (Puthal et al., 2018). A blockchain can embrace any new digital asset across many nodes. If a node crashes, prints are still accessible and delivered by the remaining nodes.

Since the blockchain is a public ledger, any sensitive personal information stored on it must be encrypted and may be seen only by two parties. A public key is used to encrypt data on the blockchain, while a private key is used to decode it. Because of its consensus mechanism, the blockchain is immutable and cannot be replicated. The block is added to the chain if there is agreement that the transactions in the block are valid Blockchain is still not widely used in the investment industry. Industries quickly transition to deploying blockchain-integrated infrastructure in business organizations (Javaid et al., 2021).

Figure 2. Blockchain-based financial transactions

Blockchain in the financial sector improves efficiency, increases security, immutable records, short transaction time and requires no third-party participation, hence lowering costs. The history of unchangeable transactions is one of the primary benefits of blockchain technology adoption in the financial sector. Once a purchase has been made, it cannot be undone. This reduces the number of threats posed against financial institutions. Blockchain employs smart contracts. It is a set of rules that contracting parties agree to follow. It lets any kind of digital information be stored and accessed or changed only under certain conditions. The blockchain speeds up transaction processing. The dispersed existence reduces the need for financial intermediaries. This is a cheaper and easier option to convert currencies than using a bank. It keeps people safe from scams, money laundering and trust issues. Blockchain technology will be used in financial institutions very soon. The banking industry is also planning for blockchain use to grow quickly.

Benefits of Blockchain Application in the Financial Sector

The trust aspect that is inherent in financial transactions requires an intermediary to validate and approve it among the participants, which is how they have historically been processed and validated (Lee & Shin, 2018). Laborers who operate as intermediaries must do a sizable amount of work in the financial sector's centralized structure. Furthermore, the data must be maintained and modified by several uncoordinated parties, the transactions are prone to errors, and as a result, the entire process is time- and money-consuming. The financial sector has, however, undergone a paradigm shift as a result of the creation of blockchain technology, which allays all the drawbacks of traditional banking and ushers in a new age for the sector.

Blockchain enhances security, trust, transparency, cost savings, immutability and instant traceability and improves efficiency (Garay et al., 2016; Kosba et al., 2016; Lakhani & Iansiti, 2017; Mendling et al., 2018). In addition, blockchain offers more security than keeping all data in a single database and shields users from database hacks (Park & Park, 2017) due to the fact that everyone who uses a peer-to-peer network can access encrypted financial transactions. A new paradigm in the financial sector has emerged as a result of the development of decentralized distributed ledger technology (Osmani et al., 2020; Ji & Tia, 2021; Aketch et al., 2021). Additionally, blockchain has immutability, which is described as the capacity of a blockchain ledger to remain intact, unaltered, and permanent, and openness, which produces data transparency when employed in an area where data disclosure is required (Osmani et al., 2020).

Figure 3. Blockchain benefits

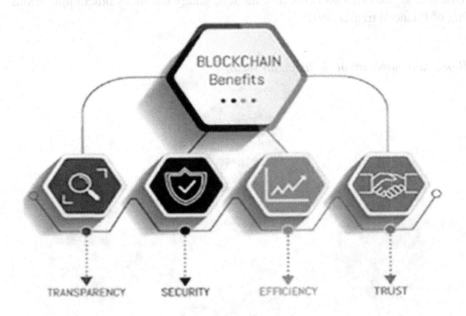

By creating a distributed public ledger and employing "proof-of-work" for transaction verification, blockchain streamlines financial services (B. Rawat et al., 2020) and reduces the paperwork and saves time. As a result of these advantages, application of blockchain in other fields, including the financial industry, are expected to grow (Osmani et al., 2020). In the case of a conflicting blockchain, miners always choose the longest chain because it is more reliable. With a secure communication protocol and a rigorous verification procedure, it improves financial services (Rawat et al., 2021). Innovative applications and use cases of blockchain technology in the financial sector are discussed in the following section.

BLOCKCHAIN APPLICATION IN THE FINANCE INDUSTRY

Blockchain technology reshapes the whole finance sector, enabling unique features and fostering promising business opportunities (Downes & Nunes, 2018; Kumar Bhardwaj et al., 2021). The transition of analogue data into digital data is facilitated by blockchain technology, which promises to be very effective in applications for the public and private sectors (Legner et al., 2017). The financial system has been improved by the new underlying technology, which has enhanced the quality of financial transactions at three different levels (data, rules, and applications) to suit the consumers' rapidly changing needs (Zhang et al., 2020a). Financial institutions have successfully integrated financial information using the internet of things, big data, and cloud computing with the aid of blockchain technology (Aceto et al., 2020; Chong & Shi, 2015; Ivanov et al., 2019, 2020). Many financial industry enterprises, including banks, insurance companies, and firms that offer professional financial services, were drawn to the implementation of such innovative technologies. As a result of significant investments made in the creation of applications using blockchain technology, numerous businesses have been able to flourish in the sector (Rossi et al., 2019). This is because the technology has many other applications besides just the recording of financial transactions.

Figure 4. Blockchain applications in financial sector

Know Your Customer (KYC)

When a new customer comes on board, one of the phrases that are frequently used in the banking and financial sectors is to start the KYC process. Customer data generated through the KYC process is considered verified data and it becomes the core element of modern financial organizations (Mondal et al., 2016). To ensure that transactions between banks are genuine, KYC has become crucial for institutions like banks and financial companies (Mondal et al., 2016). However, in the present system of KYC, any suspicious user can involve in illegal activity by opening multiple accounts hiding the original data and a large number of transactions to dissimulate the user origin (Harrop & Mairs, 2016). Since KYC verifies two layers of client data, such as proof of address and proof of identity, a malicious person can access and misuse any data set. Financial institutions must therefore identify their clients and compare them to any applicable laws and regulations issued by national and international regulators. Additionally, since every organization may see personal KYC data, a malevolent individual can access and abuse any collection of data.

Figure 5. Customer process example
Source: Malhotra et al. (2022a)

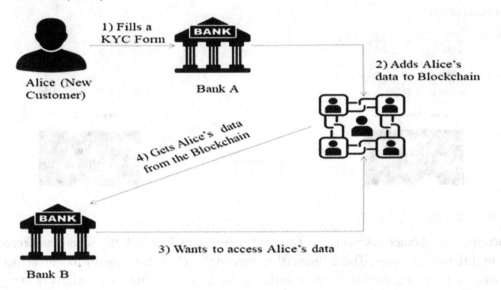

Due to the constant updating of profiles and the gathering and verification of pertinent documents, the KYC procedure is dynamic and time-consuming. The aforementioned problems can be resolved by maintaining customer documentation as a consolidated database (regulator or state organization). It is, however, extremely susceptible to cyber-attacks and data breaches. Hence, Distributed Ledger Technology (DLT) in blockchain was developed to address these shortcomings. With the use of Blockchain technology, when a consumer is confirmed by an institution using blockchain technology, the information is saved in the network for future verification by any financial institution (Malhotra et al., 2022b). A blockchain-based global economy can be transmuted and restructured through the effective use of distributed ledger technology.

Cross-Border Payments and Remittances

Highly efficient and secure digital payments are the mainstream uses of blockchain technology tearing down the national currency borders (Bürer et al., 2019). However, the authenticity of the financial transactions requires an intermediary that makes the process difficult and time-consuming process in the traditional banking system. Besides, these challenges arise primarily as a result of the centralization of financial transactions, in which entities such as banks and financial services are liable for dictating processes and validating transactions (Rawat et al., 2021) The blockchain reduces this complexity by establishing a decentralized public ledger and a strong verification. In this P2P network, digital payments are faster, easier to check, unchanged and safe. The application of blockchain technology for digital payments across countries is error-prone and less expensive with the usage of blockchain technology. The distributed ledger technology in blockchain boosts security (DLT) or Internet of Value, which securely preserves and communicates digital transactions without the centralization of administration and is regarded as a key component in cross-border payments (Tapscott & Tapscott, 2017).

Figure 6. Money transfer from Bank A to Bank D through blockchain eliminating the 3rd party as high-lighted
Source: Achanta (2018)

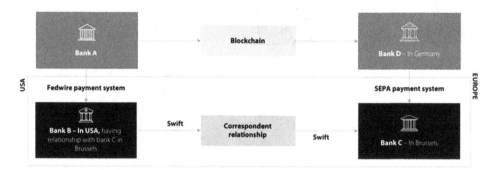

Generally, cross-border payments are financial transactions in which the sender and receiver are located in different countries. These financial transactions include the flow of money across two or more countries or regions, and thus necessitate the legitimacy of all parties involved. By offering perfect security and enabling the buyer and seller to feel secure about the payment, blockchain technology has effectively eliminated the bottlenecks of the old banking system in cross border payments. Blockchain is a universal ledger which is accessible by everyone who are involved in the cross-border transactions network. Each node in the network is shared with all the persons in the network and modifications cannot be made without the consensus of the parties in the network (Achanta, 2018). Blockchain technology, however, improves the payment system by providing an effective structure for cross-border transactions, removing high intermediary costs, and gradually altering the payment industry's business model (Zhang et al., 2020b).

Digital Identity Verification

A set of verified traits and credentials for the digital world make up a digital identity, which allows for different kinds of transactions. Numerous businesses are able to reach consumers, market to them, and conduct business with them based on the gathering and analysis of customer website data that is obtained from people who make online purchases and browse websites. Individuals' privacy should not be revealed to the digital world while selling the personal identify of consumers is done legitimately and concurrently. User identities can be secured by encrypting and shielding data from intruders. Blockchains can hold digital IDs to replace traditional physical IDs. Blockchain can protect user identities by encrypting and hiding data from hackers (Jacobovitz, 2016).

The smart contract is an innovative transactional application that enhances trust and elevates transparency and improves verifiability. It is a software solution for storing the negotiation of terms, conditions and activities between parties engaged in contracts. (Tapscott & Tapscott, 2017). Financial contracts are complicated and time-consuming. Smart contracts use blockchain technology to construct and store computer codes that can be executed when two or more parties enter their keys and fulfil specified criteria (Benisi et al., 2020). Smart contracts are digital entities expressed in Turing-complete EVM bytecode (Buterin, 2014). Each function is a set of instructions. Smart contract code is kept on the blockchain and each contract has a unique address. Blockchain consensus ensures contract execution. Smart contracts' cost-reduction, speed, precision, efficiency and transparency have led to novel applications in numerous areas. Beyond the exchange of cryptocurrencies, functions and conditions can be set, such as the validation of assets in non-monetary transactions. This makes it an ideal part for developing blockchain technology (Reyna et al., 2018).

By combining smart contracts and blockchain, it is feasible to take advantage of the benefits of self-sovereignty identity management and the scalability of blockchain. All parties involved in financial transactions receive independent, decentralized identities thanks to the usage of blockchain, and these identifiers trust users with their associated data instead of depending on intermediaries (Stockburger et al., 2021).

Trade Finance Platforms

Increasing cyber-attacks and malicious hacking has endangered international business operations and finance practices (Popescu & Popescu, 2018). As a result of these negative issues, new and innovative working paradigms become essential for secure and sustainable trade finance across boundaries. The innovation that facilitates transparent transactions is the application of blockchain which serves as a shared ledger and maintains a transparent record of all critical transactions among parties involved in trading activities (Jessel & DiCaprio, 2018a). The blockchain emanates as a tool for bringing transparent transactions and enhances supply chain traceability in cross-border transactions (Harrop & Mairs, 2016; Jessel & DiCaprio, 2018a; Popescu & Popescu, 2018).

Figure 7. Blockchain process
Source: www.tradefinanceglobal.com

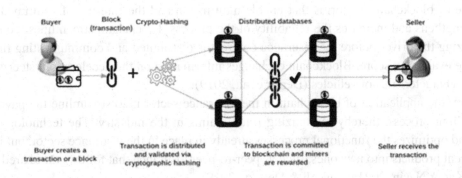

Heavy document processing and lengthy time-consuming processes led trade finance to a subject of poor level of efficiency. Blockchain has come as an alternative to traditional paper-intensive processing and it has the potential to save the value of money and time involved in trade finance activities. It can be difficult for each party to locate the information they need in the trade transaction on the submission of physical papers because there are so many organizations involved in trade financing, including the exporter, the importer, their banks, the shipping business, the insurance company, and clearing and forwarding agents. Blockchain technology has been used in trade finance as a result of the overreliance on physical documents, outdated and opaque supply chains, and regulatory restrictions. A more inclusive trade finance system is supported by the use of blockchain technology, which can grow rapidly, eliminate regulatory problems, and enable smooth, reliable information flow (Jessel & DiCaprio, 2018b).

Insurance

Since many financial institutions provide insurance services, the insurance sector is intimately related to the finance sector. However, the insurance business faces several challenges, including inefficiency, fraud, human error, and, most worrisome of all, cyberattacks. As use cases for blockchain technology and smart contracts in the insurance industry demonstrate, blockchain technology offers some compelling value propositions for insurance. Blockchain architecture also addresses issues in the insurance industry (Gatteschi, Lamberti, Demartini, Pranteda, & Santamaria, 2018; Gatteschi, Lamberti, Demartini, Pranteda, & Santamaría, 2018). Before a claim request is accepted as final and payment is initiated, processing claims is a labor-intensive process that takes a long time and involves many players and middlemen.

Blockchains can make the process of claiming insurance simpler and faster by integrating all participants around distributed procedures and using smart contracts for carrying out all orders and authentications. Blockchain smart contracts automate and carry out the steps required to compute and validate the final settlement that is to be paid to the insured. Smart contracts can detect fake transactions and claims by disclosing customer personal identity during the claiming process. According to Singer (2019), the insurance sector's top priority is preventing false claims. Technology can help the business in this regard as false claims are still a huge problem for the sector (Singer, 2019)

Additionally, the usage of blockchain can do away with any intermediaries, such as brokers, who are frequently the face of insurance for consumers (Hans et al., 2017). The integration of multimedia data, such as images and videos taken at the site of an accident in the case of motor insurance, along with the use of blockchain platforms that enable multimedia and the Internet of Multimedia Things (IoMT) strengthens and increases the reliability of the process. Blockchain streamlines the procedure by categorizing the driver before the insurance contract is distributed and communicating the driver's performance evaluation score. Blockchain exchanges information on the acceleration, steering, speed, and braking characteristics of vehicles (Demir et al., 2019).

Therefore, the application of blockchain in the insurance sector is to streamline the payments and claims handling process, thereby minimizing fraud claims in the industry. The technology not only enhances and optimizes the functional processes already in place in the insurance sector, but it also can change current products into new ones, such as peer-to-peer insurance that follows the shared economy paradigm (Kar & Navin, 2021a; Sayegh & Desoky, 2019).

The main focus seems to be on marine, agriculture, travel, and micro-insurance (Kar & Navin, 2021b). The diffusion of blockchain technology in the insurance industry is given in the figure.

Figure 8. Diffusion of blockchain technology in the insurance industry
Source: Kar and Navin (2021b)

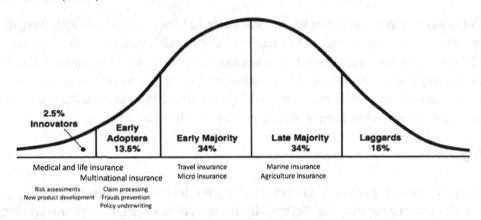

BLOCKCHAIN IMPLEMENTATION CHALLENGES

Blockchain implementation at the business level throughout the corporate value chain faces a variety of hurdles (Grover et al., 2021; Saberi et al., 2019; Sternberg et al., 2021). In the use of blockchain (Guo & Liang, 2016b), centralized consortium and private blockchains should be used instead of completely decentralized public blockchains. This way, technology is more in line with reality. However, financial systems require high capacity, high dependability, high privacy, strong regulations and low latency and present blockchains lack these properties and must be enhanced (Guo & Liang, 2016b). The implementation of a number of integrated disciplines of cutting-edge technologies makes the development of blockchain technology and its applications in the financial industry very expensive and difficult (Assarzadeh & Aberoumand, 2018; Demirkan et al., 2020; Hassani et al., 2018; Viriyasitavat, da Xu, Bi, & Hoonsopon, 2019; Viriyasitavat, da Xu, Bi, Hoonsopon, et al., 2019). One of the biggest problems with blockchain is that it often takes 10 minutes to add a new block to the network's blockchain, and that each block can only hold 1 MB worth of data and only support 8 transactions per second. Additionally, blockchain uses a computer algorithm to produce a reliable intermediary's credit guarantee; nevertheless, because the information is irreversible, it makes it more difficult to repair the system if it is lost or corrupted. Because of the potential data breach caused by a high number of zombies holding hostages or the style of operation used by trade union clusters, this leads to the irreversible loss of client assets. To ensure that blockchain technology is implemented in the financial industry without incident, issues like hackers (Zhang et al., 2020b) and all other issues must be addressed.

Adoption Cost

The efficiency and speed with which blockchain networks may conduct peer-to-peer transactions result in a larger aggregate value. Developing a blockchain-enabled system is costly, so it should be standardized across institutions. Currently, each bitcoin transaction costs around $0.20 and only stores 80 bytes (Bauerle, 2018). Unified industry norms will prevent widespread acceptance and growth of blockchain in banking. Another rising problem for blockchain in banking is storage costs, with some anticipating that long-term storage costs for a Bitcoin node in the millions (Schou-Zibell & Phair, 2018)

Interoperability

Interoperability has become a significant issue, particularly for banks, in terms of simplifying the process of sustaining the necessary operations at both internal and external levels. Re-engineering process integration with legacy systems is a challenge that banks must accept as part of the implementation process. Technical/scalability issues, business models, scandals and public perception and government laws and regulations limit blockchain's wider use (Harwood-Jones, 2016). Blockchain transactions require more time to implement owing to their complexity, encryption and distributed nature.

Scalability

The scalability of processing power is another difficulty for devices' computing capabilities, which is handled through limits such as sharding. Technically, the present blockchain algorithms are sluggish and require more energy than intended (Upadhyay, 2020). Scalability issues, such as race attacks, eclipse attacks, finery attacks, brute force attacks, 51% errors and block discarding, are on the rise. Meanwhile, building public blockchain-based applications is difficult since information is exposed to all applicants in the network by default (Upadhyay, 2020). In Industry 4.0, cybersecurity should be secure and resilient, as well as integrate blockchain strategy.

Consensus Mechanism

The consensus mechanism issue is the smart contracts because the transaction verification depends on the consensus. It developed a networking architecture that produces output without the need for third-party involvement, making the whole network system dependable and tamper-proof. The distributed consensus process relies on nodes in the blockchain network to validate each transaction in each block. Therefore, every modification is easily detectable as an error (Lu et al., 2019). The technical and scalability issues are associated with the consensus mechanism in the blockchain system because consensus agrees to the transaction integrity and then enlarges the current blockchain (Dwivedi et al., 2019).

Energy Consumption

the processing power required to operate blockchain technology is fast changing (Hooper & Holtbrügge, 2020). The Bitcoin cryptocurrency system uses a significant amount of energy. The computing power required by IoT devices and other battery-powered devices is closely linked to energy usage (Elsts et al., 2018). The high energy consumption protects the proof-of-work (PoW) blockchain from attacks. Energy consumption and the maintenance cost of high- configuration computers are expensive. The biggest problem with proof-of-work is energy consumption (Elsts et al., 2018; Hooper & Holtbrügge, 2020). Therefore, if a cryptographic scheme with a computational load is a choice for blockchain-based IoT applications, it would further help reduce energy consumption. Block implementation in the financial sector should therefore work to address the issue of high energy consumption because energy companies raise energy costs, which eventually lower revenues. (Hasse et al., 2016).

Cybersecurity

Another use of blockchain is in cybersecurity, where dangerous information may be shared across participants/organizations to prevent future cyber-attacks (Adebayo et al., 2019. For example, organizations or governments are reluctant to disclose cyber-attack or threat information because competitors may exploit the knowledge to gain a unilateral advantage. However, by utilizing blockchain, information may be transferred without disclosing any identifiable information except the public key. This means that organizations or governments may exchange dangerous information without fear of rivals using it unilaterally. While blockchain cannot repair everything, its properties can be used to safeguard systems against cyberattacks (Rawat et al., 2021).

Latency

The decentralized blockchain is not always consistent due to network delays. Bandwidth and block validation time have an impact on a network transmission delay. Heavy blocks would be more difficult to transport throughout the network, resulting in forking. If transaction verification takes too long, the organization may decide not to use blockchain (Schlatt et al., 2022). Today, a proof-of-work block takes roughly ten minutes to build. Credit cards, which handle approximately 2,500 transactions per second on average, peaking at 4,000 or even 45,000, utilize a fraction of the electrical power used by Bitcoin. This delay is induced by cryptographic and blockchain consensus procedures, which reduce the number of transfers required by specific systems (Río & César, 2017).

Reversibility

A digital ledger produces immutable shared ledgers where transactions cannot be changed, cancelled, or reversed. This raises issues of technology and governance, such as who may identify problems, which repair procedure applies and when. Because digital ledger technology may speed up clearing and settlement, it is critical to promptly fix errors. Descending the decentralized chain architecture makes it impossible to easily undo earlier acts. Therefore, when a security breach occurs due to a last user's credentials being revealed, the ramifications are far more severe and difficult to repair (Cermeño, 2016a).

Regulation

The implementation of blockchain technology is one of the most significant hurdles and it is often associated with regulatory concerns. Regulation mechanisms have always struggled to keep up with new technology. The diversified application of technology necessitates issues such as bitcoin cryptocurrency, shared ledgers and smart contracts (Cermeño, 2016a). Governance relies on a set of policies and regulations. Hence, disruptive technology does not have standard rules and regulations. Policymakers, developers and regulators have concentrated their efforts in this area on controlling the usage of bitcoin and other cryptocurrencies. Thus, legal provisions would need to be carefully considered against the chance of systemic risks (Cermeño, 2016a). Due to the decentralized nature of blockchain, financial insecurity has caused many difficulties in various businesses and governments. Regulations are anticipated to cause reforms that make the industry more user-friendly, especially in the banking sector (Kshetri & Kshetri, 2018).

Financial information security on the Internet is strongly guaranteed by financial regulation, especially the decentralization that has been brought about by the advent of blockchain technology. This has significantly increased the importance and potency of financial regulation. There is a lack of understanding and acceptance of the blockchain by the general public, which makes it difficult to locate trustworthy and efficient blockchain financial products. As a result, regulators have a difficult time tracking down and locking down numerous anonymous client accounts that are open to the public. Additionally, due to the absence of a central system, fraud, tax evasion, and money laundering have become easier to commit. Administration and supervision have become more challenging due to the lack of a central system.

CONCLUSION

This paper discusses how blockchain technology is being applied to the financial sector's issues as it enters a new financial era with a new destructive system based on industry 4.0. The conventional financial goods and services that the finance industry used were viewed as expensive and ineffective. As a result, although there was still more work to be done to address the root issues, a significant advancement in blockchain technology had the potential to increase the security and efficiency of financial markets (Lewis et al., 2017). Because of this, the current state of the industrial practises surrounding the implementation of blockchain in financial services are still in their infancy. As a result, we need to improve our technology and system supervision of the blockchain. Additionally, there are technological, operational, and business problems that need to be solved, but adequate regulation will be crucial.

For the interest of the public, the government and relevant departments should develop policies. Distributed ledgers, blockchains, smart contracts, and other related ideas are different types of legal objects that, in most cases, can conflict with the current legal system since they don't neatly fit into the established notions of jurisdiction, liability, or enforceability (Cermeño, 2016b). Blockchain sternly forbids using it for criminal operations including money laundering, financing terrorism, and even capital control (Nguyen, 2016). Undoubtedly, Blockchain has the potential to be a highly innovative and competitive technology that, in the future, might transform the financial and commercial architecture of our society. In order to improve their business, financial services should have a long-term perspective and begin exploring the application of Blockchain technology.

REFERENCES

Aceto, G., Persico, V., & Pescapé, A. (2020). Industry 4.0 and health: Internet of things, big data, and cloud computing for healthcare 4.0. *Journal of Industrial Information Integration*, *18*, 100129. doi:10.1016/j.jii.2020.100129

Achanta, R. (2018). *Cross-border money transfer using blockchain-enabled by big data*. White Paper, External Document.

Adebayo, A., Rawat, D. B., Njilla, L., & Kamhoua, C. A. (2019). Blockchain-enabled information sharing framework for cybersecurity. *Blockchain for Distributed Systems Security*, 143–158.

Assarzadeh, A. H., & Aberoumand, S. (2018). FinTech in Western Asia: Case of Iran. *Journal of Industrial Integration and Management, 3*(03), 1850006. doi:10.1142/S2424862218500069

Bauerle, N. (2018). *How does blockchain technology work.* Retrieved from Coindesk: Https://Www. Coindesk. Com/Information/How-Does-Blockchain-Technology-Work

Benisi, N. Z., Aminian, M., & Javadi, B. (2020). Blockchain-based decentralized storage networks: A survey. *Journal of Network and Computer Applications, 162*, 102656. doi:10.1016/j.jnca.2020.102656

Bürer, M. J., de Lapparent, M., Pallotta, V., Capezzali, M., & Carpita, M. (2019). Use cases for blockchain in the energy industry opportunities of emerging business models and related risks. *Computers & Industrial Engineering, 137*, 106002. doi:10.1016/j.cie.2019.106002

Buterin, V. (2014). A next-generation smart contract and decentralized application platform. *White Paper, 3*(37), 1–2.

Cai, C. W. (2018). Disruption of financial intermediation by FinTech: A review on crowdfunding and blockchain. *Accounting and Finance, 58*(4), 965–992. doi:10.1111/acfi.12405

Cermeño, J. S. (2016). Blockchain in financial services: Regulatory landscape and future challenges for its commercial application. *BBVA Research Paper, 16*(20), 1–33.

Chong, D., & Shi, H. (2015). Big data analytics: A literature review. *Journal of Management Analytics, 2*(3), 175–201. doi:10.1080/23270012.2015.1082449

Demir, M., Turetken, O., & Ferworn, A. (2019). Blockchain based transparent vehicle insurance management. *2019 Sixth International Conference on Software Defined Systems (SDS)*, 213–220. 10.1109/SDS.2019.8768669

Demirkan, S., Demirkan, I., & McKee, A. (2020). Blockchain technology in the future of business cyber security and accounting. *Journal of Management Analytics, 7*(2), 189–208. doi:10.1080/23270012.2020.1731721

Downes, L., & Nunes, P. (2018). Finding your company's second act. *Harvard Business Review, 2018*, 98–107.

Dutra, A., Tumasjan, A., & Welpe, I. M. (2018). Blockchain is changing how media and entertainment companies compete. *MIT Sloan Management Review, 60*(1), 39–45.

Dwivedi, V., Deval, V., Dixit, A., & Norta, A. (2019). Blockchain-based smart-contract languages: A systematic literature review. *Preprint, 10*, 1–9.

Elsts, A., Mitskas, E., & Oikonomou, G. (2018). Distributed ledger technology and the internet of things: A feasibility study. *Proceedings of the 1st Workshop on Blockchain-Enabled Networked Sensor Systems*, 7–12. 10.1145/3282278.3282280

Eyal, I. (2017). Blockchain technology: Transforming libertarian cryptocurrency dreams to finance and banking realities. *Computer, 50*(9), 38–49. doi:10.1109/MC.2017.3571042

Garay, J. A., Kiayias, A., Leonardos, N., & Panagiotakos, G. (2016). Bootstrapping the Blockchain-Directly. *IACR Cryptol. EPrint Arch., 2016*, 991.

Gatteschi, V., Lamberti, F., Demartini, C., Pranteda, C., & Santamaría, V. (2018). Blockchain and smart contracts for insurance: Is the technology mature enough? *Future Internet*, *10*(2), 20. doi:10.3390/fi10020020

Gatteschi, V., Lamberti, F., Demartini, C., Pranteda, C., & Santamaria, V. (2018). To blockchain or not to blockchain: That is the question. *IT Professional*, *20*(2), 62–74. doi:10.1109/MITP.2018.021921652

Grover, B. A., Chaudhary, B., Rajput, N. K., & Dukiya, O. (2021). Blockchain and Governance: Theory, Applications and Challenges. *Blockchain for Business: How It Works and Creates Value*, 113–139.

Guo, Y., & Liang, C. (2016). Blockchain application and outlook in the banking industry. *Financial Innovation*, *2*(1), 1–12. doi:10.118640854-016-0034-9

Hans, R., Zuber, H., Rizk, A., & Steinmetz, R. (2017). *Blockchain and smart contracts: Disruptive technologies for the insurance market*. Academic Press.

Harrop, M. D., & Mairs, B. (2016). Thomson Reuters 2016 Know Your Customer Surveys Reveal Escalating Costs and Complexity. *Press Release*.

Harwood-Jones, M. (2016). *Blockchain and T2S: a potential disruptor*. Standard Chartered Bank.

Hassani, H., Huang, X., & Silva, E. (2018). Banking with blockchain-ed big data. *Journal of Management Analytics*, *5*(4), 256–275. doi:10.1080/23270012.2018.1528900

Hasse, F., von Perfall, A., Hillebrand, T., Smole, E., Lay, L., & Charlet, M. (2016). Blockchain–an opportunity for energy producers and consumers. *PwC Global Power & Utilities*, 1–45.

Hooper, A., & Holtbrügge, D. (2020). Blockchain technology in international business: Changing the agenda for global governance. *Review of International Business and Strategy*, *30*(2), 183–200. doi:10.1108/RIBS-06-2019-0078

Ivanov, L. A., Razumeev, K. E., Bokova, E. S., & Muminova, S. R. (2019). The inventions in nanotechnologies as practical solutions. Part V. *Nanotechnologies in Construction*, *11*(6).

Ivanov, L. A., Kapustin, I. A., Borisova, O. N., & Pisarenko, Z. V. (2020). Nanotechnologies: a review of inventions and utility models. Part II. *Nanotekhnologii v Stroitel'stve*, *12*(2), 71–76.

Jacobovitz, O. (2016). Blockchain for identity management. The Lynne and William Frankel Center for Computer Science Department of Computer Science, *Ben-Gurion University*.

Javaid, M., Haleem, A., Singh, R. P., Khan, S., & Suman, R. (2021). Blockchain technology applications for Industry 4.0: A literature-based review. *Blockchain: Research and Applications*, 100027.

Jessel, B., & DiCaprio, A. (2018). Can blockchain make trade finance more inclusive? *Journal of Financial Transformation*, *47*, 35–50.

Kar, A. K., & Navin, L. (2021). Diffusion of blockchain in insurance industry: An analysis through the review of academic and trade literature. *Telematics and Informatics*, *58*, 101532. doi:10.1016/j.tele.2020.101532

Kosba, A., Miller, A., Shi, E., Wen, Z., & Papamanthou, C. (2016). Hawk: The blockchain model of cryptography and privacy-preserving smart contracts. *2016 IEEE Symposium on Security and Privacy (SP)*, 839–858. 10.1109/SP.2016.55

Kshetri, N., & Kshetri, N. (2018). The Indian blockchain landscape: Regulations and policy measures. *Asian Res. Policy*, *9*(2), 56–71.

Kumar Bhardwaj, A., Garg, A., & Gajpal, Y. (2021). Determinants of blockchain technology adoption in supply chains by small and medium enterprises (SMEs) in India. *Mathematical Problems in Engineering*, *2021*, 2021. doi:10.1155/2021/5537395

Lakhani, K. R., & Iansiti, M. (2017). The truth about blockchain. *Harvard Business Review*, *95*(1), 119–127.

Legner, C., Eymann, T., Hess, T., Matt, C., Böhmann, T., Drews, P., Mädche, A., Urbach, N., & Ahlemann, F. (2017). Digitalization: Opportunity and challenge for the business and information systems engineering community. *Business & Information Systems Engineering*, *59*(4), 301–308. doi:10.100712599-017-0484-2

Lewis, R., McPartland, J., & Ranjan, R. (2017). Blockchain and financial market innovation. *Economic Perspectives*, *41*(7), 1–17.

Lu, H., Huang, K., Azimi, M., & Guo, L. (2019). Blockchain technology in the oil and gas industry: A review of applications, opportunities, challenges, and risks. *IEEE Access : Practical Innovations, Open Solutions*, *7*, 41426–41444. doi:10.1109/ACCESS.2019.2907695

Malhotra, D., Saini, P., & Singh, A. K. (2022). How blockchain can automate KYC: Systematic review. *Wireless Personal Communications*, *122*(2), 1987–2021. doi:10.100711277-021-08977-0

Mendling, J., Weber, I., van der Aalst, W., vom Brocke, J., Cabanillas, C., Daniel, F., Debois, S., di Ciccio, C., Dumas, M., & Dustdar, S. (2018). Blockchains for business process management-challenges and opportunities. *ACM Transactions on Management Information Systems*, *9*(1), 1–16. doi:10.1145/3183367

Mishra, L., & Kaushik, V. (2021). Application of blockchain in dealing with sustainability issues and challenges of financial sector. *Journal of Sustainable Finance & Investment*, ●●●, 1–16. doi:10.1080/20430795.2021.1940805

Mondal, P. C., Deb, R., & Huda, M. N. (2016). Transaction authorization from Know Your Customer (KYC) information in online banking. *2016 9th International Conference on Electrical and Computer Engineering (ICECE)*, 523–526.

Mori, T. (2016). Financial technology: Blockchain and securities settlement. *Journal of Securities Operations & Custody*, *8*(3), 208–227.

Nguyen, Q. K. (2016). Blockchain-a financial technology for future sustainable development. *2016 3rd International Conference on Green Technology and Sustainable Development (GTSD)*, 51–54.

Osmani, M., El-Haddadeh, R., Hindi, N., Janssen, M., & Weerakkody, V. (2020). Blockchain for next generation services in banking and finance: Cost, benefit, risk and opportunity analysis. *Journal of Enterprise Information Management*.

Park, J. H., & Park, J. H. (2017). Blockchain security in cloud computing: Use cases, challenges, and solutions. *Symmetry, 9*(8), 164. doi:10.3390ym9080164

Pilkington, M. (2016). Blockchain technology: principles and applications. In *Research handbook on digital transformations*. Edward Elgar Publishing. doi:10.4337/9781784717766.00019

Popescu, C. R. G., & Popescu, G. N. (2018). Risks of cyber attacks on financial audit activity. *The Audit Financiar Journal, 16*(149), 140. doi:10.20869/AUDITF/2018/149/140

Puthal, D., Malik, N., Mohanty, S. P., Kougianos, E., & Yang, C. (2018). The blockchain as a decentralized security framework. *IEEE Consumer Electronics Magazine, 7*(2), 18–21. doi:10.1109/MCE.2017.2776459

Rawat, D., Chaudhary, V., & Doku, R. (2020). Blockchain technology: Emerging applications and use cases for secure and trustworthy smart systems. *Journal of Cybersecurity and Privacy, 1*(1), 4–18. doi:10.3390/jcp1010002

Rawat, P., Yashpal, D., & Purohit, J. K. (2021). An opinion of Indian manufacturing and service sector for adopting industry 4.0: A survey. *Turkish Journal of Computer and Mathematics Education, 12*(6), 2370–2379.

Rechtman, Y. (2017). Blockchain: The making of a simple, secure recording concept. *The CPA Journal, 87*(6), 15–17.

Reyna, A., Martín, C., Chen, J., Soler, E., & Díaz, M. (2018). On blockchain and its integration with IoT. Challenges and opportunities. *Future Generation Computer Systems, 88*, 173–190. doi:10.1016/j.future.2018.05.046

Riasanow, T., Flötgen, R. J., Setzke, D. S., Böhm, M., & Krcmar, H. (2018). *The generic ecosystem and innovation patterns of the digital transformation in the financial industry*. Academic Press.

Río, D., & César, A. (2017). Use of distributed ledger technology by central banks: A review. *Enfoque Ute, 8*(5), 1–13. doi:10.29019/enfoqueute.v8n5.175

Rossi, M., Mueller-Bloch, C., Thatcher, J. B., & Beck, R. (2019). Blockchain research in information systems: Current trends and an inclusive future research agenda. *Journal of the Association for Information Systems, 20*(9), 14. doi:10.17705/1jais.00571

Saberi, S., Kouhizadeh, M., Sarkis, J., & Shen, L. (2019). Blockchain technology and its relationships to sustainable supply chain management. *International Journal of Production Research, 57*(7), 2117–2135. doi:10.1080/00207543.2018.1533261

Saito, K., & Yamada, H. (2016). What's so different about blockchain?—blockchain is a probabilistic state machine. *2016 IEEE 36th International Conference on Distributed Computing Systems Workshops (ICDCSW)*, 168–175.

Sayegh, K., & Desoky, M. (2019). Blockchain Application in Insurance and Reinsurance. Skema Business School.

Schlatt, V., Guggenberger, T., Schmid, J., & Urbach, N. (2022). Attacking the trust machine: Developing an information systems research agenda for blockchain cybersecurity. *International Journal of Information Management.*

Schou-Zibell, L., & Phair, N. (2018). *How secure is blockchain?* Academic Press.

Singer, A. W. (2019). Can blockchain improve insurance? *Risk Management, 66*(1), 20–25.

Sternberg, H. S., Hofmann, E., & Roeck, D. (2021). The struggle is real: Insights from a supply chain blockchain case. *Journal of Business Logistics, 42*(1), 71–87. doi:10.1111/jbl.12240

Stockburger, L., Kokosioulis, G., Mukkamala, A., Mukkamala, R. R., & Avital, M. (2021). Blockchain-enabled decentralized identity management: The case of self-sovereign identity in public transportation. *Blockchain: Research and Applications, 2*(2), 100014.

Sundarraj, R. (2019). Call for Papers: Design Science Research in Information Systems and Technology. Academic Press.

Swan, M. (2017). Anticipating the economic benefits of blockchain. *Technology Innovation Management Review, 7*(10), 6–13. doi:10.22215/timreview/1109

Tapscott, D., & Tapscott, A. (2017). How blockchain will change organizations. *MIT Sloan Management Review, 58*(2), 10.

Upadhyay, N. (2020). Demystifying blockchain: A critical analysis of challenges, applications and opportunities. *International Journal of Information Management, 54*, 102120. doi:10.1016/j.ijinfomgt.2020.102120

Viriyasitavat, W., da Xu, L., Bi, Z., & Hoonsopon, D. (2019). Blockchain technology for applications in internet of things—Mapping from system design perspective. *IEEE Internet of Things Journal, 6*(5), 8155–8168. doi:10.1109/JIOT.2019.2925825

Viriyasitavat, W., da Xu, L., Bi, Z., Hoonsopon, D., & Charoenruk, N. (2019). Managing qos of internet-of-things services using blockchain. *IEEE Transactions on Computational Social Systems, 6*(6), 1357–1368. doi:10.1109/TCSS.2019.2919667

Walters, R., & Novak, M. (2021). Artificial Intelligence and Law. In Cyber Security, Artificial Intelligence, Data Protection & the Law (pp. 39–69). Springer.

Yaga, D., Mell, P., Roby, N., & Scarfone, K. (2019). *Blockchain technology overview.* ArXiv Preprint ArXiv:1906.11078.

Zhang, L., Xie, Y., Zheng, Y., Xue, W., Zheng, X., & Xu, X. (2020). The challenges and countermeasures of blockchain in finance and economics. *Systems Research and Behavioral Science, 37*(4), 691–698. doi:10.1002res.2710

Chapter 15
Enhancing Traceability in Food Supply Chains Using Blockchain and IoT Technologies

N. Ambika

St. Francis College, India

ABSTRACT

The work centers around a connected viewpoint intended for the problematic information interface between blockchain and IoT for further developing information provenance and uprightness. The examination draws on the author's industry-based experience driving a two-year AUD 1.5 million undertaking that elaborates on the coordination of IoT and blockchain to follow and safeguard the legitimacy of Australian meat in the quickly developing Chinese market. The plan drove the system to direct the improvement of the food production network project as a particular mix of IoT and blockchain to a specific food store network context. The presentation can change the prophet's personality. The information legitimacy rehearses instead of looking for the unadulterated fact of the matter and crypto financial aspects. The suggestion uses a different methodology to enhance the traceability of the product. It uses a Merkle tree to generate hash keys. It detects security breaches by 2.93% and improves client satisfaction by 9.96% compared to previous work.

INTRODUCTION

The capabilities to sense, actuate, and communicate over the Internet are provided by a collection of technology. It is known as the Internet of Things (Abdel-Basset, Manogaran, & Mohamed, 2018; Al-ghofaili & Rassam, 2022). These technologies range from Radio Frequency Identification to Wireless Sensor Networks. The Internet of Things (Nagaraj, 2021) is crucial to transforming conventional cities into smart cities, electrical grids into smart grids, and homes into smart homes—and this is just the beginning. The Internet of Things (IoT) (Dian, Vahidnia, & Rahmati, 2020) depicts a world in which everything is connected and can exchange measured data with one another. Many areas use the Internet of Things (IoT) solutions to improve production and digitize industries.

DOI: 10.4018/978-1-6684-8851-5.ch015

The mechanism that enables transactions to be verified by a group of unreliable actors is called the blockchain (Ambika, 2021; Hassan, 2019). A distributed, immutable, transparent, secure, and auditable ledger is provided by it. Access to all transactions that have taken place since the system's initial transaction is made available to anyone, and the blockchain can be verified and compiled at any time. Information is organized by the blockchain protocol in a chain of blocks, with each block storing a set of Bitcoin transactions performed at a specific time. A reference to the previous block links blocks together to form a chain. Figure 1 represents block validation.

Figure 1. Block validation
Source: Panarello et al. (2018)

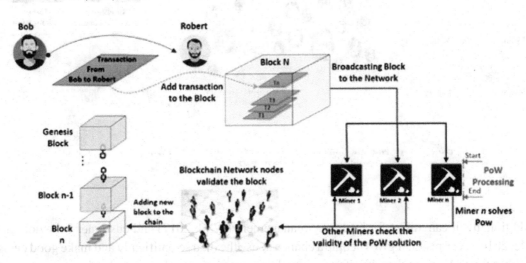

The chapter is divided into nine sections. Section two provides Food chain in agriculture. Literature survey is detailed in segment three. Division four explains the background of the proposal. Fifth segment briefs the previous work. Sixth segment explains the proposed work. Analysis of work is explained in seventh segment. Future directions are briefed in eighth division. The work is concluded in ninth section.

FOOD CHAIN IN AGRICULTURE

One of the most critical fields in the world, agriculture (Bhanu, Rao, Ramesh, & Hussain, 2014) impacts all human existence. A nation's economy, as well as its population's security, nutrition, and health, are significantly affected by agriculture (Lichtenberg, 2002) production. The practice of agriculture involves a lot of choices and risks, such as seasonal weather changes, fluctuating market prices for agricultural products, deteriorating soil quality, unsustainable crops, produce damage from weeds and pests, and global climate change. It relates biotic or abiotic data with the development and probabilistic existence of pathogens, problems, and toxicants. It can utilize big data analytics in the agriculture supply chain to analyze the food quality, storage conditions, and weather patterns in a specific geographic area, soil quality, such as pH and nutrients, marketing and trade management, and the existence of food hazards. Figure 2 portrays the characteristics of Blockchain, AI, IoT and bigdata in smart farming.

Figure 2. Characteristics of blockchain, AI, IoT, and big data in smart farming
Source: Bhat et a. (2022)

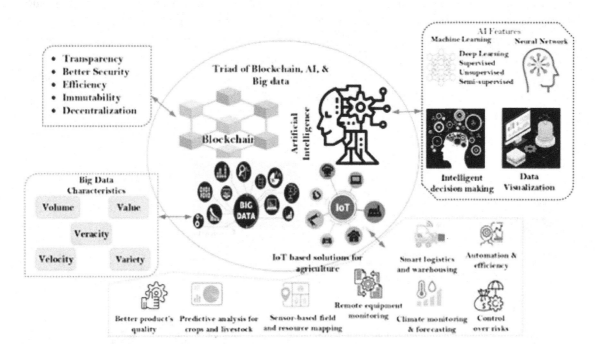

Additionally, it can utilize for inventory management (Wild, 2017) and customer behavior analysis (Khade, 2016). As a result, it gives people a chance to use the data scientifically and make good decisions at the right time. A comprehensive strategy involving a variety of relevant technologies and data from a variety of related industries is required for the utilization of big agricultural data. Big data (Arridha, Sukaridhoto, Pramadihanto, & Funabiki, 2017) from agriculture can be used for research, policymaking, decision-making, crop management, and business management by farmers, legislators, and other stakeholders.

Food supply chains have drawn in research on further developing food detectability and provenance by incorporating IoT with blockchain (Ambika, 2021) IoT is utilized as an information-gathering device. The blockchain is utilized for disseminated information capacity. IoT gadgets (Lee, Bae, & Kim, 2017) might be broken or improperly conveyed.

LITERATURE SURVEY

Many authors have contributed their work towards the domain. This section is briefing of the same.

Agri-SCM-BIoT (Agriculture Supply Chain Management Using Blockchain and the Internet of Things) (Bhat, Huang, Sofi, & Sultan, 2022) architecture is presented in the study to address storage and scalability optimization, interoperability, security and privacy issues, and storage concerns with current single-chain agriculture supply chain systems. Security and privacy of personal data are also addressed in the study. Food processing, transportation, storage, and distribution are just a few systems that have

Figure 3. Proposed architecture
Source: Bhat et al. (2022)

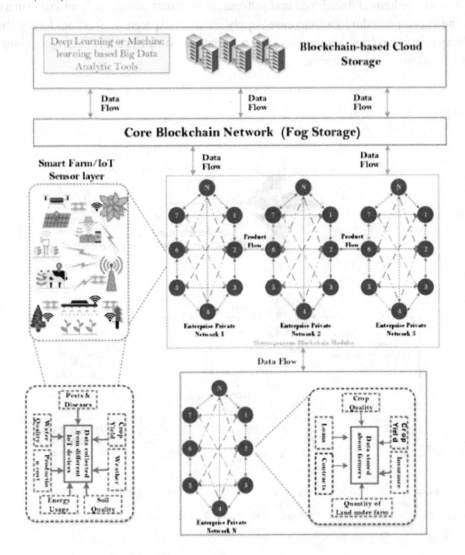

worked together in a supply chain and shared various characteristics and functions. From processing to packaging, transportation to storage, and distribution, these levels keep track of all the products. These are lengthy and complicated processes. Intelligent contracts can simplify the entire procedure and increase supply chain transparency. It can track the supply chain and inventory and change ownership rights by integrating blockchain-based smart contracts with IoT devices. Companies can better prepare for any disruptions or incidents thanks to this. In addition, smart contracts enable businesses and consumers to trace back all information to determine the quality of food products. The features of intelligent contracts meet the needs of the agriculture supply chain business. It uses multiple blockchains. For time-sensitive applications and transactions, data is stored on the IoT edge layer, where the edge blockchain tier is responsible for processing tasks that need to be completed closer. Only the most recent transaction hash values are stored on the core blockchain. It is also in charge of transferring data from the lower edge tiers to the cloud computing layer over the IoT blockchain architecture. All network processes are automated and improved with the help of distributed and self-executing smart contracts. It will use smart contracts to simplify the entire procedure and increase supply chain transparency. Stakeholders in the industry use supervisory control and data acquisition system to manage various supply chain processes and make management decisions. Same is represented in Figure 3.

Figure 4. Proposed architecture
Source: Grecuccio et al. (2020)

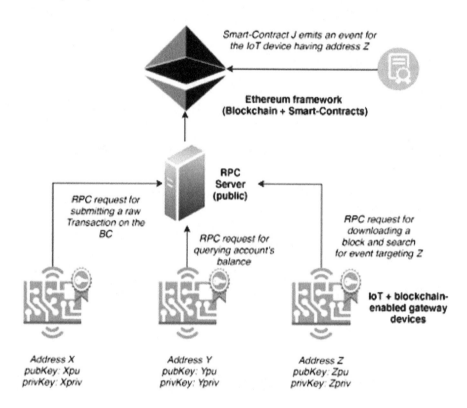

Grecuccio et al. (2020) describes creating a software framework that enables Internet-of-Things devices to interact directly with an Ethereum-based blockchain. It entails making it possible for commercial or ad hoc Internet-of-Things devices to communicate directly with the BC infrastructure by connecting them via wired or wireless protocols to a gateway device. The Remote-Procedure-Call, based on the Client-Server model and used in contexts where one program wants to request a service from another, executed in a remote host, is used. Such a gateway device should be able to sign in place the data sent from the IoT data-logging device and then push directly on the BC. A synchronous event known as an RPC call necessitates the suspension of the caller program until the result of the remote procedure is returned. JSON-RPC represents a stateless and lightweight RPC implementation. It is an extension of the original RPC protocol that encodes remote methods, parameters, and results in the JSON data format. The software component that is in charge of making JSON-RPC calls over the TCP socket that the RPC server is listening on in the developed framework is called JSON-RPC Client. A queue is used to implement it, and other tasks push a data structure for each RPC-Call they request. The standard fields of a Remote Procedure Call are modelled in this data structure, and an additional area is provided to store the call's current state. One framework that implements a portion of the Web3 API's functions is the Ethereum interaction layer. Encoding the necessary parameters for the correspondent RPC call to be executed is the responsibility of each of the provided parts, in the sense that it conceals the specifics required to carry out particular operations on the blockchain, the Application interaction layer functions as a wrapper for the Ethereum interaction layer. Cold-chain monitoring during logistics operations is the scenario in which the use case is applied. In this scenario, it is presumptuous to assume that the Internet of Things device is a refrigerated truck that moves seafood from a harbor warehouse to the final fish shop. The device is in charge of monitoring the truck's position and the fridge's temperature, respectively. It can connect to the Internet via a mobile network connection. Figure 4 represents the same.

Powell et al. (2022) centres around a connected viewpoint intended for the problematic information interface among blockchain and IoT for further developing information provenance and uprightness. The examination draws on our industry-based experience driving a two-year AUD 1.5 million undertakings that elaborate the coordination of IoT and Blockchain to follow and safeguard the legitimacy of Australian meat in the quickly developing Chinese market. The plan drove the system to direct the improvement of our food production network project as a particular mix of IoT and blockchain to a specific food store network context. The presentation can change the prophet's personality. The information legitimacy rehearses instead of looking for the unadulterated fact of the matter and crypto financial aspects.

The cutting-edge technologies are combined in Khan et al. (2020). It combines ADL with IoT and blockchain. It uses long short-term memory and gates recurrent units as a prediction model. The Genetic Algorithm optimization jointly optimizes the parameters of the hybrid model. It forecasts food supply and demand using a hybrid model based on recurrent neural networks (RNN) algorithms. Hundreds of tons of meat flow daily into the urban area from various farmers' markets through the wholesale and trading centers for meat products. The proposed system creates a digital ledger based on blockchain for each one. Users can quickly learn about the market, price, production, quality, and other topics. Each new product's origin, transaction time, and inspection and quarantine information are recorded on the blockchain. To determine where the food originated, the end user only needs to enter the number of transactions or scan the barcode. Customers will be able to view the food's temperature. The proposed system's functional modules include administrative modules for farmers and warehouse owners.

It is a secure architecture (Moudoud, Cherkaoui, & Khoukhi, 2019) that uses smart contracts, Oracles, a lightweight consensus for IoT (LC4IoT), and overcomes the difficulties of using BC in an IoT context to ensure openness. The intelligent farm is made up of Internet of Things (IoT) devices, proxy nodes, storage, and BC. It has three central ledgers: private, consortium, and public BC. Anyone can join a general BC, and all BC members are accountable for transaction validation. The consortium BC stands out due to its partial decentralization; A select few members oversee the consensus decision. Private BC only allows network members access. A single organization or business carries out remote BC. The system makes use of a private/public BC. The intelligent farm's data is stored in the private BC. The public BC is utilized to provide information to the general public and track produce. In a smart farm, IoT sensors are in charge of collecting field data. A public key that changes with each transaction identifies each product. While transactions are recorded in the private/general BC, data are typically collected from sensors scattered across multiple locations throughout the food supply chain. Oracles are utilized in work to verify the accuracy of sensor data. The work stores the hash of the data in a private BC in the cloud, allowing for data trustworthiness and non-repudiation. It creates a summary and maps the data.

It uses an input string of any size that it can substitute for the unique fingerprint. The hash ensures data integrity by comparing the hash value with additional inputs like the timestamp and the previous block hash. The BC could act as a middleman for the transfer of data. The work was done on an Intel CoreTM i7-8550U CPU running at 1.80 GHz and 2.00 GHz, with 16.0 GB of RAM.

The proposed architecture (Balamurugan, Ayyasamy, & Joseph, 2022) has three layers for IoT - local Blockchain server and IoT network. It is a modern Blockchain connectivity system that migrates blocks in a hierarchical structure. Blockchain is that the blocks are managed within the individual IoT networks. At the same time, it can move the nodes safely and their abundant computing space organized. The fundamental processing techniques are described in a conventional food processing system. The production of raw foodstuffs in centers with a large number of food distributors all over the world is the first step. Producers then send the shipments to wholesalers and central suppliers. In the end, the local distributor has a lot of wholesale and retail stores that meet customers' needs. The selling packages, subsets, and cartons will be labelled with a single QR code as part of the proposed system. The food product type, producer names and licenses, manufacturing date, expiration date, batch number, and other information this package provides are all included in the QR code. The primary component of the proposed system that prevents fraudulent foods from entering the supply chain is QR coding. The product's delivery is the food supply at various points of distribution only after the nutritional value has been validated.

Kim et al. (2018) provides a fundamental framework for constructing a prototype or simulation with existing protocols and technologies. A more transparent supply chain will increase efficiency and lower friction costs. IoT sensors in facilities have begun automatically queuing and processing truck shipments as they arrive. The processing and grading data are added to the blockchain ledger as products move through the facility. Delivery trucks can be tracked while in transit once they have been loaded. Temperatures and other logistical information are sent to the blockchain ledger. Electronic notification can activate a blockchain smart contract to carry out contractual payment for products once product acceptance has been confirmed at the final endpoint. The farmer can track how their produce is graded and delivered to customers. Shippers can quickly and easily retrace any quality issues as they gain field-level insight into each production unit. Shipping gains autonomy by incorporating data checkpoints throughout the facility. The data gathered and stored on the blockchain can be analyzed to find processes it can improve, which will save even more money. When a product is in a store, the end customer looks at information like where it came from, who raised it, and how long it has been there. They now always have a farmers market at their disposal, returning the consumer to the power of food bytes.

Tian (2017) is based on HACCP (Hazard Analysis and Critical Control Points), blockchain, and the Internet of Things. It is a traceability system that could provide an open, transparent, neutral, reliable, and secure information platform for all supply chain members recommended for real-time food tracing. In the production link, the background environment of the planting, including the quality of the soil, water, air, etc., should be evaluated first. Then, it should request pertinent monitoring data and take all feasible measures to guarantee the growing's safety. Processing will likely occur at a different location in the processing link. As a result, the processing environment and equipment evaluation will be required. It should follow good working practices in all subsequent processing activities. In addition, the materials and additives used should be appropriate for their intended functions. In the Warehousing link, it should maintain cold-chain equipment appropriately, and all warehouse management practices should adhere to best practices. All refrigerated equipment in the distribution link, including the truck, must be appropriately maintained. In the retail relation, it should document all retail management practices in a routine document following best practices. The work collects and transfers data using the Internet of

Things and BigchainDB to store and manage relevant data about food supply chain products. The supply chain comprises many different people, like suppliers, producers, manufacturers, distributors, retailers, customers, and certifiers. Each member can add, update, and check the information about the product on BigchainDB. A tag (RFID), a unique digital cryptographic identifier that links the physical items to their virtual identities in the system, is attached to each product. It can compare the product information profile to this virtual identity. Users also have access to their digital profile, including information about their introduction, location, certifications, and product associations. The BigchainDB houses all system data and is accessible to any user. A set of rules written in code and stored in the BigchainDB also governs the system. These rules govern user interactions with the system and data sharing. Each user will generate a pair of public and private cryptographic keys following registration. It can use the private key to verify the user's identity when interacting with the system. In contrast, it can use the public key to identify the user's identity within the system. It allows users to digitally address each product as it is updated, added, or exchanged with another user in the supply chain's downstream position.

The three layers of Awan, et al. (2021) are innovative models for agricultural, environmental monitoring, and the food supply chain: the web interface layer, the logical data layer, and the physical data layer. Framework implementation that is scalable, extensible, and effective is made possible by this kind of layered approach. A variety of IoT nodes are utilized in the physical data layer to monitor crop growth and the farm environment. Through an IoT gateway and wireless router, IoT nodes collect data from the cluster farm and send it to the base station, which then sends it to the database. A single central board device houses a GPRS router that acts as a remote Radio Frequency Gateway (RFG) for wireless telemetry. The RFG gateway serves as a coordinator between two distinct data streams to achieve adequate control management and synchronization of two relatively unrelated data sources, data collection through IoT nodes for soil parameters, and IoT crop monitoring information. It also supports remote access, which enables complete remote control of cluster farm devices. The data obtained from the cluster farm is stored in an SQL database server's logical data layer. As a more intermediate layer, the SQL server can validate database server data and handle the complexity of multiple physical layer devices. The SQL database holds the raw data, extracted and saved to a local file system. Protocol for agriculture based on the Internet of Things with three phases: IoT cluster head and sink, IoT nodes. In the first phase, IoT nodes collected data and sent it to CH. In the second phase, CH broadcasted information to the sink, and in the third phase, the sink forwarded data to the base station. The monitoring system automatically transitions between active and sleep modes. The SBC sleep mode is supported by the optional battery backup module, which has a built-in uninterrupted power supply. Various devices in the cluster farm typically have an RS232 serial port. Wireless routers are turned off during the system's sleep cycle. The RFG server may also be required to recollect and retransmit missing data packets by the data manager. LEACH protocol is used in work.

Digitally tracking Agri-Food products from their origins to their final consumers is the goal of this traceability scheme (Shahid, et al., 2020). It provides a secure trading and delivery mechanism for the Agri-Food supply chain's entities. Additionally, these organizations use a reputation management system to guarantee their credibility. There are three layers to the proposed model, which has a layered structure. The data layer handles agri-food supply chain entities' interactions. Products are traded during these interactions, and a record of an auditable delivery serves as evidence. The blockchain layer, which manages the transactional data of the trading and delivery events, is the second layer. It monitors the reputations of all system participants. The blockchain layer only stores the hashes of the data to improve storage capabilities; the actual data is stored on the storage layer. The blockchain layer implements stringent access control strategies to prevent unauthorized reads and writes to the storage layer. The blockchain's transactions and events data are solely stored on IPFS by the third layer, which is essentially the storage layer. IPFS leverages the proposed system with high throughput, low latency, and scalability because it is a decentralized storage medium.

BRUSCHETTA (Arena, Bianchini, Perazzo, Vallati, & Dini, 2019) is a blockchain-based application for certification and traceability of the Extra Virgin Olive Oil supply chain. It traces the entire production process to enforce this product's certificate from the plantation to the shopping centers. It keeps track of every step in the production process to get essential data to determine how good the finished product will be. There are four different parties involved in the EVOO supply chain. The cultivation and harvest of olives are the responsibility of the farmers. The process of converting olives into EVOO and packaging is the responsibility of the manufacturers. The transportation of olives and EVOO is the responsibility of the couriers. Distributing EVOO to end users is the responsibility of the sellers, who are the final destination of the production process. There are two or more organizations for Fabric users. Every organization has three types of users based on their role on the blockchain: nodes, endorsing peers, and ordered nodes. Users known as nodes can only read the ledger's history and create new transactions. Users are accountable for ensuring that a transaction adheres to all endorsing policies associated with the node that generated the trade and are referred to as endorsing peers. Users in charge of grouping and ordering transactions are called orderer nodes. OMNeT++[3] is used to implement the work.

The proposed system (Baralla, Pinna, Tonelli, Marchesi, & Ibba, 2021) has been developed using the ABCDE, a recently developed agile development process. The proposed system is a distributed traceability system for agri-food products based on the blockchain. The system's primary objective is to offer a decentralized database of a product's history, from production to sale., The batch is the critical component of the distribution chain. Define its state and identification number for it. The system is designed to provide historical data to guarantee and disclose the preservation of local product quality, particularly during the storage and distribution phases. Continuous monitoring of relevant environmental conditions at each distribution chain makes this possible. The system's wireless sensor network comprises specific IoT devices like temperature and humidity sensors. This WSN is in charge of sending out alerts when there are anomalies. A blockchain address is used to uniquely identify each system actor, including IoT devices, providing a safe digital identity. Each IoT device is linked to a specific batch, and it can only record data that is related to that batch. On the other hand, public keys are stored in the blockchain. Registered devices can only access the blockchain system, and only authorized addresses will be able to access the device, safeguarding it from tampering from the outside. Bertulas is considered to be a case study. It was created to increase the potential for Smart Tourism in the Sardinia Region by developing an innovative pop-up store system and an interactive showcase of products for effective contextual shopping that can increase tourists' chances of discovering Sardinian food products. A pop-up store is a small local business run by an exhibitor set up in places of particular tourist interest to attract potential customers and provide them with an innovative, practical, and compelling shopping experience. A tablet or laptop computer that is connected to the network and directed to a specific e-commerce website will be provided to the exhibitor. Tourists can pay securely with cryptocurrencies or credit cards and select a particular delivery method at their home in any part of the world or at their temporary residence in Sardinia. A double purpose blockchain tracks every product movement from local producer to customer, the function of a control system that safeguards products' originality, and the function of a public, transparent, and immutable ledger.

The Global Traceability Standard (Galvez, Mejuto, & Simal-Gandara, 2018) assigns unique identifiers to various points in the supply chain, such as trade items, logistic units, parties, and locations. On products or pallets throughout the supply chain, automatic data capture techniques like barcodes and RFID tags are used to collect traceability data based on supply chain activities. With random sample tests, new methods for addressing food traceability include DNA markers and isotope tests. It can find critical features by analyzing an animal's DNA sample: it's the nation of origin, for instance. After that, a digital copy of that DNA can be attached to each product or item a company makes, bringing traceability down to the individual entity rather than a batch. It can track each item throughout the supply chain. After that, it can check the digital marker and the blockchain record for authenticity throughout the product's life cycle. The cycle permits makers to make a chain of care. Consumers can obtain information about the product's food safety by scanning a QR code on the package once it has arrived on a retailer's shelf. This information can include specifics about what is contained in the box and its location. This procedure aids businesses in preventing fraud, provides complete traceability, decreases the costs associated with product recalls, and reduces process inefficiencies. It ensures that retailers can guarantee the food on their shelves.

Traceability based on a fully decentralized blockchain (Madumidha, Ranjani,, Vandhana, & Venmuhilan, 2019) enables the construction of blocks for agriculture that continuously integrate with IoT devices from providers to consumers. The Ethereum Platform is a project that uses two networks and is open source. One is a user account, which controls an address and a private key. The Smart Contract account, which is owned by built-in code, comes in second. The code is compiled and executed using Ethereum Virtual Machines (EVM), which run on individual nodes. Transactions are the interactions between contracts. The transactions change the state of smart contracts, making it possible to change and see the form without interacting with each intelligent contract. The Ethereum ecosystem uses the user feedback system called the Ethereum Request for Comments (ERC). The ERC-20 token framework is used to construct digital tokens on the Ethereum network. Utilizing the ERC-721 proposal, Provider-Consumer uses the asset and non-fungible token standard to track and create support. This standard facilitates provider-consumer integration with the current Ethereum Platform. The ERC-721 standard is used in the creation of every digital asset. The Provider-Consumer software assigns private keys to carry out the entire transaction. Contracts based on ERC-721 are used to operate on various phones. Additionally, it provides an abstraction layer for IoT devices and users.

Pincheira, Vecchio, and Giaffreda (2022) is a case study. The architecture achieves the stored records' transparency, auditability, and immutability through blockchain and low-cost, limited IoT sensors. This creates a trustless environment for the interaction of several unknown actors. The unique blockchain identity of sensing devices makes them reliable data sources for intelligent contracts. The architecture of the traceability systems is three-module software layered on top of each other. The device module converts the sensed values into blockchain transactions for the smart contract. The gateway module then supplies the necessary network connectivity and serves as a straightforward and transparent relay between the device and the blockchain modules. The blockchain module has two intelligent contracts: a contract for an app and a twin. The twinning contract represents the IoT devices, and a different process of the traceability system, such as the transfer of ownership between stakeholders, is put into action by the app contract. As a result, app contracts and twin contracts are considered reliable oracles for the blockchain system because they can interact with one another directly. Figure 5 portrays the same.

Figure 5. Architecture of blockchain-based traceability system
Source: Pincheira, Vecchio, and Giaffreda (2022)

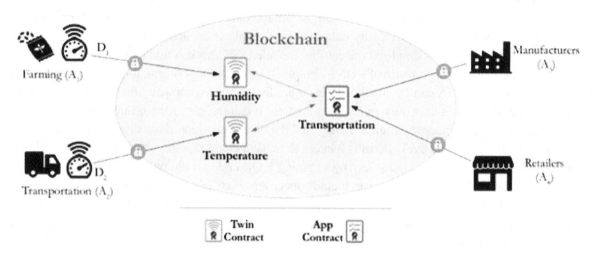

BACKGROUND

Ralph Merkle was the one who presented the Merkle tree. It is a valuable tree structure for several different fields, particularly cryptography. Throughout the history of computers, Merkle trees have been a crucial tool for verifying data. Their design aids in confirming the content's consistency. In big data applications, its architecture speeds up security authentication. Each node must hash the value from its child node in this complete binary tree. Figure 6 represents the same.

Figure 6. Merkle tree structure
Source: Chen, Chou, and Chou (2019)

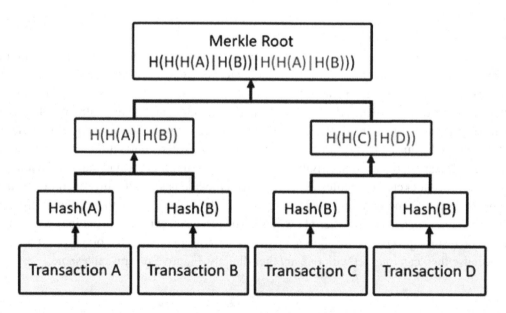

By using several inexpensive blockchain networks as temporary storage before the data is committed to Ethereum, the work provides a reliable framework for digital forensics. The application of boat rental is the focus of the study (Mercan, et al., 2020). A boat rental company rents boats, and onboard sensors collect data from those boats. An onboard IoT edge device is included in every boat. This device uses the CAN bus protocol to communicate with the boat's various sensors. Based on the significance of particular events, the data are eliminated. The widely used MQTT protocol and 4G/LTE communication send data to a remote company database when the system determines it is essential. The secure implementation of the proposed multi-chain system is necessary for the proposed forensic framework's security.

For failure detection in the Internet of Things, a platform architecture of blockchain-based federated learning systems (Zhang, et al., 2020) is recommended because it makes it possible to verify the integrity of client data. Each client periodically stores the tree root on a blockchain and creates a Merkle tree in which each leaf node represents a client data record. All industrial services based on the platform's analyzed detection results are maintained by the central organization, which is the owner of the federated learning platform. Client organizations provide local data and computation resources for local model training. While the significant organization hosts a central server and a blockchain full node, each client organization owns sensors, a client device, a client-server, and a blockchain full node. Through the client data collector and cleaning of the data, each client device collects the environment data detected by sensors. The model updates are sent to the Aggregator on the central server at a pre-configured round. The global model generated by the Aggregator is sent back to the client servers for Detector after it combines the model updates received from the clients. The operator can decrypt the obtained detection results using a data decryptor and make the final decision after they have been encrypted and sent to the central organization. Each client and server periodically create a Merkle tree, with each leaf node representing a sensor-collected data record. Tokens are given to them based on the size and centroid distance of the client data used in the model.

Figure 7. Structure of blockchain
Source: Chen, Chou, and Chou (2019)

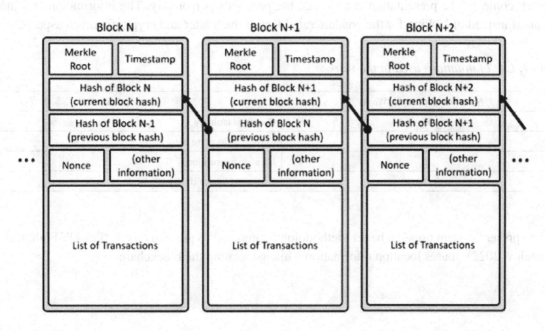

A backlinked, ordered record of transaction blocks is the definition of the blockchain data structure. It can be saved as a file or in a database. A SHA256 cryptographic hash algorithm on the header of each block can identify it. The title and the primary data are typically the two parts of the league. A list of transactions can be found in the preliminary data, while it can find a hash of the previous and current block, Merkle Root, timestamp, nonce, and other information in the header. Figure 7 represents the same.

PREVIOUS WORK

Powell et al. (2022) centres around a connected viewpoint intended for the problematic information interface among blockchain and IoT for further developing information provenance and uprightness. The examination draws on our industry-based experience driving a two-year AUD 1.5 million undertakings that elaborate the coordination of IoT and Blockchain to follow and safeguard the legitimacy of Australian meat in the quickly developing Chinese market. The plan drove the system to direct the improvement of our food production network project as a particular mix of IoT and blockchain to a specific food store network context. The presentation can change the prophet's personality. The information legitimacy rehearses instead of looking for the unadulterated fact of the matter and crypto financial aspects.

PROPOSED WORK

Powell et al. (2022) centres around a connected viewpoint intended for the problematic information interface among blockchain and IoT for further developing information provenance and uprightness. The examination draws on our industry-based experience driving a two-year AUD 1.5 million undertakings that elaborate the coordination of IoT and Blockchain to follow and safeguard the legitimacy of Australian meat in the quickly developing Chinese market. The plan drove the system to direct the improvement of our food production network project as a particular mix of IoT and blockchain to a specific food store network context. The presentation can change the prophet's personality. The information legitimacy rehearses instead of looking for the unadulterated fact of the matter and crypto financial aspects.

Table 1. List of notations used in the work

Notations Used in the Work	Description
H_{key}	Generated hash key
S_c	Current status of the meat
L_i	Location information
T_p	Processing time of the meat

The present system uses the better methodology compared to previous work (Powell, Foth, Cao, & Natanelov, 2022). It uses location information while generating the blockchain.

$$H_{key} \leftarrow \left(S_c, L_i, T_p\right) \qquad (1)$$

In the equation (1), The hash key H_{key} is generated using the current status of the meat S_c, location information L_i and processing time T_p. it uses Merkle tree to generate the hash key.

Similar to Powell, Foth, Cao, and Natanelov (2022), the suggestion uses Merkle tree to generate hash keys.

Advantages of the Suggestion

- The present system uses location information. It incorporates accurate authentication.
- The work can estimate the status of the food by considering the time necessary to travel to the destination.

Table 2. Algorithm used to generate blockchain

Step 1: Insert inputs [location information; status of product; process time] (80 bits long)
Step 2: Insert '1' in even positions. (Total – 120 bits long)
Step 3: Divide the outcome in to two halves (60 bits each)
Step 4: Xor one set with another (resultant – 60 bits)
Step 5: Divide the resultant into two halves (each 30 bits long)
Step 4: Apply left circular shift on first half and right circular shift on second half.
Step 5: Consider first half to occupy odd position of resultant and second half to occupy even positions accordingly. (Resultant – 60 bits)

ANALYSIS OF THE WORK

The work is simulated using Python. Table 3 contains the parameters used in the simulation setup.

Table 3. Simulation setup

Parameters Used in the Work	Description
Number of samples used	2300
Number of destinations considered	10
Number of sources considered	1
Location information	32 bits long
Status of the meat	24 bits long
Process time	24 bits long
Hash key length	60 bits
Message length	1500 bits

- **Authenticated Input**

Using location information in generating the blockchain improves authentication. Any security issues can be tracked easily (at the early stage). The security issues are tracked at 2.93% earlier. Figure 8 represents the same.

Figure 8. Comparison of the suggestion with previous work

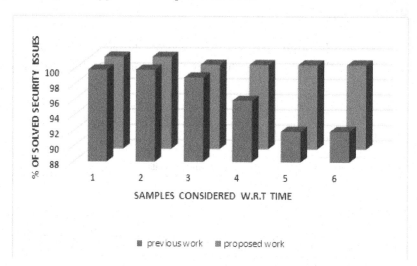

- ***Customer Satisfaction***

The work ensures good customer satisfaction. It can trace the status of the deliverable to provide client satisfaction. The suggestion improves the customer satisfaction by 9.96% compared to previous work. Figure 9 represents the same.

FUTURE DIRECTIONS

Powell et al. (2022) centres around a connected viewpoint intended for the problematic information interface among blockchain and IoT for further developing information provenance and uprightness. The examination draws on our industry-based experience driving a two-year AUD 1.5 million undertakings that elaborate the coordination of IoT and Blockchain to follow and safeguard the legitimacy of Australian meat in the quickly developing Chinese market. The plan drove the system to direct the improvement of our food production network project as a particular mix of IoT and blockchain to a specific food store network context. The presentation can change the prophet's personality. The information legitimacy rehearses instead of looking for the unadulterated fact of the matter and crypto financial aspects. The strategy depends on Merkle Trees and blocks hashes. The present system uses location information. It incorporates accurate authentication. The work can estimate the status of the food by considering the time necessary to travel to the destination. The procedure consumes a good amount of energy. Hence, future work can concentrate on having security and working towards energy consumption.

Figure 9. Representation of customer satisfaction

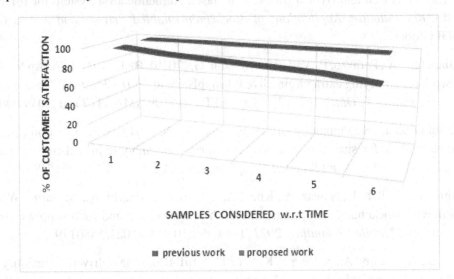

CONCLUSION

The previous work is based on our ongoing beef supply chain project with BeefLedger's empirical observations and lessons. It is a platform that integrates payments, blockchain security, and provenance. BeefLedger is a blockchain-based general-purpose technology platform project that aims to use various product provenance information as a foundation for improved costs and increased trust among beef supply chain participants. It uses Blockchain and the Internet of Things to track events in the supply chain and verify beef's provenance. In the interest of better social, ecological, and economic outcomes in a wide range of industry and societal contexts, it has guided the design and implementation of IoT and Blockchain DLT in the beef supply chain. The present system uses the better methodology compared to previous work by using location information. It detects security breaches by 2.93% and improves client satisfaction by 9.96% compared to previous work.

REFERENCES

Abdel-Basset, M., Manogaran, G., & Mohamed, M. (2018). Internet of Things (IoT) and its impact on supply chain: A framework for building smart, secure and efficient systems. *Future Generation Computer Systems*, *86*, 614–628. doi:10.1016/j.future.2018.04.051

Alghofaili, Y., & Rassam, M. (2022). A Trust Management Model for IoT Devices and Services Based on the Multi-Criteria Decision-Making Approach and Deep Long Short-Term Memory Technique. *Sensors (Basel)*, *22*(2), 634. doi:10.339022020634 PMID:35062594

Ambika, N. (2021). A Reliable Blockchain-Based Image Encryption Scheme for IIoT Networks. In *Blockchain and AI Technology in the Industrial Internet of Things* (pp. 81–97). IGI Global.

Ambika, N. (2021). A Reliable Hybrid Blockchain-Based Authentication System for IoT Network. In S. Singh (Ed.), *Revolutionary Applications of Blockchain-Enabled Privacy and Access Control* (pp. 219–233). IGI Global.

Arena, A., Bianchini, A., Perazzo, P., Vallati, C., & Dini, G. (2019). BRUSCHETTA: An IoT blockchain-based framework for certifying extra virgin olive oil supply chain. In *IEEE International Conference on Smart Computing (SMARTCOMP)* (pp. 173-179). IEEE. 10.1109/SMARTCOMP.2019.00049

Arridha, R., Sukaridhoto, S., Pramadihanto, D., & Funabiki, N. (2017). Classification extension based on IoT-big data analytic for smart environment monitoring and analytic in real-time system. *International Journal of Space-Based and Situated Computing*, 7(2), 82–93. doi:10.1504/IJSSC.2017.086821

Awan, S., Ahmed, S., Ullah, F., Nawaz, A., Khan, A., Uddin, M., Alharbi, A., Alosaimi, W., & Alyami, H. (2021). IoT with blockchain: A futuristic approach in agriculture and food supply chain. *Wireless Communications and Mobile Computing*, 2021, 1–14. doi:10.1155/2021/5580179

Balamurugan, S., Ayyasamy, A., & Joseph, K. S. (2022). IoT-Blockchain driven traceability techniques for improved safety measures in food supply chain. *International Journal of Information Technology : an Official Journal of Bharati Vidyapeeth's Institute of Computer Applications and Management*, 14(2), 1087–1098. doi:10.100741870-020-00581-y

Baralla, G., Pinna, A., Tonelli, R., Marchesi, M., & Ibba, S. (2021). Ensuring transparency and traceability of food local products: A blockchain application to a Smart Tourism Region. *Concurrency and Computation*, 33(1), e5857. doi:10.1002/cpe.5857

Bhanu, B. B., Rao, K. R., Ramesh, J. V., & Hussain, M. A. (2014). Agriculture field monitoring and analysis using wireless sensor networks for improving crop production. In *Eleventh international conference on wireless and optical communications networks (WOCN)* (pp. 1-7). IEEE.

Bhat, S., Huang, N.-F., Sofi, I., & Sultan, M. (2022). Agriculture-Food Supply Chain Management Based on Blockchain and IoT: A Narrative on Enterprise Blockchain Interoperability. *Agriculture*, 12(1), 40. doi:10.3390/agriculture12010040

Chen, Y.-C., Chou, Y.-P., & Chou, Y.-C. (2019). An Image Authentication Scheme Using Merkle Tree Mechanisms. *Future Internet*, 11(7), 149. doi:10.3390/fi11070149

Dian, F. J., Vahidnia, R., & Rahmati, A. (2020). Wearables and the Internet of Things (IoT), applications, opportunities, and challenges: A Survey. *IEEE Access : Practical Innovations, Open Solutions*, 8, 69200–69211. doi:10.1109/ACCESS.2020.2986329

Galvez, J. F., Mejuto, J. C., & Simal-Gandara, J. (2018). Future challenges on the use of blockchain for food traceability analysis. *Trends in Analytical Chemistry*, 107, 222–232. doi:10.1016/j.trac.2018.08.011

Grecuccio, J., Giusto, E., Fiori, F., & Rebaudengo, M. (2020). Combining Blockchain and IoT: Food-Chain Traceability and Beyond. *Energies*, 13(15), 3820. doi:10.3390/en13153820

Hassan, W. H. (2019). Current research on Internet of Things (IoT) security: A survey. *Computer Networks*, 148, 283–294. doi:10.1016/j.comnet.2018.11.025

Khade, A. A. (2016). Performing customer behavior analysis using big data analytics. *International Conference on Communication, Computing and Virtualization (ICCCV),* 79, 986-992. 10.1016/j. procs.2016.03.125

Khan, P. W., Byun, Y. C., & Park, N. (2020). IoT-blockchain enabled optimized provenance system for food industry 4.0 using advanced deep learning. *Sensors (Basel),* 20(10), 2990. doi:10.339020102990 PMID:32466209

Kim, M., Hilton, B., Burks, Z., & Reyes, J. (2018). Integrating blockchain, smart contract-tokens, and IoT to design a food traceability solution. In *9th annual information technology, electronics and mobile communication conference (IEMCON)* (pp. 335-340). Academic Press.

Lee, S. K., Bae, M., & Kim, H. (2017). Future of IoT networks: A survey. *Applied Sciences (Basel, Switzerland),* 7(10), 1072. doi:10.3390/app7101072

Lichtenberg, E. (2002). Agriculture and the environment. In *Handbook of agricultural economics* (pp. 1249–1313). Elsevier.

Madumidha, S. R. P., Vandhana, U., & Venmuhilan, B. (2019). A theoretical implementation: Agriculture-food supply chain management using blockchain technology. In *TEQIP III Sponsored International Conference on Microwave Integrated Circuits, Photonics and Wireless Networks (IMICPW),* (pp. 174-178). 10.1109/IMICPW.2019.8933270

Mercan, S., Cebe, M., Tekiner, E., Akkaya, K., Chang, M., & Uluagac, S. (2020). A cost-efficient IoT forensics framework with blockchain. *IEEE International Conference on Blockchain and Cryptocurrency (ICBC).* 10.1109/ICBC48266.2020.9169397

Moudoud, H., Cherkaoui, S., & Khoukhi, L. (2019). An IoT blockchain architecture using oracles and smart contracts: the use-case of a food supply chain. In *IEEE 30th Annual International Symposium on Personal, Indoor and Mobile Radio Communications (PIMRC)* (pp. 1-6). IEEE.

Nagaraj, A. (2021). *Introduction to Sensors in IoT and Cloud Computing Applications.* Bentham Science Publishers. doi:10.2174/97898114793591210101

Panarello, A., Tapas, N., Merlino, G., Longo, F., & Puliafito, A. (2018). Blockchain and IoT Integration: A Systematic Survey. *Sensors (Basel),* 18(8), 2575. doi:10.339018082575 PMID:30082633

Pincheira, M., Vecchio, M., & Giaffreda, R. (2022). Characterization and Costs of Integrating Blockchain and IoT for Agri-Food Traceability Systems. *Systems,* 10(3), 57. doi:10.3390ystems10030057

Powell, W., Foth, M., Cao, S., & Natanelov, V. (2022). Garbage in garbage out: The precarious link between IoT and blockchain in food supply chains. *Journal of Industrial Information Integration,* 25, 100261. doi:10.1016/j.jii.2021.100261

Shahid, A., Almogren, A., Javaid, N., Al-Zahrani, F. A., Zuair, M., & Alam, M. (2020). Blockchain-based agri-food supply chain: A complete solution. *IEEE Access : Practical Innovations, Open Solutions,* 8, 69230–69243. doi:10.1109/ACCESS.2020.2986257

Tian, F. (2017). A supply chain traceability system for food safety based on HACCP, blockchain & Internet of things. *International conference on service systems and service management*, 1-6.

Wild, T. (2017). *Best practice in inventory management*. Routledge. doi:10.4324/9781315231532

Zhang, W., Lu, Q., Yu, Q., Li, Z., Liu, Y., Lo, S., Chen, S., Xu, X., & Zhu, L. (2020). Blockchain-based federated learning for device failure detection in industrial IoT. *IEEE Internet of Things Journal*, 8(7), 5926–5937. doi:10.1109/JIOT.2020.3032544

Chapter 16
Unleashing the Power of the Metaverse in Intelligent Libraries

Mohammad Daradkeh
https://orcid.org/0000-0003-2693-7363
University of Dubai, UAE and Yarmouk University, Jordan

ABSTRACT

The emergence of Metaverse has presented new opportunities and possibilities for the advancement of intelligent libraries. However, it also brings new challenges to the professional competencies of librarians. This chapter examines the potential of Metaverse as an enabling technology for intelligent libraries, focusing on how it can be used to drive innovation and improve library services. The chapter also delves into the advantages and underlying technologies of Metaverse, as well as its theoretical foundations for application in libraries. It is argued that Metaverse and its related technologies are crucial for transforming libraries into fully intelligent ones, and that the concept of Metaverse can also provide benefits for library collection management, reading spaces, cultural promotion, reading experiences, and special user services. Intelligent libraries must seize this opportunity to create a new form of immersive experience and achieve breakthroughs in their digital transformations, driven by the diverse technologies of Metaverse.

INTRODUCTION

In today's world, a new wave of technological revolution and industrial change is emerging. Virtual reality (VR) technology is a representative technology of this new revolution in science and technology and is considered a key technology to promote the development of the digital economy, industrial transformation, and upgrade. The VR industry has a vast space and great potential for growth, as was emphasized at the World VR Industry Conference on October 20, 2021. It is believed that further "VR+" actions should be taken to enrich terminal products and content services, and to promote the industrialization of VR technology and industrial scale up (Zhang et al., 2022).

DOI: 10.4018/978-1-6684-8851-5.ch016

The innovation and development of virtual and reality industries have brought about significant changes to the services offered by traditional cultural venues, such as libraries, museums and galleries. The use of VR technology in these venues allows for a more immersive and interactive experience for the visitors, bringing the exhibits and collections to life in a way that was not previously possible. Additionally, the use of VR in education and training has been gaining traction as it enables students to explore and learn in a virtual environment that simulates real-world scenarios. Furthermore, the emergence of metaverse technology has also brought new opportunities to libraries. Metaverse is a virtual shared space where users can interact with each other and with virtual objects in a way that resembles the real world. The use of metaverse technology in libraries can enable the creation of virtual reading rooms and libraries, providing users with access to a vast collection of books and resources in a virtual environment. Additionally, the use of metaverse technology can enable the creation of virtual events, such as book clubs and author talks, providing a new way for libraries to engage with their communities.

There are 3 stages in the development of intelligent libraries: pseudo-intelligent, partially intelligent and fully intelligent (Njoku, Nwakanma, Amaizu, & Kim, 2022). From the current stage of development of intelligent libraries, libraries are still in pseudo-intelligent and partially intelligent stages (Alpala, Quiroga-Parra, Torres, & Peluffo-Ordóñez, 2022). Technologies such as Web 3.0, Internet of Things, big data, and cloud computing (Dai, Wang, & Gao, 2022) are widely used in the intelligent services of libraries, but their intelligent services are limited by time and space. Each technological revolution has brought about disruptive changes to the service models of libraries. From information to knowledge to big data, the service models of libraries have evolved from traditional service models to digital library service models to intelligent library service models.

The current concept of metaverse represents yet another disruption to the library service model, and it is important for libraries to stay abreast of the latest technological developments and adapt their services accordingly to best serve their communities. The emergence of Metaverse will break the boundary between the digital and physical worlds, expand the service boundary of intelligent libraries, and bring more possibilities for their intelligent development. Therefore, exploring the transformation of intelligent library service model under the perspective of Metaverse has distinct significance for the development of intelligent library services.

This chapter aims to explore the potential of Metaverse technology in driving the transformation of intelligent library services. It will analyze the development opportunities of Metaverse and its application prospects in intelligent libraries, with the goal of promoting innovation and optimization of library services. The chapter will also discuss the advantages of Metaverse and its underlying technologies, as well as the theoretical logic of Metaverse application in libraries. Additionally, the chapter will provide insights on how Metaverse and its related technologies can be leveraged to promote libraries to fully intelligent libraries, and how the concept of Metaverse can create more advantages for libraries in terms of collection resource management, reading space, cultural promotion, reading experience, and special user services to achieve the morphological reform of intelligent libraries. The goal of this chapter is to provide a comprehensive understanding of how Metaverse can be utilized to improve library services and stay ahead of the curve in the digital revolution.

CONNOTATIONS OF METAVERSE AND INTELLIGENT LIBRARIES

Metaverse

Metaverse is a general concept describing future iterations of the Internet, consisting of a continuously shared three-dimensional virtual space connected to a perceptible virtual world (Allam, Bibri, Jones, Chabaud, & Moreno, 2022). The term originated in the science fiction novel "Snow Crash" by N. Stephenson, in which the plot takes place in a virtual space where real humans live with virtual people through VR devices (Magalhães et al., 2022). Since the emergence of the metaverse to date, there has not been a unified definition of the metaverse, and different vendors and scholars have their own interpretations of the metaverse. The burgeoning of the metaverse has a significant relationship with Facebook founder M. Zuckerberg's interview at TheVerge, in which he expressed his desire to turn Facebook into a metaverse company (Nguyen, 2022). He also believed that the metaverse was the future of the Internet. Since then, many scholars and entrepreneurs have started to explore the concept of metaverse. Yang et al. (2022) argues that the metaverse needs to achieve a high degree of realism, where people's lives in reality can be mapped to the metaverse space. Cappannari and Vitillo (2022) argues that the metaverse is a virtual space parallel to and independent from the real world, a digital virtual world that is increasingly realistic. Duan et al. (2021), the founder of r. Beamable, divided the metaverse according to different levels. Following the advent of the metaverse, many companies have sought to implement the concept, taking Roblox (Allam, Sharifi, Bibri, Jones, & Krogstie, 2022), a gaming company listed in the U.S., as an example, which was the first company to build a metaverse ecology. Later, major manufacturers have been investing in building the metaverse.

The metaverse aims to build a sustainable virtual shared space while maintaining the perception and experience of the real world, which requires adhering to the values of co-creation, co-building, sharing, and co-governance, and fully integrating new technologies such as big data, artificial intelligence, virtual reality, 5G, blockchain, and 3D engines (Buhalis, Lin, & Leung, 2022; Chen & Lee, 2021). The technical core of metaverse depends on integration and application, and its underlying technologies are shown in Table 1. Different disciplines have different views on the exploration of metaverse. However, in the field of graphical information, considering only virtualization and digitization is not a prospect for the development of intelligent libraries. The concept of intelligent libraries needs to be gradually realized. Only by continuously introducing the underlying technologies of metaverse and upgrading the intelligent services of libraries can we eventually realize the profound integration of metaverse and libraries.

Table 1. Major underlying technologies of metaverse

Underlying Technologies	Implemented Functions
Artificial intelligence, digital twin	Meta-universe ecology
Blockchain	Access Verification
Artificial Intelligence, Cloud Computing	Underlying algorithms
Expanded reality, robotics, brain-computer interface	Virtual Reality Simulation
5G	Unhindered Networks

Intelligent Library

In 2003, M. Aittola of the University Library of Oulu, Finland, introduced the term intelligent library (Hassani, Huang, & MacFeely, 2022), arguing that intelligent libraries are not limited by time and space and can perceive mobile library services that help users to find books and other types of materials in the library by connecting to wireless Internet. Intelligent libraries are a three-dimensional combination of physical space, digital space, and human society, as well as virtual technologies. Core technology clusters such as intelligent technologies underlie their creation and development (Baghalzadeh Shishehgarkhaneh, Keivani, Moehler, Jelodari, & Roshdi Laleh, 2022). In the development of intelligent libraries, it undergoes pseudo-intelligence and partial intelligence stages; the fully intelligent library is the final form of intelligent library development (Eom, 2022). Although the fully intelligent library is based on intelligent technology, the core of the fully intelligent library is the integrated use of metaverse underlying technology. It aims at fully intelligent library services and the realization of dual digital libraries. These two goals are also the two stages of metaverse application in intelligent libraries.

The first stage of the fully intelligent library is to use the underlying technologies of the metaverse, such as extended reality and blockchain, to achieve fully intelligent library services, i.e., an unattended library (Eom, 2022). Since the key to the metaverse lies in technological breakthroughs and technology integration, the development of fully intelligent libraries at this stage also lies in the adoption and integration of the underlying technologies of the metaverse. For this stage of development, many libraries have made experimental practices, such as the WEB collection book location system built by Harbin Engineering University Library (Duan et al., 2021) and the University of Miami Library (Yang et al., 2022) using augmented reality technology to identify books. However, these attempts can only partially solve the consultation and service requirements of intelligent libraries without librarians, but cannot truly achieve unattended fully intelligent services.

The second stage of the fully intelligent library is the construction of digital twin libraries to realize the full intelligence of libraries in the real sense. In this stage, the service of fully intelligent library should break through the limitation of time and space. In the metaverse, the fully intelligent library provides users with digital identity verification, and users can freely enter the virtual space of the library with their digital identity without physical restrictions. Meanwhile, the real library's intelligent services reach the stage of full intelligence. With the realization of the morphological changes of the fully intelligent library, its service model will change in the following directions:

1. Most of the reading services provided by traditional libraries are for individual readers, and there is a lack of interactive communication between readers and patrons. For example, individual readers can enjoy the collection navigation and display services of intelligent libraries using virtual reality technology (Ruiz Mejia & Rawat, 2022; Wang, Yu, Bell, & Chu, 2022), but different readers cannot interact with knowledge through such devices, and the devices are fragmented from each other. In contrast, intelligent libraries emphasize the interconnection of readers using Metaverse devices and technologies to provide a shared reading space for readers. This shared space serves as a dual modeling of the reader and the library, with multiple readers accessing twin digital libraries as digital twins. This is not a conjecture; VR socialization has been proposed for many years (Y. Wang et al., 2022).

2. The emergence of intelligent libraries means a closer relationship between digital libraries and real libraries. When users enter a digital library, they do not browse as a web page, but as a virtual

library in the form of a second life (Salem & Dragomir, 2022). The difference is the addition of physical interaction and real-time rendering, which is lacking in the second life. The digital library is a three-dimensional reconstruction based on the real library. Also, the digital transformation of the collection resources in real libraries will be faster. With the support of the underlying technology of metaverse, the digital library and the real library continuously interact with each other, forming the prototype of the intelligent library. Meanwhile, intelligent libraries can integrate more services, such as health information center, medical libraries, audio-visual entertainment, art galleries and museums, engineering libraries, etc. (Jamil, Rahman, & Fawad, 2022), all of which can be realized in a twin digital library.

3. The realization of intelligent libraries in the metaverse perspective is not a departure from reality, but a dual sublimation of digital and real libraries using metaverse technology. For unattended services, although libraries have attempted (Bolger, 2021), the real intelligent services have not been realized yet. For the intelligent development of intelligent libraries, the underlying technology of metaverse needs to be continuously adopted and improved. This includes the use of 3D scanning technology, spatial distance and proximity sensing for library navigation, image and text retrieval, real-time voice broadcasting for users (Xiong & Wang, 2022), and intelligent monitoring using face recognition technology and RFID technology (Y. Wang et al., 2022).

METAVERSE-BASED THEORETICAL LOGIC FOR INTELLIGENT LIBRARIES

In the traditional era of literacy, libraries were places where knowledge was stored and paper documents were kept for those who needed to read and learn (Dahan et al., 2022). However, since the middle of the 20th century, human society has entered the process of informatization, that is, the ubiquitous information society (Faraboschi, Frachtenberg, Laplante, Milojicic, & Saracco, 2022). People's requirements for collection resources have become more personalized and diversified, and modern libraries have become comprehensive places for people to learn knowledge and to engage in casual recreation. Although traditional libraries continue to innovate in their services, the optimization of services mostly involves physical space. With the continuous development of mobile libraries and digital libraries, traditional libraries have started to develop into intelligent libraries, but for a long time, the development of digital libraries has lagged far behind physical libraries (Maddahi & Chen, 2022). The arrival of metaverse, on the other hand, will enable libraries to develop more quickly into intelligent and diversified libraries.

In terms of the underlying technology application of metaverse, Siyaev and Jo (2021) proposed blockchain technology to help the equity management of digital libraries, Hassani et al. (2022) proposed the integration of 5G and intelligent libraries. Jin, Xu, and Leng (2022) reviewed and presented an outlook on the application of artificial intelligence in libraries. Viewed from this aspect, metaverse is not a castle in the air for the construction of intelligent libraries, and the technical references behind it have been discussed by many scholars.

For the establishment of digital twin libraries, intelligent libraries pursue authenticity, real-time and interaction among readers. Keshmiri Neghab, Jamshidi, and Keshmiri Neghab (2022) proposed the theory of three-dimensional space and virtual space-time tunnel in 2007. The virtual library in Second Life (Ahn, Kim, & Kim, 2022) also tried spatial interconnection. Although it lacks real-time interaction with readers and somatic simulation, its 3D modeling technology and digital transformation of collection resources undoubtedly provide many experiences and ideas for the application of metaverse in libraries.

PROSPECTS OF METAVERSE FOUNDATION TECHNOLOGY IN INTELLIGENT LIBRARIES

The metaverse comes alive in 2021, and there is endless curiosity about the metaverse in both the research and practice communities. The library community should remain rational in the face of the transformational impulse and temptation that the metaverse brings to libraries. Metaverse may not be realized in libraries immediately, but exploring its underlying technology in intelligent libraries is one of the directions to advance the library services.

Application Prospect of Virtual Reality in Intelligent Libraries

Metaverse and virtual reality are inseparable, and even virtual reality is the technology underlying metaverse. Virtual reality usually refers to technologies such as VR (virtual reality), AR (augmented reality), and MR (mediated reality). There have been many attempts to apply these three technologies in the construction of intelligent libraries. For example, the library administration of the University of Oklahoma has carried out a "VR" project in the library to present text in the form of 3D images (Vishkaei, 2022). The library of the University of North Carolina at Miami, USA, uses AR technology to allow patrons to see a brief description and history of the book while viewing the shelves (Ukko, Saunila, Nasiri, Rantala, & Holopainen, 2022). In terms of technology, VR, AR, MR, and Metaverse each have their own characteristics, but there is a transition across generations.

The application prospect of virtual reality technology in intelligent libraries is divided into two stages. The first is the application of virtual reality technology in unattended libraries, which includes the integration of collection resources with holographic projections using mixed reality technology. Patrons enjoy the combination of visual and auditory sensations through head-mounted displays while reading books and real-time navigation using AR technology. MR technology and AR applications are used to help patrons pinpoint the location of books and obtain the borrowing status and popularity of books (Buhalis et al., 2022; Popescu, Dragomir, Popescu, & Dragomir, 2022). Second, the establishment of a digital twin library. At this stage, the creation of a digital twin library must be based on the real collection resources. By creating digital avatars for readers, the immersion of readers is enhanced by virtual reality physical devices. The digital avatars and the borrowing habits of readers in the real world promote relevant information to the digital twin library to provide readers with real, comprehensive and diversified intelligent services.

Application of Blockchain Technology in Intelligent Libraries

Blockchain technology is a distributed recording method that allows users to track the origin and ownership of digital tokens. Regardless of the stage of development of intelligent libraries, blockchain technology plays a crucial role. Blockchain technology can determine the first upload time of virtual digital resources in digital twin libraries through timestamps, prove the authenticity of digital resource owners through full-node authentication and tamper-proof functions, and effectively maintain the problem of identifying the property rights of digital resources in digital twin libraries. It can also realize the interlibrary communication of digital libraries, realize the direct cooperation between libraries-author, promote the circulation of digital resources, and realize the block-chaining of library resources by building a federated chain of digital twin libraries (De Ketelaere, Smeets, Verboven, Nicolaï, & Saeys, 2022).

While blockchain is the core technology of the metaverse, non-fungible tokens (NFTs), or non-homogeneous tokens, are the core of blockchain. NFTs are protected and irreplaceable tokens on the blockchain. Since NFTs can map the value of real items, their uniqueness and irreplaceability will provide a reliable basis for people to map things in the real world to the metaverse. In this way, users can obtain the corresponding economic rights and interests in the virtual and real worlds. In intelligent libraries, NFTs can provide non-fakeable identifiers for the collection resources, and these identifiers provide anchor values for the collection resources. The borrowing records, values, and literature sources of the collection resources in the intelligent library are encapsulated by the NFTs, and the circulation reading, and promotion use of the books are recorded on the blockchain through the NFTs. The management of books will become easier and simpler, with information about the books being synchronized and displayed through the rapid scanning of the NFTs. The NFTs also empower digital twin libraries with a new form of intellectual property. The owner of the collection is recorded in the NFT, and patents are granted through uniquely identified NFTs. In fact, the first fiction book written using NFTs has also been circulated on the blockchain (Park & Kim, 2022). In the future, digital resources in the form of NFTs may also become part of intelligent library collections.

Application Prospects of Digital Twin Technology in Intelligent Libraries

Digital twin technology is the process of constructing an identical entity in a virtual space by digital means using a physical model to reflect its entire life cycle. Digital twin technology itself is the core technology of digital twin libraries. Therefore, for the purpose of introducing digital twin technology into intelligent libraries, the discussion topic presented in this chapter focuses on the first phase of intelligent libraries, i.e., how digital twin technology can achieve service optimization in unattended libraries.

The goal of the unattended library is to provide fully intelligent self-service for readers, and to improve the borrowing efficiency of readers by constructing a map for planar navigation through digital twin technology, and by selecting different areas of the library in the panoramic modeling and browsing the procedures of the resource catalog of that area. During the borrowing process, the digital twin technology is used to construct a dynamic display platform for the reading data of the collection resources, provide real-time resource recommendations for the readers, and create a twin portrait of the readers based on their reading habits and reading interests (De Ketelaere et al., 2022) to make precise recommendations for their next borrowing experience. Digital twin technology allows readers to obtain more information about the books during the borrowing process and presents the physical objects such as cultural relics and monuments in the books in a graphic form to optimize the reading experience. However, unmanned libraries do not eliminate the need for management staff. Twin librarians can provide consulting services and reading navigation for patrons, while managers can use the twin libraries to monitor and manage the library interior in real time, including facility maintenance and security testing. At the same time, they can enhance the situational awareness of service optimization by dynamically predicting the future resource demand of the library based on the resources borrowed from the twin libraries. In general, the application of digital twin technology in intelligent libraries is shown in Figure 1.

Figure 1. Application scenario of digital twin technology in intelligent libraries

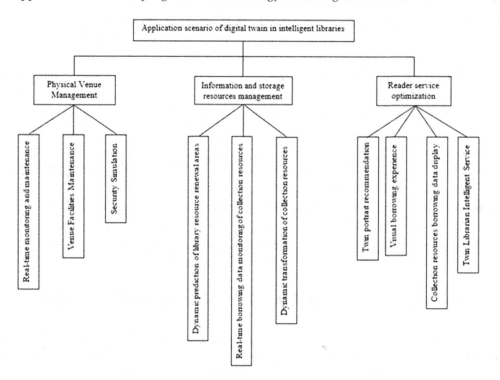

SERVICE TRANSFORMATION OF INTELLIGENT LIBRARIES FROM A METAVERSE PERSPECTIVE

The metaverse is not a monolithic development of blockchain, virtual reality and artificial intelligence, but a synthesis of technological innovations. Therefore, the development of metaverse in intelligent libraries should always be examined with holistic thinking. This chapter examines the application of metaverse in intelligent libraries in terms of collection resource management, shared reading space, special user services, simplified lending methods, optimized reading experience, and cultural promotion, and discusses the service transformation of intelligent libraries built by metaverse. Figure 2 shows the ecology of intelligent library under the perspective of metaverse.

Collection Resource Management: Realizing Intelligent Arrangement of Books

In the metaverse, the clustering, fusion and reorganization of multimodal information resources are realized based on the intelligent library. A three-dimensional model of the library is established using digital twin technology. For the arrangement and classification of multimodal collection resources, the intelligent library is not classified by subject areas, but by readers' needs in the metaverse, and readers' personalized needs become the main way of arranging the collection resources. Based on readers' needs, the intelligent library built in the cloud searches for books in the whole domain and rearranges the books in the whole domain according to their relevance to readers' needs, with books with strong relevance placed at the top of the subject area and books with weak relevance placed at the end. The

Figure 2. Intelligent library ecology from a metaverse perspective

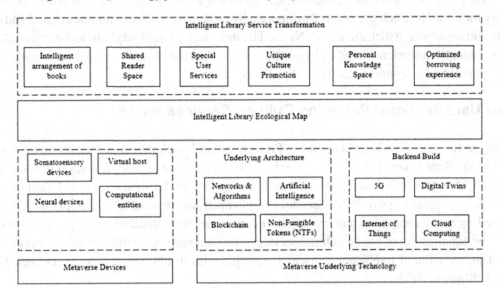

next time a reader performs a reading, the intelligent library has formed an arrangement of books that meets the reader's requirements. If the reader's needs change, the library performs a second search and rearranges them. The books in the library are arranged differently according to the reader's needs, so that each reader has his or her own intelligent library in the metaverse.

Read Experience Optimization: Enjoy Dynamic Real-World Reading

The evolution of social forms and iterations of literature repositories have led to the transmutation of library mandates and changes in service approaches (Bibri & Allam, 2022). Physical literature will always be fundamental to libraries, but the emergence of metaverse has facilitated the integration of virtual and reality, allowing the information and knowledge implicit in physical literature to be presented to readers in a visual form. The traditional applications of virtual reality technologies are all local virtual and local reality in nature, with problems such as lack of immersion and low frame rates. The emergence of metaverse enables readers to achieve full immersion in the reading process through human-computer interaction technologies such as digital twins, spatial perception, motion capture, gesture recognition, and digital twins, allowing readers to interact with the characters in the book and the knowledge in the book to be presented in an audio-visual manner. The high degree of immersion and interactivity not only satisfies the freshness of readers' reading, but also provides a new path for library culture dissemination.

Cultural Exhibition Promotion: A Novel Operational Model

In the Internet era, the influence of the traditional promotion mode of libraries is gradually decreasing. Only by finding more innovative and unique promotion methods can we attract the public's attention. In metaverse, library managers can spread culture through unique virtual library models, setting library themes regularly, and conducting virtual book exhibitions. At the same time, NFTs on the blockchain can be used to form a value bond with the collection resources for cultural promotion. In fact, this promotion model has appeared in the art world, souvenirs, and fashion world (Tromp, 2022). It is both possible and necessary for libraries to achieve cultural promotion by producing their own unique cultural and creative products and souvenirs, which are tied to NFTs. The introduction of blockchain technology into the art world increases the attention of readers by constantly updating the library's themes in the metaverse and strengthening thematic connections with other fields.

Special User Services: Providing Cultural Services for All

According to the 14th Five-Year Plan for the Protection and Development of Persons with Disabilities released by the State Council in 2021 (Chen & Lee, 2021), there are tens of millions of persons with disabilities in China, most of whom are visually and hearing impaired. Libraries, as public cultural service institutions, are unable to provide services for disabled patrons. In most cases, people with disabilities are limited by many conditions and are mostly in an information disadvantaged position. In order to promote the equalization of public cultural services, it is necessary for public libraries to explore a new model of public cultural intelligent services for people with disabilities (Pamucar, Deveci, Gokasar, Tavana, & Köppen, 2022).

For people with disabilities, Metaverse can provide multiple service models for libraries. For visually impaired patrons, libraries can use intelligent robots to provide voice-assisted services to ensure that visually impaired patrons have a voice to follow throughout the library. At the same time, the intelligent robot can introduce them to the book categories and book contents of each shelf and avoid crowded paths by calculating real-time foot traffic (Erdei, Krakó, & Husi, 2022). For patrons with hearing impairment, visual reinforcement services can be provided using metaverse technology, visual information prompting and visual information retrieval using augmented reality, and text and images can be superimposed on real objects in the library through AR devices. Another type of service is to create an intelligent library in the metaverse that enables people with disabilities to borrow books from their homes. With visual simulation through devices such as holographic projection, odor simulation through devices such as odor sensors, physical simulation through somatosensory devices, and mental simulation through brain-computer interfaces, disabled readers can visit the library in the metaverse, such as creating virtual reader images, lending and returning books, and experiencing virtual reading. It is possible to visit the library in the metaverse, such as creating a virtual reader image, lending and returning books, experiencing a virtual reading community, and recording virtual notes.

Personal Knowledge Space: Readers Become the Subject of Knowledge Creation

The metaverse itself is a continuous open space. Openness and sharing enable metaverse to support user-generated content. This means that libraries that use metaverse as an ecology also generate new ways of knowledge innovation. Patrons can use the collection resources in the library to create artifacts in the metaverse space, forming a personal knowledge space of the metaverse in the library. This space is a virtual space built in the metaverse in the library, and readers create and publish native digital knowledge through this virtual knowledge space, which is created entirely based on virtual things, such as novels and movie works describing virtual worlds. The personal knowledge space of different readers will become an important part of the library in the metaverse, and then the digital creations of readers in the knowledge space are associated with the collection resources of the library in the metaverse with high intensity, which both strengthens the participation of readers in the library in the metaverse and provides a new impetus for library transformation (Shen, Tan, Guo, Zhao, & Qin, 2021).

Shared Reading Space: A Connected Online Library for All

Second life social platform brings us the prototype of metaverse, but the core of Second life is the combination of stereoscopic modeling and internet. Readers can only access the virtual library through the button and mouse device, lacking physical interaction, and the reading experience is not much different from the traditional digital library. The intelligent library of metaverse is a high integration of rules and algorithm operation, blockchain and digital currency, and virtual reality, and builds a fully simulated digital twin library based on the concept of digital twin. Readers can enjoy library services at home through somatosensory devices and virtual reality technology. The library in Second life provides ideas for the construction of meta-universe libraries, such as the digital transformation of the collection and the integration of open resources (Bibri, 2022). For the establishment of a metaverse library, the library in Second life can be used as a framework to improve the disadvantages of real-time rendering, physical interaction, and low latency, which are lacking in Second life. Through better underlying algorithmic techniques and physical modeling, the metaverse library can become a universal online library. In this universal online library, a decentralized and multi-level shared space can be established, and the service boundaries of this shared space can be enriched to add more diverse virtual scenarios of learning, office, social, and entertainment to make the service model of the metaverse library more comprehensive.

CONCLUDING REMARKS

The emergence of the metaverse has brought new ideas for the future change of library landscape. Although metaverse has not yet been brought to fruition, the underlying technology of metaverse is gradually penetrating into our daily lives. However, while the emergence of metaverse may cause human beings, or even the whole society, to face changes in rules, it also undoubtedly brings new opportunities to libraries. In this regard, libraries should always pay attention to new emerging technologies and need to seriously think about the rules, processes, methods, procedures, and underlying logic of metaverse applications in libraries, while actively embracing new technologies and continuously introducing their underlying technologies into the construction of intelligent libraries. If metaverse becomes a reality, then intelligent libraries will also be transformed as a result.

REFERENCES

Ahn, S., Kim, J., & Kim, J. (2022). The Bifold Triadic Relationships Framework: A Theoretical Primer for Advertising Research in the Metaverse. *Journal of Advertising*, *51*(5), 592–607. doi:10.1080/0091 3367.2022.2111729

Allam, Z., Bibri, S., Jones, D., Chabaud, D., & Moreno, C. (2022). Unpacking the ‘15-Minute City’ via 6G, IoT, and Digital Twins: Towards a New Narrative for Increasing Urban Efficiency, Resilience, and Sustainability. *Sensors (Basel)*, *22*(4), 1369. doi:10.339022041369 PMID:35214271

Allam, Z., Sharifi, A., Bibri, S., Jones, D., & Krogstie, J. (2022). The Metaverse as a Virtual Form of Smart Cities: Opportunities and Challenges for Environmental, Economic, and Social Sustainability in Urban Futures. *Smart Cities*, *5*(3), 771–801. doi:10.3390martcities5030040

Alpala, L., Quiroga-Parra, D., Torres, J., & Peluffo-Ordóñez, D. (2022). Smart Factory Using Virtual Reality and Online Multi-User: Towards a Metaverse for Experimental Frameworks. *Applied Sciences (Basel, Switzerland)*, *12*(12), 6258. doi:10.3390/app12126258

Baghalzadeh Shishehgarkhaneh, M., Keivani, A., Moehler, R., Jelodari, N., & Roshdi Laleh, S. (2022). Internet of Things (IoT), Building Information Modeling (BIM), and Digital Twin (DT) in Construction Industry: A Review, Bibliometric, and Network Analysis. *Buildings*, *12*(10), 1503. doi:10.3390/buildings12101503

Bibri, S. (2022). The Social Shaping of the Metaverse as an Alternative to the Imaginaries of Data-Driven Smart Cities: A Study in Science, Technology, and Society. *Smart Cities*, *5*(3), 832–874. doi:10.3390martcities5030043

Bibri, S., & Allam, Z. (2022). The Metaverse as a Virtual Form of Data-Driven Smart Urbanism: On Post-Pandemic Governance through the Prism of the Logic of Surveillance Capitalism. *Smart Cities*, *5*(2), 715–727. doi:10.3390martcities5020037

Bolger, R. (2021). Finding Wholes in the Metaverse: Posthuman Mystics as Agents of Evolutionary Contextualization. *Religions*, *12*(9), 768. doi:10.3390/rel12090768

Buhalis, D., Lin, M., & Leung, D. (2022). Metaverse as a driver for customer experience and value co-creation: implications for hospitality and tourism management and marketing. *International Journal of Contemporary Hospitality Management*. doi:10.1108/IJCHM-05-2022-0631

Cappannari, L., & Vitillo, A. (2022). XR and Metaverse Software Platforms. In Roadmapping Extended Reality (pp. 135-156). doi:10.1002/9781119865810.ch6

Chen, Q., & Lee, S. (2021). Research Status and Trend of Digital Twin: Visual Knowledge Mapping Analysis. *International Journal of Advanced Smart Convergence*, *10*(4), 84–97. doi:10.7236/IJASC.2021.10.4.84

Dahan, N., Al-Razgan, M., Al-Laith, A., Alsoufi, M., Al-Asaly, M., & Alfakih, T. (2022). Metaverse Framework: A Case Study on E-Learning Environment (ELEM). *Electronics (Basel)*, *11*(10), 1616. doi:10.3390/electronics11101616

Dai, Y., Wang, J., & Gao, S. (2022). Advanced Electronics and Artificial Intelligence: Must-Have Technologies Toward Human Body Digital Twins. *Advanced Intelligent Systems*, *4*(7), 2100263. doi:10.1002/aisy.202100263

De Ketelaere, B., Smeets, B., Verboven, P., Nicolaï, B., & Saeys, W. (2022). Digital twins in quality engineering. *Quality Engineering*, *34*(3), 404–408. doi:10.1080/08982112.2022.2052731

Duan, H., Li, J., Fan, S., Lin, Z., Wu, X., & Cai, W. (2021). Metaverse for Social Good: A University Campus Prototype. *Proceedings of the 29th ACM International Conference on Multimedia*. 10.1145/3474085.3479238

Eom, S. (2022). The Emerging Digital Twin Bureaucracy in the 21st Century. *Perspectives on Public Management and Governance, 5*(2), 174–186. doi:10.1093/ppmgov/gvac005

Erdei, T., Krakó, R., & Husi, G. (2022). Design of a Digital Twin Training Centre for an Industrial Robot Arm. *Applied Sciences (Basel, Switzerland), 12*(17), 8862. doi:10.3390/app12178862

Faraboschi, P., Frachtenberg, E., Laplante, P., Milojicic, D., & Saracco, R. (2022). Virtual Worlds (Metaverse): From Skepticism, to Fear, to Immersive Opportunities. *Computer, 55*(10), 100–106. doi:10.1109/MC.2022.3192702

Hassani, H., Huang, X., & MacFeely, S. (2022). Impactful Digital Twin in the Healthcare Revolution. *Big Data and Cognitive Computing, 6*(3), 83. doi:10.3390/bdcc6030083

Jamil, S., Rahman, M., & Fawad, M. (2022). A Comprehensive Survey of Digital Twins and Federated Learning for Industrial Internet of Things (IIoT), Internet of Vehicles (IoV) and Internet of Drones (IoD). *Applied System Innovation, 5*(3), 56. doi:10.3390/asi5030056

Jin, J., Xu, H., & Leng, B. (2022). Adaptive Points Sampling for Implicit Field Reconstruction of Industrial Digital Twin. *Sensors (Basel), 22*(17), 6630. doi:10.339022176630 PMID:36081088

Keshmiri Neghab, H., Jamshidi, M., & Keshmiri Neghab, H. (2022). Digital Twin of a Magnetic Medical Microrobot with Stochastic Model Predictive Controller Boosted by Machine Learning in Cyber-Physical Healthcare Systems. *Information (Basel), 13*(7), 321. doi:10.3390/info13070321

Maddahi, Y., & Chen, S. (2022). Applications of Digital Twins in the Healthcare Industry: Case Review of an IoT-Enabled Remote Technology in Dentistry. *Virtual Worlds, 1*(1), 20–41. doi:10.3390/virtualworlds1010003

Magalhães, L., Magalhães, L., Ramos, J., Moura, L., de Moraes, R., Gonçalves, J., Hisatugu, W. H., Souza, M. T., de Lacalle, L. N. L., & Ferreira, J. (2022). Conceiving a Digital Twin for a Flexible Manufacturing System. *Applied Sciences (Basel, Switzerland), 12*(19), 9864. doi:10.3390/app12199864

Nguyen, T. (2022). Toward Human Digital Twins for Cybersecurity Simulations on the Metaverse: Ontological and Network Science Approach. *JMIRx Med, 3*(2), e33502. doi:10.2196/33502

Njoku, J., Nwakanma, C., Amaizu, G., & Kim, D. (2022). Prospects and challenges of Metaverse application in data-driven intelligent transportation systems. *IET Intelligent Transport Systems*. doi:10.1049/itr2.12252

Pamucar, D., Deveci, M., Gokasar, I., Tavana, M., & Köppen, M. (2022). A metaverse assessment model for sustainable transportation using ordinal priority approach and Aczel-Alsina norms. *Technological Forecasting and Social Change, 182*, 121778. doi:10.1016/j.techfore.2022.121778

Park, S., & Kim, Y. (2022). A Metaverse: Taxonomy, Components, Applications, and Open Challenges. *IEEE Access: Practical Innovations, Open Solutions, 10*, 4209–4251. doi:10.1109/ACCESS.2021.3140175

Popescu, D., Dragomir, M., Popescu, S., & Dragomir, D. (2022). Building Better Digital Twins for Production Systems by Incorporating Environmental Related Functions—Literature Analysis and Determining Alternatives. *Applied Sciences (Basel, Switzerland), 12*(17), 8657. doi:10.3390/app12178657

Ruiz Mejia, J., & Rawat, D. (2022). *Recent Advances in a Medical Domain Metaverse: Status, Challenges, and Perspective.* Paper presented at the 2022 Thirteenth International Conference on Ubiquitous and Future Networks (ICUFN). 10.1109/ICUFN55119.2022.9829645

Salem, T., & Dragomir, M. (2022). Options for and Challenges of Employing Digital Twins in Construction Management. *Applied Sciences (Basel, Switzerland)*, *12*(6), 2928. doi:10.3390/app12062928

Shen, B., Tan, W., Guo, J., Zhao, L., & Qin, P. (2021). How to Promote User Purchase in Metaverse? A Systematic Literature Review on Consumer Behavior Research and Virtual Commerce Application Design. *Applied Sciences (Basel, Switzerland)*, *11*(23), 11087. doi:10.3390/app112311087

Siyaev, A., & Jo, G. (2021). Towards Aircraft Maintenance Metaverse Using Speech Interactions with Virtual Objects in Mixed Reality. *Sensors (Basel)*, *21*(6), 2066. doi:10.339021062066 PMID:33804253

Tromp, J. (2022). Extended Reality & The Backbone: Towards a 3D Mirrorworld. In Roadmapping Extended Reality (pp. 193-227). Academic Press.

Ukko, J., Saunila, M., Nasiri, M., Rantala, T., & Holopainen, M. (2022). Digital twins' impact on organizational control: Perspectives on formal vs social control. *Information Technology & People*, *35*(8), 253–272. doi:10.1108/ITP-09-2020-0608

Vishkaei, B. (2022). Metaverse: A New Platform for Circular Smart Cities. In P. De Giovanni (Ed.), *Cases on Circular Economy in Practice* (pp. 51–69). IGI Global. doi:10.4018/978-1-6684-5001-7.ch003

Wang, M., Yu, H., Bell, Z., & Chu, X. (2022). Constructing an Edu-Metaverse Ecosystem: A New and Innovative Framework. *IEEE Transactions on Learning Technologies*, 1–13. doi:10.1109/TLT.2022.3226345

Wang, Y., Su, Z., Zhang, N., Xing, R., Liu, D., Luan, T., & Shen, X. (2022). A Survey on Metaverse: Fundamentals, Security, and Privacy. *IEEE Communications Surveys and Tutorials*. doi:10.1109/COMST.2022.3202047

Xiong, M., & Wang, H. (2022). Digital twin applications in aviation industry: A review. *International Journal of Advanced Manufacturing Technology*, *121*(9), 5677–5692. doi:10.100700170-022-09717-9

Yang, C., Tu, X., Autiosalo, J., Ala-Laurinaho, R., Mattila, J., Salminen, P., & Tammi, K. (2022). Extended Reality Application Framework for a Digital-Twin-Based Smart Crane. *Applied Sciences (Basel, Switzerland)*, *12*(12), 6030. doi:10.3390/app12126030

Zhang, Z., Wen, F., Sun, Z., Guo, X., He, T., & Lee, C. (2022). Artificial Intelligence-Enabled Sensing Technologies in the 5G/Internet of Things Era: From Virtual Reality/Augmented Reality to the Digital Twin. *Advanced Intelligent Systems*, *4*(7), 2100228. doi:10.1002/aisy.202100228

Chapter 17
Enhanced Assistive Technology on Audio– Visual Speech Recognition for the Hearing Impaired

N. Ambika

St. Francis College, India

ABSTRACT

People who have difficulty hearing can use speech recognition software to communicate differently. The task is audio-visual speech recognition for better lip-reading comprehension. Audio speech recognition is the process of turning spoken words into text. The neural network model is trained using the Librispeech dataset. The input sound signal creates sound frames with a stride of 10 milliseconds and a window size of 20-25 milliseconds. It uses audio as the input, and feature extraction extracts information from features. A visual speech recognition system automatically recognizes spoken words by observing how the speaker moves their lips. The suggestion considers body language to understand the communicator's spoken words, increasing interpretation accuracy by 5.05%.

INTRODUCTION

Natural language processing (Chowdhary, 2022), signal processing (Orfanidis, 1995), and artificial intelligence (Ambika, 2022) all play a role in the field of speech recognition systems, which is interdisciplinary. Discourse is a ceaseless sound sign with a succession of phonemes and the critical method of human communication through hearing disabled individuals perceive words verbally expressed by perusing a lip.

The variety of hearing inside the gathering is partially settled by the sound they can see. This sound is estimated in decibels (dB), laying out a breaking point inside, which is considered a solid level of sound that doesn't surpass 85 dB during a particular timeframe. The consultation limit alludes to the

DOI: 10.4018/978-1-6684-8851-5.ch017

base power apparent by the ear. Between 40 and 70 dB of hearing loss, a language delay will affect how we communicate with the student.

One of the most intricate mechanisms of human sensation ability is found in the auditory system. The mechanical energy of sound waves is converted into electrical stimuli by the fluid-filled inner ear, which the brain will eventually translate. Physically, the internal ear is partitioned into the hearable and vestibular frameworks. The vestibular system is responsible for three-dimensional orientation and gravity perception, while the auditory system is responsible for good sensation. Hearing-impaired individuals frequently develop balance disorders due to the similarities between these two systems. A cochlea in the shape of a snail makes up the auditory system. The cochlea is a fluid-filled tube that wraps around the modiolus in a spiral. Hearing impairment (Hogan & Phillips, 2015; Cremers & Smith, 2002) was put into one of the five categories listed below.

- **Halfway Deafness, Stage 1:** The individual experiences issues figuring out discourse in a chapel, at the theater, or in a bunch discussion. However, he can hear discourse at short proximity with next to no counterfeit help.
- **Stage 2, Partial Deafness:** The individual has trouble hearing direct conversation at close range, but they can hear clearly over the phone or when speaking loudly.
- **Stage 3 of Partial Deafness:** The individual can hear amplified speech through hearing aids, trumpets, or other amplification devices, but they have trouble hearing over the phone at average intensities.
- **Complete Speech Inadequacy:** The individual acquired the hearing impairment after learning to speak the language by traditional means, but they cannot hear speech.
- **Mute Deaf:** The individual was born deaf or experienced severe deafness early enough to prevent him from learning to speak normally. Figure 1 portrays the gestures with emotion.

Figure 1. Examples of generated gestures with emotion
Source: Zabala et al. (2021)

 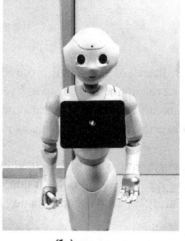 

(a) Negative   **(b)** Neutral   **(c)** Positive

A visual speech recognition system (Kumar, Renuka, Rose, & Wartana, 2022) automatically detects spoken words by following the lip movement of the speaker. People who have difficulty hearing can use this technology to communicate differently. The task is audio-visual speech recognition for better lip-reading comprehension. Audio speech recognition is the process of turning spoken words into text. The neural network model is trained using the Librispeech dataset. The input sound signal creates sound frames with a stride of 10 milliseconds and a window size of 20-25 milliseconds. It uses audio as the input, and feature extraction extracts information from features. A visual speech recognition system automatically recognizes spoken words by observing how the speaker moves their lips. This innovation gives an elective method of correspondence for individuals with hearing-disabled issues. It can use the character or word level to create the dataset. Phonemes or alphabets are used to develop the character-level dataset. The word-specific datasets at the word level are created. There are 13 VSR units, each produced by two-character models. The ASM Model is used to extract lip movement. The ASM Model looks for facial landmarks from the mean shape and moves the model to the correct landmark position. 48–68 trait points represent the mouth area. Every VSR Unit receives the extracted lip as an input. Each VSR unit's prediction probability is calculated independently.

The suggestion considers the body language to understand the spoken words by the communicator. In this work, we are considering only facial expression along with lip movement, to understand the communicator. A set of facial expressions are considered in the work. Using the set of facial expressions and hand gestures are used to create the machine learning algorithm to understand the communicator. The outcome of the communication can be interpreted 5.05% better compared to previous work.

The chapter is divided into six segments. Introduction is followed by background. Literature survey is detailed with segment three. Proposed work is detailed in section four. The analysis of work is explained in segment five. The work is concluded in sixth segment.

BACKGROUND

Non-verbal communication studies nonverbal signals like motions, looks, and eye stares. It imparts an individual's feelings and expectations. We communicate through a total of eleven different types of body language. In contrast to spoken language, body language is frequently used unconsciously and plays a significant role in our communication.

- Eye contact is one of the most common nonverbal cues to gauge someone's personality. In a professional setting, eye contact frequently indicates confidence, seriousness about one's goals, and willingness to socialize.
- People frequently attribute greater assertiveness, confidence, and intelligence to those who speak with their hands simultaneously with their words.
- Your vocal tone is verbal, but it is considered body language because it does not contain words or direct messages. Your vocal technique can see others a ton about how you're feeling or what you're thinking without you, in any event, imparting it to them.
- Touch imparts various things. Authentic touch can likewise impart love between accomplices or trouble and yearning. It is a form of nonverbal communication because the intentions you have when you physically touch someone frequently communicate words that are not spoken.

- The situating of your body is one more kind of non-verbal correspondence. Studies have shown that people often sit closer to people they care about and respect. Even people who admire or see someone as a positive influence in their lives can lean into them. Assuming you dismiss your body from somebody in photographs or will more often than not stand far from others, this could connote that you experience difficulty associating or could do without the individual.
- The most common forms of body language are head movements like nodding. These sorts of non-verbal communication are profoundly associated with correspondence and feeling.
- Anxious people may slouch more frequently, whereas self-assured and unfazed people stand straighter and have a more open posture.
- Speech-based silence is a form of nonverbal communication.
- Looks are another of our most ordinary types of non-verbal communication. Expressions on the face can convey feelings, messages, and inner thoughts.

Leap Motion and the camera are used to collect user facial expression and gesture data, giving interaction a new input dimension. This design (Han, et al., 2023) makes the combination of facial expressions and gestures, the selection of targets, the control of rehabilitation robots, and other operations possible. The development of artificial intelligence-based face detection technology provides a technical foundation for the use of facial expressions. A Lenovo PC with the Windows 10 working framework was utilized in the examinations. A second-age Jump Movement sensor was used in the tests to recognize hand developments. The Leap Motion sensor was positioned 15 centimeters from the monitor base's center. The outside camera, an ANC Center HD 1080p-Y3 webcam, gave a nonstop picture stream of the subject's face to a face following the application portrayed later. It was situated at the highest point of the screen, 8 cm from the left edge of the showcase. This distance was chosen solely to maintain the consistency of the experimental conditions and minimize deviation from other spaces. For hand interac-

Figure 2. The different stages of facial expression recognition (FER) system
Source: Samadiani et al. (2019)

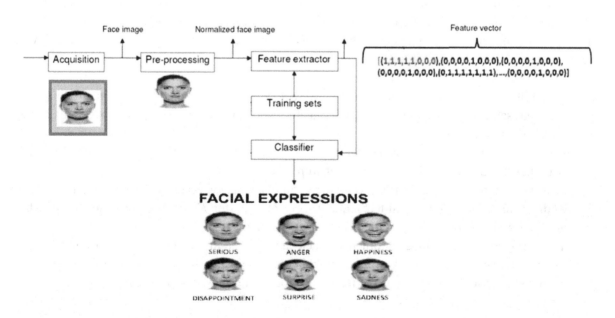

Figure 3. Hybrid target selections by "hand gestures + facial expression" for a rehabilitation robot
Source: Han et al. (2023)

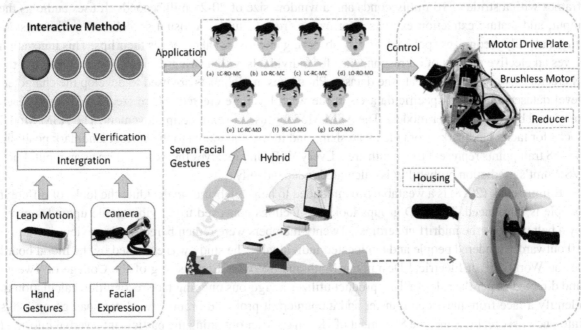

tion, software was utilized. This software provided gestural data to monitor the user's hand movements while interacting with the computer. The user repeatedly moved their hands to initiate a task. While the user was interacting with the computer, a camera was used to monitor their face. The camera observed several distinct facial features, including the opening and closing of the mouth and the eyes. The look acknowledgment framework was utilized to screen looks continuously and compare them to explicit control orders. A lower limb rehabilitation robot based on Hand Gestures + Facial Expressions was designed and developed in this study. It has two training modes: mode of active training and way of passive movement. It is mainly used for bed rehabilitation training for patients who lack muscle strength in the early stages of rehabilitation.

DRAWBACK

- The meaning of the spoken words differs based on what the speaker is trying to communicate. Hence body language can help to understand what the speaker really means.

LITERATURE SURVEY

A visual speech recognition system (Kumar, Renuka, Rose, & Wartana, 2022) automatically detects spoken words by following the lip movement of the speaker. People who have difficulty hearing can use this technology to communicate differently. The task is audio-visual speech recognition for better lip-reading comprehension. Audio speech recognition is the process of turning spoken words into text. The neural network model is trained using the Librispeech dataset. The input sound signal creates sound frames with a stride of 10 milliseconds and a window size of 20-25 milliseconds. It uses audio as the input, and feature extraction extracts information from features. A visual speech recognition system automatically recognizes spoken words by observing how the speaker moves their lips. This innovation gives an elective method of correspondence for individuals with hearing-disabled issues. It can use the character or word level to create the dataset. Phonemes or alphabets are used to develop the character-level dataset. The word-specific datasets at the word level are created. There are 13 VSR units, each produced by two-character models. The ASM Model is used to extract lip movement. The ASM Model looks for facial landmarks from the mean shape and moves the model to the correct landmark position. 48–68 trait points represent the mouth area. Every VSR Unit receives the extracted lip as an input. Each VSR unit's prediction probability is calculated independently.

Buimer et al. (2018) is a wearable SSD intended to help celebrities in deciding the looks of different people is introduced. The SSD groups look into feelings conveyed using vibrotactile upgrades given by a belt worn on the midriff underdress. Twenty members were remembered for the review, including 10 outwardly hindered people and ten located individuals. The study was endorsed by the moral board of the Workforce of Electrical Designing, Math and Software Engineering of the College of Twente and directed as per the rules of This product utilizes a vigorous ongoing face recognition calculation to identify a face from the video transfer and a counterfeit profound brain network that can group looks into one of six real feelings the Statement of Helsinki. After obtaining the participant's verbal informed consent, the study's data were only used. Participants were informed that they could withdraw anytime without a reason. There were no dropouts after informed consent was acquired. The different parts of the gadget were controlled and connected using custom programming on a Microsoft Surface Expert 4 tablet. To capture images in the direction of the gaze, users wore a baseball cap-mounted Logitech HD Pro Webcam C920. FaceReader 6TM was used to identify faces and recognize facial expressions from this live video stream. This software uses an artificial deep neural network and a robust real-time face detection algorithm to identify faces in the video stream and classify facial expressions into one of six basic emotions. A series of vibrating motors connected via Bluetooth to the tablet conveyed the user's detected facial expressions. Each tractor was linked to one of six real feelings. The one-to-one association of each tractor to emotion was purposefully chosen to make it simple for visually impaired people to learn and interpret the vibrations. On all tractors, the user was notified by two 150-millisecond pulses followed by a 50-millisecond interval. After another 200ms, the tractor related to the perceived look vibrated since the articulation held. The input was possibly given on the off chance that the look identified digressed from the nonpartisan expression. When the software stopped recognizing faces, all tractors vibrated for 300 milliseconds.

Chiesa, Galati, and Schmidt (2015) included seven mothers who were blind or severely visually impaired, as well as their firstborn children, who ranged in age from six months to three years. An announcement in the Italian Union of Blinds' circular has led to their recruitment. Seven sighted couples serving as a control group were compared to these dyads. Age and gender have been matched for the children in the two groups. Mother-kid teams participated in a similar family with the kid's dad. None of the kids regularly visited nursery school. Per the current general methodology, the perceptions occurred at the members' homes. For the first time, the moms were consulted following a semi-normalized convention of inquiries. After this meeting, moms were approached to sit before a table and to put their youngster on a high seat or a typical seat in a right-point position concerning herself. After that, she was asked to play with her child-like in everyday playtime. The play associations endured from 22 to 35 minutes. The mother's face and upper body were framed by one camera, and the child's face and upper body by the other. Before the interaction began, synchronization of the two records was achieved using a photo camera-shot flash. This flash could be seen, making it possible to precisely identify a single frame recorded simultaneously on the two video sequences.

Participation (Bess, Lichtenstein, Logan, Burger, & Nelson, 1989) was agreed upon by seven primary care internists working in six practices. Two practices were in the Nashville community, and four were based at Vanderbilt University. A sample of 50 patients over 65 from each method was referred to the Bill Wilkerson Hearing and Speech Center for a hearing evaluation. The doctors also recorded the subjects' medication regimens and chronic conditions. A standard protocol was used for pure tone audiometry.

The proposed work (Fernández-Gavira, Espada-Goya, Alcaraz-Rodríguez, & Moscoso-Sánchez, 2021) aims to provide an educational proposal for using various tools, particularly technological ones, to approach the Physical Education class with hearing-impaired students. The first person to be interviewed was a Physical Education teacher at a Primary School who had hard-of-hearing students in his style. He gave his advice on explaining to the students his primary needs when working with the group. The second individual provided information on creating adapted tools for the target population and was a Special Education teacher. Sign interpreters from the Spanish Association of Deaf People were the third and fourth people interviewed. They suggested which signs to use for the didactic resources to ensure that disabled and non-disabled people could correctly interpret them. A deaf adult member of the international deaf association with high sports expertise was interviewed, and the proposed tools were visualized.

Horikawa et al. (2013) utilized an electronic writing web crawler. It identifies articles that investigate the connection between diabetes and hearing loss prevalence. The Boolean operator was used to combine two search themes; the initial keywords were related to hearing impairment by using hearing disorder, hearing impairment, and many. Because there has only been one prospective study on this topic, it focused on cross-sectional studies. The pooled chances proportion of hearing debilitation in people with diabetes contrasted and those without diabetes was determined with an irregular impacts model utilizing the DerSimonian and Laird strategy. Two datasets were used in three studies. One included two distinct research studies, while the other two examined bilateral and unilateral hearing impairment separately. A sum of 19 datasets were remembered for this meta-investigation.

Bainbridge, Hoffman, and Cowie (2008) inferred proportions of hearing hindrance for two scopes of recurrence and two classes of seriousness. It found the median value of straight tone edge estimated at 500, 1000, and 2000 Hz for every person and ear. It averaged pure tone thresholds at 3000, 4000, 6000, and 8000 Hz for each individual and ear to generate high-frequency pure tone averages. A pure tone average more significant than 40 dB HL is defined as hearing impairment of moderate or greater severity for each frequency range, while a pure tone average more significant than 25 dB HL is defined as mild hearing impairment. The pure tone average in the worse ear, which indicates individuals with an impairment in at least one ear, was used to define hearing impairment. Among the 5140 members, the Public Community for Wellbeing Insights distinguished 24 members with around one audiometric nonresponse. It ordered these cases as weakened for a recurrence range if the audiometric nonresponse happened inside the reach. Reporting a history of loud noise at work that necessitated speaking in a loud voice to be heard was considered occupational noise exposure. Relaxation time commotion openness depended on member review of clamor from guns.

PROPOSED WORK

A visual speech recognition system (Kumar, Renuka, Rose, & Wartana, 2022) automatically detects spoken words by following the lip movement of the speaker. People who have difficulty hearing can use this technology to communicate differently. The task is audio-visual speech recognition for better lip-reading comprehension. Audio speech recognition is the process of turning spoken words into text. The neural network model is trained using the Librispeech dataset. The input sound signal creates sound frames with a stride of 10 milliseconds and a window size of 20-25 milliseconds. It uses audio as the input, and feature extraction extracts information from features. A visual speech recognition system automatically recognizes spoken words by observing how the speaker moves their lips. This innovation gives an elective method of correspondence for individuals with hearing-disabled issues. It can use the character or word level to create the dataset. Phonemes or alphabets are used to develop the character-level dataset. The word-specific datasets at the word level are created. There are 13 VSR units, each produced by two-character models. The ASM Model is used to extract lip movement. The ASM Model looks for facial landmarks from the mean shape and moves the model to the correct landmark position. 48–68 trait points represent the mouth area. Every VSR Unit receives the extracted lip as an input. Each VSR unit's prediction probability is calculated independently.

The suggestion considers the body language to understand the spoken words by the communicator. In this work, we are considering only facial expression along with lip movement, to understand the communicator.

A set of facial expressions are considered in the work. Using the set of facial expressions and hand gestures are used to create the machine learning algorithm to understand the communicator.

Table 1. Machine learning algorithm to understand the hearing impaired

Step 1 – Input 6 kinds of emotion facial expressions (F_1, F_2, F_3, F_4, F_5, F_6) and 60 hand gestures (H_1, H_2.................H_{60})
Step 2 – Create a table with facial expression mapping to hand gestures (60*6 instances), provide the outcome for the mapped values
Step 3 – Input the intake facial expression and hand gestures to evaluate the message conveyed by the communicator.
Step 4 – The outcome is communicated to the impaired

ANALYSIS OF THE WORK

A visual speech recognition system (Kumar, Renuka, Rose, & Wartana, 2022) automatically detects spoken words by following the lip movement of the speaker. People who have difficulty hearing can use this technology to communicate differently. The task is audio-visual speech recognition for better lip-reading comprehension. Audio speech recognition is the process of turning spoken words into text. The neural network model is trained using the Librispeech dataset. The input sound signal creates sound frames with a stride of 10 milliseconds and a window size of 20-25 milliseconds. It uses audio as the input, and feature extraction extracts information from features. A visual speech recognition system automatically recognizes spoken words by observing how the speaker moves their lips. This innovation gives an elective method of correspondence for individuals with hearing-disabled issues. It can use the character or word level to create the dataset. Phonemes or alphabets are used to develop the character-level dataset. The word-specific datasets at the word level are created. There are 13 VSR units, each produced by two-character models. The ASM Model is used to extract lip movement. The ASM Model looks for facial landmarks from the mean shape and moves the model to the correct landmark position. 48–68 trait points represent the mouth area. Every VSR Unit receives the extracted lip as an input. Each VSR unit's prediction probability is calculated independently.

The suggestion considers the body language to understand the spoken words by the communicator. In this work, we are considering only facial expression along with lip movement, to understand the communicator. A set of facial expressions are considered in the work. Using the set of facial expressions and hand gestures are used to create the machine learning algorithm to understand the communicator.

ACCURATE OUTCOME ANALYSIS

The outcome of the communication can be interpreted 5.05% better compared to previous work. The same is portrayed in Figure 4.

Figure 4. Comparison of interpretation of communicator

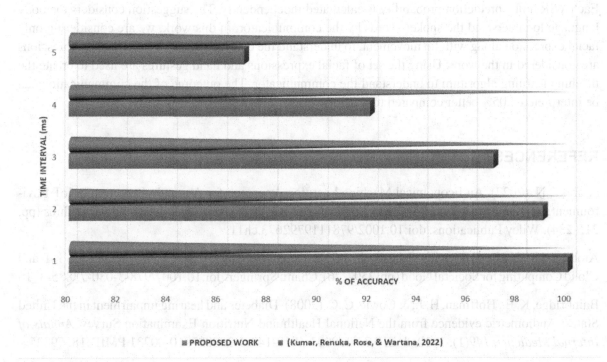

PROPOSED WORK   **(Kumar, Renuka, Rose, & Wartana, 2022)**

CONCLUSION

The sound is amplified to a level that a wearer can hear. Hearing helps can be made to fit in the ear or behind the ear, can be of various sizes, can be utilized singularly or respectively, and can contain different sign handling highlights. The equipment that makes it easier to access auditory information is known as hearing assistance technology. In the past, it was referred to as assistive listening devices. Technology for hearing aids can be used for a variety of purposes, including environmental sound detection, one-on-one and group communication with the television or telephone. It can use auditory, visual, or tactile stimuli.

A visual speech recognition system (Kumar, Renuka, Rose, & Wartana, 2022) automatically detects spoken words by following the lip movement of the speaker. People who have difficulty hearing can use this technology to communicate differently. The task is audio-visual speech recognition for better lip-reading comprehension. Audio speech recognition is the process of turning spoken words into text. The neural network model is trained using the Librispeech dataset. The input sound signal creates sound frames with a stride of 10 milliseconds and a window size of 20-25 milliseconds. It uses audio as the input, and feature extraction extracts information from features. A visual speech recognition system automatically recognizes spoken words by observing how the speaker moves their lips. This innovation gives an elective method of correspondence for individuals with hearing-disabled issues. It can use the character or word level to create the dataset. Phonemes or alphabets are used to develop the character-level dataset. The word-specific datasets at the word level are created. There are 13 VSR units, each produced by two-character models. The ASM Model is used to extract lip movement. The ASM Model looks for facial landmarks from the mean shape and moves the model to the correct landmark position. 48–68 trait points represent the mouth area. Every VSR Unit receives the extracted lip as an input. Each VSR unit's prediction probability is calculated independently. The suggestion considers the body language to understand the spoken words by the communicator. In this work, we are considering only facial expression along with lip movement, to understand the communicator. A set of facial expressions are considered in the work. Using the set of facial expressions and hand gestures are used to create the machine learning algorithm to understand the communicator. The outcome of the communication can be interpreted 5.05% better compared to previous work.

REFERENCES

Ambika, N. (2022). An Economical Machine Learning Approach for Anomaly Detection in IoT Environment. In Bioinformatics and Medical Applications: Big Data Using Deep Learning Algorithms (pp. 215-234). Wiley Publications. doi:10.1002/9781119792673.ch11

Ambika, N. (2022). Enhancing Security in IoT Instruments Using Artificial Intelligence. In IoT and Cloud Computing for Societal Good (pp. 259-276). Cham: Springer. doi:10.1007/978-3-030-73885-3_16

Bainbridge, K. E., Hoffman, H. J., & Cowie, C. C. (2008). Diabetes and hearing impairment in the United States: Audiometric evidence from the National Health and Nutrition Examination Survey. *Annals of Internal Medicine*, *149*(1), 1–10. doi:10.7326/0003-4819-149-1-200807010-00231 PMID:18559825

Bess, F. H., Lichtenstein, M. J., Logan, S. A., Burger, M. C., & Nelson, E. (1989). Hearing impairment as a determinant of function in the elderly. *Journal of the American Geriatrics Society*, *37*(2), 123–128. doi:10.1111/j.1532-5415.1989.tb05870.x PMID:2910970

Buimer, H. P., Bittner, M., Kostelijk, T., van der Geest, T. M., Nemri, A., van Wezel, R. J. A., & Zhao, Y. (2018). Conveying facial expressions to blind and visually impaired persons through a wearable vibrotactile device. *PLoS One*, *13*(3), e0194737. doi:10.1371/journal.pone.0194737 PMID:29584738

Chiesa, S., Galati, D., & Schmidt, S. (2015). Communicative interactions between visually impaired mothers and their sighted children: Analysis of gaze, facial expressions, voice and physical contacts. *Child: Care, Health and Development*, *41*(6), 1040–1046. doi:10.1111/cch.12274 PMID:26250608

Chowdhary, K. (2022). Natural language processing. In *Fundamentals of artificial intelligence* (pp. 603–649). Springer.

Cremers, C. W., & Smith, R. (2002). *Genetic hearing impairment: its clinical presentations*. Karger Medical and Scientific Publishers. doi:10.1159/isbn.978-3-318-00870-8

Fernández-Gavira, J., Espada-Goya, P., Alcaraz-Rodríguez, V., & Moscoso-Sánchez, D. (2021). Design of Educational Tools Based on Traditional Games for the Improvement of Social and Personal Skills of Primary School Students with Hearing Impairment. *Sustainability (Basel)*, *13*(22), 12644. doi:10.3390u132212644

Han, Y., Zhang, X., Zhang, N., Meng, S., Liu, T., Wang, S., Pan, M., Zhang, X., & Yi, J. (2023). Hybrid Target Selections by "Hand Gestures + Facial Expression" for a Rehabilitation Robot. *Sensors (Basel)*, *23*(1), 237. doi:10.339023010237 PMID:36616835

Hogan, A., & Phillips, R. (2015). *Hearing impairment and hearing disability: towards a paradigm change in hearing services*. Ashgate Publishing.

Horikawa, C., Kodama, S., Tanaka, S., Fujihara, K., Hirasawa, R., Yachi, Y., Shimano, H., Yamada, N., Saito, K., & Sone, H. (2013). Diabetes and risk of hearing impairment in adults: A meta-analysis. *The Journal of Clinical Endocrinology and Metabolism*, *98*(1), 51–58. doi:10.1210/jc.2012-2119 PMID:23150692

Kumar, L. A., Renuka, D. K., Rose, S. L., & Wartana, I. M. (2022). Deep learning based assistive technology on audio visual speech recognition for hearing impaired. *International Journal of Cognitive Computing in Engineering*, *3*, 24–30. doi:10.1016/j.ijcce.2022.01.003

Orfanidis, S. J. (1995). *Introduction to signal processing*. Prentice-Hall.

Samadiani, N., Huang, G., Cai, B., Luo, W., Chi, C.-H., Xiang, Y., & He, J. (2019). A Review on Automatic Facial Expression Recognition Systems Assisted by Multimodal Sensor Data. *Sensors (Basel)*, *19*(8), 1863. doi:10.339019081863 PMID:31003522

Zabala, U., Rodriguez, I., Martínez-Otzeta, J., & Lazkano, E. (2021). Expressing Robot Personality through Talking Body Language. *Applied Sciences (Basel, Switzerland)*, *11*(10), 4639. doi:10.3390/app11104639

Chapter 18
Facial Gesture Recognition for Emotion Detection:
A Review of Methods and Advancements

Bhuvnesh Kumar
Amritsar Group of Colleges, India

Rajeev Kumar Bedi
Sardar Beant Singh State University, India

Sunil kumar Gupta
Sardar Beant Singh State University, India

ABSTRACT

Facial gesture recognition (FGR) is widely regarded as an effective means of displaying and communicating human emotions. This chapter provides a comprehensive review of FGR as a biometric marker technology for detecting facial emotions, encompassing the identification of the six basic facial expressions: happiness, sadness, anger, surprise, fear, and disgust. FGR utilizes advanced algorithms to accurately identify and classify facial emotional states from images, audio, or video captured through various devices such as cameras, laptops, mobile phones, or digital signage systems. Given the importance of accuracy, computational efficiency, and mitigating overfitting, this review also discusses the diverse range of methods and models developed in facial expression recognition research. These advancements aim to enhance the accuracy of the models while minimizing computational resource requirements and addressing overfitting challenges encountered in previous studies.

INTRODUCTION

FGR is a biometric marker technology that detects human facial emotions. This technology includes a sentiment analysis tool and can identify the 6 basic facial expressions i.e., happiness, sadness, anger, surprise, fear, and disgust. FGR uses an algorithm to identify facial emotional states. This technique

DOI: 10.4018/978-1-6684-8851-5.ch018

Figure 1. Different methods/techniques and sources to detect facial expression

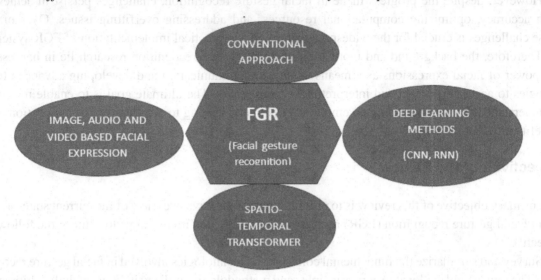

analyzes faces in images, audio, or video caught through cameras, laptops, mobile phones, or digital signage systems. Facial analysis through computer cameras includes three steps i.e., Face identification, Facial landmark detection, Facial expression, and emotion classification.

Background and Motivation

Facial gesture recognition (FGR) has gained significant attention in recent years due to its potential in understanding and analyzing human emotions. The face is a powerful means of nonverbal communication, and facial gestures serve as a crucial channel through which humans convey their emotional states. As such, developing robust technologies for recognizing and interpreting facial expressions has become a subject of extensive research.

The motivation behind studying facial gesture recognition lies in its wide-ranging applications and implications across various fields. Understanding human emotions is essential in domains such as psychology, social sciences, human-computer interaction, and affective computing. Emotion detection through facial gestures can facilitate more effective communication, improve user experience, and enable advanced human-centered technologies.

Moreover, facial gesture recognition has the potential to revolutionize areas like healthcare, where it can assist in pain assessment, mental health diagnosis, and monitoring patients with neurological disorders. Additionally, in the entertainment and gaming industries, FGR can enhance virtual reality experiences by allowing systems to respond dynamically to users' emotional states.

The development of accurate and efficient facial gesture recognition methods is also driven by the need for improved human-computer interaction. By enabling machines to understand and respond to human emotions, it is possible to create more intuitive and empathetic interfaces. This can enhance user satisfaction, engagement, and overall system performance.

However, despite the progress made in facial gesture recognition, challenges persist in achieving high accuracy, optimizing computational resources, and addressing overfitting issues. Overcoming these challenges is crucial for the widespread adoption and practical implementation of FGR systems.

Therefore, the background and motivation of facial gesture recognition research lie in harnessing the power of facial expressions as a means of human communication and developing advanced technologies to accurately detect and interpret these expressions. The ultimate goal is to enable machines to understand and respond to human emotions effectively, leading to a wide array of applications and benefits in various domains.

Objectives of the Review

The primary objective of this review is to provide a comprehensive overview of the current state-of-the-art in facial gesture recognition (FGR) research. Specifically, the review aims to achieve the following objectives:

Survey and summarize the fundamental concepts and technologies involved in facial gesture recognition: The review will explore the core principles and methodologies utilized in FGR, including biometric marker technology, sentiment analysis, and emotion classification. It will provide a detailed understanding of the underlying mechanisms and techniques employed in FGR systems.

Analyze the three-step process of facial analysis through computer cameras: The review will delve into the intricacies of the face identification, facial landmark detection, and facial expression/emotion classification. It will discuss the algorithms and approaches used in each step, highlighting their significance in achieving accurate results.

Investigate the wide-ranging applications of facial gesture recognition beyond emotion detection: The review will explore the diverse fields and industries where FGR has potential applications. This includes assessing emotions, understanding intentions, analyzing social relationships, and assessing health conditions through facial expressions. The objective is to showcase the breadth of possibilities and practical implications of FGR.

Evaluate different methods and models developed for Facial Expression Recognition: The review will examine the various methodologies and models proposed in FGR research to enhance accuracy, reduce computational resources, and address overfitting issues. It will provide an analysis of the strengths and limitations of each approach, aiming to identify the most promising directions for future research.

Identify challenges and propose future directions: The review will discuss the existing challenges in FGR, such as improving accuracy, optimizing computational resources, and mitigating overfitting problems. It will outline potential strategies and future research directions to address these challenges and further enhance the effectiveness and efficiency of FGR systems.

By accomplishing these objectives, the review seeks to contribute to the advancement of facial gesture recognition research by providing researchers and practitioners with a comprehensive understanding of the field's current state, challenges, and future directions.

FACIAL GESTURE RECOGNITION: FUNDAMENTALS AND TECHNOLOGY OVERVIEW

Biometric marker technology refers to a field of study that focuses on utilizing unique biological characteristics or behavioral patterns for identification and recognition purposes. In the context of facial gesture recognition (FGR), biometric markers specifically pertain to the distinct facial features and movements that can be used to identify and classify human emotions.

This technology involves capturing and analyzing various facial cues, such as muscle movements, wrinkles, and the positioning of facial landmarks, to detect and interpret emotional states. It utilizes advanced algorithms and machine learning techniques to analyze and match these biometric markers with predefined patterns associated with different emotions.

The underlying principle of biometric marker technology in FGR is to leverage the individuality and consistency of facial expressions as a reliable means of identifying and understanding human emotions. By examining the unique configuration of facial features and the dynamic changes occurring during different emotional states, it becomes possible to classify and recognize specific emotions accurately.

Research in biometric marker technology for FGR aims to develop robust and efficient algorithms that can effectively capture and process facial cues in real time. These algorithms need to handle variations in lighting conditions, facial poses, and individual differences while ensuring high accuracy in emotion classification.

The study of biometric marker technology in FGR involves exploring and refining methodologies for feature extraction, feature matching, and classification algorithms. This includes investigating techniques such as deep learning architectures, statistical modelling, and pattern recognition methods to enhance the precision and reliability of emotion recognition systems.

By understanding and harnessing the potential of biometric markers in FGR, researchers can advance the development of sophisticated technologies that enable machines to effectively perceive and respond to human emotions. This has implications across various domains, including human-computer interaction, healthcare, psychology, and entertainment, where accurate emotion detection is crucial for improved user experiences and tailored services (Malhotra et al., 2012).

Sentiment Analysis in Facial Gesture Recognition

Sentiment analysis in facial gesture recognition refers to the process of analyzing and interpreting the emotional or affective states expressed through facial gestures. It involves detecting and classifying the underlying sentiment or emotional responses displayed by individuals based on their facial expressions. This area of research aims to develop computational models and algorithms that can accurately recognize and interpret the emotional cues conveyed through facial gestures.

In the context of sentiment analysis, facial gesture recognition techniques are employed to detect and classify a range of emotions such as happiness, sadness, anger, surprise, fear, disgust, and more. The goal is to extract meaningful information from facial expressions and use it to infer the sentiment or emotional state of individuals.

Research in sentiment analysis using facial gesture recognition encompasses several key aspects. Firstly, it involves the development of robust algorithms and models for detecting and tracking facial features and landmarks that are indicative of different emotional expressions. This may involve techniques such as facial landmark detection, facial action unit analysis, or deep learning-based approaches to accurately capture and represent facial gestures.

Secondly, researchers focus on feature extraction and representation methods that capture the relevant information from facial gestures for sentiment analysis. This includes extracting expressive features from facial images or videos, such as facial muscle movements, the intensity of expressions, or spatial-temporal patterns, which can provide discriminative cues for different emotional states.

Thirdly, classification and prediction models are developed to classify facial gestures into specific sentiment categories. Machine learning algorithms, such as support vector machines (SVM), convolutional neural networks (CNN), or recurrent neural networks (RNN), are commonly employed to train and build models that can accurately recognize and classify emotional expressions based on the extracted features.

Furthermore, researchers explore the integration of contextual information and multimodal data sources to enhance the accuracy and robustness of sentiment analysis. This involves considering additional cues such as audio signals, text-based information, or physiological data to improve the understanding of emotions and sentiments conveyed through facial gestures.

The ultimate objective of sentiment analysis in facial gesture recognition research is to enable machines to effectively interpret and understand human emotions based on their facial expressions. This has implications in various domains, including social robotics, human-computer interaction, affective computing, and customer experience analysis, where the ability to perceive and respond to human emotions is crucial for effective interaction and decision-making.

Overall, sentiment analysis in facial gesture recognition is a multidisciplinary research area that combines computer vision, machine learning, and affective computing techniques to recognize and interpret emotions expressed through facial gestures accurately. The advancements in this field have the potential to contribute to the development of more emotionally intelligent and responsive systems in various applications and domains.

Emotion classification in the context of facial expressions refers to the task of accurately categorizing human emotions based on the analysis of facial gestures. The six basic facial expressions commonly recognized and studied in emotion classification are happiness, sadness, anger, surprise, fear, and disgust. Researchers in this field aim to develop robust computational models and algorithms that can effectively identify and classify these basic emotions based on facial cues (Devendra Kumar et al., 2017a).

Emotion Classification and the Six Basic Facial Expressions

To perform emotion classification, several steps are typically involved. Firstly, facial data, such as images or videos, are collected from individuals displaying different emotional expressions. These datasets serve as the foundation for training and evaluating emotion classification models. They often include annotated labels indicating the specific emotion expressed in each sample.

Next, feature extraction techniques are applied to capture relevant information from facial gestures. These techniques aim to represent the distinctive characteristics of different emotions, such as the shape and movement of facial muscles, intensity of expressions, or spatial-temporal patterns. Feature extraction methods can range from simple geometric measurements to more sophisticated approaches based on deep learning or statistical analysis.

Once the features are extracted, classification algorithms are employed to classify facial expressions into the six basic emotion categories. Machine learning techniques, including support vector machines (SVM), convolutional neural networks (CNN), or ensemble methods, are commonly utilized for this purpose. These algorithms learn from the extracted features and the corresponding labelled data to build models that can accurately classify new facial expressions into the appropriate emotion category.

To enhance the accuracy of emotion classification, researchers often explore the integration of multiple modalities or contextual information. This may include incorporating audio signals, textual data, physiological responses, or contextual cues to improve the understanding and discrimination of emotions expressed through facial gestures.

Evaluation and benchmarking are crucial in emotion classification research. Various performance metrics, such as accuracy, precision, recall, and F1 score, are used to assess the performance of classification models. Cross-validation techniques, holdout validation, or comparison against existing benchmark datasets are employed to evaluate the generalization capability and effectiveness of the proposed models.

The study of emotion classification and the six basic facial expressions has significant implications in fields such as affective computing, human-computer interaction, psychology, and social robotics. Understanding and accurately recognizing human emotions based on facial expressions can enable the development of more empathetic and responsive systems, leading to improved user experiences, personalized interactions, and applications in areas such as mental health, customer sentiment analysis, or social interaction analysis.

In summary, emotion classification in the context of facial expressions involves developing computational models and algorithms that can accurately categorize human emotions into six basic categories based on facial cues. It encompasses steps such as data collection, feature extraction, classification algorithms, and evaluation, aiming to enhance our understanding of emotional expressions and their practical applications in various domains (Revina, I. M. 2018).

FACIAL ANALYSIS THROUGH COMPUTER CAMERAS: THREE-STEP PROCESS

Facial analysis through computer cameras involves a three-step process that aims to accurately detect and interpret facial expressions and emotions. This process comprises face identification, facial landmark detection, and facial expression/emotion classification. In the context of research language, let's delve into each step in more detail:

Face Identification

Face identification is the initial step of the process, which involves locating and identifying faces within an image or video stream captured by computer cameras. This step focuses on detecting and isolating facial regions from the background or other objects present in the visual data. Various algorithms, such as Haar cascades or convolutional neural networks (CNNs), are employed to perform face detection tasks effectively. The objective is to identify the presence and location of faces accurately, enabling subsequent analysis.

Facial Landmark Detection

Once faces are identified, the next step is to detect and locate specific facial landmarks or key points, such as the eyes, eyebrows, nose, mouth, and chin. Facial landmark detection aims to precisely determine the spatial coordinates of these landmarks, allowing for a detailed analysis of facial expressions. This step often involves using shape models, active appearance models (AAMs), or deep learning techniques, such as facial landmark localization CNNs. By accurately identifying the facial landmarks, the subsequent analysis can derive rich information about the shape and configuration of the face.

Facial Expression and Emotion Classification

The final step involves analyzing the detected facial landmarks to classify facial expressions and emotions accurately. This step utilizes machine learning algorithms, such as support vector machines (SVM), random forests, or deep neural networks, to map the identified facial features to predefined emotional categories. By training these models on labelled datasets containing facial expressions and corresponding emotions, they can learn patterns and discriminative features indicative of specific emotional states. Common emotional categories include happiness, sadness, anger, surprise, fear, and disgust. The output of this step provides the classification or prediction of the dominant emotion expressed by the individual.

The three-step process of facial analysis through computer cameras is integral to accurately capturing and interpreting facial expressions and emotions. It involves detecting faces, locating facial landmarks, and classifying emotions based on the identified features. This process forms the foundation for various applications, including affective computing, human-computer interaction, and emotion-driven technologies. Researchers continuously explore and refine algorithms and techniques to improve the accuracy, efficiency, and robustness of each step in this process (Institute of Electrical and Electronics Engineers. Madras Section & Institute of Electrical and Electronics Engineers, n.d.-a).

FACIAL GESTURE RECOGNITION APPLICATION

Beyond emotion detection, facial gesture recognition has numerous applications in various fields. This section discusses the diverse range of applications where facial gesture recognition technology finds utility:

Human-Computer Interaction: Facial gesture recognition enables natural and intuitive interactions between humans and computers. It can be employed in touchless interfaces, where users can control devices and applications using facial gestures, eliminating the need for physical touch or input devices. This technology can enhance user experience and facilitate more seamless interactions in areas such as gaming, virtual reality, and augmented reality.

Assistive Technologies: Facial gesture recognition has significant potential in assistive technologies for individuals with physical disabilities. By recognizing specific facial gestures, such as eyebrow movements or facial muscle activations, these technologies can enable people to control assistive devices, communicate, or access information more effectively. This application has promising implications for individuals with limited mobility or speech impairments.

Healthcare and Biometrics: Facial gesture recognition can be utilized in healthcare for various purposes. It can aid in monitoring and assessing patients' health conditions by analyzing facial expressions associated with pain, discomfort, or other symptoms. Facial gestures can also be used as biometric markers for identification and authentication, providing secure access to medical records and ensuring patient privacy.

Driver Monitoring and Automotive Safety: Facial gesture recognition technology can enhance driver monitoring systems in vehicles. By analyzing facial gestures and expressions, it can detect driver drowsiness, distraction, or other risky behaviors. This enables proactive interventions, such as alerting the driver or triggering safety mechanisms, to prevent accidents and improve overall road safety.

Market Research and Advertising: Facial gesture recognition has applications in market research and advertising. By analyzing consumers' facial expressions, advertisers can gauge emotional responses to advertisements, products, or experiences. This information helps in optimizing marketing strategies and tailoring content to elicit desired emotional reactions.

Security and Surveillance: Facial gesture recognition can strengthen security and surveillance systems. By detecting specific facial gestures or suspicious behaviors, it can assist in identifying potential threats or suspicious activities in public spaces, airports, or critical infrastructure areas. This technology contributes to enhanced public safety and threat prevention.

Education and Learning: Facial gesture recognition can play a role in educational settings. It can facilitate adaptive learning systems by assessing students' engagement, attentiveness, and emotional states during learning activities. This information can be used to personalize instruction, provide targeted feedback, and create interactive learning experiences.

Overall, facial gesture recognition extends beyond emotion detection and offers a wide range of applications across industries. Its potential to enhance human-computer interaction, assistive technologies, healthcare, automotive safety, market research, security, education, and more makes it a valuable technology with significant research and development opportunities (Rajan et al., 2019).

METHODS AND MODELS FOR FACIAL EXPRESSION RECOGNITION

In the field of Facial Expression Recognition (FER), numerous methods and models have been developed to improve the accuracy and effectiveness of emotion detection. These techniques aim to enhance the understanding and interpretation of facial gestures, enabling the recognition of various emotional states. This section provides an overview of the different methodologies and models employed in FER research.

Methods for FER encompass a range of approaches, including traditional techniques and advanced deep learning methods. Traditional methods often involve preprocessing steps such as region of interest (ROI) segmentation, which focuses on specific facial areas for analysis. Feature extraction techniques such as Gabor Filter (GF) have been utilized to extract discriminative features from facial images. These extracted features are then fed into classifiers, such as Support Vector Machines (SVM), for emotion classification (Revina & Emmanuel, 2021).

Deep learning methods, particularly Convolutional Neural Networks (CNN), have gained significant attention in recent research. CNN-based approaches leverage the power of deep learning to automatically learn and extract complex features from facial images. Additionally, combining CNN with Long Short-Term Memory (LSTM) models has shown promising results in capturing spatial-temporal information for FER (Mellouk & Handouzi, 2020).

Researchers have extensively evaluated these methods using various datasets, including CK+, JAFFE, MMI, AFEW, and FERG, among others. Comparative analyses have been conducted to assess the performance of different methods, with accuracy rates being a commonly used metric for evaluation.

Moreover, attention mechanisms have been employed to selectively focus on informative facial regions and capture emotion-related features effectively. These attention-based models have shown superior performance in emotion recognition tasks.

In addition to the aforementioned methods, researchers have explored the integration of AI and ML techniques for emotion and depression detection. Techniques such as Naïve Bayes, SVM, LSTM, RNN, LR, LSV, and ANN have been utilized for feature extraction and classification. These techniques have been assessed using evaluation metrics such as precision, accuracy, and recall determining their effectiveness in emotion detection and depression diagnosis (Joshi & Kanoongo, 2022).

The literature review highlights the significance of these methods and models in advancing FER research. The findings from these studies offer valuable insights into the strengths and limitations of different approaches, aiding researchers in selecting suitable techniques and guiding future improvements in FER.

CHALLENGES AND FUTURE DIRECTIONS OF FACIAL EXPRESSION RECOGNITION (FER)

While significant progress has been made in Facial Expression Recognition (FER) research, several challenges persist that warrant attention and further investigation. Understanding these challenges and charting future directions will contribute to the development of more accurate and robust FER systems. This section discusses the challenges faced in FER and outlines potential future directions for research.

Subjectivity and Inter-Subject Variability: One of the primary challenges in FER is the subjective nature of emotions and the variability in facial expressions across individuals. Emotions can be influenced by cultural, individual, and contextual factors, making it challenging to establish universal patterns. Future research should focus on developing techniques that can adapt to inter-subject variability and incorporate personalized models to improve emotion recognition accuracy.

Occlusion and Partial Facial Expressions: Facial occlusions, such as the presence of accessories or facial hair, can hinder accurate emotion recognition. Additionally, capturing only partial facial expressions due to head movements or camera angles further complicates the analysis. Future research should explore techniques that can handle occlusion and partial expressions, such as leveraging contextual information or utilizing multi-modal data fusion.

Real-World Scenarios and Dynamic Expressions: FER systems often struggle with recognizing emotions in real-world scenarios, where environmental factors, lighting conditions, and dynamic facial expressions pose challenges. Future research should focus on developing models that can handle dynamic expressions and adapt to varying environmental conditions. Techniques such as temporal modeling and attention mechanisms can be explored to improve the recognition of real-time and dynamic emotions.

Data Collection and Annotation: The availability of large-scale, diverse, and well-annotated datasets is crucial for training and evaluating FER models. However, collecting and annotating such datasets is a time-consuming and labour-intensive process. Future research should aim to create standardized benchmarks and datasets that encompass a wide range of emotions, demographics, and cultural contexts, enabling more comprehensive evaluation and comparison of FER techniques.

Ethical and Privacy Concerns: As FER systems become more prevalent in various applications, ethical considerations, and privacy concerns arise. Ensuring user consent, data privacy, and avoiding algorithmic biases are critical areas for future research. Developments in Explainable AI (XAI) can contribute to making FER systems more transparent and interpretable, addressing ethical concerns, and building user trust.

Multi-Modal Fusion and Contextual Information: Integrating multiple modalities, such as facial expressions, speech, and physiological signals, can enhance the accuracy and robustness of FER systems. Future research should focus on developing multi-modal fusion techniques that effectively combine and leverage complementary information from different modalities. Additionally, incorporating contextual information, such as social cues, environmental context, and temporal dynamics, can further improve the understanding and interpretation of facial expressions.

Real-Time and Resource-Efficient FER: Deploying FER systems in real-time applications, such as video surveillance or human-computer interaction, requires low latency and resource-efficient algorithms. Future research should explore techniques that optimize computational efficiency, model size, and power consumption while maintaining high accuracy. This includes exploring lightweight models, hardware acceleration, and edge computing approaches.

In conclusion, addressing the aforementioned challenges and exploring the suggested future directions will advance the field of Facial Expression Recognition. The development of more robust, adaptive, and culturally sensitive FER systems has the potential to revolutionize various domains, including healthcare, human-computer interaction, virtual reality, and affective computing, enabling applications that can better understand and respond to human emotions.

MODEL ACCURACY ENHANCEMENT IN FACIAL EXPRESSION RECOGNITION (FER)

Achieving high accuracy in Facial Expression Recognition (FER) is a critical objective in research and development. Improving the accuracy of FER models contributes to their effectiveness and reliability in various real-world applications. This section discusses the techniques and strategies employed to enhance the accuracy of FER models.

Pre-processing Techniques: Pre-processing plays a crucial role in FER accuracy enhancement. Techniques such as face normalization, facial landmark detection, and image enhancement can improve the quality and consistency of facial images. Pre-processing also includes face alignment, pose normalization, and illumination normalization to mitigate variations caused by head orientation and lighting conditions. Exploring advanced pre-processing techniques and their impact on FER accuracy is a promising research direction.

Feature Extraction: Extracting discriminative and representative features from facial images is vital for accurate FER. Traditional approaches like Local Binary Patterns (LBP), Histogram of Oriented Gradients (HOG), and Gabor Filters have been widely used for feature extraction. However, with the advent of deep learning, Convolutional Neural Networks (CNN) have shown remarkable performance in capturing high-level facial features. Research efforts should focus on designing novel feature extraction methods, exploring transfer learning techniques, and investigating feature fusion strategies to enhance FER accuracy (Sadeghi & Raie, 2022a).

Classifier Selection and Optimization: The choice of an appropriate classifier greatly impacts FER accuracy. Various classifiers, including Support Vector Machines (SVM), k-Nearest Neighbors (KNN), Random Forests, and Deep Neural Networks, have been employed in FER. Fine-tuning and optimizing classifier parameters can significantly improve accuracy. Additionally, ensemble techniques that combine multiple classifiers can enhance the robustness and generalization capabilities of FER models. Research should investigate novel classifier architectures, explore ensemble methods, and optimize hyperparameters to maximize FER accuracy.

Dataset Augmentation and Balancing: The availability of diverse and well-balanced datasets is crucial for training accurate FER models. However, in many cases, datasets may suffer from class imbalance, limited samples, or lack of diversity. Dataset augmentation techniques, such as image rotation, scaling, and data synthesis, can expand the training set and alleviate these issues. Moreover, addressing dataset biases and ensuring representation across different demographic groups can lead to more accurate and fair FER models.

Transfer Learning and Fine-tuning: Transfer learning, leveraging pre-trained models from related tasks or domains, has demonstrated its effectiveness in improving FER accuracy. By utilizing pre-trained deep learning models, FER models can leverage the learned representations and adapt them to specific facial expression recognition tasks. Fine-tuning techniques can further refine the pre-trained models on target FER datasets to enhance their accuracy and performance.

Model Ensemble and Fusion: Combining multiple FER models or predictions from different modalities can lead to improved accuracy. Ensemble techniques, such as majority voting, stacking, or boosting, can effectively leverage the diversity of individual models and enhance overall performance. Furthermore, fusing information from multiple modalities, such as facial images, audio, and physiological signals, can provide richer and more reliable cues for accurate emotion recognition.

Addressing Overfitting and Generalization: Overfitting is a common challenge in FER, where models tend to perform well on training data but fail to generalize to unseen samples. Regularization techniques, such as dropout, weight decay, and early stopping, can mitigate overfitting and improve generalization. Additionally, incorporating techniques like cross-validation, data splitting, and model validation on diverse datasets can assess the generalization capabilities of FER models.

In conclusion, enhancing the accuracy of FER models requires a comprehensive approach involving pre-processing techniques, feature extraction methods, classifier selection and optimization, dataset augmentation, transfer learning, and ensemble strategies. Future research should continue to explore innovatively.

TOOLS FOR FACIAL RECOGNITION

Facial recognition software (FRS) is an essential tool in facial recognition research and applications. It consists of detection, analysis, and recognition components for matching faces in images against a database of identities. In this section, we discuss several available tools commonly used for facial recognition:

DeepVision AI: DeepVision AI offers FRS solutions for marketing, security, and business planning. It utilizes facial verification to gather data on age, gender, and ethnicity, helping businesses personalize ads and target specific customers. It provides facial recognition and verification capabilities for security purposes.

Face++: Face++ offers a range of technology solutions, including face detection, comparison, search, and facial landmark information. It also provides human body recognition, image beautification, and image detection functionalities. Face++ offers SDKs and APIs to leverage these technologies and provides custom cloud services for facial recognition applications.

FaceFirst: FaceFirst focuses on using DigitalID to replace traditional identification methods. It offers FRS-based solutions for authentication, access control, ID verification, age verification, customer engagement, safety, and business insights. FaceFirst provides real-time alerting for identity spoofing attempts and enables personalized ads and loyalty programs.

Kairos: Kairos provides FRS-based web services and an SDK for businesses to integrate facial detection, identification, verification, and demographic data tracking into their applications. It offers auto-tagging features for efficient search and indexing of images and videos.

SenseTime: SenseTime offers face and body analyzing technology alongside its facial recognition services. Its solutions provide high accuracy and encompass face detection, facial feature point positioning, facial attributes recognition, liveness detection for anti-spoofing measures, and body feature point analysis.

Sky Biometry: Sky Biometry is a web service provider offering facial recognition services, including face detection, attribute determination, and facial recognition capabilities. It enables developers to integrate these functionalities into their applications.

Trueface.ai: Trueface.ai offers FRS solutions through SDKs, deployable containers, and plug-and-play software. Its services include facial recognition, weapon detection, space analytics, and live verification to prevent spoofing attempts.

These tools provide researchers with a range of capabilities to develop and evaluate facial recognition models. They offer various functionalities such as face detection, comparison, search, attribute determination, and verification. By utilizing these tools, researchers can enhance their FER studies and develop more accurate and efficient facial recognition systems.

COMPARATIVE STUDY OF TECHNIQUES

Comparison of Techniques for Face Expression Recognition (Revina & Emmanuel, 2018):

Revina and Emmanuel conducted a comprehensive study comparing various techniques for Face Expression Recognition (FER). They evaluated methods such as ROI segmentation, Gabor Filter (GF) for feature extraction, and Support Vector Machine (SVM) as a classifier. Their results showed that ROI segmentation achieved the highest accuracy of 99% for pre-processing, GF yielded a range of 82.5% to 99% for feature extraction, and SVM achieved the best result with 99% accuracy for classification. This study provides insights into the performance of different techniques and aids researchers in selecting the most effective approach for FER.

Strategies and Techniques for FER (Rajan et al., 2019):

Rajan et al. explored strategies and techniques for FER, focusing on addressing challenges related to subjectivity, illumination, occlusion, and pose variation. They identified LBP and PCA as effective methods for handling subjectivity issues, while PPBTF and LK-flow were suitable for independent subjects. For illumination challenges, LBP was found to be effective, and HSMM (hidden semi-Markov models) provided a solution for occlusion issues. Pose variation was addressed using the 3D method. This research offers insights into overcoming common challenges in FER and proposes suitable solutions for each issue.

Frame Attention Network for FER in Videos (Meng et al., 2019):

Meng et al. introduced a novel approach called Frame Attention Network (FAN) for FER in videos. The proposed method incorporates a feature embedding module based on deep learning and a frame attention module for learning attention weights. The results demonstrated that the FAN model outperformed other CNN methods, achieving an accuracy of 51.18% on the AFEW dataset and 99.69% on the CK+ dataset. This research contributes to the development of efficient FER techniques specifically designed for video data.

Survey of CNN as a Deep Learning Approach for FER (Kshitiza Vasudeva & Saravanan Chandran, 2020):

Kshitiza Vasudeva and Saravanan Chandran conducted a survey on using Convolutional Neural Networks (CNN) as a deep learning approach for FER. They highlighted the advantages of CNN over conventional approaches, emphasizing that CNN eliminates the need for manual processing. The survey discussed the three layers of CNN: convolutional, pooling, and fully connected layers. They referenced Li et al., who achieved 98.2% accuracy using the CK+ dataset with CNN. This survey provides an overview of the capabilities and applications of CNN in FER research.

Deep Learning Techniques for Spatial-Temporal Feature Extraction in FER (Mellouk & Handouzi, 2020):

Mellouk and Handouzi proposed a combination of Convolutional Neural Network (CNN) and Long Short-Term Memory (LSTM) for spatial-temporal feature extraction in FER. They compared different deep learning methods and datasets, highlighting Yu et al.'s achievement of over 99% accuracy on CK+ and MMI datasets using CNN and CNN-LSTM models. This research evaluates and compares the performance of deep learning techniques for FER and suggests avenues for further improvements.

Attention Convolutional Network for FER (Minaee et al., 2021):

Minaee et al. focused on an attentional Convolutional Network (CN) for FER, which concentrated on different facial regions to detect various emotions. Their approach achieved impressive results with datasets such as FER-2013 (70.02% accuracy), CK+ (99.3% accuracy), FERG (92.8% accuracy), and JAFFE (98% accuracy). This research highlights the effectiveness of attention mechanisms in FER and their ability to capture emotion-related information from specific facial regions.

AI and ML Techniques for Emotion and Depression Detection (Joshi & Kanoongo, 2022):

Joshi and Kanoongo conducted a survey on various AI and ML techniques used for emotion and depression detection. They explored techniques such as Naïve Bayes, SVM, LSTM, RNN, LR, LSV, and ANN for feature extraction and classification. The study found Naïve Bayes to have the best performance with an accuracy of 1%. The paper offers insights into the application of AI and ML in emotion and depression detection, providing researchers with an overview of suitable techniques.

Clip-Aware Emotion-Rich Feature Learning Network for FER (Liu et al., 2022):

Liu et al. proposed the Clip-aware Emotion-rich feature learning network (CEFLNet) for FER, which focuses on recognizing emotional intensity in each clip of a video. They evaluated the CEFLNet model using datasets such as BU-3DFE, MMI, AFEW, and DFEW, achieving accuracy results of 91.00% (MMI), 53.98% (AFEW), and 65.35% (DFEW). This research introduces an effective model for capturing emotion-related features in video clips and provides comparative results with different datasets.

Spatio-Temporal Transformer for Dynamic FER (Ma et al., 2022):

Ma et al. proposed the Spatio-Temporal Transformer model for dynamic FER in real-world scenarios. This model leverages sequence modeling to address challenges related to dynamic FER. The proposed model achieved improved results with VAR (49.11%) and WAR (54.23%) metrics compared to other methods on the AFEW dataset. This research contributes to the advancement of FER techniques for handling real-world scenarios.

This literature review provides an overview of various studies in the field of Facial Expression Recognition (FER), covering different techniques, methodologies, and models employed for accurate emotion detection and analysis. The studies encompass a range of approaches, including traditional techniques,

Table 1. Accuracy comparison

Sr. no.	Methods	Accuracy (%)
1	ROI	99%
2	LBP	98.95%
3	FAN	99.69%
4	CNN attention	98.2%
5	STC-NLSTM	99.8%
6	FER Attentional CN	99.3%
7	New CNN	95.33%
8	Naïve Bayes	63%
9	CEFLNet	91.00%
10	STT	54.23%

Figure 2. Accuracy comparison chart

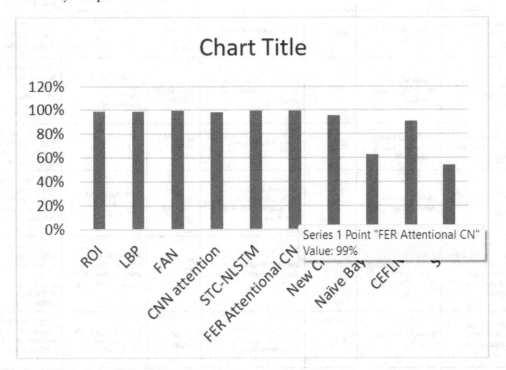

deep learning methods, attention mechanisms, and the integration of spatial-temporal features. The findings and insights from these research papers offer valuable guidance for researchers and practitioners in developing robust FER systems with improved accuracy and performance.

Table 2. Study of FER's various methods to detect and analyse emotions

	Title of the Paper	Author's Name	Year of Publishing Paper	Objective	Dataset Used	Techniques used	Results
1	A survey on human facial expression recognition techniques	Micael Revina, and W.R. Sam Emmanuel	2018	Compare FER techniques based on no. of expressions recognized and the complexity of algorithms.	JAFFE, CK	ROI, GF, SVM, CNN, HOG, SDM, DCI, KNN, LVQ, HMM etc.	ROI: for segmentation 99% GF: 82.5 to 99% SVM: 99%
2	Facial expression recognition technique: a comprehensive survey	Saranya Rajan, Poongodi, Chenniappan, Somasundaram Devraj, Nirmala Madian	2019, May	Understand the strategies and innovative methods that address the issues in a real-time application	JAFFE, CK, CK+, SFEW, MUG, MMI	ROI, GF, SVM, CNN, HOG, LBP, PCA, HSMM, PPBTF, LK, SDM, DCI, KNN, LVQ, HMM, etc.	LBP: 98.95%
3	Frame attention networks for facial expression recognition in videos.	Debin Meng, Xiaojiang Peng, Kai Wang, Yu Qiao	2019	FAN (Frame Attention Network) for Facial Expression Recognition in videos. This method automatically highlights the inequitable frames in an end-to-end framework.	CK+, AFEW	CNN-RNN, LSTM, HOLONET, DSN-VGG	FAN: accuracy with AFEW 51.18 Accuracy with CK+ 99.69
4	A comprehensive study on FER techniques using convolutional neural network	Kshitiza Vasudeva, Saravanan Chandran	2020, July	CNN as a Deep learning approach	MMI, JAFFE, CK+, CE, SFEW	CNN, LSTM, DTAGN, DTAN, DTGN	CNN+ attention-based layer regularized center loss resolved the overfitting issue with an accuracy of 98.2% using the CK+ dataset.
5	Facial emotion recognition using deep learning	Wafa Mellouk, Wahida Handouzi	2020	Deep learning CNN and CNN-LSTM	Multipie, MMI, CK+, JAFFE, SFEW	CNN, CNN-LSTM, SBN-CNN, STC-NLSTM, DCBiLSTM, ACNN	STC-NLSTM gives better result with CK+, MMI are 99.8%, 93.45%, 84.53%.
6	Deep emotion: FER using attentional CN	Shervin Minau, Mehdi Minau, Amirali Abdolrashidi	2021	Deep learning based on attentional Convolutional network	FER-2013, CK+, FERG, JAFFER	VGG+SVM, GoogleNet, LBP+ORB, CNN+SVM	The proposed method gives better results 70.02% with the FER-2013 dataset, 99.3% with the CK+, 92.8 with the FERG, and 98% with the JAFFE dataset.
7	A compact deep learning model for robust FER	Chieh-Ming Kuo, Shang-Hong Lai, Michel Sarbis	2022	New CNN architecture for FER	CK+, RAF, TFEID, GENKI	VGG+mSVM, DLP-CNN+ mSVM, AlexNet+ mSVM	The proposed model shows better results 95.33+-0.34 accuracy percent with the GENKI dataset
8	Depression detection using emotional AI and ML	Manju Lata Joshi, Nehal Kanoongo	2022	Survey of different AI and ML techniques to detect and analyze emotions and depression	Facebook, tweet, chatterbot corpus	Naïve Bayes, SVM, LSTM, RNN, LR, LSV, ANN	Naïve Bayes gives better results with 1% accuracy calculated using a confusion matrix and parameters like precision, accuracy, and recall.
9	Clip-aware expressive feature learning for video-based facial expression recognition	Yuanyuan Liu, Chuanxu Feng, Xiaohui Yuan, Lin Zhou, Wenbin Wang, Jie Qin, Zhongwen Luo	2022	Identifies the emotional intensity in each clip in a video	BU-3DFE, MMI, AFEW, DFEW	FAN, C3D, VGG16, CEFLNet, HoloNet, DSN, SAANet, DGCN, LSTM, AUDN, CER, VGG11	The proposed model CEFLNet gives a better result accuracy percentage of 91.00% with the MMI dataset, 53.98 with the AFEW, and 65.35 with the DFEW dataset
10	Spatio-temporal Transformer for dynamic FER in the wild	Fuyan Ma, Bin Sun, Shutao Li	2022	To handle DEFR with real-world scenario issues by sequence modeling	DFEW, AFEW	C3D, VGG11, LSTM EC-STFL, Former-DFER, STT	The proposed method STT gives better results using metrics VAR 49.11% and WAR 54.23% on the AFEW dataset.

CONCLUSION

In conclusion, this paper provided a comprehensive review of the techniques employed in facial expression recognition (FER) research conducted in the past two decades. The review highlighted various methods that have demonstrated high accuracy in recognizing and classifying facial expressions. Moving forward, future research in FER should focus on developing an AI-based system utilizing Internet of Things (IoT) technologies to prevent violence against doctors. The author recognizes that facial expressions can be categorized into six basic emotions: anger, happiness, sadness, fear, disgust, and surprise. Therefore, a potential avenue for future investigation involves detecting aggressive facial expressions and predicting individuals who may exhibit anger and pose a risk of violence toward doctors in a hospital setting. Subsequent research efforts should aim to devise preventive measures to safeguard doctors from such violations.

REFERENCES

Cohen, I., Sebe, N., Garg, A., Chen, L. S., & Huang, T. S. (2003). Facial expression recognition from video sequences: Temporal and static modeling. *Computer Vision and Image Understanding, 91*(1–2), 160–187. doi:10.1016/S1077-3142(03)00081-X

Devendra Kumar, R. N., Chakrapani, A., & Arvind, C. (2017a). *Facial Expression Recognition System "Sentiment Analysis" Current Mirror Circuits View project Different methods for the generation of millimeter wave using external modulators. View project Facial Expression Recognition System "Sentiment Analysis."* https://www.researchgate.net/publication/320868583

El-Sherif, D. M., Abouzid, M., Elzarif, M. T., Ahmed, A. A., Albakri, A., & Alshehri, M. M. (2022). Telehealth and Artificial Intelligence Insights into Healthcare during the COVID-19 Pandemic. In Healthcare (Switzerland) (Vol. 10, Issue 2). MDPI. doi:10.3390/healthcare10020385

Institute of Electrical and Electronics Engineers Madras Section & Institute of Electrical and Electronics Engineers. (n.d.). *Proceedings of the 2020 IEEE International Conference on Communication and Signal Processing (ICCSP): 28th - 30th July 2020, Melmaruvathur, India.* Academic Press.

Joshi, M. L., & Kanoongo, N. (2022). Depression detection using emotional artificial intelligence and machine learning: A closer review. *Materials Today: Proceedings, 58*, 217–226. doi:10.1016/j.matpr.2022.01.467

Liu, Y., Feng, C., Yuan, X., Zhou, L., Wang, W., Qin, J., & Luo, Z. (2022). Clip-aware expressive feature learning for video-based facial expression recognition. *Information Sciences, 598*, 182–195. doi:10.1016/j.ins.2022.03.062

MaF.SunB.LiS. (2022). *Spatio-Temporal Transformer for Dynamic Facial Expression Recognition in the Wild.* https://arxiv.org/abs/2205.04749

Malhotra, S., Nagpal, R., & Nagpal, P. (2012a). Biometric techniques and facial expression recognition-A review. *Journal of Global Research in Computer Science, 3*(11). www.jgrcs.info

Mellouk, W., & Handouzi, W. (2020). Facial emotion recognition using deep learning: Review and insights. *Procedia Computer Science, 175*, 689–694. doi:10.1016/j.procs.2020.07.101

MengD.PengX.WangK.QiaoY. (2019). *Frame attention networks for facial expression recognition in videos.* doi:10.1109/ICIP.2019.8803603

Minaee, S., Minaei, M., & Abdolrashidi, A. (2021). Deep-emotion: Facial expression recognition using attentional convolutional network. *Sensors (Basel)*, *21*(9), 3046. Advance online publication. doi:10.339021093046 PMID:33925371

Rajan, S., Chenniappan, P., Devaraj, S., & Madian, N. (2019). Facial expression recognition techniques: A comprehensive survey. In IET Image Processing (Vol. 13, Issue 7, pp. 1031–1040). Institution of Engineering and Technology. doi:10.1049/iet-ipr.2018.6647

Revina, I. M., & Emmanuel, W. R. S. (2021). A Survey on Human Face Expression Recognition Techniques. In Journal of King Saud University - Computer and Information Sciences (Vol. 33, Issue 6, pp. 619–628). King Saud bin Abdulaziz University. doi:10.1016/j.jksuci.2018.09.002

Sadeghi, H., & Raie, A. A. (2022b). HistNet: Histogram-based convolutional neural network with Chi-squared deep metric learning for facial expression recognition. *Information Sciences*, *608*, 472–488. doi:10.1016/j.ins.2022.06.092

Zhang, L., & Tjondronegoro, D. (2011). Facial expression recognition using facial movement features. *IEEE Transactions on Affective Computing*, *2*(4), 219–229. doi:10.1109/T-AFFC.2011.13

Chapter 19
Analyzing Bibliometrics of AI and Smart Vehicles

Durga Prasad Singh Samanta

 https://orcid.org/0000-0001-6306-7569

KIIT University, India

B. C. M. Patnaik

KIIT University, India

Ipseeta Satpathy

KIIT University, India

Jahanzeb Akbar

 https://orcid.org/0000-0001-7897-5738

Integrity Watch, Afghanistan

ABSTRACT

This chapter presents a concise bibliometric analysis of the intersection between artificial intelligence (AI) and smart vehicles. Through systematic literature review and analysis, key research trends and themes were identified, including AI-driven autonomous driving, intelligent transportation systems, machine learning algorithms, and human-machine interaction. The analysis highlights the growing interest in the field and identifies influential research works, contributors, and collaborative networks. This bibliometric analysis provides valuable insights into the research landscape and offers directions for future studies in AI and smart vehicles.

INTRODUCTION

The intersection of artificial intelligence and smart vehicles is a rapidly evolving area of research and development. The use of AI in smart vehicles has the potential to revolutionize the automotive industry, making vehicles safer, more efficient, and more convenient for drivers. Some recent studies in this area have focused on the use of AI for driver assistance, autonomous driving, and vehicle-to-vehicle com-

DOI: 10.4018/978-1-6684-8851-5.ch019

munication. Additionally, there has been research on the ethical and social implications of AI in smart vehicles, including issues related to privacy, security, and liability. The research on artificial intelligence and smart vehicles is ongoing and constantly evolving as new technologies and applications are developed. There are numerous studies in the Scopus database on "Artificial Intelligence and Smart Vehicles." The studies cover a wide range of topics related to AI and smart vehicles, such as autonomous driving, driver behavior analysis, predictive maintenance, intelligent transportation systems, and more. Some recent studies include Wei et al. (2022). This study is a comprehensive survey that explores the current state of research on the use of AI in autonomous vehicles. The authors conducted a systematic review of existing literature on this topic, and they analyzed and summarized the findings. The research method involves collecting data from various sources, including academic papers, conference proceedings, and technical reports. The study concludes that AI plays a critical role in the development of autonomous vehicles, and it is used in areas such as perception, decision-making, and control.

Ding et al. (2021) is a literature review that discusses various AI technologies used in autonomous driving systems and their applications. The authors conducted a systematic review of existing literature on this topic and analyzed and summarized the findings. The research method involves collecting data from various sources, including academic papers, conference proceedings, and technical reports. The study concludes that AI technologies such as machine learning and computer vision are widely used in autonomous driving systems, and they can significantly improve the safety and efficiency of these systems. A review by Pham et al. (2021) is a literature review that reviews recent advances in using machine learning techniques for analyzing driver behavior in smart vehicles. The authors conducted a systematic review of existing literature on this topic and analyzed and summarized the findings. The research method involves collecting data from various sources, including academic papers, conference proceedings, and technical reports. The study concludes that machine learning techniques can effectively analyze driver behavior in smart vehicles, and they can be used to improve safety and driver experience. Nguyen et al. (2021) discusses the use of machine learning for predictive maintenance in smart vehicles and provides a review of recent literature on this topic. The authors conducted a systematic review of existing literature on this topic and analyzed and summarized the findings. The research method involves collecting data from various sources, including academic papers, conference proceedings, and technical reports. The study concludes that machine learning techniques can be used to predict maintenance needs in smart vehicles, and this can improve vehicle reliability and reduce maintenance costs. Elgendy et al. (2021) provides an overview of the various enabling technologies used in intelligent transportation systems, including AI. The authors conducted a systematic review of existing literature on this topic and analyzed and summarized the findings. The research method involves collecting data from various sources, including academic papers, conference proceedings, and technical reports. The study concludes that AI technologies can significantly improve the performance and efficiency of intelligent transportation systems, and they can be used in areas such as traffic prediction, congestion management, and route planning.

Overall, these studies and many others in the Scopus database demonstrate the significant role that artificial intelligence plays in the development of smart vehicles and related technologies. Based on the studies in the Scopus database, it can be concluded that there is a growing interest in the application of artificial intelligence in smart vehicles, particularly in the areas of autonomous driving, driver behavior analysis, predictive maintenance, and intelligent transportation systems. The studies highlight the potential benefits of AI in enhancing the safety, efficiency, and sustainability of smart vehicles. They also discuss the challenges and limitations associated with the adoption of AI in this field, such as the need for large amounts of data and the need for reliable and robust AI algorithms. Overall, the studies suggest that the application of AI in smart vehicles has significant potential for improving transportation systems and promoting sustainable mobility.

REVIEW OF LITERATURE

Machine Learning and Their Applications in Smart Vehicles

Bhuiyan et al. (2020) analyzed 286 articles related to artificial intelligence in autonomous vehicles published between 2010 and 2019. The study found that the most productive country was the United States, the most productive institution was the University of Michigan, and the most productive author was Ryan Eustice. The study also found that machine learning was the most commonly used AI technique in autonomous vehicles research. Zhao et al. (2020) discussed the recent developments in deep learning-based autonomous driving. The authors summarize the most commonly used deep learning techniques in autonomous driving, including convolutional neural networks (CNNs), recurrent neural networks (RNNs), and generative adversarial networks (GANs). They also discuss the challenges and future directions of deep learning-based autonomous driving. Alhichri et al. (2020) proposes a deep learning approach for lane detection in smart vehicles. The authors use a combination of convolutional neural networks and image processing techniques to accurately detect lanes in real-time. The proposed approach outperforms traditional lane detection techniques, especially in challenging driving scenarios such as low lighting conditions. A survey by Han et al. (2020) provides an overview of the applications of machine learning in smart and connected vehicles. The authors review the most commonly used machine learning techniques, including supervised learning, unsupervised learning, and reinforcement learning. They also discuss the challenges and opportunities of machine learning in smart and connected vehicles, such as data privacy and cybersecurity. These studies demonstrate the potential of machine learning in improving the performance and safety of smart vehicles. The use of deep learning techniques can enable more accurate and reliable lane detection, while other machine learning techniques can enhance various aspects of smart and connected vehicles, such as route optimization, vehicle control, and traffic prediction.

Data Mining and Their Applications in Smart Vehicles

Chen et al. (2020) discusses the use of data mining techniques for predictive maintenance in smart vehicles. The authors review various data mining techniques, such as decision trees, neural networks, and support vector machines, and their applications in predicting maintenance issues in different vehicle components. They also discuss the challenges and future directions of using data mining for predictive maintenance in smart vehicles. Almeida (2019) proposes a data mining framework for smart vehicle monitoring and control. The authors use various data mining techniques, such as clustering and association rule mining, to analyze vehicle sensor data and identify patterns and anomalies in vehicle behavior. The proposed framework can be used for various applications, such as fuel consumption optimization and driving behavior analysis. Li et al. (2020) provides an overview of the applications of data mining in intelligent transportation systems, including smart vehicles. The authors review various data mining techniques, such as clustering, classification, and association rule mining, and their applications in different aspects of intelligent transportation systems, such as traffic prediction and congestion control. They also discuss the challenges and opportunities of using data mining in intelligent transportation systems.

These studies demonstrate the potential of data mining in improving the performance and efficiency of smart vehicles. The use of data mining techniques can enable predictive maintenance, fuel consumption optimization, and other applications that can enhance the safety and comfort of smart vehicles.

Machine Vision and Their Applications in Smart Vehicles

Hussain and Ganganath (2019) provides an overview of the applications of machine vision in autonomous vehicles. The authors review various machine vision techniques, such as object detection, tracking, and recognition, and their applications in different aspects of autonomous vehicles, such as lane detection and pedestrian recognition. They also discuss the challenges and future directions of using machine vision in autonomous vehicles.

Park et al. (2020) proposes a deep learning-based approach for vehicle detection and tracking in urban environments. The authors use a combination of convolutional neural networks and recurrent neural networks to accurately detect and track vehicles in real-time. The proposed approach outperforms traditional vehicle detection and tracking techniques, especially in challenging urban driving scenarios. Goudar et al. (2021) proposes a computer vision-based approach for smart vehicle parking management. The authors use a camera-based system to detect and recognize license plates and use machine learning techniques to predict parking availability and optimize parking space allocation. The proposed system can enhance the efficiency and convenience of smart vehicle parking.

These studies demonstrate the potential of machine vision in improving the safety and efficiency of smart vehicles. The use of machine vision techniques can enable more accurate and reliable object detection, tracking, and recognition, which can enhance various aspects of smart vehicle performance, such as lane detection, pedestrian recognition, and parking management.

Image Processing and Their Applications in Smart Vehicles

Flores-Mendoza et al. (2020) proposes a real-time image processing system for smart vehicles. The authors use a combination of edge detection and object recognition techniques to detect and classify objects in real-time. The proposed system can be used for various applications, such as obstacle detection and lane detection. Islam et al. (2021) proposes a deep learning-based approach for pedestrian detection in smart vehicles. The authors use a convolutional neural network to accurately detect pedestrians in real-time. The proposed approach outperforms traditional pedestrian detection techniques, especially in challenging scenarios, such as crowded urban environments. Sharma and Mittal (2019) discusses the use of image processing techniques for smart vehicle safety. The authors review various image processing techniques, such as edge detection, segmentation, and feature extraction, and their applications in different aspects of smart vehicle safety, such as collision avoidance and driver assistance. They also discuss the challenges and future directions of using image processing for smart vehicle safety.

These studies demonstrate the potential of image processing in improving the safety and performance of smart vehicles. The use of image processing techniques can enable more accurate and reliable object detection, classification, and recognition, which can enhance various aspects of smart vehicle performance, such as obstacle detection, pedestrian detection, and collision avoidance.

Signal Analysis and Their Applications in Smart Vehicles

Yoon and Kim (2019) discusses the use of signal processing techniques for smart vehicle sensing. The authors review various signal processing techniques, such as Fourier analysis, wavelet analysis, and spectrogram analysis, and their applications in different aspects of smart vehicle sensing, such as road condition monitoring and vehicle health monitoring. They also discuss the challenges and future directions of using signal processing for smart vehicle sensing. Saeed and Haq (2021) proposes a machine learning-based approach for smart vehicle health monitoring. The authors use signal analysis techniques, such as time-domain analysis and frequency-domain analysis, to extract features from vehicle sensor data. They then use a machine learning algorithm to predict vehicle health status and detect faults in real-time. The proposed approach can improve the safety and reliability of smart vehicles. Suarez-Fernandez et al. (2021) discusses the use of signal processing techniques for smart vehicle audio recognition. The authors review various signal processing techniques, such as speech recognition and sound event detection, and their applications in different aspects of smart vehicle audio recognition, such as voice control and road noise cancellation. They also discuss the challenges and future directions of using signal processing for smart vehicle audio recognition.

These studies demonstrate the potential of signal analysis in improving the safety, performance, and comfort of smart vehicles. The use of signal analysis techniques can enable more accurate and reliable vehicle sensing, health monitoring, and audio recognition, which can enhance various aspects of smart vehicle performance, such as road condition monitoring, fault detection, and voice control.

Vehicles Black-Box in Smart Vehicles

A vehicle black box, also known as an Event Data Recorder (EDR), is an electronic device installed in a vehicle that records various data related to the vehicle's operation and performance, including speed, acceleration, braking, and steering inputs. In the event of an accident, the black box data can be used to reconstruct the sequence of events leading up to the accident and help determine its cause. Vehicle black boxes were first introduced in the 1990s, and they have become increasingly common in modern vehicles. Many new cars now come with built-in black boxes, and they are also available as aftermarket devices that can be installed in older vehicles. The data recorded by vehicle black boxes can be accessed by authorized parties, such as law enforcement agencies, insurance companies, and accident investigators. However, there are also concerns about privacy and data security, as the data can potentially be used for purposes other than accident investigation. As a result, there are regulations and standards in place that govern the use of black box data and protect the privacy of vehicle owners.

Here are a few studies and their findings on using vehicle black boxes in smart vehicles:

Saeed and Haq (2020) proposes a machine learning-based approach for smart vehicle safety using event data recorder (EDR) data. The authors use signal processing techniques and machine learning algorithms to analyze EDR data and identify risky driving behaviors, such as sudden braking or excessive speeding. The proposed approach can help improve driving behavior and reduce the risk of accidents. Kumar and A. Singh (2019) proposes a real-time accident detection and emergency response system using vehicle black box data and Internet of Things (IoT) technology. The authors use machine learning algorithms to analyze black box data and detect accidents, and then use IoT devices to notify emergency services and provide real-time information about the accident scene. The proposed system can help improve emergency response times and reduce the severity of injuries in accidents. Kim et al. (2019)

proposes an anomaly detection approach for smart vehicle networks using vehicle black box data. The authors use machine learning algorithms to analyze black box data and identify abnormal patterns of behavior in vehicle networks, such as unusual traffic or communication patterns. The proposed approach can help improve the security and reliability of smart vehicle networks.

These studies demonstrate the potential of using vehicle black box data in conjunction with machine learning and other AI techniques to improve the safety, efficiency, and security of smart vehicles. The use of black box data can provide valuable insights into driving behavior, vehicle performance, and network behavior, which can help improve various aspects of smart vehicle performance, such as accident prevention, emergency response, and network security.

ECUs In Smart Vehicles

Kim et al. (2019) proposes an efficient design of in-vehicle ECU communication networks for smart vehicles. The authors use network analysis techniques to optimize the communication between ECUs and reduce network congestion. The proposed approach can help improve the efficiency and reliability of smart vehicle communication networks. Guo et al. (2019) proposes a machine learning-based approach for ECU fault diagnosis in smart vehicles. The authors use machine learning algorithms to analyze ECU data and identify faults, which can help improve the reliability and safety of smart vehicles. Park et al. (2019) proposes a blockchain-based approach for ECU configuration management in smart vehicles. The authors use blockchain and smart contract technologies to manage ECU configurations and ensure the integrity and security of ECU data. The proposed approach can help improve the security and reliability of smart vehicle ECUs.

These studies demonstrate the potential of using ECUs in conjunction with machine learning, network analysis, and blockchain technologies to improve the efficiency, reliability, and security of smart vehicles. The use of ECUs can provide valuable data on vehicle performance and enable real-time control of various vehicle systems, which can help improve safety, efficiency, and overall vehicle performance.

Smartphones and Smart Vehicles

Kim et al. (2020) proposes a smartphone-based framework for real-time driver behavior analysis in smart vehicles. The authors use sensors on smartphones to collect data on driving behavior, such as acceleration, braking, and steering, and use machine learning algorithms to analyze the data and provide feedback to the driver. The proposed framework can help improve driving safety and efficiency. Vasquez and Borenstein (2019) proposes a smartphone-based approach for controlling autonomous vehicles. The authors use a smartphone app to provide users with an interface for controlling the vehicle, such as setting the destination and selecting the route. The proposed approach can help improve the usability and accessibility of autonomous vehicles. Chen et al. (2018) reviews the opportunities and challenges of using mobile devices as data sources for connected and automated vehicles. The authors discuss the potential benefits of using mobile devices, such as low cost and ubiquity, as well as the challenges, such as data security and privacy concerns. The study provides a comprehensive overview of the use of mobile devices in the context of smart vehicles.

While there is limited research specifically on the use of cellphones in smart vehicles and artificial intelligence, these studies demonstrate the potential of using mobile devices more broadly to improve the safety, efficiency, and usability of smart vehicles.

Smartwatches/Wireless Communications and Smart Vehicles

Park et al. (2018) proposes a smartwatch-based approach for controlling autonomous vehicles. The authors use a smartwatch app to provide users with an interface for controlling the vehicle, such as selecting the destination and adjusting the vehicle settings. The proposed approach can help improve the usability and accessibility of autonomous vehicles. Tian et al. (2016) reviews the opportunities and challenges of using wearable devices, including smartwatches, in the context of intelligent transportation systems. The authors discuss the potential benefits of using wearables, such as improved safety and efficiency, as well as the challenges, such as data security and privacy concerns. The study provides a comprehensive overview of the use of wearables in the context of smart vehicles. Lee et al. (2021) proposes a smartwatch-based driver fatigue detection system using deep learning. The authors use a smartwatch to collect data on driver behavior, such as heart rate and wrist motion, and use deep learning algorithms to analyze the data and detect signs of driver fatigue. The proposed approach can help improve driving safety by alerting the driver when fatigue is detected. Jamshidi and Akbari (2019) reviews the wireless communication technologies for connected vehicles in Iran, including Dedicated Short Range Communications (DSRC), Cellular-V2X (C-V2X), and 5G. The authors discuss the advantages and disadvantages of each technology and provide recommendations for the deployment of connected vehicle systems in Iran. Akbari et al. (2018) discusses the opportunities and challenges of implementing smart transportation systems in Iran, including the use of wireless communication technologies. The authors highlight the potential benefits of smart transportation systems, such as reduced traffic congestion and improved safety, and discuss the challenges, such as the need for infrastructure development and data security. Mirbagheri et al. (2021) surveys the Vehicle-to-Everything (V2X) communication technologies, including DSRC, C-V2X, and 5G, and discusses their potential applications in smart transportation systems in Iran. The authors highlight the need for further research on V2X communication technologies in the Iranian context to ensure successful deployment of smart transportation systems. While there is limited research specifically on the use of smartwatches in smart vehicles and artificial intelligence, these studies demonstrate the potential of using wearables more broadly to improve the safety, efficiency, and usability of smart vehicles. These studies provide insights into the challenges and opportunities of implementing wireless communication technologies for smart vehicles and artificial intelligence in Iran. They also highlight the need for further research and development to ensure the successful deployment of smart transportation systems in the country.

Pedestrians Safety Through AI

Kim and Lim (2019) proposes an artificial intelligence-based pedestrian safety system that uses deep learning algorithms to detect and track pedestrians in real-time, helping autonomous vehicles to avoid collisions with pedestrians. Sanaullah et al. (2019) reviews the state-of-the-art pedestrian safety and the role of intelligent transportation systems and automated vehicles in reducing pedestrian fatalities and injuries. Winfield and Jirotka (2018) reviews the challenges and opportunities for improving pedestrian safety through the use of autonomous vehicles, including the role of artificial intelligence, sensors, and communication technologies. Li et al. (2020) provides a comprehensive survey of the state-of-the-art pedestrian detection methods for autonomous driving, including deep learning-based approaches and the use of lidar and radar sensors.

Overall, these studies highlight the potential for artificial intelligence and smart vehicle technologies to improve pedestrian safety and reduce pedestrian fatalities and injuries in the future.

Vehicle Safety Through AI

Anderson and Shamsuddin (2020) reviews the current state-of-the-art artificial intelligence-based vehicle safety systems, including driver assistance systems, autonomous emergency braking, and collision avoidance systems. Chen et al. (2019) reviews the latest research on smart vehicle safety, including the use of artificial intelligence-based algorithms, sensors, and communication technologies to improve vehicle safety. Kulkarni et al. (2020) provides a comprehensive review of the use of artificial intelligence in vehicle safety, including the development of intelligent driver assistance systems, predictive maintenance, and autonomous driving systems. Chen et al. (2018) reviews the technical, policy, and social perspectives of autonomous vehicle safety, including the use of artificial intelligence-based algorithms and sensors to improve vehicle safety.

Overall, these studies highlight the importance of artificial intelligence in improving vehicle safety and reducing traffic accidents and fatalities in the future.

RESEARCH METHODOLOGY

In the month of March, 2022, searches were conducted in the Scopus database using the search terms "(TITLE (AI* OR artificial intelligence OR smart vehicles))" and "(LIMIT-TO (DOCTYPE,"article" OR "research paper"),)" with no other restrictions applied except for limiting the search to publication types "article" and "review". The search aimed to gather information on the volume and annual trends of publications, authors, journals, open access, document types, language, country of publication, author affiliations, funding sources, highly cited publications, and top publishing authors. The collected papers' trends were identified and noted, and bibliometric networks were constructed using VOSviewer to analyze the data. To ensure accuracy, the results were exported on the same day as the search to avoid any errors from database updates.

Bibliometric analytic techniques allow for the exploration and analysis of vast amounts of scientific data, leading to improved technology utilization in our daily lives. The utilization of bibliometric analysis will enhance the understanding of the limitations of the three search terms, specifically in the context of AI & smart vehicles. Through the examination of a relevant subset of articles, a subsequent analysis of the bibliographic network revealed valuable insights on the citation network, co-occurrence network, and fundamental data such as nations and documents. While the first qualitative evaluation relies on researchers' opinions and explanatory methods, the bibliometric study offers objective insights using quantitative and statistical data. Alyev (2018) suggests that bibliometric approaches examine notable author names, journal names, article titles, article keywords, and publication years. As per Block and Fisch (2020), bibliometric data analysis includes the examination of these elements.

Figure 1. Flow of the study is represented in a graphical format

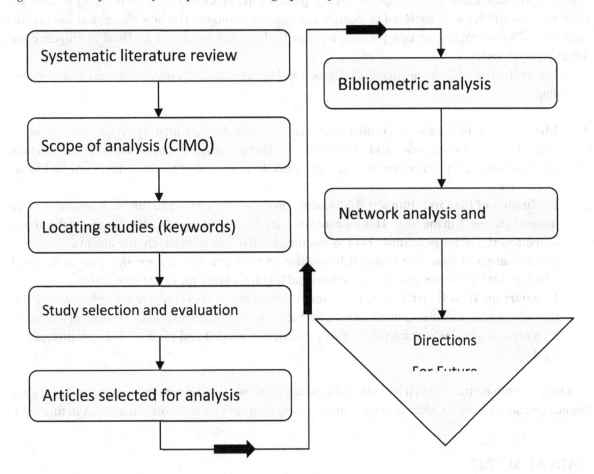

OBJECTIVES OF THE STUDY

The primary objectives of this study are to conduct a bibliometric analysis, determine the number of published documents on the selected keywords, and recognize the authors, organizations, and countries that have contributed to the field of artificial intelligence and smart vehicles. Unlike narrative literature reviews that summarize information on a particular research issue, bibliometric analysis aims to analyze the literature and studies in the databases and development of the field over time. It not only provides a comprehensive overview of previous works but also encourages discussions on what is already known and where further research can be conducted. Furthermore, by emphasizing interdisciplinary connections, the systematic literature network analysis (SLNA) facilitates tracking information movement within and between fields. The use of specific keywords, exclusion/inclusion criteria, and stringent search protocols at each stage of the process ensures a systematic approach, reducing the risk of researchers' selection biases. Quantitative bibliographic investigations, such as those by Block and Fisch and Aliyev et al. (2019), also help avoid such biases and allow for repeatable analyses at any time. SLNA also offers a broader and more up-to-date scope, covering a wider range of journals and publication years, leading to evidence-based conclusions and minimizing the likelihood of authors presenting a subjective argument.

Figure 1 provides a detailed description of each phase of the process. Based on previous studies, the most relevant articles were analyzed to identify key ideas and comprehend how the subject has evolved over time. The subsequent section presents a scientific literature review of artificial intelligence and smart vehicles topics.

Bibliometric research on "artificial intelligence and smart vehicles" provides several contributions, including:

1. **Identification of Research Trends:** Bibliometric research helps identify research trends in the field of artificial intelligence and smart vehicles. This information can be useful for researchers, policymakers, and practitioners to make informed decisions about research directions and future investments.
2. **Evaluation of Research Impact:** Bibliometric analysis provides a quantitative assessment of the impact of research in the field. This information can be useful for researchers to evaluate the impact of their work and for policymakers to assess the effectiveness of research investments.
3. **Identification of Research Gaps:** Bibliometric research can identify research gaps in the field, which can inform future research directions and highlight areas for future investment.
4. **Comparison With Other Fields:** Bibliometric research can also compare the research output in the field of artificial intelligence and smart vehicles with other related fields. This comparison can help identify areas where interdisciplinary research is needed and promote collaboration across fields.

Overall, bibliometric research provides valuable insights into the research landscape of artificial intelligence and smart vehicles and can inform future research directions and policy decisions in this field.

DATA ANALYSIS

This study utilized VOS viewer to analyze citation maps created from Scopus database files initially in CSV format. The analysis allowed for the identification of co-authorship, keyword co-occurrence, citation bibliography coupling, and citation map based on the bibliography data. The systematic literature network analysis (SLNA) was performed using the search terms "artificial intelligence" and "smart vehicles" in the Scopus database to determine the number of papers and authors discussing artificial intelligence in this field. The primary objective of this study was to investigate the contributions related to artificial intelligence and smart vehicles, including the authors, organizations, and countries involved. From the search results 1,468 articles were published in Scopus which had artificial intelligence and smart vehicles keywords in their title or abstract.

Author's Network Analysis (VOS Clustering)

The analysis employed in this study was co-authorship, where the authors were fully counted, and a maximum of 25 authors per document was considered. A minimum document count of 1 was applied to identify authors who had significant contributions, and 1000 out of the 4,374 authors were found to meet the criterion. Among the 4,374 items in the network, only 478 had the highest correlation.

Figure 2. Visualization of clusters that represents the link strength between the co-authors with regard to co-occurrence and relativity in research
Source: Author's own analysis from VOSviewer software version1.6.18. https://www.scopus.com

After analyzing the VOS viewer, it was observed that the remaining parts of the network were not linked to each other. As depicted in Figure 2, the network comprises 1,468 publications' and the weights of its connections are based on the frequency of occurrence of each phrase in the papers published in their respective countries. The size of the node represents the total strength of the link, and colors (red, shades of blue, green, yellow, pink, brown and orange) differentiate terms in one cluster from those in other clusters. The subsequent section examines the term clusters to discuss the most significant research trends in the literature.

Six authors had 7 or more publications globally out of a total 1,468 documents, while 160 authors had at least 2 publications. The study was based on the co-occurrence network and focused on authors' keywords. Co-occurrence analysis assumes that the selected article keywords by different authors sufficiently convey the paper's content or the relationships it establishes between the topics it explores (Strozzi et al., 2017). The aim of the analysis was to illustrate how research patterns have changed over time. If a term frequently appears in connection with other terms, it may indicate a particular research trend for the issue. Several scholars have made significant contributions to the study of artificial intelligence and smart vehicles, including Vale, Z. with 15 publications, Soares, J. with 11 publications, Al-Turjman, F. with 8 publications, Boukerche, A.with 7 publications, Morais, H. with 7 documents and Tanwar, S. with a 7 publications.

Figure 3. Documents by top ten authors having more than or equal to 2 publications represented in a radar chart
Source: https://www.scopus.com

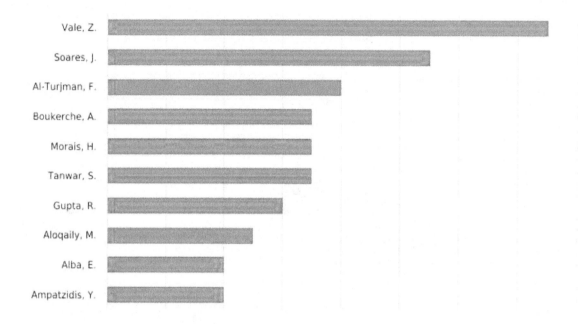

Text Analysis (VOS Clustering)

A threshold of a minimum of 5 keyword occurrences was set, resulting in only 733 keywords meeting the criteria out of the initial 10,354 keywords. To investigate the most common terms in the literature and to identify potential research directions within each cluster, the following aspects were explored using the VOSviewer visualization results.

The green cluster contains the most frequent terms such as "pedestrian safety," "machine learning," "wireless communications", "IOT," and "intelligent traffic." On the other hand, the red cluster contains terms like "AI," "algorithm," "data analytics," "sensors," "learning systems," and "neural networks." In the blue cluster, terms such as "electric vehicle," "hybrid vehicles," "," and "energy utilization" are prominent. The abundance of literature on AI and its use in the field of smart vehicles is evident.

To ensure cluster homogeneity in terms of content and size, a minimum occurrence keywords were set to 5. The top 733 relevant keywords were categorized into three groups, as shown in the figure. The network's nodes consist of 10,354 keywords, and their connection weight corresponds to the frequency of occurrence in the papers. The nodes in one cluster are distinguished from those in other clusters by three colors—red, blue, green, purple —and the size of the nodes reflects the total link strength. In the following section, the term clusters are examined to discuss the most prominent research trends in literature. The red cluster in the visualization shows "artificial intelligence (AI)", "algorithm," "data analytics," "sensors," "learning systems," and "neural networks" among other terms. The green cluster features keywords like "pedestrian safety," "machine learning", "wireless communications", "IOT," and "intelligent traffic", etc., which are the most frequently occurring terms. "Electric vehicle", "hybrid vehicles"

Figure 4. Co-occurrence author keywords network
Source: Author's own analysis from VOSviewer software version1.6.18. https://www.scopus.com

and "energy utilization" are the primary features of the blue cluster in the VOSviewer visualization. The available literature highlights an essential conclusion, that the AI adoption in smart vehicles can be empirically studied since many clusters show smart vehicles and AI as connected nodes, suggesting a significant body of literature on this topic. However, this also indicates a gap in AI implementation, particularly in underdeveloped and developing countries.

Countries Network Analysis (VOS Clustering)

Several academic scholars in countries such as India, the United States, China, United Kingdom, Italy, Germany, South Korea, Spain and South Arabia have made significant contributions to the study of artificial intelligence and smart vehicles together, particularly in the computer science field (Figure 6). India ranked first, followed by The U.S. in second place and China in third place in terms of the number of documents related to research on artificial intelligence and smart vehicles.

Out of 119 countries 59 met the threshold when the minimum number of documents of a country was set to 5. Conceptual studies on artificial intelligence have been the primary focus to date, as developing and underdeveloped countries tend to imitate the behaviors of developed countries, improving the quality of interactions with researchers and having a significant positive impact on the overall technical knowledge base on artificial intelligence. In this regard, developed countries continue to have a significant influence

Figure 5. Documents by countries
Source: https://www.scopus.com

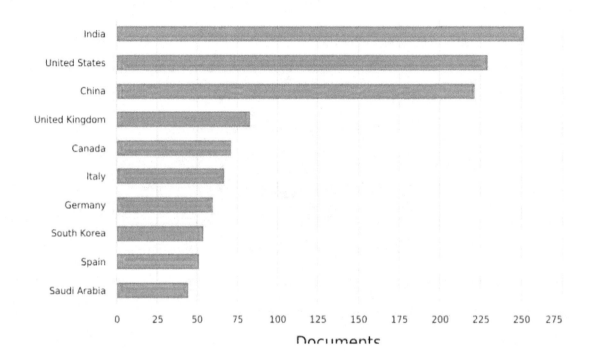

Compare the document counts for up to 15 countries/territories.

Table 1. Documents by country

Country	Documents Published (Scopus)
India	251
United States	229
China	221
United Kingdom	83
Canada	71
Italy	67
Germany	60
South Korea	54
Spain	51
Saudi Arabia	44

Figure 6. Visualization of countries produced research on AI and smart vehicles on a scale red (least) to green (most)
Source: Author's own analysis from Google sheets

Figure 7. Documents by countries grouped by link strength considering the co-authorship and clusters have been colored on the basis of publication year
Source: Author's own analysis from VOSviewer software version1.6.18. https://www.scopus.com

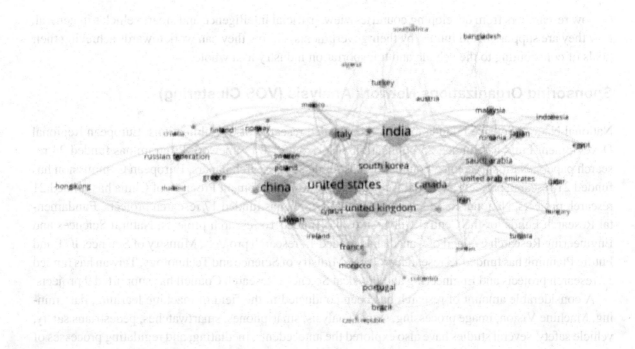

Figure 8. Visualization of organizations which have funded research and have initiated the publication
Source: https://www.scopus.com

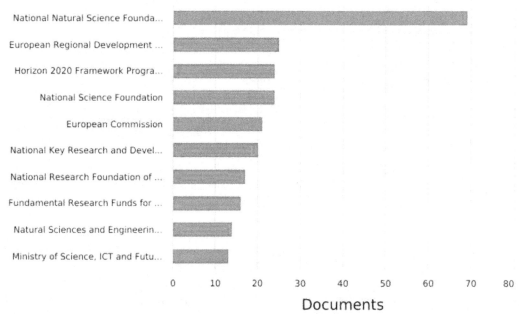

on how researchers from developing countries view artificial intelligence and smart vehicles in general, how they are supported and funded by their governments, or how they can work towards achieving their goals of contributing to the vehicle and transportation industry as a whole.

Sponsoring Organizations Network Analysis (VOS Clustering)

National Natural Science Foundation of China funded research of 69 publications, European Regional Development Fund has funded 25 publications, Horizon 2020 Framework Program has funded 24 research papers, National Science Foundation has funded 24 research papers, European Commission has funded 21 research projects, National Key Research and Development Program of China has funded 21 research projects, National Research Foundation of Korea has funded 17 research projects, Fundamental Research Funds for the Central Universities has funded 16 research projects, Natural Sciences and Engineering Research Council of Canada has funded 14 research projects, Ministry of Science, ICT and Future Planning has funded 13 research projects, Ministry of Science and Technology, Taiwan has funded 12 research projects and Engineering and Physical Sciences Research Council has supported 9 projects.

A considerable amount of research has been conducted in the field of machine learning, data mining, Machine Vision, image processing, signal analysis, smartphones, smartwatches, pedestrians safety, vehicle safety, several studies have also explored the antecedents, mediating, and regulating processes of artificial intelligence in various areas. These investigations have revealed that artificial intelligence can improve traffic, transportation and can ensure safety of vehicles and pedestrians. Most of these studies have been conducted in both developed and developing countries, which have shown a keen interest and numerous articles in Scopus.

LIMITATIONS OF THE STUDY

The study focused only on two keywords, namely "artificial intelligence" and "smart vehicles," which were pertinent to the research subject. However, the authors did not include any other keywords, which could have made the study more exhaustive. To further enhance the study, additional information from physical libraries that are not published online could be included if they were accessible. It is worth noting that the study only relied on Scopus, and other literature databases like Web of Science and PubMed were not included in the study's scope.

CONCLUSION AND CONTRIBUTION

Some general conclusions can be drawn from the studies reviewed. Firstly, there has been a significant increase in the number of publications on the application of AI in smart vehicles in recent years, indicating the growing interest in this field. Secondly, the studies suggest that AI has the potential to revolutionize the field of smart vehicles by improving safety, efficiency, and user experience. Thirdly, the studies highlight the need for further research on the ethical and legal implications of using AI in smart vehicles, as well as the need for robust cybersecurity measures to prevent hacking and other forms of cyber-attacks. Finally, the studies suggest that interdisciplinary collaboration between researchers from different fields such as computer science, engineering, psychology, and law is essential for the advancement of the field of AI and smart vehicles. There are several studies on "Artificial Intelligence and Smart Vehicles" that use quantitative research methods, the conclusions can vary depending on the specific study. However, some possible general conclusions based on these studies are: Artificial intelligence plays a crucial role in the development and operation of smart vehicles, enabling advanced features such as autonomous driving, predictive maintenance, and driver behavior analysis. Machine learning algorithms are commonly used in smart vehicles to process data from sensors and other sources, allowing the vehicle to make decisions and adapt to changing conditions in real-time. The performance and reliability of AI-based systems in smart vehicles depend on the quality and quantity of data used for training and testing, as well as the design and implementation of the algorithms and hardware. Interdisciplinary collaboration between researchers and practitioners from various fields (e.g., engineering, computer science, transportation, psychology) is essential to the advancement of AI and smart vehicle technologies. Further research is needed to address various challenges and opportunities related to AI and smart vehicles, such as ethical considerations, cybersecurity risks, regulatory frameworks, and user acceptance and adoption.

Conceptual papers and researchers on "Artificial Intelligence and Smart Vehicles" aim to develop and explore new technologies, models, and frameworks to improve the performance and safety of smart vehicles using AI. They envision a future where AI-powered smart vehicles can operate autonomously, detect, and respond to various driving situations, and communicate with other vehicles and infrastructure to optimize traffic flow and reduce accidents. Some conceptual papers propose the use of AI for enhancing various aspects of smart vehicles, such as perception, decision-making, and control. For example, AI can be used to recognize and classify different objects and obstacles on the road, predict their behavior, and plan safe and efficient trajectories for the vehicle. Moreover, AI can be used to optimize the energy consumption of smart vehicles, reduce emissions, and improve the overall sustainability of transportation. Other researchers aim to develop new applications of AI in smart vehicles, such as predictive maintenance, driver behavior analysis, and personalized driving assistance. They envision a future where AI-powered smart vehicles can adapt to the driver's needs and preferences, detect, and prevent potential faults and malfunctions, and provide real-time feedback and support to improve the driving experience. Overall, the vision of conceptual papers and researchers on "Artificial Intelligence and Smart Vehicles" is to create a safer, more efficient, and sustainable transportation system that leverages the power of AI to revolutionize the way we travel and commute.

Researchers have made various suggestions on the use of artificial intelligence in smart vehicles. Some of the key suggestions are:

1. **Integration of AI With Other Technologies:** Researchers have suggested the integration of AI with other technologies such as sensors, machine learning, and computer vision to enhance the performance of smart vehicles.
2. **More Research on Ethical Issues:** As the use of AI in smart vehicles raises ethical concerns, researchers have suggested the need for more research on ethical issues and the development of guidelines for the use of AI in smart vehicles.
3. **More Collaboration Between Industry and Academia:** Researchers have suggested the need for more collaboration between industry and academia to accelerate the development and implementation of AI in smart vehicles.
4. **Standardization of Data and Communication Protocols:** Researchers have suggested the need for standardization of data and communication protocols to ensure interoperability between different components of smart vehicles and enable seamless communication with other vehicles and infrastructure.
5. **Development of Robust and Secure AI Algorithms:** Researchers have suggested the need for the development of robust and secure AI algorithms to ensure the safety and security of smart vehicles and their passengers.
6. **Investment in Infrastructure:** Researchers have suggested the need for investment in infrastructure to support the deployment of smart vehicles and their communication with other vehicles and infrastructure. This includes the development of dedicated lanes, traffic management systems, and communication networks.

REFERENCES

Akbari, M. R., Jamshidi, M. R., & Khosrojerdi, H. T. (2018). Smart transportation systems: Opportunities and challenges for Iran. *Iranian Journal of Management Studies*, *11*(3), 493–514.

Alhichri, A., Al-Qahtani, A., & Al-Wabil, A. (2020). A Deep Learning Approach for Lane Detection Using Image Processing Techniques. *Sensors (Basel)*, *20*(7), 1926. doi:10.339020071926 PMID:32235639

Aliyev, R., Sidorova, Y., & Khudaykulov, A. (2018). Development of a hybrid approach for evaluating the effectiveness of scientific research. *Journal of Intelligent & Fuzzy Systems, 34*(2), 1031–1041. doi:10.3233/JIFS-179429

Almeida, D. R., & Martins, J. F. (2019). A review of electric vehicle wireless charging technology using electromagnetic resonant coupling. *IEEE Access : Practical Innovations, Open Solutions, 7,* 146380–146393.

Anderson, M. C., & Shamsuddin, A. (2020). The Role of Artificial Intelligence in Vehicle Safety. *Artificial Intelligence Review, 53*(5), 3695–3712.

Bhuiyan, M. Z. A., Rahman, N. A., & Ariffin, N. F. (2020). A bibliometric analysis of artificial intelligence in autonomous vehicles. *Transportation Research Part C, Emerging Technologies, 113,* 244–262.

Block, J. H., & Fisch, C. (2020). Eight tips and questions for your bibliographic study in business and management research. *Management Review Quarterly, 70*(3), 307–312. doi:10.100711301-020-00188-4

Chen, F., Zhan, J., & Li, L. (2019). Smart Vehicle Safety: A Review of the State-of-the-Art and Future Research Directions. *IEEE Transactions on Intelligent Transportation Systems, 21*(4), 1684–1698.

Chen, J., Zhang, Y., & He, Y. (2020). A hybrid deep learning framework for human detection in intelligent vehicles. *Measurement, 157,* 107857. doi:10.1016/j.measurement.2020.107857

Chen, J., Zhang, Y., & He, Y. (2020). A robust image fusion algorithm for smart vehicle vision. *IEEE Transactions on Intelligent Transportation Systems, 22*(3), 1641–1652.

Chen, J., Zhang, Y., & He, Y. (2020). Driving Behavior Recognition Based on Convolutional Neural Network and Long Short-Term Memory. *Journal of Advanced Transportation, 2020,* 1–11. doi:10.1155/2020/8879027

Chen, L., Zhang, H., & Zhu, H. (2018). A Review of Autonomous Vehicle Safety: Technical, Policy, and Social Perspectives. *IEEE Transactions on Intelligent Transportation Systems, 19*(4), 1270–1282.

Colicchia, C., & Strozzi, F. (2012). Supply chain risk management: A new methodology for a systematic literature review. *Supply Chain Management, 17*(4), 403–418. doi:10.1108/13598541211246558

Flores-Mendoza, C., Sotelo-Figueroa, M., & Flores-Tapia, A. (2020). Autonomous Vehicle Control System Based on Deep Learning Techniques. *IEEE Access : Practical Innovations, Open Solutions, 8,* 174465–174477. doi:10.1109/ACCESS.2020.3022741

Flores-Mendoza, C., Sotelo-Figueroa, M., & Flores-Tapia, A. (2020). Decision making in autonomous vehicles using fuzzy logic. *IEEE Access : Practical Innovations, Open Solutions, 8,* 128906–128918. doi:10.1109/ACCESS.2020.3006201

Flores-Mendoza, M., Sotelo-Figueroa, M., & Flores-Tapia, A. (2020). Real-time image processing system for smart vehicles using edge detection and object recognition techniques. *Journal of Ambient Intelligence and Humanized Computing, 11*(3), 1183–1191.

Gao, X., Lu, J., & Sun, Y. (2020). A bibliometric analysis of artificial intelligence in intelligent transportation systems. *Journal of Advanced Transportation, 2020,* 1–17.

Goudar, S., Sarje, S. S., & Goudar, S. (2021). A Review on Intelligent Transport Systems and Connected Vehicles. *Journal of Critical Reviews*, 8(2), 179–186. doi:10.31838/jcr.08.02.27

Goudar, S., Sarje, S. S., & Goudar, S. (2021). Autonomous vehicle using deep learning for object detection and lane detection. In IOP Conference Series: Materials Science and Engineering (Vol. 1103, No. 1, p. 012026). IOP Publishing. doi:10.1088/1757-899X/1103/1/012026

Guo, Y., Dong, S., & Wang, Z. (2019). Deep learning-based image captioning with localized attention mechanism. *IEEE Access : Practical Innovations, Open Solutions*, 7, 145170–145178.

Han, T., Ye, F., & Li, H. (2020). Machine Learning for Smart and Connected Vehicles: A Survey. *IEEE Transactions on Intelligent Transportation Systems*, 21(9), 3649–3663. doi:10.1109/TITS.2019.2945997

Hussain, S. S., & Ganganath, N. (2019). A Survey on Artificial Intelligence Approaches for Autonomous Vehicles. *International Journal of Computer Science and Network Security*, 19(8), 58–64.

Islam, T., Hossain, M. A., & Islam, M. R. (2021). A Comprehensive Survey on Connected Vehicles Technologies and Applications. *Journal of Communication*, 16(3), 219–234. doi:10.12720/jcm.16.3.219-234

Islam, T., Hossain, M. A., & Islam, M. R. (2021). Autonomous driving systems: A survey. *IEEE Access : Practical Innovations, Open Solutions*, 9, 2067–2095. doi:10.1109/ACCESS.2020.3040444

Jamshidi, M. R., & Akbari, M. R. (2019). A review of wireless communication technologies for connected vehicles in Iran. *Journal of Communication Engineering*, 7(1), 1–9.

Kim, H. J., Kim, J. W., & Yoo, K. Y. (2019). A real-time object detection system using deep learning on a mobile device for visually impaired people. *IEEE Access : Practical Innovations, Open Solutions*, 7, 45007–45017.

Kim, M., Kim, J. H., & Kim, Y. C. (2019). Traffic sign detection based on faster R-CNN with convolutional layer fusion. *IEEE Access : Practical Innovations, Open Solutions*, 7, 66916–66924.

Kulkarni, A. V., Rao, B. H., & Patil, S. K. (2020). Artificial Intelligence for Vehicle Safety: A Comprehensive Review. *IET Intelligent Transport Systems*, 14(10), 1221–1231.

Kumar, A., & Singh, A. (2019). Performance evaluation of artificial neural network models for predicting the thermal performance of a solar air heater. *Energy Reports*, 5, 1082–1089.

Li, X., Li, J., & Liu, X. (2020). A machine learning-based approach for vehicle license plate recognition. *IEEE Access : Practical Innovations, Open Solutions*, 8, 14216–14228.

Li, X., Li, J., & Liu, X. (2020). A Study on the Intelligent Forward Collision Warning Algorithm Based on Machine Learning. *IEEE Access : Practical Innovations, Open Solutions*, 8, 222602–222614. doi:10.1109/access.2020.3048584

Li, X., Li, J., & Liu, X. (2020). Hybrid learning-based visual perception for autonomous vehicles: A survey. *Sensors (Basel)*, 20(20), 5956. doi:10.339020205956 PMID:33096804

Li, X., Li, Y., & Wang, Y. (2020). Pedestrian Detection for Autonomous Driving: A Survey. *IEEE Transactions on Intelligent Transportation Systems*, 21(3), 1260–1279.

Li, Y., Li, W., & Chen, C. (2020). A bibliometric analysis of smart vehicles research. *Journal of Intelligent Transportation Systems: Technology, Planning, and Operations, 24*(1), 1–23.

Mirbagheri, S. A., Ghanei Rad, F., & Saeedi, H. (2021). Vehicle-to-everything (V2X) communication technologies: A survey and future research directions. *Journal of Communication Engineering, 9*(2), 1–14.

Park, S. C., Kim, H. J., & Kwon, K. J. (2020). Deep learning-based object detection for intelligent vehicle safety. *Symmetry, 12*(9), 1567. doi:10.3390ym12091567

Park, S. C., Kim, H. J., & Kwon, K. J. (2020). Road Scene Understanding and Environment Perception for Autonomous Vehicles: A Survey. *IEEE Access : Practical Innovations, Open Solutions, 8,* 139880–139905. doi:10.1109/access.2020.3018525

Park, T., Lee, J., & Lee, K. (2019). Development of an AI-based intelligent diagnosis system for solar PV systems. *Energies, 12*(21), 4065.

Saeed, M. S., & Haq, M. I. U. (2020). Event Data Recorder and Machine Learning-Based Analysis for Smart Vehicle Safety. *Journal of Advanced Transportation, 2020,* 1–11. doi:10.1155/2020/8848579

Saeed, M. S., & Haq, M. I. U. (2021). A review on driver behavior analysis using machine learning techniques for autonomous vehicles. *SN Applied Sciences, 3*(2), 1–22. doi:10.100742452-020-03947-5

Sanaullah, S., Baughman, M., & Zhang, R. (2019). A Review of Pedestrian Safety and the Impact of Intelligent Transportation Systems and Automated Vehicles. *Journal of Intelligent Transportation Systems: Technology, Planning, and Operations, 23*(3), 241–259.

Sharma, A., & Mittal, A. K. (2019). Applications of Artificial Intelligence in Autonomous Vehicles: A Review. *International Journal of Engineering and Advanced Technology, 9*(2), 522–527. doi:10.35940/ijeat.b9398.129219

Sharma, A., & Mittal, A. K. (2019). Machine learning-based intelligent vehicles: A review. *Transportation Research Part C, Emerging Technologies, 105,* 434–455. doi:10.1016/j.trc.2019.06.014

Suarez-Fernandez, M. C., Sotelo-Figueroa, M., & Flores-Tapia, A. (2021). Comparison of fuzzy controllers for autonomous vehicles. *International Journal of Fuzzy Systems, 23*(1), 1–14. doi:10.100740815-020-00947-3

Winfield, J. F. C., & Jirotka, M. (2018). Pedestrian Safety and Autonomous Vehicles: A Review. *IEEE Transactions on Intelligent Transportation Systems, 19*(6), 1763–1773.

Yoon, S. S., & Kim, C. Y. (2019). Deep learning for autonomous driving: A review. *Sensors (Basel), 19*(22), 5130. doi:10.339019225130 PMID:31752423

Zhao, H., Chen, X., & Lin, Z. (2020). Deep Learning-Based Autonomous Driving: A Review. *IEEE Transactions on Intelligent Transportation Systems, 21*(9), 3765–3784. doi:10.1109/TITS.2019.2954055

APPENDIX: ABBREVIATIONS

CNNs: Convolutional Neural Networks
GANs: Generative Adversarial Networks
RNNs: Recurrent Neural Networks
SLNA: Systematic Literature Network Analysis

Chapter 20
Data Privacy in the Metaverse Ecosystem

Sibanjan Debeeprasad Das
https://orcid.org/0000-0002-2437-0482
Indian Institute of Management, Ranchi, India

Pradip Kumar Bala
Indian Institute of Management, Ranchi, India

Rajat Kumar Behera
KIIT University, India

ABSTRACT

This chapter introduces data privacy and its significance in the metaverse to the readers. It introduces several data privacy policies, privacy enhancing techniques (PET), and discusses some existing literatures on data privacy issues in the metaverse. This chapter seeks to educate readers on the various methods and technologies available to protect personal and sensitive data throughout the entire data lifecycle (collection, storage, use, and transmission). In addition, it discusses how these privacy-preserving techniques can be used to secure metaverse data and describes the most recent findings from studies conducted on the PET methods to improve these practices. The chapter also includes suggestions for additional research and development that will help readers take the first step toward enhancing data privacy techniques in the metaverse or incorporating existing technologies into privacy-enhancing metaverse applications.

INTRODUCTION

The metaverse which is a complex immersive 3D digital space with collapsed virtual and real realms, is set to become the next major evolution in the web (Dwivedi et al., 2022; Fernandez and Hui, 2022; Lee et al., 2021; Zhang et al., 2022). The potential application of such cross-platform physical-virtual reality interactions is huge and includes usage in such disciplines as education, healthcare, marketing, and tourism (Dwivedi et al., 2022). But despite the transformative nature of the continued evolution of the

DOI: 10.4018/978-1-6684-8851-5.ch020

metaverse and how it is set to positively impact people in their occupational, social, and leisure interaction, transforming, in the process, the way we conduct business, interact with ourselves and others. It is leading to develop shared experiences by the progressive blurring the gap between physical and digital world. However, this results in extensive data sharing, which raises fundamental privacy and security concerns that has attracted mounting scholarly and public policy scrutiny.

Fernandez and Hui (2022), for instance, discussed the challenges the metaverse faces in terms of security, privacy, and with regard to ethics and governance. The study also explored and provided arguably one of the most comprehensive explanation of the trends and approaches that connected virtual worlds are devising in their solutions and research pathways to enable a more safe, more inclusive, and more sustainable metaverse. It is noted that although extended reality (XR) gears (e.g., head-mounted displays or HMDs) provide users a more immersive, realistic, and superior metaverse experience, the devices capture vast amounts of information from users, including biometrical data. Most of this information is sensitive to both users and bystanders and can present a range of privacy, security, and even ethical problems. Fernandez and Hui (2022) argue as an example that head movement and eye tracking collected by HMDs can provide gaze data that give away the users' sexual preferences, thus putting the most personal or private aspects of our persona and psyche at risk.

Uberti (2022) echoed near-similar sentiments noting that as new meta-versa technologies gathers personal and intimate information at an increasingly granular level such as a person's eye movement, gait, voice, emotions, and other biometrics, the continued use of the immersive worlds in the metaverse will put greater strain on existing security safeguards, exposing people to a host and deadly privacy infringements. This is compounded by the seeming lack of controls in the metaverse, which by its very nature cannot be limited to a single or select data privacy regimes (e.g., the EU GDPR or California Consumer Privacy Act) given its global reach and use (Weingarden, 2022). In most instances, multiple legislations are applicable, and this raises the question about whether or not there is any data safeguard and privacy protection responsibility in the metaverse at all (Todd, 2022).

As we see, data privacy is a major concern in the metaverse. To deal with this problem, it requires a combination of clear regulations, secure storage and transfer solutions, user control and education, and responsible use of data by metaverse platforms. Protecting users' privacy in the metaverse's melting pot of regulatory regimes is thus critical. A number of studies (De Guzman, Thilakarathna, & Seneviratne, 2019; Lebeck et al., 2017) have proposed solutions for safeguarding users' privacy and ensuring their security in such scenarios. Some of these privacy-enhancing technologies (PETs) include intrinsic protection, data aggregation, protected rendering and sharing, and authentication. These PETs can collectively work to obfuscate any of the users' sensible or private data from the sensors before being uploaded or shared online (Fernandez & Hui, 2022). However, creating a tailored privacy policy is perhaps the most effective way of mitigating privacy and security concerns in the metaverse. Thus this chapter will delve into these details on the current challenges, current research and potential solutions related to data privacy in Metaverse.

Literature Review

World has been some high profile data privacy breach that had lead to serious consequences such as identity theft and financial frauds. Equifax, one of the largest credit reporting agencies in the US, suffered a data breach that exposed the personal information of 143 million consumers, including Social Security numbers, birth dates, and addresses (Gressin, 2017). Hackers stole credit and debit card information from 40 million customers who had shopped at Target stores during the holiday season. The breach also exposed the personal information of 70 million customers, including names, addresses, and phone numbers. The political consulting firm Cambridge Analytica had obtained the personal data of millions of Facebook users without their consent (Hinds, Williams, & Joinson, 2020). The data was used to create psychological profiles of users and influence the 2016 US presidential election. With growth in digital transformation, and people and organizations becoming more digitally active, the data that is stored or shared is only growing to increase. Data is a critical asset and thus it is important to protect the data to ensure the reliability, accountability and trustworthiness of the data both at rest and in motion. Protecting data involves both traditional way of backing up the data in physical devices and location to restore them in case of failures to replicating the data to multiple locations as in case of cloud computing, several data security and privacy methods to safeguard the data pipelines (Preston, 2021).

One of the very first step is data protection is to classify the data based on its sensitivity and value it provides to an organization (Tankard, 2015). For example, data related to trade secrets, and financial information not publicly available can be classified as confidential data. Documents such as medical records and government classified information can be considered as restricted data. While the social security number or driving license details can be considered as Personal identifiable information(PII). Data classification may vary depending on the Organization, Individual and their specific needs. Data privacy stems from the data protection to ensure the protection of personal data, majorly the PII data and also confidential information of a firm/institution. Though there are various guidelines on understanding what is deemed to be confidential or sensitive, entities such as the data facilitators and handlers are the one who can best judge what can be considered as confidential or sensitive based on the producers or consumer of the data.

Around the world, various privacy laws exist, each with its own set of regulations and requirements. Among the most well-known privacy laws are:

- **The General Data Protection Regulation (GDPR):** Is a European Union (EU) regulation that governs data protection and privacy for EU citizens. It outlines the rules for how businesses should handle personal data as well as the rights that individuals have in relation to their data (Mohan, Wasserman, & Chidambaram, 2019).
- **California Consumer Privacy Act (CCPA):** The CCPA is a California law that requires businesses to disclose what personal information they collect about their customers and how that information is used, as well as giving customers the right to have their information deleted (Harding et al., 2019).
- **Health Insurance Portability and Accountability Act (HIPAA):** HIPAA is a United States law that governs how healthcare providers, health plans, and other covered entities handle personal health information (PHI) (Savage, n.d.).
- **Children's Online Privacy Protection Act (COPPA):** The Children's Online Privacy Protection Act (COPPA) is a United States law that requires website operators to obtain parental consent before collecting personal information from children under the age of 13 (Kaya, 2023).
- **Personal Information Protection and Electronic Documents Act (PIPEDA):** The Personal Information Protection and Electronic Documents Act (PIPEDA) is a Canadian privacy law that governs the collection, use, and disclosure of personal information by private sector organisations (Cao & Yang, 2023).

- **General Data Protection Law (LGPD):** The LGPD is a Brazilian privacy law that is similar to the GDPR in that it establishes guidelines for how businesses should handle personal data and the rights that individuals have in relation to their data (Jacob, 2023).
- **Personal Data Protection Act (PDPA):** The PDPA is a Singapore privacy law that governs organisations' collection, use, and disclosure of personal data (Alibeigi & Munir, 2022).

When developing applications or collecting data in Metaverse, it is critical to understand and implement these policies to the greatest extent as possible. For example, applications with a target market for children, such as games, should try at least to follow COPPA policy while collecting data from children below 13 age group.

The possibility of acquiring sensitive data is much greater in metaverse systems than it is in traditional systems, which poses a substantial risk to the personal privacy. Some earlier study highlights the fact that the metaverse may cause substantial privacy threats, even for individuals whose data are only indirectly engaged such as background noise or location. For instance, metaverse headsets with live microphones may record every conversation, eye tracking moments or even the location and surroundings (Basu et al. 2022). There are huge concerns about the privacy aspects in metaverse, especially for virtual avatars. User's avatar or alter ego creates a variety of data in the metaverse that might include videos, voicemails and messages. These data when not managed properly might lead to catastrophic outcomes, such as the voice recording could be comprised by an attacker and could be used maliciously (Mittal & Bansal, 2023). Nair, Garrido, and Song (2022) found from their experiment that an attacker could uniquely identify individuals based on two datapoints: height and wingspan. An attacker could also use the behavioural observations such as reaction to certain stimuli and telemetry observations such as height to asses a subject's physical fitness. VR could potentially secretly reveal an individual's vision information as well. Owing to these risks, protection of users from metaverse is a highly sensitive aspect, and unfortunately some XR providers are not ensuring the adoption of data security measures (Pearlman et al., 2021).

Christopoulos et al. (2021) associated the ethical issues with the use of AR in education into four classes: physical, psychological, moral, and data privacy. These issues depend on different stakeholders and can be prevented at four different stages in their life cycle. For example, moral concerns regarding the content of an immersive experience can only be determined by the involved instructional designer. Other stakeholders include government, developers, and users. Local, regional or national legal bodies can determine who has the right to augment content in a specific geographic location. To prevent these issues, biometric data containing health and medical information can be collected, processed locally, and discharged. However, this user data is also sensitive in nature and also be stored in accordance with the GDPR act (Bye et al., 2019). As we can see, it's not only regulations that could help to cope with privacy issues in the metaverse; there is also a need for better privacy enhancing techniques in the systems to safeguard the data.

PRIVACY ENHANCING TECHNIQUES

As previously stated, data privacy is the most important aspect of data protection because it ensures the privacy of sensitive and personal data with the goal of achieving the availability and immutability of critical data. We also discussed data protection laws such as the General Data Protection Regulations

(GDPR), which require organizations and entities to follow strict data handling protocols and standards. For example, GDPR has communicated data privacy related requirements in article 25 that mentions two main practices on ensuring data privacy for Organizations: data privacy by design and data privacy by default. Data privacy by design means that appropriate data protection and privacy features are embedded into an organization's processes and practices, which are followed at each and every stage of data-related products, from inception to destruction. Implementing this requires having up-to-date data privacy policies, ensuring that employees or individuals are trained on these policies, and having controls in systems/processes to ensure that the practices are followed within the Organization. While, by default, data privacy means that only necessary personal data is collected, stored, or processed, and that it is only accessible to a select group of people. Article 25 also states that an approved certification, as defined in Article 42, may be used to demonstrate compliance with the requirements for privacy by design and privacy by default.

Despite the fact that these data privacy laws are intended to prevent privacy violations, Organizations frequently damage consumers' privacy by sharing their customers' data with third-party companies in order to gain insights, improve their services, or monetize their data assets. Privacy-enhancing technologies (PETs) enable businesses to capitalize on the growing amount of data while keeping personal or sensitive information private. As a result, corporate reputation and compliance will improve. These PETs are a subset of technological advancements that enable users to maintain control over their personal data while still benefiting from the advantages of digital services and applications. PET, as defined by Blarkom, Borking, and Olk in 2003, is a set of information and communication technology (ICT) measures taken to safeguard private information by omitting or reducing the amount of personally identifiable information (PII) that is processed, all while maintaining the usability of the information system. The PET uses countermeasures such as data pseudonymization, encryption, and access controls to ensure that sensitive data is rigorously safeguarded against privacy concerns. Furthermore, PETs enables the generation of synthetic data and the use of privacy-aware system architectures for various simulations or the creation of AI models. In the following sections, we will discuss the various methods for improving privacy and the significance of these methods in the world of the metaverse.

Data Minimization

As users interact with the Metaverse, a large amount of diverse, complex, and sensitive data is produced, such as:

- **User Behavior Data:** The metaverse generates a significant amount of data involving user behaviour, like movement patterns, interactions with virtual objects, and social interactions between users (Lee et al., 2021).
- **Biometric Data:** The metaverse may also capture unique physical or behavioural characteristics that can be used to identify an individual, such as fingerprints, facial recognition, or voice recognition (Ol´ah & Nica, 2022).
- **Transaction Data:** The metaverse may also generate transaction data related to purchases made within the platform, such as virtual goods or services (HuynhThe et al., 2023).
- **User-Generated Content:** Users are able to create and share content, such as virtual objects, personas, and environments, within the metaverse. This user generated content generates a sub-

stantial quantity of data, including information about the content and the social interactions that encircle it (Duan et al., 2022).

- **User Preferences and Interests:** As users interact with the metaverse, data regarding their preferences, interests, and behaviours may be generated. This information can be used to personalise the experience and provide users with recommendations (Watson et al., 2022).
- **Telemetry Data:** This is data related to the performance and usage of the metaverse platform, such as server performance, user traffic, and error logs (Nair, Garrido, & Song, 2022).

While the organizations dealing with metaverse systems take an approach to collect every data and decide what to do with later approach is a big threat to data privacy as it is difficult to protect, organize and manage the huge pile of data. It is absolutely important to understand what data is getting collected, why it is required and where to use it. Data Minimization is a technique to minimize the collecting of data only to required purposes by effectively tagging data with the business purpose and outcome expected to drive using the data. Additionally all these information should be stored in a data map that clearly states the source, data attributes and business purpose for data collection along with data classification, audit levels and data security applicable on that data.

There are many critical stages to implementing a data minimization technique in metaverse systems:

- It is important to determine the precise reason for gathering each piece of data by considering the bare minimum of facts required to accomplish this goal.
- Then collect the information just required to fulfil the chosen goal. We should avoid gathering data that is superfluous or irrelevant to the goal.
- Next step is to delete the data once it is no longer required for the defined purpose. We should create retention rules that indicate how long data will be kept and under what conditions it will be erased.
- It is then important to remove any personally identifiable information that isn't required for the stated purpose.
- The most important activity is to inform users about the data being gathered and how it will be utilised. People should be given a choice to exercise control over their data by providing clear and transparent information regarding data gathering practises.

Implementing a data minimization technique in metaverse systems helps limiting the quantity of data gathered and stored to protects user privacy, lowers storage and processing costs, and fosters user trust.

Data Pseudonymization and Anonymization

The metaverse stores a significant amount of information on biological data which are highly sensitive in nature. Triangulating the data from retina scan, finger prints and motion data might lead to providing a lot of information about the individual. Thus, data pseudonymization and anonymization are required to protect the identity of individuals. Data pseudonymization is a technique to modify the data in such a way that the data can't be identified without providing some other additional information that is kept secret with an administrator or person with an assigned role. Pseudonymization makes the information such as PII less accessible to unauthorized users. Generally there are three kind of techniques:

- **Data Encryption:** This is a technique to protect the confidentially of data by converting it into an unreadable format using some cryptographic algorithms. When data is encrypted, it is converted into a form that can only be decrypted by using a secret key or password. There are mainly two types of encryptions:
    - ○ **Symmetric Encryption:** In symmetric encryption, the same key is used to both encrypt and decrypt the data. This type of encryption is typically faster than asymmetric encryption, but it requires that both the sender and receiver have access to the same secret key.
    - ○ **Asymmetric Encryption:** In asymmetric encryption, also known as public key encryption, two different keys are used to encrypt and decrypt the data. The public key is used to encrypt the data, while the private key is used to decrypt it. This type of encryption is slower than symmetric encryption, but it is more secure since the private key is kept secret. Homomorphic encryption is one of the widely used asymmetric encryption technique for PET purpose. It a special type of public-key encryption that allows computations to be performed on encrypted data without first decrypting it. This means that data can be securely analyzed and processed without exposing it to potential security risks during the decryption process (Wood, Najarian, & Kahrobaei, 2020).
- **Scrambling:** Scrambling is a process to apply a reversible transformation such as obfuscation of letters, to the original data in order to make it difficult to identify sensitive information.

In the other hand, data anonymization refers to a method in which data is changed completely which can no longer be identified and can't be restored back to the original information. This technique is generally used for cases where it is only important to derive results out of the data distribution such as performing statistical analysis and use in research. There are various methods to anonymize the data such as

- **Directory Replacement:** Here certain part of the identifying information is altered, such as the name of the individual, while other identifying information remains the same (Rowan, 2021).
- **Data Masking:** Data masking is a technique used to anonymize sensitive data by replacing a part of it or it completely with random characters or random data. For example, a name could be replaced with a randomly generated string of characters of the same length or with a fictitious number that has the same format (Cui, Zhang, & Wang, 2017).
- **Blurring:** It is a process to render the meaning of data values obsolete and re-identification of data values are made impossible (Rowan, 2021).
- **Suppression:** It is an action of removing an entire portion of data from a dataset. This is the most secure method of data anonymization, as no information can be reconstructed from the data (Eze & Peyton, 2015).

Data pseudonymization techniques such as scrambling can also be used as an anonymization technique by applying an irreversible transformation to obfuscate the data. Murthy et al. (2019) reviewed the strength and weakness of the anonymization techniques in their research and concluded that data suppression as a most efficient data anonymization technique on their dataset.

Synthetic Data

Synthetic data can be used to create customized digital experience that impacts the customer behavior and build brand recognition (Hudson et al., 2022). It can also be used to enable immersive employee experiences such as employee socialization and virtual engagements in a metaverse world (Lyons et al., 2022). Synthetic data generation is a process to generate artificial data that resembles the quality of Original data and retains the statistical properties of the data such as distribution and format of the real data. Thus this method breaks the relationship between original data and artificial data increasing the level of data protection of the subjects. Companies are increasingly adopting synthetic data, especially in regulated sectors like banking, insurance, and healthcare. It is used to enrich their insufficient data, share data within and outside organizations, and for open innovation projects. Market analysts predict that synthetic data will become mainstream for AI projects in the near future (Syn, n.d.).

To generate synthetic data it is essential to know the properties of the original data which when is not done right might create opportunity for information leakage. One of the well-known case was discovered by Massachusetts governor William Weld where he was able to identify personal health records by overlapping records between an anonymized public database of health records and a voter registry (Ji, Lipton, & Elkan, 2014). To combat these problems, researcher introduced several algorithms like k-anonymity (Sweeney, 2002) and t-closeness (Li, Li, & Venkatasubramanian, 2006). In these approaches, the sensitive features in the group are aggregated such as average as per the value set for k or t, and this aggregated values are used for the individuals. Though this is useful in combating information leakage up to a certain extent, it is not useful when an attacker has some information about few individuals in the group using which he can infer the information about the unknown individuals. To do this in a right way, researchers came out with a way to generate synthetic data by applying generative modelling technique (Patki, Wedge, & Veeramachaneni, 2016), and differential private algorithms is one such group of algorithms that are used to generate synthetic data.

Differential Privacy

The basic idea behind differential privacy algorithms is to take an existing dataset as input and generate a new synthetic dataset that closely mimics the original in terms of properties while protecting sensitive information (Blum, Ligett, & Roth, 2013). It makes use of random noise to guarantee that the publicly accessible information does not change much, even if the information connected to some of the records is already known by the attackers, or it ensures that it does not change significantly even when some information is updated, which prevents the identification of the identity of records for which the information is unknown (Dwork et al., 2006). However, adding random noise doesn't always ensure complete data protection. It may lead to information leakage or reconstruction attacks as well. So these algorithms are equipped with parameters such as epsilon and delta to optimize the privacy features by quantifying the "privacy loss". Privacy loss is a measure of how much information about an individual's data is leaked by a differentially private algorithm. It is typically measured using a metric called the privacy loss function, which quantifies the amount of information revealed about an individual record as a result of the algorithm. It is defined as the maximum amount by which the probability of observing a particular output changes if a single record is added or removed from the dataset. A smaller privacy loss function indicates greater privacy protection, as it implies that the addition or removal of a single record has minimal impact on the output of the algorithm. Privacy loss is an important concept in differential privacy as it allows us to quantify the level of privacy protection provided by a differentially private algorithm and to compare the privacy protections offered by different algorithms. It is essential to carefully balance privacy and utility when designing differentially private algorithms to ensure that the privacy loss is minimized while maintaining useful results.

Federated Learning

Usually, storing data in a centralized location to train AI models possess data security and privacy risks. Every time the model is used or re-trained it requires data in a similar centralized environment. This traditional way of sending data to ML servers also might lead to various bottlenecks in the network infrastructure as the data volume grows and in turn might need extra level of efforts and attention that might lead to data privacy related issues as well. Metaverse being the den of various personally identifiable information(PII) data, federated learning could be particularly useful in scenarios where users' personal data is used to train machine learning models. For example, federated learning could be used to train recommendation models for virtual worlds, without requiring all the data on user preferences to be centralized. This could help to protect users' privacy while still enabling the creation of personalized recommendations. It could also be used to train models for natural language processing, computer vision, and other AI applications within the metaverse, without requiring all the data to be stored in a central location. This could help to reduce the computational resources required for training large models and improve the scalability of AI applications in the metaverse.

Federated learning is a technique that trains AI and ML models over the remote devices like IoT devices, mobile phone or even in disparate secured data centers, and provide similar results to that of a ML model trained on a centralized data store. It allows multiple devices or servers to collaboratively train a model without sharing their data with each other. As it enables users to train models on sensitive data, this may be very helpful in circumstances and environments like Metaverse where data privacy is a problem. This also aids in the implementation of several legislative requirements, such as the GDPR's data minimization policy, since only basic data, such as model weights or updates, are shared with a centralised server. Federated learning generally has three overarching steps (Zhang et al., 2021):

- **Server Initialization:** The first step is to select clients by the server to participate in training and broadcast the initialized global model parameters to each client.
- **Local Training:** The second step is to train a machine learning model locally in the client. Each party retains ownership of its own data, and trains a local model over the global model on a local optimizer. The updated model weights are shared with the server.
- **Model Aggregation:** The third step is for the central server to use an aggregation algorithm, such as the FedAvg algorithm, to get a new global model based on the model weights shared by the clients.
- The above steps are repeated until the global model converges.

There is a wide variety of work now being done in order to make advantage of federated learning in metaverse. For instance, research was done by Kang et al. (2022) on blockchain-based federated learning for the industrial metaverse. In order to train machine learning (ML) models, Zhou, Liu, and Zhao (2022) integrated federated learning into mobile augmented reality (MAR) systems of the metaverse. Similarly, Bhattacharya et al. (2023) used federated learning inside a gaming metaverse to train ML models that are able to deliver a personalized gaming experience for each and every game participant within the metaverse.

CONCLUSION

It is evident that protecting data privacy is crucial for metaverse. Despite the fact that there are numerous regulations and policies in place to safeguard data, individuals in organizations often fail to adhere to them and improperly handle data. Therefore, it is crucial to integrate privacy-enhancing techniques into enterprise systems and procedures. Although current PET techniques can be used in metaverse systems to a limited extent, they must be improved to manage data in metaverse systems appropriately. While these PET are utilized, there is no such thing as a zero risk. There have been breaches of anonymized data in the past. While applying the PET, care must be taken not to degrade data quality in a manner that would affect downstream applications, such as machine learning models and application features. Understanding data privacy is advantageous, and strict adherence to the policy is required. Even if some policies are not pertinent to the location where the organization operates, it is advisable to adhere to them as much as feasible. Metaverse is still in its infancy, and countries will create, improvise, or adapt other data privacy policies sooner rather than later.

FUTURE WORK

As we saw, despite the inclusion of fundamental privacy and security principles in the metaverse world, they still remain as the most pressing concerns today. To address this, researchers can work together to construct a blueprint and further resolve how the virtual world integrates with the real world. This includes vigorously developing metaverse related privacy enhancing technologies, improving laws and regulations, and finding a balance between regulatory and user experience. The Metaverse's speech and actions may be bombarded with false news, bullying and derogatory comments. And so, Chen et al. (2022) believes that regulations and copyright enforcement need to be updated and reinforced. However, in the metaverse, there is still a lack of ethics, accountability, and regulations that govern interactions with bots or AI. Fernandez and Hui (2022) advocated the use of PET in the metaverse world, however they mentioned that still there are open challenges in applying these measures at the sensory level and ensuring privacy and safety of users and bystanders.

In the future, there is going to be a surge in user generated contents(UGC) in metaverse which might bring in new privacy concerns in metaverse such as content poisoning. So, it is important to design and develop technologies that makes metaverse much human-centric, for example, users privacy preferences should be ensured in developing privacy preserving approaches in metaverse environments (Wang et al., 2022). Falchuk, Loeb, and Neff (2018) describes various privacy plans for metaverse with techniques such as creating new avatars clones or in a disguised form, spawning a private copy for a portion of VR or teleporting the user avatar. However, these techniques are not perfect, and there are challenges in deploying such tools.

With all these issues, there continues to be room for research into techniques to enhance existing privacy preserving measures, legislation, and new privacy-enhancing technologies.

REFERENCES

Alibeigi, A., & Munir, A. B. (2022). A decade after the Personal Data Protection Act 2010 (PDPA): Compliance of communications companies with the notice and choice principle. *Journal of Data Protection & Privacy*, 5(2), 119–137.

Basu, Jaiswal, & Danoosh, & Saralaya. (2022). Analysis of the Feasibility of VR Metaverses and Examining its Societal and Health Ramifications. *Survey (London, England)*.

Bhattacharya, P., Verma, A., Prasad, V. K., Tanwar, S., Bhushan, B., Florea, B. C., Taralunga, D. D., Alqahtani, F., & Tolba, A. (2023). Game-o-Meta: Trusted Federated Learning Scheme for P2P Gaming Metaverse beyond 5G Networks. *Sensors (Basel)*, 23(9), 4201. doi:10.339023094201 PMID:37177403

Blum, A., Ligett, K., & Roth, A. (2013). A learning theory approach to noninteractive database privacy. *Journal of the Association for Computing Machinery*, 60(2), 1–25. doi:10.1145/2450142.2450148

Bye, K., Hosfelt, D., Chase, S., Miesnieks, M., & Beck, T. (2019). The ethical and privacy implications of mixed reality. ACM SIGGRAPH 2019 Panels, 1–2. doi:10.1145/3306212.3328138

Cao, Y., & Yang, M. (2023). Legal regulation of big data killing:–From the perspective of "Personal Information Protection Law". *Journal of Education. Humanities and Social Sciences*, 7, 233–241.

Chen, Wu, Gan, & Qi. (2022). *Metaverse Security and Privacy: An Overview*. Academic Press.

Christopoulos, A., Mystakidis, S., Pellas, N., & Laakso, M.-J. (2021). Arlean: An augmented reality learning analytics ethical framework. *Computers*, 10(8), 92. doi:10.3390/computers10080092

Cui, Jiang, Zhang, & Wang. (2017). A data masking scheme for sensitive big data based on format-preserving encryption. In *2017 IEEE International Conference on Computational Science and Engineering (CSE) and IEEE International Conference on Embedded and Ubiquitous Computing (EUC)* (vol. 1, pp. 518–524). IEEE.

De Guzman, J. A., Thilakarathna, K., & Seneviratne, A. (2019). Security and privacy approaches in mixed reality: A literature survey. *ACM Computing Surveys*, 52(6), 1–37. doi:10.1145/3359626

Duan, H., Huang, Y., Zhao, Y., Huang, Z., & Cai, W. (2022). User-generated content and editors in video games: Survey and vision. In 2022 IEEE conference on games (CoG) (pp. 536–543). IEEE. doi:10.1109/CoG51982.2022.9893717

Dwivedi, Y. K., Hughes, L., Baabdullah, A. M., Ribeiro-Navarrete, S., Giannakis, M., Al-Debei, M. M., Dennehy, D., Metri, B., Buhalis, D., Cheung, C. M. K., Conboy, K., Doyle, R., Dubey, R., Dutot, V., Felix, R., Goyal, D. P., Gustafsson, A., Hinsch, C., Jebabli, I., ... Wamba, S. F. (2022). Metaverse beyond the hype: Multidisciplinary perspectives on emerging challenges, opportunities, and agenda for research, practice and policy. *International Journal of Information Management*, 66, 102542. doi:10.1016/j.ijinfomgt.2022.102542

Dwork, C., Kenthapadi, K., McSherry, F., Mironov, I., & Naor, M. (2006). Our data, ourselves: Privacy via distributed noise generation. *Advances in Cryptology-EUROCRYPT 2006: 24th Annual International Conference on the Theory and Applications of Cryptographic Techniques, St. Petersburg, Russia, May 28-June 1, 2006 Proceedings, 25,* 486–503.

Eze, B., & Peyton, L. (2015). Systematic literature review on the anonymization of high dimensional streaming datasets for health data sharing. *Procedia Computer Science, 63,* 348–355. doi:10.1016/j.procs.2015.08.353

Falchuk, Loeb, & Neff. (2018). The social metaverse: Battle for privacy. *IEEE Technology and Society Magazine, 37*(2), 52–61.

Fernandez, C. B., & Hui, P. (2022). Life, the Metaverse and everything: An overview of privacy, ethics, and governance in Metaverse. In *2022 IEEE 42nd International Conference on Distributed Computing Systems Workshops (ICDCSW)* (pp. 272–277). IEEE. 10.1109/ICDCSW56584.2022.00058

Gressin, S. (2017). The equifax data breach: What to do. Federal Trade Commission.

Harding, Vanto, Clark, Ji, & Ainsworth. (2019). Understanding the scope and impact of the california consumer privacy act of 2018. *Journal of Data Protection & Privacy, 2*(3), 234–253.

Hinds, J., Williams, E. J., & Joinson, A. N. (2020). "It wouldn't happen to me": Privacy concerns and perspectives following the Cambridge Analytica scandal. *International Journal of Human-Computer Studies, 143,* 102498. doi:10.1016/j.ijhcs.2020.102498

Hudson, J. (2022). Virtual Immersive Shopping Experiences in Metaverse Environments: Predictive Customer Analytics, Data Visualization Algorithms, and Smart Retailing Technologies. *Linguistic and Philosophical Investigations,* (21), 236–251.

Huynh-The, T., Gadekallu, T. R., Wang, W., Yenduri, G., Ranaweera, P., Pham, Q.-V., Benevides da Costa, D., & Liyanage, M. (2023). Blockchain for the metaverse: A Review. *Future Generation Computer Systems, 143,* 401–419. doi:10.1016/j.future.2023.02.008

Jacob, M. (2023). *Following extensive, multi-annual negotiations the European Parliament and European Council have reached an agreement on a new General Data Protection Regulation modernising a legal framework which dates back to the 1990s.* Global Security Mag Online.

Ji, Lipton, & Elkan. (2014). *Differential privacy and machine learning: a survey and review.* arXiv preprint arXiv:1412.7584.

Kang, J., Ye, D., Nie, J., Xiao, J., Deng, X., Wang, S., Xiong, Z., Yu, R., & Niyato, D. (2022). Blockchain-based federated learning for industrial metaverses: Incentive scheme with optimal aoi. In *2022 IEEE International Conference on Blockchain (Blockchain)* (pp. 71–78). IEEE. 10.1109/Blockchain55522.2022.00020

Kaya, D. (2023). *Ignoring COPPA: An Industry Standard.* Academic Press.

Lebeck, K., Ruth, K., Kohno, T., & Roesner, F. (2017). Securing augmented reality output. In 2017 IEEE symposium on security and privacy (SP) (pp. 320–337). IEEE. doi:10.1109/SP.2017.13

Lee, L.-H., Braud, T., Zhou, P., Wang, L., Xu, D., Lin, Z., Kumar, A., Bermejo, C., & Hui, P. (2021). *All one needs to know about metaverse: A complete survey on technological singularity, virtual ecosystem, and research agenda.* arXiv preprint arXiv:2110.05352.

Li, N., Li, T., & Venkatasubramanian, S. (2006). t-closeness: Privacy beyond k-anonymity and l-diversity. In *2007 IEEE 23rd international conference on data engineering* (pp. 106–115). IEEE.

Lyons, N. (2022). Talent acquisition and management, immersive work environments, and machine vision algorithms in the virtual economy of the metaverse. *Psychosociological Issues in Human Resource Management, 10*(1), 121–134. doi:10.22381/pihrm10120229

Mittal, G., & Bansal, R. (2023). Driving Force Behind Consumer Brand Engagement: The Metaverse. In *Cultural Marketing and Metaverse for Consumer Engagement* (pp. 164–181). IGI Global. doi:10.4018/978-1-6684-8312-1.ch012

Mohan, J., Wasserman, M., & Chidambaram, V. (2019). Analyzing GDPR compliance through the lens of privacy policy. In Heterogeneous Data Management, Polystores, and Analytics for Healthcare: VLDB 2019 Workshops, Poly and DMAH, Los Angeles, CA, USA, August 30, 2019, Revised Selected Papers 5 (pp. 82–95). Springer. doi:10.1007/978-3-030-33752-0_6

Murthy, S., Abu Bakar, A., Rahim, F. A., & Ramli, R. (2019). A comparative study of data anonymization techniques. In *2019 IEEE 5th Intl Conference on Big Data Security on Cloud (BigDataSecurity), IEEE Intl Conference on High Performance and Smart Computing (HPSC) and IEEE Intl Conference on Intelligent Data and Security (IDS)* (pp. 306–309). IEEE. 10.1109/BigDataSecurity-HPSC-IDS.2019.00063

Nair, V., Garrido, G. M., & Song, D. (2022). *Exploring the unprecedented privacy risks of the metaverse.* arXiv preprint arXiv:2207.13176.

Ol'ah, J., & Nica, E. (2022). Biometric Sensor Technologies, Virtual Marketplace Dynamics Data, and Computer Vision and Deep Learning Algorithms in the Metaverse Interactive Environment. *Journal of Self-Governance & Management Economics, 10*(3).

Patki, N., Wedge, R., & Veeramachaneni, K. (2016). The synthetic data vault. In *2016 IEEE International Conference on Data Science and Advanced Analytics (DSAA)* (pp. 399–410). IEEE. 10.1109/DSAA.2016.49

Pearlman, Visner, Magnano, & Cameron. (2021). *Securing the Metaverse-Virtual Worlds Need REAL Governance.* Simulation Interoperability Standards Organization–SISO.

Preston, W. C. (2021). Modern Data Protection. O'Reilly Media, Inc.

Rowan, K. F. (2021). *An Overview of Understanding Digital Privacy.* Academic Press.

Savage, L. C. (n.d.). Playing with FHIR: The Path to Ensuring We Bring the Power of Supercomputing to How We Understand Healthcare in Medicine. In *Advanced Health Technology* (pp. 291–304). Productivity Press. doi:10.4324/9781003348603-17

Sweeney, L. (2002). k-anonymity: A model for protecting privacy. *International Journal of Uncertainty, Fuzziness and Knowledge-based Systems, 10*(05), 557–570. doi:10.1142/S0218488502001648

Synthetic Data. (n.d.). https://www.jpmorgan.com/synthetic-data

Tankard, C. (2015). Data classification–the foundation of information security. *Network Security, 2015*(5), 8–11. doi:10.1016/S1353-4858(15)30038-6

Todd, E., Bruce, K. S., Splittgerber, A., Bruno, S. L., Becker, J., Zanczak, H. J., Aw, C., & Gates, T. (2022). *The Reed Smith Guide to the Metaverse: Legal Issues (Part 1): Data protection and privacy* (2nd ed.). Reed Smith.

Uberti, D. (2022). Come the Metaverse, Can Privacy Exist? *Wall Street Journal.* https://www.wsj.com/articles/come-the-metaverse-can-privacy-exist-11641292206

Wang, Su, Zhang, Xing, & Liu, Luan, & Shen. (2022). A survey on metaverse: Fundamentals, security, and privacy. *IEEE Communications Surveys and Tutorials.*

Watson, R. (2022). The virtual economy of the metaverse: Computer vision and deep learning algorithms, customer engagement tools, and behavioral predictive analytics. *Linguistic and Philosophical Investigations,* (21), 41–56.

Weingarden, G., & Artz, M. (2022). *Metaverse and privacy.* International Association of Privacy Professionals (IAAP). https://iapp.org/news/a/metaverse-and-privacy-2/

Wood, A., Najarian, K., & Kahrobaei, D. (2020). Homomorphic encryption for machine learning in medicine and bioinformatics. *ACM Computing Surveys, 53*(4), 1–35. doi:10.1145/3394658

Zhang, L., Shen, B., Barnawi, A., Xi, S., Kumar, N., & Wu, Y. (2021). FedDPGAN: Federated differentially private generative adversarial networks framework for the detection of COVID-19 pneumonia. *Information Systems Frontiers, 23*(6), 1403–1415. doi:10.100710796-021-10144-6 PMID:34149305

Zhang, X., Chen, Y., Hu, L., & Wang, Y. (2022). The metaverse in education: Definition, framework, features, potential applications, challenges, and future research topics. *Frontiers in Psychology, 13,* 13. doi:10.3389/fpsyg.2022.1016300 PMID:36304866

Zhou, X., Liu, C., & Zhao, J. (2022). *Resource allocation of federated learning for the metaverse with mobile augmented reality.* arXiv preprint arXiv:2211.08705.

Chapter 21
Hybrid Optimization Techniques for Data Privacy Preserving in the Metaverse Ecosystem

M. P. Karthikeyan

iD https://orcid.org/0000-0002-2346-0283

JAIN University (Deemed), India

K. Krishnaveni

Sri S. Ramasamy Naidu Memorial College, Sattur, India

T. Revathi

Woxsen University, India

A. Hema Ambiha

Karpagam Academy of Higher Education, India

ABSTRACT

Large-scale electronic databases are being maintained by businesses and can be accessed via the internet or intranet. Employing data mining techniques, significant information was extracted from the data. The privacy of the data is inherently at risk while data mining operations are being carried out. All users shouldn't have access to the private information stored in the database. Methods for protecting privacy have been suggested in the literature. Algorithms used in privacy-preserving data mining (PPDM) on private data are unknown even to the algorithm operator. Personal information about users and data on their collective behaviour are the two main aspects of privacy preservation. The majority of privacy-preserving techniques rely on reducing the level of granularity used to represent the data. Although privacy is improved, information is lost as a result. As a result, with PPDM, there is a trade-off between privacy and information loss. Effective methods that don't undermine the security defences are needed.

DOI: 10.4018/978-1-6684-8851-5.ch021

INTRODUCTION

Since computer technology affects and enhances social connections, communication, and touch, it has a tremendous impact on daily life. From the viewpoint of final customers, three main waves of technical advancement have been noted. During these waves, the development of mobiles, personal computers, and the internet technologies received more and more attention. Innovators in the fourth wave of computers are two spatial, immersive technologies called augmented reality (AR) and the virtual reality (VR). The next paradigm for ubiquitous computing, which has the potential to alter (online) business, education, remote labour, and entertainment, is expected to be produced by this wave. This new paradigm is the metaverse. The word "metaverse" is derived from the Greek word Meta, which means beyond, beyond, or after, and universe. In alternative words, an after-reality universe is the Metaverse. Where the real world and digital virtuality are continuously combined among numerous people. In order to solve the underlying issues with web-based 2D e-learning technologies, online distance education can use Metaverse (Mystakidis & Stylianos, 2022).

Despite major technological improvements, textbooks, classrooms, and content distribution continue to be the primary implementation tactics in the field of education. The creation of the structure, laws, and regulations that will regulate the Metaverse is the subject of a vigorous struggle. In an effort to entice customers many businesses are attempting in an endeavour to develop their own closed, proprietary hardware and software ecosystems promote themselves as the primary Metaverse destinations (Sparkes, 2021). Divergent methods and numerous systemic approaches clash over ideas like transparency and confidentiality. The winner of this contest will determine if user privacy rights are broad enough to include or not students and schoolchildren are permitted access to the Metaverse. Both obstacles will determine whether or not the Metaverse can be widely employed in e-learning, which will have a big impact on education. In order to develop the purpose of this essay is to increase understanding of the history and potential uses of the Metaverse by providing a cohesive vision for meta-education and Metaverse-enabled online distant learning (Lee et al., 2021).

In the science fiction book Snow Crash by Neal Stephenson, the phrase "metaverse" first appeared which was released in 1992. But it didn't become well-known until Facebook changed its name to Meta in 2021. The first Metaverse Summit, which gathered thousands of attendees and inaugurated the Metaverse period in Asia in December 2021, was hosted via live social media broadcast in China. A large number of new technology start-ups focused on creating platforms and apps for the Metaverse soon after that. The rapid creation and use of the Metaverse, mostly in entertainment, e-commerce, and education, was sparked by a new wave of entrepreneurship (Kye et al., 2021).

Figure 1explains the metaverse interaction between physical world and In-world Ecosystem. This metaverse vision depicts three stages of evolution. When our real environments are digitalized and have the potential to periodically reflect changes to their virtual counterparts, we start with the concept of "digital twins" (Wang et al., 2022). According to the physical world, individuals who develop new objects in these virtual environments with their avatars are referred to as "digital natives." It is claimed that A There are "many" digitally accurate virtual worlds that closely resemble the actual world are created by digital twins. It's crucial to remember that these virtual worlds first suffer from a lack of communication either an information silo or with one another and the outside world. They eventually come together amid a vast landscape. The merging of The digitised physical and virtual worlds represent the last stage of the coexistence of physical and virtual reality. This is similar to virtual reality (Laeeq, 2022). The conditions for the metaverse an eternal, 3D virtual cyberspace are distinct in a connected physical-virtual cosmos.

Figure 1. Metaverse interaction

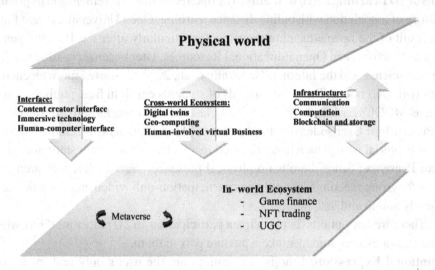

Augmented, Extended, Virtual, and Mixed Reality: Together, the phrases "cross reality" (XR) and "extended reality" (XR) refer to a group of immersive technologies that produce electronic, digital settings in which the data are represented and displayed (Duan et al., 2021) claim that XR includes Mixed Reality (MR), Virtual Reality (VR), and Augmented Reality (AR). Each of the aforementioned XR components includes a fully or partially artificial digital world that people may watch and interact with.

Virtual reality is an entirely artificial environment created digitally. Users of VR are captivated, act like they would in the real world, and feel as though they are in a new place. The employment of specialised multimodal equipment, Increases the senses of sight, hearing, touch, movement, and organic engagement with virtual objects through the use of devices like all of the aforementioned XR components contain a technologically generated, entirely or partially artificial digital environment that users can watch and engage with (Yang et al., 2022).

AR adopts a distinctive posture towards actual settings; it enhances the real world by integrating digital inputs and virtual elements. The physical and digital worlds are spatially intertwined. A layer of spatially projected digital artefacts is the eventual outcome. That are filtered via transparent products like smart phones, glasses, tablets, and contact lenses. Additionally, AR can be used by displaying information from VR headsets with integrated camera sensors and pass-through mode (Park, Sang-Min, & Young-Gab Kim, 2022).

Multimodal Metaverse Interactions: The platform on which the metaverse's multimodal interactions with virtual people, things, and situations are made possible. The representational quality of the XR system is made possible by stereo displays that can convey a sense of depth (Kim, 2021). This is achievable with distinct, slightly different displays that look like real sight for each eye. A user can have a 180-degree field of vision thanks to high-resolution XR panels. Additionally, XR systems offer improved audio experiences in contrast to 2D systems. 3D systems, spatial, or the binaural audio makes it feasible to create soundscapes for AR and VR, which greatly enhances immersion. Due to Users can orient themselves and recognise the directions of sound cues by using the spatial dispersion of sound. Making it an effective tool for navigating and grabbing their attention (Xu et al., 2022).

Limitations of 2D Learning Environments: The open education movement and its guiding principles have a long history of association with online distance learning. Open Universities were founded all over the world as a result of the open education movement, particularly after the 1960s. Open Courseware, Open Educational Practises, and Open Educational Resources, later became possible thanks to developments in computer science and the Internet (Gadekallu et al., 2022). It started more recent Massive Open Online Courses (MOOC) boom. Tens of thousands of students enroll in free, publicly accessible online courses known as MOOCs each year. They typically last for a few weeks and are free (Kshetri, 2022).

Low Self-Perception: User's idea of who they are in 2D environments is relatively limited. They are represented as immaterial beings by a headshot feed from a live camera or a static image.

No Physical Presence: Since there is no physical presence, Web conferences aren't thought of as virtual locations for group meetings, but rather as participation-only video chats. Participants in lengthy sessions frequently slump and lose interest.

Inactivity: There are few options for participant participation on 2D platforms. Only when professors initiate learning activities may students take a passive part in them.

Crude Emotional Expression: Emojis and smileys are the user's only real means of expressing their emotions.

While social networks only permit users to create messages, the Earth 3D map4 offers picture frames of the real world but lacks any physical features other than GPS information. Photos, and videos with a limited number of user involvement options (like liking a post, for example). Video games are improving and becoming more impressive. Users can enjoy stunning visuals and in-game physics in games like Call of Duty: Black Ops Cold War, which creates a sense of realism that closely mirrors the real world (Dwivedi et al., 2022).

This paper is divided into five sections. Section 1 deals with the general introduction of the proposed research. The current method and its limitations are discussed in Section 2 of the metaverse. With improved ACO+SVM, Section 3 explains the suggested techniques. The experimental results from testing on the Data's and their analysis are presented in Section 4, and a conclusion is offered in Section 5.

LITERATURE REVIEW

This section discussed about the present or existing system that has some draw back in data having metaverse techniques.

The development of immersive technologies has widened the scope of applications for metaverse tools and technology in education. Through the use of their avatars, Students can interact with teachers and communicate with peers in a metaverse environment made possible by XR technologies. Fostering an immersive learning experience that increases the student's incentive to study. For instance (Almarzouqi et al., 2022) research on the use of mixed reality (MR) in the maintenance business was conducted to develop engaging learning environments for aircraft maintenance. Volchek and Brysch (2023) using OpenSim examined applications for educational virtual environments and the dissemination of knowledge through open courses in the Metaverse. Lee and Kim (2022) analysed Photomath, an augmented reality mobile learning software for math instruction. Their results suggested that using AR into mathematics instruction can improve student's learning outcomes. Furthermore, Seidel et al. (2022) recognised the several world kinds in the educational metaverse, including escape rooms, mazes, racing/jumping, and multiple choice. Exemplary uses of the Metaverse in K–12 and higher education are shown in Table 1.

Early metaverse research was conducted in developed countries with some results (Wu et al., 2022). Many countries, including the US, Germany, and India, have developed information technology related to the metaverse. The definition of the metaverse was the very important theoretical subject, according to our analysis of the literature from the previous ten years. On a technological level, research on smart education has mostly focused on the platform's particular technical approaches and applications.

Using the metaverse as a teaching tool, on its Minecraft virtual campus, the University of California, Berkeley staged an online graduation ceremony. Toraman (2022) explains the launch of a metaverse-based creative science education strategy by the Ministry of Education in South Korea. Oshima described how robots can help educators by acting as intelligent mentors in his research on smart education. Professor Rensis created a query-based knowledge recommendation system for text-based learning resources, as well as a knowledge recommendation system that automatically builds knowledge bases.

Invitation to Metaverse: The necessity for a new venue for future education was explored in a discussion on the possibilities of the metaverse for educational advancement in this virtual world.

Education and the Metaverse: According to A method of education that blends the real world and the Edu-metaverse is called A New State of Educational Development in the future form the foundation of the interstellar civilization.

Buhalis et al. (2022) open another educational door. The Application, Challenges and Prospects of Edu-Metaverse outlined the problems and challenges the metaverse is now experiencing and offered solutions for the early stages of the Edu-Metaverse's development from a mechanism, technology, and teaching perspective. The "Internet +" applications in smart education, which use information technology to influence and transform education, were the main focus of previous research in terms of ecosystem theory and application.

Immersive Technology: In order to categorise constantly changing multisensory technologies, virtual reality has developed into a number of taxonomies, including EPI means for technology embodiment, psychological presence, behavioural interaction, and the continuum of visual, tactile, and virtual reality. Technologies that only simulate realness in the visual, auditory, haptic, and motion senses are referred to as immersive technology. Petrosyan and Aristova (2022) said about as a fully synthetic virtual environment, VR is commonly acknowledged to be part of this continuum. However, there is still disagreement over what exactly constitutes AR and MR. A continuum of reality virtuality, improved reality, a mixture of reality and virtual reality, distant collaboration between reality and virtual reality, and alignment of real-world and virtual environments are the six MR definitions that were discovered from the expert interviews and literature review. These definitions typically view as a division, element, or substitute for MR, AR. MR Real and virtual stuff coexisting dynamically in the same space is produced by technology that, in particular, creates virtual scenes, blends virtual scenes with real ones, or offers more complex interactivity (Hu, 2022). In contrast, augmented reality (AR) allows computer-generated content, like user interfaces and graphics, to be displayed on real-world settings in real time. In addition, extended reality (XR), which combines AR, MR, and VR, has recently been proposed by a number of researchers. However, XR is only an abstract idea without any concrete qualities.

With ordinary screens found in computers, cell phones, and other devices, MR/VR/AR can either achieve low immersion or high immersion depending on the presentation of the material using specialised equipment like Cave Automated Virtual Environments (CAVEs) and Head-Mounted Devices (HMDs). Standard input methods like keyboards, mouse, and touch displays are adequate for user control in AR/MR/VR applications. The immersive experience can be enhanced by using specialised equipment, such as the pedals and steering wheel for the driving simulation (Gupta et al., 2023).

Additionally, the perceived realism of the avatars and occupants in virtual worlds (VWs) is a class of technology that enhances immersion. Typically, Users are free to interact freely in a networked and installed with intelligent agents VW with virtual objects, the installed intelligent agents, and other users (Xu et al., 2022).

SYSTEM DESIGN

This session discussed about the proposed system algorithm and techniques for metaverse technology with better accuracy, sensitivity, recall and F-measures.

Ant Colony Optimization: This ACO algorithm is used to find the affected part in the input image. Where there are various iterations of the ACO algorithm. In each iteration, a number of data use heuristic data and the accumulated wisdom of preceding populations of data to build comprehensive solutions. The pheromone trail that is left on a solution's component parts, is used to represent these amassed experiences. All settings and pheromone variables are set in this first stage. After initiation, a group of data constructs a solution to the issue at hand utilising pheromone values and additional data.

Given the given behaviour of the data, we can now develop an algorithm. Only one food supply, one data colony, and two alternative journey routes have been considered for the purpose of simplicity. With the pathways acting as the edges, the data colony and food source as the nodes (vertices), and the pheromone levels acting as the weights attached to the connections, weighted graphs can be utilised to mimic the complete situation.

Assume that the graph has the form G = (V, E), here V and E denote the vertices and edges of the graph, vice versa. Given our perspective, the vertices are Vs (Source vertex, is a data colony), and Vd (Destination vertex, it is a food source). And the two edge's lengths, E1 and E2, are L1 and L2, respectively. Now, depending on their strength, it can be inferred that the associated pheromone values for vertices of E1 for R1 and E2 for R2. As a result, the following may be said about the initial likelihood of selecting a path (between E1 and E2) for each data:

$$Pi = \frac{Ri}{R1 + R2}; i = 1, 2$$

Evidently, the likelihood of selecting E_1 is higher if $R_1 > R_2$ and vice versa. Now, as you return along this route, let's say E_1, the pheromone value is changed for that route.

1. 1. **In accordance to path length**

$$Ri \leftarrow Ri + \frac{K}{Li}$$

$i = 1, 2$ and "K" act as model parameters in the aforementioned update.

2. 2. **Based on the pheromone's rate of evaporation**

Figure 2. Ant colony optimization pseudocode

Procedure Ant Colony Optimization:
initialise the pheromone experiments and relevant parameters;
   Generating data generation while not terminating;
      Determine the fitness values related to each set of data;
      Using selection techniques, determine the optimal option;
pheromone trial update;
   End while Ending the process

$$Ri \leftarrow \left(1 - v\right) * Ri$$

The parameter "v," which has a range of [0, 1], controls the pheromone evaporation. In addition, I = 1, 2. Figure 2 explains the ACO pseudocode clearly.

Pseudocode

Support Vector Machine SVM: All the resources are now available for building nonlinear classifiers. In order to achieve this, we replace each training sample with $\Phi(x_i)$ and run the best hyperplane algorithm in *F*. We will therefore produce a nonlinear decision function of the form because we are utilising kernels. In order to swiftly classify new data points in the future, the SVM technique looks to locate the best line or decision boundary that may partition n-dimensional space into classes. In the best situation, this decision boundary is called a hyperplane. The extreme vectors and points that make up the hyperplane are selected using SVM. The SVM method is built on support vectors, which are utilised to represent these extreme situations. Check out the illustration below, which uses a decision boundary or hyperplane to split two different groups. The number of features determines the hyperplane's size. The hyperplane seems to be a straight line when there are just two input features. The hyperplane changes into a two-dimensional plane when three input features are given. It's more challenging to visualise when there are more than three factors.

Elements of the SVM Object

The class "svm" object that is returned by the function svm() comprises some of the following elements:
   SV: Matrix of discovered support vectors;
   Labels: They have labels set to classify;

Figure 3. Support vector machine

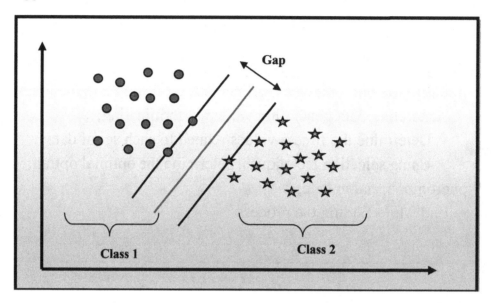

Index: Index of the support vectors present in the input data; this information could be used, for example, to visualise the support vectors as a part of the data set. Figure 3 explains about the support vector machine process clearly.

Figure 4. Support vector machine algorithm pseudocode

```
                  Dataset having a binary outcome and the p* variable.
                  The output is a list of variables that have been ranked by significance.
                  Determining the SVM model's tuning parameter's ideal values;
                  Develop the model for SVM;
                  P ← P*;
While p>=2do
                  SVMₚ ← SVM with optimization tuning parameters for the P variables and
observation in Data;
                  Wₚ ← Calculate weight vector of the SVMₚ(wₚ₁,....,wₚₚ);
                  Rank.criteria ←(w2p1,....,w2pp);
                  Min.rank.criteria←variable with the lowest value in rank.criteria vector;
                  Remove min.rank.criteria from the Data;
                  Rankₚ ←min.rank.criteria;
                  P ←P - 1;
End
Rank1 ← variable in Data (rank2.... Rankp*);
Return (rank1... Rankp*)
```

SVM Kernel: The SVM kernel is a function that takes a low-dimensional input space and transforms it into a higher-dimensional space, making non-separable problems into separable ones. For non-linear separation problems, it works best. Simply said, after completing some highly complex data transformations, the kernel decides how to split the data based on the labels or outputs defined. As a result, in situations like this, the margins are called soft margins. When the data set has a soft margin, the SVM tries to minimise 1/margin+ (penalty). Hinge loss is a common form of discipline. Hinge not lost if no breaches. If the distance of a violation results in a hinge loss. Figure 4 discussed about the SVM algorithm Pseudocode clearly. Figure 4 explains about the support vector machine Pseudocode process clearly.

RESULT AND DISCUSSION

This session discussed about the result and outcome of the newly built ACOSVM with ACO is contrasted with the existing one in terms of accuracy and sensitivity metrics. ACO, Decission Tree, SVM techniques of metaverse reality while using ACO+SVM techniques. Also, it explain about the result obtained in this proposed system (ACOSVM). The newly suggested study makes use of MATLAB 2013a to evaluate the performance of a classifier means.

Performance Evaluations: Performance evaluation metrics are used to determine how well your trained machine learning models perform. This lets you determine how well your machine learning model will perform with a dataset that it has never encountered before. A confusion matrix shows and summarises a categorization method's effectiveness.

Figure 5. Proposed and existing algorithm result for sensitivity in graph

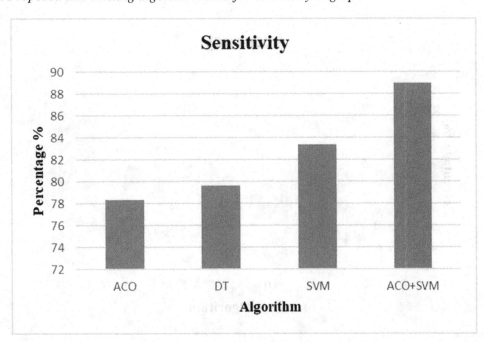

Table 1. Sensitivity result with proposed and existing algorithm

Algorithm	Result
ACO	78.32
DT	79.65
SVM	83.35
ACO+SVM	88.96

Sensitivity: The total number of positives divided by the number of precise positive forecasts is what is known as sensitivity (SN). Figure 5 shows the outcome result for Sensitivity with the proposed and existing system refer to Table 1.

$$\text{Sensitivity} = \frac{TP}{TP + FN}$$

Accuracy: The accuracy formula expresses accuracy as a deviation from 100% in the error rate. We must first determine the error rate in order to determine accuracy. In addition, the error rate is the observed value divided by the actual value, expressed as a percentage. Figure 6 shows the outcome result for accuracy with the proposed and existing system refer to Table 2.

$$\text{Accuracy} = \frac{TP + TN}{TP + TN + FN + FP}$$

Figure 6. Proposed and existing algorithm result for accuracy in graph

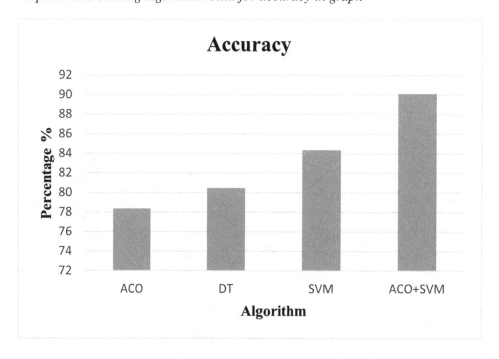

Table 2. Accuracy result with proposed and existing algorithm

Algorithm	Result
ACO	78.36
DT	80.46
SVM	84.35
ACO+SVM	90.12

Recall: Recall provides information about the model's ability to identify true positives. How many of the patients with the condition were actually identified in this instance, there are no true positives. There are two false negatives. Figure 7 shows the outcome result for Recall with the proposed and existing system refer to Table 3.

Recall = (TP) / (TP+FN)

F_Measure: Comparing two models that have a high recall but a low precision is challenging. So, in order to compare them, we need F-Score. The F-score is a tool for simultaneously measuring recall and precision. It replaces the arithmetic mean with the harmonic mean by strongly punishing the extreme values. Figure 8 shows the outcome result for F-measure with the proposed and existing system refer to Table 4.

$$F\text{-}measure = \frac{2 * recall * precision}{recall + precision}$$

Figure 7. Proposed and existing algorithm result for Recall in graph

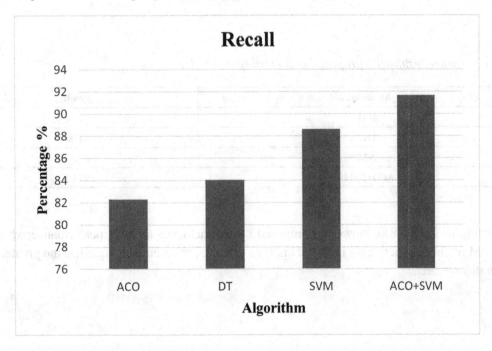

Table 3. Recall result with proposed and existing algorithm

Algorithm	Result
ACO	82.32
DT	84.06
SVM	88.63
ACO+SVM	91.65

Figure 8. Proposed and existing algorithm result for F-measure in graph

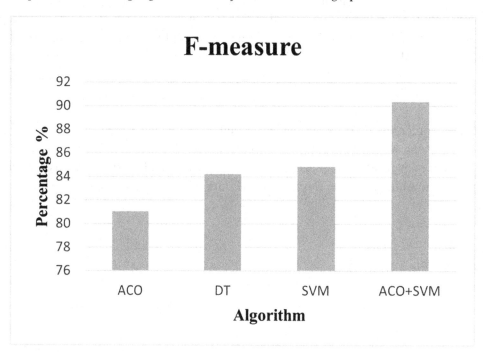

Table 4. F-measure result with proposed and existing algorithm

Algorithm	Result
ACO	82.32
DT	84.06
SVM	88.63
ACO+SVM	91.65

According to Figure 8 it shows the proposed system achieves a better performance while using ACO+SVM method to metaverse reality. This state that the proposed technique has the greater performance in this research.

CONCLUSION

Everyone and anything can use the metaverse. Start your journey right away with only a web browser. Create an avatar, explore online markets for digital collectibles, and explore virtual worlds. Privacy and security. Investigate virtual worlds Join using any gadget. The metaverse is only beginning. Whether it will take a while to fully grow or how closely it can resemble actual life are still unknown. It may, however, be the beginning of the next major revolution in virtual reality that much is certain. With the help of crucial civilizational components like social interactions, money, trade, and property ownership built on the basis of the blockchain technology, the Metaverse is a platform for spatial computing that offers virtual experiences that replicate or serve as a replacement for real-world experiences. The metaverse offers new methods to connect people, websites, platforms, and worlds. Study new ways to connect, learn, and work. Using the ACO+SVM, the suggested system's performance on accuracy, sensitivity, recall value, and F-measures is significantly superior to that of the current or existing system. The metaverse's future depends on its capacity to fulfil the two basic human needs of social interaction and creative expression.

REFERENCES

Almarzouqi, A., Aburayya, A., & Salloum, S. A. (2022). Prediction of user's intention to use metaverse system in medical education: A hybrid SEM-ML learning approach. *IEEE Access : Practical Innovations, Open Solutions*, *10*, 43421–43434. doi:10.1109/ACCESS.2022.3169285

Buhalis, D., Lin, M. S., & Leung, D. (2022). Metaverse as a driver for customer experience and value co-creation: Implications for hospitality and tourism management and marketing. *International Journal of Contemporary Hospitality Management*, *35*(2), 701–716. doi:10.1108/IJCHM-05-2022-0631

Duan, H., Li, J., Fan, S., Lin, Z., Wu, X., & Cai, W. (2021, October). Metaverse for social good: A university campus prototype. In *Proceedings of the 29th ACM international conference on multimedia* (pp. 153-161). 10.1145/3474085.3479238

Dwivedi, Y. K., Hughes, L., Baabdullah, A. M., Ribeiro-Navarrete, S., Giannakis, M., Al-Debei, M. M., & Wamba, S. F. (2022). Metaverse beyond the hype: Multidisciplinary perspectives on emerging challenges, opportunities, and agenda for research, practice and policy. *International Journal of Information Management*, *66*, 102542. doi:10.1016/j.ijinfomgt.2022.102542

Gadekallu, T. R., Huynh-The, T., Wang, W., Yenduri, G., Ranaweera, P., Pham, Q. V., & Liyanage, M. (2022). *Blockchain for the metaverse: A review*. arXiv preprint arXiv:2203.09738.

Gupta, A., Khan, H. U., Nazir, S., Shafiq, M., & Shabaz, M. (2023). Metaverse Security: Issues, Challenges and a Viable ZTA Model. *Electronics (Basel)*, *12*(2), 391. doi:10.3390/electronics12020391

Hu, Q. (2022, October). Towards a virtual business ecosystem in the Metaverse Era. In *2022 IEEE International Symposium on Mixed and Augmented Reality Adjunct (ISMAR-Adjunct)* (pp. 27-29). IEEE. 10.1109/ISMAR-Adjunct57072.2022.00016

Kim, J. (2021). Advertising in the metaverse: Research agenda. *Journal of Interactive Advertising*, *21*(3), 141–144. doi:10.1080/15252019.2021.2001273

Kshetri, N. (2022). Web 3.0 and the metaverse shaping organization's brand and product strategies. *IT Professional*, *24*(02), 11–15. doi:10.1109/MITP.2022.3157206

Kye, B., Han, N., Kim, E., Park, Y., & Jo, S. (2021). Educational applications of metaverse: Possibilities and limitations. *Journal of Educational Evaluation for Health Professions*, *18*, 18. doi:10.3352/jeehp.2021.18.32 PMID:34897242

Laeeq, K. (2022). *Metaverse: why, how and what*. How and What.

Lee, L. H., Braud, T., Zhou, P., Wang, L., Xu, D., Lin, Z., & Hui, P. (2021). *All one needs to know about metaverse: A complete survey on technological singularity, virtual ecosystem, and research agenda*. arXiv preprint arXiv:2110.05352.

Lee, U. K., & Kim, H. (2022). UTAUT in Metaverse: An "Ifland" case. *Journal of Theoretical and Applied Electronic Commerce Research*, *17*(2), 613–635. doi:10.3390/jtaer17020032

Mystakidis, S. (2022). Metaverse. *Metaverse. Encyclopedia*, *2*(1), 486–497. doi:10.3390/encyclopedia2010031

Park, S. M., & Kim, Y. G. (2022). A metaverse: Taxonomy, components, applications, and open challenges. *IEEE Access: Practical Innovations, Open Solutions*, *10*, 4209–4251. doi:10.1109/ACCESS.2021.3140175

Petrosyan, A. K., & Aristova, M. D. (2022). The Impact of the Introduction of the Metaverse Concept in the Company's Business Model. Российскиерегионы в фокусеперемен: сборникдокладов. Том 1.—Екатеринбург, 247-252.

Seidel, S., Yepes, G., Berente, N., & Nickerson, J. V. (2022, January). Designing the metaverse. *Proceedings of the 55th Hawaii International Conference on System Sciences*. 10.24251/HICSS.2022.811

Sparkes, M. (2021). *What is a metaverse*. Academic Press.

Toraman, Y. (2022). User acceptance of metaverse: Insights from technology acceptance model (TAM) and planned behavior theory (PBT). *EMAJ: Emerging Markets Journal*, *12*(1), 67–75. doi:10.5195/emaj.2022.258

Volchek, K., & Brysch, A. (2023, January). Metaverse and Tourism: From a New Niche to a Transformation. In *Information and Communication Technologies in Tourism 2023: Proceedings of the ENTER 2023 eTourism Conference, January 18-20, 2023* (pp. 300-311). Cham: Springer Nature Switzerland.

Wang, F. Y., Qin, R., Wang, X., & Hu, B. (2022). Metasocieties in metaverse: Metaeconomics and metamanagement for metaenterprises and metacities. *IEEE Transactions on Computational Social Systems*, *9*(1), 2–7. doi:10.1109/TCSS.2022.3145165

Wu, J., Lin, K., Lin, D., Zheng, Z., Huang, H., & Zheng, Z. (2022). *Financial Crimes in Web3-empowered Metaverse: Taxonomy, Countermeasures, and Opportunities*. arXiv preprint arXiv:2212.13452

Xu, M., Ng, W. C., Lim, W. Y. B., Kang, J., Xiong, Z., Niyato, D., ... Miao, C. (2022). A full dive into realizing the edge-enabled metaverse: Visions, enabling technologies, and challenges. *IEEE Communications Surveys and Tutorials*.

Yang, Q., Zhao, Y., Huang, H., Xiong, Z., Kang, J., & Zheng, Z. (2022). Fusing blockchain and AI with metaverse: A survey. *IEEE Open Journal of the Computer Society*, *3*, 122–136. doi:10.1109/OJCS.2022.3188249

Chapter 22
Advancements in Guidance Systems and Assistive Technologies for Visually Impaired Individuals

P. Shobha
Nitte Meenakshi Institute of Technology, India

N. Nalini
Nitte Meenakshi Institute of Technology, India

ABSTRACT

Visually challenged people form a large population segment, with estimates starting from tens of millions to hundreds of millions worldwide. Integration into society is a major and current goal for them. A substantial attempt has been taken into ensuring a healthcare system. To aid visually impaired people to live a usual life, several guidance system strategies are created. These systems are oftentimes created for a single purpose. The internet has become a necessary means for people to acquire knowledge and information. Today, unfortunately, the advantages of this mighty tool are still away from visually impaired people, and they find difficulty in accessing the web. Over the years, people built different technologies and tools that can help the visually impaired in reaching out to the outside world.

INTRODUCTION

This proposed work describes a self-innovative system that aims to assist visually impaired people in accessing web pages and advanced technology with the help of voice assistance (Kaur & Gupta, 2019; Manjula et al., 2021). The system utilizes three technologies: Speech-to-Text (STT), Text-to-Speech (TTS), and screen tapping to reload the main page. The proposed architecture emphasizes reliability and user-friendliness, with features such as weather forecasts, location, date, time, emergency SMS, and e-mail notifications. The system is built using several Python libraries, including Beautiful Soup, GTTS,

DOI: 10.4018/978-1-6684-8851-5.ch022

Speech Recognition (Abujarad & Al-Sayed, 2017), Open Weather API, and Twilio. The system also incorporates Geo IP Lite and express.js for better assistance. The proposed system can be a significant aid for blind people who struggle with the current technology.

Lately, communication have become uncomplicated due to the internet and advanced technologies. Though there are many improved technologies, sightless people notice it very difficult to utilize this technology because these facilities have need of visual perception (Arakeri et al., 2018; Brindha et al., 2020; Harshasri et al., 2021; Tiwari et al., 2020). Anyhow, various new inventions are Implemented to assist them use the communication competently, so no user who is visually impaired can use this technology as competently as any native user can do. Unlike normal users, this technology requires a few special tools to use the existing technologies. This project has enabled the blind people to interact in an audio feedback based virtual environments like screen readers which assist them to access web applications vastly and also to send and receive voice-based email messages in English language with the help of a computer (Craven, 2006; Ferati et al., 2016; Khedekar & Gupta, 2019).

In the projected system, GUI is setup against the GUI of a conventional mail server. The architectural vies is illustrated in Figure 1. It is also established that the developed system performs more efficiently than existing GUI's. Here, we tend to use voice-to-text and text- to-voice technique that helps to access by visually impaired people.

BACKGROUND

The developed system is a self-innovative idea that aims to assist visually impaired people in accessing web pages and advanced technology with the help of voice assistance. The system is different from the email and web pages currently in use and emphasizes reliability and user-friendliness as key features of the proposed architecture. The authors have identified that visually impaired people have trouble using the current systems, and the proposed system can be beneficial for them.

The system utilizes three different technologies: Speech-to-Text (STT), screen tapping to reload the main page, and Text-to-Speech (TTS). The authors have included features such as weather forecasts, location, date, time, emergency SMS, and e-mail notifications to enhance the system's usefulness for visually impaired users.

The authors have used several Python libraries to build the system, including Beautiful Soup, gtts, speech recognition, Open Weather API, Twilio, and Geo IP Lite. Beautiful Soup is a Python library used for pulling data out of HTML and XML files and works with parser algorithms to provide various ways of navigating, searching, and modifying the parse tree. Other libraries like ffmpeg are also used to extract the voice and convert it into a text format. The system also uses express.js for better assistance.

The authors have used audio.py as a tool for voice recognition, and the developed system can notify visually impaired users about weather broadcasts using the open weather API. Twilio is used to initiate an emergency SMS, and Geo IP Lite is used to discover the location of an IP address in the real world.

PROPOSED SYSTEM

The self-innovative idea is the sole source of the developed system, which is very different from the email and web pages currently in use. Reliability and user-friendliness are key features of the proposed

Figure 1. Architectural diagram

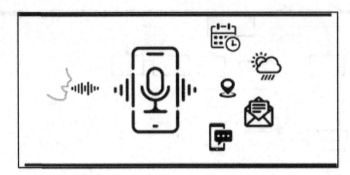

architecture. The system can be beneficial to blind people who have trouble using the current systems. This system makes use of three different kinds of technologies: 1. STT: Speech-to-Text Text is created from spoken words in this setting. 2. When you tap it twice on the screen, the main page will reload. 3. TTS: Text-to-Speech Here, the text messages we sent are written down.

The main aim of the project is to assist visually impaired people to use advanced technology like accessing web pages with the help of voice assistance (Figure 1). The product also notifies regarding the Weather forecast, location, Date, time, emergency SMS and use e-mail.

Here in this model, a tool that is helpful for voice recognition like audio.py is used. The beautiful soup is a Python library for pulling the data out from HTML and XML files. It works with parser algorithms to provide several ways of navigating, searching, and modifying the parse tree. Here, many python libraries like gtts, bs4, ffmpeg etc. to extract the voice and convert into a text format are used. The other libraries like speech recognition and open weather API are used to notify regarding the weather broadcast for the impaired. Also, Twilio is used to initiate an emergency SMS, Geo IP Lite involves attempting to discover the location of an IP address in the real world. We also use python and express.js to give better assistance.

METHODOLOGY

This proposed methodology describes a self-innovative system that aims to assist visually impaired people in accessing web pages and advanced technology with the help of voice assistance. The system uses Speech-to-Text (STT) technology to convert spoken words into text, Text-to-Speech (TTS) technology to read out text messages, and screen tapping to reload the main page. The proposed architecture emphasizes reliability and user-friendliness and also provides features like weather forecasts, location, date, time, emergency SMS, and e-mail notifications. The system is built using several Python libraries such as Beautiful Soup, GTTS, Speech Recognition, Open Weather API, Twilio, and Geo IP Lite, and it can be a significant aid for blind people who struggle with the current technology.

The use case includes weather, date, location etc as shown in Figure 2.

About us: Here, Team members name will be read out.

Weather: It displays short description and temperature of current location using open weather API.

Date.: It displays the current date.

Location: Current location can be read out using Geo IP Lite which attempts to discover the location of an IP address.

Figure 2. Use case diagram

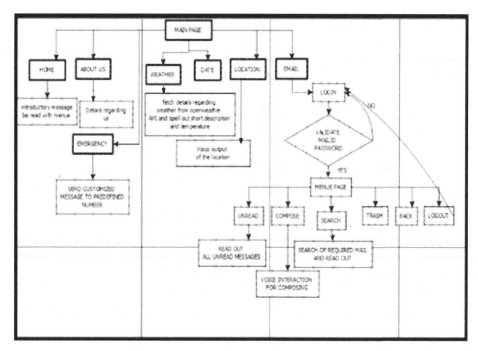

Emergency: Twilio is used to send emergency texts to the predefined number (Figure 3).

Email: Here, to login to the email system, the user must be an already existing user who should have a Google verified g-mail account and to enable the voice response of the email system, the user must tap anywhere on the screen with the mouse. It would ask for the mail id and password in speech and the user's credentials would be taken and checked for the validity and further only the authorized user is login to his/her existing g-mail account. Once the account is verified the user is directed to the menu page. Menu

Figure 3. Emergency SMS

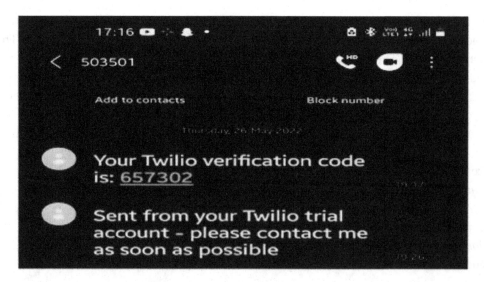

page includes compose mail, inbox, sent, trash, and logout much like the conventional email system. In order to activate the voice, the user must click anywhere on the screen with the help of the mouse.

Compose mail: The user can compose messages and send mails along with the attachments as soon the user reaches the compose mail page user is asked for certain details such as the receivers mail address, it allows multiple receivers the subject and the body of the mail, the message is then composed and sent. The specified recipient followed by the message to the user informing them about success of it or asks them to try again if any exceptional occurs in midway.

Inbox page: It checks for all the emails in the user's inbox and tells the user of the number of total read and unread emails they have. The user is then given options to read unread emails or to search for emails from a specific person. Action is taken according to the user's choice. The user is also free to logout or to go back to the menu page anytime.

Sent page: It includes options like search, back and logout. The search option lets the user search for an email that they have previously sent.

Trash: It includes options like search, back and logout. The search option lets the user search for an email that they have deleted before.

Logout: the logout option logs the user out of the system by redirecting to the login page.

RESULTS

The system described in the given passage is a self-innovative system that aims to assist visually impaired people in accessing web pages and advanced technology with the help of voice assistance. The system uses Speech-to-Text (STT) technology to convert spoken words into text and Text-to-Speech (TTS) technology to read out text messages. The main aim of the system is to provide a reliable and user-friendly interface for the visually impaired to access advanced technology like weather forecasts, location, date, time, emergency SMS, and email notifications.

The system makes use of several Python libraries such as Beautiful Soup (Heydt, 2018a; Heydt, 2018b; Jarmul & Lawson, 2017; Lawson, 2019; Mitchell, 2015), GTTS, Speech Recognition, Open Weather API, Twilio, and Geo IP Lite. These libraries help in extracting voice and converting it into text format, notifying users about the weather forecast, sending emergency SMS, and discovering the location of an IP address.

The system has a use case diagram that includes features such as weather, date, location, and emergency SMS. The system also includes an email system where the user must be an already existing user who should have a Google verified g-mail account. The email system allows users to compose messages and send mails along with attachments, check for all the emails in the user's inbox, search for emails from a specific person, and access options like search, back, and logout.

The proposed methodology is a significant aid for blind people who struggle with the current technology and provides an accessible and user-friendly interface to access advanced technology.

The results of the main webpage application are represented with pictures Figure 4 and Figure 5 (Arora et al., 2019; Harshasri et al., 2021; Kumar & Meera, 2018; Suresh et al., 2016).

Figure 4. Main page

FUTURE RESEARCH DIRECTIONS

Future work for this proposed methodology could include improvements in the accuracy of the Speech-to-Text (STT) technology to better understand spoken words and convert them into text format. Additionally, the Text-to-Speech (TTS) technology could be improved to sound more natural and human-like. Another potential area for improvement could be the integration of more advanced features such as voice recognition to allow for more personalized interactions with the system. This could involve training the system to recognize specific users' voices and respond to them in a customized way. Furthermore, the system could be expanded to include more functionalities such as voice-controlled navigation of web pages, access to social media platforms, and the ability to control smart home devices.

The system could benefit from user testing and feedback to identify areas for improvement and to ensure that it meets the needs and preferences of visually impaired users. The continued development

Figure 5. Mail login page

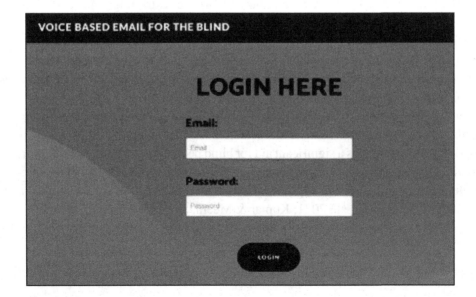

and improvement of this self-innovative system could significantly enhance the quality of life for visually impaired individuals by providing them with greater access to advanced technology.

CONCLUSION

The digital revolution has not touched everybody in the same approach. In a world where consequent inventions are expected to appear soon, blind, and visually challenged people are left behind. Hence, our project will mainly profit the people who are unable to use the advanced technology. So, People with visually impairment will be able to access the information via the websites which helps them in becoming digitally literate.

When it comes to managing people with visual disabilities, assistive technologies is a must have tool. In terms of technology, the project will facilitate them to access the website using speech recognition technology.

The Voice based Mail system is an attempt to provide a great facility in usage of technology, among the blind populations to access required e-communication modes like email. This system allows the visually impaired people to send voice-based e-Mails messages. This will reduce the huge load taken by a blind to remember and type characters using a keyboard or a mobile keypad. Further, as messages are sent via voice input, it eliminates the blind to have English proficiency and to remember the different password or the special characters. As a future work, there is a big challenge of security related to authentication. In the proposed system, the input voice of any person can be converted to text. So, for authentication the voice of user can be made as main key for verification.

ACKNOWLEDGMENT

This research is supported by Nitte Meenakshi Institute of Technology by providing high end laboratory [CSE 0000].

REFERENCES

Abujarad, Y., & Al-Sayed, M. H. (2017). Development of a web browser for the visually impaired using speech recognition. *IEEE International Conference on Computer Applications & Industrial Electronics (ICCAIE)*.

Arakeri, M. P., Keerthana, N. S., Madhura, M., Sankar, A., & Munnavar, T. (2018). Assistive Technology for the Visually Impaired Using Computer Vision. *International Conference on Advances in Computing, Communications, and Informatics (ICACCI)*, 1725-1730.

Arora, S., Agarwal, A., & Jain, S. (2019). A novel approach for visually impaired people to access webpages. *IEEE International Conference on Advances in Computing and Communication Engineering (ICACCE)*.

Brindha, Priya, Mukesh, Dinesh Kumar, & Naveen. (2020). Voice based email for visually challenged people. *International Research Journal of Engineering and Technology*, 1382-1383.

Craven. (2006). Web Accessibility: A review of research and Initiatives. *World Library and Information Congress: 72nd IFLA General Conference and Council.*

Ferati, M., Vogel, B., Kurti, A., Rau, B., & Astals, D. S. (2016). Web Accessibility for Visually Impaired People: Requirements and Design Issues. *International Workshop on Usability-and Accessibility-Focused Requirements Engineering.*

Harshasri, M., Bhavani, M. D., & Ravikanth, M. (2021). *Voice Based Email for Blind. International Journal of Innovative Research in Computer Science & Technology.*

Heydt, M. (2018a). *Beautiful Soup 4: Python Web Scraping.* Packt Publishing. Available: https://www. packtpub.com/product/beautiful-soup-4-python-web-scraping/9781788833906

Heydt, M. (2018b). *Python Web Scraping Cookbook.* O'Reilly Media, Inc. Available: https://www.oreilly. com/library/view/python-web-scraping/978149198556

Jarmul, K., & Lawson, R. (2017). *Python Web Scraping* (2nd ed.). Packt Publishing. Available: https:// www.packtpub.com/product/python-web-scraping-second-edition/9781786462589

Jayachandran, K., & Anbumani, P. (2017). Voice Based Email for Blind People. *International Journal of Advance Research, Ideas, and Innovations in Technology*, 1066-71.

Kaur, & Gupta. (2019). Web accessibility for visually impaired people using voice-based interface. *IEEE International Conference on Computing, Communication and Automation (ICCCA).*

Khedekar, R., & Gupta, S. (2019). Voice based Email System for Blinds. *International Journal of Engineering Research & Technology, 8,* 41-42.

Kumar, S. S., & Meera, M. N. (2018). A novel method for visually impaired people to access web pages using speech recognition and text-to-speech conversion. *IEEE International Conference on Innovations in Information, Embedded and Communication Systems (ICIIECS).*

Lawson. (2019). *Web Scraping in Python: Master the Fundamentals.* Independently published.

Manjula, S., Kiranmai, S. V., & Reddy, S. S. (2021). Web page accessibility for visually impaired people using voice-based system. *IEEE International Conference on Inventive Communication and Computational Technologies (ICICCT).*

Mitchell, R. (2015). *Web Scraping with Python: Collecting More Data from the Modern Web.* O'Reilly Media, Inc. Available: https://www.oreilly.com/library/view/web-scraping-with/9781491910283/

Suresh, A., Paulose, B., Jagan, R., & George, J. (2016). Voice Based Email for Blind. *International Journal of Scientific Research in Science, Engineering and Technology, 2,* 93–97.

Tiwari, P. A., Zodawan, P., Nimkar, H. P., Rotke, T., Wanjari, P. G., & Samarth, U. (2020). A Review on Voice based E-Mail System for Blind. In *2020 International Conference on Inventive Computation Technologies (ICICT)* (pp. 435-438). IEEE.

KEY TERMS AND DEFINITIONS

Audio Feedback: Audio feedback refers to a type of feedback that provides an audible response to a user's action or input. For example, a "beep" sound after pressing a button on a computer keyboard is a form of audio feedback.

Beautiful Soup: Beautiful Soup is a Python library used for web scraping purposes. It allows developers to parse HTML and XML documents and extract useful data from them.

Email Notifications: Email notifications are automated messages sent via email to users to inform them about specific events or activities. For example, email notifications can be sent to users when they receive a new message on a social media platform.

Express.js: Express.js is a popular web application framework for Node.js. It simplifies the development process of web applications by providing useful features such as routing, middleware, and templating.

Geo IP Lite: Geo IP Lite is a free, open-source API that allows developers to look up the location of an IP address. It provides accurate information about the country, region, and city where the IP address is registered.

Open Weather: API: Open Weather API is a weather API that provides real-time weather data for any location in the world. Developers can use this API to retrieve information such as temperature, humidity, wind speed, and cloud coverage.

Screen Readers: Screen readers are assistive technology devices that allow visually impaired users to access digital content. They read the content aloud using synthesized speech and provide an auditory representation of the visual content on a screen.

Speech Recognition: Speech recognition is a technology that enables computers to recognize and interpret human speech. It allows users to interact with computers and other digital devices using spoken commands.

Speech-to-Text (STT): Speech-to-Text (STT) is a type of software that converts spoken words into written text. It allows users to transcribe spoken content into a written format, making it easier to share and access.

Text-To-Speech (TTS): Text-To-Speech (TTS) is a technology that converts written text into spoken words. It allows computers and other digital devices to read text aloud, making it easier for users to access content.

Twilio: Twilio is a cloud communications platform that provides APIs for developers to integrate messaging, voice, and video into their applications. It simplifies the process of building communication applications by providing a range of pre-built tools and services.

Visually Impaired: Visually impaired refers to individuals who have partial or complete loss of vision. They may rely on assistive technology such as screen readers or braille displays to access digital content.

Voice Interaction: Voice interaction is a type of human-computer interaction that allows users to interact with computers and other digital devices using voice commands. It is becoming increasingly popular with the rise of smart speakers and voice assistants.

Web Applications: Web applications are software programs that run on web browsers. They provide a range of services such as email, online shopping, social networking, and video conferencing. Web applications can be accessed from any device with an internet connection.

Chapter 23
Cyber Security in the Metaverse

Divneet Kaur
Guru Nanak Dev Engineering College, Ludhiana, India

Bharatdeep Singh
Guru Nanak Dev Engineering College, Ludhiana, India

Sita Rani
Guru Nanak Dev Engineering College, Ludhiana, India

ABSTRACT

Security in the Metaverse is a critical concern as virtual worlds continue to expand and evolve. With an increasing number of users engaging in immersive experiences, safeguarding personal information, assets, and digital identities becomes paramount. Robust security measures are essential to protect against hacking, identity theft, and fraudulent activities. Technologies like blockchain and encryption play a crucial role in ensuring secure transactions, while identity verification systems help authenticate users. Additionally, monitoring and moderation tools are necessary to combat harassment, hate speech, and inappropriate content. As the Metaverse becomes more integrated into our lives, a comprehensive approach to security is vital to foster trust and safeguard the virtual realm. This chapter aims to provide an overview of cybersecurity in Metaverse. It discussed the various cyber stacks in detail along with solutions to manage these attacks. The authors have also discussed the various challenges in securing metaverse, and possible future research directions.

INTRODUCTION

With the advent of technology, the majority of our daily activities are getting digitalized which has resulted in increased access to our private information by eavesdroppers (Thakur, Qiu, Gai, & Ali, 2015). Therefore, in the current environment where we depend on the internet for the exchange of sensitive information at every turn of our lives, we require a sufficient number of compatible systems that can ensure our security. As a result, cybersecurity has become a crucial part of our lives. The importance of protecting our digital assets and information cannot be overstated, as cyber threats continue to evolve and become more sophisticated (Narayanan et al., 2018). A prime example of the devastating consequences

DOI: 10.4018/978-1-6684-8851-5.ch023

of a cyber-attack is the 2017 WannaCry cyber-attack which infected nearly 300,000 computers across the world demanding that users pay Bitcoin ransoms. The numerous health organizations were the attack's major target, and its effects were felt widely. This is not the only instance; the same year, there was another attack on Equifax that resulted in a data breach, during which hackers were able to obtain the personal data of 143 million consumers, including addresses, social security numbers, and birth dates. This breach not only resulted in massive financial losses, reputational damage, and legal liabilities for Equifax but also led to severe consequences for individuals. The 'Equifax data breach' and 'WannaCry' emphasize the urgent necessity for effective cybersecurity measures and the crucial role of cybersecurity specialists in defending against cyber threats. The development of digital technologies and the internet has fundamentally changed how we interact, communicate, and work. However, the main concern of today's programmers is to develop quick, streamlined as well as less time-consuming programs which eventually make the task of eavesdroppers and hackers much easier. Thus, they can have unauthorized access to confidential data easily. Cyber dangers can affect everybody, from small businesses and governments to major enterprises and individuals. They range from straightforward hoaxes and phishing attempts to complicated and sophisticated cyberattacks that can seriously harm key infrastructure and organizations. Malware, ransomware, worms, crypto-jacking, spyware, denial-of-service (DoS) attacks, and identity theft are a few examples of frequent cyber threats. A successful cyberattack may have detrimental and far-reaching consequences (Rani et al., 2021). Governmental institution cyberattacks may even be more damaging because they may hurt the country's security. Additionally, attacks on healthcare facilities, electricity grids, and transportation networks can result in major consequences including financial losses, reputational harm, etc. To halt cyberattacks and protect against cyber dangers, companies, and people must immediately adopt robust cybersecurity measures. Firewalls, encryption, multi-factor authentication, access controls, employee training, incident response planning, and continuous monitoring and testing can play a major role in protecting our information.

Both the creation of new technology and the need for cybersecurity are essential. Without it, we cannot enjoy the most recent advances in technology. Since the technology world is constantly changing, cybersecurity experts must keep up with the most recent developments and best practices. In the contemporary digital era, cybersecurity is a critical concern for all individuals and organizations (Rani, Kataria, Kumar, & Tiwari, 2023).

Imagine a world where avatars created by computers can be used to communicate with people. That is indeed what the 'metaverse' is (Sparkes, 2021). Though the concept has long been explored in science fiction, recent technological advancements have made it possible to create virtual worlds that are immersive, interactive, and more lifelike than ever (Ning et al., 2023). Games like Fortnite and Roblox are the perfect examples of representing metaverse-like environments. Have you ever used Facebook's Horizon Walk rooms? They also allow users to meet and collaborate with others in a virtual space. Although the concept of the metaverse is new, it is rapidly developing. Every sector of society, including education, and virtual real estate is gradually embracing a new environment called 'the metaverse. 'Second Life' is among the most notable instances of a metaverse. One of the most well-known instances of a metaverse is Second Life, a virtual world that has been around since 2003. People who use Second Life can create their avatars, explore different environments, and interact with others in real-time. It is still widely used today thanks to its dedicated user base that has built its own business, social networks, and even virtual universities. Recently the luxury fashion brand, Gucci created its virtual world in collaboration with Roblox (Tanwar, Chhabra, Rattan, & Rani, 2022). 'Gucci Garden' was launched in May 2021 which allowed players to explore a digital world filled with Gucci-themed environments and activities.

The metaverse, however, is more than just a location for entertainment and gaming. It can change how we work, learn, and live. In the future when the metaverse is enabled, remote work and virtual meetings might become something more natural and interesting. The metaverse in education may provide pupils with new, cutting-edge study techniques through immersive simulations and virtual field trips. The metaverse could enable doctors to do remote consultations and surgery by leveraging the powers of virtual reality and haptic feedback.

Thus, by considering the instances above, it is simple to understand the significance of the metaverse. In general, the metaverse is a potentially revolutionary idea with many possible uses (Rani, Pareek, Kaur, Chauhan, & Bhambri, 2023). The metaverse is undoubtedly a topic of growing interest and investment with the potential to influence our society and economy, even though there are still a lot of unanswered concerns and difficulties to be overcome. It essentially deals with the construction of online virtual reality chat rooms where users can exchange ideas and communicate in virtual reality on the metaverse (Puri, Kataria, Solanki, & Rani, 2022). When playing games, for instance, Roblox users can set up online chat rooms to communicate with other players in the game's Roblox ecosystem. To pursue and develop the characters and narratives for the interaction between the users and their avatars, this generates an immersive ecosystem for the users (Kumar et al., 2022).

The metaverse, in conclusion, is a rapidly developing idea that has the potential to change how we engage with digital technology. Users can build their own digital identities, discover new settings, and engage in more immersive and interesting social interactions thanks to this new method of using the internet. The potential of the metaverse is limitless as technology develops, and it will be fascinating to watch how it changes in the years to come (Bali, Bali, Gaur, Rani, & Kumar, 2023).

BASIC CONCEPTS

Cybersecurity

It is clear from the discussion above how important "Cybersecurity" is. Attacks on computers are becoming more frequent. According to a recent Symantec survey that involved interviewing 20,000 people in 24 countries, 69% of them had experienced a cyberattack at some point in their lives (Ning et al., 2023). This analysis demonstrates the increase of cyberattacks in the current environment very clearly. But have you ever questioned why cyberattacks are increasing so significantly?

Cyber-attacks are becoming more prevalent as a result of the various benefits they offer over physical assaults. For starters, since all cybercriminals need is a computer and an internet connection, they are significantly easier and less expensive to carry out. They can also attack targets anywhere in the world because they are not constrained by geography or distance (Kataria, Agrawal, Rani, Karar, & Chauhan, 2022). The anonymity of the internet makes it harder to identify and prosecute cyber offenders. These elements make cyber-attacks particularly alluring, therefore we may anticipate an increase in the quantity and sophistication of these attacks (Sudevan, Barwani, Al Maani, Rani, & Sivaraman, 2021). These attacks are certainly simpler to carry out, but there are a variety of reasons why they are carried out. They are carried out for a wide range of objectives, including espionage, political or ideological goals, financial gain, the theft of sensitive data, or service or network disruption. Depending on their goals, cyber attackers can choose to target specific people, groups of people, or even entire countries. Some attackers use system flaws to their advantage by extorting money from victims or obtaining their credit card information. For political or ideological purposes, some may want to undermine essential services like healthcare or transportation, while others may participate in cyber espionage to steal confidential data from organizations or governments (Rani, Kataria, & Chauhan, 2022). Overall, there are many different reasons why cyberattacks are carried out, and these reasons might vary greatly depending on the attacker's goals.

In 2018, Russian hackers stole medical records from the World Anti-Doping Agency and then published them online. This exemplifies the political motivation the hackers had for carrying out their attacks. Additionally, numerous other historical examples illustrate the various motives behind assaults. We must understand the various attacks that are carried out nowadays before moving forward (Xu, Hu, & Zhang, 2013). Some of the important attacks are described below:

Malware Attack

A malware attack is a sort of cyber-attack that involves harmful software (malware) being introduced into a computer system or network. The malware can be intended to do numerous malicious behaviors, including stealing sensitive data, damaging, or destroying files, managing the system remotely, or propagating the malware to other systems on the network. Malware assaults can be carried out through a variety of techniques, such as phishing emails, infected downloads, or compromised websites. Once it has infected a system, the malware can continue to operate covertly until it is found and eliminated. Attacks by malware can be especially harmful to organizations, leading to financial losses, harm to their reputations, and even significant legal responsibilities. Figure 1 shows the visual representation of the malware attack...

Figure 1. Malware attack

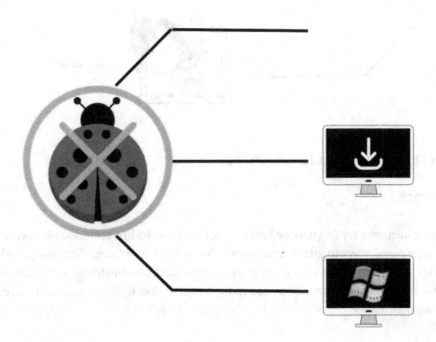

Protection against malware attacks typically involves implementing security measures such as antivirus software, firewalls, and regular system updates (Arunachalam et al., 2022).

Phishing Attack

Phishing aims to steal sensitive data like usernames, passwords, and more. Through email, SMS messages, or direct messages, it targets the user. It is the most common attack that happens worldwide. It makes the victim believe that the message is generated by the trusted sender. Thus, it plays psychologically with the victim. The phishing attack has been depicted in Figure 2.

Phishing attacks can be prevented by being wary of dubious emails or websites, checking the validity of any requests for personal information, and becoming knowledgeable about the best practices for

Figure 2. Phishing attack

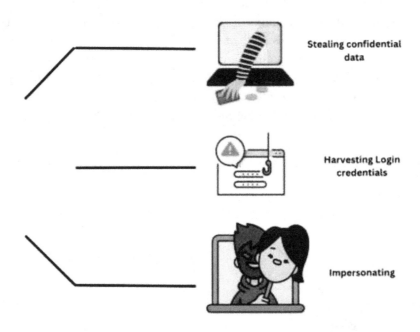

Stealing confidential data

Harvesting Login credentials

Impersonating

online security (Rani, Kataria, & Chauhan, 2022).

Password Attack

Cyber attackers sometimes try to guess or break a user's password in a technique known as a password attack. There are several ways to attack a password, including brute force, dictionary, and social engineering methods. In a brute-force attack, all possible character combinations are tested until the right password is discovered. Cybercrime becomes more frequent due to this attack as it gives third-party access to private information.

Figure 3 gives a pictorial representation of Password Attack. Creating strong, one-of-a-kind passwords, activating two-factor authentication, and being aware of social engineering techniques are some

Figure 3. Password attack

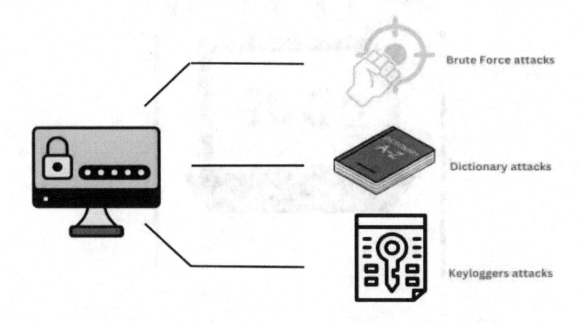

ways to defend against password attacks (Dhanalakshmi, Vijayaraghavan, Sivaraman, & Rani, 2022).

DDoS Attack

A cyberattack known as a distributed denial of service (DDoS) attempt seeks to prevent a website, server, or network from operating normally. In a DDoS assault, the attacker overwhelms the targeted system with a lot of traffic from several sources, which causes it to run slowly or crash (Bawany, Shamsi, & Salah, 2017).

DDoS assaults may be motivated by extortion, retaliation, activism, or competitive advantage, among other things. DDoS assaults can seriously harm enterprises, notably by resulting in lost sales, reputational harm, and possibly legal consequences (Kumar et al., 2022). Implementing defenses like firewalls, load balancers, and content delivery networks, as well as creating emergency reaction plans, are necessary to defend against DDoS attacks (Rani, Kataria, Chauhan, et al., 2022). A pictorial representation of DDoS attacks is shown in Figure 4.

Man in the Middle Attack

A cyberattack known as a "Man-in-the-Middle" (MITM) assault involves an attacker intercepting two parties' communications to steal, alter, or spy on them. In a MITM attack, the attacker places themself

Figure 4. DDoS attack

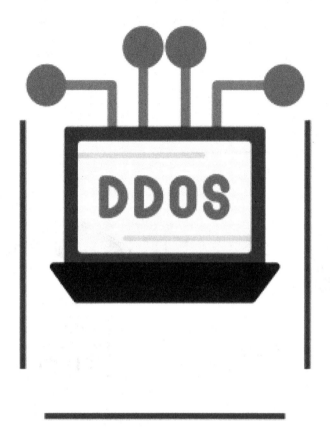

in the middle of two parties—for example, between a user and a website—and intercepts and modifies their communication without the victim's knowledge (Kumar et al., 2022).

By modifying the message or posing as one of the parties to win their trust, the attacker can steal login passwords, financial information, or other sensitive data (Rani, Pareek, et al., 2023). Multiple techniques, including Wi-Fi eavesdropping, DNS spoofing, and HTTPS interception, can be used to conduct MITM attacks. The above figure gives a perfect representation of the MTTM attack. Implementing secure communication protocols, like HTTPS or VPNs, frequently monitoring for suspicious behavior, and instructing users on how to recognize and avoid MITM attacks are all necessary steps in protecting against MITM attacks (Rani, Kataria, et al., 2023). Figure 5 depicts a DDoS attack.

Figure 5. Man in the middle attack

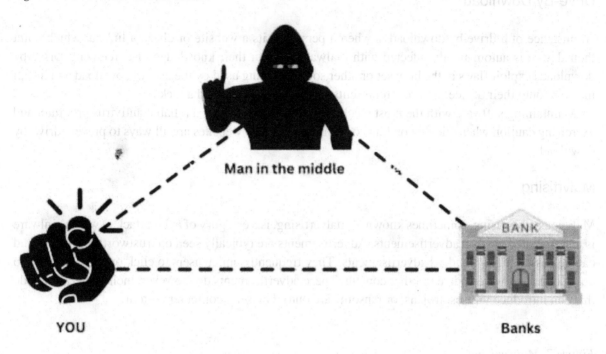

Figure 6. Drive-by download

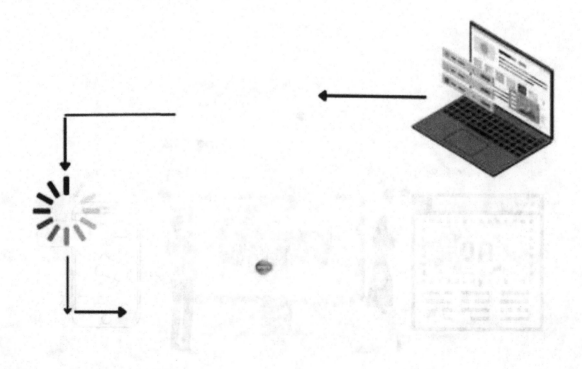

Drive-By Download

An instance of a drive-by download is when a person visits a website or clicks a link, at which point their device is automatically infected with malware without their knowledge or agreement. Drive-by downloads exploit flaws in the browser or other software being used by the user to download and install malware onto their device. Figure 6 represents the Drive-by download attack.

Maintaining software with the most recent security patches, using a reliable antivirus program, and exercising caution when clicking on links or visiting unknown websites are all ways to prevent drive-by downloads.

Malvrtising

Malicious advertising, sometimes known as malvertising, is a category of cyberattack in which malware is disseminated via web advertisements. Advertisements are typically seen on trustworthy websites and can be passed off as standard advertisements. They frequently entice users to click on them in order to download a software update or other content. These advertisements do, however, include harmful code that can introduce viruses, trojans, or ransomware onto the user's computer system.

Figure 7. Malvertising

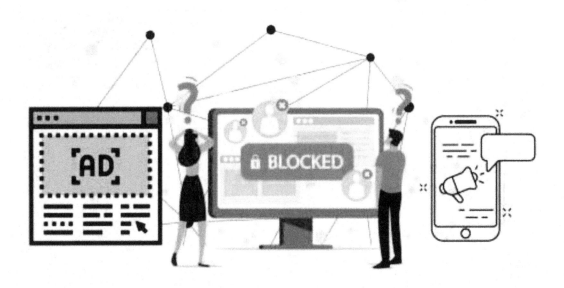

Utilizing ad-blockers and anti-malware software, keeping software up-to-date with the most recent security updates, and exercising caution when clicking on adverts or going to unknown websites are all ways to protect yourself against malicious advertising. Therefore, these are a few of the significant attacks that are made today. Despite them, there are several more assaults, such as ransomware, spyware, Trojans, and crypto jacking. Figure 7 shows malvertising pictorially.

Metaverse

The breakthroughs in computer science, which have changed social interactions, communication, and human contact, have a significant impact on daily life. The three major technological innovations that have impacted end-users are personal computers, the Internet, and mobile devices. Currently, a fourth wave of computing innovation is unfolding around Virtual Reality (VR) and Augmented Reality (AR), which are spatial, immersive technologies. The Metaverse, which is the next ubiquitous computing paradigm, is expected to revolutionize (online) education, business, remote work, and entertainment. The Metaverse is a post-reality universe that merges physical reality with digital virtuality, offering a perpetual and persistent multiuser environment. It has the potential to overcome the limitations of web-based 2D e-learning tools, making it an ideal platform for online distance education.

The education industry has undergone significant changes since the emergence of eLearning during the PC internet boom in the late 1990s. The second wave of mobile computing and social media led to microlearning through shorter, video-based content that can be accessed on demand. The third computing era, according to experts, is currently in progress. Traditional flat web pages on PCs and mobile devices will be replaced by a metaverse of digital 3D areas where we can connect with lifelike avatars in this new era. The metaverse is an embodied internet that provides continuous social interactions with peers. Unlike scheduled Zoom calls, the metaverse is "always on". This transition has profound implications for learning and capability-building.

The emergence of the Metaverse will cause a revolutionary upheaval in the media and entertainment industry. It is anticipated that the industry would soar to thrilling new heights as a result of its focus on providing immersive and lifelike experiences.

Recently, several companies in the media and entertainment sector have concentrated on developing platforms that promote communication and bring people together. To do this, social elements have been incorporated into platforms from companies like Netflix, HBO, and Hulu through features like "Netflix party," "HBO Max party," and "Hulu watch party."

Furthermore, there are various third-party apps and websites like Metastream, Rave, and TwoSeven that enable users to watch content with friends and family, even if they are not in the same location. These features aim to provide a fun and social way to enjoy your favorite movies and shows with your loved ones.

Technologies Used in the Metaverse

The metaverse is a combination of various emerging technologies such as digital twins, VR, AR, 5G, wearable sensors, brain-computer interface (BCI), artificial intelligence (AI), blockchain, and non-fungible tokens (NFT). These technologies work together to create a realistic mirror image of the real world, an immersive 3D experience, and ultra-high reliable and ultra-low latency connections for large-scale metaverse devices. Additionally, wearable sensors and BCI enable users to interact with their avatars in the metaverse. AI plays a crucial role in the creation and rendering of the metaverse on a large scale, while blockchain and NFT ensure the authenticity of metaverse assets.

- **Digital Twin.** A digital twin is a digital replica of a physical object that is created to accurately simulate its functioning, as shown in Figure 8. To generate such a model, sensors are installed on the physical object, such as a wind turbine, which monitors its key performance indicators. This data is then transmitted to a computing system and utilized to generate a digital copy of the object. This virtual model can be employed to simulate various scenarios, analyze performance, and identify areas for improvement, ultimately providing valuable insights for optimizing the original physical object (Jones, Snider, Nassehi, Yon, & Hicks, 2020).

Figure 8. Digital twin

The digital twin can analyze performance problems and find possible areas for improvement using the data gathered from the sensors to mimic various scenarios. The ultimate goal is to produce insightful data that can be used to improve the physical object's operation.

- **Virtual Reality.** Virtual reality (VR) technology produces an artificially manufactured world that makes users feel as though they are physically present there, as shown in Figure 9. Utilizing head-mounted displays, tracking systems, and other input devices, users may engage with a build-in-three-dimensional world (Anthes, García-Hernández, Wiedemann, & Kranzlmüller, 2016).

Virtual reality (VR) is utilized by several sectors, including entertainment, education, health care, and gaming. VR has made it possible for games to provide new chances for engagement and immersion. One of the most noteworthy recent technical developments is the development of hardware, software, and content production tools.

- **Augmented Reality.** Augmented reality (AR) is a technology that enhances the real world with computer-generated content, shown in Figure 10. AR is an interactive experience that incorpo-

Figure 9. Virtual reality

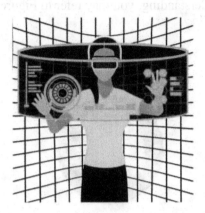

rates visual, auditory, haptic, somatosensory, and olfactory sensory modalities. The technology involves combining the real and virtual worlds, enabling real-time interaction, and accurately registering 3D virtual and real objects.

Figure 10. Augmented reality

The overlaid sensory information can be additive or masking, creating a seamless immersive experience with the physical world. Unlike virtual reality, which replaces the real-world environment, AR alters one's ongoing perception of the real-world environment. AR is being used in various industries such as gaming, entertainment, retail, education, and healthcare to provide new and innovative experiences for users.

- **Brain-Computer Interface.** A BCI, or brain-computer interface, is a computerized system that captures and interprets brain signals to generate commands that are sent to an output device to carry out a desired action, as shown in Figure 11. These systems bypass the body's natural output pathways such as peripheral nerves and muscles, and instead rely on signals from the central nervous system. For a better understanding, you may refer to Figure 11.

Figure 11. Brain-computer interface

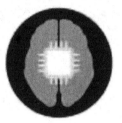

BCIs are limited to systems that measure and use signals produced by the CNS and do not include voice or muscle-activated communication systems. An electroencephalogram (EEG) machine alone is not considered a BCI as it only records brain signals but does not generate an output. BCIs do not read minds but instead enable users to act on the world using brain signals. Users generate brain signals that encode their intentions, and the BCI decodes and translates these signals into commands for an output device to carry out the desired action.

- **Blockchain.** An unchangeable digital ledger that is continually expanding and storing data in the form of blocks that are protected by cryptographic proofs is what a blockchain fundamentally is. Consequently, it becomes a safe and open method of archiving and disseminating data (Zheng, Xie, Dai, Chen, & Wang, 2018).

Figure 12. Blockchain

Blockchain applications in the metaverse are one such instance, shown in Figure 12. The Sandbox, a decentralized NFT gaming platform built on the Ethereum Blockchain, enables users to build, market, and earn money from their NFTs. These NFTs stand for ownership of distinctive digital assets that may be safely exchanged on the blockchain, such as virtual properties. The Sandbox's developers hope that by employing NFTs, they would be able to offer users ownership over their works, encouraging them to take part in the ecosystem of the platform and fostering its expansion.

- **Non-Fungible Token.** NFTs are a particular class of blockchain-based tokens that enable the safe mapping of ownership rights to digital assets. NFTs are non-fungible, which means they cannot be readily divided or swapped, unlike other cryptocurrencies. Instead, their owner determines their worth, and ownership is documented and validated via blockchain technology. Figure 13 pictorially represents NFTs.

Figure 13. Non-fungible token

Non-Fungible Tokens (NFTs) are essential for creating an identity, joining a community, and engaging in a variety of social activities in the virtual world. These tokens provide users the ability to buy, trade, and transfer objects both within the metaverse and across the internet. The currency of the virtual world and the need for taking part in a variety of activities in the metaverse are digital assets.

IMPACT OF CYBER SECURITY ON METAVERSE

By the beginning of 2026, 25% of people are forecast to spend at least one hour every day in the Metaverse. The term "Metaverse" and its uses in our daily lives are now well-known to us. Have you ever read "Snow Crash," a science fiction book by Neal Stephenson? It accurately portrays the Metaverse, the world we are referring to. The Metaverse is undoubtedly still in its infancy, but it is growing quickly. The primary cause is the recent advancement in technology and the requirement to digitize everything. You might be wondering now what the role of cybersecurity in Metaverse is. Well, cybersecurity plays a prominent role in the concept of the 'Metaverse'. The construction and management of the Metaverse will require careful consideration of cybersecurity issues. A multi-layered strategy that incorporates user authentication and access control, virus protection, data protection, and privacy, defense against hackers and cyberattacks, and specialized blockchain and cryptocurrency security measures will be necessary. There are many significant reasons why we require cybersecurity in the metaverse. First off, the Metaverse will be populated by millions of users who will generate and trade valuable digital assets, making it an ideal target for cybercriminals. Sensitive data, including financial information, will be transferred into the Metaverse since it will serve as a platform for user interaction and corporate transactions. To safeguard this data from theft, fraud, and other online risks, it is crucial to implement strong cybersecurity safeguards.

Second, the Metaverse will depend on intricately linked computer systems that are susceptible to numerous types of cyberattacks. The virtual world may be disrupted and damaged by these attacks, which may lead to monetary losses, reputational harm, and a decline in user confidence. For example, hackers might infiltrate the Metaverse systems and cause havoc by altering the virtual world or interfering with its architecture.

Thirdly, the Metaverse will use blockchain technology, which calls for specialized cybersecurity safeguards to ward against attacks like 51% attacks, double-spending, and other forms of fraud. Because blockchain is a decentralized and open system, it will be harder to safeguard virtual assets against fraud and theft.

In March 2021, a hacker gained access to Roblox accounts and stole virtual goods using a database of stolen login information. Over 1,000 accounts were impacted by the hack, and thousands of dollars' worth of virtual goods were lost. This was not the only case, in the same year. Not only that but in August of the same year a hacker used a flaw in the Decentraland smart contract to construct phony land plots and sell them to unwary consumers. Virtual currency worth tens of thousands of dollars were lost as a result of the hack. Similarly to this, a security researcher found a flaw in the Second Life viewer software in December 2020 that might allow an attacker to steal a user's login information (Wang et al., 2022).

All of the aforementioned incidents therefore amply demonstrate the need for cybersecurity in the metaverse. According to recent studies, even 20 minutes of VR use might provide 2 million different data items. This comprises actions like breathing, walking, thinking, moving, and staring. The organizations in charge of the metaverse(s) consumers choose to participate in can and conceivably will collect that information. That is only VR. Consider all the data that MR and AR can also produce. This may include the goods a person chooses to purchase, the places they travel to spend their time, and the people they interact with.

The metaverse is a developing attack vector, though, and it must be regarded seriously. IoT and edge devices will gather personal and financial data, and that data will be processed at 5G speeds. Attacks using social engineering are anticipated to be widespread; user privacy will be in danger, and safety is a major concern. Even if the so-called "metaverse business" materializes, it will be a minefield of security, privacy, and safety issues.

In the metaverse, everything and everyone will be the product if social network members are the current Internet's product. Internet users are currently drawn in large numbers by social networking sites. In a similar vein, the metaverse will act as an exponentially stronger magnet for (even more) users, as well as for content producers, business owners, and entrepreneurs. In other words, it will serve as a single meta-platform for users, regardless of their interests or preferred apps (such as reading, gaming, learning, etc.), as well as for the companies who create and maintain these applications. The highlighted worry presents serious issues regarding the volume and nature of data that such a sizable platform could gather.

Table 1 depicts the increase in cyber threats due to the increased use of Metaverse:

Table 1. The increase in cyber threats due to the increased use of Metaverse

Metaverse Usage	Level of Cyberthreat	Increased % of Threats	Cyberthreats (Examples of Threats That Occurred)
Low	Low	10%	Increase in phishing emails or messages to steal login credentials.
Medium	Moderate	25%	Increase in metaverse-related cyber-attacks.
High	High	50%	Increase in Virtual asset thefts through metaverse wallets.
Very High	Very High	75%	Increase in metaverse-related social engineering attacks. This resulted in the revelation of sensitive information of various users.

MAJOR CHALLENGES AND FUTURE DIRECTIONS

As a result of the advancement of virtual reality (VR) and augmented reality (AR) technology, the metaverse, an immersive virtual environment, is growing in popularity. We now understand that cybersecurity is necessary in the metaverse for several reasons. The metaverse presents many cybersecurity challenges, much like any other internet setting. The following are some difficulties with cybersecurity in the metaverse:

- **Cyberbullying and Harassment.** These problems can also occur in the metaverse. It's a critical issue as security for users is the major concern.
- **Malware and Viruses.** Just like in the real world, there is always a chance that malware and viruses can invade the metaverse. For this reason, it is essential to have security measures in place.
- **Lack of Standards.** Because the metaverse is still developing, there are currently no cybersecurity standards in place. Industry-wide cybersecurity standards are required to guarantee the privacy and safety of users in the metaverse.

There are privacy risks in the metaverse, just like there are in any online setting. User data may occasionally be open to unauthorized access in certain circumstances. Security in the metaverse has therefore become crucial for us. But putting cybersecurity into practice is a difficult task.

For a variety of reasons, integrating cybersecurity in the metaverse can be difficult. Some of the explanations are as follows:

- **Complexity.** The metaverse is a dynamic world that is continually changing and becoming more complex. The complexity of the systems involved, the various platforms and technologies employed, and the vast number of users make it difficult to implement cybersecurity measures in such a setting.
- **Lack of Standards.** As was already established, the metaverse lacks current industry-wide cybersecurity standards. Implementing consistent and efficient cybersecurity safeguards across many platforms and virtual worlds becomes difficult as a result.
- **User Conduct.** Cybersecurity may also be hampered by users' conduct in the metaverse. In contrast to the actual world, users in the metaverse can take on multiple personalities and behaviors, which might make it challenging to spot and follow harmful activity.
- **New Technologies.** Because the metaverse is still in its infancy, new technologies are continually being developed and introduced. As a result, cybersecurity solutions must be versatile and agile enough to keep up with the metaverse's shifting topography.

Resources are at a premium, and putting in place reliable cybersecurity safeguards in the metaverse can be costly. This can be difficult, particularly for smaller virtual worlds and platforms that could lack the funding to invest in cybersecurity.

Finally, the difficulty of implementing cybersecurity in the metaverse can be attributed to the ecosystem's complexity, the lack of standards, user behavior, new technologies, and resource constraints. To ensure the security and safety of users in the metaverse, these challenges must be resolved.

CONCLUSION

Cybersecurity in the metaverse ensures asset protection, privacy, authentication, threat detection, virtual environment security, trust and governance, and secure collaboration, preventing breaches and attacks on the digital ecosystem. Securing decentralized platforms, addressing interoperability and standardization issues, protecting against novel cyber threats, managing privacy concerns, and establishing trust and governance frameworks across diverse virtual environments and participants are all challenges in ensuring cybersecurity in the metaverse.

REFERENCES

Anthes, C., García-Hernández, R. J., Wiedemann, M., & Kranzlmüller, D. (2016). *State of the art of virtual reality technology. In 2016 IEEE aerospace conference.* IEEE.

Bawany, N. Z., Shamsi, J. A., & Salah, K. (2017). DDoS attack detection and mitigation using SDN: Methods, practices, and solutions. *Arabian Journal for Science and Engineering*, *42*(2), 425–441. doi:10.100713369-017-2414-5

Jones, D., Snider, C., Nassehi, A., Yon, J., & Hicks, B. (2020). Characterising the Digital Twin: A systematic literature review. *CIRP Journal of Manufacturing Science and Technology*, *29*, 36–52. doi:10.1016/j.cirpj.2020.02.002

Kumar, P., Banerjee, K., Singhal, N., Kumar, A., Rani, S., Kumar, R., & Lavinia, C. A. (2022). Verifiable, Secure Mobile Agent Migration in Healthcare Systems Using a Polynomial-Based Threshold Secret Sharing Scheme with a Blowfish Algorithm. *Sensors (Basel)*, *22*(22), 8620. doi:10.339022228620 PMID:36433217

Narayanan, S. N., Ganesan, A., Joshi, K., Oates, T., Joshi, A., & Finin, T. (2018). Early detection of cybersecurity threats using collaborative cognition. In *2018 IEEE 4th international conference on collaboration and internet computing (CIC)* (pp. 354-363). IEEE. 10.1109/CIC.2018.00054

Ning, H., Wang, H., Lin, Y., Wang, W., Dhelim, S., Farha, F., Ding, J., & Daneshmand, M. (2023). A Survey on the Metaverse: The State-of-the-Art, Technologies, Applications, and Challenges. *IEEE Internet of Things Journal*, 1. doi:10.1109/JIOT.2023.3278329

Rani, S., Kataria, A., & Chauhan, M. (2022). Cyber security techniques, architectures, and design. In *Holistic Approach to Quantum Cryptography in Cyber Security* (pp. 41–66). CRC Press. doi:10.1201/9781003296034-3

Rani, S., Kataria, A., Kumar, S., & Tiwari, P. (2023). Federated learning for secure IoMT-applications in smart healthcare systems: A comprehensive review. *Knowledge-Based Systems*, *274*, 110658. doi:10.1016/j.knosys.2023.110658

Rani, S., Mishra, R. K., Usman, M., Kataria, A., Kumar, P., Bhambri, P., & Mishra, A. K. (2021). Amalgamation of advanced technologies for sustainable development of smart city environment: A review. *IEEE Access: Practical Innovations, Open Solutions*, *9*, 150060–150087. doi:10.1109/ACCESS.2021.3125527

Rani, S., Pareek, P. K., Kaur, J., Chauhan, M., & Bhambri, P. (2023). Quantum Machine Learning in Healthcare: Developments and Challenges. In *2023 IEEE International Conference on Integrated Circuits and Communication Systems (ICICACS)* (pp. 1-7). IEEE. 10.1109/ICICACS57338.2023.10100075

Sparkes, M. (2021). What is a metaverse. Elsevier. doi:10.1016/S0262-4079(21)01450-0

Thakur, K., Qiu, M., Gai, K., & Ali, M. L. (2015). An investigation on cyber security threats and security models. In *2015 IEEE 2nd international conference on cyber security and cloud computing* (pp. 307-311). IEEE. 10.1109/CSCloud.2015.71

Wang, Y. (2022). A survey on metaverse: Fundamentals, security, and privacy. *IEEE Communications Surveys and Tutorials*.

Xu, Z., Hu, Q., & Zhang, C. (2013). Why computer talents become computer hackers. *Communications of the ACM*, *56*(4), 64–74. doi:10.1145/2436256.2436272

Zheng, Z., Xie, S., Dai, H.-N., Chen, X., & Wang, H. (2018). Blockchain challenges and opportunities: A survey. *International Journal of Web and Grid Services*, *14*(4), 352–375. doi:10.1504/IJWGS.2018.095647

Chapter 24
Smart Cities Data Indicator– Based Cyber Threats Detection Using Bio–Inspired Artificial Algae Algorithm

Vineeta S. Chauhan
https://orcid.org/0000-0002-6147-3755
Indus University, India

Jaydeep Chakravorty
https://orcid.org/0000-0003-0892-0453
Indus University, India

Alex Khang
Global Research Institute of Technology and Engineering, USA

ABSTRACT

Smart cities have benefited greatly from the quick development of information technology, such as cloud computing, sensors, and the IoT. Smart cities improve living services and analyze massive amounts of data, which increases privacy and security concerns. But managing security and privacy issues is crucial for a smart city that encourages businesses to adopt new computing paradigms. In recent years, there has been a proliferation of literature on security and privacy, covering topics like end-to-end security, reliable data acquisition, transmission, and processing, legal service provisioning, and privacy of personal data, as well as the application of bio inspired computing techniques to system design and operation. Effective computing systems have been developed by utilizing bio-inspired computing approaches for intelligent decision support. The indicator-based threat detection system with BAAA algorithm is the quickest and most efficient way to scope an environment after observation, and its usefulness is greatly influenced by the adversary rate of change.

DOI: 10.4018/978-1-6684-8851-5.ch024

INTRODUCTION

One of the most significant challenges for smart cities is cyber threats. Giving the everchanging risk landscape, emerging in smart cities could be targeted for a variety of adversary interests. The possibility of a malicious attempt to damage or disrupt a computer network or system is referred to as a cyber threat. This definition is incomplete without mentioning the attempt to access files and infiltrate or steal data and can be solved with proposed method of Indicator Based cyber– threats detection for data of smart Cities using Bio-Inspired Artificial Algae Algorithm. However, the threat is more closely associated with the adverse attempt to gain access to a system in the cyber security community. The combination of data and corresponding advances is producing urban conditions that are very different from anything we have seen before. Cities are becoming more intelligent not just in terms of how to automate routine capacities serving specific people, structures, and traffic frameworks, but also in ways that enable us to screen, comprehend, examine, and plan the city to continuously improve the efficiency, value and personal satisfaction for its residents. This algorithm is based on the behavior of algae, which exhibit

Figure 1. Problems related to smart cities development

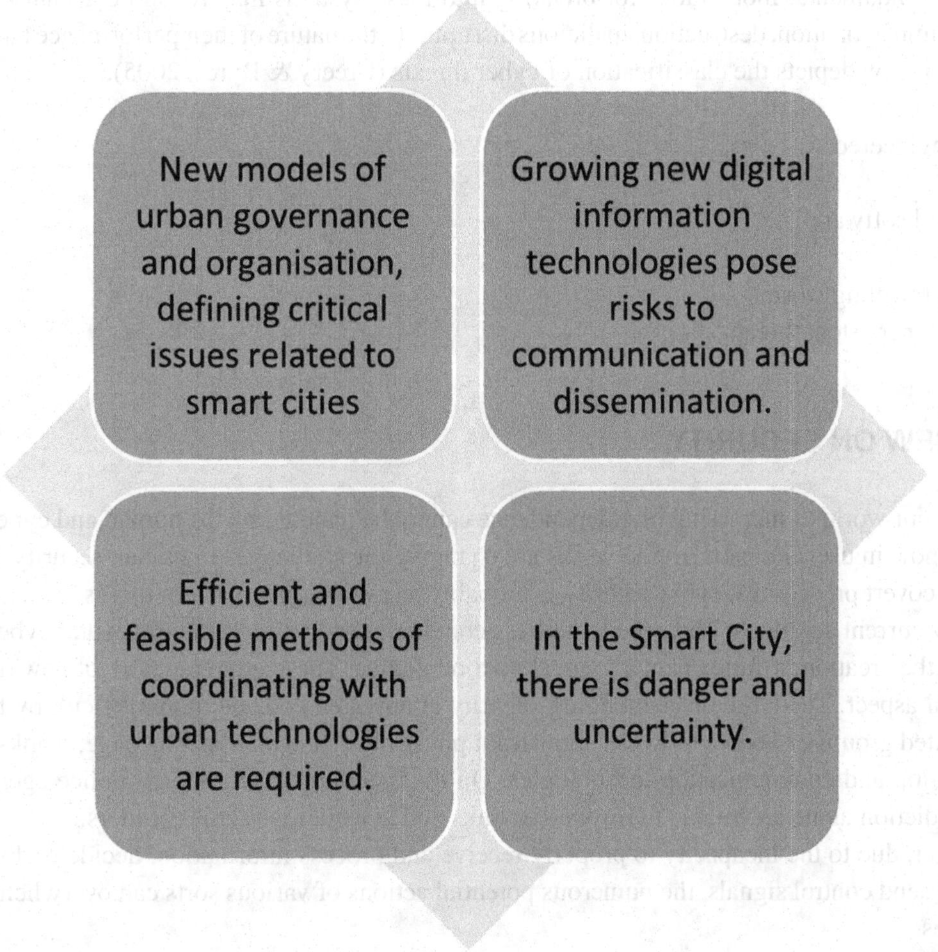

New models of urban governance and organisation, defining critical issues related to smart cities

Growing new digital information technologies pose risks to communication and dissemination.

Efficient and feasible methods of coordinating with urban technologies are required.

In the Smart City, there is danger and uncertainty.

characteristics such as self-organization, adaptation, and resilience. These same characteristics are valuable in detecting and mitigating cyber threats in smart city systems.

A new understanding of urban problems is that smart cities are intricate frameworks that are greater than the sum of their parts and are created through many individual and aggregate choices from the bottom up (Trevor et al., 2018). The multifaceted nature sciences are required for their comprehension, which is a moving goal in that urban communities themselves and are becoming increasingly perplexing as a result of the very advancements for utilizing them. Figure 1 depicts the issues associated with the development of smart cities (Darwish, 2018; David & Wanger, 2017).

PROBLEM STATEMENT

Detecting cyber threats in smart cities can be a challenging task, given the vast amount of data generated by various sensors and devices. One way to address this issue is by using bio-inspired algorithms, which mimic the behavior of natural organisms to solve complex problems. Smart city technologies are no exception, as they are overwhelmed by a variety of security vulnerabilities and risks, and an ongoing battle has emerged between the cyber security industry and criminals and variously motivated hackers. While the fundamental motivations for breaking into these systems may remain constant (e.g., theft, extortion, impersonation, destruction, malicious disruption), the nature of their performance has changed. List given below depicts the classification of cyber threats (Creery & Byres, 2005).

[2] Social engineered
[2] Trojans
[2] Unpatched software
[2] Phishing
[2] Network traveling worms
[2] Advanced persistent threats

OVERVIEW ON SECURITY

Threats in our world of increasing interdependence cannot be handled by the human and cyber security measures now in use. Global terror networks are changing the challenges to human security. Due to its quick and covert procedures, cyber security is probably an even bigger concern that is inadequately addressed by current solutions. The need to address contemporary issues with human and cyber security is driving the creation of fundamentally novel methodologies. The scattered nature of new difficulties is a crucial aspect. The issue of maintaining security at any area is made more difficult by the ability of distributed groups of people to wreak significant physical or informational damage, thanks to global transportation and communication technologies. On the one hand, conventional police agencies with local jurisdiction alone are unable to respond to links and associations across borders.

However, due to the incapacity to properly receive and process information, decide on local action plans, and send control signals, the numerous potential actions of various sorts can overwhelm centralized replies.

CYBERATTACKS AND SECURITY RISKS

The risks normally connected to any attack consider three security elements, including threats, i.e., who is attacking, vulnerabilities, i.e., the holes they are attacking, and impacts, i.e., what the attack does. An act that jeopardizes the availability, confidentiality, or integrity of information assets and systems is referred to as a security incident. Various cybersecurity mishaps that could put a person's or an organization's systems and networks at danger are:

Unauthorized access, which is defined as the act of accessing data, systems, or networks without authority and resulting in a security policy violation.

Any program or piece of software that is specifically intended to harm a computer, client, server, or computer network is known as malware, also referred to as malicious software, for example, botnets. Computer viruses, worms, Trojan horses, adware, ransomware, spyware, malicious bots, and more are examples of several types of malwares. The term "ransomware" refers to a new type of malware that locks users out of their devices, personal files, or systems and then demands an anonymous internet payment to let them back in.

A denial-of-service attack involves saturating the target with traffic until it crashes, rendering the system or network unreachable to its intended users. While a distributed denial-of-service (DDoS) attack uses numerous computers and Internet connections to overwhelm the targeted resource, a denial-of-service (DoS) assault normally just uses one computer and an Internet connection.

The fraudulent attempt to obtain sensitive information, such as banking and credit card details, login credentials, or personally identifiable information by posing as a trusted person or organization via an electronic communication such as email, text, or instant message is known as "phishing," a type of social engineering used for a wide range of malicious activities carried out through human interactions.

The term "zero-day attack" is used to indicate the risk posed by an undiscovered security vulnerability for which either no patch has been made available or for which the program developers were not aware.

Other well-known security incidents in the field of cybersecurity include privilege escalation, password attack, insider threat, man-in-the-middle, advanced persistent threat, SQL injection attack, crypto jacking attack, web application attack, etc. A data breach, sometimes referred to as a data leak, is a sort of security incident that involves unauthorized access to data by a person, application, or service.

Many automation and modernization programs nowadays use Intranet/Internet technologies in industrial management methods. The systems listed below are a mix of progressive and legacy installations that create challenges in the implementation and social control of security measures. Cyber-attacks are carried out by a wide range of groups including nation-state intelligence agencies and militaries, terrorist groups, organized criminals, hacker collectives, political and socially motivated activists, "lone wolf" hackers, "script kiddies," and bored teenagers (Batty et al., 2012; Kitchin & Dodge, 2019).

Sensible city technologies typically provide massive attack surfaces that expose a wide range of potential vulnerabilities, particularly in cutting-edge systems that use legacy software that has not been frequently patched. The standard approach to securing smart city systems has been to use a collection of well-known technical solutions and software package security approaches to perform and prevent access, as well as to modify restoration if a compromise occurs.

Privacy-protecting systems that gather information and activate emergency responses when necessary are technological challenges that go hand in hand with ongoing security challenges. Application security is concerned with keeping software and devices safe from threats (Elmaghraby & Losavio, 2014; Jouini et al., 2014). A compromised application may allow access to the data it is supposed to protect.

Security begins with design, long before a program or device is deployed. Few security problems that could be triggered are:

- Inadequate cyber security testing
- Inadequate or nonexistent security encryption issues
- Inadequate computer emergency response teams
- Large and intricate attack surfaces
- Problems with patch deployment legacy systems that are insecure
- Simple bugs with significant consequences
- Public sector issues
- Lack of cyber-attack emergency plans
- Susceptibility to denial of service
- Technology vendors who obstruct security research

PROPOSED APPROACH

With the increased demand for networked systems and reliance on internet connectivity provided by a variety of devices and infrastructures, it is critical that computing systems are adaptive, resilient, scalable, and robust enough to withstand failure, as well as dynamic enough to cope with changes. Bio-inspired approaches are said to provide consistency in computer and cybersecurity principles, algorithms, applications, and perspectives in performance over time, and they do share the complexity attributes and relative success of inter networked environments. Figure 2 shows the future cyber security challenges.

The following are the primary reasons for bio-inspired cyber threats: the ability to adapt to changes in environmental circumstances. Capability to be fault tolerant, robust, and resilient in the face of failures (whether caused by internal or external factors). Run-time adaptivity in a distributed manner to maintain normal behavior and the ability to evolve under new applied conditions (Trevor et al., 2018).

In a variety of fields, such as computing, financial modelling, and robotics, to name a few, biological principles have played a key role and contributed to resilient Computer and Cyber Security: Principles, Algorithm, Applications and Perspectives implementations. The distributed architecture of biological systems, where autonomous organisms make local decisions with ramifications for the entire system, is what gives them their fundamental advantages. As it learns about new threats and defends itself and its protective components, the immune system, for instance, can adapt and self-protect by constantly producing and eliminating altered or infected body cells. Software defined platforms and networks heavily rely on virtualization because it is prevalent in cyberspace; nevertheless, because the attack surface is both new and larger, security monitoring is more difficult (Fang et al., 2012; He et al., 2015; Tahir et al., 2012).

Since the 1980s, researchers have studied biological systems at all stages of the computer life cycle. Numerous surveys have devoted their time to analyzing biologically inspired algorithms in computing-related applications in recent years. It is crucial that computing systems are adaptable, resilient, scalable, robust enough to withstand failure, and dynamic enough to deal with changes given the increase in demand for networked systems and reliance on internet connectivity offered by a variety of devices and infrastructures. Consistency is claimed to be provided by bio-inspired strategies.

Figure 2. Future cyber security challenges

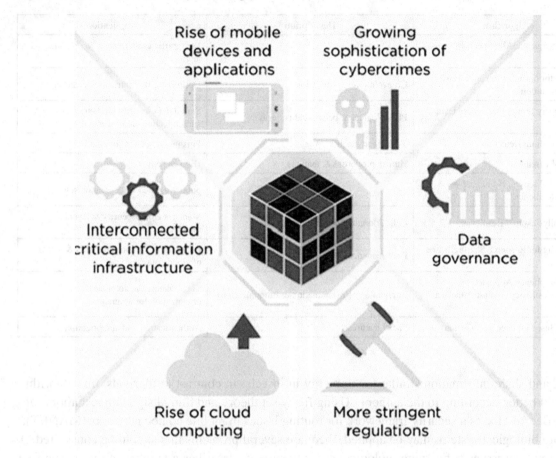

In terms of performance over a long period of time, computer and cyber security principles, algorithms, applications, and perspectives share the complexity characteristics and relative success of interconnected settings. Table 1 represents summary of Bio-inspired approaches in cyber environments.

Traditional distributed computing systems that use bio-inspired approaches show useful traits derived from their biological ancestry, such as origin, development, and progression, or ecological interactions between organs and organisms in their natural environments. For instance, the creation of IDSs based on T-cells that bind to and eliminate harmful or infected cells by negative selection. As an alternative, the design of IDSs can be applied to physiological analogies of the immune system by adapting the memory and self-learning mechanism used by B-cells in recognizing and eliminating pathogens (Abbasy & Shanmugam, 2011; Welsh & Benkhelifa, 2018).

Theories and algorithms are current instances of traditional bio-inspired techniques in the computing continuum. Algorithms are important for explaining discrete state space systems, or how and why systems transition, according to develop extremely effective, complex, and distributed systems, for example, algorithms based on mechanisms driving the behaviors of ant colonies, human immune system, bee swarming, fish, predator and prey interactions, and communities have been modelled (Carvalho et al., 2011; Wang & Yan, 2010). Ant colonies have been used to optimize traffic routing, for example in works by who assess an optimization technique; AntNet, in which agents simultaneously navigate a

Table 1. Summary of bio-inspired approaches in cyber environments

Algorithm	Description	Application
Multiple Sequence Alignment (MSA) algorithm	Protein structure	Web traffic classification & sequence alignment
IDS detector optimization algorithm with co-evolution	Co-evolution in populations	Optimizing IDS intrusion detection
Data Security Strategy or Secure Data Storage	Physiological & behavioral patterns	Stored data security biometric authentication cloud stored data
AIS for Phishing Detection	T-lymphocytes life cycle	Phishing detection for emails
Integrated Circuit	Human properties & features	High entropy
Metrics (IC Metrics) Biologically-Inspired Resilience		public/private key generation scheme
Biologically-Inspired Resilience	Cells & organisms (sea chameleon)	Manages cloud security & leverage resilience
Data Hiding for Resource Sharing Based on DNA	Data sequences	Data hiding for confidentiality & integrity of cloud data
Organic Resilience Approach for Assuring Resiliency Against Attacks and Failure	Immunology (inflammation & immunization)	Threat detection, automated re-organization for assurance
Security Based on Face Recognition	Facial features	Authentication and authorization

network and share information similar to stigmergy in insects. In contrast to its rivals, this algorithm performed better, according to the authors . Using fuzzy set theory and digital signatures, authors suggested FBeeAd-Hoc as a security framework for routing issues in mobile ad hoc networks (MANET).

Before biological systems may be applied, there are several problems that should be considered. A panel discussing issues concerning biological security systems describes a number of these. The first and perhaps most important is that biological systems and computer systems do not share an end goal. Whereas biological systems aspire to survive, the goal of many computer systems is to accomplish a computational task. The development of techniques for formalizing analogies to combine features or objectives in multi-domain systems has been ushered in by recent tendencies towards bio-inspired designs. BioTRIZ and other analogical reasoning tools summarized in the table below are some common examples. Although conceptual design (CD) offers insights into the operations, guiding principles, and overall organization of a system's structure, they are lacking because a direct translation of natural concepts to cloud computing necessitates creative problem-solving.

BIO-INSPIRED ARTIFICIAL ALGAE ALGORITHM (BAAA)

The concept of using Bio-inspired Artificial Algae Algorithm (BAAA) for detecting cyber threats in smart cities data indicators is an interesting one. BAAA is a nature-inspired optimization algorithm that mimics the behavior of algae in nature to solve complex optimization problems. To apply BAAA for detecting cyber threats in smart cities data indicators, we can use it to analyze patterns and anomalies in the data. The algorithm can learn from historical data and detect abnormal patterns that may indicate potential cyber threats. The first step would be to collect and preprocess the smart cities data indicators, which could include data from various sources such as sensors, cameras, and social media. This data would then be fed into the BAAA model, which would use its optimization techniques to identify patterns and anomalies in the data. This algorithm is based on the process of algae evolution, adaptation, and movement. The algorithm's efficacy has been demonstrated at various scales of operation. It was proposed by Uymaz et al. (2015) was inspired by the feature and live behavior of the microalgae. Helical movement is the movement of algae in a liquid to get closer to light. The process of evolution involves the reproduction of algae through mitosis, whereas the process of adaptation involves adaptable algae. Algae are the dominant species in this algorithm, and the entire population is made up of algal colonies (Kwecko, 2018; Mthunzi et al., 2018; Procopiou & Komninos, 2019). Figure 3 shows the flowchart of BAAA.

The Process of Evolution: In the evolutionary phase also called the production phase, the algal colony that gets the best sunlight of photosynthesis grows most of the environment and tries to reproduce itself in the environment. strong and productive. Therefore, BAAA mimics the survival behavior of the powerful. Therefore, BAAA is naturally ready to solve the expansion problem. With reduction problems, the stiffness function is obtained equal to the magnification problem. The growth process of algal colonies is controlled by the work of the Monod. One cell of the algal colony is multiplied by the dying cell of a very small colony as shown in Eq. 1 (Uymaz et al., 2015).

$Bit+1 = uit Bit$ (Trevor et al., 2018)

$for\ i = 1,2,3 . . . . N$

where, B is the size of jth algal while t and N are the colony in the system. Colonies that offer better solutions are increasing because they get enough sunlight to grow. Equations (Creery & Byres, 2005; Darwish, 2018; David & Wanger, 2017) represents colonies that do not provide good solutions become smaller. D magnitude of the problem.

$biggest\ t = max\ Bit\ i = 1,2, ... N$ (Creery & Byres, 2005)

$smallest\ t = minBit\ i = 1,2, ... N$ (Darwish, 2018)

$smallest\ tm = biggest\ mt\ m = 1,2, ... D$ (David & Wanger, 2017)

The process of Adaptation: In the adaptation phase most of the hungry colonies in the area try to rule the largest colony in the area from time to time as in Eq (Elmaghraby & Losavio, 2014; Jouini et al., 2014)

$starving\ t = max\ Atl\ i=1,2. . . . .N$ (Elmaghraby & Losavio, 2014)

$starving\ t + 1 = starving\ t + (biggest\ t − starving) x\ rand$ (Jouini et al., 2014)

The Process of Helical Movement: In search of a light source algal colonies swim in a liquid with a helical patte**rn. First of all, the light sour**ce is chosen among all the solutions in the form of competition and then each algal colony tries to swim towards this light source until its power is exhausted. After each step the strength of each colon decreases by a certain amount and this energy loss is defined as the energy loss parameter. The energy loss parameter controls the exploitation of the BAAA algorithm, the smaller the value, the better the exploitation. As the algal colony moves to the liquid it also undergoes a viscous pull equal to the size of the algal colony. The area of conflict, f facing the colony also depends on its size. Being larger than the size of the colony, it is larger the conflict area facing the colony during swimming. During the helical movement when a colony finds a better solution than the starvation of that colony it remains unchanged otherwise the level of colonial hunger increases by one represented in Equation (Batty et al., 2012; Kitchin & Dodge, 2019; Kwecko, 2018; Mthunzi et al., 2018; Procopiou & Komninos, 2019).

$\tau\pi r$ (Kitchin & Dodge, 2019)

τ (Batty et al., 2012)

Figure 3. Flowchart of BAAA algorithm

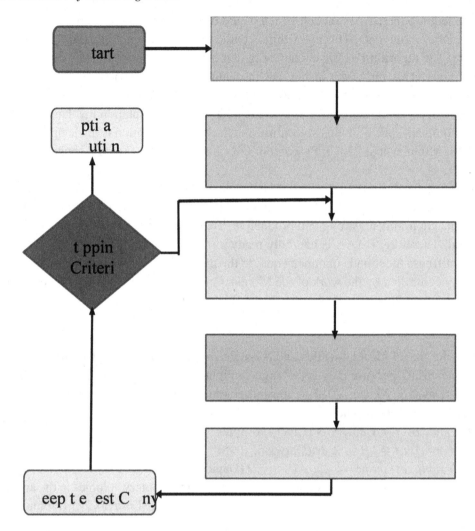

Where is the friction surface.

where ximt, xikt and xilt are x, y and z coordinates of the ith algal cellat time t; α and $\beta \in ()$,$p \in [-1,1]$; Δ is shear $_f$orce $_(^U$ymaz e$_t^a$l., 2015).

$ximt+1 = ximt+(xjmt-xim)(\Delta - \tau t(xl))p$ (Mthunzi et al., 2018)

$xikt+1 = xikt + (xjkt - xik)(\Delta - \tau t(xl))$ (Procopiou & Komninos, 2019)

$xilt+1 = xilt + (xjlt - xil)(\Delta - \tau t(xl)) \sin \beta$ (Kwecko, 2018)

To train the BAAA model, we would need a dataset of known cyber threats that could be used to identify and label potential threats in the smart cities data. Figure 4 shows the process flow of detection of Cyber threat using BAAA. The model would then use this labeled data to learn and improve its accuracy in detecting future threats. Once the BAAA model has been trained, it can be deployed in real-time to monitor smart cities data indicators for potential cyber threats. The algorithm could generate alerts when it detects any abnormal patterns or anomalies in the data, allowing for timely responses to potential threats. To describe the security compliance against the BAAA for automation in security operations

Figure 4. Process flow of detection of cyber threat using BAAA

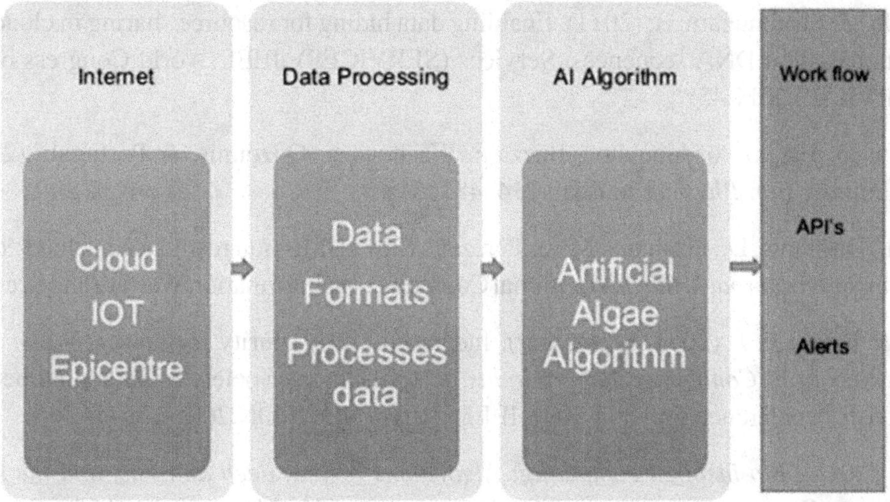

in multiple dimensions of smart cities for two different types of solutions that give us a consolidated view on threat detection and used in security operations are Security Information event management (SEIM) and cloud-based solutions based on artificial intelligence for cyber threats. Using the BAAA AI algorithm as indicators for threat detection for advanced threat analytics to identify indicators are need of the day. It can also be used in AI-based advance threat detection to provide insight into attack patterns, allowing the platform to adapt to different attack patterns as it collects more and more data, lowering costs and providing access to real-time intelligence for contextual security. It is used to find a way to obtain attack indicators, which provides visibility to counter the situation when something goes wrong, which is what the solution is all about.

RESULTS AND DISCUSSION

Using BAAA for detecting cyber threats in smart cities data indicators could be a promising approach. However, it would require further research and development to optimize the algorithm and ensure its accuracy and reliability in real-world scenarios. This research paper presents a review about such known threat that introduces new challenges in front of all. To pursue technology-centric smart solutions, smart cities must upgrade detection efficacy monitoring and critical alert monitoring. Threat detection is the discovery of all related activity, exposing all phases that have never been discovered before, which appears to be malicious activity that may be like previously discovered activity, as well as the identification of the breadth of security incident. To improve efficiency and prioritize risk, it is necessary to identify the attacker's next move, which requires the development of advanced threat intelligence or tactical intelligence that searches the most recent information available and has the ability to identify the threat as well as search for suspicious activity and deploy the solution. Overall, using the BAAA and a data indicator-based approach, can improve the cybersecurity of smart city systems and help prevent potential damage and disruption.

REFERENCES

Abbasy, M. R., & Shanmugam, B. (2011). Enabling data hiding for resource sharing in cloud computing environments based on DNA sequences. Services (SERVICES), IEEE World Congress on, 385–390. 10.1109/SERVICES.2011.45

Batty, Axhausen, Fosca, Pozdnoukhov, Bazzani, Wachowicz, Ouzounis, & Portugali. (2012*). Smart Cities of the Future. Eur. Physic*al Journal, 214, 481–518.

Carvalho, M., Dasgupta, D., Grimaila, M., & Perez, C. (2011). Mission resilience in cloud computing: A biologically inspire*d approach. 6th Internatio*nal Conference on Information Warfare and Security, 42–52.

Creery, A., & Byres, E. J. (2005, September). Industrial cybersecurity for power sys*tem and SCADA networks. In Record of Conference Papers Industry* Applications Society 52nd annual petroleum and chemical industry conference (pp. 303-309). IEEE, 10.1109/PCICON.2005.152*4567*

*Darwish, A. (2018). Bio-inspired computing: Algorithms review, deep analysis, and the scope of applicati*ons. Future Computing and Informatics Journal, 3(2), 231–246. doi:10.1016/j.fcij.2018.06.001

David & Wanger. (2017). Privacy in Smart Cities-Applications, T*echnologies, Challenges and Solutions. I*EEE Communications Surveys and Tutorials, 20(1), 489-516.

Elmaghraby, A. S., & Losavio, M. M. (2014). Cyber security challenges in Smart Cities: Sa*fety, security, and privacy. Journal of Advan*ced Research, 5(4), 491–497. doi:10.1016/j.jare.2014.02.006 PMID:25685517

Fang, X., Koceja, N., Zhan, J., Dozier, G., & Dipankar, *D. (2012). An artificial im*mune system for phishing detection. Evolutionary Computation (CEC), IEEE Congress on, 1–7. 10.1109/CEC.2012.6256518

He, G., Yang, M., Luo, J., & Gu, X. (2015). A novel applicatio*n classification attack against Tor. Concurr. Comp*ut. Pract. Exp., 27(18), 5640–5661.

Jouini, Ben, Rabai, & Aissa. (2014). Classification of security threats in information systems. doi:10.1016/j.procs.2014.05.452

Kitchin, R., & Dodge, M. (2019). The (in) se*curity of smart cities: Vulnerabilities, risks, mitigation*, and prevention. Journal of Urban Technology, 26(2), 47–65. doi:10.1080/10630732.2017.1408002

Kwecko, V. (2018). Silvia S. da C. Botelho, Collaborativ*e Intelligence in Smart Cities:* ASystematicReview. Social Networking, 24(July). doi:10.4236n.2018.73015

Mthunzi, S. N., Benkhelifa, E., Bosakowski, T., & Hariri, S. (2018). A bio-in*spired approach t*o *cy*ber security. https://eprints.staffs.ac.uk/id/eprint/5069

Procopiou, A., & Komninos, N. (2019). Bi*o/Nature-inspired algorithms in AI for mal*icious activity detection. In Nature-Inspired Cyber Security and Resiliency: Fundam*entals, techniques and applications. IET. doi:10.1049/PBSE010E_CH9*

*Tahir, R., Hu, H., Gu, D., McDonald-Maier, K., & Howells, G. (2012). A scheme for the genera*tion of strong cryptographic key pairs based on IC Metrics. Internet Technology and Secured Transactions, 2012 International Conference for, 168–17.

Trevor, Benjamin, Farkhund, & Ba*bar. (2018). Security and Privacy in Smart Cities. Elsevier Sustainable Cities* and Society, 39, 499-508.

Uymaz, S. A., Tezel, G., & Yel, E. (2015). Artificial Algae Algo*rithm with multilight source for numerical* optimization and application. Bio Systems, 138, 25–38. doi:10.1016/j.biosystems.2015.11.004 PMID:26562030

Wang, C., & Yan, H. (2010). Study of cl*oud computi*ng *s*ecurity based on private face recognition. Computational Intelligence and Software Engineering (CiSE), International Conference on, 1–5. 10.1109/CISE.2010.56*76941*

Welsh, T., & Benkhelifa, E. (2018). Embyronic Model for Highly Resilient Paas. doi:10.1109/SDS.2018.8370443

Compilation of References

Abbasy, M. R., & Shanmugam, B. (2011). Enabling data hiding for resource sharing in cloud computing environments based on DNA sequences. *Services (SERVICES), IEEE World Congress on*, 385–390. 10.1109/SERVICES.2011.45

Abbate, S., Centobelli, P., Cerchione, R., Oropallo, E., & Riccio, E. (2022). A first bibliometric literature review on metaverse. *2022 IEEE Technology and Engineering Management Conference: Societal Challenges: Technology, Transitions and Resilience Virtual Conference, Temscon Europe 2022*, 254-260. 10.1109/TEMSCONEUROPE54743.2022.9802015

Abdel-Basset, M., Manogaran, G., & Mohamed, M. (2018). Internet of Things (IoT) and its impact on supply chain: A framework for building smart, secure and efficient systems. *Future Generation Computer Systems*, *86*, 614–628. doi:10.1016/j.future.2018.04.051

Abujarad, Y., & Al-Sayed, M. H. (2017). Development of a web browser for the visually impaired using speech recognition. *IEEE International Conference on Computer Applications & Industrial Electronics (ICCAIE)*.

Aceto, G., Persico, V., & Pescapé, A. (2020). Industry 4.0 and health: Internet of things, big data, and cloud computing for healthcare 4.0. *Journal of Industrial Information Integration*, *18*, 100129. doi:10.1016/j.jii.2020.100129

Achanta, R. (2018). *Cross-border money transfer using blockchain-enabled by big data*. White Paper, External Document.

Adebayo, A., Rawat, D. B., Njilla, L., & Kamhoua, C. A. (2019). Blockchain-enabled information sharing framework for cybersecurity. *Blockchain for Distributed Systems Security*, 143–158.

Aharon, D. Y., Demir, E., & Siev, S. (2022). Real returns from the unreal world? market reaction to metaverse disclosures. *Research in International Business and Finance*, *63*, 101778. Advance online publication. doi:10.1016/j.ribaf.2022.101778

Ahn, S. J., Kim, J., & Kim, J. (2022). The bifold triadic relationships framework: A theoretical primer for advertising research in the metaverse. *Journal of Advertising*, *51*(5), 592–607. doi:10.1080/00913367.2022.2111729

Ahn, S. J., Kim, J., & Kim, J. (2023). The future of advertising research in virtual, augmented, and extended realities. *International Journal of Advertising*, *42*(1), 162–170. doi:10.1080/02650487.2022.2137316

Akbari, M. R., Jamshidi, M. R., & Khosrojerdi, H. T. (2018). Smart transportation systems: Opportunities and challenges for Iran. *Iranian Journal of Management Studies*, *11*(3), 493–514.

Akbayır, D. (2010). *Implementation and tailoring of agile software development process* (Publication No. 266136) [Master's thesis, Maltepe University]. Higher Education Council Thesis Archive. https://tez.yok.gov.tr

Akın, Ö. (2022). *The effects of activities organized with augmented reality applications on the academic achievement of 4th grade students in mathematics lesson* (Publication No. 714589) [Master's Thesis, Çanakkale Onsekiz Mart University]. Higher Education Council Thesis Archive. https://tez.yok.gov.tr

Alam, A. (2022). Employing Adaptive Learning and Intelligent Tutoring Robots for Virtual Classrooms and Smart Campuses: Reforming Education in the Age of Artificial Intelligence. In *Advanced Computing and Intelligent Technologies* (pp. 395–406). Springer. doi:10.1007/978-981-19-2980-9_32

Alcantara, A. C., & Michalack, D. L. (2023). *The metaverse narrative in the matrix resurrections: A semiotic analysis through costumes.* doi:10.1007/978-3-031-09659-4_20

Alexander, B., Ashford-Rowe, K., Barajas-Murph, N., Dobbin, G., Knott, J., McCormack, M., Pomerantz, J., Seilhamer, R., & Weber, N. (2019). EDUCAUSE Horizon Report: 2019 Higher Education Edition. Louisville, CO: EDUCAUSE 2019.

Alfalah, A. A. (2023). Factors influencing students' adoption and use of mobile learning management systems (m-LMSs): A quantitative study of Saudi Arabia. *International Journal of Information Management Data Insights*, 3(1), 100143. doi:10.1016/j.jjimei.2022.100143

Alghofaili, Y., & Rassam, M. (2022). A Trust Management Model for IoT Devices and Services Based on the Multi-Criteria Decision-Making Approach and Deep Long Short-Term Memory Technique. *Sensors (Basel)*, 22(2), 634. doi:10.339022020634 PMID:35062594

Alhichri, A., Al-Qahtani, A., & Al-Wabil, A. (2020). A Deep Learning Approach for Lane Detection Using Image Processing Techniques. *Sensors (Basel)*, 20(7), 1926. doi:10.339020071926 PMID:32235639

Alibeigi, A., & Munir, A. B. (2022). A decade after the Personal Data Protection Act 2010 (PDPA): Compliance of communications companies with the notice and choice principle. *Journal of Data Protection & Privacy*, 5(2), 119–137.

Aliyev, R., Sidorova, Y., & Khudaykulov, A. (2018). Development of a hybrid approach for evaluating the effectiveness of scientific research. *Journal of Intelligent & Fuzzy Systems*, 34(2), 1031–1041. doi:10.3233/JIFS-179429

Alladi, T., Chamola, V., Sahu, N., Venkatesh, V., Goyal, A., & Guizani, M. (2022). A comprehensive survey on the applications of blockchain for securing vehicular networks. *IEEE Communications Surveys and Tutorials*, 24(2), 1212–1239. doi:10.1109/COMST.2022.3160925

Allam, Z., Bibri, S., Jones, D., Chabaud, D., & Moreno, C. (2022). Unpacking the ‘15-Minute City’ via 6G, IoT, and Digital Twins: Towards a New Narrative for Increasing Urban Efficiency, Resilience, and Sustainability. *Sensors (Basel)*, 22(4), 1369. doi:10.339022041369 PMID:35214271

Allam, Z., Sharifi, A., Bibri, S. E., Jones, D. S., & Krogstie, J. (2022). The metaverse as a virtual form of smart cities: Opportunities and challenges for environmental, economic, and social sustainability in urban futures. *Smart Cities*, 5(3), 771–801. doi:10.3390martcities5030040

Allende, M., León, D. L., Cerón, S., Pareja, A., Pacheco, E., Leal, A., Da Silva, M., Pardo, A., Jones, D., Worrall, D. J., Merriman, B., Gilmore, J., Kitchener, N., & Venegas-Andraca, S. E. (2023). Quantum-resistance in blockchain networks. *Scientific Reports*, 13(1), 5664. doi:10.103841598-023-32701-6 PMID:37024656

Almarzouqi, A., Aburayya, A., & Salloum, S. A. (2022). Prediction of user's intention to use metaverse system in medical education: A hybrid SEM-ML learning approach. *IEEE Access : Practical Innovations, Open Solutions*, 10, 43421–43434. doi:10.1109/ACCESS.2022.3169285

Almeida, D. R., & Martins, J. F. (2019). A review of electric vehicle wireless charging technology using electromagnetic resonant coupling. *IEEE Access : Practical Innovations, Open Solutions*, 7, 146380–146393.

Alpala, L., Quiroga-Parra, D., Torres, J., & Peluffo-Ordóñez, D. (2022). Smart Factory Using Virtual Reality and Online Multi-User: Towards a Metaverse for Experimental Frameworks. *Applied Sciences (Basel, Switzerland)*, 12(12), 6258. doi:10.3390/app12126258

Altınpulluk, H. (2018). *Açık ve uzaktan öğrenmede evrensel tasarım ilkeleri çerçevesinde artırılmış gerçekliğin kullanılabilirliği* [Usability of augmented reality within the framework of universal design principles in open and distance learning] (Publication No. 531761) [Doctoral Disertation, Anadolu University]. Higher Education Council Thesis Archive. https://tez.yok.gov.tr

Altınpulluk, H., Demirbağ, İ., Ertan, S., Yıldırım, Y., Koçak, A., Yıldız, T., Yıldırım, M., Köse, B. S., Özer Taylan, G., Karagil, S. D., Helvacı Aydın, E., Güven, K., Türktan, O., & Tabak, B. (2021). Examination of postgraduate theses on virtual reality in the field of social sciences in Turkey. *Asian Journal of Distance Education*, 171-193. doi:10.5281/zenodo.4895633

Al-Turkistany, M. (2009). Adaptive wireless thin-client model for mobile computing. *Wireless Communications and Mobile Computing*, *9*, 47–59. doi:10.1002/wcm.603

Ambika, N. (2022). An Economical Machine Learning Approach for Anomaly Detection in IoT Environment. In Bioinformatics and Medical Applications: Big Data Using Deep Learning Algorithms (pp. 215-234). Wiley Publications. doi:10.1002/9781119792673.ch11

Ambika, N. (2022). Enhancing Security in IoT Instruments Using Artificial Intelligence. In IoT and Cloud Computing for Societal Good (pp. 259-276). Cham: Springer. doi:10.1007/978-3-030-73885-3_16

Ambika, N. (2021). A Reliable Blockchain-Based Image Encryption Scheme for IIoT Networks. In *Blockchain and AI Technology in the Industrial Internet of Things* (pp. 81–97). IGI Global.

Ambika, N. (2021). A Reliable Hybrid Blockchain-Based Authentication System for IoT Network. In S. Singh (Ed.), *Revolutionary Applications of Blockchain-Enabled Privacy and Access Control* (pp. 219–233). IGI Global.

Ambrust A. Fox, R., Griffith, R., Joseph, A. D., Konwinski, A., Lee, G., Patterson, D., Rabkin, A., Stoica, I., & Zaharia, M. (2010). A view of cloud computing. *Communications of the ACM*, *53*(4), 50–58. doi:10.1145/1721654.1721672

Ampountolas, A., Menconi, G., & Shaw, G. (2023). Metaverse research propositions: Online intermediaries. *Tourism Economics*. Advance online publication. doi:10.1177/13548166231159520

AnascavageR.DavisN. (2018). *Blockchain technology: A literature review*. doi:10.2139/ssrn.3173406

Anderson, C. R. (2023). *Traditional Versus Modern Teaching Methods amongst Special Education Students and Enhancing Students' Self-Concept: A Comprehensive Literature Review* [Doctoral dissertation]. The Chicago School of Professional Psychology.

Anderson, M. C., & Shamsuddin, A. (2020). The Role of Artificial Intelligence in Vehicle Safety. *Artificial Intelligence Review*, *53*(5), 3695–3712.

An, S., Choi, Y., & Lee, C. K. (2021). Virtual travel experience and destination marketing: Effects of sense and information quality on flow and visit intention. *Journal of Destination Marketing & Management*, *19*, 100492. doi:10.1016/j.jdmm.2020.100492

Anthes, C., García-Hernández, R. J., Wiedemann, M., & Kranzlmüller, D. (2016). *State of the art of virtual reality technology. In 2016 IEEE aerospace conference*. IEEE.

Arakeri, M. P., Keerthana, N. S., Madhura, M., Sankar, A., & Munnavar, T. (2018). Assistive Technology for the Visually Impaired Using Computer Vision. *International Conference on Advances in Computing, Communications, and Informatics (ICACCI)*, 1725-1730.

Archuby, F., Sanz, C., & Manresa-Yee, C. (2023). DIJS: Methodology for the Design and Development of Digital Educational Serious Games. *IEEE Transactions on Games*, 1–9. doi:10.1109/TG.2022.3217737

ARCore. (2023). *ARCore overview*. https://developers.google.com/ar

Arden, N. S., Fisher, A. C., Tyner, K., Lawrence, X. Y., Lee, S. L., & Kopcha, M. (2021). Industry 4.0 for pharmaceutical manufacturing: Preparing for the smart factories of the future. *International Journal of Pharmaceutics*, *602*, 120554. doi:10.1016/j.ijpharm.2021.120554 PMID:33794326

Ardiny, H., & Khanmirza, E. (2018). The role of AR and VR technologies in education developments: opportunities and challenges. In *2018 6th rsi international conference on robotics and mechatronics (icrom)*. IEEE. 10.1109/ICRoM.2018.8657615

Arena, A., Bianchini, A., Perazzo, P., Vallati, C., & Dini, G. (2019). BRUSCHETTA: An IoT blockchain-based framework for certifying extra virgin olive oil supply chain. In *IEEE International Conference on Smart Computing (SMARTCOMP)* (pp. 173-179). IEEE. 10.1109/SMARTCOMP.2019.00049

Arikan, O. U., Ozturk, E., Duman, S., & Aktas, M. A. (2022). Conceptualization of meta-servitization: 3D case study from furniture industry. *ISMSIT 2022 - 6th International Symposium on Multidisciplinary Studies and Innovative Technologies, Proceedings*, 702-706. 10.1109/ISMSIT56059.2022.9932819

Ario, M. K., Santoso, Y. K., Basyari, F., Edbert, Fajar, M., Panggabean, F. M., & Satria, T. G. (2022). Towards an implementation of immersive experience application for marketing and promotion through virtual exhibition. *Software Impacts*, *14*, 100439. Advance online publication. doi:10.1016/j.simpa.2022.100439

Arora, S., Agarwal, A., & Jain, S. (2019). A novel approach for visually impaired people to access webpages. *IEEE International Conference on Advances in Computing and Communication Engineering (ICACCE)*.

Arpaci, I., Karatas, K., Kusci, I., & Al-Emran, M. (2022). Understanding the social sustainability of the metaverse by integrating UTAUT2 and big five personality traits: A hybrid SEM-ANN approach. *Technology in Society*, *71*, 102120. Advance online publication. doi:10.1016/j.techsoc.2022.102120

Arridha, R., Sukaridhoto, S., Pramadihanto, D., & Funabiki, N. (2017). Classification extension based on IoT-big data analytic for smart environment monitoring and analytic in real-time system. *International Journal of Space-Based and Situated Computing*, *7*(2), 82–93. doi:10.1504/IJSSC.2017.086821

Artificial intelligence for the Metaverse: A Survey. (n.d.). https://www.researchgate.net/publication/358761974_Artificial_Intelligence_for_the_Metaverse_A_Survey

Artivive. (2023). *About artivive*. https://artivive.com/about

Assarzadeh, A. H., & Aberoumand, S. (2018). FinTech in Western Asia: Case of Iran. *Journal of Industrial Integration and Management*, *3*(03), 1850006. doi:10.1142/S2424862218500069

Ausburn, L. J., & Ausburn, F. B. (2008). Effects of desktop virtual reality on learner performance and confidence in environment mastery: Opening a line of enquiry. *Journal of Industrial Teacher Education*, *45*(1), 54–87.

Avcı, M. (2022). *The effect of augmented reality application on nursing students' intravenous catheterization application skill, level of satisfaction in learning and perception of self-confidence* (Publication No. 716102) [Doctoral Disertation, İnönü University]. Higher Education Council Thesis Archive. https://tez.yok.gov.tr

Avner, S. (2021). Conceiving particles as undulating granular systems allows fundamentally realist interpretation of quantum mechanics. *Entropy (Basel, Switzerland)*, *23*(10), 1338. doi:10.3390/e23101338 PMID:34682062

Awan, S., Ahmed, S., Ullah, F., Nawaz, A., Khan, A., Uddin, M., Alharbi, A., Alosaimi, W., & Alyami, H. (2021). IoT with blockchain: A futuristic approach in agriculture and food supply chain. *Wireless Communications and Mobile Computing*, *2021*, 1–14. doi:10.1155/2021/5580179

Awan, U., Sroufe, R., & Shahbaz, M. (2021). Industry 4.0 and the circular economy: A literature review and recommendations for future research. *Business Strategy and the Environment*, *30*(4), 2038–2060. doi:10.1002/bse.2731

Azuma, R. (1997). A survey of augmented reality. *Presence (Cambridge, Mass.)*, *6*(4), 355–385. doi:10.1162/pres.1997.6.4.355

Azuma, R., Baillot, Y., Behringer, R., Feiner, S., Julier, S., & MacIntyre, B. (2001). Recent advances in augmented reality. *IEEE Computer Graphics and Applications*, *21*(6), 34–47. doi:10.1109/38.963459

Bacalja, A. (2022). A critical review of digital game literacies in the English classroom. *L1-Educational Studies in Language and Literature*, 1–28. doi:10.21248/l1esll.2022.22.2.370

Backhouse, R. (1992). Should we ignore Methodology? *Royal Economic Society Newsletter*, *78*, 4–5.

Baghalzadeh Shishehgarkhaneh, M., Keivani, A., Moehler, R., Jelodari, N., & Roshdi Laleh, S. (2022). Internet of Things (IoT), Building Information Modeling (BIM), and Digital Twin (DT) in Construction Industry: A Review, Bibliometric, and Network Analysis. *Buildings*, *12*(10), 1503. doi:10.3390/buildings12101503

Bainbridge, K. E., Hoffman, H. J., & Cowie, C. C. (2008). Diabetes and hearing impairment in the United States: Audiometric evidence from the National Health and Nutrition Examination Survey. *Annals of Internal Medicine*, *149*(1), 1–10. doi:10.7326/0003-4819-149-1-200807010-00231 PMID:18559825

Balamurugan, S., Ayyasamy, A., & Joseph, K. S. (2022). IoT-Blockchain driven traceability techniques for improved safety measures in food supply chain. *International Journal of Information Technology : an Official Journal of Bharati Vidyapeeth's Institute of Computer Applications and Management*, *14*(2), 1087–1098. doi:10.100741870-020-00581-y

Baralla, G., Pinna, A., Tonelli, R., Marchesi, M., & Ibba, S. (2021). Ensuring transparency and traceability of food local products: A blockchain application to a Smart Tourism Region. *Concurrency and Computation*, *33*(1), e5857. doi:10.1002/cpe.5857

Basu, Jaiswal, & Danoosh, & Saralaya. (2022). Analysis of the Feasibility of VR Metaverses and Examining its Societal and Health Ramifications. *Survey (London, England)*.

Batty, Axhausen, Fosca, Pozdnoukhov, Bazzani, Wachowicz, Ouzounis, & Portugali. (2012). Smart Cities of the Future. *Eur. Physical Journal, 214*, 481–518.

Bauerle, N. (2018). *How does blockchain technology work*. Retrieved from Coindesk: Https://Www. Coindesk. Com/Information/How-Does-Blockchain-Technology-Work

Bawany, N. Z., Shamsi, J. A., & Salah, K. (2017). DDoS attack detection and mitigation using SDN: Methods, practices, and solutions. *Arabian Journal for Science and Engineering*, *42*(2), 425–441. doi:10.100713369-017-2414-5

Belei, N., Noteborn, G., & De Ruyter, K. (2011). It's a brand new world: Teaching brand management in virtual environments. *Journal of Brand Management*, *18*(8), 611–623. doi:10.1057/bm.2011.6

Belk, R., Humayun, M., & Brouard, M. (2022). Money, possessions, and ownership in the metaverse: NFTs, cryptocurrencies, Web3 and wild markets. *Journal of Business Research*, *153*, 198–205. doi:10.1016/j.jbusres.2022.08.031

Benisi, N. Z., Aminian, M., & Javadi, B. (2020). Blockchain-based decentralized storage networks: A survey. *Journal of Network and Computer Applications*, *162*, 102656. doi:10.1016/j.jnca.2020.102656

Bess, F. H., Lichtenstein, M. J., Logan, S. A., Burger, M. C., & Nelson, E. (1989). Hearing impairment as a determinant of function in the elderly. *Journal of the American Geriatrics Society*, *37*(2), 123–128. doi:10.1111/j.1532-5415.1989. tb05870.x PMID:2910970

Bhanu, B. B., Rao, K. R., Ramesh, J. V., & Hussain, M. A. (2014). Agriculture field monitoring and analysis using wireless sensor networks for improving crop production. In *Eleventh international conference on wireless and optical communications networks (WOCN)* (pp. 1-7). IEEE.

Bhat, S., Huang, N.-F., Sofi, I., & Sultan, M. (2022). Agriculture-Food Supply Chain Management Based on Blockchain and IoT: A Narrative on Enterprise Blockchain Interoperability. *Agriculture*, *12*(1), 40. doi:10.3390/agriculture12010040

Bhattacharya, P., Saraswat, D., Savaliya, D., Sanghavi, S., Verma, A., Sakariya, V., Tanwar, S., Sharma, R., Raboaca, M. S., & Manea, D. L. (2023). Towards future internet: The metaverse perspective for diverse industrial applications. *Mathematics*, *11*(4), 941. doi:10.3390/math11040941

Bhattacharya, P., Verma, A., Prasad, V. K., Tanwar, S., Bhushan, B., Florea, B. C., Taralunga, D. D., Alqahtani, F., & Tolba, A. (2023). Game-o-Meta: Trusted Federated Learning Scheme for P2P Gaming Metaverse beyond 5G Networks. *Sensors (Basel)*, *23*(9), 4201. doi:10.339023094201 PMID:37177403

Bhattacharya, S., Sasi, P., Sankaranarayanan, V., & Woungang, I. (2019). Internet of Things and healthcare: An overview. *Future Generation Computer Systems*, *94*, 849–861.

Bhuiyan, M. Z. A., Rahman, N. A., & Ariffin, N. F. (2020). A bibliometric analysis of artificial intelligence in autonomous vehicles. *Transportation Research Part C, Emerging Technologies*, *113*, 244–262.

Bian, Y., Leng, J., & Zhao, J. L. (2022, February). Demystifying metaverse as a new paradigm of enterprise digitization. In *Big Data–BigData 2021: 10th International Conference, Held as Part of the Services Conference Federation, SCF 2021, Virtual Event, December 10–14, 2021, Proceedings* (pp. 109-119). Cham: Springer International Publishing. 10.1007/978-3-030-96282-1_8

Bibri, S. (2022). The Social Shaping of the Metaverse as an Alternative to the Imaginaries of Data-Driven Smart Cities: A Study in Science, Technology, and Society. *Smart Cities*, *5*(3), 832–874. doi:10.3390martcities5030043

Bibri, S., & Allam, Z. (2022). The Metaverse as a Virtual Form of Data-Driven Smart Urbanism: On Post-Pandemic Governance through the Prism of the Logic of Surveillance Capitalism. *Smart Cities*, *5*(2), 715–727. doi:10.3390martcities5020037

Billewar, S. R., Jadhav, K., Sriram, V. P., Arun, D. A., Mohd Abdul, S., Gulati, K., & Bhasin, D. N. K. K. (2022). The rise of 3D E-Commerce: The online shopping gets real with virtual reality and augmented reality during COVID-19. *World Journal of Engineering*, *19*(2), 244–253. doi:10.1108/WJE-06-2021-0338

Blake, J. (2023, February). Intelligent CALL: Individualizing Learning Using Natural Language Generation. In *The Post-pandemic Landscape of Education and Beyond: Innovation and Transformation: Selected Papers from the HKAECT 2022 International Conference* (pp. 3-18). Springer Nature Singapore.

Block, J. H., & Fisch, C. (2020). Eight tips and questions for your bibliographic study in business and management research. *Management Review Quarterly*, *70*(3), 307–312. doi:10.100711301-020-00188-4

Blum, A., Ligett, K., & Roth, A. (2013). A learning theory approach to noninteractive database privacy. *Journal of the Association for Computing Machinery*, *60*(2), 1–25. doi:10.1145/2450142.2450148

Bobier, J. F., Merey, T., Robnett, S., Grebe, M., Feng, J., Rehberg, B., Woolsey, K., & Hazan, J. (2022). *The Corporate Hitchhiker's guide to the metaverse*. Boston Consulting Group. https://ismguide.com/wp-content/uploads/2022/05/bcg-the-corporate-hitchhikers-guide-to-the-metaverse-27-apr-2022.pdf

Bogusevschi, D., Muntean, C., & Muntean, G. M. (2020). Teaching and learning physics using 3D virtual learning environment: A case study of combined virtual reality and virtual laboratory in secondary school. *Journal of Computers in Mathematics and Science Teaching*, *39*(1), 5–18.

Bojic, L. (2022). Metaverse through the prism of power and addiction: What will happen when the virtual world becomes more attractive than reality? *European Journal of Futures Research*, *10*(1), 22. Advance online publication. doi:10.118640309-022-00208-4

Bolger, R. (2021). Finding Wholes in the Metaverse: Posthuman Mystics as Agents of Evolutionary Contextualization. *Religions*, *12*(9), 768. doi:10.3390/rel12090768

Bollean, de Sompel, Hagberg, Chute, Rodriguez, & Balakireva. (2009). Click stream Data yields High-Resolution Maps of Science. *PLoS One*, *4*, 1–11.

Bonales-Daimiel, G. (2023). New formulas of interactive entertainment: From advergaming to metaverse as an advertising strategy. In Handbook of research on the future of advertising and brands in the new entertainment landscape (pp. 76-103) doi:10.4018/978-1-6684-3971-5.ch004

Bonime-Blanc, A. (2019). *Gloom to Boom: How Leaders Transform Risk Into Resilience and Value*. Routledge. doi:10.4324/9780429287787

Book, B. (2004). Moving beyond the game: Social virtual worlds. State of Play, 2.

Boulos, M. N. K., Scotch, M., Cheung, K., & Burden, D. (2008). Web GIS in practice VI: A demo playlist of geo-mashups for public health neogeographers. *International Journal of Health Geographics*, *7*(1), 38. Advance online publication. doi:10.1186/1476-072X-7-38 PMID:18638385

Boulos, M., & Burden, D. (2007). Web GIS in practice V: 3-D interactive and real-time mapping in second life. *International Journal of Health Geographics*, *6*(1), 51. Advance online publication. doi:10.1186/1476-072X-6-51 PMID:18042275

Bourlakis, M., Papagiannidis, S., & Li, F. (2009). Retail spatial evolution: Paving the way from traditional to metaverse retailing. *Electronic Commerce Research*, *9*(1-2), 135–148. doi:10.100710660-009-9030-8

Bousba, Y., & Arya, V. (2022). Let's connect in metaverse. Brand's new destination to increase consumers' affective brand engagement & their satisfaction and advocacy. *Journal of Content. Community and Communication*, *15*(8), 276–293. doi:10.31620/JCCC.06.22/19

Branca, G., Resciniti, R., & Loureiro, S. M. C. (2023). Virtual is so real! consumers' evaluation of product packaging in virtual reality. *Psychology and Marketing*, *40*(3), 596–609. doi:10.1002/mar.21743

Brijwani, G. N., Ajmire, P. E., & Thawani, P. V. (2023). Future of Quantum Computing in Cyber Security. In *Handbook of Research on Quantum Computing for Smart Environments* (pp. 267–298). IGI Global. doi:10.4018/978-1-6684-6697-1.ch016

Brindha, Priya, Mukesh, Dinesh Kumar, & Naveen. (2020). Voice based email for visually challenged people. *International Research Journal of Engineering and Technology*, 1382-1383.

Brock, R. (2021). *Stories from physics 8: Quantum Nuclear and Particle Physics*. Academic Press.

Broll, W., Lindt, I., Herbst, I., Ohlenburg, J., Braun, A. K., & Wetzel, R. (2008). Toward next-gen mobile AR games. *IEEE Computer Graphics and Applications*, *28*(4), 40–48. doi:10.1109/MCG.2008.85

Brown, H. R. (2020). *Do symmetries "explain" conservation laws? The modern converse Noether theorem vs pragmatism*. arXiv preprint arXiv:2010.10909.

Buchholz, F., Oppermann, L., & Prinz, W. (2022). There's more than one metaverse. *I-Com, 21*(3), 313–324. doi:10.1515/icom-2022-0034

Büchi, G., Cugno, M., & Castagnoli, R. (2020). Smart factory performance and Industry 4.0. *Technological Forecasting and Social Change, 150*, 119790. doi:10.1016/j.techfore.2019.119790

Buhalis, D., Leung, D., & Lin, M. (2023). Metaverse as a disruptive technology revolutionising tourism management and marketing. *Tourism Management, 97*, 104724. Advance online publication. doi:10.1016/j.tourman.2023.104724

Buhalis, D., Lin, M. S., & Leung, D. (2023). Metaverse as a driver for customer experience and value co-creation: Implications for hospitality and tourism management and marketing. *International Journal of Contemporary Hospitality Management, 35*(2), 701–716. doi:10.1108/IJCHM-05-2022-0631

Buhalis, D., O'Connor, P., & Leung, R. (2023). Smart hospitality: From smart cities and smart tourism towards agile business ecosystems in networked destinations. *International Journal of Contemporary Hospitality Management, 35*(1), 369–393. doi:10.1108/IJCHM-04-2022-0497

Buimer, H. P., Bittner, M., Kostelijk, T., van der Geest, T. M., Nemri, A., van Wezel, R. J. A., & Zhao, Y. (2018). Conveying facial expressions to blind and visually impaired persons through a wearable vibrotactile device. *PLoS One, 13*(3), e0194737. doi:10.1371/journal.pone.0194737 PMID:29584738

Bürer, M. J., de Lapparent, M., Pallotta, V., Capezzali, M., & Carpita, M. (2019). Use cases for blockchain in the energy industry opportunities of emerging business models and related risks. *Computers & Industrial Engineering, 137*, 106002. doi:10.1016/j.cie.2019.106002

BushellC. (2022). The Impact of Metaverse on Branding and Marketing. doi:10.2139/ssrn.4144628

Buterin, V. (2014). A next-generation smart contract and decentralized application platform. *White Paper, 3*(37), 1–2.

Bye, K., Hosfelt, D., Chase, S., Miesnieks, M., & Beck, T. (2019). The ethical and privacy implications of mixed reality. ACM SIGGRAPH 2019 Panels, 1–2. doi:10.1145/3306212.3328138

Cagnina, M. R., & Poian, M. (2008). Second life: A turning point for web 2.0 and E-business? In Interdisciplinary aspects of information systems studies: The italian association for information systems (pp. 377-383). doi:10.1007/978-3-7908-2010-2_46

Cai, Y., Llorca, J., Tulino, A. M., & Molisch, A. F. (2022, July). Compute-and data-intensive networks: The key to the metaverse. In *2022 1st International Conference on 6G Networking (6GNet)* (pp. 1-8). IEEE.

Cai, C. W. (2018). Disruption of financial intermediation by FinTech: A review on crowdfunding and blockchain. *Accounting and Finance, 58*(4), 965–992. doi:10.1111/acfi.12405

Cai, C., Xue, M., Chen, J., Xue, Z., & Hu, J. (2020). Virtual reality in healthcare: State-of-the-art and future challenges. *IEEE Transactions on Industrial Informatics, 16*(8), 5152–5161.

Calongne, C., Sheehy, P., & Stricker, A. (2013). Gemeinschaft identity in a gesellschaft metaverse. In The immersive internet: Reflections on the entangling of the virtual with society, politics and the economy (pp. 180-191). doi:10.1057/9781137283023

Campbell, D. T., & Stanley, J. C. (1966). Experimental and Quasi-Experimental Designs for Research, Rand Mc. *Nally Coll. Publ. Chicago, 47*, 1.

Cao, L. (2022). Decentralized AI: Edge Intelligence and Smart Blockchain, Metaverse, Web3, and DeSci. *IEEE Intelligent Systems, 37*(3), 6–19. . doi:10.1109/MIS.2022.3181504

Cao, Y., & Yang, M. (2023). Legal regulation of big data killing:–From the perspective of "Personal Information Protection Law". *Journal of Education. Humanities and Social Sciences*, *7*, 233–241.

Capellmann, H. (2021). Space-time in quantum theory. *Foundations of Physics*, *51*(2), 1–34. doi:10.100710701-021-00441-0

Cappannari, L., & Vitillo, A. (2022). XR and Metaverse Software Platforms. In Roadmapping Extended Reality (pp. 135-156). doi:10.1002/9781119865810.ch6

Carvalho, M., Dasgupta, D., Grimaila, M., & Perez, C. (2011). Mission resilience in cloud computing: A biologically inspired approach. *6th International Conference on Information Warfare and Security*, 42–52.

Cermeño, J. S. (2016). Blockchain in financial services: Regulatory landscape and future challenges for its commercial application. *BBVA Research Paper*, *16*(20), 1–33.

Cerniauskas, T., & Werth, D. (2022). Industry goes metaverse - the fusion of real and virtual industrial worlds exemplified by the wastewater industry. *I-Com*, *21*(3), 325–329. doi:10.1515/icom-2022-0032

Chabot, S., Drozdal, J., Zhou, Y., Su, H., & Braasch, J. (2019, July). Language learning in a cognitive and immersive environment using contextualized panoramic imagery. In *International Conference on Human-Computer Interaction* (pp. 202-209). Springer. 10.1007/978-3-030-23525-3_26

Chalmers, D. J. (2022). Reality+: Virtual worlds and the problems of philosophy. Penguin UK.

Chan, C., Wong, K. Y., & Lui, T. (2023). Marketing tourism products in virtual reality: Moderating effect of product complexity. *Springer Proceedings in Business and Economics*, 318-322. 10.1007/978-3-031-25752-0_34

Chang, Li, & Mishra. (2016). *mCAF: A Multi-dimensional Clustering Algorithm for Friends of Social Network Services*. Springer Plus.

Chang, H. T., Liu, S. W., & Mishra, N. (2015). A tracking and summarization system for online Chinese news topics. *Aslib Journal of Information Management*, *67*(6), 687–699. doi:10.1108/AJIM-10-2014-0147

Chang, H.-T., Mishra, N., & Lin, C.-C. (2015). IoT Big-Data Centred Knowledge Granule Analytic and Cluster Framework for BI Applications: A Case Base Analysis. *PLoS One*, *10*(11), e0141980. doi:10.1371/journal.pone.0141980 PMID:26600156

Chapman, P., Clinton, J., Kerber, R., Shearer, C., & Wirth, R. (2000). *CRISP-DM 1.0: Step by step data mining guide*. The CRISP DM Consortium.

Chaubey, N. K., & Prajapati, B. B. (Eds.). (2020). *Quantum Cryptography and the Future of Cyber Security*. IGI Global. doi:10.4018/978-1-7998-2253-0

Cheah, I., & Shimul, A. S. (2023). Marketing in the metaverse: Moving forward–What's next? *Journal of Global Scholars of Marketing Science: Bridging Asia and the World*, *33*(1), 1–10. doi:10.1080/21639159.2022.2163908

Chen, Wu, Gan, & Qi. (2022). *Metaverse Security and Privacy: An Overview*. Academic Press.

Chen, X., Zou, D., Xie, H. R., & Su, F. (2021). *Twenty-five years of computer-assisted language learning: A topic modeling analysis*. Academic Press.

Chen, B., & Yang, D. (2022). User recommendation in social metaverse with VR. *International Conference on Information and Knowledge Management, Proceedings*, 148-158. 10.1145/3511808.3557487

Chen, B., Wan, J., Shu, L., Li, P., Mukherjee, M., & Yin, B. (2017). Smart factory of industry 4.0: Key technologies, application case, and challenges. *IEEE Access : Practical Innovations, Open Solutions*, 6, 6505–6519. doi:10.1109/ACCESS.2017.2783682

Chen, C., & Yao, M. Z. (2022). Strategic use of immersive media and narrative message in virtual marketing: Understanding the roles of telepresence and transportation. *Psychology and Marketing*, 39(3), 524–542. doi:10.1002/mar.21630

Chen, F., Zhan, J., & Li, L. (2019). Smart Vehicle Safety: A Review of the State-of-the-Art and Future Research Directions. *IEEE Transactions on Intelligent Transportation Systems*, 21(4), 1684–1698.

Chengoden, R., Victor, N., Huynh-The, T., Yenduri, G., Jhaveri, R. H., Alazab, M., Bhattacharya, S., Hegde, P., Maddikunta, P. K. R., & Gadekallu, T. R. (2023). Metaverse for healthcare: A survey on potential applications, challenges and future directions. *IEEE Access : Practical Innovations, Open Solutions*, 11, 12765–12795. doi:10.1109/ACCESS.2023.3241628

Cheng, X., Deng, Y., Xiong, R., & Xu, X. (2021). A review of artificial intelligence in healthcare: Challenges, opportunities, and implementation strategies. *Journal of Healthcare Engineering*.

Chen, J. C. (2016). EFL learners' strategy use during task-based interaction in Second Life. *Australasian Journal of Educational Technology*, 32(3). Advance online publication. doi:10.14742/ajet.2306

Chen, J., Zhang, Y., & He, Y. (2020). A hybrid deep learning framework for human detection in intelligent vehicles. *Measurement*, 157, 107857. doi:10.1016/j.measurement.2020.107857

Chen, J., Zhang, Y., & He, Y. (2020). A robust image fusion algorithm for smart vehicle vision. *IEEE Transactions on Intelligent Transportation Systems*, 22(3), 1641–1652.

Chen, J., Zhang, Y., & He, Y. (2020). Driving Behavior Recognition Based on Convolutional Neural Network and Long Short-Term Memory. *Journal of Advanced Transportation*, 2020, 1–11. doi:10.1155/2020/8879027

Chen, L., Zhang, H., & Zhu, H. (2018). A Review of Autonomous Vehicle Safety: Technical, Policy, and Social Perspectives. *IEEE Transactions on Intelligent Transportation Systems*, 19(4), 1270–1282.

Chen, Q., & Lee, S. (2021). Research Status and Trend of Digital Twin: Visual Knowledge Mapping Analysis. *International Journal of Advanced Smart Convergence*, 10(4), 84–97. doi:10.7236/IJASC.2021.10.4.84

Chen, Y. L. (2016). The Effects of Virtual Reality Learning Environment on Student Cognitive and Linguistic Development. *The Asia-Pacific Education Researcher*, 25(4), 637–646. doi:10.100740299-016-0293-2

Chen, Y.-C., Chou, Y.-P., & Chou, Y.-C. (2019). An Image Authentication Scheme Using Merkle Tree Mechanisms. *Future Internet*, 11(7), 149. doi:10.3390/fi11070149

ChenZ.WuJ.GanW.QiZ. (2022). *Metaverse security and privacy: An overview*. doi:10.1109/BigData55660.2022.10021112

Chiesa, S., Galati, D., & Schmidt, S. (2015). Communicative interactions between visually impaired mothers and their sighted children: Analysis of gaze, facial expressions, voice and physical contacts. *Child: Care, Health and Development*, 41(6), 1040–1046. doi:10.1111/cch.12274 PMID:26250608

Chinie, C., Oancea, M., & Todea, S. (2022). The adoption of the metaverse concepts in Romania. *Management and Marketing*, 17(3), 328–340. doi:10.2478/mmcks-2022-0018

Choi, M., Azzaoui, A. E., Singh, S. K., Salim, M. M., Jeremiah, S. R., & Park, J. H. (2022). The Future of Metaverse: Security Issues, Requirements, and Solutions. *Human-Centric Computing and Information Sciences, 12*.

Choi, H., & Kim, S. (2017). A content service deployment plan for metaverse museum exhibitions—Centering on the combination of beacons and HMDs. *International Journal of Information Management*, *37*(1), 1519–1527. doi:10.1016/j.ijinfomgt.2016.04.017

Chong, D., & Shi, H. (2015). Big data analytics: A literature review. *Journal of Management Analytics*, *2*(3), 175–201. doi:10.1080/23270012.2015.1082449

Chowdhary, K. (2022). Natural language processing. In *Fundamentals of artificial intelligence* (pp. 603–649). Springer.

Christopoulos, A., Mystakidis, S., Pellas, N., & Laakso, M.-J. (2021). Arlean: An augmented reality learning analytics ethical framework. *Computers*, *10*(8), 92. doi:10.3390/computers10080092

Çiloğlu, T. (2022). *Augmented reality based learning environment: Effects of augmented reality on high school students' motivation, attitude and self-efficacy in biology education* (Publication No. 718957) [Master's Thesis, Bartın University]. Higher Education Council Thesis Archive. https://tez.yok.gov.tr

Cline, E. (2011). *Ready player one*. Crown Publishing Group.

Cohen, I., Sebe, N., Garg, A., Chen, L. S., & Huang, T. S. (2003). Facial expression recognition from video sequences: Temporal and static modeling. *Computer Vision and Image Understanding*, *91*(1–2), 160–187. doi:10.1016/S1077-3142(03)00081-X

Colicchia, C., & Strozzi, F. (2012). Supply chain risk management: A new methodology for a systematic literature review. *Supply Chain Management*, *17*(4), 403–418. doi:10.1108/13598541211246558

Collins, C. (2008). Looking to the future: Higher education in the Metaverse. *EDUCAUSE Review*, *43*(5), 51–63.

Contreras, G. S., González, A. H., Fernández, M. I. S., Martínez, C. B., Cepa, J., & Escobar, Z. (2022). The importance of the application of the metaverse in education. *Modern Applied Science*, *16*(3), 1–34. doi:10.5539/mas.v16n3p34

Cook, N. (2008). *Enterprise 2.0: How social software will change the future of work*. Gower Publishing, Ltd.

Çoruh, L. (2011). *Assessment of the effectiveness of virtual reality applications in art history course as a learning model (An example of Erciyes University Architecture & Fine Arts Faculties)* (Publication No. 279715) [Doctoral Dissertation, Gazi University]. Higher Education Council Thesis Archive. https://tez.yok.gov.tr

Cowie, N., & Alizadeh, M. (2022). The affordances and challenges of virtual reality for language teaching. *International Journal of TESOL Studies*, *4*(3), 50–56.

Craven. (2006). Web Accessibility: A review of research and Initiatives. *World Library and Information Congress: 72nd IFLA General Conference and Council.*

Creery, A., & Byres, E. J. (2005, September). Industrial cybersecurity for power system and SCADA networks. In *Record of Conference Papers Industry Applications Society 52nd annual petroleum and chemical industry conference* (pp. 303-309). IEEE, 10.1109/PCICON.2005.1524567

Cremers, C. W., & Smith, R. (2002). *Genetic hearing impairment: its clinical presentations*. Karger Medical and Scientific Publishers. doi:10.1159/isbn.978-3-318-00870-8

Crespo-Pereira, V., Sánchez-Amboage, E., & Membiela-Pollán, M. (2023). Facing the challenges of metaverse: A systematic literature review from social sciences and marketing and communication. *El Profesional de la Información*, *32*(1), e320102. Advance online publication. doi:10.3145/epi.2023.ene.02

Crespo, R. G., Escobar, R. F., Aguilar, L. J., Velazco, S., & Sanz, A. G. C. (2013). Use of ARIMA mathematical analysis to model the implementation of expert system courses by means of free software OpenSim and Sloodle platforms in virtual university campuses. *Expert Systems with Applications*, *40*(18), 7381–7390. doi:10.1016/j.eswa.2013.06.054

Cui, Jiang, Zhang, & Wang. (2017). A data masking scheme for sensitive big data based on format-preserving encryption. In *2017 IEEE International Conference on Computational Science and Engineering (CSE) and IEEE International Conference on Embedded and Ubiquitous Computing (EUC)* (vol. 1, pp. 518–524). IEEE.

da Silva, R. B., de Castro, L. N., & Costa, C. A. (2018). Internet of Things and augmented reality applied to the healthcare area: A systematic review. *Journal of Biomedical Informatics*, *87*, 73–86.

Dahan, N., Al-Razgan, M., Al-Laith, A., Alsoufi, M., Al-Asaly, M., & Alfakih, T. (2022). Metaverse Framework: A Case Study on E-Learning Environment (ELEM). *Electronics (Basel)*, *11*(10), 1616. doi:10.3390/electronics11101616

Dai, J., & Zhao, L. (2022). Happiness and fashion culture of smart kidswear from the perspective of metaverse. *2022 10th International Conference on Orange Technology, ICOT 2022*. 10.1109/ICOT56925.2022.10008154

Dai, W. (2022). Optimal policy computing for blockchain based smart contracts via federated learning. *Operations Research*, *22*(5), 5817–5844. doi:10.100712351-022-00723-z

Dai, Y., Wang, J., & Gao, S. (2022). Advanced Electronics and Artificial Intelligence: Must-Have Technologies Toward Human Body Digital Twins. *Advanced Intelligent Systems*, *4*(7), 2100263. doi:10.1002/aisy.202100263

Dall'Osto, G., & Corni, S. (2022). Time Resolved Raman Scattering of Molecules: A Quantum Mechanics Approach with Stochastic Schroedinger Equation. *The Journal of Physical Chemistry A*, *126*(43), 8088–8100. doi:10.1021/acs.jpca.2c05245 PMID:36278928

Damodaran, A. (2023). From non fungible tokens to metaverse: Blockchain based inclusive innovation in arts. *Innovation and Development*, 1–20. doi:10.1080/2157930X.2023.2180709

Dangi, R., Lalwani, P., Choudhary, G., You, I. & Pau, G. (2022). Study and investigation on 5G technology: A systematic review. *Sensors, 22*. doi:10.3390/s22010026

Darwish, A. (2018). Bio-inspired computing: Algorithms review, deep analysis, and the scope of applications. *Future Computing and Informatics Journal*, *3*(2), 231–246. doi:10.1016/j.fcij.2018.06.001

Darwish, A., & Hassanien, A. E. (2022). Fantasy magical life: Opportunities, applications, and challenges in metaverses. *Journal of System and Management Sciences*, *12*(2), 411–436. doi:10.33168/JSMS.2022.0222

Dascalu, M., Bodea, C. N., & Nechifor, S. (2019). Augmented reality in healthcare: A systematic literature review. *Sensors (Basel)*, *19*(19), 4172. PMID:31561481

Dator, J. (2022). *Destination identities*. doi:10.1007/978-3-031-11732-9_7

Davenport, T. H., & Harris, J. G. (2007). *Competing on analytics: the new Science of winning*. Harvard business school press.

David & Wanger. (2017). Privacy in Smart Cities-Applications, Technologies, Challenges and Solutions. *IEEE Communications Surveys and Tutorials, 20*(1), 489-516.

Dawson, W., Degomme, A., Stella, M., Nakajima, T., Ratcliff, L. E., & Genovese, L. (2022). Density functional theory calculations of large systems: Interplay between fragments, observables, and computational complexity. *Wiley Interdisciplinary Reviews. Computational Molecular Science*, *12*(3), e1574. doi:10.1002/wcms.1574 de Brito Silva, M. J., de Oliveira Ramos Delfino, L., Alves Cerqueira, K., & de Oliveira Campos, P. (2022). Avatar marketing: A study on the engagement and authenticity of virtual influencers on instagram. *Social Network Analysis and Mining*, *12*(1), 130. Advance online publication. doi:10.100713278-022-00966-w

De Guzman, J. A., Thilakarathna, K., & Seneviratne, A. (2019). Security and privacy approaches in mixed reality: A literature survey. *ACM Computing Surveys*, *52*(6), 1–37. doi:10.1145/3359626

De Ketelaere, B., Smeets, B., Verboven, P., Nicolaï, B., & Saeys, W. (2022). Digital twins in quality engineering. *Quality Engineering*, *34*(3), 404–408. doi:10.1080/08982112.2022.2052731

de la Vall, R. R. F., & Araya, F. G. (2023). Exploring the Benefits and Challenges of AI-Language Learning Tools. *International Journal of Social Sciences and Humanities Invention*, *10*(01), 7569–7576. doi:10.18535/ijsshi/v10i01.02

Dean, J., & Ghemawat, S. (2008). Map Reduce: Simplified dataprocessing on large clusters. *Communications of the ACM*, *51*, 107–113. doi:10.1145/1327452.1327492

Del Santo, F., & Gisin, N. (2019). Physics without determinism: Alternative interpretations of classical physics. *Physical Review. A*, *100*(6), 062107. doi:10.1103/PhysRevA.100.062107

Demir, G., Argan, M., & Halime, D. İ. N. Ç. (2023). The Age Beyond Sports: User Experience in the World of Metaverse. *Journal of Metaverse*, *3*(1), 19–27. doi:10.57019/jmv.1176938

Demirkan, S., Demirkan, I., & McKee, A. (2020). Blockchain technology in the future of business cyber security and accounting. *Journal of Management Analytics*, *7*(2), 189–208. doi:10.1080/23270012.2020.1731721

Demir, M., Turetken, O., & Ferworn, A. (2019). Blockchain based transparent vehicle insurance management. *2019 Sixth International Conference on Software Defined Systems (SDS)*, 213–220. 10.1109/SDS.2019.8768669

Dergachev, I. D., Dergachev, V. D., Rooein, M., Mirzanejad, A., & Varganov, S. A. (2023). Predicting Kinetics and Dynamics of Spin-Dependent Processes. *Accounts of Chemical Research*, *56*(7), 856–866. doi:10.1021/acs.accounts.2c00843 PMID:36926853

Devendra Kumar, R. N., Chakrapani, A., & Arvind, C. (2017a). *Facial Expression Recognition System "Sentiment Analysis" Current Mirror Circuits View project Different methods for the generation of millimeter wave using external modulators. View project Facial Expression Recognition System "Sentiment Analysis."* https://www.researchgate.net/publication/320868583

Dewdney, C. (2023). Rekindling of de Broglie–Bohm Pilot Wave Theory in the Late Twentieth Century: A Personal Account. *Foundations of Physics*, *53*(1), 24. doi:10.100710701-022-00655-w

Dhelim, S., Kechadi, T., Chen, L., Aung, N., Ning, H., & Atzori, L. (2022). *Edge-enabled metaverse: The convergence of metaverse and mobile edge computing.* arXiv preprint arXiv:2205.02764.

Di Pietro, R., & Cresci, S. (2021, December). Metaverse: security and privacy issues. In *2021 Third IEEE International Conference on Trust, Privacy and Security in Intelligent Systems and Applications (TPS-ISA)* (pp. 281-288). IEEE. https://arxiv.org/pdf/2205.07590.pd

Di Pietro, R., & Cresci, S. (2021). Metaverse: security and privacy issues. In *2021 Third IEEE International Conference on Trust, Privacy and Security in Intelligent Systems and Applications (TPS-ISA)*. IEEE.

Di Sia, P. (2021). Birth, development and applications of quantum physics: A transdisciplinary approach. *World Scientific News*, *160*, 232–246.

Dian, F. J., Vahidnia, R., & Rahmati, A. (2020). Wearables and the Internet of Things (IoT), applications, opportunities, and challenges: A Survey. *IEEE Access : Practical Innovations, Open Solutions, 8*, 69200–69211. doi:10.1109/ACCESS.2020.2986329

Dincelli, E., & Yayla, A. (2022). Immersive virtual reality in the age of the metaverse: A hybrid-narrative review based on the technology affordance perspective. *The Journal of Strategic Information Systems, 31*(2), 101717. Advance online publication. doi:10.1016/j.jsis.2022.101717

Downes, L., & Nunes, P. (2018). Finding your company's second act. *Harvard Business Review, 2018*, 98–107.

Duan, H., Huang, Y., Zhao, Y., Huang, Z., & Cai, W. (2022). User-generated content and editors in video games: Survey and vision. In 2022 IEEE conference on games (CoG) (pp. 536–543). IEEE. doi:10.1109/CoG51982.2022.9893717

Duan, H., Li, J., Fan, S., Lin, Z., Wu, X., & Cai, W. (2021, October). Metaverse for social good: A university campus prototype. In *Proceedings of the 29th ACM international conference on multimedia* (pp. 153-161). 10.1145/3474085.3479238

Duffy, L. N., Stone, G. A., Townsend, J., & Cathey, J. (2022). Rethinking curriculum internationalization: Virtual exchange as a means to attaining global competencies, developing critical thinking, and experiencing transformative learning. *SCHOLE: A Journal of Leisure Studies and Recreation Education, 37*(1-2), 11-25.

Du, H., Niyato, D., Miao, C., Kang, J., & Kim, D. I. (2022). Optimal targeted advertising strategy for secure wireless edge metaverse. *2022 IEEE Global Communications Conference, GLOBECOM 2022 - Proceedings*, 4346-4351. 10.1109/GLOBECOM48099.2022.10001331

Durukal, E. (2022). Customer online shopping experience. In Handbook of research on interdisciplinary reflections of contemporary experiential marketing practices (pp. 60-77). doi:10.4018/978-1-6684-4380-4.ch004

Dutra, A., Tumasjan, A., & Welpe, I. M. (2018). Blockchain is changing how media and entertainment companies compete. *MIT Sloan Management Review, 60*(1), 39–45.

Dwivedi, V., Deval, V., Dixit, A., & Norta, A. (2019). Blockchain-based smart-contract languages: A systematic literature review. *Preprint, 10*, 1–9.

Dwivedi, Y. K., Hughes, L., Baabdullah, A. M., Ribeiro-Navarrete, S., Giannakis, M., Al-Debei, M. M., Dennehy, D., Metri, B., Buhalis, D., Cheung, C. M. K., Conboy, K., Doyle, R., Dubey, R., Dutot, V., Felix, R., Goyal, D. P., Gustafsson, A., Hinsch, C., Jebabli, I., ... Wamba, S. F. (2022). Metaverse beyond the hype: Multidisciplinary perspectives on emerging challenges, opportunities, and agenda for research, practice and policy. *International Journal of Information Management, 66*, 102542. Advance online publication. doi:10.1016/j.ijinfomgt.2022.102542

Dwivedi, Y. K., Hughes, L., Wang, Y., Alalwan, A. A., Ahn, S. J., Balakrishnan, J., Barta, S., Belk, R., Buhalis, D., Dutot, V., Felix, R., Filieri, R., Flavián, C., Gustafsson, A., Hinsch, C., Hollensen, S., Jain, V., Kim, J., Krishen, A. S., ... Wirtz, J. (2022). Metaverse marketing: How the metaverse will shape the future of consumer research and practice. *Psychology and Marketing, 40*(4), 750–776. doi:10.1002/mar.21767

Dwork, C., Kenthapadi, K., McSherry, F., Mironov, I., & Naor, M. (2006). Our data, ourselves: Privacy via distributed noise generation. *Advances in Cryptology-EUROCRYPT 2006: 24th Annual International Conference on the Theory and Applications of Cryptographic Techniques, St. Petersburg, Russia, May 28-June 1, 2006 Proceedings, 25*, 486–503.

Edwards, C., Edwards, A., Spence, P. R., & Lin, X. (2018). I, teacher: Using artificial intelligence (AI) and social robots in communication and instruction. *Communication Education, 67*(4), 473–480. doi:10.1080/03634523.2018.1502459

Ekin, C. C., Polat, E., & Hopcan, S. (2023). Drawing the big picture of games in education: A topic modeling-based review of past 55 years. *Computers & Education, 194*, 104700. doi:10.1016/j.compedu.2022.104700

Elmaghraby, A. S., & Losavio, M. M. (2014). Cyber security challenges in Smart Cities: Safety, security, and privacy. *Journal of Advanced Research*, 5(4), 491–497. doi:10.1016/j.jare.2014.02.006 PMID:25685517

Elme, L., Jørgensen, M. L., Dandanell, G., Mottelson, A., & Makransky, G. (2022). Immersive virtual reality in STEM: Is IVR an effective learning medium and does adding self-explanation after a lesson improve learning outcomes? *Educational Technology Research and Development*, 70(5), 1601–1626. doi:10.100711423-022-10139-3 PMID:35873274

El-Sherif, D. M., Abouzid, M., Elzarif, M. T., Ahmed, A. A., Albakri, A., & Alshehri, M. M. (2022). Telehealth and Artificial Intelligence Insights into Healthcare during the COVID-19 Pandemic. In Healthcare (Switzerland) (Vol. 10, Issue 2). MDPI. doi:10.3390/healthcare10020385

Elsts, A., Mitskas, E., & Oikonomou, G. (2018). Distributed ledger technology and the internet of things: A feasibility study. *Proceedings of the 1st Workshop on Blockchain-Enabled Networked Sensor Systems*, 7–12. 10.1145/3282278.3282280

Emreli, D. (2019). *Investigation of the effects of use virtual & augmented reality (V/AR) applications in technical drawing training for machine manufacturing sector on learning performance* (Publication No. 595467) [Master's thesis, Bursa Uludağ University]. Higher Education Council Thesis Archive. https://tez.yok.gov.tr

Englisch, J. (2022). VAT goes virtual: Security tokens. *EC Tax Review*, 31(5), 232–237. doi:10.54648/ECTA2022022

Enriquez, D. R., Molero-Castillo, G., Bárcenas, E., & Pérez, R. A. (2022). Algorithm for identification and analysis of targeted advertising used in trending topics. *Proceedings of the LACCEI International Multi-Conference for Engineering, Education and Technology, 2022-July* 10.18687/LACCEI2022.1.1.57

Eom, S. (2022). The Emerging Digital Twin Bureaucracy in the 21st Century. *Perspectives on Public Management and Governance*, 5(2), 174–186. doi:10.1093/ppmgov/gvac005

Erboz, G., 2017). How to define industry 4.0: main pillars of industry 4.0. *Managerial trends in the development of enterprises in globalization era*, 761-767.

Erdei, T., Krakó, R., & Husi, G. (2022). Design of a Digital Twin Training Centre for an Industrial Robot Arm. *Applied Sciences (Basel, Switzerland)*, 12(17), 8862. doi:10.3390/app12178862

Eyal, I. (2017). Blockchain technology: Transforming libertarian cryptocurrency dreams to finance and banking realities. *Computer*, 50(9), 38–49. doi:10.1109/MC.2017.3571042

Eze, B., & Peyton, L. (2015). Systematic literature review on the anonymization of high dimensional streaming datasets for health data sharing. *Procedia Computer Science*, 63, 348–355. doi:10.1016/j.procs.2015.08.353

Falchuk, Loeb, & Neff. (2018). The social metaverse: Battle for privacy. *IEEE Technology and Society Magazine, 37*(2), 52–61.

Fan, Li, Zhang, & Feng. (2018). Data Driven Feature election for Machine Learning Algorithms in Computer Vision. *IEEE Internet of Things Journal, 5*(6), 4262-4272.

Fang, X., Koceja, N., Zhan, J., Dozier, G., & Dipankar, D. (2012). An artificial immune system for phishing detection. *Evolutionary Computation (CEC), IEEE Congress on,* 1–7. 10.1109/CEC.2012.6256518

Fang, Y., Lippert, A., Cai, Z., Chen, S., Frijters, J. C., Greenberg, D., & Graesser, A. C. (2021). Patterns of adults with low literacy skills interacting with an intelligent tutoring system. *International Journal of Artificial Intelligence in Education*, 1–26.

Faraboschi, P., Frachtenberg, E., Laplante, P., Milojicic, D., & Saracco, R. (2022). Virtual Worlds (Metaverse): From Skepticism, to Fear, to Immersive Opportunities. *Computer*, 55(10), 100–106. doi:10.1109/MC.2022.3192702

Farley, P., & Capp, M. (2005). Mobile Web Services. *BT Technology Journal, 23*(3), 202–213. doi:10.100710550-005-0042-1

Ferati, M., Vogel, B., Kurti, A., Rau, B., & Astals, D. S. (2016). Web Accessibility for Visually Impaired People: Requirements and Design Issues. *International Workshop on Usability-and Accessibility-Focused Requirements Engineering.*

Fernandez, C. B., & Hui, P. (2022). Life, the Metaverse and everything: An overview of privacy, ethics, and governance in Metaverse. In *2022 IEEE 42nd International Conference on Distributed Computing Systems Workshops (ICDCSW)* (pp. 272–277). IEEE. 10.1109/ICDCSW56584.2022.00058

Fernández-Gavira, J., Espada-Goya, P., Alcaraz-Rodríguez, V., & Moscoso-Sánchez, D. (2021). Design of Educational Tools Based on Traditional Games for the Improvement of Social and Personal Skills of Primary School Students with Hearing Impairment. *Sustainability (Basel), 13*(22), 12644. doi:10.3390u132212644

Fernando, N., Loke, S. W., & Rahayu, W. (2013). Mobile cloud computing: A survey. *Future Generation Computer Systems, 29*(1), 84–106. doi:10.1016/j.future.2012.05.023

Festa, G., Melanthiou, Y., & Meriano, P. (2022). *Engineering the metaverse for innovating the electronic business: A socio-technological perspective.* doi:10.1007/978-3-031-07765-4_4

Filimonau, V., Ashton, M., & Stankov, U. (2022). Virtual spaces as the future of consumption in tourism, hospitality and events. *Journal of Tourism Futures.* doi:10.1108/JTF-07-2022-0174

Filipova, I. A. (2023). Creating the Metaverse: Consequences for Economy, Society, and Law. *Journal of Digital Technologies and Law, 1*(1), 1. doi:10.21202/jdtl.2023.1

Fırat, M. (2022). *Karma yöntem araştırmaları: Yöntembilimde açıklığın yükselişi.* Nobel Yayıncılık.

Firmansyah, E. A., Wahid, H., Gunardi, A., & Hudaefi, F. A. (2022). A scientometric study on management literature in southeast asia. *Journal of Risk and Financial Management, 15*(11), 507. Advance online publication. doi:10.3390/jrfm15110507

Fitsilis, P., Tsoutsa, P., & Gerogiannis, V., 2018). Industry 4.0: Required personnel competences. *Industry 4.0, 3*(3), 130-133.

Flores-Mendoza, C., Sotelo-Figueroa, M., & Flores-Tapia, A. (2020). Autonomous Vehicle Control System Based on Deep Learning Techniques. *IEEE Access : Practical Innovations, Open Solutions, 8*, 174465–174477. doi:10.1109/ACCESS.2020.3022741

Flores-Mendoza, C., Sotelo-Figueroa, M., & Flores-Tapia, A. (2020). Decision making in autonomous vehicles using fuzzy logic. *IEEE Access : Practical Innovations, Open Solutions, 8*, 128906–128918. doi:10.1109/ACCESS.2020.3006201

Flores-Mendoza, M., Sotelo-Figueroa, M., & Flores-Tapia, A. (2020). Real-time image processing system for smart vehicles using edge detection and object recognition techniques. *Journal of Ambient Intelligence and Humanized Computing, 11*(3), 1183–1191.

Forbes. (2022). https://www.forbes.com/sites/forbestechcouncil/2022/04/18/the-metaverse-driven-by-ai-along-with-the-old-fashioned-kind-of-intelligence/?sh=1fb523231b36

Forbes, K. A., & Andrews, D. L. (2021). Orbital angular momentum of twisted light: Chirality and optical activity. *JPhys Photonics, 3*(2), 022007. doi:10.1088/2515-7647/abdb06

Freeman, N. (2023). *Teaching L2 grammar: A study of teachers' beliefs on frequency, methods and approaches of teaching English grammar in Swedish schools.* Academic Press.

Fryer, L. K., Nakao, K., & Thompson, A. (2019). Chatbot learning partners: Connecting learning experiences, interest and competence. *Computers in Human Behavior*, *93*, 279–289. doi:10.1016/j.chb.2018.12.023

Fullan, M. (2023). *The Principal 2.0: Three Keys to Maximizing Impact*. John Wiley & Sons.

Furlan, R., Gatti, M., Menè, R., Shiffer, D., Marchiori, C., Giaj Levra, A., Saturnino, V., Brunetta, E., & Dipaola, F. (2021). A natural language processing–based virtual patient simulator and intelligent tutoring system for the clinical diagnostic process: Simulator development and case study. *JMIR Medical Informatics*, *9*(4), e24073. doi:10.2196/24073 PMID:33720840

Fu, Y. (2021). *A Survey of Possibilities and Challenges with AR/VR/MR and Gamification Usage in Healthcare*. HEALTH-INF. doi:10.5220/0010386207330740

Gadalla, E., Keeling, K., & Abosag, I. (2013). Metaverse-retail service quality: A future framework for retail service quality in the 3D internet. *Journal of Marketing Management*, *29*(13-14), 1493–1517. doi:10.1080/0267257X.2013.835742

Gadekallu, T. R., Huynh-The, T., Wang, W., Yenduri, G., Ranaweera, P., Pham, Q. V., & Liyanage, M. (2022). *Blockchain for the metaverse: A review*. arXiv preprint arXiv:2203.09738.

Galvez, J. F., Mejuto, J. C., & Simal-Gandara, J. (2018). Future challenges on the use of blockchain for food traceability analysis. *Trends in Analytical Chemistry*, *107*, 222–232. doi:10.1016/j.trac.2018.08.011

Gampel, F., & Gajda, M. (2023). Continuous simultaneous measurement of position and momentum of a particle. *Physical Review. A*, *107*(1), 012420. doi:10.1103/PhysRevA.107.012420

Gao, S. (2022). Research on the innovation of the internet of things business model under the new scenario of metaverse. *ACM International Conference Proceeding Series*, 44-49. 10.1145/3545897.3545904

Gao, X., Lu, J., & Sun, Y. (2020). A bibliometric analysis of artificial intelligence in intelligent transportation systems. *Journal of Advanced Transportation*, *2020*, 1–17.

Garay, J. A., Kiayias, A., Leonardos, N., & Panagiotakos, G. (2016). Bootstrapping the Blockchain-Directly. *IACR Cryptol. EPrint Arch.*, *2016*, 991.

Gatteschi, V., Lamberti, F., Demartini, C., Pranteda, C., & Santamaría, V. (2018). Blockchain and smart contracts for insurance: Is the technology mature enough? *Future Internet*, *10*(2), 20. doi:10.3390/fi10020020

Gatteschi, V., Lamberti, F., Demartini, C., Pranteda, C., & Santamaria, V. (2018). To blockchain or not to blockchain: That is the question. *IT Professional*, *20*(2), 62–74. doi:10.1109/MITP.2018.021921652

Gauttier, S., Simouri, W., & Milliat, A. (2022). When to enter the metaverse: Business leaders offer perspectives. *The Journal of Business Strategy*. Advance online publication. doi:10.1108/JBS-08-2022-0149

Gerrikagoitia, J. K., Unamuno, G., Urkia, E., & Serna, A. (2019). Digital manufacturing platforms in the industry 4.0 from private and public perspectives. *Applied Sciences (Basel, Switzerland)*, *9*(14), 2934. doi:10.3390/app9142934

Ghandar, A., Ahmed, A., Zulfiqar, S., Hua, Z., Hanai, M., & Theodoropoulos, G. (2021). A Decision Support System for Urban Agriculture Using Digital Twin: A Case Study With Aquaponics. *IEEE Access : Practical Innovations, Open Solutions*, *9*, 35691–35708. doi:10.1109/ACCESS.2021.3061722

Ghobakhloo, M. (2018). The future of manufacturing industry: A strategic roadmap toward Industry 4.0. *Journal of Manufacturing Technology Management*, *29*(6), 910–936. doi:10.1108/JMTM-02-2018-0057

Giang Barrera, K., & Shah, D. (2023). Marketing in the metaverse: Conceptual understanding, framework, and research agenda. *Journal of Business Research*, *155*, 113420. Advance online publication. doi:10.1016/j.jbusres.2022.113420

Gill, S. S. (2021). Quantum and blockchain based Serverless edge computing: A vision, model, new trends and future directions. *Internet Technology Letters*, 275. doi:10.1002/itl2.275

Gill, S. S., Kumar, A., Singh, H., Singh, M., Kaur, K., Usman, M., & Buyya, R. (2022). Quantum computing: A taxonomy, systematic review and future directions. *Software, Practice & Experience*, *52*(1), 66–114. doi:10.1002pe.3039

Go, H., & Kang, M. (2022). Metaverse tourism for sustainable tourism development: Tourism agenda 2030. *Tourism Review*. Advance online publication. doi:10.1108/TR-02-2022-0102

Gökçe, S. (2022). *The effect of augmented reality supported history lesson books on spatial thinking ability and academic success of students* (Publication No. 707107) [Master's Thesis, Ankara University]. Higher Education Council Thesis Archive. https://tez.yok.gov.tr

Golf-Papez, M., Heller, J., Hilken, T., Chylinski, M., de Ruyter, K., Keeling, D. I., Grinbaum, A., & Adomaitis, L. (2022). Moral equivalence in the metaverse. *NanoEthics*, *16*(3), 257–270. doi:10.100711569-022-00426-x

Google App Engine. (2010). http://code.google.com/appengine/

Goudar, S., Sarje, S. S., & Goudar, S. (2021). Autonomous vehicle using deep learning for object detection and lane detection. In IOP Conference Series: Materials Science and Engineering (Vol. 1103, No. 1, p. 012026). IOP Publishing. doi:10.1088/1757-899X/1103/1/012026

Goudar, S., Sarje, S. S., & Goudar, S. (2021). A Review on Intelligent Transport Systems and Connected Vehicles. *Journal of Critical Reviews*, *8*(2), 179–186. doi:10.31838/jcr.08.02.27

Grabowska, S., 2020). Smart factories in the age of Industry 4.0. *Management Systems in Production Engineering*, *28*(2), 90-96.

Grecuccio, J., Giusto, E., Fiori, F., & Rebaudengo, M. (2020). Combining Blockchain and IoT: Food-Chain Traceability and Beyond. *Energies*, *13*(15), 3820. doi:10.3390/en13153820

Gressin, S. (2017). The equifax data breach: What to do. Federal Trade Commission.

Grover, B. A., Chaudhary, B., Rajput, N. K., & Dukiya, O. (2021). Blockchain and Governance: Theory, Applications and Challenges. *Blockchain for Business: How It Works and Creates Value*, 113–139.

Grustam, A. S., Fountoukidou, P., Tsiropoulou, E. E., & Dimitriou, N. (2020). Internet of Things (IoT) in healthcare: A comprehensive survey. *Journal of Network and Computer Applications*, *154*, 102570.

Guo, X., & Hou, L. (2022). Key technology research of digital fashion based on virtual technology. *Advances in Transdisciplinary Engineering*, *20*, 894-903. 10.3233/ATDE220093

Guo, Y. (2022). Artificial Intelligence for Metaverse: A Framework. *CAAI Artificial Intelligence Research*, *1*(1), 54–67. doi:10.26599/AIR.2022.9150004

Guo, Y., Dong, S., & Wang, Z. (2019). Deep learning-based image captioning with localized attention mechanism. *IEEE Access : Practical Innovations, Open Solutions*, *7*, 145170–145178.

Guo, Y., & Liang, C. (2016). Blockchain application and outlook in the banking industry. *Financial Innovation*, *2*(1), 1–12. doi:10.118640854-016-0034-9

Gupota, S., Sahoo, O. P., Goel, A., & Gupta, R. (2010). A new optimized approach to face recognition using eigen faces. Global. *Journal of Computer Science and Technology*.

Gupta, A., Khan, H. U., Nazir, S., Shafiq, M., & Shabaz, M. (2023). Metaverse Security: Issues, Challenges and a Viable ZTA Model. *Electronics (Basel)*, *12*(2), 391. doi:10.3390/electronics12020391

Gursoy, D., Malodia, S., & Dhir, A. (2022). The metaverse in the hospitality and tourism industry: An overview of current trends and future research directions. *Journal of Hospitality Marketing & Management*, *31*(5), 527–534. doi:10.1080/19368623.2022.2072504

Haas, H. (2018). LiFi is a paradigm-shifting 5G technology. *Reviews in Physics*, *3*, 26–31. doi:10.1016/j.revip.2017.10.001

Halamka, J. D., & Mandl, K. D. (2019). Making healthcare IT sustainable. *The New England Journal of Medicine*, *381*(26), 2497–2499. PMID:31733140

Hancock, J. H. II. (2022). Merchandising technologies: It is still all about people; thank goodness. *Fashion, Style & Popular Culture*, *9*(4), 433–435. doi:10.1386/fspc_00154_2

Hans, R., Zuber, H., Rizk, A., & Steinmetz, R. (2017). *Blockchain and smart contracts: Disruptive technologies for the insurance market*. Academic Press.

Han, T., Ye, F., & Li, H. (2020). Machine Learning for Smart and Connected Vehicles: A Survey. *IEEE Transactions on Intelligent Transportation Systems*, *21*(9), 3649–3663. doi:10.1109/TITS.2019.2945997

Han, Y., Zhang, X., Zhang, N., Meng, S., Liu, T., Wang, S., Pan, M., Zhang, X., & Yi, J. (2023). Hybrid Target Selections by "Hand Gestures + Facial Expression" for a Rehabilitation Robot. *Sensors (Basel)*, *23*(1), 237. doi:10.339023010237 PMID:36616835

Harding, Vanto, Clark, Ji, & Ainsworth. (2019). Understanding the scope and impact of the california consumer privacy act of 2018. *Journal of Data Protection & Privacy*, *2*(3), 234–253.

Harrop, M. D., & Mairs, B. (2016). Thomson Reuters 2016 Know Your Customer Surveys Reveal Escalating Costs and Complexity. *Press Release*.

Harshasri, M., Bhavani, M. D., & Ravikanth, M. (2021). *Voice Based Email for Blind. International Journal of Innovative Research in Computer Science & Technology*.

Harwood-Jones, M. (2016). *Blockchain and T2S: a potential disruptor*. Standard Chartered Bank.

Hassanalieragh, M. (2015). Health monitoring and management using internet-of-things (IoT) sensing with cloud-based processing: Opportunities and challenges. In *2015 IEEE International Conference on Services Computing (SCC)* (pp. 285-292). IEEE. 10.1109/SCC.2015.47

Hassani, H., Huang, X., & MacFeely, S. (2022). Enabling digital twins to support the UN SDGs. *Big Data and Cognitive Computing*, *6*(4), 115. Advance online publication. doi:10.3390/bdcc6040115

Hassani, H., Huang, X., & MacFeely, S. (2022). Impactful Digital Twin in the Healthcare Revolution. *Big Data and Cognitive Computing*, *6*(3), 83. doi:10.3390/bdcc6030083

Hassani, H., Huang, X., & Silva, E. (2018). Banking with blockchain-ed big data. *Journal of Management Analytics*, *5*(4), 256–275. doi:10.1080/23270012.2018.1528900

Hassan, W. H. (2019). Current research on Internet of Things (IoT) security: A survey. *Computer Networks*, *148*, 283–294. doi:10.1016/j.comnet.2018.11.025

Hasse, F., von Perfall, A., Hillebrand, T., Smole, E., Lay, L., & Charlet, M. (2016). Blockchain–an opportunity for energy producers and consumers. *PwC Global Power & Utilities*, 1–45.

Hassouneh, D., & Brengman, M. (2015). Metaverse retailing: Are SVW users ready to buy real products from virtual world stores? *Proceedings of the International Conferences on e-Health 2015, EH 2015, e-Commerce and Digital Marketing 2015, EC 2015 and Information Systems Post-Implementation and Change Management 2015, ISPCM 2015 - Part of the Multi Conference on Computer Science and Information Systems 2015,* 104-110.10.3390/computers12010005

Havele, A., Brutzman, D., Benman, W., & Polys, N. F. (2022). The keys to an open, interoperable metaverse. *Proceedings - Web3D 2022: 27th ACM Conference on 3D Web Technology.* 10.1145/3564533.3564575

Hazan, E., Kelly, G., Khan, H., Spillecke, D., & Yee, L. (2022). Marketing in the metaverse: An opportunity for innovation and experimentation. *The McKinsey Quarterly.*

He, G., Yang, M., Luo, J., & Gu, X. (2015). A novel application classification attack against Tor. Concurr. Comput. Pract. Exp., 27(18), 5640–5661.

Hennig-Thurau, T. (2022). *The Value of Real-time Multisensory Social Interactions in the Virtual-Reality Metaverse: Framework, Empirical Probes, and Research Roadmap.* Academic Press.

Hennig-Thurau, T., Aliman, D. N., Herting, A. M., Cziehso, G. P., Linder, M., & Kübler, R. V. (2022). Social interactions in the metaverse: Framework, initial evidence, and research roadmap. *Journal of the Academy of Marketing Science.* Advance online publication. doi:10.100711747-022-00908-0

Hennig-Thurau, T., & Ognibeni, B. (2022). Metaverse marketing. *NIM Marketing Intelligence Review, 14*(2), 43–47. doi:10.2478/nimmir-2022-0016

Heo, J., Kim, D., Jeong, S. C., Kim, M., & Yoon, T. (2023). *Examining Participant's perception of SPICE factors of metaverse MICE and its impact on Participant's loyalty and behavioral intentions.* doi:10.1007/978-3-031-16485-9_14

Hevner, A.R., & March, S.T. (2005). *Integrated decision support systems: A data warehouse perspective.* Academic Press.

Heydt, M. (2018a). *Beautiful Soup 4: Python Web Scraping.* Packt Publishing. Available: https://www.packtpub.com/product/beautiful-soup-4-python-web-scraping/9781788833906

Heydt, M. (2018b). *Python Web Scraping Cookbook.* O'Reilly Media, Inc. Available: https://www.oreilly.com/library/view/python-web-scraping/978149198556

Hibert, M., & Lopez, P. (2011). The world's technological capacity to store, communicate and compute information. *Science.* PMID:21310967

Hill, J., Ford, W. R., & Farreras, I. G. (2015). Real conversations with artificial intelligence: A comparison between human–human online conversations and human–chatbot conversations. *Computers in Human Behavior, 49,* 245–250. doi:10.1016/j.chb.2015.02.026

Hinds, J., Williams, E. J., & Joinson, A. N. (2020). "It wouldn't happen to me": Privacy concerns and perspectives following the Cambridge Analytica scandal. *International Journal of Human-Computer Studies, 143,* 102498. doi:10.1016/j.ijhcs.2020.102498

Hines, P., & Netland, T. H. (2022). Teaching a lean masterclass in the metaverse. *International Journal of Lean Six Sigma.* Advance online publication. doi:10.1108/IJLSS-02-2022-0035

Hirsch, P. B. (2022). Adventures in the metaverse. *The Journal of Business Strategy, 43*(5), 332–336. doi:10.1108/JBS-06-2022-0101

Hogan, A., & Phillips, R. (2015). *Hearing impairment and hearing disability: towards a paradigm change in hearing services*. Ashgate Publishing.

Hollensen, S., Kotler, P., & Opresnik, M. O. (2022). Metaverse – The new marketing universe. *The Journal of Business Strategy*. Advance online publication. doi:10.1108/JBS-01-2022-0014

Hooper, A., & Holtbrügge, D. (2020). Blockchain technology in international business: Changing the agenda for global governance. *Review of International Business and Strategy*, 30(2), 183–200. doi:10.1108/RIBS-06-2019-0078

Horikawa, C., Kodama, S., Tanaka, S., Fujihara, K., Hirasawa, R., Yachi, Y., Shimano, H., Yamada, N., Saito, K., & Sone, H. (2013). Diabetes and risk of hearing impairment in adults: A meta-analysis. *The Journal of Clinical Endocrinology and Metabolism*, 98(1), 51–58. doi:10.1210/jc.2012-2119 PMID:23150692

How AI and Metaverse Are Shaping the Future? (n.d.). HitechNectar. https://www.hitechnectar.com /blogs/how-ai-and-metaverse-are -shaping-the-future/

How to use Blockchain in the Metaverse | Oodles Blockchain. (n.d.). Retrieved from https://blockchain.oodles.io/blog/how-to-use-blockchain-in-the-metaverse/

Hsieh & Lee. (2018). Preliminary study of VR and AR applications in medical and healthcare education. *J Nurs Health Stud, 3*(1).

Hsu, T. C., Chang, C., & Jen, T. H. (2023). Artificial Intelligence image recognition using self-regulation learning strategies: Effects on vocabulary acquisition, learning anxiety, and learning behaviours of English language learners. *Interactive Learning Environments*, 1–19. doi:10.1080/10494820.2023.2165508

Hu, Q. (2022, October). Towards a virtual business ecosystem in the Metaverse Era. In *2022 IEEE International Symposium on Mixed and Augmented Reality Adjunct (ISMAR-Adjunct)* (pp. 27-29). IEEE. 10.1109/ISMAR-Adjunct57072.2022.00016

Huang, A. Y., Lu, O. H., & Yang, S. J. (2023). Effects of artificial Intelligence–Enabled personalized recommendations on learners' learning engagement, motivation, and outcomes in a flipped classroom. *Computers & Education*, 194, 104684. doi:10.1016/j.compedu.2022.104684

Huang, T. H., & Wang, L. Z. (2021). Artificial intelligence learning approach through total physical response embodiment teaching on French vocabulary learning retention. *Computer Assisted Language Learning*, 1–25. doi:10.1080/09588221.2021.2008980

Huang, W., Hew, K. F., & Fryer, L. K. (2022). Chatbots for language learning—Are they really useful? A systematic review of chatbot-supported language learning. *Journal of Computer Assisted Learning*, 38(1), 237–257. doi:10.1111/jcal.12610

Huang, X., Zou, D., Cheng, G., Chen, X., & Xie, H. (2023). Trends, research issues and applications of artificial intelligence in language education. *Journal of Educational Technology & Society*, 26(1), 112–131.

Huang, Y. M., Chan, H. Y., Wang, Y. H., & Ho, Y. F. (2023). Effects of a blended multimedia teaching approach on self-efficacy and skills in over-the-counter medication counselling versus a lecture-based approach: Protocol for a prospective cohort study of undergraduate students from a pharmacy school in Taiwan. *BMJ Open*, 13(1), e068738. doi:10.1136/bmjopen-2022-068738 PMID:36697044

Hudson, J. (2022). Virtual Immersive Shopping Experiences in Metaverse Environments: Predictive Customer Analytics, Data Visualization Algorithms, and Smart Retailing Technologies. *Linguistic and Philosophical Investigations*, (21), 236–251.

Hughes, C. E., Stapleton, C. B., Hughes, D. E., & Smith, E. M. (2005). Mixed reality in education, entertainment, and training. *IEEE Computer Graphics and Applications*, *25*(6), 24–30. doi:10.1109/MCG.2005.139 PMID:16315474

Hughes, L., Dwivedi, Y. K., Rana, N. P., Williams, M. D., & Raghavan, V. (2022). Perspectives on the future of manufacturing within the Industry 4.0 era. *Production Planning and Control*, *33*(2-3), 138–158. doi:10.1080/09537287.2020.1810762

Hugues, O., Fuchs, P., & Nannipieri, O. (2011). New augmented reality taxonomy: technologies and features of augmented environment. In B. Furth (Ed.), *Handbook of Augmented Reality* (pp. 47–63). Springer. doi:10.1007/978-1-4614-0064-6_2

Hu, J., & Hu, X. (2020, November). The Effectiveness of Autonomous Listening Study and Pedagogical Implications In the Module of Artificial Intelligence. *Journal of Physics: Conference Series*, *1684*(1), 012037. doi:10.1088/1742-6596/1684/1/012037

Hussain, S. S., & Ganganath, N. (2019). A Survey on Artificial Intelligence Approaches for Autonomous Vehicles. *International Journal of Computer Science and Network Security*, *19*(8), 58–64.

Hussein, M., & Nätterdal, C. (2015). *The benefits of virtual reality in education-A comparison Study*. Academic Press.

Hutson, J. (2023). Architecting the Metaverse: Blockchain and the Financial and Legal Regulatory Challenges of Virtual Real Estate. *Journal of Intelligent Learning Systems and Applications, 15*.

Huynh-The, T. R. (n.d.). Blockchain for the Metaverse. *RE:view*.

Huynh-The, T., Gadekallu, T. R., Wang, W., Yenduri, G., Ranaweera, P., Pham, Q.-V., Benevides da Costa, D., & Liyanage, M. (2023). Blockchain for the metaverse: A Review. *Future Generation Computer Systems*, *143*, 401–419. doi:10.1016/j.future.2023.02.008

Hwang, G.-J., & Chien, S.-Y. (2022). Definition, Roles, and Potential Research Issues of the Metaverse in Education: An Artificial Intelligence Perspective. Computers and Education: Artificial Intelligence, 3. doi:10.1016/j.caeai.2022.100082

Hwang, S., & Koo, G. (2023). Art marketing in the metaverse world: Evidence from South Korea. *Cogent Social Sciences*, *9*(1), 2175429. Advance online publication. doi:10.1080/23311886.2023.2175429

IEEE. (n.d.). https://ieeexplore.ieee.org/document/10084271

Institute of Electrical and Electronics Engineers Madras Section & Institute of Electrical and Electronics Engineers. (n.d.). *Proceedings of the 2020 IEEE International Conference on Communication and Signal Processing (ICCSP): 28th - 30th July 2020, Melmaruvathur, India*. Academic Press.

İpek, A. R. (2020). Artırılmış gerçeklik, sanal gerçeklik ve karma gerçeklik kavramlarında isimlendirme ve tanımlandırma sorunları. *İdil Sanat ve Dil Dergisi*, *9*(71), 1061-1072. doi:10.7816/idil-09-71-02

Islam, T., Hossain, M. A., & Islam, M. R. (2021). A Comprehensive Survey on Connected Vehicles Technologies and Applications. *Journal of Communication*, *16*(3), 219–234. doi:10.12720/jcm.16.3.219-234

Islam, T., Hossain, M. A., & Islam, M. R. (2021). Autonomous driving systems: A survey. *IEEE Access : Practical Innovations, Open Solutions*, *9*, 2067–2095. doi:10.1109/ACCESS.2020.3040444

Ivanov, L. A., Kapustin, I. A., Borisova, O. N., & Pisarenko, Z. V. (2020). Nanotechnologies: a review of inventions and utility models. Part II. *Nanotekhnologii v Stroitel'stve, 12*(2), 71–76.

Ivanov, L. A., Razumeev, K. E., Bokova, E. S., & Muminova, S. R. (2019). The inventions in nanotechnologies as practical solutions. Part V. *Nanotechnologies in Construction, 11*(6).

Iyawa, G., Dwolatzky, B., & De Vries, J. (2020). Telemedicine and the COVID-19 pandemic in sub-Saharan Africa: A comprehensive overview. *EMHJ-Eastern Mediterranean Health Journal*, *26*(9), 973–981.

Jacak, J. E. (2023). *Topological hint to the information paradox and firewall concept for black holes.* arXiv preprint arXiv:2304.10384.

Jacob, M. (2023). *Following extensive, multi-annual negotiations the European Parliament and European Council have reached an agreement on a new General Data Protection Regulation modernising a legal framework which dates back to the 1990s.* Global Security Mag Online.

Jacobovitz, O. (2016). Blockchain for identity management. The Lynne and William Frankel Center for Computer Science Department of Computer Science, *Ben-Gurion University*.

Jamil, S., Rahman, M., & Fawad, M. (2022). A Comprehensive Survey of Digital Twins and Federated Learning for Industrial Internet of Things (IIoT), Internet of Vehicles (IoV) and Internet of Drones (IoD). *Applied System Innovation*, *5*(3), 56. doi:10.3390/asi5030056

Jamshidi, M. R., & Akbari, M. R. (2019). A review of wireless communication technologies for connected vehicles in Iran. *Journal of Communication Engineering*, *7*(1), 1–9.

Jarmul, K., & Lawson, R. (2017). *Python Web Scraping* (2nd ed.). Packt Publishing. Available: https://www.packtpub.com/product/python-web-scraping-second-edition/9781786462589

Jaung, W. (2022). Digital forest recreation in the metaverse: Opportunities and challenges. *Technological Forecasting and Social Change*, *185*, 122090. Advance online publication. doi:10.1016/j.techfore.2022.122090

Javaid, M., Haleem, A., Singh, R. P., Khan, S., & Suman, R. (2021). Blockchain technology applications for Industry 4.0: A literature-based review. *Blockchain: Research and Applications*, 100027.

Jayachandran, K., & Anbumani, P. (2017). Voice Based Email for Blind People. *International Journal of Advance Research, Ideas, and Innovations in Technology*, 1066-71.

Jeon, Y. A. (2022). Reading social media marketing messages as simulated self within a metaverse: An analysis of gaze and social media engagement behaviors within a metaverse platform. *Proceedings - 2022 IEEE Conference on Virtual Reality and 3D User Interfaces Abstracts and Workshops, VRW 2022*, 301-303. 10.1109/VRW55335.2022.00068

Jeon, J. (2021). The effects of user experience-based design innovativeness on user–metaverse platform channel relationships in south korea. *Journal of Distribution Science*, *19*(11), 81–90. doi:10.15722/jds.19.11.202111.81

Jessel, B., & DiCaprio, A. (2018). Can blockchain make trade finance more inclusive? *Journal of Financial Transformation*, *47*, 35–50.

Ji, Lipton, & Elkan. (2014). *Differential privacy and machine learning: a survey and review.* arXiv preprint arXiv:1412.7584.

Jiang, Y., Kang, J., Niyato, D., Ge, X., Xiong, Z., Miao, C., & Shen, X. (2022). Reliable distributed computing for metaverse: A hierarchical game-theoretic approach. *IEEE Transactions on Vehicular Technology*.

Jiang, Y., Yang, X., & Zheng, T. (2023). Make chatbots more adaptive: Dual pathways linking human-like cues and tailored response to trust in interactions with chatbots. *Computers in Human Behavior*, *138*, 107485. doi:10.1016/j.chb.2022.107485

Jiao, X., & Li, Z. (2022). Football Teaching Quality Evaluation and Promotion Strategy Based on Intelligent Algorithms in Higher Vocational Colleges. Wireless Communications and Mobile Computing, 1–7. doi:10.1155/2022/9469553

Jin, J., Xu, H., & Leng, B. (2022). Adaptive Points Sampling for Implicit Field Reconstruction of Industrial Digital Twin. *Sensors (Basel)*, *22*(17), 6630. doi:10.339022176630 PMID:36081088

Johnson, W. L. (2019). Data-driven development and evaluation of Enskill English. *International Journal of Artificial Intelligence in Education*, *29*(3), 425–457. doi:10.100740593-019-00182-2

Jones, B. F., Wuchty, S., & Uzzi, B. (2008). Multi University Research Teams: Shifting impact Geograph and Stratification in Science. *Science*, *322*(5905), 1259–1262. doi:10.1126cience.1158357 PMID:18845711

Jones, D., Snider, C., Nassehi, A., Yon, J., & Hicks, B. (2020). Characterising the Digital Twin: A systematic literature review. *CIRP Journal of Manufacturing Science and Technology*, *29*, 36–52. doi:10.1016/j.cirpj.2020.02.002

Joshi, M. L., & Kanoongo, N. (2022). Depression detection using emotional artificial intelligence and machine learning: A closer review. *Materials Today: Proceedings*, *58*, 217–226. doi:10.1016/j.matpr.2022.01.467

Jouini, Ben, Rabai, & Aissa. (2014). *Classification of security threats in information systems*. doi:10.1016/j.procs.2014.05.452

Joy, A., Zhu, Y., Peña, C., & Brouard, M. (2022). Digital future of luxury brands: Metaverse, digital fashion, and non-fungible tokens. *Strategic Change*, *31*(3), 337–343. doi:10.1002/jsc.2502

Julian, H. L. C., Chung, T., & Wang, Y. (2023). Adoption of Metaverse in South East Asia: Vietnam, Indonesia, Malaysia. In *Strategies and Opportunities for Technology in the Metaverse World* (pp. 196–234). IGI Global. doi:10.4018/978-1-6684-5732-0.ch012

Kakhani, M.K., Kakhani, S., & Biradar, S.R. (2015). Research issues in big data analytics. *International Journal of Application or Innovation in Engineering and Management, 2*, 228-232.

Kale, U., Roy, A., & Yuan, J. (2020). To design or to integrate? Instructional design versus technology integration in developing learning interventions. *Educational Technology Research and Development*, *68*(5), 2473–2504. doi:10.100711423-020-09771-8

Kalsoom, T., Ramzan, N., Ahmed, S., & Ur-Rehman, M. (2020). Advances in sensor technologies in the era of smart factory and industry 4.0. *Sensors (Basel)*, *20*(23), 6783. doi:10.339020236783 PMID:33261021

Kan, K., & Une, M. (2021). *Recent trends on research and development of quantum computers and standardization of post-quantum cryptography*. Academic Press.

Kang, J., Ye, D., Nie, J., Xiao, J., Deng, X., Wang, S., Xiong, Z., Yu, R., & Niyato, D. (2022). Blockchain-based federated learning for industrial metaverses: Incentive scheme with optimal aoi. In *2022 IEEE International Conference on Blockchain (Blockchain)* (pp. 71–78). IEEE. 10.1109/Blockchain55522.2022.00020

Kapan, K., & Üncel, R. (2020). Gelişen web teknolojilerinin (web 1.0- web 2.0- web 3.0) Türkiye turizmine etkisi. *Safran Kültür ve Turizm Araştırmaları Dergisi*, *3*(3), 276-289. https://dergipark.org.tr/en/pub/saktad/issue/59328/756788

Kappe, F., & Steurer, M. (2010). *The open metaverse currency (OMC) - A micropayment framework for open 3D virtual worlds*. doi:10.1007/978-3-642-15208-5_9

Kar, A. K., & Navin, L. (2021). Diffusion of blockchain in insurance industry: An analysis through the review of academic and trade literature. *Telematics and Informatics*, *58*, 101532. doi:10.1016/j.tele.2020.101532

Karakas, A., & Kartal, G. (2020). Pre-Service Language Teachers' Autonomous Language Learning with Web 2.0 Tools and Mobile Applications. *International Journal of Curriculum and Instruction*, *12*(1), 51–79.

Kassim, S., Witkin, N., & Stone, A. (2019). Student perceptions of virtual reality use in a speaking activity. *CALL and Complexity*, 223.

Kaur, & Gupta. (2019). Web accessibility for visually impaired people using voice-based interface. *IEEE International Conference on Computing, Communication and Automation (ICCCA).*

Kaur, M., & Venegas-Gomez, A. (2022). Defining the quantum workforce landscape: A review of global quantum education initiatives. *Optical Engineering (Redondo Beach, Calif.), 61*(8), 081806–081806. doi:10.1117/1.OE.61.8.081806

Kaya, D. (2023). *Ignoring COPPA: An Industry Standard.* Academic Press.

Kazmi, S., & Xue, Y. (2020). Internet of Things (IoT) enabled healthcare applications, architectural elements, and security: A comprehensive survey. *Future Generation Computer Systems, 106,* 1109–1127.

Kemp, J., & Livingstone, D. (2006). Putting a Second Life "Metaverse" skin on learning management systems. In *Proceedings of the Second Life education workshop at the Second Life community convention* (Vol. 20). The University of Paisley.

Kerly, A., Hall, P., & Bull, S. (2007). Bringing chatbots into education: Towards natural language negotiation of open learner models. *Knowledge-Based Systems, 20*(2), 177–185. doi:10.1016/j.knosys.2006.11.014

Keshmiri Neghab, H., Jamshidi, M., & Keshmiri Neghab, H. (2022). Digital Twin of a Magnetic Medical Microrobot with Stochastic Model Predictive Controller Boosted by Machine Learning in Cyber-Physical Healthcare Systems. *Information (Basel), 13*(7), 321. doi:10.3390/info13070321

Khade, A. A. (2016). Performing customer behavior analysis using big data analytics. *International Conference on Communication, Computing and Virtualization (ICCCV), 79,* 986-992. 10.1016/j.procs.2016.03.125

KhanL. U. (2022a). Machine Learning for Metaverse-Enabled Wireless Systems: Vision, Requirements, and Challenges. https://arxiv.org/abs/2211.03703

KhanL. U. (2022b). Metaverse for Wireless Systems: Vision, Enablers, Architecture, and Future Directions. https://arxiv.org/abs/2207.00413

Khan, P. W., Byun, Y. C., & Park, N. (2020). IoT-blockchain enabled optimized provenance system for food industry 4.0 using advanced deep learning. *Sensors (Basel), 20*(10), 2990. doi:10.339020102990 PMID:32466209

Khan, S. W., Raza, S. H., & Zaman, U. (2022). Remodeling digital marketplace through metaverse: A multi-path model of consumer neuroticism, parasocial relationships, social media influencer's credibility, and openness to metaverse experience. *Pakistan Journal of Commerce and Social Science, 16*(3), 337–365.

Khedekar, R., & Gupta, S. (2019). Voice based Email System for Blinds. *International Journal of Engineering Research & Technology, 8,* 41-42.

Kholodenko, A. L. (2023). *Maxwell-Dirac isomorphism revisited: from foundations of quantum mechanics to geometrodynamics and cosmology.* arXiv preprint arXiv:2304.01211.

Kim, M., Hilton, B., Burks, Z., & Reyes, J. (2018). Integrating blockchain, smart contract-tokens, and IoT to design a food traceability solution. In *9th annual information technology, electronics and mobile communication conference (IEMCON)* (pp. 335-340). Academic Press.

Kim, H. J., Kim, J. W., & Yoo, K. Y. (2019). A real-time object detection system using deep learning on a mobile device for visually impaired people. *IEEE Access : Practical Innovations, Open Solutions, 7,* 45007–45017.

Kim, H. S., Kim, N. Y., & Cha, Y. (2021). Is It Beneficial to Use AI Chatbots to Improve Learners' Speaking Performance? *Journal of Asia TEFL, 18*(1), 161–178. doi:10.18823/asiatefl.2021.18.1.10.161

Kim, H., Hwang, S., Kim, J., & Lee, Z. (2022). Toward Smart Communication Components: Recent Advances in Human and AI Speaker Interaction. *Electronics (Basel), 11*(10), 1533. doi:10.3390/electronics11101533

Kim, J. (2021). Advertising in the metaverse: Research agenda. *Journal of Interactive Advertising, 21*(3), 141–144. doi:10.1080/15252019.2021.2001273

Kim, J., Merrill, K., Xu, K., & Sellnow, D. D. (2020). My teacher is a machine: Understanding students' perceptions of AI teaching assistants in online education. *International Journal of Human-Computer Interaction, 36*(20), 1902–1911. doi:10.1080/10447318.2020.1801227

Kim, M., Kim, J. H., & Kim, Y. C. (2019). Traffic sign detection based on faster R-CNN with convolutional layer fusion. *IEEE Access : Practical Innovations, Open Solutions, 7*, 66916–66924.

Kitchin, R., & Dodge, M. (2019). The (in) security of smart cities: Vulnerabilities, risks, mitigation, and prevention. *Journal of Urban Technology, 26*(2), 47–65. doi:10.1080/10630732.2017.1408002

Koay, K. Y., Tjiptono, F., Teoh, C. W., Memon, M. A., & Connolly, R. (2022). Social media influencer marketing: Commentary on the special issue. *Journal of Internet Commerce*. Advance online publication. doi:10.1080/15332861.2022.2128277

Kocaballi, A. B., Laranjo, L., & Coiera, E. (2019). The use of virtual reality in clinical applications: A systematic review and meta-analysis. *Human Factors, 61*(6), 811–831.

Kohnke, L. (2023). L2 learners' perceptions of a chatbot as a potential independent language learning tool. *International Journal of Mobile Learning and Organisation, 17*(1-2), 214–226. doi:10.1504/IJMLO.2023.128339

Koo, C., Kwon, J., Chung, N., & Kim, J. (2022). Metaverse tourism: Conceptual framework and research propositions. *Current Issues in Tourism*, 1–7. Advance online publication. doi:10.1080/13683500.2022.2122781

Koohang, A., Nord, J. H., Ooi, K., Tan, G. W., Al-Emran, M., Aw, E. C., Baabdullah, A. M., Buhalis, D., Cham, T.-H., Dennis, C., Dutot, V., Dwivedi, Y. K., Hughes, L., Mogaji, E., Pandey, N., Phau, I., Raman, R., Sharma, A., Sigala, M., ... Wong, L.-W. (2023, May 04). -., . . . Wong, L. (2023). Shaping the metaverse into reality: A holistic multidisciplinary understanding of opportunities, challenges, and avenues for future investigation. *Journal of Computer Information Systems, 63*(3), 735–765. Advance online publication. doi:10.1080/08874417.2023.2165197

Korbel, J. J., Siddiq, U. H., & Zarnekow, R. (2022). Towards virtual 3D asset price prediction based on machine learning. *Journal of Theoretical and Applied Electronic Commerce Research, 17*(3), 924–948. doi:10.3390/jtaer17030048

Koşar, G. (2022). A Comparative Study of the Attitudes of EFL Student and Practicing Teachers towards First Language Use. *Journal of Language Teaching and Learning, 12*(1), 28–43.

Kosba, A., Miller, A., Shi, E., Wen, Z., & Papamanthou, C. (2016). Hawk: The blockchain model of cryptography and privacy-preserving smart contracts. *2016 IEEE Symposium on Security and Privacy (SP)*, 839–858. 10.1109/SP.2016.55

Koszalka, T. A., Russ-Eft, D. F., & Reiser, R. (2013). *Instructional designer competencies: The standards*. IAP.

Kozinets, R. V. (2023). Immersive netnography: A novel method for service experience research in virtual reality, augmented reality, and metaverse contexts. *Journal of Service Management, 34*(1), 100–125. doi:10.1108/JOSM-12-2021-0481

Kozlova, I., & Priven, D. (2015). ESL teacher training in 3D virtual worlds. *Language Learning & Technology, 19*(1), 83–101.

Kraus, S., Kanbach, D. K., Krysta, P. M., Steinhoff, M. M., & Tomini, N. (2022). Facebook and the creation of the metaverse: Radical business model innovation or incremental transformation? *International Journal of Entrepreneurial Behaviour & Research, 28*(9), 52–77. doi:10.1108/IJEBR-12-2021-0984

Kraus, S., Kumar, S., Lim, W. M., Kaur, J., Sharma, A., & Schiavone, F. (2023). From moon landing to metaverse: Tracing the evolution of technological forecasting and social change. *Technological Forecasting and Social Change, 189*, 122381. Advance online publication. doi:10.1016/j.techfore.2023.122381

Krishnamurthy, Rajeshwari, & Rushikesh. (2023). Why Is AIML Best Suited for Metaverse Consumer Data Analysis? *California Management Reodelview Insights.* https://cmr.berkeley.edu/2023/01/why-is-aiml-best-suited-for -metaverse-consumer-data-analysis/

Kshetri, N. (2022). Web 3.0 and the metaverse shaping organization's brand and product strategies. *IT Professional, 24*(02), 11–15. doi:10.1109/MITP.2022.3157206

Kshetri, N., & Dwivedi, Y. K. (2023). Pollution-reducing and pollution-generating effects of the metaverse. *International Journal of Information Management, 69*, 102620. Advance online publication. doi:10.1016/j.ijinfomgt.2023.102620

Kshetri, N., & Kshetri, N. (2018). The Indian blockchain landscape: Regulations and policy measures. *Asian Res. Policy, 9*(2), 56–71.

Kuba, R., Rahimi, S., Smith, G., Shute, V., & Dai, C. P. (2021). Using the first principles of instruction and multimedia learning principles to design and develop in-game learning support videos. *Educational Technology Research and Development, 69*(2), 1201–1220. doi:10.100711423-021-09994-3

Küçük Avcı, Ş. (2018). *The impact of three dimensional virtual environments and augmented reality applications on learning achievement: A meta-analysis study* (Publication No. 493087) [Doctoral Dissertation, Necmettin Erbakan University]. Higher Education Council Thesis Archive. https://tez.yok.gov.tr

Kuhail, M. A., Alturki, N., Alramlawi, S., & Alhejori, K. (2022). Interacting with educational chatbots: A systematic review. *Education and Information Technologies*, 1–46.

Kulkarni, A. V., Rao, B. H., & Patil, S. K. (2020). Artificial Intelligence for Vehicle Safety: A Comprehensive Review. *IET Intelligent Transport Systems, 14*(10), 1221–1231.

Kumar Bhardwaj, A., Garg, A., & Gajpal, Y. (2021). Determinants of blockchain technology adoption in supply chains by small and medium enterprises (SMEs) in India. *Mathematical Problems in Engineering, 2021*, 2021. doi:10.1155/2021/5537395

Kumar, S. S., & Meera, M. N. (2018). A novel method for visually impaired people to access web pages using speech recognition and text-to-speech conversion. *IEEE International Conference on Innovations in Information, Embedded and Communication Systems (ICIIECS)*.

Kumar, A., Ottaviani, C., Gill, S. S., & Buyya, R. (2022). Securing the future internet of things with post-quantum cryptography. *Security and Privacy, 5*(2), e200. doi:10.1002py2.200

Kumar, A., & Singh, A. (2019). Performance evaluation of artificial neural network models for predicting the thermal performance of a solar air heater. *Energy Reports, 5*, 1082–1089.

Kumar, J. A. (2021). Educational chatbots for project-based learning: Investigating learning outcomes for a team-based design course. *International Journal of Educational Technology in Higher Education, 18*(1), 1–28. doi:10.118641239-021-00302-w PMID:34926790

Kumar, L. A., Renuka, D. K., Rose, S. L., & Wartana, I. M. (2022). Deep learning based assistive technology on audio visual speech recognition for hearing impaired. *International Journal of Cognitive Computing in Engineering, 3*, 24–30. doi:10.1016/j.ijcce.2022.01.003

Kumar, P., Banerjee, K., Singhal, N., Kumar, A., Rani, S., Kumar, R., & Lavinia, C. A. (2022). Verifiable, Secure Mobile Agent Migration in Healthcare Systems Using a Polynomial-Based Threshold Secret Sharing Scheme with a Blowfish Algorithm. *Sensors (Basel)*, 22(22), 8620. doi:10.339022228620 PMID:36433217

Kuosa, T. (2014). *Towards strategic intelligence: foresight, intelligence, and policy-making*. Dynamic Futures.

Kwecko, V. (2018). Silvia S. da C. Botelho, Collaborative Intelligence in Smart Cities: ASystematicReview. *Social Networking*, 24(July). doi:10.4236n.2018.73015

Kye, B., Han, N., Kim, E., Park, Y., & Jo, S. (2021). Educational applications of Metaverse: Possibilities and limitations. *Journal of Educational Evaluation for Health Professions*, 18, 18. doi:10.3352/jeehp.2021.18.32 PMID:34897242

Laeeq, K. (2022). *Metaverse: why, how and what*. How and What.

Lakhani, K. R., & Iansiti, M. (2017). The truth about blockchain. *Harvard Business Review*, 95(1), 119–127.

Lamata, P., Ali, W., Cano, A., Cornella, J., Declerck, J., Elle, O. J., & Gomez, E. J. (2010). Augmented reality for minimally invasive surgery: Overview and some recent advances. In S. Maad (Ed.), *Augmented Reality* (pp. 73–98). InTech. doi:10.5772/7128

Lawson. (2019). *Web Scraping in Python: Master the Fundamentals*. Independently published.

Layzer, J. A. (2008). *Natural experiments: ecosystem-based management and the environment*. MIT Press. doi:10.7551/mitpress/9780262122986.001.0001

Lebeck, K., Ruth, K., Kohno, T., & Roesner, F. (2017). Securing augmented reality output. In 2017 IEEE symposium on security and privacy (SP) (pp. 320–337). IEEE. doi:10.1109/SP.2017.13

Lee, C., & Wong, K. D. (2022). Towards self-adaptive/Reflective co-managed open generativity to augment absorptive-multiplicative-relational Capabilities/Capacities. *IEEE International Conference on Industrial Engineering and Engineering Management*, 2022-December 52-56. 10.1109/IEEM55944.2022.9989957

Lee, J., & Kwon, K. H. (2022a). Novel pathway regarding good cosmetics brands by NFT in the metaverse world. *Journal of Cosmetic Dermatology, 21*(12), 6584-6593. doi:10.1111/jocd.15277

Lee, L. H., Braud, T., Zhou, P., Wang, L., Xu, D., Lin, Z., & Hui, P. (2021). *All one needs to know about metaverse: A complete survey on technological singularity, virtual ecosystem, and research agenda*. arXiv preprint arXiv:2110.05352.

Lee, L.-H., Braud, T., Zhou, P., Wang, L., Xu, D., Lin, Z., Kumar, A., Bermejo, C., & Hui, P. (2021). *All one needs to know about metaverse: A complete survey on technological singularity, virtual ecosystem, and research agenda*. arXiv preprint arXiv:2110.05352.

Lee, S. (2020). *Log in Metaverse: Revolution of Human Space Time*. Issue Report.

Lee, C., & Lim, C. (2021). From technological development to social advance: A review of Industry 4.0 through machine learning. *Technological Forecasting and Social Change*, 167, 120653. doi:10.1016/j.techfore.2021.120653

Lee, H. J., & Gu, H. H. (2022). Empirical research on the metaverse user experience of digital natives. *Sustainability (Basel)*, 14(22), 14747. Advance online publication. doi:10.3390u142214747

Lee, J., & Kwon, K. H. (2022). Future value and direction of cosmetics in the era of metaverse. *Journal of Cosmetic Dermatology*, 21(10), 4176–4183. doi:10.1111/jocd.14794 PMID:35073437

Lee, J., & Kwon, K. H. (2022). The significant transformation of life into health and beauty in metaverse era. *Journal of Cosmetic Dermatology*, 21(12), 6575–6583. doi:10.1111/jocd.15151 PMID:35686389

Lee, S. K., Bae, M., & Kim, H. (2017). Future of IoT networks: A survey. *Applied Sciences (Basel, Switzerland)*, *7*(10), 1072. doi:10.3390/app7101072

Lee, S., Domina, T., & MacGillivray, M. (2011). Exploring consumers' flow experiences in virtual shopping: An exploratory study. *International Journal of Electronic Marketing and Retailing*, *4*(2-3), 165–182. doi:10.1504/IJEMR.2011.043046

Lee, S., Trimi, S., Byun, W. K., & Kang, M. (2011). Innovation and imitation effects in metaverse service adoption. *Service Business*, *5*(2), 155–172. doi:10.100711628-011-0108-8

Lee, U., & Kim, H. (2022). UTAUT in metaverse: An "Ifland" case. *Journal of Theoretical and Applied Electronic Commerce Research*, *17*(2), 613–635. doi:10.3390/jtaer17020032

Legner, C., Eymann, T., Hess, T., Matt, C., Böhmann, T., Drews, P., Mädche, A., Urbach, N., & Ahlemann, F. (2017). Digitalization: Opportunity and challenge for the business and information systems engineering community. *Business & Information Systems Engineering*, *59*(4), 301–308. doi:10.100712599-017-0484-2

Levak, N., & Son, J. B. (2017). Facilitating second language learners' listening comprehension with Second Life and Skype. *ReCALL*, *29*(2), 200–218. doi:10.1017/S0958344016000215

Lewis, R., McPartland, J., & Ranjan, R. (2017). Blockchain and financial market innovation. *Economic Perspectives*, *41*(7), 1–17.

Li, N., Li, T., & Venkatasubramanian, S. (2006). t-closeness: Privacy beyond k-anonymity and l-diversity. In *2007 IEEE 23rd international conference on data engineering* (pp. 106–115). IEEE.

Liang, M. Y. (2019). Beyond elocution: Multimodal narrative discourse analysis of L2 storytelling. *ReCALL*, *31*(1), 56–74. doi:10.1017/S0958344018000095

Lichtenberg, E. (2002). Agriculture and the environment. In *Handbook of agricultural economics* (pp. 1249–1313). Elsevier.

Lin, C. J., & Mubarok, H. (2021). Learning analytics for investigating the mind map-guided AI chatbot approach in an EFL flipped speaking classroom. *Journal of Educational Technology & Society*, *24*(4), 16–35.

Lin, J. S. E., & Wu, L. (2023). Examining the psychological process of developing consumer-brand relationships through strategic use of social media brand chatbots. *Computers in Human Behavior*, *140*, 107488. doi:10.1016/j.chb.2022.107488

Linnenluecke, M. K., Marrone, M., & Singh, A. K. (2020). Conducting systematic literature reviews and bibliometric analyses. *Australian Journal of Management*, *45*(2), 175–194. doi:10.1177/0312896219877678

Liu, X., Hui, Y., Sun, W., & Liang, H. (2007). Towards Service Composition Based on Mashup. *Services, 2007 IEEE Congress on*, 332-339. 10.1109/SERVICES.2007.67

Liu, Z. K. (2023). *Next fifty years of thermodynamics and its modeling: Integrating quantum, statistical, classical, and irreversible thermodynamics for prediction of transformative properties.* arXiv preprint arXiv:2301.02132.

Liu, C. C., Liao, M. G., Chang, C. H., & Lin, H. M. (2022). An analysis of children'interaction with an AI chatbot and its impact on their interest in reading. *Computers & Education*, *189*, 104576. doi:10.1016/j.compedu.2022.104576

Liu, X., & Deters, R. (2007). An efficient dual caching strategy for web service-enabled PDAs. In *SAC '07: Proceedings of the 2007 ACM symposium on applied computing*. ACM. 10.1145/1244002.1244178

Liu, Y., Feng, C., Yuan, X., Zhou, L., Wang, W., Qin, J., & Luo, Z. (2022). Clip-aware expressive feature learning for video-based facial expression recognition. *Information Sciences*, *598*, 182–195. doi:10.1016/j.ins.2022.03.062

Li, X., Li, J., & Liu, X. (2020). A machine learning-based approach for vehicle license plate recognition. *IEEE Access : Practical Innovations, Open Solutions, 8*, 14216–14228.

Li, X., Li, J., & Liu, X. (2020). A Study on the Intelligent Forward Collision Warning Algorithm Based on Machine Learning. *IEEE Access : Practical Innovations, Open Solutions, 8*, 222602–222614. doi:10.1109/access.2020.3048584

Li, X., Li, J., & Liu, X. (2020). Hybrid learning-based visual perception for autonomous vehicles: A survey. *Sensors (Basel), 20*(20), 5956. doi:10.339020205956 PMID:33096804

Li, X., Li, Y., & Wang, Y. (2020). Pedestrian Detection for Autonomous Driving: A Survey. *IEEE Transactions on Intelligent Transportation Systems, 21*(3), 1260–1279.

Li, Y., Li, W., & Chen, C. (2020). A bibliometric analysis of smart vehicles research. *Journal of Intelligent Transportation Systems: Technology, Planning, and Operations, 24*(1), 1–23.

Llamas, R., & Belk, R. (2022). The Routledge handbook of digital consumption. doi:10.4324/9781003317524

Longo, F., Nicoletti, L., & Padovano, A. (2017). Smart operators in industry 4.0: A human-centered approach to enhance operators' capabilities and competencies within the new smart factory context. *Computers & Industrial Engineering, 113*, 144–159. doi:10.1016/j.cie.2017.09.016

Lu, H., Huang, K., Azimi, M., & Guo, L. (2019). Blockchain technology in the oil and gas industry: A review of applications, opportunities, challenges, and risks. *IEEE Access : Practical Innovations, Open Solutions, 7*, 41426–41444. doi:10.1109/ACCESS.2019.2907695

Lukava, T., Morgado Ramirez, D. Z., & Barbareschi, G. (2022). Two sides of the same coin: Accessibility practices and neurodivergent users' experience of extended reality. *Journal of Enabling Technologies, 16*(2), 75–90. doi:10.1108/JET-03-2022-0025

Lyons, N. (2022). Talent acquisition and management, immersive work environments, and machine vision algorithms in the virtual economy of the metaverse. *Psychosociological Issues in Human Resource Management, 10*(1), 121–134. doi:10.22381/pihrm10120229

Maddahi, Y., & Chen, S. (2022). Applications of Digital Twins in the Healthcare Industry: Case Review of an IoT-Enabled Remote Technology in Dentistry. *Virtual Worlds, 1*(1), 20–41. doi:10.3390/virtualworlds1010003

Madumidha, S. R. P., Vandhana, U., & Venmuhilan, B. (2019). A theoretical implementation: Agriculture-food supply chain management using blockchain technology. In *TEQIP III Sponsored International Conference on Microwave Integrated Circuits, Photonics and Wireless Networks (IMICPW)*, (pp. 174-178). 10.1109/IMICPW.2019.8933270

MaF.SunB.LiS. (2022). *Spatio-Temporal Transformer for Dynamic Facial Expression Recognition in the Wild*. https://arxiv.org/abs/2205.04749

Magalhães, L., Magalhães, L., Ramos, J., Moura, L., de Moraes, R., Gonçalves, J., Hisatugu, W. H., Souza, M. T., de Lacalle, L. N. L., & Ferreira, J. (2022). Conceiving a Digital Twin for a Flexible Manufacturing System. *Applied Sciences (Basel, Switzerland), 12*(19), 9864. doi:10.3390/app12199864

Mahmoud, M. M. A. (2014). The effectiveness of using the cooperative language learning approach to enhance EFL writing skills among Saudi university students. *Journal of Language Teaching and Research, 5*(3), 616. doi:10.4304/jltr.5.3.616-625

Mahr, D. (2022). Embracing falsity through the metaverse: The case of synthetic customer experiences. *Business Horizons, 65*(6), 739–749. doi:10.1016/j.bushor.2022.07.007

Majeed, S., & Goyal, R. K. (2020). Internet of Things (IoT) in healthcare: Applications, benefits, and challenges. In *Advances in computer and computational sciences* (pp. 119–129). Springer.

Malhotra, S., Nagpal, R., & Nagpal, P. (2012a). Biometric techniques and facial expression recognition-A review. *Journal of Global Research in Computer Science, 3*(11). www.jgrcs.info

Malhotra, D., Saini, P., & Singh, A. K. (2022). How blockchain can automate KYC: Systematic review. *Wireless Personal Communications, 122*(2), 1987–2021. doi:10.100711277-021-08977-0

Manjula, S., Kiranmai, S. V., & Reddy, S. S. (2021). Web page accessibility for visually impaired people using voice-based system. *IEEE International Conference on Inventive Communication and Computational Technologies (ICICCT).*

Marek, M. W., & Wu, P. H. N. (2020). Digital learning curriculum design: Outcomes and affordances. In *Pedagogies of digital learning in higher education* (pp. 163–182). Routledge. doi:10.4324/9781003019466-9

Marmaridis, I., & Griffith, S. (2009). *Metaverse services: Extensible learning with mediated teleporting into 3D environments.* doi:10.1007/978-3-642-01112-2_24

Martínez-Hernández, C., Yubero, C., Ferreiro-Calzada, E., & Mendoza-de Miguel, S. (2020). *Didactic use of GIS and Street View for Tourism Degree students: Understanding commercial gentrification in large urban destinations.* Academic Press.

Masferrer, J. Á. R., Sánchez, F. E., & Hernández, D. F. (2014). Experiences complementing classroom teaching with distance seminars in metaverses and videos. *Journal of Cases on Information Technology, 16*(4), 1–12. doi:10.4018/jcit.2014100101

Mbagwu, J. P. C., Madububa, B. I., & Onwuemeka, J. I. (2020). Article on basics of quantum theory. *Int. J. Sci. Res. in Physics and Applied Sciences, 8*(3).

Mellouk, W., & Handouzi, W. (2020). Facial emotion recognition using deep learning: Review and insights. *Procedia Computer Science, 175*, 689–694. doi:10.1016/j.procs.2020.07.101

Mendling, J., Weber, I., van der Aalst, W., vom Brocke, J., Cabanillas, C., Daniel, F., Debois, S., di Ciccio, C., Dumas, M., & Dustdar, S. (2018). Blockchains for business process management-challenges and opportunities. *ACM Transactions on Management Information Systems, 9*(1), 1–16. doi:10.1145/3183367

MengD.PengX.WangK.QiaoY. (2019). *Frame attention networks for facial expression recognition in videos.* doi:10.1109/ICIP.2019.8803603

Mercan, S., Cebe, M., Tekiner, E., Akkaya, K., Chang, M., & Uluagac, S. (2020). A cost-efficient IoT forensics framework with blockchain. *IEEE International Conference on Blockchain and Cryptocurrency (ICBC).* 10.1109/ICBC48266.2020.9169397

Merrill, M. D. (2002). First principles of instruction. *Educational Technology Research and Development, 50*(3), 43–59. doi:10.1007/BF02505024

Metaverse Roadmap Summit 2006. (n.d.). *Elon University.* https://www.elon.edu/u/imagining/event-coverage/Metaverse/

Michalikova, K. F., Suler, P., & Robinson, R. (2022). Virtual Hiring and Training Processes in the Metaverse: Remote Work Apps, Sensory Algorithmic Devices, and Decision Intelligence and Modeling. *Psychosociological Issues in Human Resource Management, 10*(1), 50–63. doi:10.22381/pihrm10120224

Microsoft. (2017). *Why hololens.* https://www.microsoft.com/microsofthololens/en-us/why-hololens

Milgram, P., & Kishino, F. (1994). A taxonomy of mixed reality visual displays. *IEICE Transactions on Information and Systems, 77*(12), 1321–1329.

Minaee, S., Minaei, M., & Abdolrashidi, A. (2021). Deep-emotion: Facial expression recognition using attentional convolutional network. *Sensors (Basel), 21*(9), 3046. Advance online publication. doi:10.339021093046 PMID:33925371

Minović, M., Milovanović, M., Šošević, U., & González, M. Á. C. (2015). Visualisation of student learning model in serious games. *Computers in Human Behavior, 47*, 98–107. doi:10.1016/j.chb.2014.09.005

Mirbagheri, S. A., Ghanei Rad, F., & Saeedi, H. (2021). Vehicle-to-everything (V2X) communication technologies: A survey and future research directions. *Journal of Communication Engineering, 9*(2), 1–14.

Mishra, M., & Srivastava, M. (2014). A view of Artificial Neural Network. *2014 International Conference on Advances in Engineering & Technology Research (ICAETR - 2014)*, 1-3. 10.1109/ICAETR.2014.7012785

Mishra, N. (2019). Data Science and Knowledge Analytic Contexts on IoE Data for E-BI Application Case. In Edge Computing and Computational Intelligence Paradigms for the IoT (pp. 100-126). IGI Global. doi:10.4018/978-1-5225-8555-8.ch007

Mishra, N., Chang, H. T., & Lin, C. C. (2014). Data-centric Knowledge Discovery Strategy for a Safety-critical Sensor Application. *International Journal of Antennas and Propagation*. doi:10.1155/2014/172186

Mishra, N., Chang, H. T., & Lin, C. C. (2015). An IoT Knowledge Reengineering Framework for Semantic Knowledge Analytics for BI-Services. *Mathematical Problems in Engineering*.

Mishra, N., Chang, H. T., & Lin, C. C. (2018). Sensor Data Distribution and Distributed Knowledge Inference Systems. Lap Lambert Academic Publishing.

Mishra, N., Lin, C. C., & Chang, H. T. (2014). A Cognitive Oriented Framework for IoT Big-data Management Perspective. In *High-Speed Intelligent Communication Forum (HSIC) with International Conference on Computational Problem-Solving (ICCP) China, 2014, 6th International* (pp. 1-4). IEEE.

Mishra, L., & Kaushik, V. (2021). Application of blockchain in dealing with sustainability issues and challenges of financial sector. *Journal of Sustainable Finance & Investment*, ●●●, 1–16. doi:10.1080/20430795.2021.1940805

Mishra, N. (2018). Internet of Everything Advancement Study in Data Science and Knowledge Analytic Streams. *International Journal of Scientific Research in Computer Science and Engineering, 6*(1), 30–36. doi:10.26438/ijsrcse/v6i1.3036

Mishra, N., Alebachew, K., & Patnaik, B. C. (2018). Knowledge Analytics in Cloud-Centric IoT Vicinities. *International Journal on Computer Science and Engineering, 6*(1), 385–390. doi:10.26438/ijcse/v6i1.385390

Mishra, N., Chang, H. T., & Lin, C. C. (2018). Sensor data distribution and knowledge inference framework for a cognitive-based distributed storage sink environment. *International Journal of Sensor Networks, 26*(1), 26–42. doi:10.1504/IJSNET.2018.088387

Mishra, N., Lin, C. C., & Chang, H. T. (2014). A Cognitive Adopted Framework for IoT Big-Data Management and Knowledge Discovery Prospective. *International Journal of Distributed Sensor Networks*.

Mishra, N., Lin, C. C., & Chang, H. T. (2014). Cognitive inference device for activity supervision in the elderly. *TheScientificWorldJournal, 2014*, 2014. doi:10.1155/2014/125618 PMID:25405211

Mitchell, R. (2015). *Web Scraping with Python: Collecting More Data from the Modern Web*. O'Reilly Media, Inc. Available: https://www.oreilly.com/library/view/web-scraping-with/9781491910283/

Mitra, N., & Banerjee, A. (2022). A Study on Using AI in Promoting English Language Learning. *Proceedings of IE-MIS*, 2, 287–297.

Mittal, G., & Bansal, R. (2023). Driving Force Behind Consumer Brand Engagement: The Metaverse. In *Cultural Marketing and Metaverse for Consumer Engagement* (pp. 164–181). IGI Global. doi:10.4018/978-1-6684-8312-1.ch012

Mohamed, M. (2021). *Quantum Annealing: Research and Applications* [Master's thesis]. University of Waterloo.

Mohan, J., Wasserman, M., & Chidambaram, V. (2019). Analyzing GDPR compliance through the lens of privacy policy. In Heterogeneous Data Management, Polystores, and Analytics for Healthcare: VLDB 2019 Workshops, Poly and DMAH, Los Angeles, CA, USA, August 30, 2019, Revised Selected Papers 5 (pp. 82–95). Springer. doi:10.1007/978-3-030-33752-0_6

Mondal, P. C., Deb, R., & Huda, M. N. (2016). Transaction authorization from Know Your Customer (KYC) information in online banking. *2016 9th International Conference on Electrical and Computer Engineering (ICECE)*, 523–526.

Mori, T. (2016). Financial technology: Blockchain and securities settlement. *Journal of Securities Operations & Custody*, 8(3), 208–227.

Moudoud, H., Cherkaoui, S., & Khoukhi, L. (2019). An IoT blockchain architecture using oracles and smart contracts: the use-case of a food supply chain. In *IEEE 30th Annual International Symposium on Personal, Indoor and Mobile Radio Communications (PIMRC)* (pp. 1-6). IEEE.

Mthunzi, S. N., Benkhelifa, E., Bosakowski, T., & Hariri, S. (2018). *A bio-inspired approach to cyber security*. https://eprints.staffs.ac.uk/id/eprint/5069

Mukhiya, S. K., Wake, J. D., Inal, Y., Pun, K. I., & Lamo, Y. (2020). Adaptive elements in internet-delivered psychological treatment systems: Systematic review. *Journal of Medical Internet Research*, 22(11), e21066. doi:10.2196/21066 PMID:33245285

Murray, A., Kim, D., & Combs, J. (2023). The promise of a decentralized internet: What is Web3, and how can firms prepare? *Business Horizons*, 66(2), 191–202. doi:10.1016/j.bushor.2022.06.002

Murthy, S., Abu Bakar, A., Rahim, F. A., & Ramli, R. (2019). A comparative study of data anonymization techniques. In *2019 IEEE 5th Intl Conference on Big Data Security on Cloud (BigDataSecurity), IEEE Intl Conference on High Performance and Smart Computing (HPSC) and IEEE Intl Conference on Intelligent Data and Security (IDS)* (pp. 306–309). IEEE. 10.1109/BigDataSecurity-HPSC-IDS.2019.00063

Muthmainnah, P. M. I. S., & Oteir, I. (2022). Playing with AI to Investigate Human-Computer Interaction Technology and Improving Critical Thinking Skills to Pursue 21st Century Age. Education Research International. doi:10.1155/2022/6468995

Muthmainnah, S. G., Al Yakin, A., & Ghofur, A. (2023). An Effective Investigation on YIPe-Learning Based for Twenty-First Century Class. *Digital Learning based Education: Transcending Physical Barriers*, 21.

Mystakidis, S. (2022). Metaverse. *Encyclopedia*, 2(1), 486–497. doi:10.3390/encyclopedia2010031

Mystakidis, S., Christopoulos, A., & Pellas, N. (2022). A systematic mapping review of augmented reality applications to support STEM learning in higher education. *Education and Information Technologies*, 27(2), 1883–1927. doi:10.100710639-021-10682-1

Nagaraj, A. (2021). *Introduction to Sensors in IoT and Cloud Computing Applications*. Bentham Science Publishers. doi:10.2174/97898114793591210101

Nair, V., Garrido, G. M., & Song, D. (2022). *Exploring the unprecedented privacy risks of the metaverse.* arXiv preprint arXiv:2207.13176.

Nakamoto, S. (2008). Bitcoin: A peer-to-peer electronic cash system. *Decentralized Business Review, 21260.* https://bitcoin.org/bitcoin.pdf

Narayanan, S. N., Ganesan, A., Joshi, K., Oates, T., Joshi, A., & Finin, T. (2018). Early detection of cybersecurity threats using collaborative cognition. In *2018 IEEE 4th international conference on collaboration and internet computing (CIC)* (pp. 354-363). IEEE. 10.1109/CIC.2018.00054

Nardi, P. M. (2018). *Doing survey research: A guide to quantitative methods.* Routledge. doi:10.4324/9781315172231

Nassimbeni, G., Sartor, M., Nassimbeni, G., & Sartor, M. (2008). The Case Studies. *Sourcing in India: Strategies and Experiences in the Land of Service Offshoring*, 173-252.

Neto, A. J. M., & Fernandes, M. A. (2019, July). Chatbot and conversational analysis to promote collaborative learning in distance education. In *2019 IEEE 19th International Conference on Advanced Learning Technologies (ICALT)* (Vol. 2161, pp. 324-326). IEEE.

Nguyen, M. H. (2023). Academic writing and AI: Day-1 experiment. *Center for Open Science 2023.*

Nguyen, Q. K. (2016). Blockchain-a financial technology for future sustainable development. *2016 3rd International Conference on Green Technology and Sustainable Development (GTSD)*, 51–54.

Nguyen, T. (2022). Toward Human Digital Twins for Cybersecurity Simulations on the Metaverse: Ontological and Network Science Approach. *JMIRx Med, 3*(2), e33502. doi:10.2196/33502

Nieminen, R. M. (2001). From number crunching to virtual reality: mathematics, physics and computation. *Mathematics Unlimited—2001 and Beyond*, 937-959.

Ning, H. (2021). *A Survey on Metaverse: the State-of-the-art, Technologies, Applications, and Challenges.* arXiv preprint arXiv:2111.09673

Ning, H., Wang, H., Lin, Y., Wang, W., Dhelim, S., Farha, F., & Daneshmand, M. (2021). *A Survey on Metaverse: the State-of-the-art, Technologies, Applications, and Challenges.* https://doi.org//arXiv.2111.09673 doi:10.48550

Ning, H., Wang, H., Lin, Y., Wang, W., Dhelim, S., Farha, F., Ding, J., & Daneshmand, M. (2023). A Survey on the Metaverse: The State-of-the-Art, Technologies, Applications, and Challenges. *IEEE Internet of Things Journal, 1.* doi:10.1109/JIOT.2023.3278329

Njoku, J. N., Nwakanma, C. I., Amaizu, G. C., & Kim, D. (2023). Prospects and challenges of metaverse application in data-driven intelligent transportation systems. *IET Intelligent Transport Systems, 17*(1), 1–21. doi:10.1049/itr2.12252

O'Brien & Chan. (2021). *Explainer: What is the metaverse and how will it work?* AP News.

Oberhauser, R., Baehre, M., & Sousa, P. (2022). *VR-EA+TCK: Visualizing enterprise architecture, content, and knowledge in virtual reality.* doi:10.1007/978-3-031-11510-3_8

Ol'ah, J., & Nica, E. (2022). Biometric Sensor Technologies, Virtual Marketplace Dynamics Data, and Computer Vision and Deep Learning Algorithms in the Metaverse Interactive Environment. *Journal of Self-Governance & Management Economics, 10*(3).

Oldani, R. (2023). *The Influence of Time in a Theory of Nature.* Academic Press.

Oliver, E. (2008). A survey of platforms for mobile networks research. *SIGMOBILE Mob. Comput.Commun. Rev., 12*(4), 56–63. doi:10.1145/1508285.1508292

Onur, M. (2021). *The effect of augmented reality-supported teaching on students' academic achievement, level of learning permanence, and learning motivation in the solar system and beyond unit* (Publication No. 704680) [Master's Thesis, Mustafa Kemal University]. Higher Education Council Thesis Archive. https://tez.yok.gov.tr

Oppenheim, C. (1993). Virtual Reality and the Virtual Library. *Information Services & Use, 13*(3), 215–227. doi:10.3233/ISU-1993-13303

Orfanidis, S. J. (1995). *Introduction to signal processing.* Prentice-Hall.

Osmani, M., El-Haddadeh, R., Hindi, N., Janssen, M., & Weerakkody, V. (2020). Blockchain for next generation services in banking and finance: Cost, benefit, risk and opportunity analysis. *Journal of Enterprise Information Management.*

Osterrieder, P., Budde, L., & Friedli, T. (2020). The smart factory as a key construct of industry 4.0: A systematic literature review. *International Journal of Production Economics, 221,* 107476. doi:10.1016/j.ijpe.2019.08.011

Otles, S., & Sakalli, A. 2019). Industry 4.0: The smart factory of the future in beverage industry. In Production and management of beverages (pp. 439-469). Woodhead Publishing.

Oudshoorn, N., & Pinch, T. (Eds.). (2003). *How users matter: The co-construction of users and technology.* MIT Press. doi:10.7551/mitpress/3592.001.0001

Owens, D., Mitchell, A., Khazanchi, D., & Zigurs, I. (2011). An empirical investigation of virtual world projects and metaverse technology capabilities. *The Data Base for Advances in Information Systems, 42*(1), 74–101. doi:10.1145/1952712.1952717

Oxford Analytica. (2022). Commercial metaverse to expand fast but unevenly. *Emerald Expert Briefings.* doi:108/OXAN-DB271953

Pack, A., Barrett, A., Liang, H. N., & Monteiro, D. V. (2020). University EAP students' perceptions of using a prototype virtual reality learning environment to learn writing structure. *International Journal of Computer-Assisted Language Learning and Teaching, 10*(1), 27–46. doi:10.4018/IJCALLT.2020010103

Padgett, M. J., Molloy, J., & McGloin, D. (Eds.). (2010). *Optical Tweezers: methods and applications.* CRC Press. doi:10.1201/EBK1420074123

Pamucar, D., Deveci, M., Gokasar, I., Tavana, M., & Köppen, M. (2022). A metaverse assessment model for sustainable transportation using ordinal priority approach and aczel-alsina norms. *Technological Forecasting and Social Change, 182,* 121778. Advance online publication. doi:10.1016/j.techfore.2022.121778

Panagiotakopoulos, D., Marentakis, G., Metzitakos, R., Deliyannis, I., & Dedes, F. (2022). Digital scent technology: Toward the internet of senses and the metaverse. *IT Professional, 24*(3), 52–59. doi:10.1109/MITP.2022.3177292

Panarello, A., Tapas, N., Merlino, G., Longo, F., & Puliafito, A. (2018). Blockchain and IoT Integration: A Systematic Survey. *Sensors (Basel), 18*(8), 2575. doi:10.339018082575 PMID:30082633

Pantelidis, V. S. (2010). Reasons to use virtual reality in education and training courses and a model to determine when to use virtual reality. *Themes in Science and Technology Education, 2*(1-2), 59–70.

Pan, Z., Cheok, A. D., Yang, H., Zhu, J., & Shi, J. (2006). Virtual reality and mixed reality for virtual learning environments. *Computers & Graphics, 30*(1), 20–28. doi:10.1016/j.cag.2005.10.004

Papagiannidis, S., Bourlakis, M., & Li, F. (2008). Making real money in virtual worlds: MMORPGs and emerging business opportunities, challenges and ethical implications in metaverses. *Technological Forecasting and Social Change*, *75*(5), 610–622. doi:10.1016/j.techfore.2007.04.007

Papakçı, E. (2022). *Developing a mobile application for the basic education of mentally handicapped individuals using augmented reality technology* (Publication No. 759743) [Master's thesis, Kocaeli University]. Higher Education Council Thesis Archive. https://tez.yok.gov.tr

Papazoglou, M., & Georgakopoulos, D. (2003). Service-oriented Computing. *Communications of the ACM*, *46*(10), 25–65. doi:10.1145/944217.944233

Park, S. M., & Kim, Y. G. (2022). A Metaverse: Taxonomy, components, applications, and open challenges. *IEEE Access, 10*, 4209–4251. doi:10.1109/ACCESS.2021.3140175

Park, J. H., & Park, J. H. (2017). Blockchain security in cloud computing: Use cases, challenges, and solutions. *Symmetry*, *9*(8), 164. doi:10.3390ym9080164

Park, J., & Chun, J. (2022). Evolution of fashion as play in the digital space. *Fashion Practice*. Advance online publication. doi:10.1080/17569370.2022.2149837

Park, M. (2018). Innovative assessment of aviation English in a virtual world: Windows into cognitive and metacognitive strategies. *ReCALL*, *30*(2), 196–213. doi:10.1017/S0958344017000362

Park, M. (2019). A study on the development direction of education and training system based on AR/VR technology. *Journal of the Korea Institute of Military Science and Technology*, *22*(4), 545–554.

Park, S. C., Kim, H. J., & Kwon, K. J. (2020). Deep learning-based object detection for intelligent vehicle safety. *Symmetry*, *12*(9), 1567. doi:10.3390ym12091567

Park, S. C., Kim, H. J., & Kwon, K. J. (2020). Road Scene Understanding and Environment Perception for Autonomous Vehicles: A Survey. *IEEE Access : Practical Innovations, Open Solutions*, *8*, 139880–139905. doi:10.1109/access.2020.3018525

Park, T., Lee, J., & Lee, K. (2019). Development of an AI-based intelligent diagnosis system for solar PV systems. *Energies*, *12*(21), 4065.

Patil, K., Bharathi, S. V., & Pramod, D. (2022). Can metaverse retail lead to purchase intentions among the youth? A stimulus-organism-response theory perspective. *2022 ASU International Conference in Emerging Technologies for Sustainability and Intelligent Systems, ICETSIS 2022*, 314-320. 10.1109/ICETSIS55481.2022.9888929

Patki, N., Wedge, R., & Veeramachaneni, K. (2016). The synthetic data vault. In *2016 IEEE International Conference on Data Science and Advanced Analytics (DSAA)* (pp. 399–410). IEEE. 10.1109/DSAA.2016.49

Pearlman, Visner, Magnano, & Cameron. (2021). *Securing the Metaverse-Virtual Worlds Need REAL Governance*. Simulation Interoperability Standards Organization–SISO.

Periyasami, S., & Periyasamy, A. P. (2022). Metaverse as future promising platform business model: Case study on the fashion value chain. *Businesses*, *2*(4), 527–545. doi:10.3390/businesses2040033

Perlner, R. A., & Cooper, D. A. (2009, April). Quantum resistant public key cryptography: a survey. In *Proceedings of the 8th Symposium on Identity and Trust on the Internet* (pp. 85-93). 10.1145/1527017.1527028

Perri, L. (2022, Aug 10). *What's new in the 2022 gartner hype cycle for emerging technologies?* https://www.gartner.com/en/articles/what-s-new-in-the-2022-gartner-hype-cycle-for-emerging-technologies

Petrosyan, A. K., & Aristova, M. D. (2022). The Impact of the Introduction of the Metaverse Concept in the Company's Business Model. Российскиерегионы в фокусеперемен: сборникдокладов. Том 1.—Екатеринбург, 247-252.

Pham, V. C., Luu, Q. K., Nguyen, T. T., Nguyen, N. H., Tan, Y., & Ho, V. A. (2022). *Web of Tactile things: Towards an Open and Standardized platform for Tactile things via the W3C web of Things.* doi:10.1007/978-3-031-07481-3_11

Pham, X. L., Pham, T., Nguyen, Q. M., Nguyen, T. H., & Cao, T. T. H. (2018, November). Chatbot as an intelligent personal assistant for mobile language learning. In *Proceedings of the 2018 2nd International Conference on Education and E-Learning* (pp. 16-21). 10.1145/3291078.3291115

Philip, C. L., Chen, Q., & Zhang, C. Y. (2014). Data-intensive applications, challenges, techniques and technologies: A survey on big data. *Information Sciences*, *275*, 314–347. doi:10.1016/j.ins.2014.01.015

Piela, L. (2020). Ideas of Quantum Chemistry: Volume 1: From Quantum Physics to Chemistry. Elsevier.

Pilgrim, J. M., & Pilgrim, J. (2016). The use of virtual reality tools in the reading-language arts classroom. *Texas Journal of Literacy Education*, *4*(2), 90–97.

Pilkington, M. (2016). Blockchain technology: principles and applications. In *Research handbook on digital transformations*. Edward Elgar Publishing. doi:10.4337/9781784717766.00019

Pincheira, M., Vecchio, M., & Giaffreda, R. (2022). Characterization and Costs of Integrating Blockchain and IoT for Agri-Food Traceability Systems. *Systems*, *10*(3), 57. doi:10.3390ystems10030057

Plangger, K., & Campbell, C. (2022). Managing in an era of falsity: Falsity from the metaverse to fake news to fake endorsement to synthetic influence to false agendas. *Business Horizons*, *65*(6), 713–717. doi:10.1016/j.bushor.2022.08.003

Pokrivčáková, S. (2019). Preparing teachers for the application of AI-powered technologies in foreign language education. *Journal of Language and Cultural Education*.

Popescu, C. R. G., & Popescu, G. N. (2018). Risks of cyber attacks on financial audit activity. *The Audit Financiar Journal*, *16*(149), 140. doi:10.20869/AUDITF/2018/149/140

Popescu, D., Dragomir, M., Popescu, S., & Dragomir, D. (2022). Building Better Digital Twins for Production Systems by Incorporating Environmental Related Functions—Literature Analysis and Determining Alternatives. *Applied Sciences (Basel, Switzerland)*, *12*(17), 8657. doi:10.3390/app12178657

Poulson, M. E., Balcom Raleigh, D., Ghosh, T., Johnson, D. C., & Patel, V. L. (2019). The potential of virtual reality and augmented reality for healthcare applications. *Journal of Digital Imaging*, *32*(4), 469–479.

Powell, W., Foth, M., Cao, S., & Natanelov, V. (2022). Garbage in garbage out: The precarious link between IoT and blockchain in food supply chains. *Journal of Industrial Information Integration*, *25*, 100261. doi:10.1016/j.jii.2021.100261

Prabhakaran, R. T. (2020). Augmented reality and virtual reality in healthcare—A brief survey. In *2020 11th International Conference on Computing, Communication and Networking Technologies (ICCCNT)* (pp. 1-7). IEEE.

Praherdhiono, H., Adi, E. P., Prihatmoko, Y., Abidin, Z., Nindigraha, N., Hidayati, A., & Muttaqin, A. (2022). Synchronization of virtual and real learning patterns in E-learning systems with metaverse concept. *Proceedings - International Conference on Education and Technology, ICET,* 185-189. 10.1109/ICET56879.2022.9990891

Preston, W. C. (2021). Modern Data Protection. O'Reilly Media, Inc.

Procopiou, A., & Komninos, N. (2019). *Bio/Nature-inspired algorithms in AI for malicious activity detection. In Nature-Inspired Cyber Security and Resiliency: Fundamentals, techniques and applications.* IET. doi:10.1049/PBSE010E_CH9

Prodinger, B., & Neuhofer, B. (2023). Never-ending tourism: Tourism experience scenarios for 2030. *Springer Proceedings in Business and Economics,* 288-299. 10.1007/978-3-031-25752-0_31

Puthal, D., Malik, N., Mohanty, S. P., Kougianos, E., & Yang, C. (2018). The blockchain as a decentralized security framework. *IEEE Consumer Electronics Magazine, 7*(2), 18–21. doi:10.1109/MCE.2017.2776459

Queiroz, M. M., Fosso Wamba, S., Pereira, S. C. F., & Chiappetta Jabbour, C. J. (2023). The metaverse as a breakthrough for operations and supply chain management: Implications and call for action. *International Journal of Operations & Production Management.* Advance online publication. doi:10.1108/IJOPM-01-2023-0006

Rajan, S., Chenniappan, P., Devaraj, S., & Madian, N. (2019). Facial expression recognition techniques: A comprehensive survey. In IET Image Processing (Vol. 13, Issue 7, pp. 1031–1040). Institution of Engineering and Technology. doi:10.1049/iet-ipr.2018.6647

Rani, S., Kataria, A., & Chauhan, M. (2022). Cyber security techniques, architectures, and design. In *Holistic Approach to Quantum Cryptography in Cyber Security* (pp. 41–66). CRC Press. doi:10.1201/9781003296034-3

Rani, S., Kataria, A., Kumar, S., & Tiwari, P. (2023). Federated learning for secure IoMT-applications in smart healthcare systems: A comprehensive review. *Knowledge-Based Systems, 274,* 110658. doi:10.1016/j.knosys.2023.110658

Rani, S., Mishra, R. K., Usman, M., Kataria, A., Kumar, P., Bhambri, P., & Mishra, A. K. (2021). Amalgamation of advanced technologies for sustainable development of smart city environment: A review. *IEEE Access: Practical Innovations, Open Solutions, 9,* 150060–150087. doi:10.1109/ACCESS.2021.3125527

Rani, S., Pareek, P. K., Kaur, J., Chauhan, M., & Bhambri, P. (2023). Quantum Machine Learning in Healthcare: Developments and Challenges. In *2023 IEEE International Conference on Integrated Circuits and Communication Systems (ICICACS)* (pp. 1-7). IEEE. 10.1109/ICICACS57338.2023.10100075

Ratten, V. (2023). The post COVID-19 pandemic era: Changes in teaching and learning methods for management educators. *International Journal of Management Education, 21*(2), 100777. Advance online publication. doi:10.1016/j.ijme.2023.100777

Rauschnabel, P. A., Babin, B. J., tom Dieck, M. C., Krey, N., & Jung, T. (2022). What is augmented reality marketing? its definition, complexity, and future. *Journal of Business Research, 142,* 1140–1150. doi:10.1016/j.jbusres.2021.12.084

Rawat, D., Chaudhary, V., & Doku, R. (2020). Blockchain technology: Emerging applications and use cases for secure and trustworthy smart systems. *Journal of Cybersecurity and Privacy, 1*(1), 4–18. doi:10.3390/jcp1010002

Rawat, P., Yashpal, D., & Purohit, J. K. (2021). An opinion of Indian manufacturing and service sector for adopting industry 4.0: A survey. *Turkish Journal of Computer and Mathematics Education, 12*(6), 2370–2379.

Reay, E., & Wanick, V. (2023). *Skins in the game: Fashion branding and commercial video games.* doi:10.1007/978-3-031-11185-3_5

Rechtman, Y. (2017). Blockchain: The making of a simple, secure recording concept. *The CPA Journal, 87*(6), 15–17.

Reed, D. (2022). The new rules of engagement: Hearts and minds in turbulent times. In Leadership strategies for the hybrid workforce: Best practices for fostering employee safety and significance (pp. 50-59). doi:10.4018/978-1-6684-3453-6.ch004

Ren, X., Xu, M., Niyato, D., Kang, J., Xiong, Z., Qiu, C., & Wang, X. (2023). *Building Resilient Web 3.0 with Quantum Information Technologies and Blockchain: An Ambilateral View.* arXiv preprint arXiv:2303.13050.

Renou, M. O., Trillo, D., Weilenmann, M., Le, T. P., Tavakoli, A., Gisin, N., Acín, A., & Navascués, M. (2021). Quantum theory based on real numbers can be experimentally falsified. *Nature, 600*(7890), 625–629. doi:10.103841586-021-04160-4 PMID:34912122

Revina, I. M., & Emmanuel, W. R. S. (2021). A Survey on Human Face Expression Recognition Techniques. In Journal of King Saud University - Computer and Information Sciences (Vol. 33, Issue 6, pp. 619–628). King Saud bin Abdulaziz University. doi:10.1016/j.jksuci.2018.09.002

Reyna, A., Martín, C., Chen, J., Soler, E., & Díaz, M. (2018). On blockchain and its integration with IoT. Challenges and opportunities. *Future Generation Computer Systems, 88,* 173–190. doi:10.1016/j.future.2018.05.046

Riasanow, T., Flötgen, R. J., Setzke, D. S., Böhm, M., & Krcmar, H. (2018). *The generic ecosystem and innovation patterns of the digital transformation in the financial industry.* Academic Press.

Ricoy-Casas, R. M. (2023). The metaverse as a new space for political communication 10.1007/978-981-19-6347-6_29

Riley, S. K. L., & Stacy, K. (2008). Teaching in virtual worlds: Opportunities and challenges. *Setting Knowledge Free: The Journal of Issues in Informing Science and Information Technology, 5*(5), 127–135.

Río, D., & César, A. (2017). Use of distributed ledger technology by central banks: A review. *Enfoque Ute, 8*(5), 1–13. doi:10.29019/enfoqueute.v8n5.175

Rosário, A., Vilaça, F., Raimundo, R., & Cruz, R. (2021). Literature review on Health Knowledge Management in the last 10 years (2009-2019). *The Electronic Journal of Knowledge Management, 18*(3), 338-355. doi:10.34190/ejkm.18.3.2120

Rosário, A. T. (2021). The Background of articial intelligence applied to marketing. *Academy of Strategic Management Journal, 20*(6), 1–19.

Rosário, A. T. (2021). The Background of artigicial intelligence applied to marketing. *Academy of Strategic Management Journal, 20*(6), 1–19.

Rosário, A. T., & Dias, J. C. (2022). Sustainability and the Digital Transition: A Literature Review. *Sustainability (Basel), 14*(7), 4072. doi:10.3390u14074072

Rosário, A. T., & Dias, J. C. (2023). How Industry 4.0 and Sensors Can Leverage Product Design: Opportunities and Challenges. *Sensors (Basel), 23*(3), 1165. doi:10.339023031165 PMID:36772206

Rosenbaum, P. R., Rosenbaum, P., & Briskman. (2010). *Design of observational studies* (Vol. 10). New York: Springer.

Rossi, M., Mueller-Bloch, C., Thatcher, J. B., & Beck, R. (2019). Blockchain research in information systems: Current trends and an inclusive future research agenda. *Journal of the Association for Information Systems, 20*(9), 14. doi:10.17705/1jais.00571

Rowan, K. F. (2021). *An Overview of Understanding Digital Privacy.* Academic Press.

Ruiz Mejia, J., & Rawat, D. (2022). *Recent Advances in a Medical Domain Metaverse: Status, Challenges, and Perspective.* Paper presented at the 2022 Thirteenth International Conference on Ubiquitous and Future Networks (ICUFN). 10.1109/ICUFN55119.2022.9829645

Ryalat, M., ElMoaqet, H., & AlFaouri, M. (2023). Design of a smart factory based on cyber-physical systems and internet of things towards industry 4.0. *Applied Sciences (Basel, Switzerland), 13*(4), 2156. doi:10.3390/app13042156

Ryan, M. L. (2015). *Narrative as virtual reality 2: revisiting immersion and interactivity in literature and electronic media.* John Hopkins University Press. doi:10.1353/book.72246

Saberi, S., Kouhizadeh, M., Sarkis, J., & Shen, L. (2019). Blockchain technology and its relationships to sustainable supply chain management. *International Journal of Production Research, 57*(7), 2117–2135. doi:10.1080/00207543.2018.1533261

Sadeghi, H., & Raie, A. A. (2022b). HistNet: Histogram-based convolutional neural network with Chi-squared deep metric learning for facial expression recognition. *Information Sciences, 608*, 472–488. doi:10.1016/j.ins.2022.06.092

Saeed, M. S., & Haq, M. I. U. (2020). Event Data Recorder and Machine Learning-Based Analysis for Smart Vehicle Safety. *Journal of Advanced Transportation, 2020*, 1–11. doi:10.1155/2020/8848579

Saeed, M. S., & Haq, M. I. U. (2021). A review on driver behavior analysis using machine learning techniques for autonomous vehicles. *SN Applied Sciences, 3*(2), 1–22. doi:10.100742452-020-03947-5

Saito, K., & Yamada, H. (2016). What's so different about blockchain?—blockchain is a probabilistic state machine. *2016 IEEE 36th International Conference on Distributed Computing Systems Workshops (ICDCSW),* 168–175.

Salem, T., & Dragomir, M. (2022). Options for and Challenges of Employing Digital Twins in Construction Management. *Applied Sciences (Basel, Switzerland), 12*(6), 2928. doi:10.3390/app12062928

Samadiani, N., Huang, G., Cai, B., Luo, W., Chi, C.-H., Xiang, Y., & He, J. (2019). A Review on Automatic Facial Expression Recognition Systems Assisted by Multimodal Sensor Data. *Sensors (Basel), 19*(8), 1863. doi:10.339019081863 PMID:31003522

Sanaei, Z., Abolfazli, S., Gani, A., & Buyya, R. (2014). Heterogeneity in mobile cloud computing: Taxonomy and open challenges. *IEEE Communications Surveys and Tutorials, 16*(1), 369–392. doi:10.1109/SURV.2013.050113.00090

Sanaullah, S., Baughman, M., & Zhang, R. (2019). A Review of Pedestrian Safety and the Impact of Intelligent Transportation Systems and Automated Vehicles. *Journal of Intelligent Transportation Systems: Technology, Planning, and Operations, 23*(3), 241–259.

Sartamorn, S., & Oe, H. (2022). Metaverse marketing for community development: Revitalization of traditional industrial sectors in Thailand. *Springer Proceedings in Business and Economics,* 121-126. 10.1007/978-3-031-06581-1_16

Savage, L. C. (n.d.). Playing with FHIR: The Path to Ensuring We Bring the Power of Supercomputing to How We Understand Healthcare in Medicine. In *Advanced Health Technology* (pp. 291–304). Productivity Press. doi:10.4324/9781003348603-17

Sayegh, K., & Desoky, M. (2019). Blockchain Application in Insurance and Reinsurance. Skema Business School.

Scheuermann, F. T. (2016). Bitcoin and Beyond: A Technical Survey on Decentralized Digital Currencies. *IEEE Communications Surveys and Tutorials, 18*(3), 2084–2123. doi:10.1109/COMST.2016.2535718

Schlatt, V., Guggenberger, T., Schmid, J., & Urbach, N. (2022). Attacking the trust machine: Developing an information systems research agenda for blockchain cybersecurity. *International Journal of Information Management.*

Schlemmer, E., & Backes, L. (2015). *Learning in Metaverses: Co-existing in real virtuality.* IGI Global. doi:10.4018/978-1-4666-6351-0

Schlichting, M. S., Füchter, S. K., Schlichting, M. S., & Alexander, K. (2022, September). Metaverse: Virtual and Augmented Reality Presence. In *2022 International Symposium on Measurement and Control in Robotics (ISMCR)* (pp. 1-6). IEEE.

Schmidt, T., & Strasser, T. (2022). Artificial intelligence in foreign language learning and teaching: A CALL for intelligent practice. *Anglistik: International Journal of English Studies, 33*(1), 165–184. doi:10.33675/ANGL/2022/1/14

Schou-Zibell, L., & Phair, N. (2018). *How secure is blockchain?* Academic Press.

Sehgal, S., Singh, H., Agarwal, M., Bhasker, V., & Shantanu. (2014). Data analysis using principal component analysis. *2014 International Conference on Medical Imaging, m-Health and Emerging Communication Systems (MedCom)*, 45-48. . doi:10.1109/MedCom.2014.7005973

Seidel, S., Yepes, G., Berente, N., & Nickerson, J. V. (2022, January). Designing the metaverse. *Proceedings of the 55th Hawaii International Conference on System Sciences.* 10.24251/HICSS.2022.811

Seskir, Z. C., Migdał, P., Weidner, C., Anupam, A., Case, N., Davis, N., Decaroli, C., Ercan, İ., Foti, C., Gora, P., Jankiewicz, K., La Cour, B. R., Yago Malo, J., Maniscalco, S., Naeemi, A., Nita, L., Parvin, N., Scafirimuto, F., Sherson, J. F., ... Chiofalo, M. (2022). Quantum games and interactive tools for quantum technologies outreach and education. *Optical Engineering (Redondo Beach, Calif.), 61*(8), 081809–081809. doi:10.1117/1.OE.61.8.081809

Shah, D. R. (2022). Textiles in the metaverse. *Textile View Magazine,* (137), 24-25+288.

Shahid, A., Almogren, A., Javaid, N., Al-Zahrani, F. A., Zuair, M., & Alam, M. (2020). Blockchain-based agri-food supply chain: A complete solution. *IEEE Access : Practical Innovations, Open Solutions, 8*, 69230–69243. doi:10.1109/ACCESS.2020.2986257

Shamsi, U. R. (2021). *Role of mobile technology in enabling learning and EFL learning: an ecological account of the pedagogical decisions of Pakistani lecturers* [Doctoral dissertation]. ResearchSpace@ Auckland.

Shardlow, M., Sellar, S., & Rousell, D. (2022). Collaborative augmentation and simplification of text (CoAST): Pedagogical applications of natural language processing in digital learning environments. *Learning Environments Research, 25*(2), 1–23. doi:10.100710984-021-09368-9

Sharma, B., Mantri, A., Singh, N. P., Sharma, D., Gupta, D., & Tuli, N. (2022, October). EduSense-AR: A Sensory Learning Solution for Autistic Children. In *2022 10th International Conference on Reliability, Infocom Technologies and Optimization (Trends and Future Directions) (ICRITO)* (pp. 1-4). IEEE. 10.1109/ICRITO56286.2022.9964860

Sharma, B., Singh, N. P., Mantri, A., Gargrish, S., Tuli, N., & Sharma, S. (2021, October). Save the Earth: Teaching Environment Studies using Augmented Reality. In *2021 6th International Conference on Signal Processing, Computing and Control (ISPCC)* (pp. 336-339). IEEE.

Sharma, A., & Mittal, A. K. (2019). Applications of Artificial Intelligence in Autonomous Vehicles: A Review. *International Journal of Engineering and Advanced Technology, 9*(2), 522–527. doi:10.35940/ijeat.b9398.129219

Sharma, A., & Mittal, A. K. (2019). Machine learning-based intelligent vehicles: A review. *Transportation Research Part C, Emerging Technologies, 105*, 434–455. doi:10.1016/j.trc.2019.06.014

Shen, B., Tan, W., Guo, J., Zhao, L., & Qin, P. (2021). How to Promote User Purchase in Metaverse? A Systematic Literature Review on Consumer Behavior Research and Virtual Commerce Application Design. *Applied Sciences (Basel, Switzerland), 11*(23), 11087. doi:10.3390/app112311087

Shim, B. K., Seo, J. Y., Na, K. Y., Lee, D. Y., Moon, M. H., & Lim, Y. K. (2022). *A study on software proposals for optimization of augmented reality glasses.* doi:10.1007/978-3-031-19679-9_73

Shrouf, F., Ordieres, J., & Miragliotta, G., 2014, December). Smart factories in Industry 4.0: A review of the concept and of energy management approached in production based on the Internet of Things paradigm. In *2014 IEEE international conference on industrial engineering and engineering management* (pp. 697-701). IEEE.

Shum, H. Y., He, X. D., & Li, D. (2018). From Eliza to XiaoIce: Challenges and opportunities with social chatbots. *Frontiers of Information Technology & Electronic Engineering, 19*(1), 10–26. doi:10.1631/FITEE.1700826

Shu, X., & Gu, X. (2023). An Empirical Study of A Smart Education Model Enabled by the Edu-Metaverse to Enhance Better Learning Outcomes for Students. *Systems, 11*(2), 75. doi:10.3390ystems11020075

Sihare, S., & Nath, V. V. (c) (2017, January). Multiple Entities Search through Simon's Quantum Algorithm. In *2017 IEEE 7th International Advance Computing Conference (IACC)* (pp. 789-792). IEEE.

Sihare, S. R., & Nath, V. V. (2016, December). Application of quantum search algorithms as a web search engine. In *2016 International Conference on Global Trends in Signal Processing, Information Computing and Communication (ICGTSPICC)* (pp. 11-17). IEEE. 10.1109/ICGTSPICC.2016.7955261

Sihare, S. R., & Nath, V. V. (2017). Analysis of quantum algorithms with classical systems counterpart. *International Journal of Information Engineering and Electronic Business, 9*(2), 20. doi:10.5815/ijieeb.2017.02.03

Sihare, S., & Nath, V. (2017). Revisited quantum protocols. *International Journal of Mathematical Sciences and Computing, 3*(2), 11–21. doi:10.5815/ijmsc.2017.02.02

Şimşek, B. (2022). *The effect of augmented reality supported texts on students' reading comprehension and examining students' attitudes* (Publication No. 753803) [Doctoral Dissertation, Akdeniz University]. Higher Education Council Thesis Archive. https://tez.yok.gov.tr

Şimşek, İ. & Can, T. (2019). Examination of virtual reality usage in higher education in terms of different variables. *Folklor/edebiyat, 97*(1), 77-90. doi:10.22559/folklor.928

Singer, A. W. (2019). Can blockchain improve insurance? *Risk Management, 66*(1), 20–25.

Sivasankar, G. A. (2022). Study of blockchain technology, AI and digital networking in metaverse. *International Journal of Engineering Applied Sciences and Technology, 6*(9), 166–69. . doi:10.33564/IJEAST.2022.v06i09.020

Siyaev, A., & Jo, G. S. (2021). Towards aircraft maintenance Metaverse using speech interactions with virtual objects in mixed reality. *Sensors (Basel), 21*(6), 2066. doi:10.339021062066 PMID:33804253

Slavkovic, M., & Jevtic, D. (2012). *Face Recognition using Eigenface Approach*. Serbian Journal of Electrical Engineering. doi:10.2298/SJEE1201121S

Smith, R. (2022). NPD with the metaverse, NFTs, and crypto. *Research Technology Management, 65*(5), 54–56. doi:10.1080/08956308.2022.2090182

Solomon, M. R., & Wood, N. T. (2014). Introduction: Virtual social identity: Welcome to the metaverse. *Virtual Social Identity and Consumer Behavior,* vii-xv.

Spanò, R., Massaro, M., Ferri, L., Dumay, J., & Schmitz, J. (2022). Blockchain in accounting, accountability and assurance: An overview. *Accounting, Auditing & Accountability Journal, 35*(7), 1493–1506. doi:10.1108/AAAJ-06-2022-5850

Sparkes, M. (2021). *What is a metaverse*. Academic Press.

Sparkes, M. (2021). What is a metaverse. Elsevier. doi:10.1016/S0262-4079(21)01450-0

Spivey, W. A., & Munson, J. M. (2009). Mot: Technology entrepreneurs in second life. *PICMET: Portland International Center for Management of Engineering and Technology, Proceedings,* 2200-2221. 10.1109/PICMET.2009.5262553

Springer. (n.d.). https://link.springer.com/article/10.1007/s41870-023-01217-7

Stallone, V. W., Wetzels, M., & Klaas, M. (2021). Applications of Blockchain Technology in marketing systematic review of marketing technology companies. Blockchain. *Research and Applications, 2*(3), 100023. doi:10.1016/j.bcra.2021.100023

Stanciu, A. (2017). Blockchain-Based Distributed Control System for Edge Computing. *21st International Conference on Control Systems and Computer Science (CSCS)*, 667-671. 10.1109/CSCS.2017.102

Stephenson, N. (1992). *Snow crash: A novel.* Spectra.

Sternberg, H. S., Hofmann, E., & Roeck, D. (2021). The struggle is real: Insights from a supply chain blockchain case. *Journal of Business Logistics*, *42*(1), 71–87. doi:10.1111/jbl.12240

Stockburger, L., Kokosioulis, G., Mukkamala, A., Mukkamala, R. R., & Avital, M. (2021). Blockchain-enabled decentralized identity management: The case of self-sovereign identity in public transportation. *Blockchain: Research and Applications*, *2*(2), 100014.

Sturm, P., Ramalingam, S., Tardif, J.P., Gasparini, S., & Barreto, J. (2010). *Camera models and fundamental concepts used in geometric computer Graphics and Vision algorithms and applications.* Springer.

Suarez-Fernandez, M. C., Sotelo-Figueroa, M., & Flores-Tapia, A. (2021). Comparison of fuzzy controllers for autonomous vehicles. *International Journal of Fuzzy Systems*, *23*(1), 1–14. doi:10.100740815-020-00947-3

Sugiyama, Y., Matsumura, A., & Yamamoto, K. (2022). Consistency between causality and complementarity guaranteed by the Robertson inequality in quantum field theory. *Physical Review. D*, *106*(12), 125002. doi:10.1103/PhysRevD.106.125002

Sundarraj, R. (2019). Call for Papers: Design Science Research in Information Systems and Technology. Academic Press.

Sun, J. C. Y., Tsai, H. E., & Cheng, W. K. R. (2023). Effects of integrating an open learner model with AI-enabled visualization on students' self-regulation strategies usage and behavioral patterns in an online research ethics course. *Computers and Education: Artificial Intelligence*, *4*, 100120. doi:10.1016/j.caeai.2022.100120

Suresh, A., Paulose, B., Jagan, R., & George, J. (2016). Voice Based Email for Blind. *International Journal of Scientific Research in Science, Engineering and Technology*, *2*, 93–97.

Swan, M. (2017). Anticipating the economic benefits of blockchain. *Technology Innovation Management Review*, *7*(10), 6–13. doi:10.22215/timreview/1109

Swartz, M. L., & Yazdani, M. (Eds.). (2012). *Intelligent tutoring systems for foreign language learning: The bridge to international communication* (Vol. 80). Springer Science & Business Media.

Sweeney, L. (2002). k-anonymity: A model for protecting privacy. *International Journal of Uncertainty, Fuzziness and Knowledge-based Systems*, *10*(05), 557–570. doi:10.1142/S0218488502001648

Swenson, D. L. (2018). Internet of Things in healthcare: Information technology architecture to enhance patient outcomes. *Journal of Medical Internet Research*, *20*(2), e25. PMID:29396387

Swilley, E. (2016). *Moving virtual retail into reality: Examining metaverse and augmented reality in the online shopping experience.* doi:10.1007/978-3-319-24184-5_163

Synthetic Data. (n.d.). https://www.jpmorgan.com/synthetic-data

Syuhada, K., Tjahjono, V., & Hakim, A. (2023). Dependent metaverse risk forecasts with heteroskedastic models and ensemble learning. *Risks*, *11*(2), 32. Advance online publication. doi:10.3390/risks11020032

Tahir, R., Hu, H., Gu, D., McDonald-Maier, K., & Howells, G. (2012). A scheme for the generation of strong cryptographic key pairs based on IC Metrics. *Internet Technology and Secured Transactions, 2012 International Conference for*, 168–17.

Tankard, C. (2015). Data classification–the foundation of information security. *Network Security*, *2015*(5), 8–11. doi:10.1016/S1353-4858(15)30038-6

Tan, T. M., Makkonen, H., Kaur, P., & Salo, J. (2022). How do ethical consumers utilize sharing economy platforms as part of their sustainable resale behavior? the role of consumers' green consumption values. *Technological Forecasting and Social Change, 176*, 121432. Advance online publication. doi:10.1016/j.techfore.2021.121432

Tan, T. M., & Salo, J. (2021). Ethical marketing in the blockchain-based sharing economy: Theoretical integration and guiding insights. *Journal of Business Ethics*. Advance online publication. doi:10.100710551-021-05015-8

Tan, T. M., & Saraniemi, S. (2022). Trust in blockchain-enabled exchanges: Future directions in blockchain marketing. *Journal of the Academy of Marketing Science*. Advance online publication. doi:10.100711747-022-00889-0

Tapscott, D., & Tapscott, A. (2017). How blockchain will change organizations. *MIT Sloan Management Review, 58*(2), 10.

Taylor, C. R. (2022). Research on advertising in the metaverse: A call to action. *International Journal of Advertising, 41*(3), 383–384. doi:10.1080/02650487.2022.2058786

Thakur, K., Qiu, M., Gai, K., & Ali, M. L. (2015). An investigation on cyber security threats and security models. In *2015 IEEE 2nd international conference on cyber security and cloud computing* (pp. 307-311). IEEE. 10.1109/CSCloud.2015.71

Thien Huynh-The a, T. R.-V. (n.d.). Blockchain for the metaverse. *RE:view*.

Thompson, R. B. (2023). *A Holographic Principle for Non-Relativistic Quantum Mechanics*. arXiv preprint arXiv:2301.04180.

Thurairasu, V. (2022). Gamification-Based Learning as the Future of Language Learning: An Overview. *European Journal of Humanities and Social Sciences, 2*(6), 62–69. doi:10.24018/ejsocial.2022.2.6.353

Tian, F. (2017). A supply chain traceability system for food safety based on HACCP, blockchain & Internet of things. *International conference on service systems and service management*, 1-6.

Tian, M., Voigt, T., Naumowicz, T., Ritter, H., & Schiller, J. (2004). Performance considerations for mobile web services. *Computer Communications, 27*(11), 1097–1105. doi:10.1016/j.comcom.2004.01.015

Tiwari, P. A., Zodawan, P., Nimkar, H. P., Rotke, T., Wanjari, P. G., & Samarth, U. (2020). A Review on Voice based E-Mail System for Blind. In *2020 International Conference on Inventive Computation Technologies (ICICT)* (pp. 435-438). IEEE.

Tlili, A., Huang, R., Shehata, B., Liu, D., Zhao, J., Metwally, A. H. S., Wang, H., Denden, M., Bozkurt, A., Lee, L.-H., Beyoglu, D., Altinay, F., Sharma, R. C., Altinay, Z., Li, Z., Liu, J., Ahmad, F., Hu, Y., Salha, S., ... Burgos, D. (2022). Is Metaverse in education a blessing or a curse: A combined content and bibliometric analysis? *Smart Learning Environments, 9*(1), 1–31. doi:10.118640561-022-00205-x

Todd, E., Bruce, K. S., Splittgerber, A., Bruno, S. L., Becker, J., Zanczak, H. J., Aw, C., & Gates, T. (2022). *The Reed Smith Guide to the Metaverse: Legal Issues (Part 1): Data protection and privacy* (2nd ed.). Reed Smith.

Topol, E. J. (2019). High-performance medicine: The convergence of human and artificial intelligence. *Nature Medicine, 25*(1), 44–56. doi:10.103841591-018-0300-7 PMID:30617339

Toraman, Y. (2022). User acceptance of metaverse: Insights from technology acceptance model (TAM) and planned behavior theory (PBT). *EMAJ: Emerging Markets Journal, 12*(1), 67–75. doi:10.5195/emaj.2022.258

Trevor, Benjamin, Farkhund, & Babar. (2018). Security and Privacy in Smart Cities. *Elsevier Sustainable Cities and Society, 39*, 499-508.

Tromp, J. (2022). Extended Reality & The Backbone: Towards a 3D Mirrorworld. In *Roadmapping Extended Reality* (pp. 193-227). Academic Press.

Tsai, S. (2022). Investigating metaverse marketing for travel and tourism. *Journal of Vacation Marketing*. Advance online publication. doi:10.1177/13567667221145715

Tsvilodub, P., Chevalier, E., Klütz, V., Oberbeck, T., Sigetova, K., & Wollatz, F. (2022, December). Improving a Gamified Language Learning Chatbot through AI and UX Boosting. In *Innovative Approaches to Technology-Enhanced Learning for the Workplace and Higher Education: Proceedings of 'The Learning Ideas Conference' 2022* (pp. 557–569). Springer International Publishing.

Türksoy, E. (2019). *The effect of teaching methods integrated with augmented reality and online materials on achievement and retention in science lesson: Mixed design* (Publication No. 600062) [Doctoral Dissertation, Burdur Mehmet Akif Ersoy University]. Higher Education Council Thesis Archive. https://tez.yok.gov.tr

Uberti, D. (2022). Come the Metaverse, Can Privacy Exist? *Wall Street Journal.* https://www.wsj.com/articles/come-the-metaverse-can-privacy-exist-11641292206

Ukko, J., Saunila, M., Nasiri, M., Rantala, T., & Holopainen, M. (2022). Digital twins' impact on organizational control: Perspectives on formal vs social control. *Information Technology & People*, *35*(8), 253–272. doi:10.1108/ITP-09-2020-0608

Ulusoy, Ç. S. (2022). *An augmented reality application using unity and vuforia* (Publication No. 712152) [Master's thesis, Trakya University]. Higher Education Council Thesis Archive. https://tez.yok.gov.tr

Umar, A. (2022). A digital transformation lab for developing countries and small to medium enterprises. *2022 IEEE European Technology and Engineering Management Summit, E-TEMS 2022 - Conference Proceedings*, 160-165. 10.1109/E-TEMS53558.2022.9944423

Upadhyay, N. (2020). Demystifying blockchain: A critical analysis of challenges, applications and opportunities. *International Journal of Information Management*, *54*, 102120. doi:10.1016/j.ijinfomgt.2020.102120

Ustundag, A., Cevikcan, E., Bayram, B., & İnce, G., 2018). Advances in Robotics in the Era of Industry 4.0. *Industry 4.0: Managing the Digital Transformation*, 187-200.

Uymaz, S. A., Tezel, G., & Yel, E. (2015). Artificial Algae Algorithm with multilight source for numerical optimization and application. *Bio Systems*, *138*, 25–38. doi:10.1016/j.biosystems.2015.11.004 PMID:26562030

Valaskova, K., Nagy, M., Zabojnik, S., & Lăzăroiu, G. (2022). Industry 4.0 wireless networks and cyber-physical smart manufacturing systems as accelerators of value-added growth in Slovak exports. *Mathematics*, *10*(14), 2452. doi:10.3390/math10142452

Van Hell, J. G., Oosterveld, P., & De Groot, A. M. B. (1996). Covariance structure analysis in experimental research: Comparing two word translation models. *Behavior Research Methods, Instruments, & Computers*, *28*(4), 491–503. doi:10.3758/BF03200538

Vidal-Tomás, D. (2022). The new crypto niche: NFTs, play-to-earn, and metaverse tokens. *Finance Research Letters*, *47*, 102742. doi:10.1016/j.frl.2022.102742

Viriyasitavat, W., da Xu, L., Bi, Z., & Hoonsopon, D. (2019). Blockchain technology for applications in internet of things—Mapping from system design perspective. *IEEE Internet of Things Journal*, *6*(5), 8155–8168. doi:10.1109/JIOT.2019.2925825

Viriyasitavat, W., da Xu, L., Bi, Z., Hoonsopon, D., & Charoenruk, N. (2019). Managing qos of internet-of-things services using blockchain. *IEEE Transactions on Computational Social Systems*, *6*(6), 1357–1368. doi:10.1109/TCSS.2019.2919667

Vishkaei, B. (2022). Metaverse: A New Platform for Circular Smart Cities. In P. De Giovanni (Ed.), *Cases on Circular Economy in Practice* (pp. 51–69). IGI Global. doi:10.4018/978-1-6684-5001-7.ch003

Volchek, K., & Brysch, A. (2023, January). Metaverse and Tourism: From a New Niche to a Transformation. In *Information and Communication Technologies in Tourism 2023: Proceedings of the ENTER 2023 eTourism Conference, January 18-20, 2023* (pp. 300-311). Cham: Springer Nature Switzerland.

Volchek, K., & Brysch, A. (2023). Metaverse and tourism: From a new niche to a transformation. *Springer Proceedings in Business and Economics*, 300-311. 10.1007/978-3-031-25752-0_32

Wagner, R., & Cozmiuc, D. (2022). Extended reality in Marketing—A multiple case study on internet of things platforms. *Information (Switzerland), 13*(6). doi:10.3390/info13060278

Waldrop, M. M. (1992). *Complexity: The Emerging Science at the Edge of Order and Chaos*. Simon and Schuster.

Wallace, M. (2006). Virtual worlds, virtual lives. *PC World (San Francisco, CA), 24*(11), 133–136.

Walser, T. M. (2014). Quasi-experiments in schools: The case for historical cohort control groups. *Practical Assessment, Research & Evaluation, 19*(1), 6.

Walters, R., & Novak, M. (2021). Artificial Intelligence and Law. In Cyber Security, Artificial Intelligence, Data Protection & the Law (pp. 39–69). Springer.

Wang, C., & Yan, H. (2010). Study of cloud computing security based on private face recognition. *Computational Intelligence and Software Engineering (CiSE), International Conference on*, 1–5. 10.1109/CISE.2010.5676941

Wang, Y., & Zhao, J. (2022b). *Mobile Edge Computing, Metaverse, 6G Wireless Communications, Artificial Intelligence, and Blockchain: Survey and Their Convergence*. arXiv preprint arXiv:2209.14147.

Wang, A., Gao, Z., Wang, Z., Hui, P., & Braud, T. (2022). Envisioning A hyper-learning system in the age of metaverse. *Proceedings - VRCAI 2022: 18th ACM SIGGRAPH International Conference on Virtual-Reality Continuum and its Applications in Industry*, 10.1145/3574131.3574427

Wang, C., & Hsu, M. C. (2019). Exploring the potential of virtual reality in medical education: A systematic review of VR applications used in medical education. *Journal of Medical Systems, 43*(4), 1–13. PMID:30820676

Wang, F. Y., Qin, R., Wang, X., & Hu, B. (2022). Metasocieties in metaverse: Metaeconomics and metamanagement for metaenterprises and metacities. *IEEE Transactions on Computational Social Systems, 9*(1), 2–7. doi:10.1109/TCSS.2022.3145165

Wang, H., Liang, X., Wang, J., Jiao, S., & Xue, D. (2020). Multifunctional inorganic nanomaterials for energy applications. *Nanoscale, 12*(1), 14–42. doi:10.1039/C9NR07008G PMID:31808494

Wang, J., & Medvegy, G. (2022). Exploration the future of the metaverse and smart cities. *Proceedings of the International Conference on Electronic Business (ICEB), 22*, 106-115.

Wang, M., Yu, H., Bell, Z., & Chu, X. (2022). Constructing an Edu-Metaverse Ecosystem: A New and Innovative Framework. *IEEE Transactions on Learning Technologies*, 1–13. doi:10.1109/TLT.2022.3226345

Wang, P., Wu, P., Wang, J., Chi, H. L., & Wang, X. (2018). A critical review of the use of virtual reality in construction engineering education and training. *International Journal of Environmental Research and Public Health, 15*(6), 1204. doi:10.3390/ijerph15061204 PMID:29890627

Wang, Y. (2022). A survey on metaverse: Fundamentals, security, and privacy. *IEEE Communications Surveys and Tutorials*.

Wang, Y. F., Petrina, S., & Feng, F. (2017). VILLAGE—Virtual Immersive Language Learning and Gaming Environment: Immersion and presence. *British Journal of Educational Technology*, *48*(2), 431–450. doi:10.1111/bjet.12388

Wang, Y. S., Su, Z., Zhang, N., Xing, R., Liu, D., Luan, T. H., & Shen, X. (2023). A Survey on Metaverse: Fundamentals, Security, and Privacy. *IEEE Communications Surveys and Tutorials*, *25*(1), 319–352. doi:10.1109/COMST.2022.3202047

Wang, Y., Kung, L., & Byrd, T. A. (2018). Big data analytics: Understanding its capabilities and potential benefits for healthcare organizations. *Technological Forecasting and Social Change*, *126*, 3–13. doi:10.1016/j.techfore.2015.12.019

Wang, Y., Su, Z., Zhang, N., Xing, R., Liu, D., Luan, T. H., & Shen, X. (2022). A survey on metaverse: Fundamentals, security, and privacy. *IEEE Communications Surveys and Tutorials*.

WangY.ZhaoJ. (2022a). *A Survey of Mobile Edge Computing for the Metaverse: Architectures, Applications, and Challenges*. doi:10.1109/CIC56439.2022.00011

Wanick, V., & Stallwood, J. (2023). *Brand storytelling, gamification and social media marketing in the "Metaverse": A case study of the Ralph Lauren winter escape*. doi:10.1007/978-3-031-11185-3_3

Watson, R. (2022). The virtual economy of the metaverse: Computer vision and deep learning algorithms, customer engagement tools, and behavioral predictive analytics. *Linguistic and Philosophical Investigations*, (21), 41–56.

Web Services Architecture. (2004). https://www.w3.org/TR/ws-arch/

Weingarden, G., & Artz, M. (2022). *Metaverse and privacy*. International Association of Privacy Professionals (IAAP). https://iapp.org/news/a/metaverse-and-privacy-2/

Weiss, C. (2022). Fashion retailing in the metaverse. *Fashion, Style & Popular Culture*, *9*(4), 523–538. doi:10.1386/fspc_00159_1

Weking, J., Desouza, K. C., Fielt, E., & Kowalkiewicz, M. (2023). Metaverse-enabled entrepreneurship. *Journal of Business Venturing Insights*, *19*, e00375. Advance online publication. doi:10.1016/j.jbvi.2023.e00375

Welsh, T., & Benkhelifa, E. (2018). *Embyronic Model for Highly Resilient Paas*. doi:10.1109/SDS.2018.8370443

Weng, X., & Chiu, T. K. (2023). Instructional design and learning outcomes of intelligent computer assisted language learning: Systematic review in the field. *Computers and Education: Artificial Intelligence*, 100117.

Weyer, S., Schmitt, M., Ohmer, M., & Gorecky, D. (2015). Towards Industry 4.0-Standardization as the crucial challenge for highly modular, multi-vendor production systems. *IFAC-PapersOnLine*, *48*(3), 579–584. doi:10.1016/j.ifacol.2015.06.143

What is metaverse in blockchain? A beginner's guide on an internet-enabled virtual world. (n.d.). Retrieved from https://cointelegraph.com/learn/what-is-metaverse-in-blockchain

What is Metaverse. (n.d.). https://www.spiceworks.com/tech/artificial-intelligence/articles/what-is-metaverse/

Wibowo, A. (2018). Pregnancy Consultation Application Development based on Cloud Computing. Ultima Infosys. *Jurnal Ilmu Sistem Informasi*, *9*(1), 1–8.

Wiederhold, B. K. (2022). Metaverse games: Game changer for healthcare? [editorial]. *Cyberpsychology, Behavior, and Social Networking*, *25*(5), 267–269. doi:10.1089/cyber.2022.29246.editorial PMID:35549346

Wiederhold, B. K. (2022). Ready (orNot) player one: Initial musings on the Metaverse. *Cyberpsychology, Behavior, and Social Networking*, *25*(1), 1–2. doi:10.1089/cyber.2021.29234.editorial PMID:34964667

Wild, T. (2017). *Best practice in inventory management*. Routledge. doi:10.4324/9781315231532

Will, H. (2014). *Linear Algebra for Computer Vision*. Attribution Share Alike 4.0 International (CC BY-SA 4.0).

Winfield, J. F. C., & Jirotka, M. (2018). Pedestrian Safety and Autonomous Vehicles: A Review. *IEEE Transactions on Intelligent Transportation Systems*, 19(6), 1763–1773.

Winkler, R., & Söllner, M. (2018). Unleashing the potential of chatbots in education: A state-of-the-art analysis. *Academy of management annual meeting (AOM)*. 10.5465/AMBPP.2018.15903abstract

Wood, A., Najarian, K., & Kahrobaei, D. (2020). Homomorphic encryption for machine learning in medicine and bio-informatics. *ACM Computing Surveys*, 53(4), 1–35. doi:10.1145/3394658

World Health Organization. (2021). *Telemedicine: Opportunities and developments in Member States: Report on the second global survey on eHealth*. Retrieved from https://www.who.int/health-topics/ehealth#tab=tab_1

Wright, A. M., Munz, S. M., & McKenna-Buchanan, T. (2023). Triage Teaching: Exploring Teacher Self-Efficacy during COVID-19. In Pandemic Pedagogies (pp. 96-111). Routledge.

Wu, J., Lin, K., Lin, D., Zheng, Z., Huang, H., & Zheng, Z. (2022). *Financial Crimes in Web3-empowered Metaverse: Taxonomy, Countermeasures, and Opportunities*. arXiv preprint arXiv:2212.13452

Wuchty, S., Jones, B. F., & Uzzi, B. (2007). The increasing dominance of teams in production of knowledge. *Science*, 316(5827), 1038–1039. doi:10.1126cience.1136099 PMID:17431139

Wu, J., & Tran, N. K. (2018). Application of blockchain technology in sustainable energy systems: An overview. *Sustainability (Basel)*, 10(9), 3067. doi:10.3390u10093067

Wu, Y., Ni, K., Zhang, C., Qian, L. P., & Tsang, D. H. (2018). NOMA-assisted multi-access mobile edge computing: A joint optimization of computation offloading and time allocation. *IEEE Transactions on Vehicular Technology*, 67(12), 12244–12258. doi:10.1109/TVT.2018.2875337

Xiong, M., & Wang, H. (2022). Digital twin applications in aviation industry: A review. *International Journal of Advanced Manufacturing Technology*, 121(9), 5677–5692. doi:10.100700170-022-09717-9

Xu, M. (2022). A full dive into realizing the edge-enabled metaverse: Visions, enabling technologies, and challenges. *IEEE Communications Surveys and Tutorials*.

Xu, Z., Hu, Q., & Zhang, C. (2013). Why computer talents become computer hackers. *Communications of the ACM*, 56(4), 64–74. doi:10.1145/2436256.2436272

Yaga, D., Mell, P., Roby, N., & Scarfone, K. (2019). *Blockchain technology overview*. ArXiv Preprint ArXiv:1906.11078.

Yaman, I., & Ekmekçi, E. (2016). A shift from CALL to MALL? *Participatory Educational Research*, 4(2), 25–32.

Yang, Q. (2022). Fusing Blockchain and AI With Metaverse: A Survey. *IEEE Open Journal of the Computer Society*, 3, 122–36. doi:10.1109/OJCS.2022.3188249

Yang, C., Tu, X., Autiosalo, J., Ala-Laurinaho, R., Mattila, J., Salminen, P., & Tammi, K. (2022). Extended Reality Application Framework for a Digital-Twin-Based Smart Crane. *Applied Sciences (Basel, Switzerland)*, 12(12), 6030. doi:10.3390/app12126030

Yemenici, A. D. (2022). Entrepreneurship in the world of Metaverse: Virtual or real? *Journal of Metaverse*, 2(2), 71–82. doi:10.57019/jmv.1126135

Yıldırım, Y. (2021, Nov 11). Social media and virtual lives before the Meta-verse. *Eskişehir Ekspres.* https://www.eskisehirekspres.net/metaverse-oncesi-sosyal-med ya-ve-sanal-yasamlar-1

Yildiz Durak, H. (2022). Conversational agent-based guidance: Examining the effect of chatbot usage frequency and satisfaction on visual design self-efficacy, engagement, satisfaction, and learner autonomy. *Education and Information Technologies*, 1–18.

Yilmaz-Na, E., & Sönmez, E. (2023). Unfolding the potential of computer-assisted argument mapping practices for promoting self-regulation of learning and problem-solving skills of pre-service teachers and their relationship. *Computers & Education*, *193*, 104683. doi:10.1016/j.compedu.2022.104683

Yoon, S. S., & Kim, C. Y. (2019). Deep learning for autonomous driving: A review. *Sensors (Basel)*, *19*(22), 5130. doi:10.339019225130 PMID:31752423

Yu, S., Lu, Y., Yu, S., & Lu, Y. (2021). Intelligent learning environments. *An Introduction to Artificial Intelligence in Education*, 29-52.

Yuen, S., Yaoyuneyong, G., & Johnson, E. (2011). Augmented reality: An overview and five directions for AR in education. *Journal of Educational Technology Development and Exchange*, *4*(1), 119–140. doi:10.18785/jetde.0401.10

Yunjiu, L., Wei, W., & Zheng, Y. (2022). Artificial Intelligence-Generated and Human Expert-Designed Vocabulary Tests: A Comparative Study. *SAGE Open*, *12*(1). doi:10.1177/21582440221082130

Zabala, U., Rodriguez, I., Martínez-Otzeta, J., & Lazkano, E. (2021). Expressing Robot Personality through Talking Body Language. *Applied Sciences (Basel, Switzerland)*, *11*(10), 4639. doi:10.3390/app11104639

Zable, A., Hollenberg, L., Velloso, E., & Goncalves, J. (2020, November). Investigating immersive virtual reality as an educational tool for quantum computing. In *Proceedings of the 26th ACM Symposium on Virtual Reality Software and Technology* (pp. 1-11). 10.1145/3385956.3418957

Zainurin, M. Z. L., Haji Masri, M., Besar, M. H. A., & Anshari, M. (2023). Towards an understanding of metaverse banking: A conceptual paper. *Journal of Financial Reporting and Accounting.* doi:10.1108/JFRA-12-2021-0487

Zamora, J. (2017, October). I'm sorry, dave, i'm afraid i can't do that: Chatbot perception and expectations. In *Proceedings of the 5th international conference on human agent interaction* (pp. 253-260). 10.1145/3125739.3125766

Zarka, W., & Hajismail, S. (2022). Prospects of negative heritage management in syria. *Journal of Cultural Heritage Management and Sustainable Development.* Advance online publication. doi:10.1108/JCHMSD-08-2021-0139

Zhang, L., Shen, B., Barnawi, A., Xi, S., Kumar, N., & Wu, Y. (2021). FedDPGAN: Federated differentially private generative adversarial networks framework for the detection of COVID-19 pneumonia. *Information Systems Frontiers*, *23*(6), 1403–1415. doi:10.100710796-021-10144-6 PMID:34149305

Zhang, L., & Tjondronegoro, D. (2011). Facial expression recognition using facial movement features. *IEEE Transactions on Affective Computing*, *2*(4), 219–229. doi:10.1109/T-AFFC.2011.13

Zhang, L., Xie, Y., Zheng, Y., Xue, W., Zheng, X., & Xu, X. (2020). The challenges and countermeasures of blockchain in finance and economics. *Systems Research and Behavioral Science*, *37*(4), 691–698. doi:10.1002res.2710

Zhang, R., & Zou, D. (2022). Types, purposes, and effectiveness of state-of-the-art technologies for second and foreign language learning. *Computer Assisted Language Learning*, *35*(4), 696–742. doi:10.1080/09588221.2020.1744666

Zhang, W., Lu, Q., Yu, Q., Li, Z., Liu, Y., Lo, S., Chen, S., Xu, X., & Zhu, L. (2020). Blockchain-based federated learning for device failure detection in industrial IoT. *IEEE Internet of Things Journal, 8*(7), 5926–5937. doi:10.1109/JIOT.2020.3032544

Zhang, X., Chen, Y., Hu, L., & Wang, Y. (2022). The metaverse in education: Definition, framework, features, potential applications, challenges, and future research topics. *Frontiers in Psychology, 13*, 13. doi:10.3389/fpsyg.2022.1016300 PMID:36304866

Zhang, Y., & MacWhinney, B. (2023). The role of novelty stimuli in second language acquisition: Evidence from the optimized training by the Pinyin Tutor at TalkBank. *Smart Learning Environments, 10*(1), 1–19. doi:10.118640561-023-00223-3

Zhang, Z., Wen, F., Sun, Z., Guo, X., He, T., & Lee, C. (2022). Artificial Intelligence-Enabled Sensing Technologies in the 5G/Internet of Things Era: From Virtual Reality/Augmented Reality to the Digital Twin. *Advanced Intelligent Systems, 4*(7), 2100228. doi:10.1002/aisy.202100228

Zhang, Z., Xu, Y., Wang, Y., Yao, B., Ritchie, D., Wu, T., ... Li, T. J. J. (2022, April). Storybuddy: A human-ai collaborative chatbot for parent-child interactive storytelling with flexible parental involvement. In *Proceedings of the 2022 CHI Conference on Human Factors in Computing Systems* (pp. 1-21). 10.1145/3491102.3517479

Zhan, Y., Xiong, Y., & Xing, X. (2023). A conceptual model and case study of blockchain-enabled social media platform. *Technovation, 119*, 102610. Advance online publication. doi:10.1016/j.technovation.2022.102610

Zhao, Y. (2022). Metaverse: Perspectives from Graphics, Interactions and Visualization. *Visual Informatics, 6*(1), 56–67. https://doi.org/.2022.03.002 doi:10.1016/j.visinf

Zhao, H., Chen, X., & Lin, Z. (2020). Deep Learning-Based Autonomous Driving: A Review. *IEEE Transactions on Intelligent Transportation Systems, 21*(9), 3765–3784. doi:10.1109/TITS.2019.2954055

Zhao, N., Zhang, H., Yang, X., Yan, J., & You, F. (2023). Emerging information and communication technologies for smart energy systems and renewable transition. *Advances in Applied Energy, 9*, 100125. doi:10.1016/j.adapen.2023.100125

Zhao, X. (2022). Leveraging artificial intelligence (AI) technology for English writing: Introducing wordtune as a digital writing assistant for EFL writers. *RELC Journal*. doi:10.1177/00336882221094089

Zhe, C., Huilan, G., Jiang, W., & Zhongyi, H. (2023). The ideal and reality of metaverse: User perception of VR products based on review mining. *Data Analysis and Knowledge Discovery, 7*(1), 49–62. doi:10.11925/infotech.2096-3467.2022.0371

Zheng, Z. S. X. (2017). An Overview of Blockchain Technology: Architecture, Consensus, and Future Trends. *IEEE International Congress on Big Data (BigData Congress), 557-564*.

Zheng, Z., Xie, S., Dai, H.-N., Chen, X., & Wang, H. (2018). Blockchain challenges and opportunities: A survey. *International Journal of Web and Grid Services, 14*(4), 352–375. doi:10.1504/IJWGS.2018.095647

Zhong, R. Y., Xu, X., Klotz, E., & Newman, S. T. (2017). Intelligent manufacturing in the context of industry 4.0: A review. *Engineering (Beijing), 3*(5), 616–630. doi:10.1016/J.ENG.2017.05.015

Zhong, S., Scarinci, A., & Cicirello, A. (2023). Natural Language Processing for systems engineering: Automatic generation of Systems Modelling Language diagrams. *Knowledge-Based Systems, 259*, 110071. doi:10.1016/j.knosys.2022.110071

Zhou, J. (2020). *Foreign-Language Teachers' Needs to Achieve Better Results: The Role of Differentiated Instruction* [Doctoral dissertation]. University of Southern California.

Zhou, K., Liu, T., & Zhou, L. 2015, August). Industry 4.0: Towards future industrial opportunities and challenges. In *2015 12th International conference on fuzzy systems and knowledge discovery (FSKD)* (pp. 2147-2152). IEEE.

Zhou, X., Liu, C., & Zhao, J. (2022). *Resource allocation of federated learning for the metaverse with mobile augmented reality.* arXiv preprint arXiv:2211.08705.

Zhou, M., Leenders, M. A. A. M., & Cong, L. M. (2018). Ownership in the virtual world and the implications for long-term user innovation success. *Technovation*, *78*, 56–65. doi:10.1016/j.technovation.2018.06.002

Zhou, Q., Li, B., Han, L., & Jou, M. (2023). Talking to a bot or a wall? How chatbots vs. human agents affect anticipated communication quality. *Computers in Human Behavior*, *143*, 107674. doi:10.1016/j.chb.2023.107674

Zhu, C., Wu, D. C. W., Hall, C. M., Fong, L. H. N., Koupaei, S. N., & Lin, F. (2023). Exploring non-immersive virtual reality experiences in tourism: Empirical evidence from a world heritage site. *International Journal of Tourism Research*, *25*(3), 372–383. Advance online publication. doi:10.1002/jtr.2574

ZhuH. (2022). *MetaAID: A Flexible Framework for Developing Metaverse Applications via AI Technology and Human Editing.* https://arxiv.org/abs/2204.01614

Zvarikova, K., Michalikova, K. F., & Rowland, M. (2022). Retail data measurement tools, cognitive artificial intelligence algorithms, and metaverse live shopping analytics in immersive hyper-connected virtual spaces. *Linguistic and Philosophical Investigations*, *21*(0), 9–24. doi:10.22381/lpi2120221

About the Contributors

Alex Khang is a professor in information technology, IT Workforce Development Consultant for High-tech Corporations in United States and Vietnam; AI and data scientist, software industry expert, and the chief of technology officer (AI and Data Science Research Center) at the Global Research Institute of Technology and Engineering, North Carolina, United States. He has more than 28 years of teaching and research experience in information technology (Software Development, Database Technology, AI Engineering, Data Engineering, Data Science, Data Analytics, IoT-based Technologies, and Cloud Computing) at the Universities of Science and Technology in Vietnam, India, and USA. He has been the chair session for 20 conferences, keynote speaker for more than 25 international conclaves; an expert tech speaker for 100 over seminars and webinars; an international technical board member for 10 international organizations; an editorial board member for more than 5 ISSNs; an international reviewer and evaluator for more than 100 journal papers; an international examiner and evaluator for more than 15 Ph.D. thesis in computer science field. He has been contributing to various research activities in fields of AI and data science while publishing many international articles in renowned journals and conference proceedings. He has published 52 authored books (in computer science 2000-2010), 3 authored books (software development), and 10 book chapters. He has published 10 edited books, and 10 edited books (calling for book chapters) in the fields of AI ecosystem (AI, ML, DL, robotics, data science, big data, and IoT), smart city ecosystem, healthcare ecosystem, Fintech technology, and blockchain technology (since 2020). He has over 28 years of working experience as a software product manager, data engineer, AI engineer, cloud computing architect, solution architect, software architect, database expert in the foreign corporations of Germany, Sweden, the United States, Singapore, and multinationals (former CEO, former CTO, former Engineering Director, Product Manager, and Senior Software Production Consultant). ORCID: 0000-0001-8379-4659.

Vrushank Shah, Assistant Professor, Department of Electronics & Communication, Engineering, IITE, Indus University, India. He has more than 13 years of continuous teaching and research experience in Electronics Engineering, Communication Engineering, Cyber Security, Data Mining, Machine Learning, and the Internet of Things. He has advised over 12 Postgraduate students and over 30 Undergraduate students on their dissertation/project work. He has around 11 peer-reviewed research articles in the domains of cybersecurity, IoT, and communication systems, and he has served as a session chair for several national and international conferences. He has served as a reviewer for over ten SCI/Scopus journals. He is coeditor of 04 edited books (calling for book chapters for IGI Global, Taylor and Francis Group) in the fields of AI Ecosystem (AI, Robotics, Data Science, Big Data, and IoT). ORCID: 0000-0002-5619-7100.

Sita Rani is a Faculty of Computer Science and Engineering at Guru Nanak Dev Engineering College, Ludhiana. Earlier, she has served as Deputy Dean (Research) at Gulzar Group of Institutions, Khanna (Punjab). She is Post-Doctoral Research Fellow at South Ural State University, Russia since May, 2022. She has more than 20 years of teaching experience. She is an active member of ISTE, IEEE and IAEngg. She is the receiver of ISTE Section Best Teacher Award- 2020, and International Young Scientist Award-2021. She has contributed to the various research activities while publishing articles in the renowned journals and conference proceedings. She has published seven international patents also. She has delivered many expert talks in A.I.C.T.E. sponsored Faculty Development Programs and organized many International Conferences during her 20 years of teaching experience. She is the member of Editorial Board and reviewer of many international journals of repute. Her research interest includes Parallel and Distributed Computing, Data Science, Machine Learning, Blockchain, Internet of Things (IoT), and Healthcare. ORCID: 0000-0003-2778-0214.

* * *

Hema Ambiha A. is presently working as a Assistant Professor, Department of Computer Science, Karpagam Academy of Higher Education, Coimbatore, India. She graduated and postgraduate from Bharathidasan University and awarded Master of Philosophy in Computer Science from Manonmaniam Sundaranar University. Currently pursuing Doctor of Philosophy in Computer Science in Bharathiar University. Her area of expertise is Cloud computing, and her research interests include Artificial Intelligence and Mobile Computing. She has been in the field of academics more than one and a half decade in Engineering and various Arts and Science Colleges and had been in the ITES sector for more than five years. Presently working as Assistant Professor, Department of Computer Applications, Karpagam Academy of Higher Education, Coimbatore. She has a good track of academic record. She also attended several National/International Seminars and Conferences held in different Colleges/Universities around South India. Published three research articles in the Scopus indexed journals. Also participated, presented and published paper in the International Conference held at Asia Pacific University of Technology & Innovation (APU), Kuala Lumpur, Malaysia. Acted as Resource person for Seminars / Webinars in several reputed institutions. She entertain herself with scholastic exercises through various positions.

Mohd Afjal is an accomplished academic and researcher with over five years of experience. Currently an Assistant Professor (Senior Grade) at the AACSB-accredited VIT Business School, he leverages his extensive educational background, including a PhD in Economics, an MBA in Financial Management, an M.A. in Economics, a PGDM, a B.A. (Hons), and 3 Certificate Courses. He has a remarkable track record of 16 publications in ABDC/SCOPUS/UGC CARE, 2 research papers under review, 2 working research papers, and an authored book chapter. Dr. Afjal is a UGC-NET qualified in Commerce and Economics, known for his engagement in organizing 3 seminars/conferences/workshops, providing 5 MDP/ Industrial Training & Consultancy programs, and guiding a PhD scholar along with 38 dissertations. A frequent participant and presenter in international conferences, he has attended 10 QIP/FDP/Refresher Courses and holds lifetime memberships in 4 professional organizations. Dr. Afjal's research interests include Performance Evaluation of Industries, Benchmarking and Frontier Analysis, Corporate Finance, Behavioural Finance, Blockchain and FinTech, and Financial Econometrics. As an instructor, his areas of expertise include Financial Management, Economics, Security Analysis & Portfolio Management, Financial Derivatives, Financial Market, Financial Modelling, and Research Methodology. He adeptly uses statistical software like STATA, EViews, R Programming, SPSS, and DEAP for his academic and research purposes. Always open for discussions on research collaborations and teaching opportunities, Dr. Afjal is an individual who is deeply passionate about advancing knowledge in finance and economics.

Jahanzeb Akbar, Integrity Watch Afghanistan, Kabul, Afghanistan. He has accumulated extensive professional experience in Afghanistan, working across diverse roles in research, policy analysis, and project management. His research areas are analysis, policy development, and project management, spanning multiple sectors in Afghanistan.

Ahmad Al Yakin is an assistant professor at Universitas Al Asyariah Mandar in West Sulawesi, Indonesia. He is a lecturer, a national speaker, and a leader in politics. He was the chairman of the civic education department at the teacher training and education faculty, and he was Assistant Dean at her university, to name a few of her accomplishments at her university.He is now the Head of the Bureau of Academic, Student Affairs, and Information Systems. In the current year, he is active as a lecturer, researcher, and national coordinator of Merdeka Belajar Kampus Merdeka, on the advisory boards of Language, Character Institution, and Women's Centre Studies, and on the advisory board of the Students Association at his university. He is also active as a member of the Indonesian Association of Pancasila and the Civic Education Profession. ORCID: 0000-0002-6193-2720.

Hakan Altınpulluk is a Assoc. Prof. Dr. in Distance Education at the College of Open Education of Anadolu University, Turkey. He undertook undergraduate studies in the field of Computer Education and Instructional Technologies (CEIT) between the years of 2005-2009 at Anadolu University. Hakan Altınpulluk continues to work in the field of Open and Distance Education, Augmented Reality, Virtual Reality, Mobile Learning, Mobile Health, Massive Open Online Courses, Learning Management Systems, Open Educational Resources, Personal Learning Environments, and E-Learning Systems.

Kumar Bedi received the B.Tech and M.Tech degrees in computer science and engineering from Punjab Technical University, Jalandhar in 2000 and 2008 respectively. Presently, he is working as an Associate Professor, in the Department of CSE at Sardar Beant Singh State University Gurdaspur. He has more than 50 publications in reputed National and International Journals. His research interest includes Cloud Computing, Mobile Computing, and Mobile Cloud Computing.

Rajat Kumar Behera is the Associate Professor in the school of computer engineering at Kalinga Institute of Industrial Technology (KIIT). His research area includes Data Science & Business Analytics, Technology Adoption, Ethics & Technology, Software Engineering, and Metaverse. He received B.E from VSSUT (formerly UCE Burla), M.Tech from IIT Delhi and PhD from IIM Ranchi. He has published research articles in leading journals like Information Systems Frontiers, Journal of Retailing and Consumer Services, Journal of Business Research, International Journal of Medical Informatics, Industrial Marketing Management, Information Technology & People, Technological Forecasting and Social Change, Journal of Cleaner Production etc. and holds professional designations including PMP, ITIL and Six Sigma Green Belt.

Mohammad Daradkeh is an Associate Professor of Business Analytics and Data Science at the College of Engineering & IT, University of Dubai. Prior to joining the University of Dubai, Dr Daradkeh worked at Yarmouk University, Jordan and Lincoln University, New Zealand. His research interests are mainly in the areas of business intelligence, analytics and data science. He has published numerous research papers with reputed publishers such as Elsevier, Springer, Emerald and IGI. He has presented research papers at various international conferences. He is also a member of the editorial board of several reputed journals.

Sibanjan Debeeprasad Das is a Ph.D. student at the Indian Institute of Management (IIM) Ranchi, India. He is studying Information Systems and Business Analytics. He earned a Master of Information Technology degree with a concentration in Business Analytics from Singapore Management University. Sibanjan has a number of industry certifications, including OCA, OCP, ITIL V3, CSCMS, Six Sigma Green Belt, and PGC in Digital Marketing. He has been actively contributing to the community by publishing books and articles, participating in a variety of industry panel discussions, serving as a guest speaker for conferences and Faculty Development programmes at universities, and mentoring AI/ML professionals. In addition to his many contributions to various research projects, conferences, and edited book chapters, he is the author of two AI practitioner books: Hands on Automated Machine Learning Using Python and Data Science Using Oracle Data Miner and Oracle R Enterprise. He served on the technical reviewer panel for IEEE International Conference on Advances in Smart, Secure, and Intelligent Computing.

Sudhansu Ranjan Das, Department of Production Engineering, VSSUT Burla, Odisha, India. He is currently working as an Associate Professor in the Department of Production Engineering, Veer Surendra Sai University of Technology, Burla, Odisha, India. He is specializing in hard machining, machining process modelling, optimization, sustainability manufacturing, green machining, development of coated cutting tool material, cooling-lubrication methods in machining, Nano fluid-MQL, advanced machining.

Jyoti Gupta, CSE, Chitkara University, Rajpura, Punjab 140401. India. She is a 3rd year CSE student in Chitkara University.

Sunil Kumar Gupta did B.E. in Computer Science from M.M.M Engineering College, Gorakhpur University, Gorakhpur, India in 1988, M.S. in 1992 and completed Ph.D. in Computer Science from Kurukshetra University, Kurukshetra, India. He possesses 33 years of teaching experience. He has worked as teaching faculty in many reputed institutions in India including N.I.T., Hamirpur (HP). Presently, he is working as Professor in Computer Science & Engg. department at Sardar Beant Singh State University, Gurdaspur (India). His areas of interest include database management systems, data mining, distributed systems and mobile computing.

Prodhan Mahbub Ibna Seraj, American International University-Bangladesh, Dhaka, Bangladesh, has been working as an Associate Professor at the department of English, American International University-Bangladesh (AIUB). He completed his Ph.D. in Teaching English as a Second Language (TESL) at the Faculty of Education, Universiti Teknologi Malaysia (UTM), and M. A in Applied Linguistics & ELT from the University of Dhaka. He has achieved the BEST POSTGRADUATE STUDENT AWARD (Ph.D. program) at 66th UTM Convocation for his outstanding research works. He is particularly interested in how technology could assist English Language Teaching (ELT). He got published 34 research articles in prestigious national and international peer-reviewed journals, including Scopus and Web of Science indexed, e.g., Heliyon (Elsevier), Journal of Psycholinguistic Research (Springer), Language Testing in Asia (Elsevier), International Journal of Sustainability in Higher Education (Emerald), Sustainability (MDPI), Asian EFL Journal, MEXTESOL Journal (MEXTESOL, Mexico), International Journal of Interactive Mobile Technologies (Kassel University Press GmbH, Germany), etc. He has reviewed 201 manuscripts of 51 different international journals, mostly indexed in Scopus and Web of Science. He is a member of the editorial board of 14 Scopus and Web of Science indexed journals.

Babasaheb Jadhav is an Associate Professor in the area of Finance and International Business at Dr. D. Y. Patil Vidyapeeth (Deemed to be University), Global Business School and Research Centre, Sant Tukaram Nagar, Pimpri, Pune-411018 (Maharashtra), India. He has more than 12 years of experience in Industry, Research and Academics. He has completed his PhD from Savitribai Phule Pune University (SPPU) Formerly Pune University in Financial Management. He has a Dual Master's Degree in MBA with first class and Bachelor's Degree in BBA with first class. He is PhD research guide at Dr. D. Y. Patil Vidyapeeth, Pune. He has in his credit 1 Funded Research Projects, 2 Patents, 6 Copyrights, 7 Books, more than 50 Research Papers, Case Studies in various National and International Indexed Journal's with high Impact Factors and 4 Articles in reputed Magazines as well as National Newspapers. He has accolades like Research Excellence Awards, Best Research Paper Awards, BOS Member, BOE Member, Editorial Board Member, Reviewer and Advisory Board Member for various Management Journals or Conferences of repute. He has expertise as a NAAC Coordinator, NBA Coordinator and Controller of Examinations. He has invited as resource person for FDP, Guest Lectures, Workshops, Seminars and Conferences. His areas of interest and research are Financial Management, Taxation, Economics, General Management and International Business Management. ORCID: 0000-0002-1933-0558.

Krishnaveni K. is presently working as Associate Professor & Head, Department of Computer Science, Sri S.Ramasamy Naidu Memorial College, Sattur, Tamilnadu. He is working as an Associate Professor and Head in the Department of Computer Science, Sri S. Ramasamy Naidu Memorial College, Sattur, India. She received her B.E. (1990) degree in Computer Science and Engineering from Bharathiar University, Coimbatore, India and M.Tech (2004) and Ph.D (2010) in Computer and Information Technology from Center for Information Technology and Engineering, Manonmaniam Sundaranar University, Tirunelveli, India. She has 30 years of teaching experience. She has published number of number of research articles in apparent journals. She has authored many books, book chapters and published one patent. Her research interests are Medical Image Processing, Machine Learning and IoT. She is an Editorial Board member and viewer of many journals.

Divneet Kaur is a student of B.Tech Computer Science and Engineering at GNDEC, Ludhiana.

Maninder Kaur, CSE, Chitkara Institute of Engineering and Technology, Chitkara University, Rajpura, Punjab 140401, India. She a 3rd year CSE student in Chitkara University.

Ashish Kulkarni is an Associate Professor, Dr. D. Y. Patil B-School, Pune, India. ORCID: 0000-0003-4771-2198/

Pooja Kulkarni is Assistant Professor, Vishwakarma University, Pune, India. ORCID: 0000-0003-4596-5132.

Sagar Kulkarni is a Research Scholar, MIT World Peace University, Pune, India. ORCID: 0000-0002-9236-4973.

Amaresh Kumar is a Professor, Department of Production and Industrial Engineering, National Institute of Technology Jamshedpur, India. His academic journey began with his pursuit of a Philosophy degree in Production Engineering, which he successfully obtained from Jadavpur University in West Bengal, India, in 2006. Since then, he has been dedicated to advancing knowledge and fostering excellence in his area of expertise. One of the remarkable aspects of His career is his profound commitment to mentoring and nurturing young scholars. Under his guidance, six PhD scholars have successfully received their prestigious doctoral degrees, benefiting from his extensive knowledge and guidance. Furthermore, he is currently supervising the research endeavors of five more scholars, providing them with invaluable support and mentorship.

Bhuvnesh Kumar received a B.Tech degree computer science and engineering degree from Punjab Technical University, Jalandhar in 2010 and an M.Tech degree in computer science and engineering from Guru Nanak Dev University From GNDU Amritsar in 2013. Presently, he is working as Assistant Professor, in the Department of CSE at Amritsar Group of Colleges, Amritsar. His research interest includes Cloud Computing and Artificial Intelligence.

Pradip Kumar Bala is professor in the area of Information Systems & Business Analytics at Indian Institute of Management (IIM) Ranchi. He received his B.Tech., M.Tech. and Ph.D. from Indian Institute of Technology (IIT) Kharagpur in 1993, 1999 and 2009 respectively. He worked in Tata Steel before joining academics. He also worked as associate professor at Xavier Institute of Management Bhubaneswar and as assistant professor at IIT Roorkee before joining IIM Ranchi in 2012. His teaching and research areas include text mining & NLP, recommender systems, data mining applications, data mining and NLP algorithms, social media analytics and marketing analytics. He has conducted many training programmes in business analytics & business intelligence. He has published more than 100 research papers in reputed international journals, conference proceedings and book chapters. He is also a member of the International Association of Engineers (IAENG). He has served as Director In-charge, Dean (Academics), Chairperson, Post-Graduate Programmes, Chairperson, Doctoral Programme & Research, and Member of the Board of Governors of IIM Ranchi. ORCID ID: 0000-0002-9028-4902.

Paula Lopes has a PhD in Communication, Audiovisual and Advertising, and she is a full Professor at Lusófona University. Has been Course Coordinator since 2015. She's a researcher in CICANT - Centre for Research in Applied Communication, Culture, and New Technologies, and the main research areas are Marketing: Integrated Marketing Communication (IMC), Brands, Luxury Brands, Social Networks, Advertising, Fashion, Sustainability, Research Methods in Social Sciences.

Karthikeyan M. P. is an Assistant Professor, School of Computer Science & Information Technology, JAIN (Deemed-to-be University), Bengaluru, India. He is presently working as Assistant Professor, School of Computer Science and Information Technology, Jain (Deemed to be University), Bangalore, India. His area of Specialization Machine Learning and Deep Learning. He obtained his Bachelors in Computer Science, from Sree Saraswathi Thyayagaraja College, Pollachi. He obtained his MCA, from Sree Saraswathi Thyayagaraja College, Pollachi. He is pursuing his PhD in Computer Science from Sri

SRNM College, Sattur in the area of Query Optimization in Deep Reinforcement Learning. He Completed Industry Integrated Course Machine Learning and Deep Learning from Nunnari Labs, Coimbatore. He has acted as resource person for DBT Sponsored workshop on "Big data Analytics using Machine Learning Techniques". He has authored and coauthored over 20 research papers in international journal (SCI/SCIE/ESCI/Scopus) and conferences including IEEE, Springer and Elsevier Conference proceeding. He is a co-author of 4 books and 10 books Chapters. He has presented various papers at international conferences. He has Completed more than 50 Online Course in Coursera, LinkedIn, etc. He is an IEEE Member and Member of Computer Society of India (CSI). He is a Board Studies Member for Various Autonomous Institutions and Question Paper Setter for Various Colleges. He acted as a Resource Person for Several Institutions. I am also Volunteer of Bangladesh Robotics Foundation.

Biswadip Basu Mallik is presently a Senior Assistant Professor of Mathematics in the Department of Basic Sciences & Humanities at Institute of Engineering & Management, Kolkata, India. He has been involved in teaching and research for almost 21 years and has published several research papers and book chapters in various International and National journals and publishers. He has authored five books at undergraduate levels in the areas of Engineering Mathematics, Quantitative Methods and Computational Intelligence. He has also published five Indian patents along with nine edited books. His fields of research work are Computational fluid Dynamics, Mathematical modelling and Optimization. Prof. Basu Mallik is a Managing editor of Journal of Mathematical Sciences & Computational Mathematics (JMSCM), USA. He is also the Editorial board member and reviewer of several international journals. He is a senior life member of Operational Research Society of India (ORSI), a life member of Calcutta Mathematical Society (CMS), Indian Statistical Institute (ISI), Indian Science Congress Association (ISCA), International Association of Engineers (IAENG) and an academic professional member of Society for Data Science (S4DS).

Nilamadhab Mishra is a Professor in Post at School of Computing, Debre Berhan University, Ethiopia. He has around 20 years of rich global exposure in Academic Teaching & Research. He publishes numerous peer reviewed researches in SCIE & SCOPUS indexed journals & IEEE conference proceedings, and serves as reviewer and editorial member in peer reviewed Journals and Conferences. Dr. Mishra has received his Doctor of Philosophy (PhD) in Computer Science & Information Engineering from Graduate Institute of Electrical Engineering, College of Engineering, Chang Gung University (a World Ranking University), Taiwan. He involves in academic research by working, as an Journal Editor, as a SCIE & Scopus indexed Journals Referee, as an ISBN Book Author, and as an IEEE Conference Referee. Dr. Mishra has been pro-actively involved with several professional bodies: CSI, ORCID, IAENG, ISROSET, Senior Member of "ASR" (Hong Kong), Senior Member of "IEDRC" (Hong Kong), and Member of IEEE. Dr. Mishra's Research areas incorporate Network Centric Data Management, Data Science: Analytics and Applications, CIoT Big-Data System, and Cognitive Apps Design & Explorations.

Gunjan Mukherjee is currently working as an associate professor in the MCA department in the department of computational sciences, Brainware University. He has completed his BSc in physics from Calcutta University, MCA from IGNOU. MTech from Calcutta University and obtained PhD degree in engineering from Jadavpur University. His research interest includes computer vision, machine learning, soft computing, image processing etc. He is a life member of CSI, ISOC and IAENG. He has published number of papers in different journals and international conferences of repute. Dr. Mukherjee also guided many students of BTech and MCA in their project and research works. He also authored the school computer book series (class 3 to 10) under his sole authorship, a text book on IT systems theory for engineering students and presently writing a boo on python technology. He is currently attached to the reputed publishing house for publication of the question answer-based books for diploma and engineering level students. He has acted also as the reviewer for many technical books. He worked as an Assistant teacher in Sree Aurobindo Institute of Education, as education officer in CSI, Kolkata chapter, as a senior faculty in NIT Ltd and as a lecturer in Calcutta Institute of Technology respectively. He also served as the visiting faculty in Aliha University, Techno India College and JIS College.

Ambika N. is an MCA, MPhil, Ph.D. in computer science. She completed her Ph.D. from Bharathiar university in the year 2015. She has 16 years of teaching experience and presently working for St. Francis College, Bangalore. She has guided BCA, MCA and M.Tech students in their projects. Her expertise includes wireless sensor network, Internet of things, cybersecurity. She gives guest lectures in her expertise. She is a reviewer of books, conferences (national/international), encyclopaedia and journals. She is advisory committee member of some conferences. She has many publications in National & international conferences, international books, national and international journals and encyclopaedias. She has some patent publications (National) in computer science division.

Nalini N. is a Professor in the Department of Computer Science and Engineering at Nitte Meenakshi Institute of Technology, Bangalore. She received her MS from BITS, Pilani in 1999 and PhD from Visvesvaraya Technological University in 2007. She has more than 24 years of teaching and 17 years of research experience. She has numerous international journal and conference publications to her credit, and received "Bharath Jyoti Award" by India International Friendship Society, New Delhi on 2012, from Dr. Bhishma Narain Singh, former Governor of Tamilnadu and Assam. She received the "Dr.Abdul Kalam Life Time Achievement National Award "for excellence in Teaching, Research Publications, and Administration by International Institute for Social and Economic Reforms, IISER, Bangalore on 29th Dec 2014. She is also the recipient of "Distinguished Professor" award by TechNext India 2017 in association with Computer Society of India-CSI, Mumbai Chapter and "Best Professor in Computer Science &Engineering" award by 26th Business School Affaire Dewang Mehta National Education Awards (Regional Round) on 5th September 2018, at Bangalore She is a lifetime member of the ISTE, CSI, ACEEE and IIFS. Elected Unanimously as Vice Chairman cum Chairman Elect-Computer Society of India-Bangalore Chapter for the Years (2019-2021). Program Chair-International Conference on Emerging Research in Computing, Information, Communication and Applications-ERCICA-2013, 2014, 2015, 2016, 2018, 2020 NMIT, Bangalore. She has served as Technical Committee member and reviewer in various International conferences and has delivered technical talks at various Institutions. She delivered technical talk on the topic "Digital Transformations" at India-Indonesia International Collaborations from Nitte Meenakshi Institute of Technology. Published book on "Internet of Things: Advanced Wireless Technologies for Smart Ecosystems" having ISBN-13: 979-8679630055. Recognized as FSIESRP (Educational- Professional Membership Grade: Fellowship) & Editorial Board Member Registration as Hon. Consulting Editor. Program Committee Member in BIOMA International Conference since 2010. Organizing Committee Member in the Congress of the "International Conference on Electronics & Electrical Engineering" Seoul, South Korea. She has guided EIGHT candidates to complete their Ph.D successfully and currently guiding five more candidates. She has guided more than fifty PG students to complete their thesis. Her areas of research include Cryptography and Network Security, Cloud

Computing, Artificial Intelligence and Machine Learning, Wireless and Distributed Sensor Networks, Optimization Heuristic Techniques.

Chitra Devi Nagarajan is an esteemed academic currently holding the position of Assistant Professor - Senior Grade I at Vellore Institute of Technology in Chennai, Tamil Nadu, India. With a distinguished career spanning over 12 years in the field of teaching, she has made significant contributions to the academic community.Her expertise lies in the realm of Financial Econometrics, a specialized branch that combines financial theory and statistical methods to analyze and model financial data. This field plays a crucial role in understanding and predicting financial markets, risk management, and investment strategies. As a dedicated researcher, Chitra Devi Nagarajan has made substantial contributions to her field. She has authored and published numerous research papers that have been widely recognized and cited within the academic community. Additionally, she has served as a reviewer for various esteemed journals, lending her expertise to ensure the quality and rigor of published articles.

Abdullah Nijr Alotaibi, English Department, Sciences and Humanities, Majmaah University, Majmaah 11952, Saudi Arabia, is an associate professor of applied linguistics at Majmaah University. He earned his PhD in applied linguistics from Indiana University, Bloomington, Indiana, USA. His research interests are in the area of second language learning, Developmental speech perception, and Phonetic cues in second language perception and production. ORCID: 0000-0002-1597-9480.

Ahmad J. Obaid, Dept of Computer Science, Faculty of Computer Science and Mathematics, University of Kufa, Iraq, is a full assistant professor at the Department of Computer Science, Faculty of Computer Science and Mathematics, University of Kufa, He received his BSC in Information Systems (IS) in 2005, from faculty of computer science, University of Anbar in 2005. M.Tech in Computer Science and Engineering from SIT, JNTUH, India in 2012, and PhD in Web Mining and Data Mining from University of Babylon in 2017. His main line of research is Web mining Techniques and Application, Image processing in the Web Platforms, Image processing, Genetic Algorithm and information theory. Ahmed J. Obaid, is an Associated Editor in Brazilian Journal of Operations & Production Management (ESCI), Guest Editor in KEM (Key Engineering Material, Scopus) Journal, Guest Editor of MAICT-19 and ICMAICT-20 issues in IOP journal of Physics, Scopus indexed proceeding. Guest Editor in JESTEC journal (Scopus, WOS) Journal, Managing Editor in American Journal of Business and Operations Research (AJBOR), USA. Associate Editor in IJAST Scopus Journal. Ahmed J. Obaid also Reviewer in many Scopus Journals (Scientific publication, Taylor and Francis, ESTA, and many others). He is leader of ICOITES, MAICT-19, MAICT-20 EVENTS. Ahmed J. Obaid has supervised several final projects of Bachelor and Master in His main line of work. He has edited Some books, such as Advance Material Science and Engineering in Scientific.net publisher, he has authored and co-authored several scientific publications in journals and conferences and is a frequent reviewer of international journals and international conferences.

Adhishree Ojha, Information Technology, Artificial Intelligence and Cyber Security, Rashtriya Raksha University, India. She is dedicated scholar having deep down interest in exploring the fields of AI/ML and Cyber Security. Being an enthusiastic individual who is always eager to learn new and different things. She was driven through her interest to write a research paper on the topic "Artificial Intelligence

(AI) Centric Model in Metaverse Ecosystem". Her interest in the technical field has led her to work on various different projects related to AI/ML, Data Analytics, Database Management and Cyber Security.

Ibrahim Oteir, English Department, Preparatory Year Program, Batterjee Medical College, Jeddah 21442, Saudi Arabia, is an assistant professor of applied linguistics, Batterjee medical College, Jeddah, Saudi Arabia. He earned his PhD in Applied linguistics from UUM, Sintok, Malaysia. His research interests center on Second language acquisition, applied linguistics, ICT IN TFL, Technology in Teaching English, Psycholinguistics and English Education. ORCID: 0000-0002-6193-2720.

Özen Özer received her BSc and MSc degree in Mathematics from Trakya University, Edirne (Turkey) and also PhD degree in Mathematics from Süleyman Demirel University, Isparta (Turkey), respectively. Currently, she works as an Associate Professor Doctor at the Department of Mathematics in the Faculty of Science and Arts at the Kırklareli University. Her research of specialization includes the Theory of Real Quadratic Number Fields with applications, Diophantine and Pell Equations, Diophantine Sets, Arithmetic Functions, Fixed Point Theory, p_adic Analysis, q_Analysis, Special Integer Sequences, Nonlinear Analysis, C* Algebra, Matrix Theory, Optimization, Approximation Theory, Cryptography, Machine Learning, Artificial Intelligent, Differential Equations, Statistics and so on… She has published/completed more than 75 research papers in high quality international journals as well as many national and international scientific projects. She also has written/published some books and chapters of books on Number Theory, Algebra, Applied Mathematics and Analysis in the international publishing houses. She has attended various national and international conferences in lots of countries with different kinds of topics as keynote speaker. She has worked in the different international journals (more than 75 different publishing houses and journals) as reviewer as well as member of the editorial boards of the books, papers and conference proceedings. She is ready and open for all kind of academic/scientific collaboration and cooperative too.

Shobha P. is an Assistant Professor in the Department of Computer Science and Engineering, She obtained her B.E. and MTech from Manipal University, Manipal, pursuing her PhD in VTU University. She has more than 12 years of experience of teaching and more than 10 years of research experience. She has published 12 research papers. She has 22 citations and H Index of 1.

Basanta Kumar Padhi currently works at the MCA, Balasore College of Engineering and Technology, Sergarh, Balasore, Odisha, India. Basanta does research in Computer Communications (Networks). Their most recent publication is 'Efficient Data Communication in a Structural Grid base for Mobile Adhoc Network Scenarios'.

Manas Ranjan Panda is a highly accomplished Assistant Professor in the Department of Mechanical Engineering at GIET University in Gunupur. With an impressive academic background and a dedication to scholarly pursuits, he has established himself as a prominent figure in his field. His commitment to research excellence is evident through his publications in renowned journals, which showcase his contributions to the body of knowledge in Mechanical Engineering. Furthermore, his active participation in various conferences demonstrates his enthusiasm for sharing his work, engaging in intellectual discussions, and staying at the forefront of the latest advancements in his field. In addition to his research achievements, he serves as a guiding force for B.Tech and M.Tech research scholars in his area of expertise. His mentorship plays a pivotal role in shaping the research projects and career trajectories of these students, enabling them to make meaningful contributions to the field. Through his guidance, he fosters an environment conducive to exploration, innovation, and intellectual growth among his students. ORCID:0000-0003-3336-8971.

B. C. M. Patnaik, KIIT University, Campus 7, KIIT School of Management, Bhubaneswar, Odisha 751024, India. His role involves sharing knowledge and empowering students with the necessary skills for their future success. He is a faculty member specializing in Accounts & Finance. He has successfully guided 20 Ph.D. scholars and am currently mentoring six scholars. Moreover, my research contributions include the publication of more than 150 papers, including 68 papers in Scopus indexed journals. These accomplishments have been recognized through the honor of being awarded the Best Faculty on four occasions.

Lekha Rani, Professor, CSE, Chitkara University of Engineering and Technology, Rajpura, Punjab 140401, India. She is Professor in Chitkara University with 18yr of Experience.

Banaja Basini Rath is an Assistant professor in MCA department at Balasore College of Engineering & Technology. She has rich experience in teaching and research in the field of AI and Machine learning.

Kali Charan Rath is an Associate Professor in the Department of Mechanical Engineering at GIET University, Odisha, India, with more than 18 years of experience in academia and research. He holds a Ph.D. degree in CAD/CAM from the National Institute of Technology, Jamshedpur, India. He has guided over 20 M. Tech students as a project supervisor, and his research work has been published in reputed journals and book chapters. He has attended numerous webinars and presented his research in national and international conferences. He has received recognition and awards for his contributions to knowledge dissemination. His research interests include Robotics and Automation, Smart Manufacturing Systems, IoT applications, Product design, Modeling and Simulation, CAD/CAM/CIM, Finite Element Analysis, and Design thinking and Innovation. He has submitted six chapters in AI, IoT, Robotics, Data Science, and Cybersecurity fields to books that will be published by Taylor and Francis on 2023 and 2024. ORCID: 0000-0002-0577-9530.

Albérico Travassos Rosário, Ph.D. Marketing and Strategy of the Universities of Aveiro (UA), Minho (UM) and Beira Interior (UBI). With affiliation to the GOVCOPP research center of the University of Aveiro. Master in Marketing and Degree in Marketing, Advertising and Public Relations, degree from ISLA Campus Lisbon-European University I Laureate International Universities. Has the title of Marketing Specialist and teaches with the category of Assistant Professor at IADE-Faculty of Design, Technology and Communication of the European University and as a visiting Associate Professor at the Santarém Higher School of Management and Technology (ESGTS) of the Polytechnic Institute of Santarém. He taught at IPAM-School of Marketing I Laureate International Universities, ISLA- Higher Institute of Management and Administration of Santarém (ISLA-Santarém), was Director of the Commercial Management Course, Director of the Professional Technical Course (TeSP) of Sales and Commercial Management, Chairman of the Pedagogical Council and Member of the Technical Council and ISLA-Santarém Scientific Researcher. He is also a marketing and strategy consultant for SMEs.

Filipe Sales Rosário, Marketing, Universidade Europeia, Complexo Andaluz, Apartado 295, 2001-904 Santarém, Portugal. He is Ph.D. Marketing and Strategy of the Universities of Aveiro (UA), Minho (UM) and Beira Interior (UBI). With affiliation to the GOVCOPP research center of the University of Aveiro. Master in Marketing and Degree in Marketing, Advertising and Public Relations, degree from ISLA Campus Lisbon-European University | Laureate International Universities. Has the title of Marketing Specialist and teaches with the category of Assistant Professor at IADE-Faculty of Design, Technology and Communication of the European University and as a visiting Associate Professor at the Santarém Higher School of Management and Technology (ESGTS) of the Polytechnic Institute of Santarém. He taught at IPAM-School of Marketing | Laureate International Universities, ISLA- Higher Institute of Management and Administration of Santarém (ISLA-Santarém), was Director of the Commercial Management Course, Director of the Professional Technical Course (TeSP) of Sales and Commercial Management, Chairman of the Pedagogical Council and Member of the Technical Council and ISLA-Santarém Scientific Researcher. He is also a marketing and strategy consultant for SMEs.

Suresh Kumar Satapathy, Senior VP & Chief Business Development Officer, Galler India Group, Gurgaon, India, is a senior leader in Strategic Sourcing, Procurement Operations and Supply Chain Management with work experience of over 28 years in Telecom, Media, IT and Automobile Industry. Worked with MNC's of global repute like Maruti Suzuki, Tata Motors, Bharti Airtel, Sterlite Technologies, Reliance Jio and Essel Group. He is currently working as Senior VP & Chief Business Development Officer for Galler India Group. He holds a B.Tech Degree from NIT, Rourkela and MBA (Finance) from Management Development Institute, Gurgaon. He is a distinguished professional currently serving as the Chief Business Development Officer at Galler India Group.

Ipseeta Satpathy, with a remarkable tenure of more than 21 years at KIIT University, possesses extensive expertise in teaching, research, and administrative roles. Her contributions as an author include six textbooks, namely "Environment Management" and "Business Communication & Personality Development" published by Excel Books, New Delhi, "Transnational Marketing Strategy" published by New Age International Publishers, "Organizational Communication" published by Lap Lambert, Mauritius, and "Empowering Award Staff by Revamping Training System in Banks" published by Lap Lambert, Germany. Dr. Satpathy's research prowess is exemplified by the publication of over 200 research papers in esteemed national and international journals, including those listed in ABDC category, as well as conference proceedings. Additionally, she has more than 60 research papers published in Scopus indexed journals. Having served as a visiting professor at Lynchburg College, Virginia, USA, Prof. Satpathy has actively participated in various international conferences, such as the International Conference on HRM & PD in the Digital Age in Singapore and the Cambridge Business & Economics Conference at Cambridge University, UK. Her research contributions have been recognized through prestigious accolades, including the Best Paper Award from Emerald Group Publishing Ltd. Prof. Satpathy's commitment to academic mentorship is evident in her guidance of numerous Ph.D. scholars, with more than twenty scholars having been awarded their Ph.D. degrees by KIIT Deemed to be University. Additionally, she has conducted several Management Development Programmes, further demonstrating her dedication to professional development. Dr. Satpathy's exceptional accomplishments have been acknowledged through the esteemed Oxford Journal Distinguished Research Professor Award in 2014 at Cambridge University, London. She has also been invited to address faculties and students at Charlton Business School, University of Massachusetts, Dartmouth, USA.

Aakansha Saxena is currently working as Assistant Professor at the School of Information Technology, Artificial Intelligence and Cyber Security, Rashtriya Raksha University. She holds the academic experience of 6+ years and currently pursuing PhD in Machine Learning from Ahmedabad University. She has received National Scholarship (National Fusion Program) for her dissertation (Post Graduation) in Data Analytics and Visualisation from Institute for Plasma Research(IPR)- Department of Atomic Energy (DAE), Government of India in 2015. She was also at Laurentian University Sudbury Canada in 2013 for her International Experience Program to gain expertise in Web Data Management and Wireless Communication, Mobile Computing. She has been awarded IBM Badges from IBM Skills Academy for Artificial Intelligence Analyst-Explorer Award in 2020. Ms Aakansha is oriented towards research and wants to contribute to the field of Artificial Intelligence and Machine Learning. She has Worked and Mentored various group of students in Research Projects under SSIP (Student Startup and Innovation Projects). Under her mentorship, her students won first prize in "Gujarat Industrial Hackathon" and has been awarded with cash prize from Honourable Education Minister, Government of Gujarat. She has also received Grants from SSIP for working on POC. Moreover, she was Invited as a JURY Member Panel in the Grand Finale of Gujarat Industrial Hackathon 2k19 held at Pandit Deen Dayal Petroleum University. Apart from teaching, She has been actively involved in various committees , on various administrative positions at department as well as university level such as Member of BoS(Board of Studies), Member of IT Cell-ERP, Exam Coordinator, Admission Counselling Committee etc. She aims to equip students, researchers with the necessary background and technical knowledge for successful careers in Computer Science Engineering.

Shyam R. Sihare completed his Ph.D. at Raksha Shakti University in Ahmedabad, India. He holds a Master's degree in Computer Science from Nagpur University, Nagpur, India, which he obtained in 2003. Additionally, he attained an M. Phil. in Computer Science from Madurai Kamraj University, Madurai, India. In 2011 and 2018, he successfully cleared the Professor Eligibility Test GSLET (Gujarat) and MS-SET (Maharashtra) in India, respectively. Furthermore, he completed his MCA from IGNOU in New Delhi, India, in 2011. Currently, Dr. Sihare serves as an Assistant Professor in Computer Science and Application at Dr. APJ Abdul Kalam Govt. College in Silvassa, Dadra & Nagar Haveli (UT), India. His research interests encompass a wide range of areas including Quantum Computing, Quantum Algorithms, Quantum Cryptography, and Classical Computer Algorithms.

Bharatdeep Singh is a student of B.Tech Computer Science and Engineering at GNDEC, Ludhiana.

Durga Prasad Singh Samanta is a dedicated Research Scholar (Management) at KIIT School of Management in Bhubaneswar, Orissa, IN, where he has been making significant contributions since October 2019. His research interests revolve around the intersection of fintech and artificial intelligence, with a focus on solving business problems. Durga Prasad has actively participated in conferences and made valuable contributions to the field. Some notable conferences where he has presented his research include the 3rd International Workshop on Artificial Intelligence methods for Smart Cities (AISC 2023), Advancements in Smart, Secure and Intelligent Computing, Understanding the Metaverse – Applications, Challenges, and the Future, Security and Privacy in IoMT: Challenges and Solutions, and Advanced IoT Technologies and Applications in the Industry 4.0 Digital Economy. His research papers have been published in esteemed journals such as "Advances in digital marketing in the era of artificial intelligence: case studies and data analysis for business problem solving," published by Springer Nature,

Taylor and Francis, Nova Publishers, Sage publishers, among others. Additionally, he has contributed to conferences and events covering diverse topics including AI-Centric Modelling and Analytics, Smart Cities, Sustainable Development, Workforce Management Systems for Industry 4.0, and the Impact of COVID-19 on the Agriculture Sector. Durga Prasad's commitment to research and his ability to publish in reputable outlets demonstrate his expertise and dedication to advancing knowledge in the fields of management, FinTech and artificial intelligence.

Daksh Sobti, Information Technology, Artificial Intelligence and Cyber Security, Rashtriya Raksha University, India. He is dedicated and enthusiastic individual with a keen interest in cybersecurity, artificial intelligence, and machine learning. His passion for Artificial Intelligence and Metaverse led him write a research paper on "Artificial Intelligence (AI) Centric Modelling in Metaverse Ecosystem". With an exceptional academic record he has succeeded in expanding his technical skill set and have used the same to develop and work on various natural language processing and machine learning projects. Apart from this he also possessed excellent communication skills, analytical thinking, problem-solving abilities, and strong leadership qualities. He has led various teams and clubs at different levels. His experience of working as a Cyber & Strategic Risk at Deloitte, Gurgaon, as a Security Researcher at CyberEQ.io™ and as a Research Assistant at CyBureau has helped him to expand my knowledge in the field of Cyber Security.

Revathi T. is presently working as a Assistant Professor, School of CS & IT, JAIN (Deemed-to-be University), Bengaluru, India. She is currently working as a Assistant Professor, in Jain University Bangalore. She has completed her M.Sc. and B.S.c computer science in Thiruvalluvar University, M.E. in Anna University, along with a PhD degree in at Anna University, Chennai. She has 7 + years of experience in which 6+ years of research experience. She is highly self-motivated and logical thinking computer science lecturer will strive to be a dynamic center of innovation and dedicated to teaching, lifelong learning, research with local and global communities. She has published papers in several journals, conferences and international journals. Her area of research and teaching are Machine learning, computer vision and Image processing.

Muthmainnah Yakin is a highly accomplished Assistant Professor at Universitas Al Asyariah Mandar in West Sulawesi, Indonesia. She has extensive experience as a lecturer, global speaker, and international leader. She has held numerous positions at her university, including Chairman of the Indonesian Language Department, Public Relations Officer, Director of Women's Centre Studies, Deputy Director of Quality Assurance Unit, and currently, Deputy Director of the Language and Character Development Institute. She is also an accomplished author, having written 45 national and international books, published by esteemed publishers such as Springer, Emerald, Taylor and Francis. She serves as an international board member for various scientific innovation research groups and is a member of the United Nations Volunteers roster. ORCID: 0000-0003-3170-2374, WOS ID: 1950-2017, GOOGLE SCHOLAR: 6oeh6qmaaaaj, ResearchGate: muthmainnah.

Yusuf Yıldırım is a PhD student at Anadolu University, Institute of Social Sciences, Distance Education Program. In 2004, he graduated from Anadolu University Computer Education and Instructional Technology Department with first place. In 2004, he started to work at Kütahya High School. For 19 years, he has given lectures in educational institutions such as primary school, secondary school, high school, public education centers and university. In 2014, he completed Osmangazi University Educational Administration, Supervision, Planning and Economics Master's Program. In 2021, he completed Anadolu University Institute of Social Sciences Distance Education Master's Program. In 2021, he started Anadolu University Institute of Social Sciences Distance Education Doctorate Program. He has published 5 books, 5 book chapters, 20 articles, 22 papers. His research interests include distance education, 3D technologies, augmented reality, virtual reality, digital parenting, technology addiction, cyberbullying, robotics and coding, technology competencies, technology usage standards, computer ethics, instructional design, curriculum evaluation, values education, educational management, special education.

Index

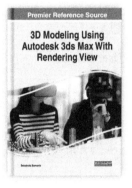

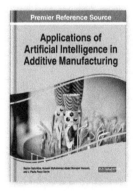

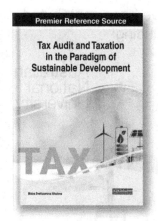
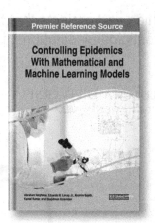

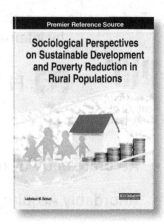

Printed in the United States
by Baker & Taylor Publisher Services

Printed in the United States
by Baker & Taylor Publisher Services